W9-DHS-299

Fire in My Bones

Contemporary Ethnography

Series Editors
Dan Rose
Paul Stoller

A complete list of books in the series
is available from the publisher.

Fire in My Bones

Transcendence and the Holy Spirit
in African American Gospel

Glenn Hinson

In collaboration with saints
from a host of churches

Photographs by Roland L. Freeman

PENN

University of Pennsylvania
Philadelphia

All royalties from this book will go to church projects designated by the saints who have served as this work's consultants and co-authors.

10 9 8 7 6 5 4 3 2 1

Published by
University of Pennsylvania Press
Philadelphia, Pennsylvania 19104-4011

The author wishes to thank the following for permission to reprint lyrics:
The label copy for "Just Rehearsal." Written by Frank Williams; published by Malaco Music Co. International copyright secured pc 1985.
The label copy for "I'd Sho' Shout It." Written by Lemuel C. Jones / John Wes Lewis. Malaco Music Co. BMI. International copyright secured pc 1987.
"Stop That Putting On" © 1969 and "I Wonder Is Everybody Happy That Shouts?" © 1946, by William Walker. Used by permission of Mirdis Walker.

Library of Congress Cataloging-in-Publication Data
Hinson, Glenn.
    Fire in my bones : transcendence and the Holy Spirit in African
American gospel / Glenn Hinson.
        p.   cm. — (Contemporary ethnography)
    Includes bibliographical references and index.
    ISBN 0-8122-3528-2 (hardcover : alk. paper). —
ISBN 0-8122-1717-9 (pbk. : alk. paper)
    1. Afro-American public worship.   2. Experience (Religion)
3. Afro-Americans—Religion.   I. Title.   II. Series.
BR563.N4H56   1999
306.6′64′008996073—dc21   99-36613
                                                 CIP

Frontispiece: The performed power of the Word. The Branchettes—Lena Mae Perry and Ethel Elliott—at the group's twenty-third anniversary at Long Branch Disciple Church, Newton Grove, North Carolina, March 10, 1996. (Photo by Roland L. Freeman.)

Contents

Illustrations

Chapter 1

Seeking Understanding

"You Got to Be in It to Feel It"

"I wish I could just expose this so greatly to you that your heart and mind would set on fire. But if you know not this . . ." Elder W. Lawrence Richardson pauses, momentarily grasping for words. How does one convey the ecstasy of rapture to one whose soul is yet unsaved? How does one describe an experience whose depths render all descriptions inadequate? The elder tries again, this time addressing process rather than feeling. "It comes quick and it goes quick." Another pause.

Our conversation is stretching into its second hour, as Elder Richardson patiently shares understandings granted him by God and confirmed by personal experience. The evening's talk, like many before it, presses into the night. He, a Primitive Baptist elder and a singer of deep intensity, sits on one side of a small kitchen table. I, a folklorist seeking understanding of a power often witnessed and sometimes felt, sit on the other. Only the muted sound of the cassette's turning wheels breaks the evening's silence. I sit expectantly, respecting the pause, waiting.

Suddenly, a cry of "Hallelujah!" explodes from Elder Richardson's lips, transforming his countenance from earnestness to undeniable joy. "Something hit me right then! Sure enough! I ain't kidding you!" The phrases tumble forth with infectious exhilaration, pressing one after another through a widening smile. "Yeah! Something hit me just that quick!"

There's no need to ask what that "something" was. If the preceding words hadn't made it clear, the overall conversation certainly had. In those few fleeting moments, Elder Richardson had experienced the emotional transport of transcendence.

"It don't stay with you," Elder Richardson continues, his words still buoyed by excitement. "And you can't keep it long. It'll hit you here, and it just—something feel funny, go all to the sole of your foot! It'll make you want to—Hallelujah!" Once again his eyes turn toward heaven and his voice rises in praise. "Sure enough!"

Now the laugh that has been building in his throat cascades forth, a blissful laugh born of beatitude rather than humor. "Amen! Now, *this* is what I'm talking about. Otherwords, you got to be *in it* to *feel it*. And if you're not *in it*, you just sit there and you look."

Elder Richardson pauses, briefly fixing his eyes on mine. Watching me watching him. I still say nothing. "But when you are *in it*," he continues, "God is never absent. When you are in the Spirit, and serving the Spirit, then God's going to let you *know* that you have been heard by Him." His heightened tone and jubilant smile suggest that the rush of joy has yet to subside. "Amen! I wouldn't have a religion that I couldn't *feel* sometimes!"[1]

Sitting in that darkened room, I listen with anticipation and awe. What moves me is not Elder Richardson's words—I've heard similar words in many services and conversations. Nor is it the seemingly spontaneous touch of the Spirit—I've often witnessed the touch in talks with sanctified believers and have heard enough testimonies to know that the Spirit heeds no boundaries of place or occasion. What moves me is the transformative power of the holy touch, a power felt both physically (the "feeling" that penetrates from head to foot) and emotionally (the rapturous infusion of joy). More important than its impact in either of these realms, however, is the Spirit's power to move the *soul*, to touch that mysterious wellspring that grants being its experiential essence. The saints of the African American sanctified community say that soul is the domain not of body or mind, but of *spirit*. And when the Spirit touches spirit, the soul rejoices in an epiphany of truth and knowledge.

Speaking of soul, Spirit, and experience draws talk into a realm rarely explored by academic inquiry. Yet these are the topics that dominate conversation among those who call themselves "saints," believers who have professed Christ as their personal savior, been saved by His holy power, and now walk the "set apart" path of sanctification. To ignore these matters is to deny the saints' experiential world, and thus to craft a portrait that speaks more to academic understandings than to the lived reality of believers. When I began this inquiry, I knew little of this reality. Like others exploring the expressive world of African American believers, I viewed testimonies, prayers, sermons, and songs as artistic vessels, as means for artfully capturing and conveying community meaning. Choosing song as my point of entry, I set out to investigate the layered dimensions of this meaning, only to be drawn inexorably into an experiential realm whose boundaries stretched far beyond aesthetics, ideology, and everyday encounter. I soon discovered that to understand the sanctified experience of song, one had to understand—and ultimately *feel*—the power of the Spirit. Otherwise, as Elder Richardson so succinctly observed, one could only "sit there and look."

That Elder Richardson would feel the holy touch while conversing quietly with a friend, the two of us sitting alone in an otherwise empty room, says something about the nature of this experience. No "ritual context" induced its occurrence; no ceremonial surround of sound, motion, and sensory saturation invoked frames of expectation and enactment; no relentless rhythms drove consciousness down an alternate path. Only quietude and conversation framed the moment. Or perhaps I should say, quietude and *conversations*. For, as Elder Richardson's words make clear, I was hearing only the voiced conversation, the words articulated by mouth and lips. At the same time, a second, silent conversation was taking place, a dialogue of praise and prayer, a communion born of meditation and conveyed by thought. The unseen partner in this conversation was the Spirit, whose response took the form of a holy touch.[2]

That touch—say the saints—finds many expressions. It can draw a saint's feet into the exhilarating steps of holy dance. It can empower a preacher's faltering words with wisdom and revelation. It can summon from the throat a shout of praise and jubilation. It can lead the tongue to revel in the phrasings of an unknown, celestial language. And it can push a singer to voice lyrics never before heard by mortal ears. Many forms, many responses, but a single source. "The Spirit is the Spirit," say the saints. "There's only one."

Tying these manifestations of Spirit together is the constant of meditative conversation. While the touch (also called the "anointing") can never be predicted, it can be *invited*, as saints focus their minds on the workings of God. Earnest praise and prayer render context irrelevant, as conversation—voiced or unvoiced—comes to power the dynamic of faith. "When praises go up," say the saints, "blessings come down." Herein lies the power of song. Song helps to focus one's thoughts, acting as a kind of cognitive lens that encourages singers and hearers alike to link lyrics with life experience, a process that believers say invariably leads to praise. This praise initiates the supernatural conversation, thus opening the mind's doors to transcendence. This is what saints mean when they talk about "singing until you feel it."

As Elder Richardson's experience suggests, song is but one of many possible vehicles of invitation. Preaching, praying, testifying, witnessing, and praising can all invoke the same invitational frame. The determining factor is not genre, but the devotional conversation that underlies it. Nonetheless, song holds a special place in the services of the saints. Believers are quick to point out the psalmist David's charge to "sing unto the Lord a new song, and his praise in the congregation of saints" (Psalm 149:1). They also cite the apostle Paul's encouragement to "sing and make melody in your heart to the Lord" (Ephesians 5:19). Does not God, they ask, surround Himself with angels, whose mouths are ever filled with songs of praise (Revelation 14:2–3)? Just as song is the primary vehicle of angelic praise, so is it a favored form among saints, marking every service with tuneful accord. Song, noted Elder Richardson in an earlier conversation, is one of the three "walking sticks" of faith, standing alongside prayer and preaching as a basic support on the heavenbound journey.[3] Without song, one stands in constant danger of stumbling down the path of error.

So in every service—be it Sunday morning worship, midweek prayer meeting, or even afternoon funeral—the saints raise their voices in jubilant praise. Stretching beyond meetinghouse walls to echo in the halls of heaven, the singing pulses with joy and exuberance, proclaiming the imminent advent of Christ's kingdom while celebrating the soul's experience of saving grace. In so doing, it fulfills the often-cited words of the psalmist: "Make a joyful noise unto the Lord, all the earth: make a loud noise, and rejoice, and sing praise" (Psalm 98:4).

Obeying the Word, the saints lift their voices in exaltation, accompanying passionate words with clapping hands, patting feet, swaying bodies. The singing stretches up, reaches out, and touches within; it simultaneously magnifies the Lord's name, heartens hearers here on earth, and welcomes the indwelling Spirit.

"Sing unto him, sing psalms unto him: talk ye of all his wondrous works. Glory ye in his holy name: let the heart of them rejoice that seek the Lord." (Psalm 105:2–3)

Though singing never stands alone, services dedicated to song are an integral part of the African American church experience. Listen to gospel radio in any African American community large enough to support AM programming, and you'll hear announcement after announcement about upcoming musical "programs" and "anniversaries." Always framed as "services" rather than as "entertainment," these events range from large "ticket programs" featuring touring professionals to modest church-auxiliary events presenting singers from local congregations. Filling weekend afternoons and evenings, they offer saints a range of musical choices to complement the Word-directed services of Sunday morning. Linking them all together is a shared format, a shared faith, and a shared desire to experience the fires of holiness.

The saints often say that singing can lead one to transcendence; for this reason, I have chosen the song program—as a site of such singing—to explore the sanctified worlds of meaning and experience. By focusing on the gospel program, I am able to move beyond the limited sphere of artist and song to consider the full range of program participants (including those not seen by mortal eyes); the richly layered contexts of faith, aesthetics and performance; the contested dynamics of expectation and experience; and the vernacular poetics of sacred enactment. This approach frees me to address not only the voices, sounds, and movements that fill every given moment, but also the ways that these expressions flow through time, coming together to yield meaningful sequences. Together, they yield a textured tapestry of music, motion, speech, and silence.

Few threads in this tapestry are unique to the gospel program; few components do not also grace other services of worship. Much the same can be said of program participants; their worship experience is certainly not circumscribed by the narrow world of musical presentation. Indeed, for many saints, the gospel program stands as but one event in a full schedule of regularly attended services. Like the program, each of these services boasts a separate title and manifest purpose ("tarrying service," "Bible study," "Women's Day service," "funeral," and so on). Each also assumes a unique expressive contour and carries its own set of norms and expectations. Yet *all* of these services serve the cardinal function of worship, and all evoke the same frame of meditative conversation. This draws them together into a devotional universe where shared repertoires of religious action forge links across genre, role, and event.

The boundaries of inclusion stretch even further when we move beyond the walls of the meetinghouse. As the saints are quick to remind us, sincere worship far transcends those bounded events designated as "services." "If the Spirit only deals with you in church," notes longtime gospel singer Lena Mae Perry, "then you need to go back and search yourself. Because if you can't live it *here* first of all," she says, pointing to her heart, "then there's no sense in you going to the church trying to do it."[4] Those who limit devotional activity to services are branded "Sunday Christians," "benchwarmers" who—in the words of one Missionary Baptist preacher—"profess but don't possess."[5] "True" saints, in contrast, are said to fill their everyday lives with praise and prayer, heeding the psalmist's call to "bless the Lord at all times" (Psalm 34:1) and the apostle Paul's charge to "pray without ceasing" (1 Thessalonians 5:17). Such worship both complements and comments upon that which occurs in church. As such, it draws yet another field of events into the gospel program's devotional universe.

The tangled world of social experience thus drives us from the particular to the collective, connecting song with sermon, prayer, testimony, holy dancing, and the silent witness of tears. Together, these acts move through a world of baptisms, funerals, prayer meetings, revivals, and the muted entreaties of the private prayer closet.[6] Paradoxically, inquiry at this more inclusive level refocuses our attention on the individual. After all, all repertoires involve choices, and all choosing indicates intent—on the part of either the believer or the controlling spirit. Every testimony, every song, every stylized step and ecstatic shout must thus be treated as a product of choice between options, with every expression becoming a statement—through contrast—about alternatives not chosen. At the same time, every devotional act reflects and implicitly remarks upon related acts in other worship settings. Hence a single song voiced at a gospel program might call to mind a testimony heard earlier that morning, a powerful sermon heard years ago over the radio, and the everyday performances of one's deceased mother who sang while she worked. All religious expression assumes this umbra of connotative reference, drawing the devotional universe together around an axis of personal experience. The step beyond singular event thus carries inquiry both *outward* to religious context and *inward* to motive and memory, thickening the descriptive texture while simultaneously grounding it in human experience.[7]

Considering connotation and memory pushes us yet further from the single event by freeing us from the boundaries of linear time. The knowledge that guides assessment and interpretation is grounded in experience rather than occasion. It draws upon the full span of lifetime encounter, upon experiences known personally and those known through the proxy of narrative, upon tradition and emotion and expectation and belief. People forge associative links not according to "logic" or cultural decree, but according to personal grammars of significance, grammars perhaps framed by culture, but always defined by individual experience. Hoping to evoke this world of association in this book, I too draw freely upon diverse conversations and performances, jumping across time and place so as to establish *my own* field of reference. My purpose in so doing is *not* to claim interpretive authority, but rather to suggest the ways that subjectivity—and by extension, the *many* subjectivities that define an audience—informs experience and interpretation at group events.[8]

With this end in mind, this study of gospel services focuses on a single event, though in so doing it draws upon many. The following chapters chronicle one service—the twentieth anniversary of the North Carolina gospel duo, the Branchettes. The discussion therein, however, travels freely from worship service to worship service, and from conversation to conversation. This strategy necessarily sacri-

1. The Branchettes—Ethel Elliott and Lena Mae Perry—close their twenty-third singing anniversary at the Long Branch Disciple Church. The two women drew their group's name from the church, identifying themselves as "branches of Long Branch." Photographer Roland L. Freeman captured this image, and those that follow, at the Branchettes' twenty-third and twenty-sixth anniversaries, on March 9 and 10, 1996, and March 14, 1999.

fices a degree of descriptive depth, distorting the flow that grants events their particular unity. At the same time, however, it achieves a measure of experiential breadth, invoking the range of encounter that frames interpretation at any given moment. Programgoers' responses to an event are always conditioned by experiences at other events; to ignore these referencing experiences is to collapse personal history into an arbitrarily delimited frame. Hence I move freely between local "anniversaries" and professional "ticket programs," between sincere performance and the most blatant showmanship, between the testimonies of the saved and the words of those whose soul's status stands in doubt. Throughout, I let my consultants make the distinctions; and throughout, I try to reference the field of these believers' experience. My goal, in the end, is not to describe a gospel program, but rather to explore the metaphysical and experiential worlds of the program's participants.

Exploring these worlds means acknowledging and adopting the sources of authority accepted by believers. The discussion that follows attempts to do just this, building its understandings from the saints' perspectives, and thus offering as substantiating evidence only the words of saints, those who present themselves as saints, prophecy, and the highest textual authority, the Bible. This is not to say that saints aren't interested in—or don't actively engage—the ideas of outsiders; their active collaboration with this book certainly suggests otherwise. But these ideas, though sometimes referenced, rarely claim much space in sanctified conversations. Honoring this choice, I've placed all contributions from church outsiders in the notes; the main text belongs to believers.

When setting out on this exploration, I searched for models that both addressed the lived complexities of culture and captured the eloquence so often voiced by culture's creators. Most appealing were those ethnographies that charted the pathways linking talk, belief, value, and art. Many of these works followed an ethnography of communication approach, one that enabled them to slide from detail to enveloping context with an ease that called to mind the effortlessness of this move in everyday practice.[9] Yet something still seemed missing. The cultural connections still seemed analytic rather than lived; the richness of consultant testimony still seemed muted by a sense of detached removal. What was missing from this matrix was any sense of the consultants' actual *experience*.

The exploration of context and communication certainly opens sundry doors of understanding. But by not addressing the subjective realm of experience, it ultimately fails to grant entry to the very domain that believers say holds the master keys to meaning—because it bypasses the realm that grounds knowledge and gives rise to faith. Recall the conversation with Elder Richardson. He was struggling with words, wrestling with the inherent inadequacy of language, attempting to describe the indescribable so as to convey meaning. Then came the holy touch. And then a rush of words, words no longer bound, words that could reference experience to impart understanding. The experience—sudden, swift, powerful—let Elder Richardson *know* that his struggle for words was not in vain. Note the certainty in his words. He didn't "suspect" that the Spirit was at hand; he didn't just "sense" a presence other than our own. He *knew* it, beyond a shadow of a doubt. Because he *felt* it. And felt it in a way that left no room for skepticism. Not in a way that was shaped *by* belief, but in a way that *gave his belief its very shape*.

Listen again to Elder Richardson's closing words: "I wouldn't have a religion that I couldn't *feel* sometimes!" Anyone who has spent time in the company of saints knows this comment well, for it pervades sanctified talk, regularly lending emphasis to sermons, testimonies, and everyday conversations. Now consider the maxim's meaning. The expressive weight of the entire sentence falls on the single stressed word, "feel." Without feeling, the saying suggests, religion would be hollow. Without feeling, it would be mere precept and doctrine, with no evidential grounding, no soul-moving power. Some kind of "feeling" clearly makes the difference.

But what *is* this feeling? The term "feeling" is, after all, rather vague. For clarification, we can turn to the maxim's often-voiced variant "I wouldn't have a God that I couldn't *feel* sometimes!" The "feeling" is of God and *is* God. At issue here is transcendent encounter, the experience of the holy, a feeling that so transcends the everyday that it grants certain knowledge and grounds ardent faith. Without addressing such encounter, and without according it the essential centrality granted it by the saints, ethnographic inquiry—like religion without feeling—would be a hollow exercise. The ethnographer, to paraphrase Elder Richardson, would be forever "sitting and looking," always watching from the outside, always cataloging behavior but never understanding essence. To avoid this, I shall begin by addressing the elusive worlds of belief and experience, grounding this inquiry in vernacular understandings and revealed knowledge before exploring the world of sanctified song.

Chapter 2

Belief, Knowledge, and Experience

"The Lord Can Be Mysterious"

The setting is antebellum Alabama; the occasion, a conversation between an African American saint and a white man whose soul's status remains uncertain. The saint, named only Jack, had been born in Africa, carried in chains across the waters, and converted to Christianity on the plantation that claimed him as property. The narrator is the plantation mistress:

"Once, just after [Jack] had been publicly shouting and proclaiming how precious he had found Jesus to his soul, a young man looking on said to him: 'Jack, don't be so certain about having Jesus with you. You only *hope* you have him, I guess.'

" 'Mr. Thomson, do you *hope* you have your hat on your head?'

" 'Hope, Jack? Why I *know* I have it on.'

" 'But you can't *see* it: it's on the back of your head.'

" 'But I can *feel* it,' returned Mr. Thomson, a little out of patience with Jack's questioning.

" 'Yes, that's just so. You *feel* it. Well, Mr. Thomson, that's just the way with Jack. I *know* I've got my Jesus in my heart. I can't see Him, but I *feel* Him. O *how* I feel Him! Bless the Lord! Bless the Lord!' And Jack went to shouting again."[1]

*   *   *   *   *

Jack's words are tellingly similar to those uttered by Elder Richardson more than a century later. Both speakers draw belief, knowledge, and experience into a single referential field, linking the three in a way that proclaims their intrinsic accord. This communion has always marked the language of the saints. And it has always drawn talk beyond words to the actuality of supernatural encounter. Here, in the realm of religious experience, lies talk's final reference point. Indeed, one could argue that the language of experience—a language grounded in subjectivity and the recognition of shared sensation—stands as the saints' primary medium for articulating both knowledge and belief.[2]

Religious experience, as both Elder Richardson and Jack attest, grants a special kind of knowing. It imparts a knowledge said to resonate with the soul, a knowledge carrying so much certainty that it denies the need for objective verification and makes all calls for public validation seem petty and irrelevant. This deep knowing is of a markedly different order from that gained in everyday encounter; indeed, it is said to make all mundane knowledge seem shallow, insubstantial, unimportant. *Worldly* knowledge, say the saints, must be *achieved*; it accrues from study, from reflection, from the heeded lessons of everyday experience. Such knowledge, grounded in the shallow wisdom of mortality, is ever subject to error and ever susceptible to the shifting winds of argument. *Spiritual* knowledge, in contrast, does not depend on the studied efforts of self. This is knowledge *imparted*, a knowing granted from outside the individual. The mind receives it with a reported flash of understanding, realizing immediately its inherent and unchanging verity. There's no doubt, no room for argument. The human spirit, recognizing holy Spirit, proclaims its truth.[3]

This knowledge, in turn, informs belief. Granting special insight into the mysteries of existence, it helps fill the frame of faith, enlivening the holy text while drawing believers directly into the process of divine revelation. This is not to say that the knowledge granted through experience necessarily *determines* belief, for in most cases it is belief that first convicts the soul and leads sinners to embrace Christ as savior. Belief stands as the foundation of Christian consciousness; it grants entrée into the world of holiness and guides believers in their journey toward sanctification. As such, belief frames all thought and action in the community of saints.

This framing places belief in a dynamic relationship with experience and knowledge. But it would be a mistake to presume that belief commands primacy in this relationship. Belief does not *decree* the interpretation of experience; nor does it *define* the meanings of granted knowledge. Divinely induced experience and knowledge are said to carry with them full understanding; they need not reference belief for verification. What belief offers is a frame for understanding, a way of situating the fleeting encounter and flash of understanding in the timelessness of celestial design. Acting only as a frame, belief does not shape sensibility; it does not—as social scientists have traditionally claimed—distort perception and twist cognition in order to satisfy established theological imperatives. This assumption grants a special primacy to belief, giving it determinative power over both experience and knowledge; in a sense, it makes the latter dependent on the former. Yet the saints grant belief no such preeminence. Their testimonies clearly establish that transcendent encounter and divine revelation are key, core experiences, ones that themselves can shape consciousness and, significantly, transform belief. At the moment of occurrence, they claim determinative precedence. The saints thus do not grant fixed primacy to any one factor in this equation of faith. Instead, they set belief, knowledge, and experience into balance, letting only the moment determine each factor's subjective weight.

Earlier, I suggested a temporal condition to this equation, noting that belief usually precedes divine encounter. Even this, however, is variable, as countless conversion accounts will attest. Although most saints first experience grace only after prayer and confession, many encounter the Spirit from positions of stolid *dis*belief. Perhaps the most referenced example of such encounter is the New Testament conversion of Saul, whose transformation from unbelieving persecutor to ardent apostle testifies to the unpredictability of celestial agency. This biblical account repeatedly finds confirmation in the testimonies of saved believers. "I used to be the most wicked man in the world," notes one saint, "but a [divine] voice converted me . . ." "I don't know why I got converted," adds another believer, "because I had been doing nearly everything they told me I ought *not* to do. I danced, played cards and done just like I wanted to do." "The first time I heard the voice it scared me," declares a third saint, "because I wasn't thinking about God and His works. But God is planning when we are asleep and when He wills He moves on His own time."[4]

By focusing on agency, this last saint's closing words strike at the heart of the issue. The saints accept as a given the fact that divine encounter can precede belief. To presume otherwise, they say, is to place limits on the power of God, suggesting that celestial agency can only operate within a worldly frame—a suggestion that the saints reject as arrogantly presumptuous. But since this presumption offers a convenient frame for disbelief, it remains a staple of secular understanding. As suggested above, the claim of necessary precedence allows doubters to argue that belief shapes believers' interpretations and experiences. What saints "know" and what they "feel"—nonbelievers contend—are little more than self-generated sensations fashioned by tradition and molded by cultural expectation. The saints are quite familiar with this argument; they often talk about how "the world" seems to find comfort in this "explanation" of their claims. This awareness, in turn, undoubtedly contributes to the ubiquity—in the church's narrative stream—of accounts detailing nonbelievers' encounters with the Spirit. Not only does each such narrative testify to the unrestricted potential of spiritual action, but it also offers an answer to "the world," letting unbelievers know that their "explanations" are simply not confirmed by community experience. If both believers *and* nonbelievers can feel the holy touch, then cause cannot be attributed to culture.

But cause *can* be attributed to supernatural agency. What else, ask the saints, could yield this instantaneous rush of joy? What else could induce an experience so intense that even the prophet Jeremiah was forced to describe it with metaphor, likening it to "a burning fire shut up in my bones" (Jeremiah 20:9)? And what else could grant such a certain knowledge that its source was divine? The answer, say the saints, has to lie beyond the mortal sphere. Even if one was not a believer before experiencing transcendence—indeed, even if one had no cultural frame within which to couch the experience, with neither suitable belief nor exposure to a Christian worldview—the answer would still be the same. For the experience would carry with it certain knowledge, and from that knowledge would spring belief. Hence the circle of faith is complete. Experience grants knowledge; knowledge informs belief; belief invites further experience. At the same time, experience confirms belief; belief provides a frame for knowledge; and knowledge explains experience. Such are the poetics of faith among sanctified believers.

* * * * *

"There are lots of folks—and educated ones, too—that say we believe in superstition," noted Rev. William Adams, a ninety-three-year-old Texas preacher, speaking in the late 1930s. "Well, it's because they don't understand. Remember [that] the Lord, in some of His ways, can be mysterious. The Bible says so. There are some things the Lord wants all folks to know, some things just the chosen few to know, and some things no one should know. Now, just because *you* don't know about some of the Lord's laws, it's not 'superstition' if some other person understands and believes in such."[5]

* * * * *

It's easy to dismiss that which you don't understand. And you won't understand, Rev. Adams asserts, until you've been granted the knowledge. Only then does one become a "steward of the mysteries of God" (1 Corinthians 4:1). This process of accessing the unknown, of gaining insight into what some saints call the "invisible manuscript," is intensely personal. Though the body of believers may offer guidance, the journey toward understanding must ultimately be realized alone. The silent conversations, the epiphanous encounters, the enacted dialogues of praise all occur between self and Spirit. Fellow saints observe, counsel, and encourage, but ultimately do not participate in this private encounter. Only the experiencing saint knows the fullness of the moment. And only by addressing this absolute subjectivity can ethnography begin to fathom the broader world of sanctified meaning. The entry point must be individual experience.

Ethnography has traditionally avoided encounter with the subjective realm of experience. Not just supernatural experience, but experience in general. Presuming singularity and idiosyncrasy in the workings of individual consciousness, ethnographers have instead focused their inquiries on the workings of culture. Here they explore expressions said to emerge from experience, probe the structures said to order it, and chart the mental pathways through which it is presumably constituted. Experience itself, however, remains but a reference point, a domain invoked but rarely addressed.

This ethnography takes a different approach. In what follows, experience serves as both point of entry and guide to understanding. Personal stories ground the discussion at every turn, while experiential testimony fuels the unfolding arguments. When this testimony steps toward the supernatural, I make no attempt to steer it back into boundaries undoubtedly more familiar to many of this book's readers. Nor do I circumscribe the reality this testimony charts, setting it apart as something "provisional," as if its truths applied only to believers. Instead, I treat this reality as wholly and unconditionally real. In so doing, I try to grant it the fullness it commands in saints' lives, and the fullness it *demands* if we are to understand those lives more fully.[6]

Chapter 3

Experiencing the Holy

"Just Like Fire Shut Up in My Bones"

"The first time I baptized here was a little before Christmas, in the creek which ran through my lot," writes Elder David George, an African American Baptist preacher, in the early 1790s. "I preached to a great number of people on the occasion, who behaved very well. I now formed the church with us six, and administered the Lord's supper in the Meeting-house before it was finished. They went on with the building, and we appointed a time every other week to hear experiences. . . . I preached at Birch Town from the fall till about the middle of December, and was frequently hearing experiences, and baptized about twenty there. Those who desired to hear the word of God, invited me from house to house, and so I preached."[1]

*　*　*　*　*

"The 'experiences' of the Negroes . . . are their own descriptions of their emotions when under the influence of religious truths and spiritual operations," writes Rev. Charles A. Raymond, a white minister, in 1863. "Sometimes these experiences are revealed in conversation, and form the subject of social gossip. But their more formal and imposing narration is reserved for what are termed 'Experience Meetings,' and which are usually held as preparatory to the Negro's 'joining the church' upon a public profession of religion. . . . I have heard hundreds, I suppose I might say thousands [of 'experiences'], in Louisiana, Mississippi, Alabama, Georgia, South Carolina, and Virginia, on the sea-board and in the mountains, and I have heard always and everywhere the same story. . . . The peculiar imagery of the light, the fire, and the loving feelings are almost inevitable."[2]

*　*　*　*　*

"One day I went behind the house and sat down to cry," testifies Sister Kelley, a Tennessee saint and centenarian, in the late 1920s. "Well, I got back there and went to sit down, and I tell you the gospel's truth, I can go and put my hand on the spot right now, where I just fell face foremost—something just struck me. 'Oooh Lord!' I cried. 'Have mercy on me, a poor hell-deserving sinner!' You heard me—I said I didn't know how to pray, but those words just came to me from nowhere. Child, I fell to crying, just like I was crazy! I felt right crazy too, praise God, but I wasn't. It was just the grace of God . . ."

"Well, I tell you child, when I got up from prayer, I felt like I was brand new. I had been washed in Jesus' blood, oh my great and holy Father! Sometimes I get to thinking about it and I get happy! Yessiree, child, if you want old sister Kelley to tell you about her religious experience, I sure can tell you that, because I've sure been through a great fight with the devil. Oooh, praise God!"[3]

* * * * *

Even as early as the 1790s, African American saints were articulating their faith in the language of experience. Indeed, following the example of their white evangelical counterparts, they had already stretched the definition of "experience" beyond its reference to the ongoingness of everyday encounter to embrace the experiential singularity of conversion and then to denote the *telling* of that experience. In the conversational world of the saints, one "experienced" life, had "the experience" of conversion, and told (rather than "told *of*") one's "experience" to the gathered faithful. Already the saints were setting aside special assemblies for public testimony, "experience meetings" where the focus was not preaching or singing, but "giving experiences." At these spirited gatherings, believers old and new testified to the wondrous workings of the Lord in bringing them from "the sea of doubt and jaws of hell" to the very "throne of grace."[4]

Most references to "experience meetings" suggest that their purpose was to provide a forum for newly converted believers to describe their conversion experience prior to their baptism and admission into the church. "I told my experience in April eleven years ago, and was baptized the third Sunday in May," recalled Georgia preacher Sol Lockheart at the turn of the twentieth century. "You have to tell your experience before you can join the church, tell what the Lord has done for you," added Georgia saint Fanny Roberts more than three decades later.[5] This public telling affirmed one's conversion, offering narrative proof of the believer's transformation. The evidence lay not so much in the simple claim of spiritual metamorphosis as in the particular detailing of the convert's experience. To demonstrate the passage from sinner to saint, one had to specify *how* the Lord had acted on one's life. For the saints, this meant describing not a process of considered thought and gradual choice, but an experience of soul-jarring intensity, a moment of knowledge and certainty, an encounter that so far transcended the mundane that it achieved the status of eminent tellability. Such encounter, wrought with drama and passion, begged to be told. And in that telling lay manifest proof of conversion. To truthfully "give one's experience," a convert first had to have had one.[6]

Many accounts of "experience meetings" frame the presenting of testimony as an act of giving, with saints telling of converts who "*give* their experience."[7] This combination of "give" and "experience" holds a telling double meaning, suggesting that what is being given is not only "experience" as story, but also "experience" as spiritual encounter. We've already encountered this phenomenon in the giving of personal testimony, where voiced talk initiates the silent conversation that invites the holy touch. This is precisely the process to which Sister Kelley refers in her abovementioned comments, when she says, "Sometimes I get to thinking about it and I get happy!" "Getting happy," in the parlance of the saints, means to feel the Spirit and to experience the infusion of holy joy that comes with the Spirit's touch. Sister Kelley, like Elder Richardson and the African-born Jack, tells of experience, thinks on that experience, and then experiences the experience anew, as the Spirit palpably joins the conversation.[8] But it is by no means only the *speaking* saint who invites this flash of ecstasy. The invitational key, remember, lies in *unvoiced* conversation. Listening saints hear and reflect and begin their own dialogues of praise. The heard words spark thought and meditation, prompting hearers to ponder the points of experiential resonance, to consider how the messages conveyed apply to their own lives and speak to their own souls. The hearer's spirit, one might say, momentarily connects with that of the speaker, drawing the two together in the recognition of shared experience. At the same time, both spirits reach out to *the* Spirit, seeking communion with the divine.

This circle of communion brings us back to the "giving" of "experience." Historical accounts that speak of "experiences" as testimonies often close by noting that the telling precipitated holy shouting—a mark of "getting happy"—among the gathered saints. "I told my experience and caused much shouting," recalls one elder saint. "The Baptists . . . all get together—all them old deacons—and they talk of their religious experience, and then they get to really feeling good," says another.[9] The testifying saint not only "gives" testimony, but also "gives" the meditative meat that fosters reflection and, potentially, experience. Hence, though believers would never say that a saint could actually "give" holy experience (this being solely the prerogative of the Spirit), the combination of terms suggests that the saint can "give" its potential. In the artful shorthand of the vernacular, this becomes "giving experience," with the play on double meaning subtly referencing the complexities of spiritual process.

The awesome experience of the holy clearly grounds reality for sanctified believers. In like manner, talk about this experience—whether conveyed through song, sermon, testimony, or simple conversation—grounds sanctified discourse. References to "feeling the Spirit," to "being born again," to "getting happy," to the "anointing," to the holy "touch," to "feeling the fire," to being "filled with the Spirit" suffuse all talk of faith, tacitly testifying to the lived centrality of holy encounter. At the same time, these references invite all talk to break the frame of the mundane, to burst the bounds of human utterance and transport the speaker to the very experiential realm being referenced.

Yet despite this dynamic of testimony and encounter, and despite the spoken centrality of experiential reference, detailed *descriptions* of actual subjective encounter are quite rare. This is not to say, of course, that vivid accounts of divine action are uncommon. Indeed, such accounts can be heard at every turn, in stories of conversion and healing and miraculous delivery. But these accounts are quite different from those that describe one's feelings *at the moment of encounter*. Testimonies and conversion accounts tend to chronicle the events leading *up to* and *away from* this moment; as narratives of action and sequence, these plotted accounts testify to the purposeful movement of God's will. In so doing, they artfully detail the subjective responses of the teller at almost every step of the story's unfolding. Even the most hardened of listeners can feel the grief, the despair, the triumph, the joy, the gratitude. The language is always direct and sensuous, drawing listeners into the union of narrative identity. But at the recounted moment of encounter, when spirit and Spirit meet, the words fall strangely silent. Instead of describing the sensations that surge through the body and flood the awestruck mind, tellers turn to metaphor and the verbal shorthand of tradition. The paramount experience thus remains undescribed.

When I began this inquiry, this descriptive void puzzled me. If the experience of anointment was so central, then why didn't its description play a more prominent role in narratives that were otherwise so filled with subjective detail? If holy encounter was so profoundly compelling, then why did saints limit its characterization to such stock phrases as "getting happy" and being "blessed by the Spirit"? Granted, some of these expressions—particularly the ubiquitous "getting happy"— do reference subjective states. But the term "happy" hardly captures the reported intensity of rapture. Where were the descriptions of *feeling*? What *was* the experience of the often-invoked "fire"?

In retrospect, my naïveté surprises me. In my quest for phenomenological understanding, I was asking for no less than a description of ecstasy. And that, my friends in the church patiently explained, entailed describing encounter with the divine. Which is impossible. Human language can no more capture the essence of holy experience than the mind can understand the mysteries of God. Again and again, I was told that the words simply don't exist. Hence all one can do is talk *around* the experience, struggling to convey meaning through metaphor and connotation.[10]

The obviousness of this explanation first became clear to me during a conversation with Rev. Samuel McCrary, a Missionary Baptist minister and longtime singing partner of Elder Richardson. When I pressed for a description of his feelings during anointment, Rev. McCrary seemed momentarily at a loss for words. After a few time-biding phrases, however, he regained his characteristic eloquence and explained that only a small part of the experience could actually be told. The rest— the mysterious essence of holy encounter—"is a thing between your soul and the Spirit of God." As he grappled with the issue of tellability, his words fell into the poetic cadences of preaching, flowing with the rhythms of conviction and faith:

You see, now we can say,
    "Well, I was converted [on] July the first,"
      and give the date,
      give the time when you was.
But you can't tell your *reaction* about it.
Some people will tell you what they heard somebody else say—
    "I was sitting in the amen corner,"
    or "was on the street,"
    or "in the cornfield,"
    or "in my house"
    or whatnot—
but they can just tell you a certain *portion* of it.
They can't tell you all of it.
Even when Jeremiah tried to describe it,
    he had to say,
      "The Word, the Spirit of God, is just like fire,"
      said, "shut up in your bones."[11]

Even the prophet Jeremiah, whose mouth had been "touched" by the hand of God, had to turn to metaphor when describing the anointing (Jeremiah 1:9). This part of the experience simply defies articulation. But everything else, as Rev. McCrary explained, can readily be told. The time, the date, the place, the situation—these details leap to the tongue, begging for expression. The rest remains untellable.

And, perhaps, without need of telling. For once saints have felt the holy touch, they *know* it. With this knowing comes the awareness that all other born-again believers have shared the experience. They too have felt the holy fire; they too know the reality of divine encounter. Why, then, struggle to describe that which is already so deeply known? Among the saints, descriptive glosses will suffice. These glosses admit the inadequacy of language while simultaneously referencing the singular encounter that draws believers into experiential communion.

As for those who have *not* felt the Spirit, close description—say the saints—would be meaningless, for these hearers have no experience in which to ground understanding. The words would not resonate with internal knowledge, and thus would not carry power. Consequently, when addressing the unsaved, the details *surrounding* encounter (rather than the experienced specifics *of* encounter) become centrally important, in that they establish an experiential common ground. By locating spiritual experience firmly in the nonbeliever's world, they affirm the commonality of hearer and teller, and thus invite belief. The rest, say the saints, will become known only when it is felt.

Three months after I posed the question about feeling to Rev. McCrary, I asked it again to another preacher, Rev. Carolyn Bryant. Reverends McCrary and Bryant both know well the Spirit's flow. And both have established reputations as gifted gospel singers. But while Rev. McCrary pastors a Missionary Baptist church in Nashville, Rev. Bryant pastors a Pentecostal fellowship—in the much smaller denomination, Bethel Church of Christ Written in Heaven—in Philadelphia. Further, Rev. McCrary hails from the generation of Rev. Bryant's parents. Nonetheless, their answers agreed in every detail. Indeed, when asked to describe the anointing, both stressed the difference between what one learns from hearing and what one knows from feeling.

"It's hard to talk about it or to tell somebody about it," explained Rev. Bryant, as she paused in the midst of preparing chicken suppers for a church benefit. This question seemed to demand a more measured response. Someone else's description, Rev. Bryant explained, can never impart understanding:

> It's just something that you have to feel.
> A lady sang a song one time,
>   and she said,
>   somebody told her about the joys that *they* had.
>   And somebody told her about the way that they *felt*.
>   But then the other part of the song said,
>   "I never knew what it was until it happened to me."
> So it's very hard to tell an individual—
>   you have to experience it.[12]

These words introduced a litany of metaphorical descriptions, as Rev. Bryant detailed how the anointing sometimes felt like a chill, sometimes like "electricity," sometimes like burning heat, sometimes like an ethereal weightlessness. But the descriptions always ended on the same note—"you have to experience the anointing to understand it."

I have since heard this sentiment expressed scores of times in scores of ways. "If you haven't ever had no experiences, you can't tell anybody anything," declares Evangelist Evelyn Gilchrist before a Pentecostal congregation in Durham, North Carolina. "You won't know, unless you actually know it yourself. But when you get that feeling, it's something that nobody can know except only you," adds veteran quartet lead and Baptist deacon Edward Denkins in Philadelphia. "You will never understand, until you've experienced it," agrees Baptist quartet singer Claude Landis from rural Creedmoor, North Carolina. "Now, if you was connected into this realm as a heir of our Lord and savior Jesus, you—you, sitting right there asking the question—Amen!—you would catch on fire too!" concludes Elder Lawrence Richardson, echoing the "you got to be *in it* to *feel it*" sentiments voiced in the opening chapter. "So by you being absent of what I'm talking about now," he continues, "I just can't expose it, [so] that you can get the insight of what I'm talking about. See, if you were part of the family—Amen—then you would *know*—Amen—what I'm talking about." All of these saints—separated by denomination and distance but joined in the fellowship of faith—stand in essential agreement. And all would concur with the prophetic words reportedly spoken by the Spirit to a Primitive Baptist elder early in the century: "Nobody can talk about the religion of God unless they've had a religious experience in it."[13]

The essential untellability of holy experience, combined with the experiential prerequisite of "membership" in the fellowship of saints (i.e., being "saved, sancti-fied, and filled with the Holy Ghost"), have led many to dismiss sanctified experi-ence as "emotionalism."[14] These observers interpret witnessed behavior entirely in terms of emotional release, arguing that the saints' felt experience is in fact a self-generated response to psychological and social pressures; as such, it becomes an artifact of emotion. Such analysis, as I've already suggested, treats testimony as emotional fantasy. In so doing, it not only ignores believer's claims, but also denies the saints' ability to differentiate between emotionally induced and supernaturally actuated experience.

If advocates of this interpretation were to question saints about this matter, they would probably be surprised at the number of believers who would agree with them. At least in part. The saints readily admit that many churchgoers mistake human emotion for holy ministration. This particularly holds true for those who have not yet been filled with the Holy Ghost. These worshipers are fooled by emotion, thinking that what they feel represents the fullness of grace. They have, in the words of one holiness evangelist, the Holy Ghost "on" them but not "in" them. But saints with the Spirit "in" them know the difference. They respond to cries of "emotionalism" by calmly noting that anointment brings a knowledge that clar-ifies all confusion. Its experienced depths reveal emotions as fleeting and inher-ently shallow, as sensations that even in their extremes can never equal the inten-sity of holy encounter. This is not to suggest, of course, that emotion doesn't accompany such encounter. Indeed, the saints say that the response to anointment is intrinsically and overwhelmingly emotional. But the emotion in this equation is *reaction* rather than *cause*. When the Spirit truly touches, emotion is the artifact of experience, rather than the other way around.

* * * * *

Friday evening marks the fifth and final night of spirited revival at Durham's Mount Calvary Holy Church. Attendance has grown steadily every evening, culmi-nating in tonight's packed church. More than two hundred believers jam the pews as the testimony service begins to roll. As saint after saint stands to offer their testi-monies, the organist—a master of keyboard subtlety—pushes their words with nu-anced improvisations and dramatic cadenzas. Most testimonies flow either from or into song, keeping the organist's deft fingers ever busy at the keys. The currents of talk and tune slow and surge, but never stop.

Again and again, the Spirit moves through the pews, traveling "from heart to heart and breast to breast," touching with a randomness that knows no mortal pattern. Some saints close their eyes and weep. Others whisper repeated refrains of "Thank you, Jesus!," their voices hushed in rapture. Still others leap from the pews in holy dance, their shoes beating out the ecstatic cadences of praise and mystery. For each saint caught by dance, the organist and drummer sound a chorus of driving rhythm. And the pews erupt with cries of encouragement and the jubilant cadences of the "holy clap." The Spirit is clearly high.

The praises stretch on for more than an hour. Every time the energy seems to wane, the presiding evangelist moves toward the pulpit. But then the Spirit strikes again, setting in motion another round of exaltation. Finally, Evangelist Deborah Yarborough—the daughter of the church's pastor—takes the microphone. Her winded voice sounds tired but exuberant, still showing the effects of a holy dance that carried her across the cross-aisle. As she begins, speaking in a quiet, conversational tone, the muffled sounds of congregational praise continue unabated. Almost immediately, however, the saints join the dialogue, punctuating the evangelist's every phrase with calls of affirmation.

The Holy Ghost has been here this evening!	(Yes!)
And more than that, the Holy Ghost is here even now.	(Yes!/Amen!)
And I tell you, if I were you,	
if I were you,	(Yes!)
and didn't have the Holy Ghost,	(Come on!)
I wouldn't let this revival close.	(Yes!/Amen!)
Because it's too free in here!	(Yes!)
Huh?	(That's right!)

The question marks a shift in both tone and response, as Evangelist Yarborough's voice grows more crisp and assertive. All signs of windedness disappear, giving way to an easy flow of word and image. Meanwhile, a lone saint starts clapping her approval. From this point forward, brief bursts of congregational clapping accent the evangelist's words.

It's moving around too good in here,	(Alright!/Yes!)
for you to go home without it.	(Amen!)
Amen, I wouldn't leave without it.	(Yes!)
I would not leave without it, if I didn't have it.	(Yes!)
Amen, and then if I had it, I'd say, "Lord,	(Lord!)
give me a double portion!	(Hallelujah!)
Give me some more of that Spirit,	(Yes Lord!)
that I may stand."	(Yes!)
'Cause I'm telling you—ain't no way in the world	
you all can have this kind of church,	(Alright!)
this good,	(Go on!)
and the devil leave you alone!	(Amen!/Tell it!)
Ain't no kind of way at all.	(Amen!)
Tomorrow morning, tonight, midnight, when-	
ever you walk out this door, all hell's going to	
break loose.	(That's right!)
And we going to find how much you got.	(Amen!)

Amen, 'cause we going to find out if you got it *in*	
you, or if you got it *on* you.	(Alright!/Amen!)
'Cause if it's *on* you, the devil will come and he'll	
knock it off of you!	(Yes!/Amen!)
And it won't be with you long.	(Whoo!)
But if it's *in* you,	(Yes!/My Lord!)
he's going to have a hard time!	(Yes!)
Huh?	(Yes!/My Lord!)
'Cause, number one, he ain't going in there after it!	(Alright!)
Because he's scared of what he might run into.	(Amen!)
If he don't do nothing but run into the Word	
where it says "Greater	(Greater!)
is He	(Is He!)
that was in me,	(That was in me!)
than he	(Than he!/Yes!)
that is in the World!"	(Yes!/Glory!)
Amen, so if I were you, I'd have it *in* me.	(Glory, glory!)
I tell you, we done had some dancing in this	
place.	(Yes!/Amen!)
But, honey, a good dance won't last long.	(No it won't!)
Amen, you can't go on a dance.	(Amen!/That's right!)
I wouldn't leave this revival with just a dance.	(Praise God!)
'Cause there's too much more in here besides a	
dance.	(You're right!)
Amen?	(Amen!)
Amen?	(Amen!)
Amen?	(Amen!)
Amen!	(Amen!)[15]

After that final, triumphant "Amen!" Evangelist Yarborough shifts her voice to the everyday tones of conversation. She mentions how good she feels, jokes about those who have to work the next morning, and announces the itinerary of the revival's featured speaker. The congregation's comments lose their focused enthusiasm, growing quieter and more restrained. Then Evangelist Yarborough calls for a selection from the choir. The pause in praise is clearly momentary. The cycle will soon start anew.

*　*　*　*　*

Evangelist Yarborough contrasts having the Holy Ghost "on you" with having Him "in you." "On you" suggests that the believer is deceived by emotion, that the feelings of fervor and passion are generated by self. This is not to imply that such feelings are in any way not "real"; the very fact that they can lead believers to shout or rise in holy dance suggests just the opposite. No, say the saints, these emotions are quite real. But they are not what many believers believe them to be. These are feelings stirred by *spirit* rather than *Spirit*; they are human responses to humanly perceived situations. As such, they are more like the emotions felt when cheering for one's favorite ball team (to use an analogy often employed by the saints) than those felt when touched by transcendence. Such feelings, say the saints, certainly have a place in church. They fuel the enthusiasm, spark the singing, enliven the praise. But they don't make a believer a saint. As one preacher is said to have declared more than a century ago, "Even a monkey can have emotional religion!"[16] Though emotion plays an important role in worship, it alone does nothing for one's soul.

When differentiating between fervent enthusiasm and the ministrations of the Spirit, saints often point out that human emotions are transient and temporary. Evangelist Yarborough, for example, declares that they "won't be with you long." Generated by self, such feelings are said to have no foundation in the soul. Instead, they are layers of affect, forming an emotive covering that rests "on" the self. The thinness of this overlay—when not fused to the soul by the fires of grace—invites the devil to "knock it off," to steal the joy and still the passion. Saints say that the devil will always try to strike when emotions are high and praise is fervent. "Ain't no way in the world you all can have this kind of church," asserts Evangelist Yarborough, "and the devil leave you alone!" Assault by Satan is taken as a given, as one of the experienced realities of holy life. Against such attack, emotions alone offer little protection.

Evangelist Yarborough makes another reference to the shallowness of emotion when she remarks that "a good dance won't last long," and then that "you can't go on a dance." The first comment, when set in the context of her earlier remarks on the transience of emotion and her subsequent statement that there's "too much more in here besides a dance," suggests that the dancing to which she refers is dancing *in self*. Such dancing springs from emotional enthusiasm rather than spiritual actuation; it is a product of will, a joyous display of praise fueled by emotion and triggered by decision. Some may think—Evangelist Yarborough implies— that such praise will guarantee entry into heaven. Not so, she declares; "you can't go on a dance." Emotional display—no matter how deeply felt—is no substitute for saving grace. The night before, the revival preacher had made the same point. "A lot of us want to go sweeping into heaven on a shout," he had preached. "But you got to get in the Word and get something of God."[17] Emotion and its behavioral signs (shouting, dancing, and so on) are simply not enough. Saints must "get something of God"; they must receive from outside of selves, must feel the power of transcendence. And they must *know* the difference between that which their own minds create and that which comes from on high. *Not* knowing invites self-deception and unsuspecting reliance on self. And this, say the saints, will never get one to heaven.

The complex relationship between experiences born of emotion and those caused by the Spirit has long been a topic of discussion among the saints. Over the years, I have heard this relationship discussed in many ways, the sheer variety of which suggests a range of concurrent interpretations. While usually agreeing on matters of process, the framing of these explanations vary widely. One of the clearest of these framings, one elegant in its simplicity, was first articulated to me by Rev. Zebedee D. Harris, pastor of Durham's Oak Grove U. A. Free Will Baptist Church. Human selfhood, he explained, is comprised of three parts—the spiritual, the mental, and the physical. The mental is the faculties of the mind; the physical is the flesh; and the spiritual is "the God part in all of us," the part that comes alive when the believer is born again. For the body to act, two of these parts must work together. That union will always overrule the powers of the third.

"In the church," Rev. Harris explained, "you often have the mental part and the physical part responding to some messages. [The listeners] are not saved. But they'll come out and tell you they enjoyed it. . . . There's something that hit them in their life. But they have not yet accepted Christ. Because they move out and forget about all what they heard."[18] These unsaved hearers feel the resonance of told experience with their own; they recognize and respond, with the mental spurring the physical into feeling and action. The flesh seeks, and finds, satisfaction in physical response. But the feeling emerges from emotion and flesh rather than spirit. And hence will last for only a moment. The hearers—those who responded so fervently in church—will soon forget.

But when the believer's spirit is saved, the entire process is transformed. For spirit seeks to please God rather than flesh. Now the spirit and the mind work together, forcing the flesh to submit to the ministrations of the Holy Spirit. The physical part, no longer in control, can now only respond; its animation—expressed in tears, in shouting, in holy dance, in tongues—comes from without rather than within. The believer's experience, in other words, comes from God rather than self.

Once again, we face the clear distinction between human and holy cause and between emotional and spiritual response. I have devoted so much space to discussing this relationship for two reasons. First, because it demonstrates that the saints themselves are acutely aware of the dangers of misinterpreting their experiences and consequently deceiving themselves about their source and significance. The saints do not, as many have suggested, uncritically interpret experience through the lens of faith. If anything, their faith makes their interpretation *more* critical, for it warns them of the power of emotions and provides tools for distinguishing between experience occasioned from within and from without. The second reason for this focus is that these issues are centrally important to understanding the gospel experience. As we shall soon discover, questions of emotion, assessment, and holy encounter lie at the very heart of gospel performance and interpretation.

Chapter 4

A Conversation

"You've Got to Open the Door"

Before turning to the gospel program, we must quickly reground our discussion in the broader poetics of faith. Earlier I suggested that the language of experience serves as the primary medium for articulating belief. Every time saints say that they "wouldn't have a religion that they couldn't feel sometimes," they reaffirm this primacy. But this *voiced* emphasis on experience in no way suggests that faith hinges on feeling. As saints are quick to point out, feeling is not always there. Transcendence touches according to the will of the Spirit rather than the choice of believers. When the touch isn't felt, belief remains. And sustains. Just as belief usually precedes the first experience of transcendence, so does it continue to inform understanding and frame reality when that experience lives only in memory and expectation.

* * * * *

In presenting saints' thoughts about belief and experience, I should first say a word about saints' talk. When discussing faith, many saints speak with a structured eloquence that sets their words quite apart from the flow of everyday exchange. Slowly, in the course of conversation, their remarks take on an increasingly poetic character, their words arranging themselves in artful phrases punctuated by dramatic pauses. These phrases, in turn, come together in passages that flow with rhetorical repetitions and poetic parallels. And these passages often take a subtle step toward melody, riding patterns of rising and falling tone that lend the talk a gentle, rolling lilt. To some, this may sound like a description of elegant preaching. It should, for the patterns of structure and sound are quite similar. But this talk is *not* preaching; nor are its purveyors all preachers. Instead, this is the talk of everyday saints, who ease into eloquence when engaging the topic of faith. The key to such talk's emergence, say the saints, is simple engagement. As one saint puts it, "The more you *get into* talking about the Word, the more the words just flow."

I attempt to convey a measure of this "flow" by transcribing my consultants' words in lines rather than block paragraphs. In so doing, I hope to entice the eye much as these words enticed the ear, thus encouraging readers to join in the talk's imaginative reconstruction. The speaker's pauses craft the lines. Parallel structures and shifting tones, in turn, shape the indentation. And the very presence of lines suggests the flow. When talk tumbles forth in a less marked manner, following the familiar cadences of conversation, I let the natural pauses of thought and emphasis decide the edges of sentence and paragraph.[1]

✶　✶　✶　✶　✶

I had been attending Bishop Frizelle Yelverton's church for many months before asking him if we could talk about some of the issues that confused me. The bishop is known throughout the Carolinas as a man gifted with deep spiritual insight. As the longtime pastor of Durham's Mount Calvary Holy Church, he has nurtured the growth of many preachers from his congregation, perhaps the most notable of whom is holiness pastor and celebrated "Queen of Gospel" Shirley Caesar. On the Sunday before our conversation, in the midst of a Spirit-filled, three-hour service, Bishop Yelverton had called me to stand before the congregation and declare the state of my soul. Though I had often spoken at services and had freely joined in the singing and praising, this focused call unnerved me. At that point, I had only witnessed the movement of the Spirit; I was one of those whom saints described as "knowing *of* the Lord" but not yet "*knowing* Him." Caught in the bishop's penetrating gaze, I fumbled for words, all the while realizing that a long journey still lay ahead.

Three days later, with my faltering remarks still echoing in my mind, I sat myself across from the bishop on his living-room couch. In our first hour of conversation, I asked most of the questions. We talked about the Spirit's role in preaching, about the different degrees of anointing, about growth in the Spirit. Then the bishop began questioning me, asking about my writing and my commitment to God. The anxiousness and uncertainty that I felt in church swept over me anew. I'll admit that I dodged a bit, all the while wondering if my active participation in services had in fact been an act of misrepresentation. Then I explained that I believed I was being called to some end, but as yet did not yet understand its nature.

Looking back, I now realize that I was searching for ordered, "rational" explanations for both the workings of the Spirit and my own feelings. I was seeking pattern and coherency, wanting to understand belief as *system* rather than as *mystery*. Bishop Yelverton recognized this immediately. Turning to me with a calm smile, he said slowly, "You don't '*understand*' God. *I* don't understand Him. But I *believe* His Word."

At this, the bishop paused, letting the words penetrate. Then he repeated the closing line: "I believe what He said. As I said a few moments ago, He says to you or I, 'Whosoever will, let him come.' "

"You come."

I wasn't sure from the bishop's voice whether the final words were part of the quotation or a separate invitation. Or both. He paused; I remained silent. When he spoke again, he talked about experience, the topic I had so eagerly pursued earlier in our conversation.

"And it's not altogether through feeling. It's through believing. It's through believing."

The final phrase was only slightly louder than a whisper. I moved forward a few inches, not wanting to miss the words. Then another pause.

"Believe in it, and then there's a time that the feeling will come. And there's a time that you won't feel nothing."

I must have looked confused at these final words, for Bishop Yelverton started to laugh. A gentle, rolling laugh. Now I *was* confused. A time without feeling? "That's right," he said, answering my question before I could voice it. And he laughed some more.

"Now, I don't understand that," I responded. I couldn't even understand why he was *laughing*. I didn't yet realize that the bishop had just flipped all of my questions about feeling into perspective. And then had given that perspective a little shake.

"You don't understand that?" Bishop Yelverton asked, the chuckle still in his voice. "Okay. There's a time that—uh . . ." He paused for a moment, and then went on.

> See, the Lord said,
>   "My Spirit shall not always strive with man."
> There's a time that you won't *feel* nothing,
>   but you yet *believe*.
> That's right.
> See, you don't get it on feeling;
>   you get it on belief.

Once again the bishop paused. As his voice gained strength, his words began to flow with the patterned eloquence so familiar from his sermons.

> He that cometh to God *must* believe
>   that He is a rewarder of them that diligently seek Him.
> Not diligently *feel* him.
> But diligently *seek* him.
> If you come,
>   you must believe.
> Belief is *all* of it.
> You got to accept Jesus Christ, or the Lord, by faith.
> That's believing.
> I didn't see Him crucified,
>   but I believe it.

I didn't see Him when He rose from the grave,
   but the Word tells me and I believe that He rose.
I didn't see Him when He ascended back to heaven on a cloud,
   but I believe He did.
And I believe He's sitting on the right-hand side of the Father.
And He's making intercession for you and I right now.
In other words, He's talking to God about me and you.

There it was, in a nutshell. Saints may *talk* a lot about feeling—they may freely testify to their experiences in "the world," they may tell and retell stories of conversion and miraculous intercession, they may even judge songs and sermons and entire services wholly in terms of how they made them *feel*—but this is all a kind of secondary discourse, a talk that rides on the taken-for-grantedness of belief. Belief is the ever-present given, the final foundation of faith, the encompassing frame for the understandings drawn from experience and revelation. You don't get saved, as Bishop Yelverton eloquently establishes, by feeling. You get saved by believing. And then, as the bishop adds, "the feeling will come."

As I was thinking on these words, the bishop continued speaking. Now his voice had grown quieter and more intimate. It was almost as if his words were following the traditional frame of a sermon, beginning with scripture, moving through exposition, and closing with an invitation. And indeed they were. After establishing the primacy of belief, Bishop Yelverton extended an invitation to experience that primacy firsthand.

There's a song we sing,
   "Somebody's Knocking at my Door."
The Word go forward—
   "He's knocking at the door."
And He said, "Whosoever will,
   whosoever open up the door,
      I will come in.
   And my father and I will sup with him."
It's left all in your hands.
You've got to open the door,
   the door of your heart,
      and invite Him in.
Come, Lord Jesus, take all of me.
Take complete control of me.
And He'll come in.
And He'll stay there.[2]

Open the door, and He'll come in. Open the door, and He'll take control. And when He takes control, say the saints, you will *know* and you will *feel*.

At every gospel program, the call for the Lord to take control goes forth in just this manner. Again and again, performers and saints in the pews ask the Spirit to "take control," to "have Your way," to "turn this service toward Your ends." How the saints actually effect this invitation—how they stir the fires of faith, achieve the accord of communion, and open the conversations of praise—will become evident only when we join the spirited worship at a gospel program.

Chapter 5

Beginnings

"Happy to Be in the House of Worship"

The Long Branch Disciple Church buzzes with anticipation as the saints prepare for the second part of the Branchettes' twentieth singing anniversary. The night before, more than two hundred had jammed the pews in this small country church to pay tribute to the honorees. The sanctuary had rung with voices of praise, despite predictions that the evening promised the worst blizzard in years. Local radio announcers had anxiously reported more than a foot of snow blanketing nearby North Carolina counties and had solemnly cautioned travelers to stay off the roads. The stilled darkness of the nearby town of Meadow gave immediacy to these warnings, bearing witness to downed power lines and scolding winds. Yet the saints had still come, confident that the Lord would protect those who went about His business. And protect them He did, for the storm had passed the church by, only dusting its grounds with a gentle whiteness. Now the saints were back, and the sun shone gloriously in the Sunday afternoon sky.

Car after car pulls onto the hardened sand of the church's ample lot, each filled with saints dressed in their Sunday finest. As newcomers jockey for positions nearest the white block church, those who have already parked are busily unloading. Open trunks reveal a bounty of bulky amplifiers, guitar and bass cases, covered cakes and cooking pans, and carefully folded choir robes shimmering through protective plastic. Small groups of saints bustle around the trunks and open car doors, preparing for the service and catching up on the news. Near the church, a young mother struggles to adjust the tie on her nattily dressed toddler while instructing her daughters to smooth out their bright crimson gowns. Across the lot an elderly deacon shouts greetings to a friend he hasn't seen since the last anniversary. A muffled cascade of laughter sounds from a small band of teenagers, as one jokingly reenacts the shout step danced by their choir director in the morning service. A few cars down, middle-aged members of a male chorus huddle to review their set, at one point breaking into harmony as they practice a passage that gave them trouble at last week's rehearsal. As I pull boxes of recording tape from my own car, an elegantly dressed church "mother" graciously welcomes me back to the anniversary. A spirit of friendly informality reigns across the lot.

2. On the second weekend of every March, the Branchettes celebrate their singing anniversary at the Long Branch Disciple Church, where they first met more than three decades ago. The church lies in rural Johnston County, at the western edge of North Carolina's coastal plain, between the towns of Meadow and Newton Grove. (Photo by Roland L. Freeman)

Much the same holds true inside the church. The golden-carpeted sanctuary hums with conversation and laughter, as programgoers gaily greet old friends and meet new ones. Family groups of three and four slowly make their way down the center aisle, their progress interrupted time and again by hugs and handshakes. A small circle of men position themselves in the vestibule, sending wives and children ahead while they pause to swap gossip and trade quips about the previous night's basketball game. At regular intervals, they move aside to allow musicians lugging heavy amplifiers to pass. Sunlight streaming in through stained glass panes bathes the sanctuary in a glow of warm amber. At the church-front, hanging on the wall over the choir loft, a computer-printed banner welcomes the saints with the words, "The Branchettes 20th Singing Anniversary."

In the cross-aisle between the pulpit and pews, two young men in powder-blue jackets and charcoal pants search for a free outlet for their amps, stepping past the high bouquets flanking the rostrum and around the silver drum kit in the aisle to its left. Another similarly dressed fellow—clearly a member of the same quartet—starts testing the four microphones resting on chrome stands below the pulpit. "Check, check, check one, check one, check," he intones monotonously, contributing a droning bass line to the church's ambient hum. Meanwhile, a young man sitting in the front left pew fingers gentle runs on the neck of his sparkling black guitar. And another amplifier clicks on, adding one more layer to the sizzling undertone of electronic hiss.

Across from the drum kit, in the right-side "amen corner," Ethel Elliott and Lena Mae Perry—the Branchettes—sit behind a wobbly card table covered with envelopes, two chrome offering plates, a spiral pad, and many small slips of paper. Stepping up to the table, a tall sister in a flowing pink gown hands Sister Elliott an envelope containing her choir's "donation" for the honorees, a cash offering recognizing the Branchettes' twenty years of service.[1] While so doing, she "registers" her choir and finds out what place they'll fill—determined on a "first come, first sing" basis—in the afternoon's program. Meanwhile, the singer's young daughter, immaculately outfitted in a matching pink gown, turns from the table to gaze at the welter of cables and tapes surrounding my recorder in the adjacent front pew. Her older brother—no more than five—has already picked up one of my unconnected microphones and is miming the performative stylings of a "hard" quartet lead, drawing the mike close to his mouth and pointedly jabbing his forefinger into the air. His mother, catching sight of these antics, casts him a stern glance. Without a word spoken, the microphone returns to the pew.

The pews behind me, meanwhile, are quickly filling up. Most of those already seated are women, virtually all of whom are clad in elegant dresses or flowing robes. The vivid hues—given passing pattern by clusters of like-garbed choir members sitting side by side—create a colorful patchwork whose form is punctuated by ribboned hats and the bright beads and bows in young girls' hair. The men's contribution to this colorful exuberance, in contrast, is decidedly subdued. Most are wearing conservatively tailored dark suits, with only the quartet members' outfits standing apart in their stylishness and sartorial symmetry. A number of men boast coats without ties; a few have no jackets at all. Only the young men sport brightly hued shirts; all others wear muted pastels and whites.

Talk in the pews is much like that outside, though markedly less boisterous. Saints' necks crane over children and pew-backs to catch the latest news or comment on the week's goings-on. Many are talking about last night's weather, sparking story after story about highway mishaps and folks caught without power. Each overheard tale seems to include voiced thanksgivings for the teller's safety. While parents talk, young children wriggle in their seats, furtively awaiting the averted eye that will free them to slip under the pew and away to excitement. Babies' cries pierce the conversational hum, while babies themselves pass from pew to pew and mother to admiring mother. In the midst of the greetings, giggles, and gossip, a few heads bow in silent prayer.

As more folks find their seats, movement to and from a door at the left of the choir loft seems to increase. Every time the door swings open, the rich aromas of baked ham and recently fried chicken float into the sanctuary. Behind the door are the fellowship hall and kitchen, where church members are preparing and setting out meats, salads, cakes, pies, and drinks brought by the Branchettes and their friends. As I discovered last night, the food is available throughout the program, free of charge. Given that many of this afternoon's singers set out for the anniversary immediately after morning services, and in some cases drove for more than an hour, the fare is certainly welcome. As its smells enter the church, they mingle with the subtle scents of perfume and cologne, lending the whole an air of earthy sweetness.

As 2:30 draws nearer, the bustling activity in the cross-aisle begins to settle down. Five boxy black amplifiers are now plugged in and ready to roar; three unsnapped guitar cases are resting under the pew besides the drums; and an electric keyboard sits atop a spare aluminum frame near the left-side "deacon's corner." A girl who couldn't be more than fourteen has taken a commanding position behind the drums, while a man who looks to be in his early twenties has strapped on a bass and joined the guitarist in the front pew. The steady flow of singers to the amen-corner table seems to have stopped, though friends of the Branchettes are still coming up to wish them well. Sauntering down the increasingly clear center aisle and smiling greetings to all who catch her eye, one of Sister Elliott's nieces hands out programs to those who didn't receive one at the door. This simple folded sheet identifies only the devotional leaders, the mistress of ceremonies, and the basic order. Neither the names nor numbers of guest groups are listed.

The air is festive, celebratory, and tinged with an edge of excitement. Less than ninety minutes earlier, many of these same saints had been praising the Lord in churches scattered across a sixty-mile radius. The Spirit had undoubtedly been high in many of those services, and folks are looking forward to His presence anew. Indeed, judging from the comments I overhear around me, many are still feeling the euphoric fulfillment of the morning's anointing. To use a phrase often heard among the saints, they "have their shouting shoes on" and are ready to reengage the communal conversation of praise.

Sister Ethel Elliott, the elder of the two Branchettes at a youthful sixty-four, stands at her place in the amen corner to open the program. "It's time," she says in a warm, conversational tone, "for us to begin our devotional service." Though her unamplified words are barely audible over the buzz of conversation, her commanding presence draws the saints' attention. Someone sitting near me whispers to no one in particular, "Shhh!"

"And after devotional service is over," Sister Elliott continues, "we'll go right on into the program." The guitars are still voicing abbreviated arpeggios, seemingly oblivious to Sister Elliott's words. And the voices in the pews, though hushing a bit, are slow to give way. Each talking saint seems intent on squeezing out a few final words. But Sister Elliott proceeds undaunted. "We're going to ask our mothers to come around and open up for us—Mother Lofton and Mother Nixon." With these words, the singer turns and sits back in the pew. The conversations and the guitarists' melodic wanderings continue, filling in the momentary pause.

But they soften a bit when Mother Eunice Nixon, one of the church's respected elders, rises to her feet. From a position near the Branchettes in the amen corner, she steps toward the center aisle. On the way, someone hands her a microphone, granting her voice an amplified dominance that Sister Elliott's lacked. Pausing in the cross-aisle, she scans the talking crowd and says slowly, "Good afternoon." The subsequent pause, as the congregation well knows, invites a response, drawing the saints into the opening act of collective dialogue. "Good afternoon," they answer, their voices a bit hesitant, as if they would like a moment more to conclude their conversations. But Mother Nixon presses her advantage, quickly taking her turn in the exchange.

"We're so happy to be back in the house of worship one more time, just to help the Branchettes celebrate another anniversary." Mother Nixon's conversational tone stylistically echoes the casual talk in the pews. Opening with the collective "we," she calls for—but does not command—the saints' attention.

"It's so good to be together for twenty years—you know, that's a *long* time." This second sentence draws the congregation's first "Amen." Dozens of heads nod in agreement. "And they said last night, they'd never had a cross word." ("Lord Jesus," says a woman sitting in the front pew.) "Now that's wonderful." ("Amen!" say a chorus of voices.) "That is *wonderful!*" ("Amen!" they say again.)

The side conversations cease as the congregation turns its attention to Mother Nixon. With a few short sentences, she has begun to move the saints from the singularity of personal concern to the communal accord of worship. Her talk begins as talk among peers, as the back-and-forth of everyday exchange. Then, without warning, it bursts into song. As the "Amens" fade, Mother Nixon launches into the old "Dr. Watts" favorite, "At the Cross."

> At last and did my savior bleed,
>   And did my sovereign die.
> Would He devote that sacred head
>   For such a worm as I?[2]

3. The anniversary opens on a quiet note, with unamplified words from Sister Ethel Elliott, one of the Branchettes. "It's time for us to begin our devotional service," she remarks. "And after devotional service is over, we'll go right on into the program." Conversations in the pews slowly draw to a close, as the saints prepare for praise. (Photo by Roland L. Freeman)

Forgoing the standard introduction, Mother Nixon presses directly into song, catching the congregation—and the musicians—a bit off guard. By the end of the second measure, hands are beginning to clap and voices are joining in. By the second line, the entire church is singing, with almost every programgoer joining in a piece that all recognize as "one of those old, soul-stirring hymn songs." At the beginning of the third line, the keyboard player starts chording the melody; two measures later, the electric bass adds its resonant contribution. The guitarist, who has been struggling to find the chords, joins the praises midway through the verse's final line. With his entry, the keyboardist switches from simple chording to rhythmic ornamentation, pushing the singing with finely articulated melodic flourishes. By the chorus, the praises are rising with spirited zeal. Hearty claps sound on every second and fourth beat, while the vibrant patting of feet punctuates every first and third. Throughout the church, saints begin to sway gently from side to side.

> O, at the cross, at the cross,
>> Where I first saw the light,
>>> And the burdens of my heart rolled away,
>> It was there by faith
>>> I received my sight,
>>>> And now I am happy all the day!

Devotional spirit builds as the saints swing into the chorus. The lyric's portrayal of conversion—with its familiar reference to a celestial light and feelings of joyous unencumbrance—strikes deeply for all who have joined the ranks of the saved. Many saints sing these words not as metaphor, but as description of lived experience. By the time they sound the chorus's final line, the singing rings with joy and jubilation. They are "happy all the day"—sing the saints—already anticipating the greater "happiness" of the holy touch.

The celestial conversations have clearly begun. And the saints have taken the first steps toward congregational accord.[3]

∗ ∗ ∗ ∗ ∗

From the moment the saints step into a gospel program, they enter church. But the "church" into which they step is more than a mere structure. Indeed, the structure itself has little bearing on the event. The program could take place in a school auditorium, a lodge hall, a civic center, an armory, a stadium. The place is of little consequence. What matters to the saints, and what defines place as "church," is the enactment of faith. Believers come not for escape or entertainment, but for worship, for joining together in prayer and praise. This shared purpose consecrates place and transforms both it and the event into "church." Hence saints talk not only about "going to church," but also about "having church," where what is "had" is deeply shared devotions and soul-stirring praise. When the Spirit moves in the midst of such praise, saints say they've "had *good* church." And "good church" is the goal of every service, be it morning worship, evening prayer meeting, or the afternoon anniversary at Long Branch Disciple Church.

"Church" is never a given in a worship service. Rather, it's something that must be achieved, a state reached through individual worship and shared focus. To "have" church, the saints must collectively seek it, and the Spirit must join the service to bring it about. "Having church" thus becomes an act of collaboration, where sincere seeking invites divine intercession and yields—if the Spirit so wills—

4. "O, at the cross, at the cross, where I first saw the light, and the burdens of my heart rolled away . . ." Mother Eunice Nixon opens devotions with an old Dr. Watts favorite, starting the hymn slowly and then quickly pushing it to a joyously up-tempo pace. (Photo by Roland L. Freeman)

holy experience. Though this process is ultimately collaborative, it begins with the saints. The seeking, the praises, the shared focus must come first; they lay the foundation for "good church." This awareness frames believers' decisions to attend services and travels with them as they step into the arena of worship. With it comes the expectation that others both know how to achieve "church" and sincerely desire to effect this end.

At the heart of these understandings lays the conviction that the Holy Spirit will move among those who earnestly engage in worship. The saints ground this conviction in Christ's promise to the disciples: "For where two or three are gathered together in my name, there am I in the midst of them" (Matthew 18:20). All services constitute such a gathering, and all thus assure the presence of the Spirit. This is not to say, however, that they insure the Spirit's movement, for spiritual *presence* does not necessarily indicate spiritual *activity*. The responsibility for inviting such activity, as suggested earlier, rests with the saints. They must worship with spirit and sincerity to set the process of "having church" into motion.

The final measure of the Spirit's movement, and thus of the quality of "church" on any given occasion, rests in the realm of experience. Believers say that behavior alone offers no guide for gauging transcendent activity, for the Spirit often manifests Himself in ways not evident to the mortal eye. Hence, one cannot assess divine involvement by the mere presence or absence of dramatic conduct like shouting or speaking in tongues. The Spirit knows no such limits; He need not show Himself in order to act. And His actions take many forms. To some He might grant insight and revelation; to others He might bring relief from the burdens of worldly worry. Neither act need ever be known by any other than the experiencing saint. To some the Spirit might grant a fleeting (and manifestly hidden) moment of ecstasy; to others He might grant only a certain awareness of His presence. All of these endowments are manifestations of the Spirit and all hinge on what is felt rather than what is seen. The full range of such private experiences, along with those that find more dramatic expression, bear witness to both the *presence* and the *movement* of the Spirit. This activity, in turn, stands as the central feature that draws worship services together under the rubric of "church." Personal encounter with the divine thus becomes the experiential leitmotif of these events, linking saints in a communion based on experiences shared only through the joint recognition of their intense individuality.

The fact of spiritual experience empowers the term "church" with a kind of predicative force, transforming it from a designation of place and event to one of events "had." The verb suggests a sense of possession and encounter, of partaking and embracing. One "has church" much as one "has an experience." The combination subtly draws the teller, the person who "has," into the construction, referencing a degree of personal engagement. Given this allusion, it should come as no surprise that saints often balance the phrase "having church" with its more explicit analogue, "having a good time in the Lord." Again and again, one hears devotional leaders linking the two expressions in direct apposition, suggesting a relationship of equivalence. The significance of this relationship becomes immediately clear. The phrase "having a good time in the Lord," frequently abbreviated to the simpler "having a good time," situates experience firmly "in the Lord," suggesting both the shared joys of worship and the personal rapture of "getting happy." If to "have church" is to "have a good time," then to "have church" is also to feel the Spirit moving.

To have the "good time in the Lord," to invite the workings of the Spirit, the saints must first join in collective praise. This is the single most important purpose of the "devotional service," the worship segment that opens most services in the sanctified church. Whether Sunday morning worship, gospel program, revival, or funeral, most services begin by drawing the full congregation together in praise, prayer, and song. This collective worship in the "devotions" sets the frame for the more focused proceedings that follow. At meetings that feature preaching (e.g., Sunday morning services and revivals), the devotional service traditionally leads into a worship sequence that begins with choir singing, swings into the sermon, and culminates in the altar call. At prayer meetings, devotions usually preface the "prayer service," when congregation members join around the altar for invocation and entreaty. And at gospel programs, devotions pave the way for the featured singing, when gifted saints fuel the already kindled devotional fires with spirited praise.[4]

When Sister Elliott stood to introduce Mother Nixon, she set the afternoon's "devotional service" into motion. Her program-opening words marked the beginning of congregational engagement, giving focus to the sundry conversations that buzzed through the church. A few sentences later, this emergent engagement became evident with the sounding of the congregation's first "Amen." Conversation with the cross-aisle was beginning to displace that across the pews. Thoughts began to turn away from "the world" and toward transcendence. And as minds and voices came together, first in a moment of dialogue and then in song, the fires of holiness began to stir. The ardent "Amens," the enthusiastic clapping, the impassioned singing all bore witness to the growing spirit of collectivity.

A song marks only the beginning of devotions. By drawing voices together in an outpouring of praise, it audibly affirms an emergent sense of congregational unity. But that unity rarely coalesces with a single act of worship. The fires are stirring but have yet to burst into flame. And so devotions continue, following praise first with the lessons of the Word, and then with prayer. At the Branchettes' anniversary, as we shall see, song led to scripture, scripture to prayer, and prayer back to song, describing an ascendant spiral of passion and praise. At the close of the second song, Sister Perry stood to welcome all who had joined the service. The welcome explicitly invited a response, leading a sister in the pews to step forth and extend thanks on behalf of the entire congregation. Sister Perry then returned to the cross-aisle to introduce the afternoon's mistress of ceremonies. This act formally closed the devotional service, ushering in the anniversary's second—and much longer—segment.

The format of devotions varies from service to service, depending on the event's function and the hosting denomination. Whatever the form, prayer and congregational song stand as constants. Both acts draw churchgoers into collective action—the first through congregational response, the second through joint creation. And both spur the silent conversations of faith—the first through example, the second through actual articulation.[5]

Other devotional acts accomplish the same ends. Many devotions, for example, include testimony services, where saints in the pews give thanks for recent blessings. Testifying saints often open their thanksgivings with song, voicing lyrics that tellingly speak to personal experiences. Fellow churchgoers, in turn, join the singing, following the testifier's lead while contributing their own cho;used emotions to the praise. Other devotions complete the three-way communion of praise, prayer, and preaching by adding a "sermonette," an abbreviated—but structurally complete—sermon delivered by a preacher.[6] Like prayer, such preaching draws the saints into communal conversation, thus sharpening devotional focus. Toward this same end, devotional leaders often call for extra prayers and, as was the case at the Branchettes' anniversary, additional songs. All of these acts serve the same essential function; all help to kindle the fires of faith, preparing the saints' hearts for the intense encounter with transcendence.

* * * * *

Elder Lawrence Richardson and I were returning from a festival appearance by the Fairfield Four when our talk turned to devotions. As was usually the case at secular festivals, the emcee had introduced the quartet with no devotional preface. On this particular day, this hadn't sat well with Elder Richardson. So he opened the performance with brief prayer and then pushed into a song whose chorus was accessible even to those unfamiliar with the tradition. In essence, he conducted an abbreviated devotional service. Though its spareness set it apart from most church devotions, this miniservice echoed the truncated versions that often open "professional" gospel programs. Elder Richardson clearly was looking to "have church." So he began by making sure that the proper frame was in place.

When I asked about his actions, Elder Richardson likened the festival performance to Sunday services. "I felt that it would bring the Spirit among us," he said; "it would dwell in the midst. As I said a few minutes ago, when you light a fire, you're going to feel some heat. And this is the beginning, by singing these songs and praising His holy name."

"So the devotions light the fire?" I asked.

"If I could refer back earthly-wise, to when it's cold," he answered, "mom or dad would tell us, say, 'Son, lay the wood in order.' "

"And say, 'In the morning, all we have to do is get up and light the fire.' "

"And from that—by lighting the fire, you know—it will bring heat in the building."

"So it is by singing praises unto God."

"God will light up the hearts and the minds of those that are there for service."[7]

* * * * *

Most sanctified Sunday services give both congregation members and church authorities an opportunity to present their singular gifts to the assembly. The same is true of most gospel programs. Both sets of services unfold as balanced celebrations of devotional artistry. And both actualize this balance in the liturgy itself, by ordaining a shifting focus of devotional authority. At one moment, the congregation members guide the service; at another, the ministers take charge. In musical programs, the performers stand in stead of the preachers. In both cases, momentary authority for management of the service shifts from group to group.

When Sister Elliott stood to open the anniversary, she initiated the congregational component of the program. Note from whence she came. Both she and Mother Nixon stepped into the cross-aisle from the pews. The same was true for every other speaker and songleader during devotions. This is traditionally the case for this program-opening segment—devotional leaders almost always hail from the congregation rather than the ranks of church authority. The second part of the program, in contrast, traditionally rests in the hands of performers and the master of ceremonies, who act, in a sense, as ministerial surrogates. Yet even these saints—though their numbers may well include ministers—maintain a stance of congregational identity, for they too step into the cross-aisle from the pews, and then return to the pews when they're finished. Hence, though they momentarily command a role of devotional authority, they ultimately rejoin the ranks as congregational coequals. The balance of devotional voices is thus ever apparent, symbolically declaring unity of purpose at every level of structure and enactment.

The saints who traditionally lead devotions are usually deacons, "deaconesses," church "mothers," and church elders—individuals whose authority stems more from strength of faith than from divine ordination. Unlike preachers, these leaders have not been formally "called" by God into service. Instead, they have moved up through the ranks of church membership to achieve positions of respect. They thus represent attainable potential, that which can be achieved by anyone who ardently pursues the path of holiness. In that their authority stems from mortal ordination, these saints command little real power over their fellow parishioners. For the most part, they are still viewed as congregational peers; the special esteem they earn recognizes their spiritual strength but does not lift them from the ranks of devotional equals. Hence, though called upon to *lead* the congregation, these saints are also *of* the congregation. Their prayers, testimonies, and songs ring with the familiarity of common circumstance and shared pursuit.

As if to spatially confirm this position of equality, devotional leaders traditionally address the assembly not from the pulpit, but from the cross-aisle between the front row of pews and the dais. This is a markedly liminal space, a narrow stretch that separates pews from pulpit and congregation from clergy. From the pulpit comes the divine will, revealed in scripture and sermon; from the pews come choruses of praise and thanksgiving, rendered in song, shout, and testimony. From the pulpit come words of exhortation, edification, and comfort; from the pews come words of adoration, gratitude, and response.[8] Between pulpit and pew lies the cross-aisle meeting ground, a space both mundane and holy. At its ends, in traditional church structures and in the minds of saints rooted in tradition, are the "deacons' corner" and the "amen corner," spaces reserved for those furthest along the path to sanctification. Here deacons, trustees, deaconesses, mothers, and missionaries keep the fires kindled and the dialogue alive with constant words of praise and encouragement. The two axes of engagement—from pulpit to pews, and deacons' corner to amen corner—define a living cross whose heart rests at the center of the cross-aisle.[9]

This centered space draws meaning from enactment and memory. Here the saints march every Sunday to deliver their offerings; here they gather for healing and special prayer; here they experience the tranquil serenity of communion. To this centered space step those wishing to profess Christ as savior; here they receive their first words of ministerial counsel; here they join the ranks of the holy. And here many first feel the consuming flames of anointment, an experience burned indelibly into their memories. The space virtually pulses with experiential echoes of harmony and rapture.

The actions of the preacher deepen the space's significance yet further. For it is here that preachers stride at the peak of their sermons, when the Spirit impels them to carry the Word beyond the pulpit. And it is here that they often extend the invitation, gazing with penetrating insight into the eyes and hearts of the congregation. Here preachers solemnly anoint supplicants with holy oil; here they triumphantly lay on the hands of healing. Here they tearfully receive backsliders back into the fold; and here they joyously extend the hand of fellowship to new members. The heart of the cross-aisle thus stands as space consecrated by the fire of the Spirit and hallowed by communion with the saints.

At one moment, the cross-aisle serves as stage for the congregation. At another, it acts as platform for preachers and Spirit. At yet another, it serves as meeting place where saints, preacher, and Spirit unite in happy epiphany. It is from this marked space that devotional leaders lead the congregation in praise. Their very placement colors the meaning of their actions; at the same time, it confers on them a role whose definition is blurred by the cross-aisle's many associations. They are at once congregational *leaders* and congregational *members*, mediating between the roles in a way that erases the distinctions. Though they clearly "lead" the devotions, they also invite the saints to share the duties of leadership, calling on them for songs, prayers, and testimonies. Devotional leaders manage, but do not dictate, the proceedings; they guide the flow while letting congregation members determine much of the content. And when others momentarily take the lead, devotional leaders—though still standing in the cross-aisle—act as regular members of the congregation, chorusing the closing lines of call-and-response lyrics, responding to saints and Spirit with cries of "Amen" and "Thank you, Jesus," and adding their testimonies to the tide of thanksgiving. When devotions close, they return to a place in the pews, spatially reaffirming their roles as congregational peers.

At the Branchettes' anniversary, Mother Nixon's informal tone and inclusive language immediately suggests her congregational identity. So also does her title (announced by Sister Elliott), as church "mothers" are among the most respected members of a congregation; esteem for their wisdom and spiritual commitment tends to cross congregational and denominational lines. If Mother Nixon had not been introduced by title (as is often the case with devotional leaders, who frequently receive no introduction), and if the assembly had not included so many church members and friends, then she would have had to rely on her words, her position in the cross-aisle, and her coactivity to establish her place among the saints. Devotional leaders usually meet this challenge by immediately engaging the congregation in song, thus effectively identifying self with the collective. Once voices have been joined in praise, the worship leader can proceed from a position of devotional equality.

Chapter 6

Scripture

"It's About Being Sincere in Your Heart"

After drawing the saints together on the chorus, Mother Nixon swings into the hymn's second verse. Within a few words, the saints are singing along, pushing the melody with nuanced improvisations and offbeat clapping. The second round of the chorus is even louder and more passionate than the first, leading Mother Nixon to repeat it a second time. Midway through the lyric, a sister sitting near the cross-aisle starts shaking a tambourine, adding a sibilant sizzle to the singing. A few seconds later, a second tambourine—this one shaken by a girl of about five—joins the music. Her playing, replete with offbeat phrasing, is as deft as that of her elder counterpart and perhaps even a bit more imaginative.

As Mother Nixon sings the last line of the chorus, she scans the congregation. Smiling at the assembly's obvious enthusiasm, she launches into yet another repetition of the refrain. By now she is swaying from side to side, her weight shifting with every other beat. The congregation echoes her movement, as whole pews sway in synchrony. The overall effect, accented by the clapping hands and accentuated by the rainbow hues, is of rippling waves of color.

Spurred by the saints' involvement, Mother Nixon lets her voice soar. Her powerful singing drives the final chorus, as she anticipates every line and voices its opening words a split second before the congregation gets to them. She sings as if she's trying to fill every moment with meaning.

> Down at the cross, at the cross,
>   Where I first saw the light,
>   And the burden of my heart, it just rolled away,
> O, it was there by faith
>   That I received my sight,
>   And now I am happy all the day!

5. "The Lord is my shepherd; I shall not want . . ." So begins Mother Edna Lofton's reading of the Twenty-third Psalm, a favorite scripture at gospel programs. Though most saints in the pews know this chapter by heart, they nonetheless silently read along in their own Bibles. (Photo by Roland L. Freeman)

At the extended final word, Mother Nixon stops clapping. Then, as the chorus closes, she utters a loud "Amen!" signaling the hymn's end. The word has hardly left her mouth before Sister Perry, still sitting in the amen corner, adds an "Amen!" of her own. A third, fourth, and fifth sister quickly join the chorus, as "Amens" cascade through the pews.

Taking the cue, the guitar and keyboard draw the melody to a ragged close, each ending it at a different point. Then, without a moment's hesitation, the two begin a quietly improvised musical meditation that buoys the "Amens" and the words that follow. Mother Nixon, meanwhile, steps back to the amen corner, as Mother Edna Lofton—another church elder—takes her place in the cross-aisle. She's carrying a large, well-worn Bible, bound in black. The music—still playing—makes for a seamless transition.

"I'm going to read for our scripture today," says Mother Lofton, pausing briefly, "the Twenty-third Psalm." Her tone, like that of Mother Nixon, is friendly and informal. But when she begins reading, her voice assumes a commanding authority.

"The Lord is my shepherd; I shall not want. He maketh me to lie down in green pastures. He leadeth me besides the still waters. He restoreth my soul."

The adults in the pews sit quietly through the reading. Not so the children. Many are already starting to fidget, squirming in their seats and looking for distraction. A young mother sitting near me hushes her daughter, who giggles while making faces at her toddler brother. A young boy, dressed in a dapper three-piece suit, escapes from his mother's pew and hurries down the aisle toward his grandfather. On the way, he passes three adolescent girls engaged in whispered conversation. A number of adults, meanwhile, are following the reading in their Bibles. Others appear somewhat distracted. Some of them, too, are whispering, apparently closing out the conversations stilled by the singing. The unity so evident moments ago seems to be dissipating.

But Mother Lofton's voice does not falter. She presses on, reciting the well-known passage more from memory than from reference to the written page. As she ends her fifth line, she draws the first responsive "Yes" from the congregation. The organ and guitar, meanwhile, continue to play softly under her words.

"He leadeth me in the path of righteousness for His name's sake. Yea, though I walk through the valley of shadow of death, I fear no evil. For thou are with me."

Someone in the deacon's corner, with head bowed, anticipates the familiar words and mutters "I fear no evil" even before Mother Lofton does. The last line draws another affirming "Yes" from the pews. The organ slowly fades into silence, leaving the guitar to sustain the words.

"Thy rod and thy staff, they comfort me."

A quick chorus of overlapping "Amens" sounds from the pews as the line closes. The devotional conversation seems to be beginning anew.

"Thou prepare a table before me in the presence of mine enemies. Thou anointeth my head with oil. My cup runneth over."

Each sentence evokes a response from the saints, though none is as sustained or jointly voiced as the earlier flurry of "Amens." "Lord, thank you," says one sister. "Uh-huh," murmurs another. "Yes," whispers a third.

"Surely goodness and mercy shall follow me, all the days of my life. And I will dwell in the house of the Lord, forever."

Mother Lofton utters the closing word with an air of finality. "Amen!" proclaims a sister in the amen corner. "Amen!" says another, and another, and another. As the responses sound, Mother Lofton steps back to the pew. And the guitarist, still seated facing the cross-aisle and pulpit, plays on.

* * * * *

Devotions pass seamlessly from song to Psalms, keeping the service's focus firmly on praise. Throughout, the softly chorded guitar lends felicitous continuity, linking sung words with words once meant to be raised in song. Such is the special appropriateness of the Psalms. After all, the psalmist David was himself a gifted musician, and his Psalms are all said to have originally been set to music. Further, many of these verses—certainly more than in any other book of the Bible—call for musical worship, encouraging believers to "sing unto the Lord a new song," to "praise him with the timbrel and dance," to "praise him with stringed instruments and organs" (Psalm 149:1, 150:4). That the Psalms are songs of praise makes them particularly well-suited for musical services directed toward this same end. Hence the appropriateness of the printed cover on the Branchettes' anniversary program, picturing a horn and a Bible opened to the Psalms. Written in the shadowed space of the instrument's mouth are the words: "Make a joyful noise unto God . . . make his praise glorious. Psalm 66:1, 2."

Most gospel program devotions that include scripture draw their readings from the Psalms. Sometimes readers draw verses from the four gospels, and less often from the Book of Acts, but rarely do they recite from any other book in the Bible. The Psalms simply seem most appropriate. Not only do they tailor scripture to the event, but they also provide tacit biblical sanction for the service. At the same time, they remind programgoers that the primary purpose of the gathering is praise.

But the praise of the Psalms differs markedly from the praise of songs. For the saints deem most songs to be the works of mortal minds. Scripture, in contrast, stands as the unmediated Word of God, a Word supernaturally dictated to the Bible writers, who penned its verses precisely as received. Again and again the Bible describes this process of revelation, telling how the prophets and disciples had but to open their mouths to find them filled with the words of God. The Book of Psalms itself details this process, explicitly attributing authorship to the divine: "I am the Lord thy God, which brought thee out of the land of Egypt; open thy mouth wide, and I will fill it" (Psalm 81:10).[1] The Bible, say the saints, is the result of many such "fillings."

As I've already suggested, the saints believe that the process of divine revelation is ongoing. The Lord continues to "fill the mouths" of anointed believers, delivering prophecy through mortally voiced sermons, prayers, songs, testimonies, and utterances in unknown tongues. But these prophetic words fail to carry the authority of scripture. Though tracing authorship to the Spirit, they address them-selves to the needs of the moment; they are bound, in essence, to the situation. Not so the Bible. The words of scripture are designed to serve as the foundation of faith for time eternal. As Bishop Frizelle Yelverton once instructed his parishioners at Durham's Mount Calvary Holy Church, they "are not mere words," but rather "are fragments of God," bearing the singular authority of timelessness.[2] Written for all the world, and not contingent on special occasion or particular mouthpiece, they offer the ultimate revelation of truth.

As such, the words of scripture carry—to quote a popular congregational song—"wonder-working power." They give guidance in times of confusion, solace in times of worry, strength in times of weakness, and direction in times of uncer-tainty. Hence their presence in devotions. Scripture grounds the service in the Word, emphasizing the goal of praise while implicitly renouncing that of enter-tainment. By opening with scripture, the saints unambiguously turn the program's path toward "church."[3]

At gospel programs, the actual placement of the reading within devotions is determined more by church tradition and congregational preference than by litur-gical demand. In most church-based programs, like that at Long Branch, devotions tend to follow the church's normal order of service. Hence at the Branchettes' anniversary, as in Sunday morning services, the scripture reading falls between song and prayer. This sequence follows praise with praise, setting the frame for entreaty and then leading into a full service of sung hosannas. In events not af-filiated with a particular church, decisions about the order—and actual makeup—of devotions rest in the hands of program hosts and devotional leaders. Many such programs leave scripture readings out altogether. This is particularly true for promoter-sponsored professional events, where devotions are usually shortened to include only introductions, song, and prayer. Since gospel programs traditionally have no place for scripture in their second part, leaving the reading out of devo-tions often means leaving it out of the service entirely.

Like singing, reading is an egalitarian act, open to all the saints. One needs no special gift to stand before the congregation and read. Unlike singing, however, reading is charged to a single speaker. Whereas the songleader invites all the saints to raise their voices, the reader reads alone. In this sense, reading resembles devo-tion's other cardinal act, praying. Praying also rests in the hands of a lone speaker. But praying tends to be delegated to saints with a special gift for prayer, to those recognized for their special God-given eloquence. Reading knows no such restric-tion. Hence it stands betwixt and between, as a solo act conducted by saints with no special qualifications (beyond, of course, the ability to read). In devotions like those at Long Branch, this composite quality insures scripture reading a strategic place between song and prayer, neatly effecting a transition from congregational control to gifted leadership. Since the post-devotional song service relies entirely on gifted performance, reading in this setting becomes the last act in which pro-gramgoers wield a controlling hand.

At the Branchettes' anniversary, a church mother stepped from the pews to read the scripture. As is usually the case with readers, she stood as a congregation member who brought no special gift to the cross-aisle. Her status as "mother," in this instance, had no bearing on the role she was asked to fill. Called solely to serve as a vehicle for divine words, she was expected to add nothing more to the reading than a few perfunctory sentences of introduction and conclusion. Beyond these brief remarks, the only demand placed upon her was that she read with some measure of clarity and flow.

The ease of meeting these qualifications opens the reader's role to the full field of church membership. In the eyes of the saints, preachers are no more qualified for this role than church mothers, mothers no more than deacons, and deacons no more than lay members. Devotional leaders are thus free to assign reading responsibilities to virtually anyone in the congregation.

The lay reader's move to the church-front underscores anew the essential communality of worship, in that it draws a programgoer with no title or obvious gifts into the center of attention. The reader thus stands as a congregational Everyone, a saint whose qualifications for the role are shared by most of those present. This sense of prosaicness tends to be accentuated by the reader's performance, which often shows signs of hesitancy and anxiety. Quite frequently, one hears scripture read with the drama and dignity that Mother Lofton brought to the Psalms. Just as commonly, however, the recitation proceeds in a monotone, with many speakers either pressing their words in an unbroken rush or delivering them with halting precision. The frequent spontaneity of the call to read gives readers no time to prepare, thus inviting a sense of nervousness. The resultant awkwardness, in turn, underlines the commonness of the reader's skill, defining the speaker as a plain-speaking peer rather than a performative paragon. The very ordinariness of presentation thus further cements the bonds of co-congregational identity.

The holiest of readings are thus presented by a congregational peer. One might well expect that this combination would evoke respect and focused attention from the saints. But this isn't always the case. Many programgoers seem to respond to the reading with an air of mild indifference, treating the words with a kind of dispassion evinced in neither song nor prayer. Recall the response to Mother Lofton's recitation. Children squirmed and giggled; teenagers whispered; adults just sat and listened. Not until Mother Lofton's fifth line did a single saint field a vocal response. Three lines later, she elicited a second rejoinder, followed by a few more as she moved toward the scripture's end. Only once did more than a single saint raise her voice in response—a rate of acknowledgment even lower than that which marked Mother Nixon's pre-song introduction. And the responses that the reading *did* evoke were, by and large, not very enthusiastic. What precisely is going on here?

One answer might lie in programgoers' familiarity with the read passages. Devotional repertoires, as suggested earlier, are rather limited, leading inevitably to frequent repetition. This duplication is deepened by the use of these same scriptures—particularly the Psalms—in devotions at other services. But repetition also marks a host of other worship acts, none of which elicit a comparable reaction. Choir songs, for example, are often repeated week after week, month after month, without ever seeming to lose their affecting power. Of course, song invites a very different kind of involvement—and touches the emotions in a very different kind of way—than speech. But saints say that song and scripture both act on the soul in the same way. Both elicit reflection; both open doors to the Spirit. And both invite active involvement. All of which suggest that the key to congregational coolness lies beyond mere familiarity.

What, then, accounts for the apparent indifference? Perhaps the answer demands a second question: what sets scripture reading apart from other devotional acts? First, there's the source of the text. Yet one would expect divine authorship to elicit a spirited, rather than spiritless, response. Second, there's the text's inherent rigidity, which leaves no room for improvisation. Yet a similar fixity also marks many songs, all of which receive a warmer reception than the readings. Third, there's the manner in which the text is conveyed, the actual performance. Herein may lie the key. As mentioned earlier, scripture reading often shows no hint of vocal dramatics and little sign of personal involvement. In essence, the act of reading lacks both style and passion. Note my focus on *act* and not text. Does the reader's lack of engagement foster a corresponding lack of engagement on the part of the congregation? Or, to pose the question differently, does the act of performance weigh so heavily as to override the stated ideal of respect for the holy text? Our search for an answer may well offer insight into the aesthetics of performance among the saints.

* * * * *

The pianist for the Greater Joy Ensemble was visibly troubled by the congregation's lack of enthusiasm. The ensemble, a chorus of nine, had opened the evening program with a brief, sweetly voiced "theme." Then, almost without pause, they pressed into a spirited song of praise. As the song's tempo accelerated, the singing grew increasingly impassioned. The lead singers were clearly "feeling the song." But the crowd just as clearly was not. Folks in the high school auditorium just sat and talked, paying only polite attention to the singers. Most of the young programgoers were waiting, it seemed, for the popular headline act, an ensemble whose upbeat "contemporary" sound particularly appealed to youth. Many simply weren't paying attention to these "local" singers. The piano player, whose fingers had forcefully pushed the song to a fiery conclusion, was clearly frustrated.

Keeping one hand on the keys, he reached to grab the mike hanging over the piano.

His words—quick, crisp, almost gruff—betrayed his aggravation.
   We didn't come here for a show tonight!
   I don't know why *you* came,
      But *we* came to praise the Lord!

Praise God!
We came to lift His name,
>and have some *church*!
But you can't have no church just sitting there!
>Nobody clapping their hands,
>Nobody patting their feet,
>Nobody saying "Amen!"
You all acting like you're dead out there!
But this ain't no cemetery.
This is a service!
Praise God!
If you want to get something out of it,
>you've got to put something into it!

This last comment draws the first audible "Amen" from the seats. At least *someone* is beginning to get into the spirit.[4]

＊　＊　＊　＊　＊

"If you want to get something out of it, you've got to put something into it." One hears this adage again and again in the church, where it takes many forms and appears in many contexts. "The more you put into it, the more you'll get out of it," say some. "The more you give, the more He gives to you," say others. "The more you feel it, the more someone else will feel it," say still others. Sometimes the words refer to life, sometimes to worship, sometimes to performance. But whatever the referent, the point is always the same: reward only follows intense, soulful involvement.

When applied to worship, the saying holds many meanings. In the private sphere, it references the silent conversation of faith, when the believer earnestly addresses the Lord. As has already been discussed, the "something put into" such conversation is devout passion; the "something received," in turn, is often the touch of transcendence. Simply put, the more intense the devotion, the greater the blessings.

Saints also apply the adage to performance. Here the terms of the equation change, shifting the hearing audience from God alone to God *and* congregation. No longer can the message remain unvoiced; now it must be vocalized for all to hear. The mode, however, must remain the same. The words must still convey intensity and passion. The spirit of delivery thus becomes a critical part of the performance. And a central part of the message. While the words carry the text, the manner in which they are voiced conveys the extra "something put in." Intensity thus becomes a kind of metacommunicative display, serving not only to ease personal focus, but also to demonstrate that focus to the congregation. And the greater the display of intensity, the more enthusiastically supportive the congregational response. Which, of course, fosters further focus. And invites greater blessings. Put simply, "the more you put into it, the more you'll get out of it."

But it's not only the performer who should "get something out of" performance. When set within the frame of conversational devotion, all performance becomes ministry, one of whose ends is to spur congregational reflection and to open dialogues with the divine. In this context, displays of passion become examples and inducements, encouraging others to strive for the intensity apparently being experienced by the performer. Recall the version of the adage that most clearly links presentation and receipt: "The more you feel it, the more someone else will feel it." To the saints in the pews, manifest passion offers evidence of the performer's concentration and sincerity. This, in turn, motivates deeper involvement of self in the devotional conversation.

The dynamics of this equation are patently clear to those who regularly share their gifts through the ministry of performance. "You got to put some effort in it," says Elder Lawrence Richardson, speaking about both singing and preaching. "You got to put some *emotion* in it, and get the eyes of the people."

"And if you do that," adds Richardson's longtime singing partner, Rev. Sam McCrary, "the more expression you use and the more sincereness you use, it will open the hearts of somebody else."

"And by the people seeing your effort and what you're doing and the meaning that you're saying to them," elaborates Elder Richardson, jumping back into the conversation, "it begins to touch. And when it touches—a lot of time you don't want to do a thing, but when the Holy Ghost touches you, like Jeremiah said, 'it was just like fire in my bones, and I couldn't hold my peace.' "[5]

Look at the words Elder Richardson and Rev. McCrary use in this exchange. To command churchgoers' attention, and to elicit the reflection that will open their hearts, performers must invest presentation with "effort," "emotion," "expression," and "sincereness." Every term suggests intense and impassioned involvement. Without these qualities, the performance risks being dismissed as "dead." And death, of course, has never been conducive to good conversation.[6]

Interestingly, nowhere in this or many other like conversations do fluency and artistic command appear as the key criteria for measuring excellence. What seems to be important is not how perfectly the words emerge or how artfully the voice shapes them, but how much feeling they convey. This was precisely the message articulated by holiness evangelist Susan Massenburg, who once preached about saints who aren't masters of fancy words, but who nonetheless speak with sincerity and spirit:

Some people can't put the words together—	(That's right.)
they don't have the education,	(Yes./Tell it!)
or they just aren't good with words.	(Go ahead!/Yes!)
But that's not what it's about—	(My Lord!)
being able to put words together.	(Yes!)
What it's about is being sincere in your heart.	(Amen!/My Lord!)[7]

Sincerity is clearly a key to competence. And sincerity shows through style—through the tone of one's voice, the expression on one's face, the movement of one's body. Together, these factors convey a sense of spirited involvement that has little to do with self-conscious artistry. They speak to the affective core of devotional performance. And in so doing, they command the attention and engagement of the gathered saints.

* * * * *

This brings us full circle to the issue of congregational response to scripture reading. Many readings, when judged against a standard of personal involvement, are quintessentially "dead." They manifest no intensity, no passion. Perhaps this happens because nervousness stifles many readers' performances, as they momentarily allow the performance expectations of the outside world to override the special criteria called into play during worship. Perhaps the shortness and fixity of the text stall efforts to infuse the reading with emotion. Or perhaps readers' sincerity simply does not show in readily discernible ways. Whatever the reason or combination thereof, many readers fail to demonstrate involvement with the text. Not surprisingly, such readers also fail to engage the congregation.

This would suggest, of course, that readers who *do* show spirit can draw the saints into lively and enthusiastic participation. This is precisely the case. Mother Lofton, who read the Psalms with a sense of conviction and subtle drama, began to move in this direction. She elicited far more responses than many in her position. I've heard others fill the words with absolute fervor, giving them a vitality that commands attention. Perhaps these readers were, as the saints say, simply "gifted to read," just as some are gifted to pray or to preach. Or perhaps their texts spoke with some special significance to their lives, leading to particularly impassioned performances. Whatever the reason, those readings drew both handclaps and spirited cries of "My Lord!" and "Jesus!" And on more than one occasion, they prompted outbreaks of shouting that literally swept through the church, even though the service was only just beginning. In these instances, the presented Word pushed the assembly further on the path to accord, continuing the ascendant journey that began with song.

This wasn't the case at the Branchettes' anniversary. Instead, one might say that the reading held the saints on a devotional plateau, neither firing their spirits nor dulling their enthusiasm. But the reading *did* close with an enthusiastic chorus of "Amens." The saints were clearly ready for the next step on their devotional journey, a step that would bring them to the very "throne of grace." Following the double dose of praise, the next act of worship would be prayer.

Chapter 7

Prayer

"The Vibrations of the Holy Spirit Go Out There"

The young guitarist picks out a spare melody while Mother Lofton moves away from the microphone and toward her seat in the amen corner. As she lowers herself to the pew, Sister Elliott, sitting nearby, pushes herself to a standing position. "We'll have prayer by our deacon," she says quietly, nodding toward the far side of the church. "Deacon Eldridge." Then, as quickly as she rose, Sister Elliott sits down.

At that same moment, a short, sturdy man stands in the deacon's corner. His smooth, unwrinkled face contrasts sharply with his closely cropped white hair, suggesting a youthfulness unsullied by decades of hard labor. His nimble steps around the drums and into the cross-aisle add to this assessment, testifying to a vitality of both body and spirit. This deacon has clearly not been slowed by age.

As Deacon Willie H. Eldridge reaches for the microphone, the bass player picks a few random notes, as if to check his tuning. The guitarist strums his strings in tacit response. The saints remain still and silent.

Now standing before the pulpit, Deacon Eldridge gazes into the pews. His eyes strike me as being full of warmth, showing no hint of pridefulness or pretension. Standing flatly on both feet, his suit hanging comfortably on his rugged frame, he conveys an air of quiet dignity. The deacon's opening words confirm this first impression.

"You all bow," he says, his voice barely rising above a whisper, "for the prayer." The words emerge more as humble request than as command. All heads lower, many falling forward into clasped hands stretched across the backs of pews. And Deacon Eldridge, with closed eyes and quiet voice, begins to pray.

"God's plan," he says slowly, "included us." The deacon pauses dramatically between the sentence's two halves, as if to invite a voiced response. One comes quickly. At sentence's end, a sister in the amen corner murmurs, "Lord Jesus."

"If you have a plan today," Deacon Eldridge continues, pausing again to break his words, "include Him." The same sister whispers "Lord Jesus" a second time.

Now the bass player catches on to Deacon Eldridge's emerging rhythm. His melodic wanderings become a series of ascending and descending arpeggios that climax at each pause. The subtly voiced notes accentuate the prayer's measured pacing, giving a sense of forward-moving inevitability to the words.

As soon as the bass sets its cadenced pattern, the guitarist adds an overlay of soft but piercing slides, making the instrument sound as if it were weeping. The guitar's plaintive cries deepen the spirit of entreaty, tacitly turning minds toward the inward conversations of prayer. Deacon Eldridge, meanwhile, seems oblivious to the instrumental additions. With eyes still closed and voice still soft, he continues the prayer.

Lord, our hope for this evening	
is that all the things	(Jesus)
for this anniversary,	(Lord Jesus)
Lord, include Him,	
Christ Jesus.	(Lord Jesus/Yes)
Because without Him,	(Yes, Lord)
there is no place.	(Jesus/Amen)
Without Him,	(Lord Jesus)
there is no way.	(Oh, my savior!)
Without Him,	(Lord Jesus)
there is no hope.	(Jesus!)

As he presses through this rhetorical triplet, Deacon Eldridge's voice begins to strengthen, slowly rising in both volume and intensity. In voiced correspondence, sisters in the pews respond with growing enthusiasm. The once-whispered calls of "Jesus" now sound with new emphasis—"Jee-sus!"

Taking this growing passion as a cue, the organist joins the devotional conversation. Faintly at first, and then with growing assertion, he improvises a melody around the words, filling every pause with sweetly voiced phrasings. This gentle commentary draws the deacon's sincere words, the saints' fervent calls, the bass's warm voicings, and the guitar's pensive cries together in a kind of worshipful harmony, yielding a seamlessness of sound that echoes the emergent communion of the saints.

So soon and very soon,	(Yeah, Lord!)
we're coming	
down to the end.	(Yes, Lord!/Yes)
To where we won't be able to come this way	(Lord Jesus/Yes!)
for another anniversary.	(Lord Jesus!/Yes)
Not even a church service.	(Lord Jesus)

As Deacon Eldridge's phrases begin to show distinct contours of tone and meaning, more saints offer responses at every pause. Many others are just as clearly responding to other, silent conversations. Some gently sway back and forth in their seats, their upper bodies marking a tempo that corresponds to neither the music nor the deacon's phrasings. Others murmur hushed words of entreaty and thanks, their muted voicings masked by the organ and amplified prayer. One elderly sister begins a slowly paced clap, her steady timing matching none of the service's ongoing rhythms. And Deacon Eldridge prays on.

So Lord, while we have	(Yes, sir)
this privilege,	(Yes, Lord!/Yes!)
Lord, let's put Him ahead,	(Oh Lord Jesus!)
Lord, in *all* things.	(All things, Lord!)
That things can be done decent	(Yes, Lord, yes, Lord!)
and in order.	(Yes, Lord!/Yes!)

A second set of six lines signals a momentary transition from entreaty to thanks, as Deacon Eldridge assumes a more forceful delivery. Repeatedly foregrounding the name of the Lord, the deacon almost shouts out the next lines. Each bursts from his mouth with equal power, giving them a staccato forcefulness that draws enthusiastic affirmation from the saints.

Lord, we thank You this evening,	(Thank You!/Yes!)
Lord, that You have given us,	(Yes, Lord!/Yes!)
Lord, strength again,	(Yeah, Lord!/Yes!)
Lord, that we were able to come into Your house.	(Jesus!)

The deacon's commanding voice rings through the church, rising high above the instruments' conversational voicings. Even with eyes closed, I can feel the passion in the pews, feel the intensity of the moment. For an instant, I raise my eyes from prayer, glancing toward the center aisle. A young sister at the end of my pew is silently weeping.

Lord, look on all of us this evening!	(Amen!/Yeah, Lord!)
My Lord. Take a second thought	(Yes!/My Lord!)
where's our hope this evening,	(Lord Jesus!)
if it's not in Him?	(Oh, my savior!)
I think about the fact You say:	(Jesus!/Oh yes!)
This day,	(Jesus!)
and all other days,	(Yeah, Lord!)
are vanity,	(Yes!/Lord Jesus!)
and vexation.	(Mmmmm!)
Lord we all are soon	(Lord!/Yes, Lord!)
Lord, to be closed,	(Yes!/Mmmmm!)
to this manner of privilege.	(Yeah, Lord!)
So we thank You this evening,	(Thank You, Jesus!)
for this time.	(Oh, my God!)

Each set of lines assumes a descending contour as the prayer turns back to entreaty. Starting high and falling low, the irregular groupings move from the singsong lilt of earlier segments to a less predictable, and more forceful, chanting. The saints' response seems uniformly enthusiastic.

And Lord, as You *always* have blessed us,	(Yes, Lord!/Jesus!)
Lord, we're looking for Your blessings again this	
evening.	(Oh, my God!/Yes!)
For Lord, not so much of Your blessings,	(Lord Jesus!)
But Lord, how much of a blessing	(Jesus/Yes)
are we giving Him?	(Lord Jesus/Yes!)
So bless us this evening.	(In the name of
	Jesus!/Yes, Lord!)
Lord, and we know You're not going to forget us.	(Lord Jesus!/Yes!)
And Lord, this is my prayer this evening,	(Jesus!)
for Christ's sake,	(Christ's sake)
Amen.	(Amen!)

Just as the deacon's voice rose as he pressed into the prayer, so does it fall as he draws to a close. The final lines cascade downward in volume and tone, carrying the prayer back to its beginnings in modesty and quietude. Deacon Eldridge's "Amen" is almost a whisper, barely audible above the crying guitar.

Not so the "Amens" called out by the saints. They ring forth from every pew, sweeping the church in a surge of simultaneity. As the first wave of response subsides, a second, quieter one eases through the congregation. "Amen," murmur some saints a second time. "Thank You, Jesus," say others. Still others, some of whose heads are just beginning to rise from the private conversations of prayer, simply whisper the name "Jesus."

The organist, guitarist, and bass player, meanwhile, continue to play as if nothing has changed. They recognize that the "Amens" signal not an ending, but merely a point of transition. The service, after all, is just beginning. As the instrumentalists keep conversation alive, Deacon Willie Eldridge—whose head is only now rising from his prayer—steps back toward his place in the pews.

* * * * *

Remember the three walking sticks of faith? Song, prayer, and preaching. Together, the three inscribe a hallowed circle of devotion. And together, they embrace the fullness of faith. Devotional services open with the first two acts in this holy threesome. Song lifts the saints' voices in praise; prayer lifts them in petition. Both acts stretch out toward God. And both set in motion conversations that are simultaneously personal and shared.

6. "Lord, we're looking for your blessings again this evening." All heads bow as the saints extend the thanks and entreaty of prayer. Waves of hushed affirmation ebb and flow through the church, testifying to the intimate connection of spiritual conversation. (Photo by Roland L. Freeman)

In singing, the sharing manifests itself in lyrics that are jointly voiced. The sung words, echoed by the whole, fashion a frame for the intimate and unspoken dialogues of reflection. In directed praying, words again fix a shared frame, though now the task of shaping that frame rests solely with the prayer leader. Think for a moment about the prayer of Deacon Eldridge. Standing at the center of congregational attention, he guides the flow of thought and theme. His words alone carry the voiced message of entreaty. As such, they provide a common reference point, offering a meditative focus for all who listen. Instead of sharing in the message's creation (as in song), the congregation receives and responds to it.

This shift transforms the relationship between the spoken words and the messages of internal dialogue. In song, the voiced message rings from many mouths. In prayer, it hails from only one. The singer need seek no further than self to hear the words of praise. The one who listens to prayer must look beyond, for in heard prayer, the message-bearing words hail from another, drawing attention away from one's own voicings. Though the self still engages in creative talk—punctuating the prayer with calls of "Jesus!" and "Yes, Lord!"—these words no longer sustain the central message. Instead, they reflect the individual's commentary on that message, conveying voiced responses to both the heard words and the self's unspoken thoughts.

Those thoughts, however, remain veiled, caught in the intimacy of personal communion . . . or in the wayward paths of distraction. None can legislate the travels of the mind. Yet the very tradition of response, the framing of all talk as *conversation*, encourages an engagement that keeps the mind on track, fostering a kind of attentiveness that, at the very least, yields appropriate responses. True, these responses might well be wholly automatic, the unthinking consequences of ingrained tradition. Some certainly are. Yet if one listens closely, one tends to hear not mechanical murmurings, but rather reasoned remarks, words that echo, complement, and advance the prayer. Most such responses testify to the listener's active conversational involvement with the prayer-giver. When the words *do* seem to part from those of the voiced prayer, they often do so with a fervor and flow that suggest their role in an altogether separate conversation, a conversation perhaps sparked by the spoken prayer, but certainly not directed by it.

This points to another difference in the engagement fostered by song and prayer. In congregational singing, thoughts tend to rise in harmony with the words, following the flow of lyric and theme. The very act of participation demands the singer's involvement—at least on some minimal level—with the lyrics; the singer must call the words to mind, confront them with thought, voice them with tongue, and hear them with ears tuned to the accord of praise. The engaged words invite contemplation; their utterance and their hearing both prompt thought. The song verses, in turn, frame this thought, maintaining a focus facilitated by the ongoing act of singing. However far the mind may wander, the very voicing of the words will draw it back, keeping thoughts tied (if only tangentially) to the lyrics.

Heard prayer does not exert this same sort of control; it allows the hearer's thoughts much greater freedom—both because the hearer is not also the speaker and because the hearer knows not what the speaker will say. In singing, congregation members know in advance the range of lyric possibilities; they know the familiar words and know which others will likely fit within the song's open frame. They thus can reflect upon the whole while singing the parts. The song—as a conceptual whole comprised of lyrics sung and those only called to mind—guides their reflection. Hence the harmony. Prayer, however, encourages listeners to think in *counterpoint* to the voiced words, to relate to the message more as a prompt than as a guide. Saints often say that the purpose of prayer is *to inspire prayer*; the voiced words invite conceptual contact, stirring individual thought and prompting conversations that leave the heard words far behind. But not so far behind that they can't continue to touch and inspire. While the unvoiced prayers proceed, the voiced words offer a constantly shifting ground for further reflection, ever raising new issues and inviting new thoughts. Believers can continue their silent conversations, giving little heed to the prayer leader, or they can selectively take cues from the spoken prayer, listening only long enough to spark a new train of thought. Thus can begin a back-and-forth movement in which reflection assumes a distinctly improvisatory form, riffing at one moment off the themes of the voiced prayer and pursuing at another the issues pressing on the heart of the believer. The spoken words provide a changing point of reference, stimulating the flow of personal thought while raising selected issues to the level of public talk. The individual saint, in turn, chooses from this talk those points deemed personally relevant, using them as a base for reflective elaboration while conducting a separate, largely unvoiced conversation.

The subtle shifts between those moments when a saint actively "follows" voiced prayer and those when that saint pursues private conversation often make themselves visibly and/or audibly apparent. Earlier, for example, I mentioned a young sister whom I saw weeping midway through Deacon Eldridge's prayer. This same sister had begun the prayer with strong words of affirmation, following the deacon's opening phrases with forceful cries of "Lord Jesus!" and "Oh my savior!" But as the deacon began to speak of times winding "down to the end," when the saints would not be able to "come this way" even to attend church, the sister's responses grew increasingly hushed. Then as the prayer moved into jubilant thanksgiving, the sister's body began to shake with muffled sobs. Was she thinking of a loved one recently gone on? Was she praying for the soul of an unrepentant sinner? Or was she thinking about something not even related to the prayer's words? There's no way to know, short of asking her. All that we can "read" from this moment is the apparent incongruity of her response: while the prayer leader offered thanks, the sister sobbed. And then, as quickly as they had begun, the tears stopped. As the prayer proceeded, the sister's words gradually returned to joyous affirmation, an affirmation now seemingly touched with triumph. "Yes, Lord!" she cried as the deacon cited the biblical verse about vexation. "Thank You, Jesus!" she called as he again offered thanks. By prayer's end, she was echoing the deacon's eloquence, caught up in a pattern of joyful counterpoint. To his "Not so much of Your blessings," she added, "Your blessings, Lord!" To his "So bless us this evening," she cried, "Bless us, Jesus!" And to his whispered "Amen," she closed with a rousing cry of the same, the smile evident in her voice. Whatever message her own prayer had conveyed, the sister closed in agreement with the voiced words of the deacon.[1]

Like chords in a jazz tune, the spoken words of the prayer leader provide a base for improvisatory soloing. Yet these solos, the personal prayers of the saints, are simultaneous and largely unsounded. This silent simultaneity infuses public prayer with its overriding sense of collectivity. Praying saints know that their fellows—as they themselves—are engaged in private entreaty; they know too that all are speaking to the same God. The resultant communion is not of voice (as in group song), but of act; not of word, but of motive. Confirming this consonance of focus are the interlocked cries of "Amen," "Yes, Lord," and "Thank You, Jesus!" that ring from the pews during public prayer. Though their diversity suggests differences of involvement and petition, the very frequency of these comments testifies to a oneness of purpose. And just as these comments thicken the texture of sound, so too do they thicken the texture of devotion, increasing each saint's awareness of others' absorption in prayer. In so doing, they tacitly encourage each saint's own rapt engagement. The chorused cries thus not only offer sounded confirmation of congregational unity; they also act through that confirmation to deepen individual involvement.

That's why prayer stands alongside song as a key component of devotions. Both acts stir the spirit of fellowship. Both turn the mind inward to self, outward to community, and upward to the divine. And both open conversation with the Spirit. For in both, it is God whom the saints address. In song, this address rises forth in praise. In prayer, it presses forth in petition. And, invariably, in thanksgiving. For whenever the saints pray, they also give thanks.

Gratitude and entreaty walk hand in hand in prayer. Saints treat the two as essential parts of the same whole, publicly recognizing that entreaty would be impossible but for the grace of God. Hence thanks constantly rise from the pews, grounding petition in the simple and special blessings of everyday existence. In a world filled with danger and uncertainty, and a world where Satan struggles to block the saints' every forward step, nothing is too insignificant to merit thanks. So praying saints thank God for "waking up this morning cloaked in our right minds," for rising "with the blood still running warm in our veins," for traveling "safely over the dangerous highways." And, as Deacon Eldridge prays, for "giving us strength again . . . to come into Your house."

Note how thanksgiving suffuses Deacon Eldridge's entire prayer. From its opening acknowledgment that God included the saints in His holy plan, to its closing thanks for the service, the prayer balances themes of gratitude and entreaty. Add to its thanks the many cries of "Thank You, Jesus!" that ring from the pews, and you begin to realize how even supplication falls within the frame of praise, joining song and Psalms in setting a tone of devotional celebration.

Bolstering this celebratory spirit is a sense that petition is ultimately less important than praise. Because, say the saints, God already knows what you need—before you even open your mouth. "He'll look past your wants and supply your needs," says the favorite adage. So when you pray, pray not for self, but for the fulfillment of God's will. Pray that you become a vessel, that *others* might be served. Pray, in other words, to become a servant to others' needs, in accordance with God's mysterious and unknowable plan.

The professed dynamic of prayer is thus one of deflection, of turning away from self and toward the needful other, ever confident that the self's needs will be met, as quartet singer Jojo Wallace once said in conversation, "according to His riches in heavenly places, and not according to our fleshly desires."[2] This confidence arises from personal experience, from the intimate knowledge that one's most pressing needs have in fact already been met, from the awareness that one's very existence is testimony to God's grace. This awareness, in turn, turns the mind anew to thanksgiving, once again setting in motion the cycle of prayer and praise. The two walk hand in hand in the sanctified world of words, gracing each other's presence in song, prayer, preaching, and even casual conversation. Whenever one is invoked, the other always stands close at hand.

* * * * *

When Deacon Eldridge stepped from the deacons' corner, he continued the cycle of shifting congregational focus that began with Sister Elliott's initial introduction. Thus far in the service, four saints have stood in the cross-aisle. Each arrived there from a place in the pews. Each stepped forth with no prefacing fanfare and only the barest of introductions. And all returned to the congregation when their duty was done. The transitions from one to another flowed with an easy informality, ever buoyed by the fluid phrasings of the musicians. These seamless shifts, in turn, underline the degree to which devotional authority rests in the hands of congregational equals. No one has yet to sit on the raised dais; no one has yet to stand behind the pulpit. Even the musicians sit in (or, in the case of the drummer, sit next to) the pews. The saints' focus thus shifts only from nave to cross-aisle, at one moment centering on the singing congregation, at another on the reader or prayer leader, and at yet another on the sound-sustaining musicians. The service clearly belongs to the collective.

Yet despite this celebration of devotional equality, those called to lead prayer nonetheless stand apart from their peers. Charged with leading congregation members to the very "throne of grace," they occupy a position of special leadership. They are, after all, the first speakers in the service to publicly and explicitly address the Lord. As such, they assume the very real responsibility of shaping the program's devotional tone. At the same time, they guide saints in the silent and shifting conversations of prayer. The ability to meet these challenges sets prayer leaders in a class apart.

So who fills this role? Believers say that every saint can lead praise, that praise comes naturally with the gifts of grace, as a "second nature" ability that flows freely from one's own never-ceasing thanksgivings. By the same token, saints say that all saved believers can lead prayer. For leading prayer is just praying out loud, giving voice to the petitions that already mark saints' everyday thoughts. If the public nature of such prayer causes hesitation, saints are enjoined to ask the Spirit to "give" them a prayer, to provide them with appropriate words and the strength to convey them. Just as the disciples are said to have asked Christ to teach them to pray (Luke 11:1), so too do many saints still publicly testify to having prayed to receive a prayer.[3] These considerations would seemingly open the role of prayer leader to all the saints.

But in practice, this isn't the case. Indeed, prayer leaders tend to come from a rather restricted group, a company that often includes preachers, deacons, deaconesses, and church mothers. At first glance, this group's makeup might suggest deference to authority, tacitly acknowledging the hierarchical politics of church administration. But a closer look reveals that the group's numbers also include saints who hold no positions of authority. When asked about this matter, saints with whom I spoke explained that the invitation to the cross-aisle hinges not on status, but rather on the "gift of prayer." Believers with this gift are said to be endowed with a special God-given talent for praying, a talent that makes itself evident not only in an eloquence of words, but also in the power of these words to touch the soul. Like the gifts of song or prophecy, this mystical endowment infuses language with affective force, enabling it to bypass the hearer's critical faculties and strike directly at the heart. The gifted and anointed prayer, say the saints, has the power to truly "move"; it stirs deep passions and sparks deep reflection. The source of this power, of course, is the Spirit. But the vessel is the gifted saint, the believer who earns the honor of the term "prayingest" (as in the comment, "She's the prayingest sister!"). Simply put, it's the "prayingest" saints who traditionally lead prayer at gospel programs.[4]

If the gift gives prayer affective power, then the intended audience clearly extends beyond God to include the congregation. The prayer leader must thus construct an appeal that not only addresses spiritual needs, but also provokes congregational reflection. Complicating this task is the prayer leader's awareness that not all in the assembly are saints. This is particularly true at gospel programs, where many come simply to enjoy the music. Or, as is the case with unsaved performers, to present their gifts and reap the worldly rewards thereof. Hence the prayer's message must stretch forth to three distinct audiences: the Lord, the saints, and those not yet walking the path of sanctification. The prayer leader is thus responsible not only for praying, but also for ministering—through that prayer—to both the saved and the unsaved.

The presence of the unsaved at gospel programs is something that most saints accept as a given. Again and again in the course of conversation, saved believers cautioned me against trusting all that I saw or heard at gospel events. Many singers, they argued, are simply not "real"; they perform more for personal gain than for praise. Much the same is said about congregation members, many of whom come to be entertained rather than uplifted. Recognizing these divisions among performers and programgoers, prayer leaders at gospel programs often explicitly address the issue of false performance and misguided purpose. Indeed, one might argue that this theme is perhaps the single most characteristic feature of their devotional prayers. Whether taking the veiled form of a call for devotional "order," or more explicitly asking that the performances be "real," the appeal for authenticity marks most program-opening invocations.

Deacon Eldridge opens his prayer at the Branchettes' anniversary with just such a call. "God's plan included us," he begins, speaking to the congregation even before explicitly addressing the Lord. "If you have a plan today, include Him." The deacon's message is simple: whatever your reason for being here, be sure that God is part of it. "Lord, our hope for this evening," he continues, shifting the address from church to heaven, "is that all the things for this anniversary, Lord, include Him, Christ Jesus." The second appeal repeats the first, though this time Deacon Eldridge brings the issue directly before the Lord. Note, however, that though he twice names the Lord as intended hearer, he still closes by referring to God in the third person, using "Him" instead of "You." In so doing, he keeps the appeal firmly within the congregational frame.

A short while later, Deacon Eldridge restates this mixed petition, again calling on the Lord, though just as clearly speaking to his human hearers: "So Lord, while we have this privilege, Lord, let's put Him ahead, Lord, in *all* things, that things can be done decent and in order." The closing call to "order" references Paul's familiar invocation, "Let all things be done decently and in order" (1 Corinthians 14:40). Invoked in this context, it serves as a clear admonition to those who would employ the showy "disorder"—the so-called "ripping and running" of singers and the counterfeit shouting of false "saints"—that characterizes inauthentic performance.

At the same time, as Deacon Eldridge explained in a later conversation, the allusion to "order" notifies those who would place self before God that their priorities are "out of order." "Without Him, it's not in order," asserted the deacon.

So many singers are leaving that out of gospel music—
    they're forgetting the spiritual part of it.
And [they're] looking at the part,
    you know, that might raise them up before the eyes of men.
And if you're raised up,
    you're supposed to be raised up by the Spirit.
[But] at that point,
    you're raising *yourself* up.
You know, whatever you're doing,
    you're looking for people to praise *you*.
In other words,
    [to] lift *you* up.
And if the people lift you up,
    where's your profit?
That's what I was saying there.[5]

Where's the profit when—as the prayer asserts—"we've come down to the end," when all things of this world are "soon to be closed"? In the time of judgment, how will singers be served by the praises of peers? Simply put, they won't. Hence the plea for authenticity—not only to avoid deceiving the song's hearers, but also to avoid endangering the singers' souls.

The centrality of this issue becomes markedly evident when one listens to program-opening prayers at other gospel events. At a gospel program at Durham's Mount Calvary Holy Church, for example, prayer leader Rachel Williams admonishes singers to leave behind "form and fashion" and renounce "outside show" so that souls might be blessed in the service. Once again, the injunction is framed as an appeal to the Lord. And once again, it asks that the program follow the Lord's will rather than that of its mortal participants:

And Father God, in the name of Jesus,	(Thank You, Jesus!)
We didn't come, Lord, for no form or fashion.	(Jesus!)
Neither did we come, Lord, for no outside show.	(Thank You!)
We come that our souls will be glorified,	(Yes!)
in Jesus' name.	(Oh, Lord)
Because we need You now, at every hour.	(Yes, Lord!)
We want You, Lord, to come in the midst of us.	(Yes, Father)
And we want You to have Your way tonight, God, in	
the service.	(Oh my Father)
Because the service, Lord, belongs to You.	(Yes, Lord)[6]

Note how Sister Williams eloquently sets forth the program's purpose by first declaring what it is *not*. In so doing, she admonishes the singers with graceful indirection, never stepping outside the frame of respectful prayer. At the same time, she deftly preempts the denials of "form and fashion" that will almost certainly be voiced by singers later in the program, letting them know that she—at least—will be looking beyond their glib disclaimers.

This same theme marks the devotional prayer of Rev. Louis Cash, whose words opened the sixteenth anniversary of Durham's Gilchrist Family. After offering thanks for the Lord's many blessings, Rev. Cash turns his words toward the singers, praying that they let self give way to Spirit:

God, we pray, God, that every group that comes forth,	
let them decrease.	(Yes)
And let the anointing of the Holy Ghost	(Amen)
increase in them.	(My Lord!)
In the name of You, God.	(In the name
	of Jesus)
That You may get the glory,	(Glory!)
the honor and the praise,	(Hallelujah!)
out of every song.	(Amen)
and I'm not lying.	(Alright)
In the name of Jesus.	(In the name
	of Jesus!)[7]

The key to Rev. Cash's call lies in the continuum of control he charts in his opening lines. "Let self decrease and Spirit increase," he prays, suggesting a closed equilibrium where one part expands only at the expense of the other. To truly allow the Spirit to "have His way" in the service, the singers must cede a portion of themselves, surrendering mortal will to that of the divine. This leaves little room for selfish performance, thus squeezing out "form and fashion" showiness and focusing all glory on the Lord. The singers, meanwhile, step from a position of self-willed creativity to one of creative collaboration, with the Spirit now joining as a partner in performance.

All of these prayers indirectly address the singers while directly addressing the Lord. And all convey the same basic message: be "real" when you sing, so that God—rather than self—might be glorified. This theme arises again and again in gospel programs, peppering the texts of testimonies, prayers, songs, and between-song commentary. But it usually appears first in the devotional prayer, where it comes framed not as admonition or denial, but as petition to the Lord. The prayer leader, in essence, calls on God to insure the singers' sincerity. Performers appearing after this point thus stand reminded that to sing with false hearts is to risk invoking the Lord's wrath.

Of course, this same admonition might well be addressed to those who lead prayer. They too are subject to the temptations of prestige and worldly acclaim. They too are susceptible to the seductions of style. And they too are prone to misuse their gift. For the gift comes as endowment rather than decree, as an ability fully subject to the whims of human will, making no demands of its own. It comes, as it were, with no strings attached, never referencing its source, never dictating its own use. To the unreflective and the unsaved, the gift seems simply a matter of "natural" competence.

For those who merit the designation "prayingest," the gift manifests itself in lyric style and affective power. These masters of artful talk fashion prayers that seem to tumble from the tongue, their crafted words pausing on their heavenbound journey just long enough to penetrate hearers' hearts. But penetration need not indicate spiritual sustenance. Nor need eloquence signify divine sanction. The affective phrasings of prayer may in fact be little more than hollow rhetoric, God-given but not God-filled. Such words, assuming the guise of godliness, carry little power.

Baptist deacon Edward Denkins, a gifted quartet singer from Philadelphia, addressed this issue with characteristic pithiness when speaking one day about proofs of spiritual presence. "Some of these people that get down to pray a prayer," he remarked, "they pray for a whole hour. And pray *fine* words! They'll start here and wind up in Georgia! But that prayer don't go no further than the ceiling."[8] Self stalls the prayer's journey, robbing its words of their power. Though ringing in the ears of the congregation, the words never reach earshot of heaven.

But such words can nonetheless stir the emotions, sparking reflection and perhaps even precipitating a shout. The words themselves, after all, can be truthful and righteous. What's lacking is spirit. Or, more precisely, Spirit. In its stead often stands a conscious attempt to transform artful words into self-serving vehicles of prestige and status. Though the phrasings of such prideful prayer-givers may *sound* inspired, the wellsprings from which they draw are ultimately those of mortal creativity and culturally constructed eloquence.[9]

＊　＊　＊　＊　＊

Baptist preacher and poet William Walker used to scold those who prayed "just to hear themselves pray" in a poem he often recited at Chicago church gatherings. The poem, "Stop That Putting On," is still sold at Chicago-area stores that specialize in gospel music. Its third stanza reads:

Some folks like to pray
   and make their voices ring out.
They'll pray for a half hour
   trying to make someone shout.
And if someone just happens to scream
   they'll change their voice and tone.
And pray like earth and heaven have passed away,
   and know they are just putting on.
Their prayer never leaves the room
   to be answered or even heard.
Because it didn't come from the heart
   just a matter of uttering words.
Whenever you need to pray
   to approach God on his throne
Be sincere in the heart
   and stop that putting on.[10]

＊　＊　＊　＊　＊

Some pray just to "make their voices ring"; others pray to sincerely address the Lord. Some prayers "never leave the room"; others wing their way to heaven. The difference rests in the distinction between style and power. More precisely, it rests in the contrast between mortal mastery (the unanointed gift) and transcendent enablement (the anointed gift). The gift, as suggested earlier, confers artistic competence; it grants a command of style, allowing eloquence to flow with ease. This eloquence, in turn, carries with it an emotional force that is deeply grounded in African American culture. Evoking a world of memories and associations, the style itself resonates loudly as symbol, speaking to the unconscious mind just as forcefully as the words speak to the conscious. In so doing, it strikes deep chords in hearers' hearts, evoking meanings that stretch far beyond the actual words conveyed.[11]

But saints say that these chords resonate in the *mind* rather than the *soul*. Recall for a moment Rev. Z. D. Harris's three-part model of the self, where the spiritual, the mental, and the physical work together to create meaning. The mental part, Rev. Harris argues, responds to words and style, interpreting spoken references, reading meanings into sound, and generating from those readings the stirrings of emotion. The physical part, in turn, translates emotion into experience, granting it a palpably physical dimension. Hence the tears, the raised hands, perhaps even the shout. All of which, say the saints, can be generated entirely by the self. But when prayer carries the substance of Spirit, when the gift flows with the anointing, the response transcends both the referential and the symbolic. Now the spiritual enters the equation, adding lyric measure to the meanings of words, deepening the cultural understandings of style, and infusing the whole with a profound sense of the sacred. The saved hearer *feels* the prayer in an entirely different way, sensing the grace that transports the words while experiencing the mystical ministrations of the Spirit. The chords that resonate now rest deep in the soul. As they vibrate through mind and body, they draw the mental and physical together in harmony, evoking a response that saints say is far deeper than mere emotion. Now the upwelling tears, the upraised hands, the joyous shout come forth not as shallow constructions of self, but as spontaneous celebrations of spirit meeting Spirit.

*   *   *   *   *

When I first talked with Elder Lawrence Richardson about prayer, I had never thought of it as an act in which the Spirit participated. Prayer had always struck me as a private act of address, a one-way communication where thanksgiving and entreaty went up and nothing came down. At least not immediately. I did believe that a response would eventually come, but I had never thought of the process as conversational, with some response—at least enough to indicate that I had been heard—coming quickly. Nor had I ever considered the possibility that the Spirit might ride, as it were, the public words of prayer, moving with them into the hearer's ear and then into the soul. That's just not the way I thought about—or experienced—prayer.

But Elder Richardson spoke of a different process, one in which prayers went up and Spirit came down. He described how the Spirit endowed the words of the anointed prayer-giver, giving them a special spin, granting them the power to touch hearer's hearts.

"When you're serving God," Elder Richardson explained, "you got to be in the Spirit. And if you are in the Spirit, God will let you know you're serving Him in spirit, and He will endow His Holy Spirit to come upon you."

I'll admit that all those references to "spirit" left me a bit confused. So I pressed for clarification, asking, "So what happens when the Spirit endows the person who is praying with Spirit? Now, that person's still talking to the Lord, isn't he? Or is he talking now to the people?"

I was thinking in either/or terms, wondering how the Spirit could be "working on" the very words that were being addressed to the Spirit. Did the Spirit's involvement turn those words from upward-directed prayer to outward-directed ministry? To whom was the anointed prayer-giver now talking?

"He's talking to the Lord," Elder Richardson clarified. "He's talking to the Lord about himself; he's talking to the Lord [about] the condition of the people. And when he is talking to the Lord, about someone—maybe they is heavy burdened—now when he's talking to the Lord, then he is endowed by His Holy Spirit."

"Now when he's talking, see, it will touch somebody else out there, who has a problem. And by them having a problem, and the prayer that is prayed for them—to God concerning whatever it may be—then God will endow the man in prayer. Then it will touch somebody else."

"See, that prayer *moves* from heart to heart and from breast to breast. It can't just be for one only. God's going to let somebody else feel it."

"So the prayer's out moving," I asked, still confused about the process, "with the Spirit's power. Now is it going to touch more people once the Spirit's in it than it did when that deacon was just saying it in self? Are folks in the congregation going to know the difference?"

"Yes!" Elder Richardson asserted emphatically. "If—they—believe." A dramatic pause separated each word, as the elder stared deep into my eyes. Another pause. "You can't be a hypocrite, and expect something when you know you're not right within yourself."

"Okay," I said, "I understand that. But what I wanted . . ."

But Elder Richardson wasn't through yet. "Hold your point," he declared, punctuating his words with a pointed finger. "Hold your point right there." His words were starting to flow now, taking on an urgency they hadn't shown mere moments before. "The spirit works in prayer like, you know, dynamite."

I *didn't* know, but I didn't say anything either.

"You light a fuse here, you know, just hssssssssss," Elder Richardson continued. "If you have a half stick of dynamite, you know, well, quite naturally it won't blast louder than a whole stick of dynamite." He paused only long enough to chuckle, and then pressed on. "So now, when you get into the prayer, this lightly will start exploding, you know. But it's not too much power there."

Now I was beginning to understand. Earlier in our conversation, Elder Richardson had said that gifted words had the power to touch, but that gifted words *endowed with Spirit* had even greater power. The half stick was those words without Spirit.

"But if you keep on and get the whole stick of the dynamite, then the blast—will—do—more—damage." Again the dramatic pauses. Again the pointed finger. And then, in a voice filled with quiet assurance, Elder Richardson concluded his analogy. "So it is with the Holy Spirit."

After this pause, Elder Richardson's words began to assume the deliberate rhythms of preaching. Starting slowly at first, and then gathering speed, his phrases rolled with the force of conviction.

If you are in Christ,
    and Christ [is] in your heart,
    and you pour out—
        I believe the word of God.
        He said, "If you call me,
            I will answer."
    And when He answers you,
        the *vibrations* of the Holy Spirit begin to just go out there—
        you know, *like the earth when it trembles!*

The elder's entire countenance had changed by this point. No longer was he simply explaining a point. Now he was preaching, and preaching in high gear. As he uttered the last line, Elder Richardson's wiry hands grasped an imaginary globe, raised it to eye level, and began to shake it with forceful determination. His upper body quivered with intensity as his words rushed forward, their pitch ever rising.

So it is that members that [are] sitting there,
    they gon—
    otherwords, they going to be doing one of these things in the seat!
They can't sit still!

Now his trembling hands had left the globe, pulled apart, and moved above his head, palms facing forward and fingers spread in a fluttery dance of praise. To heighten the effect, Elder Richardson began to pump his legs up and down, beating out the rapid rhythms of sanctification. For a moment, he seemed caught up in rapture. But his piercing eyes never left mine. And his voice never slowed.

Why?
The power of God is beginning to mix
    itself
        into the hearts of those—
I'm talking about true born into the gospel!
I'm talking about Jesus Christ, the only begotten son!

The words trembled with tuneful passion, leaping melismatically at every point of emphasis. The hands, meanwhile, had fallen to chest-level, with palms facing heaven and fingers tightening as if to squeeze each stressed syllable.

Sometimes you can say, "Je-e-sus"—
    it's so much power in "Jesus,"
        that somebody'll answer!
So it is with prayer.

Suddenly, with little warning, the words reached resolution. Elder Richardson smiled as he spoke that final line, his voice once again quiet and calm. I just sat there, saying nothing, thinking about those "vibrations" that ride the words of prayer. The words themselves don't change. But they gain a mystical, affective force, a force infused by the Spirit. This force does far more than merely augment meaning, for it carries understandings that transcend both the literal and stylistic meanings of performed prayer. In the words of Elder Richardson, it "mixes" itself directly in the hearts of believers. Note that there's no mention of mind. Only heart. Or, by extension, soul. When I asked Elder Richardson about this later in our conversation, he confirmed that the omission was purposeful. "The vibrations shake the mind, but *speak* to the heart," he explained. "Spirit connects with Spirit. And when you're connected with Jesus Christ, you will be lighted within your *heart*."[12]

* * * * *

The mystical "vibrations" of the Spirit transform both the experience of praying and that of hearing prayer. They do not, however, necessarily change the process of authorship. The words can still be those of the prayer-giver, emerging as products of mortal (albeit divinely gifted) competence. As Elder Richardson explains, the Spirit simply *adds to* these words, cloaking them in an aura of transcendence. In the words of Baptist deacon Edward Denkins, the Spirit "puts a little process on them," transforming affective texture but not actual text.[13] The anointed prayer-giver experiences this transformation in much the same manner as the saints in the pews—as a receiver of spiritual ministrations. The fact of receipt, however, need not change the process of creation, other than perhaps to inspire deeper thanksgivings or to prompt differently informed entreaty. The Spirit's contribution thus rests in the affective, rather than the textual, realm.

Proofs of the Spirit's participation in prayer lay entirely in the experiential arena. Saints testify to "feeling" the power of the words, to experiencing the mystical touch of transcendence, to finding selves drawn into the Spirit-willed movements of praise. Elder Richardson's comment about saints not being able to sit still through prayer echoes similar observations that have been voiced for generations, calling to mind an account from almost 130 years earlier when enslaved believers asked the plantation master to remove the backrails from their prayer-house benches so that they might have "room enough to pray."[14] The blessed "vibrations" reach out, touch, and set into motion, flowing through the congregation in holy confirmation of the Spirit's presence. Though not every saint will feel the touch, all will recognize the telltale "signs of the Spirit" in those whom the Lord has chosen to bless.

The regular co-occurrence of spiritual signs and the gifted words of prayer raises anew the question of style and symbolic meaning. Earlier I suggested that the very *sound* of prayer—the cadenced phrasings, the tonal elevation, the taut delivery—invokes a world of associations. Chief among these, at least in sanctified fellowships, is a perceived link between speech style and spiritual state. Simply put, many worshipers associate the heightened style of delivery with divine empowerment.

This perceived connection finds its most telling confirmation in sermons, where this same heightened style often emerges after the point of "elevation," when preachers are said to start receiving ideas and words from on high. Again the voice eases from a conversational to a poetic mode. Again the words pattern themselves into short, cadenced phrases. And again these phrases assume a distinctly melodic lilt, taking on tonal contours that lend the whole a chant-like character. In the sermon, these features emerge most markedly when the preacher moves into "high gear" and the Spirit is said to take greater control of the preaching voice. At this same time, the Spirit often makes itself manifest in a variety of other ways. Preachers cry out; sisters shout; deacons weep; mothers leap into the holy dance. Once again, speech style and signs of the Spirit coincide.[15]

The same style of delivery also marks other acts of worship. Testimonies frequently slide into the fluent phrasings of elevated style, as do the impromptu exhortations that devotional leaders often voice when advancing the service from one point to another (bridging for example, prayer and testimony, or perhaps song and song). In both instances, those who use this style tend to be saints with a reputation for holiness, those whose deep faith has supposedly earned them a "right" to the gift. With this "right" comes a presumed closeness to the Spirit, a presumption that frequently grounds itself in the speakers' display of spiritual signs. The testifying mother often breaks into a shout; the exhorting deacon often launches into the quickstep rhythms of holy dance; the praise-evoking evangelist often bursts into a shouted litany of "Thank You, Jesus!" The style and the Spirit seem to walk hand in hand. Though one does not *always* accompany the other, they certainly co-occur often enough to cement a firm association between them.[16]

Simple co-occurrence, of course, does not establish causality. The fact that stylistic elevation often accompanies apparent or experienced spiritual signs testifies to coincidence rather than cause. When questioned on this issue, most saints are quick to reject any inherent connection. As suggested earlier, they recognize that not all those who bear the stylistic gift are anointed.

Then again, not all worshipers are saints. Not all those who attend services are saved. And many of those attending only *think* themselves saved, but in fact have not yet crossed that threshold.[17] These worshipers have no certain way of differentiating between anointed and unanointed speech. They hear the flowing words, but don't feel the vibrations. They find their emotions stirred, but know not the stirring of the soul. They might even shout, but do so only in self, *willing* an emotional release rather than *responding* to the indwelling Spirit. For many of these worshipers, the style/Spirit connection slips from coincidence to causality. Believing that the Spirit actuates the style, they assume that the style (as vehicle of the Spirit) precipitates the shouts. And for the unanointed, the style might do precisely this. After all, if they are shouting from emotion, if they have—as Evangelist Yarborough suggested—the Holy Ghost *on* them rather than *in* them, then they might well be responding to style. For these believers, personal experience offers proof of causality.

So what bearing does all this have on the opening prayer? In most gospel programs, the elevated style makes its first appearance during prayer. Coming this early in the service, the style stands as a sign of things to come, auguring the intensity of holy accord. Saved believers hearing the shift into chant are immediately reminded (if only subconsciously) of revelation, transcendence, and past experiences with the Spirit. For them, the shift operates as symbol, connotatively calling to mind the sacred flow of anointment. Unsaved believers might also think of transcendence, though many would hear the shift more as signifier than as symbol, taking it as indication of the Spirit's actual presence. Others among the unsaved might hear the style as mere rhetorical device. But even they would likely associate the sound with sanctified behavior, particularly if they are regular servicegoers. They would not, however, necessarily draw any causal conclusions.

For all these worshipers, the emergence of heightened style invokes a particular interpretive frame. Though these frames differ for different worshipers, all of them somehow point to transcendence. All turn the mind to spiritual action. And all, in turn, guide devotional reflection, providing a backdrop against which the speaker's words are heard and the hearers' private prayers are constructed. The prayer-giver thus influences the unvoiced prayers of the congregation not only through word and theme, but also through style.

Before turning away from issues of style and meaning, mention should be made of the role that *intensity* plays in this soulful drama. When listening to Deacon Eldridge, one cannot help but be struck by the sheer passion of his prayer. What begins as conversational flow gradually turns to impassioned torrent, as words surge forth with ever-increasing speed and power. Also caught in this rising current is the prayer's pitch, which climbs throughout the prayer until finally settling in the upper reaches of the deacon's vocal range. This tonal rise, culminating in a sharp narrowing of tonal compass, is one of the key characteristics of heightened speech. It's also the characteristic that most clearly testifies to vocal intensity, since maintaining this elevated tone demands that most speakers manifestly strain their voices. The exertion required to achieve this end becomes evident in the tautness of speakers' delivery, the hoarseness of their speech, and the sheer force with which words press from their mouths. All signs point to complete, soulful engagement. This engagement, in turn, offers a model for the congregation, tacitly encouraging saints in the pews to delve deeper and more ardently into worship. The adage "if you want something out of it, you've got to put something into it" virtually shouts its way into the foreground of consciousness. Heightened style thus commands not only the hearers' attention, but also their commitment. Just as it suggests the potential of spiritual presence, so too does it testify to the potential of intense, personal engagement.

The themes of devotional prayers vary from speaker to speaker and occasion to occasion. But the tone and intensity of these prayers show a consistency that crosses the full spectrum of worship events. This is certainly the case for gospel programs. Even in the most crassly commercial "ticket programs"—where devotions include only an abbreviated introduction, a few verses of song, and a prayer—the prayer usually rings forth with passion and sincerity. Indeed, in such programs it often extends longer than the congregational singing. No matter how "dead" the crowd or how "entertainment"-oriented the event, the prayer seems to emerge unscathed, demanding programgoers' attention and enjoining singers to give God all the glory.

✳   ✳   ✳   ✳   ✳

"The environment of prayer is the foundation of the world," a Baptist deacon once told me.[18] It certainly provides the foundation for the gospel program. Public prayer initiates the program's formal conversation with the Lord, opening the service with explicit entreaty and thanks. At the same time, it encourages private, unvoiced communion, eliciting reflection and inspiring personal prayer. Prayer supplements song with a message of thanksgiving, setting the service off on a path of devotional celebration. At the same time, it explicitly asks the Spirit to guide the proceedings and calls on saints to open their hearts to that guidance. Prayer's style symbolically alludes to the touch of transcendence, while its words overtly invite that touch. And its delivery offers a model for intense, worshipful engagement. Prayer indeed provides a foundation for worship. At the Branchettes' anniversary, the first act to build on this foundation is congregational song.

Before turning to song, however, perhaps we should assess the Spirit's role in the service thus far. Elder Richardson's words suggest the possibility of transcendent involvement in prayer, describing one form of spiritual intercession. Yet we have no way of knowing whether the Spirit so moved in this particular service. What we *do* know is that "spiritual signs" and displays of passion offer no certain guide to actual experience and thus cannot be trusted as indicators of divine presence. No matter how impassioned the prayer or how enthusiastic the response, these witnessed behaviors tell us nothing about the holy touch. That knowledge will come only from the testimonies of saints. But as of yet, we have not actually asked any of the saints at this anniversary about their experience. That's clearly the next step in our journey toward fuller understanding.

Chapter 8

A Conversation

"It's the Words of Him That's Speaking Through Me"

Almost a year after the Branchettes' twentieth anniversary, Deacon Willie Eldridge and I met at Long Branch Disciple Church to talk about prayer. We arranged the meeting over the phone and both pulled into the church's sandy lot at about the same time. After shaking hands and exchanging pleasantries, Deacon Eldridge unlocked the church doors and moved toward the amen corner, where he lit a small wall heater. As the wintry night had left a deep chill in the sanctuary, the two of us huddled around the warmth. With coats still on, we stretched our hands before the welcome flames.

Up to this point, I hadn't really spoken at length with Deacon Eldridge. Though I'd seen him a number of times in church and talked with him over the telephone, we had never sat down together to discuss matters of faith. But as I prepared to speak with him about my transcription of his prayer, other church members encouraged me to partake more fully of his wisdom. "He's a real rock of the church," one member had declared, "someone who knows his Bible and lives by it." So when I called Deacon Eldridge to arrange our meeting, I asked if we could spend some time talking about the workings of prayer. He responded with characteristic humility, saying simply that he'd gladly share whatever limited understandings the Lord had granted him.

In the chilled emptiness of the church, we began by talking about the words he had prayed with such passion almost a year earlier. Following a transcription while the tape played, we moved line by line through the prayer, listening and stopping and then listening again.

Throughout this process, Deacon Eldridge responded almost as if he were hearing the prayer for the first time. Given the passage of time, this didn't strike me as particularly unusual. What *did* strike me, however, was the deacon's repeated uncertainty about the meanings he had been trying to convey. He kept rephrasing the prayed lines, sometimes adding words to fill out a thought, sometimes changing words that didn't seem to make sense, sometimes departing from the text altogether to clarify an opaque reference. Even more intriguing were Deacon Eldridge's comments about correcting the prayer's orientation. With no prompting from me, he kept remarking that lines openly addressed to God (such as "So Lord, while we have this privilege, Lord, let's put Him ahead . . .") seemed in fact to be directed at the congregation. Intended audience seemed to shift from heaven to earth even in the course of single lines.

When we finished listening to the recording, I asked Deacon Eldridge about the actual *experience* of praying. I knew from earlier conversations that many saints, when speaking about prayer, describe a process of spiritual involvement that extends far beyond the "vibrations" discussed in the last chapter. Reflecting on Deacon Eldridge's uncertainty about meanings and orientations, I wondered whether he too sometimes experienced this sense of heightened spiritual involvement. When I posed the question, he immediately described a process of divine enablement in which his role as author decreased while that of the Spirit increased. The exchange that ensued is worth printing in full, if only to convey the sense of experiential certainty that permeates Deacon Eldridge's remarks. As he makes quite clear, he knows precisely from whence came the words of his prayer.[1]

"I've heard some folks talk about [how] when they pray—especially when they're leading prayer in front of a congregation—how sometimes the words just seem to flow," I began, turning the conversation away from transcription and toward matters of process. "Sometimes how the words—it's almost as if they don't have to think about the words, but rather that those words just, just seem to come on out of their own accord. Is that an experience you're familiar with?"

Deacon Eldridge didn't hesitate for a second. Almost before I had finished, he was already answering, his voice full of quiet conviction. While he spoke, I couldn't help but notice the intensity that burned in his deeply set eyes. Fixing on me and never wavering, they underscored his words with a message of unfaltering certainty.

"Yes, I am," he said gently. "Because, the most of the time [when] I get up to pray, I don't know what I'm going to say. So to me, it's *given*. By Him. Because, see, through in doing all things like that, if we don't rely on Him, we got to, sort of, make it up. Make us up a program or a prayer. And if we would do that, we [would] praise directly from what we have made up. And, you know, a lot of times you can get up there and *forget* what *you* have made up. Then you look back at Him, and you're using *your* prayer. *Then*, where will you fit, in trying to deliver a prayer?"

Not wanting to break his train of thought, I murmured a simple "uh-huh." His question was rhetorical, and its answer obvious. Using one's own prayer left one subject to the whims of memory and the conceits of self-interest. But using that which was "given" insured both efficacy and flow.

"See," he continued, still speaking about self-made prayer, "that will show you up as not being in the Spirit. You're just in self. You're just delivering something out of self. So the most of the time I get up to pray, I don't have no idea of what I

7. Members of Long Branch Disciple Church speak of Deacon Willie Eldridge as "one of the prayingest men" they've every encountered. He, in turn, attributes his gift for prayer entirely to the Spirit. "It's not *my* words," he explains. "It's the words of Him that's speaking through me. . . . All I do is just open my mouth. And He delivers." (Photo by Roland L. Freeman)

am going to say. Now, I could have thought of *these* words in the beginning, and that's this: 'God's plans included us. Do our plans include Him?' And from that point on, I didn't know what I was going to say. Definitely not."

Almost a year later, here was the connection to the anniversary prayer. And perhaps an explanation for Deacon Eldridge's interpretive uncertainties upon hearing it back. Only the opening phrases were products of forethought. Beyond this formulaic preface, the deacon let the words come of their own accord, not thinking about them in advance, not stopping them as they flowed. Composition was spontaneous.

After a brief pause, Deacon Eldridge continued, extending his explanation beyond the single example. "And in *all* prayers, I never know what I'm going to say, altogether. Not only prayers—testimonies too. I know that I want to tell the people what He have done for *me*. But a lot of times I get up and start to testifying, [and] things come to me that I hadn't even thought about, that He have done for me. So, [in] these things, we depend on Him. *Not* on ourselves. So this is something that comes to you, as you stand before a congregation, or whatever. And whenever you rely on Him, things will work out right."

The deacon's soft voice had yet to waver; his eyes had yet to break their focused gaze. His words still conveyed a sense of gentle certainty, not as if he were trying to convince me, but rather as if the reported flow were a simple fact, an experienced given. Yet despite this matter-of-factness, the described process was clearly different from the compositional practices of everyday conversation. Deacon Eldridge kept distancing the *source* of the words, separating source from self, speaking of thoughts that "came" from somewhere else, of words that were "given" from the outside. As the pause after his last statement lengthened, I chose to probe this sense of external authorship.

"Now when you say it 'comes' to you," I asked, stumbling as I framed the question, "could you describe that process a little bit?"

"Well, the way I would describe that—I know it don't come exactly, I would say, as [if] He is standing talking to us. This comes through the Spirit, the Holy Spirit. Just like the Holy Spirit can be *on* us, but do we see it?"

"Not at all," I replied.

"So [in] these things, it's not that He's *speaking* to us," Deacon Eldridge continued, pointing slightly to his mouth and stressing the word "speaking" to indicate the audible act of talking. "But the Holy Spirit is speaking to us and telling us." (This "speaking" and "telling" were soft, quiet, as if to suggest a process of a very different nature.) "Because for me to utter these words that I uttered, not knowing what I was going to say, the Spirit—and it had to be the Holy Spirit—spoke *through* me. It's not *my* words. It's the words of Him that's speaking through me. Because, you know, it's not our works. It's the works of *Him*. But He *uses us* as a *vessel*. So we're just only a vessel."

Compositional agency is thus no longer an issue. Deacon Eldridge describes the words not as "coming" to his mind from the hidden wellsprings of consciousness, but as coming *to* him from the Spirit and passing *through* him as water would a vessel. Just as that water is neither product nor part of the vessel, so too are the words neither product nor part of the mind. Though they perhaps pass *through* that mind (which "hears" them as a silent voice), they are not its creation.

As the deacon explained this process, his words grew more animated and poetic, aligning themselves in structures of rhetorical apposition. The Spirit's not speaking out loud; He's speaking in mind. I don't speak; He speaks through me. They're not my words; they're His words. Again and again, Deacon Eldridge stressed the point, making certain that I understood that this was a process apart, a supernatural enablement, an encounter with transcendence. Yet the enabling had its conditions. After a long pause, the deacon continued, his voice once again quiet.

"But you got to be in the position that He can use you as that vessel. Because, see, so many times, so many of us, we don't have the Holy Spirit. And we have no thoughts of Him. And He can't use us as a vessel to *deliver* a thought, or a message, from Him."

"That's just like a preacher. If he haven't been called and anointed by the Spirit of God, he can preach all he want to. But then again I would say [that even] there a lot of times—you know, the devil can preach. But he can't live it."

"Uh-huh," I responded, thinking about his tacit reference to misused gifts. With the unanointed preacher, the preachings can be gifted but still flow from self. Or, as he suggests, the enabling may come from Satan, who is *also* a spirit. "Right," I added quietly.

"So people can—you can look on a person, a lot of times, and know—if you are anointed—that they are not anointed. That's a preacher. So that's the best I can describe that. The words come from Him. I was just a vessel. Delivering His message. That's the only thing I can say."

In speaking of preachers, Deacon Eldridge briefly raised the issue of spiritual discernment, noting that the anointed can often see through the guise of the unanointed. But then he returned to matters of enablement, repeating his deference to divine authorship. I chose to pursue the latter path and asked for fuller description.

"Now when you stand before the congregation, and you offer those words, do you get the *thoughts*, and then put them into words? Do the words themselves come to your mind as you say them? How . . ."

"I understand what you mean," Deacon Eldridge replied gently. "They come to my mind. As I open my mouth. Because, you know, whenever I got to stop and think, I'm still in self. So the words flow *through me*. It's not my thoughts [that] are trying to figure out what's going to come next. Because they're there. All I do is just open my mouth. And *He* delivers."

After a long pause, I pressed further: "So you're actually not even consciously taking part in the . . ."

"No," interjected the deacon.

". . . in the construction of that prayer?"

"No sir."

"And the words are just, coming of their own . . ."

"Coming on their own. Because, when I pray, in most all instances, I never know what I'm going to say. It just comes to me. As I attempt to deliver a prayer."

The process that Deacon Eldridge describes is clearly *more* than simple inspiration, where thoughts come from outside the self and are then translated by the self into inspired pronouncements. The act of translation is missing here. The words come to, flow through, and go out. Without addition. Without change. That which is uttered is the Word of God, mediated (at least ideally) only by the mechanisms of the human voice. If the self does not intervene, authorship of the message's content rests solely with the Spirit.

As I've already suggested, saints who describe this process of divine authorship most often link it with preaching. Many, including Deacon Eldridge, also tie it to testimony. In both cases, the rationale for divine intervention seems clear. In preaching, the Lord steps in to instruct, exhort, counsel, comfort, encourage, and persuade. The preached words, whether anointed or not, are addressed to the congregation. In testimony, the Lord intercedes to counsel, console, and encourage by having saints publicly recount the workings of grace in their lives. Though testimony is formally framed as an act of thanksgiving, with words addressed to the Lord, most saints agree that its intended audience in fact includes all those with ears to hear. In its role as public witness, testimony, like preaching, invites divine intercession. Both acts address themselves to human hearers.

But not so praying. At least not so overtly. As I suggested in the previous chapter, prayer by its very nature addresses itself to God. Though public voicing adds an inherent element of ministry, prayer's principal functions are entreaty and thanksgiving. When the Spirit "rides" the words, as Elder Richardson explained, the ministerial function intensifies, sending the words both upward to heaven *and* outward to the pews. Yet those words, however blessed, are not necessarily the voicings of the Spirit. Though perhaps inspired and anointed, they can still be products of the mortal mind. Deacon Eldridge, however, speaks of prayers where the words themselves—words ostensibly directed *to* the Lord—in fact come *from* the Lord. To confirm that this is what happens, I asked the deacon the same question I had posed to Elder Richardson: who precisely is talking to whom?

"One thing that's always intrigued me, interested me about that process," I began. "You are praying to the Lord . . ."

"Uh-huh," the deacon affirmed.

". . . before the congregation."

"That's right."

"And yet at the same time as you're praying, the words are being given you *by* the Lord, in order to pray back *to* the Lord."

"Uh-huh."

"Is that what's going on, essentially?"

"Well," Deacon Eldridge responded, with what sounded like a sigh. "Let me see if I could clear that up to you. *Not* for the words to go back to the Lord, because He gives the words."

"Right," I added.

"But to me, it would be that the Lord delivers this prayer *through* you, to tell the *people*. To pray to the *people* what I want them to hear. Or what I want them to know. It's not that they're going back to Him."

"Right."

"Because He delivers them."

"Right."

"And regardless of whether you go back or don't go back, He knows the prayer. The prayer is His in the beginning. All I got to do is humble myself and do what He asks *me* to do. That's all."

And that *was* all, for here was the answer to my question. Simply put, when the author changes, so too does the prayer's function and direction. But not its frame. The words still *textually* address the Lord, though *functionally* they now address the congregation. Once again, I asked the deacon to confirm this understanding.

"So in essence, the prayer—the public prayer—becomes almost an act of ministry? In that the Lord is giving these words to you, so that they might be heard by the congregation."

"Right," said Deacon Eldridge, his voice sounding relieved that I'd finally understood.

"And that the congregation might then reflect upon them and take them to their heart."

"That's true. That's the message."

"Okay," I concluded. "And that's essentially the same thing that happens in— sometimes in testimony, in preaching . . ."

"Right."

". . . for a called and anointed preacher . . ."

"Uh-huh. [An] anointed preacher."

". . . and I imagine sometimes in singing, perhaps, as well."

"Well, [in] singing, you know, a message can be delivered through singing. Yes. Don't forget that. Because there have been a lot of people uplifted in a song. Even, as you said a while ago, as you stated just a few minutes ago, there have been a lot of people that took and looked back into their lives and took another step, through song."

"Right," I added.

"So, it's not that everybody has to be uplifted through the prayer," Deacon Eldridge explained. "Same thing—some people through a song, some people through a prayer. Some can be uplifted through a testimony. Some can be uplifted through a sermon. But then again too, the Word said, '*Without* the Word of God, none of us can come to Him. None of us can make this journey.'"

"But, I believe," he continued, "as we have stated, those words that come through these various other things, is the Word of God. Whether it's through a song, prayer, or testimony. Of course, then again too, it says, 'the preaching of the foolishness of the gospel is high.' Well said." Then Deacon Eldridge chuckled.[2]

Genre clearly poses no barrier to revelation. The words can flow in song, prayer, testimony, and preaching. Though they may sound like "foolishness" to the unsaved, to the saints they carry the power to "uplift" and nourish the spirit.

The deacon's comments led me to ask about the ways in which revelation is actually received. "Well now," I began, "this sort of communication, this sort of message from the Lord, is a message which comes to you internally. So that as you're praying, for example, you're hearing it, and saying it."

"Uh-huh," the deacon affirmed.

"And the words," I continued, "the words—unknown to you—are flowing . . ."

"That's right."

". . . from your mouth. Have there been instances in your own life where the Word of the Lord came to you in a different way?"

"Well, I would put that this way," responded Deacon Eldridge, hesitating slightly. "Yes. But I'm going to go say this now, before I say that. One thing you're about to say there, I believe—I was expecting you to ask me if [in] every prayer that I've ever delivered, if the words flowed."

"Well, that's a good question," I added quickly. "Let's talk about that one."

"But, not so," he stated firmly. "That's why I *know*, [that] without the Spirit of the Lord, a prayer—the first thing about it—is *worthless*."

He paused to let the words sink in, and then continued. "Because so many times, maybe you have attempted—not only a prayer—to perform certain things. I know one time they asked me to get up and speak on Men's Day. So I used quite a bit of time trying to prepare myself, picking up different things from different books and so forth, to put together. But when I stood up, you know what happened?"

"You're mind went blank," I ventured, recalling similar stories I'd heard from preachers who told how the Spirit pulled them away from their prepared notes.

"That's right," Deacon Eldridge declared. "Every bit of it left me. And I went the way that He led me to go. And He give me the message. And I delivered the message. And it was well done. But what happened in the beginning, I was going to prepare *my* message. But I found out my message wasn't going to do."

"So," he added, "He don't have to come to you the very same *way* every time. But whatever way He come to you is right. He don't never come to you in a way that's wrong. Whatever way is right."

"So there are times," I asked, "when you've been asked to lead prayer and haven't felt that flow?"

"Oh yes." Again his words conveyed a sense of certainty. "Yes. But it's been quite some time. But that really teaches me, or gives me experience to know, [that] without the Spirit of the Lord, we're not able to do anything that's successful."

"When you say it's been quite some time," I responded, "does that mean that when you were younger in the Lord, that the flow came less than it does now?"

"Well, I put that this way," the deacon responded, again with something of a sigh. "Not exactly young—well, it could be young in the Lord too. But *until* the Holy Spirit, until you're born again—I believe John 3 and 3 says, 'Except a man be born again, he cannot even *see* the kingdom of God.' And I believe Matthew 6 and 33, it tells us to 'Seek ye first the kingdom of God, and *His* righteousness, and all other things will fall in place.' So until we decided to start seeking Him, through *all* things—it could have been [that] a lot of times things didn't fall into place, as they should. Because *we* were in the way. So, that's what I meant by that, you know. So whenever the Holy Spirit, or the Spirit of the Lord, come upon you, it's a difference."

In essence, Deacon Eldridge rejected the frame that I'd set forth suggesting that the anointed flow came with spiritual maturity. At issue isn't maturity, the deacon asserted, but conversion. A simple before and after. Before being born again, all talk necessarily rises from self. After being born again, all talk stands ready to submit to the will of the Spirit. Once the relationship is established, the potential for divine intercession is *always* there.

So much for potential. But what of those times when the words are *not* provided? Are these prayers, to use Deacon Eldridge's own term, "worthless"? And what of the prayers prayed by believers who are sincerely seeking but not yet saved? Or by those who *think* that they are saved, but in fact are not? Are these prayers just so many sounding words?

"Now when you prayed without the guidance of the Lord," I asked, hoping to pursue these questions, "when you prayed without those words coming to you . . ."

"Uh-huh," said the deacon, nodding his head.

". . . you speak of those prayers as being prayers in self. And yet those prayers are sincere. Can people in the congregation nonetheless be moved, be led to reflect, be touched by those words? Even though those words were not given to you by the Spirit?"

"Well, let's put that this way," Deacon Eldridge responded, pausing a bit to gather his words. "It's been a many a sermon preached by people that, a lot of times, was not called and anointed . . ."

"Right," I added, filling in the pause.

". . . by God. But you know, God is able to do *anything*. So God don't fail. If these things are delivered to the people that He, He seek the people to be moved from this, they can be moved. Because I don't care who's standing before us, we all are not judges to know who's saved and to know who's not saved. So, if I prayed a prayer, or anybody prayed a prayer, a lot of times that, maybe, weren't exactly given through the Lord, it can be effective to the people as far as they might accept the words."

"Because," I added, testing my understanding, "with the Lord being able to do all things, the Lord can . . ."

"That's right," added the deacon.

". . . insure their effectiveness."

"That's right," he agreed. "That's true."

As suggested in the previous chapter, spiritual efficacy does not hinge on the prophetic provision of words. Nor does it hinge on the spiritual state of the speaker. Words may be uttered in sincerity or in hypocrisy; they may be spoken to glorify God or to glorify self. However they are used, whatever their original purpose, the words are still subject to divine direction. Put simply, the Lord can intervene and *use* those words to serve His ends. The vibrations can ride, the message can touch, the soul can stir. All because the Spirit *wills* the words to carry power. The final key to spiritual efficacy thus lies not with speaker, style, or message, but with Spirit. For if the Spirit so wills, even the words of the unanointed will become as the Spirit's own, touching and uplifting with as much power as if they had been uttered by the Spirit Himself.

This issue led me back to Deacon Eldridge's comments about praying without the anointing. He said there had been times when he prayed without the flow, and he suggested that this was certainly true before he was saved. I wondered whether he could remember the first time he *did* experience the anointing of words.

"Can you recall," I began, "and this is a big jump—can you recall your first experience with having those words provided for you, be it in testimony, in prayer, in whatever? Can you recall the first time that you felt that the Spirit [was] giving you those words?"

"Well, I can't give you the specific day," Deacon Eldridge answered slowly, "or the specific place, or the specific time. But I do know that, I can tell you—I *could* feel a difference."

"Because I've known a time, I believe whenever I was maybe first made a deacon, I was—[I] believe we had a chairman deacon here—and as far as praying, I was sort of shy from praying. At least, the most of the time, maybe I'd be up in the choir stand to sing with the choir, so maybe I wouldn't be asked to pray. Because see, the Lord—to me—*He was not giving me a prayer and I didn't have nothing!*" The deacon chuckled as he recalled singing to avoid being called to pray. But as he continued, his words grew faster and more emphatic, pushing forth with the power of deep conviction.

"So I was afraid that I wouldn't pray to suit the people. *But now, I don't pray to suit the people, because I know whom I'm praying to!* I pray the prayer of Him. And if I pray the prayer that *He* gives me, I don't worry about suiting the people. It's the right prayer." The deacon's closing sentence was once again quietly calm. Voiced with an air of finality, it led to a long pause. I nodded and moved to turn off the recorder. Then Deacon Eldridge began again, offering the conversation's coda.

"So that's what I can remember. And I can't tell you the specific time. But I do know this much—that whenever I got in that position that He could use me, there was a difference. Because see, one thing, we got to do something ourselves. First. We got to get ourselves out of the way, so He *will* come in. Now, He *could* come in. But so He *will* come in. And prepare us. But we got to do something ourselves."

Like so many other conversations about spiritual activity, this one ended with a call for personal practice. As Deacon Eldridge pointed out, the Spirit can act with or without the willful engagement of the individual. But to optimize the potential for such action, the believer must first invite the Spirit in. This invitation entails reducing concern for self so that the Spirit's way might be eased. Again the model is one of equilibrium: only as the self decreases can the Spirit increase. In the arena of prayer, this means focusing away from the pettiness of individual desire and turning all thoughts to the will of the Lord. In the broader arena of life, it means turning away from the ways of the world and walking the narrow path of sanctification. In both realms, the responsibility for taking the first step rests firmly with the individual.

As Deacon Eldridge uttered his closing words, he drew his hands together in a gentle gesture of finality. The steadiness of his gaze suggested that what needed to be said had been said. After a long pause, I turned off the recorder, and we began to speak of other things.

Chapter 9

Song

"Sing Till the Power of the Lord Comes Down"

"Glory to God! Glory to God!" Joining in the hosannas that close Deacon Eldridge's prayer, Mother Eunice Nixon stands in the amen corner and moves toward the cross-aisle. Her outstretched arm receives the microphone from the deacon while murmured "Amens" still whisper through the sanctuary and the guitar still quietly weeps. Without a moment's hesitation, she addresses the church, her tone once again warm and conversational.

"This next song," she says slowly, glancing toward the musicians, "is dedicated to the Branchettes." The guitarist and bass player are still playing the melody they had settled into during the prayer. At Mother Nixon's glance, however, they bring it to a quick close. At the same moment, saints in the pews fill the impending silence with words of affirmation, calling out "Yes" and "Lord Jesus." As Mother Nixon continues, her words assume the purposeful rhythms of conversation.

> When you get Christ in your life,   (Lord Jesus!)
>   and no matter how far you go,   (So true!)
>   no matter *where* you go,   (Amen!)
> don't let nobody turn you around!

A wave of assent ripples through the pews, the saints clearly approving Mother Nixon's choice of song. "Yeah," they cry. "Amen!" "That's right!" The bass player, meanwhile, stills the subtle chording with which he had punctuated each of Mother Nixon's lines. Now he waits for her to set a new rhythm.

The wait is not long. Someone in the front pew passes Mother Nixon a tambourine, and she immediately begins to sing, striking the jingling frame on the second beat. By the fourth, she's joined by clapping from the pews. An enthusiastic chorus of voices is already sounding the familiar spiritual, singing with an exuberance that testifies to the song's aptness for an anniversary. Before the third line has even begun, a sister in the amen corner is pushing the lyrics with an offbeat clap.

Turn you round,
TURN YOU ROUND,
DON'T LET NOBODY TURN YOU ROUND!

The guitarist is the first musician to join the praises, opening the second verse with an understated, rather ragged version of the melody. A few bars later, the bass lays a fluently voiced foundation, inspiring the guitarist to a clearer phrasing of the chorused words. The congregation, meanwhile, joyfully repeats the opening lines, preparing the way for Mother Nixon's solo lead.

TURN YOU ROUND,
TURN YOU ROUND,
DON'T LET NOBODY TURN YOU ROUND!

Mother Nixon launches the next verse by double-timing the tambourine, pushing the tempo with a driving sizzle. Her resonant voice soars above the accompaniment as she passionately cries out the lyrics. The guitarist matches her note for note.

Don't let nobody turn you around,
TURN YOU ROUND
Don't let nobody turn you around,
TURN YOU ROUND
Don't let nobody
TURN YOU ROUND,
KEEP YOUR FEET ON SOLID GROUND!

Midway through the verse, the keyboards leap in, sounding the synthesized voicings of chorded piano. Now freed from its supportive role, an emboldened bass pushes to the melodic foreground, wrapping its warm notes around Mother Nixon's every word. Meanwhile, a second tambourine adds its sibilant pulse to the thickening rhythms.

Don't let nobody turn you around,
TURN YOU ROUND
Don't let nobody turn you around,
TURN YOU ROUND
Don't let nobody
TURN YOU ROUND,
KEEP YOUR FEET ON SOLID GROUND!

The entire church moves with the joy of jubilant praise. Old and young alike sing with a full-voiced enthusiasm that rings from the block walls and presses

8. "Don't let nobody turn you round! Keep your feet on solid ground!" The raised voices of the congregation push the singing to a passionate peak, transforming the song's message from sober counsel to joyful affirmation. Here members of St. Amanda Missionary Baptist Church's Gospel Choir—seated behind the kente-garbed Grace A.M.E. Mass Choir—add the sizzle of tambourines. (Photo by Roland L. Freeman)

against the restraints of the song's tempo. The sharp reports of slapping palms and the resonant thrum of rapping feet further nudge the rhythm, quickening it at a pace both imperceptible and undeniable. Mother Nixon, caught up in the wave of rejoicing, closes her eyes and presses into the next set of verses.

My hope is built on nothing less,
    DON'T LET NOBODY TURN YOU ROUND
Than Jesus' blood and righteousness.
    DON'T LET NOBODY TURN YOU ROUND
Friends may come and friends may go,
    DON'T LET NOBODY TURN YOU ROUND
But there's one thing I'd like you to know,
    DON'T LET NOBODY TURN YOU ROUND
They'll build you up just to let you down.
    DON'T LET NOBODY TURN YOU ROUND
Just keep your feet on solid ground!
    DON'T LET NOBODY TURN YOU ROUND

Midway through the verse, a young sister behind me starts clapping in triplets, lending the singing an air of rolling acceleration. Looking away from the cross-aisle, I notice that the sisters in the amen corner are swaying in loose unison. As I turn, I see that the same holds true for much of the congregation, with whole pews moving in harmony, the saints' upper bodies and clapping hands describing an impassioned arc of devotion.

As Mother Nixon swings into the chorus, she personalizes the lyric, transforming the song from advice to testimony. As soon as the shift becomes evident, a sister sitting near the cross-aisle cries out, "Alright! Alright!"

I ain't going to let nobody turn me around!
    TURN ME ROUND
I ain't going to let nobody turn me around!
    TURN ME ROUND
I ain't going to LET NOBODY
    TURN ME ROUND,
KEEP YOUR FEET ON SOLID GROUND!

Each solo line of this testimonial verse evokes a shouted response, with a brother in the deacon's corner calling out "Yeah!" during the second, and a sister in the pews crying "Alright!" during the third. A chorus of sisters helps Mother Nixon conclude that third line, spontaneously adding their testimonies to hers.

After a brief bridging flourish from the keyboards, Mother Nixon repeats the core verses, closing once again with the shift into testimony. Cries of affirmation are now ringing forth freely, punctuating and personalizing the sung lines. "Go ahead!" "Yes Lord!" Hands clap, bodies sway, upraised arms wave, and eyes shine with a spirit of irrepressible joy.

Finally ready to close the song, Mother Nixon swings into the chorus one last time. As she nears the verse's end, she lays down the microphone and steps away from the center aisle. But the spirit in the church is simply too high to stop, so she reprises the testimonial verse, her unamplified voice still filled with enough fire to climb high above the instruments' soulful phrasings.

Recognizing that the end is near, the guitar and keyboard players both cut their volume and slightly slow the tempo. But then Mother Nixon launches into the chorus a second time. The congregational tambourines quickly push the rhythm right back up, keeping the passion palpably alive. As the verse closes, dozens of voices join Mother Nixon in chorusing "Don't let nobody turn you around," almost shouting the words so as to give the line a staccato forcefulness. Then Mother Nixon slides once again into the testimonial refrain.

As she begins, she glances toward the instrumentalists and stills her tambourine. The organist reads her cue and starts to ease out of the song, leaving the lead to the guitar. The guitarist, in turn, guides the congregation to a slow conclusion, stretching out the final word with a sweetly voiced flourish. At the song's close, Mother Nixon smiles radiantly at the congregation. Her delicate, flushed face seems lit from within, as if holding in the very fires of holiness.

Even before many have stopped singing, the church is already ringing with handclaps and fervent cries of thanksgiving. "Glory!" calls a mother in the amen corner. "Amen! Amen!" cries a sister from the pews behind me. "Thank You, Jesus!" shouts a brother from the rear of the church. Among the voices raised in praise is that of Mother Nixon, who slowly steps back to her place in the amen corner. Throughout, the guitarist keeps on playing, quietly improvising a melody to welcome the cross-aisle's next speaker.

* * * * *

Mother Nixon's song is by no means hers alone. Though she opens and she leads, the song belongs as much to the congregation as it does to her. The singers in the pews take the song, transform it, and mold it to their will, filling it along the way with spirit and fire. What begins as solo performance quickly becomes spirited dialogue, and then moves beyond even that, transcending the bounds of tuneful talk in a vibrant celebration of artful simultaneity.

As the song eases into the congregation's hands, the focused lead dissolves, losing its singular authority and becoming but one of many voices guiding performance. Much the same holds true for the authority of words, which wanes so as to open conversational leadership to tune, motion, rhythm, and the entire range of vocalized sound. In performance, the conversational arena widens far beyond the restrictive boundaries of language.

Within this widened arena, new leads emerge and just as quickly vanish, momentarily crystallizing conversational focus while contributing to the song's surging flow. Like overlapping voices in a spirited conversation, these leads are both sequential and simultaneous, lending the whole a layered thickness that invites both contribution and response. The rights of leadership, of creative, response-eliciting contribution, are open to all; the very act of participation grants this potential. At the same time, participation invites ever-deepening conversational involvement, encouraging saints to creatively "play off" of each other's devotional contributions. Congregational song thus offers every worshiper the option of both creating and responding, both soloing and sustaining.[1] A saint's slow sway sets those around her to swaying in synchrony; a sister's low moan finds extension and embellishment in the moans of nearby others; a brother's breathless cry of "Hallelujah!" sparks supportive calls of "Praise God!" and "Thank You, Jesus!" In like manner, steady handclapping from one pew elicits offbeat accenting from another, while the percussive phrasings of the bass prompt a swooping, melismatic improvisation from the lead singer. At any given moment, any saint can initiate, follow, or transform that act of following by creating anew. Always pressing for greater fulfillment, worshipers thus transform the simple conversations of words and melody into triumphant celebrations of waving and swaying, moaning and weeping, handclapping and foot tapping and the worshipful uplifting of eyes.

Within this frame of joint creativity, the saints' professed goal is to "come to one accord." "Accord," in this context, references something far deeper than a simple state of harmony. When the saints speak of "coming to accord," they mean recreating in spirit and mood the focused reverence that prevailed among the apostles on the day of Pentecost. Such deep devotion never "just happens." Rather, it must be actively *achieved*. To attain this state of devotional consonance, saints must purge from their minds the tumbling confusions of idle thought and worldly concern. Their goal is nothing less than a congruity of consciousness, a shared focus that one preacher describes as "hearts beating in unison . . . [and] in tune."[2] Achieving this mystical communion, in turn, is said to invite the Holy Ghost into the gathering, much as it did on that day when "tongues of fire" were first visited upon the apostles. To "come to one accord" is thus to create the optimal conditions for visitation by the Spirit.

This brings us right back to song. Saints say that congregational singing offers one of the most direct paths toward achieving the oneness of accord. Singing crafts a consonance of sound and motion that both prefigures and evokes a consonance of spirit. It audibly declares a singleness of congregational purpose; its very harmonies announce a sharing of ends and actions. At the same time, by drawing individuals into performance, congregational singing immerses believers in a creative realm that both demands engagement and prompts thought. Song's power emerges from this special meeting of self and collective, a coming together that frees the mind for meditation while sustaining the voice on a sea of sound. On one level, the experience is intensely personal, the self responding to song with reflection. On another, it's deeply communal, the self surrendering to the flow of praise. And on a third, it is personal in its very communality, the self adding its soul-shaped contribution to the interlocking effervescence. This coupling of meditation, communion, and creation yields an experience whose intensity and duration are matched by no other worship act. Only congregational song can predictably evoke and sustain the multilayered fullness of praise.[3]

This is precisely why song plays such an integral role in the devotional service. When most saints enter the service, their minds are still rambling the paths of mundane existence. Recall for a moment the conversations overheard just prior to the Branchettes' anniversary. Folks talked about the wintry weather, the basketball game, the morning's "peculiar" shout. They fiddled with amplifiers, tended to babies, exchanged the day's gossip. They entered, in other words, as individuals still caught in the webs of worldly concern. The purpose of devotions is to clear away these webs and to replace them with a single, shared focus on worship. Hence the devotional reliance on song. By drawing all together in a joint act of praise, singing stirs the spirit of communality and puts worshipers in what holiness bishop Frizelle Yelverton calls "the attitude to worship."

"Nobody ought to have to tell [saints] to praise," says Bishop Yelverton, talking about song and devotions. "Ordinarily, they ought to be a-praising. But a lot of times, we have them praising the Lord in order to get them in the *attitude to worship*. Because the Bible says we are to worship Him in spirit and in truth. See? You just don't worship the Lord any kind of way. But you got to be in the spirit to worship. And you can't worship Him in the spirit if the spirit's not in the individual. You've got to have that."[4]

For worship to be effective, for the Spirit to flow among the saints, believers must first achieve a spirit of worshipful union. Doing so means putting aside *individual* concerns and replacing them with *collective* conviction. Singing initiates this process, sweeping away trifling talk and errant thought while rerouting attention onto a common track, the "attitude to worship." As churchgoers themselves declare in song, singing facilitates this spirit of collective concentration:

We have come into His house,
    gathered in His name, to worship Him. [Repeat]
We have come into His house,
    gathered in His name, to worship Christ our Lord.
Worship Him, worship Christ our Lord.

Let's forget about ourselves,
    concentrate on Him, and worship Him. [Repeat]
Let's forget about ourselves,
    concentrate on Him, and worship Christ our Lord.
Worship Him, worship Christ our Lord.

Hence song's frequent appearance at times when congregational focus seems to be lacking. This is precisely why preachers who face "dead" congregations often call for a song before their sermons. And why praise leaders caught in "dry" services exhort churchgoers to sing and "put some spirit in the house." All of these efforts seek to foster a spirit of devotional collectivity by engaging churchgoers in collective action. Put simply, they seek to bring the congregation to accord.

* * * * *

During his long tenure as a Baptist deacon, quartet veteran Edward Denkins led more than his share of devotions. Talking to me in his seventy-ninth year, he was still strong of voice and sound of mind. Not only did he still sing with resonant power, but he still opened services with an enthusiasm that would shame most saints many years his junior. One afternoon, while we were discussing the Spirit's role in quartet performance, he offered a few words on congregational singing. His comments, marked by the deliberate pauses of reflective testimony, succinctly capture the special power of congregational song.

> Song is the Psalms,
>   is the light.
> Song gives you a feeling of togetherness.
> We can all sing together,
>   where we all can't talk at the same time.
> [If we] do,
>   we don't know what neither one's saying.
> When you got a group of people,
>   and they're singing an old familiar hymn,
>   together,
> there's a *vibration* that goes through the congregation,
>   that only you can understand and feel.
>   Cause you're together.
> Then there's lots of times [when] you can sing all day long,
>   and nothing happens.[5]

Devotional singing draws the congregation together, setting in motion the incipient "vibrations" of accord. But as Deacon Denkins points out, the process is by no means automatic. The simple act of singing does not spontaneously turn minds toward praise. For that to happen, the singing must be fueled by a will to worship. Accord comes only when saints actively seek it. And this seeking begins not with the congregation, but with the individual.

* * * * *

Singing demands a kind of engagement that few other acts of worship require. Most segments of the service ask only that worshipers engage the words and actions of distanced others. Though such engagement can be both active and creative (particularly when it involves transcendent conversation), it can also be wholly passive. Singing doesn't offer that option. Nor does it offer hearers the relatively prosaic role of respondents. Instead, singing demands creative participation, forcing singers to craft words to tune and tune to the melodies that fill the air. From the moment their mouths open in song, singers assume the responsibilities of performance, fully aware that their voices will affect the texture of the harmonized whole. The act of singing transforms worshipers from engaged audience members to artful actors.

Only testimony makes similar demands upon members of the congregation. But testimony—at least in its spoken form—is a solitary act, one that calls the speaker to *individually* address the full congregation. The testifier, in essence, chooses the role of devotional soloist. Moreover, since testimonies proceed sequentially, the constraints of time usually limit their number. This means that in most services, most saints do *not* have the opportunity to testify. Congregational singing, in contrast, sweeps the entire church into performance, drawing all together in an outpouring of praise that offers a range of opportunities for creative contribution. Singers can seize the lead, elaborate the rhythms, embellish the harmonies, follow in unison. Free to solo or accompany or solo while accompanying, congregational singers control the measure of their participation, ever adjusting engagement to meet the experience of the moment.

Whatever form their participation takes, singers are nonetheless engaged in the activity of singing. As suggested earlier, this alone demands a measure of thoughtful involvement. This involvement, in turn, prompts reflection. Singers, after all, are not merely voicing sounds. They are articulating words, words crafted into poetic messages of praise, words whose very familiarity bears witness to their ongoing relevance. In devotions, these words ring from songs that need no inscription in books, from pieces with long histories in the church. Their lyrics jump quickly to the tongue, freeing memory from the labors of retrieval while calling to mind the full range of associations linked to the songs. When the lyrics flow with ease, the tongue can roll each word, savoring its sound while letting the mind ponder its meaning.

As the mouth sings, so do the ears hear, taking in the words chorused by the assembly. These too pique the mind, leading to a layering of thought that listens to both self and singing other. The lyrics, borne on waves of passion, press themselves into consciousness, seeking relevance in memory, finding resonance in experience. Fueled by emotion and faith, the words strain for connection, struggling to ground the sung message in personal experience. With each connection, with each moment of resonance, the mind focuses a bit more, turning away errant thoughts while turning toward the contemplative fullness of worship. Saints say that only when this focus begins does one stop *hearing* the lyrics and start *feeling* them. No longer mere words, they now present themselves as piercing fragments of understanding. As they penetrate ever deeper into consciousness, the singer finds ever more reasons to praise.

The internal focus of praise, in turn, manifests itself in clearly voiced passion, transforming singing from exercise to exaltation. The difference makes itself palpably evident in the congregation. Saints singing with understanding are singing in the depths of spirit; their voices ring with a fullness that seems powered from within, as if driven by the soul rather than the tongue. Theirs are the voices that set the "vibrations" pulsing through the pews, "vibrations" that, as Deacon Denkins suggested, are both *felt* and *understood* by fellow saints. The *feeling* issues from a simple reading of voiced emotions; the *understanding*, however, issues from a deep sense of recognition, a resonating of spirit with spirit. This recognition draws the understanding saint even deeper into praise, cycling yet more passion into the singing while evoking the incipient consonance of accord.

For the individual saint, song serves as a vehicle of focus, a means of achieving an internal accord that sets all thoughts on parallel paths of praise. For the sanctified congregation, song serves as a vehicle of communion, a means of achieving an external accord that draws all minds to devotional congruence. Both forms of accord prepare the way for the Spirit, clearing away worldly concerns and inviting the Spirit's touch.

This is precisely the process to which saints refer when they sing the devotional standard "Let Us Sing Till the Power of the Lord Comes Down":

> Let us sing till the power of the Lord comes down.
> Let us sing till the power of the Lord comes down.
>> Lift up your head,
>>> Don't be afraid,
> Let us sing till the power of the Lord comes down.[6]

It is also the process referenced in the even more familiar congregational piece "My Soul Couldn't Rest Contented," one verse of which reads:

> Well, I singed and I singed,
>> Well, I singed all night long.
> Well, I singed and I singed,
>> Until I found the Lord.

The former song invokes the collective "us," clearly referencing the singing congregation. The latter testifies to the experience of "I," just as clearly referencing the singing individual. Both identify singing as a potent vehicle of devotional focus and spiritual invitation.

       *   *   *   *   *

The Spirit was high that Sunday morning at Mount Calvary Holy Church. I had arrived near the end of Bible Study and even then could feel the difference. The talk just seemed more intent, more earnestly focused, than usual. When Bishop Yelverton called the saints forward for altar prayer, this intensity found voice in an ardent chorus of affirmation and praise. As the bishop's voice rode the poetic cadences of spiritual elevation, kneeling saints wept and waved and added their prayers to his, yielding a spirited cacophony of cries and voices. The members of Mount Calvary were clearly ready to "have church."

And "have church" they did. Even before most saints had found their way back to the pews, a young deaconess was raising the service's first song, the joyous "Oh, How I Love Jesus." The song stretched on and on, its lead passed from sister to singing sister. In the midst of the praises that marked its close, a sister sitting near the front launched into an impassioned rendition of "Jesus, Jesus, How I Love Him." Again the congregation chorused the song with fervent exuberance. Again the lead passed from mouth to mouth. Next came "What a Mighty God We Serve," "To Be Like Jesus," and "I Love Him Because He First Loved Me," each song following quickly on the heels of the last, leaving no time between for spoken testimony. By now the organist and drummer had joined the praises and were filling each break with imaginatively improvised phrasings, drawing the songs and thanks and claps into a single devotional whole.

After a particularly spirited version of "There's a Song in My Heart that the Angels Can Sing," the elderly lead, one of the church mothers, offered a soulful testimony that culminated in a loud "Whoooo!" and a joyful holy dance. When the double-timed congregational clapping slowed and a group of sisters helped the still-praising mother to her seat, a woman in the same pew started singing the congregational favorite "When I Think of the Goodness of Jesus." Two more shouts, the second followed by a hoarsely whispered litany of "Thank You, Jesus," punctuated the singing. When the song closed, one of the devotional leaders, a young deaconess, felt the Spirit's touch and launched into fast-stepping praise across the full length of the cross-aisle. As the dance subsided, she breathlessly started singing "I Feel Like Praising, Praising Him."

By this point, devotions had stretched on for more than an hour. While the closing words to the last song still echoed in the air, Evangelist Rachel Green mounted the pulpit to formally move the service forward. Still sounding winded from her own shout during "When I Think of the Goodness of Jesus," she addressed the saints with a hoarse and clearly elated voice.

"Like the song says," she began, referencing the very song to which she had shouted, "When I think . . ." "When I think!" echoed the congregation. "That's right!" cried some. "My Lord!" called others.

". . . Of the *goodness*!" The evangelist was forcefully enunciating every word, straining for volume, struggling to be heard over the praising saints. Despite the effort, joy shone from her face. Again the assembly echoed her words, adding cries of "Praise God!" and "Hallelujah!"

". . . Of Jesus!" Evangelist Green clapped her hands together, and the amplified sound boomed through the church, punctuating the clapping that already accompanied her words. "Jesus!" cried the saints. "Thank You, Jesus!"

"And *all* that He's done for me!" The words rang forth in rapt witness, their very tone testifying to the joy welling up in Evangelist Green's soul. "Thank You, Jesus!" cried a host of saints. "All that He's done!" echoed others. "Tell it, tell it!"

"My very *soul* cries out 'Halle—' Whoooo!" The final "Hallelujah" never left Evangelist Green's mouth. In its place came a piercing shout, as the Spirit descended and blessed her with the anointing touch. Instantly, her hands shot into the air and her feet leapt into dance, beating out the ecstatic rhythms of holy joy. Before the congregation could even clap their encouragement, a sister in the choir loft shouted and also began to dance. Almost instantaneously, a deacon in the front pew was propelled to his feet, as was an elderly sister near the back of the church. Within seconds, four more saints were caught up in the rapture, shouting His praises and dancing the rhapsodic steps of holiness. The Spirit was clearly flowing.

But it was Evangelist Green who held my attention. In the sequence that climaxed in her second shout, she had embodied the process of reflective focus. First in song, and then in quoted lyrics. "When I think of the goodness of Jesus," she declared, vocally focusing on the act of thought, "and *all* that He's done for me, my soul cries out, 'Hallelujah!' " There it was, captured in word and act—the focus, the praise, the implicit invitation, and the touch. Evangelist Rachel Green had sung the words, pondered their meaning, and then felt the Spirit. Moments later, she *spoke* the words, thought again on their meaning, and again felt the Spirit. The same statement, in different forms, led to the same end. Melody clearly wasn't critical to the process. The factors that remained constant (and the elements that apparently "mattered") were the act of reflection and the sustenance of a community united in praise.

As I scribbled this account in my field notebook, I couldn't help but wonder whether saints would interpret Evangelist Green's public enactment of focus as a kind of modeling that had been purposely engineered by the Spirit. If the Spirit brought on the shout, then wouldn't a shout as strategically timed as this one send a clear message to all observers about the dynamics of praise? When I later posed this question to some Mount Calvary members, they indicated that they had paid no special attention to this incident; they recalled only that the Spirit had been particularly high during devotions. On considering the sequence I described, however, one saint declared that the episode probably *did* send a message—and an explicitly purposeful one—to those who the Spirit deemed *needed to hear that message*. For the saints, he noted, the message would have simply re-stated basic knowledge. But for outsiders, it could convey new understandings and thus would stand apart. "The Spirit never acts without purpose," added a young sister who had joined the conversation. "He clearly wanted someone to hear." Pausing briefly and then turning to me with a smile, she continued, "And you heard, didn't you?"[7]

*   *   *   *   *

The young sister's comments raise anew the issue of congregational diversity. My portraits of singing at Long Branch and Mount Calvary suggest full congregational involvement, posing every churchgoer as actively engaging song and its messages. The surging passion of performance certainly tends to convey this impression. But beneath this apparent collectivity lurks a miscellany of thoughts and motives and degrees of engagement. Not everyone joins in the singing. Of those who do, not everyone sings with a mind toward worship. And of those who, in their own way, *do* seek this end, not everyone treats song as a means toward accord. Or as a vehicle of reflection. Appearances, simply put, are deceptive. The outward evidences of collectivity in no way prove its actual presence.

Let's look again, for example, at the issue of reflection. There's little doubt that many worshipers never really think about the lyrics that they sing. This is particularly true for songs that are deeply familiar, songs that saints have sung for years and continue to sing on a regular basis. These are precisely the songs most often chorused by congregations at gospel programs, where the audience mix demands a measure of familiarity. Many churchgoers admit that they often sing such pieces by rote, mouthing—but not really thinking about—the words. As is the case with such time-honored recitations as the Lord's Prayer and the Pledge of Allegiance, meaning tends to get vested in the whole rather than in its parts.[8] Hence, while the song as a unit might carry significance, the words themselves lose their meaningful particularity. Reflection, in turn, often gets lost in the gloss.[9]

Contributing to rote performance—and sometimes inhibiting performance altogether—is a simple unwillingness to actively engage in worship. This kind of diffidence particularly plagues gospel programs, where audiences invariably include members who seek entertainment rather than worship. Saints tend to look askance at such "pleasure-seekers," claiming that most of them come from the ranks of the unsaved, and criticizing them for treating devotions as meaningless rituals that simply delay the "real" action. Yet as Bishop Frizelle Yelverton reminds us, even the saved don't always come to church prepared to praise. Tired from a long week of work, many saints attend programs looking to relax, to be entertained, *and* to worship. They've spent their days teaching school, toiling at computer terminals, operating backhoes, cooking someone else's food. Now they want to enjoy the fruits of someone else's labor. So they'll come to a program, sit through the devotions, and then delight to the sweet sounds of other people's singing. Though still *hoping* for a blessing, these saints do not actively *seek* it. In essence, they want to reap the benefits of accord without actually contributing to its creation. To paraphrase a remark often made by devotional leaders, they arrive with "dead batteries" and expect the performers to give them a "Holy Ghost charge."

Every gospel audience includes some "dead batteries." Some programs, however, attract far more than others. Commercial "ticket programs," for example, tend to draw more than smaller events sponsored by church auxiliaries or local nonprofessional ensembles. Indeed, many saints claim that at most commercial programs, and particularly at those featuring full bills of professional touring groups, unsaved audience members actually outnumber the saved. Whether or not this is the case, the presence of programgoers who are unwilling to meet the demands of worship has a decided impact on devotions. While some saints are struggling to achieve accord, these others are merely going through the motions, responding more out of habit than conviction. When their numbers are many, their listless presence takes a particularly telling toll on congregational singing. Muffling the sound of the entire assembly, their languor spreads just as contagiously as the fervor of heartfelt praise. Instead of ringing with enthusiasm, the hymns drag with disinterest, trudging laboriously to their ends. When this happens, even in the most commercial programs, devotional leaders will often take to the microphone and try to "raise some spirit" among the congregation. The problem they face, of course, is that many in the assembly don't see themselves as members of a *congregation*. As far as they're concerned, they're simply here as *audience*.

* * * * *

Most folks had put in a long day's work on that steamy summer Monday, and when they trickled into the Civic Center for the thirty-first anniversary of Durham's Famous Jordanaires, they looked and acted tired. The hall's oppressive humidity only dampened spirits further, as did the program's tardy opening. So when the devotional leader, a local deacon, finally mounted the stage, the audience seemed fidgety, impatient, distracted. The deacon immediately called for an "Amen," hoping to begin the conversations of worship. Less than ten people answered. Again he called for an "Amen"; again the programgoers failed to respond. So he invoked the Psalms, chiding the congregation for their silence and reminding them that the Book enjoins them to "make a joyful noise." Still no response.

Clearly frustrated, the deacon began peppering his remarks with questions, closing every few lines with a interrogative "Huh?" or a response-demanding "Is that right?" Though a few programgoers answered, most continued talking among themselves. The only obvious recourse was song. So the deacon called the audience to their feet, pointedly appealing to cultural disposition to win their participation. "You all know, we Black folk, we've got rhythm in our bones!" he declared. "I want you all to stand with me, if you will, [and] help me to sing this song!" He then launched into an impassioned rendition of "I Will Trust in the Lord."

But the passion remained largely with the deacon. No musicians mounted the stage to back him up. And only a handful of audience members joined the singing. After three powerfully voiced verses, he closed the song and called for prayer. Again the passion sounded forth, as the deacon's voice rode the poetic cadences of spiritual elevation. Though a few cries of "Yes Lord" and "In the name of Jesus" rang from the sparsely filled hall, the prayer emerged largely as a solo effort. After the final "Amen," the deacon called a second devotional leader to the stage and stepped off to the side.

But the second speaker never appeared. As the seconds ticked inexorably by, audience members resumed the conversations that the singing had stilled. Thirty seconds, a minute, a minute and a half, and still no voice from the stage. Finally, at the two-minute mark, one of the Jordanaires bounded onto the platform. Still dressed in his street clothes, he grabbed a microphone and called for backup from musicians seated in the audience. As a drummer hesitantly approached the drum kit and a guitarist moved toward an amplifier, the singer reprised "I Will Trust in the Lord." Shouting "Come on!" after each opening line, he sang with both spirit and conviction. By the second verse, two other singers had joined him at the mike, adding sweet harmonies to his booming lead. But most of the audience still seemed content to just listen. After three barely accompanied verses, the lead signaled the musicians to lower their volume, and then began to scold the programgoers:

> I don't know what you come to do today,
>   but I do know *I did come* to serve the Lord!
> I'm not crying some excuse!
>   Cause God's been good to me!
>   And I know He's been good to you.

Momentarily turning away from the mike, the songleader murmured, "Bring me down a little bit on the drums." Then he once again addressed the crowd.

> Now I don't think nobody worked no harder than I did today!
> I was up—
>   maybe some of you was up—
>   at four o'clock.
>   And I was working [at] about that time, too.
> But now,
>   God has been good to me.
> I don't know what He's done for you,
>   but I *know* what He's done for me!
> I'm not setting in judge[ment] of nobody.
>   But I come here to serve God tonight!
> If nobody don't want to sing this evening,
>   don't sing!
> If all the groups don't show up,
>   *I'll sing!*
> But you know what?

As if answering his own question, the songleader slid right back into song, pulling the instruments with him as he sang, "I'm going to treat everybody right . . ." While the musicians closed the line, he prefaced the next with tacit admonition, shouting, "I don't know about you, but . . ." Then he jumped back to the song, again singing, "I'm going to treat everybody right . . ."

As the amplified sounds of voice and guitars echoed off the distant walls, a few more programgoers joined the singing. But it would take two more songs before devotional leaders felt that the audience was "ready" to hear the first of the featured groups. The hoped-for accord simply wasn't happening.[10]

＊ ＊ ＊ ＊ ＊

Up to this point, I've suggested that devotional services "belong" to the congregation and that they unfold as celebrations of congregational equality. As the saints say, devotions proceed "with no big 'I's' and little 'you's.' " But this only holds true when congregations accept the responsibilities of worship. Without churchgoers' active participation, the spirit of equality gives way to one of hierarchy, opening a chasm of presumed righteousness between the devotional parties.

This is precisely the breach so tellingly evident in the scolding delivered at the Jordanaires' anniversary. Though the songleader steps onto the stage from a seat in the audience, he nonetheless peppers his remarks with explicit me/you oppositions. "I don't know why *you* came," he begins, "but *I* came to serve the Lord!" "If *you* don't want to sing this evening," he continues, "then *I'll* sing!" "I don't know about *you*," he concludes, "but *I'm* going to treat everybody right." At every step, the songleader declares his *distance* from the programgoers, proclaiming in effect that he doesn't want to be identified with an audience that won't praise the Lord.

Such self-distancing simultaneously denies equality and decrees a position of authority. Suddenly, the stature afforded by the stage and the dominance afforded by amplification loom large in the hierarchical drama, lending symbolic weight to the songleader's exhortations. For a moment, the speaker dons the mantle of the preacher. For a moment, he stands apart. But the role-shift is decidedly temporary. Note *how* the speaker establishes the distance: first he charts a devotional high ground, and then he challenges the congregation to meet him there. The hierarchy is thus wholly provisional; once the saints actively engage in worship, once they become participants instead of onlookers, it dissolves. So too dissolve the trappings of ministerial authority. When the singer at the Jordanaires' anniversary concluded his reprimand, he reassumed the role of songleader. When the song ended, he returned the mike to the deacon and walked back into the audience. Having returned from whence he came, he was once again a member of the congregation.

This cycle of shifting roles recurs in both the devotional and song services at gospel programs. Whenever praises rise halfheartedly, whenever voices are mute and bodies still, worship leaders turn to exhortation, momentarily acting as proxies for preachers. This role shift proves particularly effective in devotions, where it starkly contradicts the rule of collectivity. Programgoers *expect* some "preaching" in the service's second half; after all, in most services, this half hosts the sermon. But devotions typically offer no place for exhortation. Dedicated to the pursuit of praise and prayer, devotions' very structure denies the hierarchy that preaching presumes. Hence the pointed effectiveness of devotional preachments. Standing apart in their presumption of authority and commanding attention by virtue of their unexpectedness, they force churchgoers to hear their message. And this, of course, is precisely their intent. By momentarily breaking the devotional frame, they work to insure that frame's fuller realization.

Exhortation is but one of many ways of eliciting fuller congregational involvement. Another method is to lead the congregation in what many saints call a "shout song." Loosely defined, a "shout song" is any piece whose driving tempo and repetitious structure encourage emotional engagement.[11] These songs are said to demand a different kind of involvement from that exacted by their slower counterparts. Their quickened pace forces singers to focus on the mechanics of singing, on voicing the rapid-fire lyrics and keeping up with the rushing tempo. There's little time to roll the words on the tongue, little time to let the mind wander the pathways of reflection. Thoughts that might otherwise turn inward turn instead to the pragmatics of production, guiding the tongue through the headlong convolutions of creative articulation. Involvement becomes more visceral than contemplative.

But visceral involvement is nonetheless a form of involvement. At issue here is not the *nature* of engagement, but rather its very existence. Put simply, shout songs *demand* the singer's involvement. They focus the mind on the task of singing. In so doing, they clear away some of the extraneous concerns that block the spirit of communion. That's why the deacon at the Jordanaires' anniversary followed the mid-tempo opener and the songleader's exhortation with a driving version of the old spiritual "Come by Here." By shifting this piece into a sizzling "shout" tempo, the deacon hoped to grab the audience's attention and finally force some involvement in the service. He knew that this kind of involvement would not necessarily lead to accord. He also knew, however, that a shout song might at least *start* the process of engagement, laying a foundation for further focus. If the focus could then be gently turned toward devotion, the engagement might ultimately yield communion.

Shout songs do more than merely focus the singer on the physical act of singing. They also draw the singer into a realm of heightened sensual engagement. The quickened rhythms sweep over the body, inviting involvement that stretches beyond the voice, seductively beckoning the self to become one with the rolling flow. Every time another set of hands claps, every time another foot adds its resonant thump, the beat grows more insistent, more tangible, more alluring. As the volume slowly rises, so too does one's awareness of the rhythm's sheer physicality. The vibrations shiver through the floorboards and pulse through the pews, subtly setting in motion even those otherwise unmoved by the singing. The body can't help but acknowledge *experiencing* the beat.

The eyes, in turn, add tacit confirmation to that which is heard and felt. Encountering a sea of rhythmic motion, they gaze upon nodding heads, swaying torsos, pumping legs, and arms repeating their sweeping arcs with ever-increasing swiftness. The witnessed bodies chart tempos and countertempos, describing rhythms that both complement and challenge those that drive the singing. The eyes also behold the subtle signs of exertion and intensity, seeing the sweating foreheads, the clenched eyelids, the hands that break the cycle of clapping to rise into the air. The nose catches slight hints of aromatic pungency; the skin registers slight rises in the room's temperature. The sensed surround seems to invite full-bodied involvement.

The saints freely acknowledge that the emotions often join the body in accepting this invitation. Responding more to the beat than to the message, the emotions rise to embrace the singing, drawing the affective self into active engagement. This is precisely the phenomenon to which Rev. Z. D. Harris referred when he spoke of "the mental part and the physical part responding in church." To invoke Rev. Harris's three-part model of the self, one might say that in shout songs, the physical seizes the lead and then draws the emotional into rapt congruence. What's often missing is the *spiritual*, leaving the emotions only worldly understandings to sustain them. But in the rapture of engagement, the self rarely pauses to question passion's source. What registers instead is passion's *strength*, which sweeps through the mind like rhythms sweep through the body, sometimes gracing the singer with fleeting epiphanies of unanchored emotional intensity.

These flashes of emotion shake the body in their struggle for expression, often pushing their way to the throat and bursting forth as joyous shouts. Singers describe this experience as fleeting and intense; they say it momentarily draws one to a subjective realm wholly apart, a space seemingly distanced from the materiality of the surround and the plodding progress of time. Responding to this moment of intensity, the experiencing believer gives voice to a shout of thanksgiving and praise. That's why saints call these pieces "shout songs."

Shouts in self are not, however, shouts in Spirit. Stirred by excitement, invoked by expectation, and shaped by example, such shouts—and the emotional epiphanies that give them rise—are willed from within rather than authored from without; they are the products of spirit "on" rather than "in" the believer. Saints are quick to make this distinction. This is not to suggest that they brand self-generated shouts less "real" than those actuated by the Spirit. Rather, they see them as *differently* real. One group gets treated as products of culture, the other as products of transcendence. The former feed the emotions; the latter feed the soul. The problem with shouts in self, as Evangelist Yarborough so eloquently pointed out, is that believers often *mistake* them for shouts in Spirit. Or they treat them as *acceptable substitutes* for the Spirit's blessings. "You can't go sweeping into heaven on just a shout," say the saints. The shout without the touch offers no nourishment for the soul. There's no contemplation, no application, no lesson learned. Just a celebration of emotion. And, returning to the rationale for the shout song that spurred this discussion, a focusing.[12]

When the deacon at the Jordanaires' anniversary launched into a "shout-time" version of "Come by Here," he was simply trying to get audience members "into the service." He was probably not attempting—or expecting—to elicit a shout. He knew that the song *might* yield that result. He also knew, however, that a far more likely outcome was a simple heightening of congregational engagement. After all, shout songs do not inevitably or predictably "trigger" shouts. They simply provide a frame of possibility. Expectation, emotional stance, degree of belief, sense of appropriateness, and a host of other variables also factor into the devotional equation. Given the anniversary audience's obvious lack of involvement and their patent unwillingness to respond even after the songleader's exhortations, the deacon probably assumed that the song would do little more than spark a spirit of praise in the congregation. If some programgoers *had* shouted out of emotion, I suspect that the deacon would have welcomed their cries as evidence of engagement. And if some had shouted from the anointing, the deacon would have had even more reason to rejoice. The latter would indicate, at least, that the Spirit was present, suggesting that accord was perhaps on its way after all.

Thus far I've linked shout songs only to the emotion-based cries of believers. I do not mean to suggest, however, that such songs are never graced by the Spirit's touch. Nor do I mean to infer that they cannot serve as instruments of devotional invitation. Nothing about these songs actively prevents soulful contemplation; nothing bars the involvement, to again reference Rev. Harris's model, of the mortal spirit. Though the "beat" might distract the mind and the emotions might inhibit reflection, the songs nonetheless offer themselves as potential vehicles for thought and accord. How such songs are actually used depends entirely on the individual. If, for example, a saint at the Jordanaires' anniversary had pondered the simple message of "Come by Here," granting the repeated call to "come by here, good Lord, come by here" a passionately personalized, here-and-now immediacy, the Spirit might well have done just that. Indeed, even if that saint had *not* initiated the dialogue of praise, the Spirit could still have touched. Grace, after all, can fall at *any* point in the service. Hence any shout, in any situation, could be divinely induced. The only saints who would know with any certainty whether the cry arose from self or Spirit would be those who had been granted the rare, mystical gift of spiritual "discernment."

Though admitting that any act of singing can invite the Spirit, many saints nonetheless argue that shout songs too easily distract attention away from the sung message. Without the message, they contend, the songs are little more than tunefully hollow shells. "You don't have to have all of this noise, or this emotion, for the spirit man to grasp that which is important," asserts Rev. Z. D. Harris, referencing the spiritual component of the three-part self. "It's that [which is] spoken by God's word or the Holy Spirit that makes connection." Jojo Wallace, the tenor singer with the Sensational Nightingales, agrees wholeheartedly. "Any time you can hear the words, and concentrate on the words and not [on] the beat or the emotions, you're on the right track. Because the only thing [that] has the power is the Word."[13]

Both of these saints target "the beat" (here addressed as "noise" by Rev. Harris, though later in the conversation he equates "noise" with "beat") and "emotion" as villains in the devotional drama. The charges of villainy, however, are entirely conditional. We need only look at actual practice to discover that Rev. Harris's services, for example, typically ring with the driving choruses of shout songs and that the Nightingales' performances often include long sequences of impassioned, "hard" singing. The problem seems to lie not in the "beat" or "emotions" per se, but rather in the reliance on rhythm and feelings *at the expense of* the articulated Word. "Feeding the emotions is fine," the saints seem to say, "as long as the soul is fed as well." And as Jojo Wallace points out, that feeding comes only when the spirit can hear and contemplate the devotional message.

＊ ＊ ＊ ＊ ＊

When I stepped into the darkened sanctuary of the First Church of Love, Faith and Deliverance, the Tuesday night devotions had already begun. The small congregation was quietly chorusing the lyrics of an old hymn, accompanied by the gentle phrasings of an organ. The singing—slow and hushed—struck me as markedly subdued. No one pushed the tempo. No one seized the lead. No one voice soared above the others. The congregation seemed serene, as if caught in a moment of rapt communion. I immediately hesitated at the vestibule, not wanting to interrupt. But as I stopped, an usher touched my arm and guided me to a seat in the front row. I joined the singing with muted voice.

The room's only light glowed from a blue cross mounted in the front wall and backlit by soft fluorescence. The pale hues that suffused the sanctuary seemed perfectly suited to the hushed singing. I remember wondering whether the lighting would change when the songs grew more spirited or when the preaching began. The light never changed. Nor, for the most part, did the spirit of the singing. And the preaching never happened.

When that first song drew to a close, a distinguished-looking brother mounted the pulpit and led the congregation in singing the nineteenth-century hymn "Blessed Quietness." Though the tempo quickened somewhat, and drums now joined the organ, the song proceeded with the same spirit of devotional quietude that marked its predecessor. The congregation chorused the slow refrain fully seven times before singing the first verse. They then repeated it nine more times, after which the songleader, speaking calmly over the organ and drums, called the saints to cry "Hallelujah!" for their blessings. As they praised the Lord with voice and clapping hands, the organist gently drew them back into the song. Now, however, he played at a noticeably faster pace than before. The scattered handclaps quickly fell into a double-timed pattern, and the saints started singing anew. They repeated the chorus *another* nine times at this quickened pace. Finally, the songleader signaled the song's close. Twice repeating the words to the refrain, he called for another round of thanksgiving.

Once again waves of quietly ardent praise whispered through the pews. As they subsided, the songleader introduced a sister from the congregation, who stepped to the cross-aisle and began to sing the hymn "I Will Make the Darkness Light." After ten minutes of solo song, the pastor of the church, Rosie Wallace Brown, stepped into the pulpit and began to meditate on the lyrics, speaking over the piano's ongoing phrasings. Clearly moved by the singing, she spoke calm and cadenced words of praise. Her every phrase, however, seemed to draw her further toward song, until finally she submitted to the flow and reprised the hymn. Like the singer before her, she infused every line with quiet passion. This, in turn, prompted the earlier soloist to stand and accompany her in a soulfully voiced duet. A few choruses later, the entire congregation joined in, sometimes voicing the words and sometimes merely humming the tune while Pastor Brown offered hushed thanksgivings. The singing stretched on for another five minutes.

So went the entire evening. Slow songs flowed seamlessly into spoken praises, which then always seemed to spark further singing. At times praise and melody stood apart; more often, however, they overlapped, with hosannas rising over the organ's choruses and punctuating every sung verse. Long stretches would pass when the entire congregation seemed caught in the raptures of praise, as hands waved slowly and tears flowed freely. Pastor Brown herself was rejoicing in the Spirit and made no effort to direct the service onto another course. Though she remained at the pulpit for another hour, she never preached. Instead, she simply encouraged the praise, gently calling on the saints to "Bless His holy name," joyously adding her own cries of "Hallelujah!" and "Thank You, Jesus!" and repeatedly whispering a rapturous "Oh ye-e-e-es!" Throughout, the organist offered wave after subtle wave of muted melody.

As the service neared its second hour, Pastor Brown extended the invitation to those who didn't yet know the Lord. While she talked, her words—still uttered in short phrases and still punctuated by her own praises—gradually began to rhyme. The organist, taking the rhymes as a cue, began to articulate a clear melody, making it apparent to all that Pastor Brown was citing lyrics to a song. With no further signal, and with the pastor still talking, saints in the pews began to sing the slow praise song, "Christ Jesus Paid the Debt That I Could Never Pay." As they chorused the familiar words, Pastor Brown moved in and out of the song, singing at one moment, commenting on the lyrics at the next, and calling for praises at a third. Finally, she drew the service to a close.

A week later, while sitting with Pastor Brown in her office, I commented on the way that song—and particularly *slow* song—had so completely dominated the service. She explained that sometimes the Lord wills precisely that. "Sometimes," she said, "we get very emotional. Very, very emotional. But we don't let that override and overrule our spirits being strengthened and ministered to. Sometimes we just dance around here . . ." She smiled broadly and began to chuckle. "Oh, you haven't seen that yet! We enjoy all of that."

"[But] other times we just sit and—perhaps someone might be on the organ ministering, and the people are just blessed and *engulfed* in the music. Other times, the Lord is just ministering to us out of the Word. Now on Tuesday night—last Tuesday, when you were here—I didn't take any particular text. I didn't even open the Bible! The Lord just took us another way. And I've learned that when the Lord is moving *His* way, we just move with the flow. For God is meeting more needs than the minister could ever know."

After a brief pause, Pastor Brown added, "Our most glorious services are when the pace has slowed up—slowed up a bit, like on Tuesday—and the people are just in the presence of God. And they can hear what the Lord is saying through song."[14]

＊　＊　＊　＊　＊

This brings us full circle to the issue of reflective engagement. I mentioned earlier that devotional services at gospel programs often open with hymns or measured spirituals. Lying at the very foundation of devotional repertoires, such songs claim a popularity that transcends boundaries of age and denomination. Some are versions of English hymns that date back to the eighteenth century, pieces like John Newton's "Amazing Grace" and Isaac Watts's ever-popular "At the Cross." Many more are Anglo-American revival hymns from the 1800s, standards like "What a Friend We Have in Jesus," "On Christ the Solid Rock I Stand," "Leaning on the Everlasting Arms," and the Fanny Crosby favorites "Jesus Keep Me Near the Cross," "Pass Me Not, Oh Gentle Savior," and "Blessed Assurance." Still others are spirituals and congregational standards whose roots rest firmly in the African American church, numbers like "Remember Me," "I Will Trust in the Lord," "Come by Here," "Don't Let Nobody Turn You Around," and "We Are Climbing Jacob's Ladder." Congregations at most gospel programs sing these songs at a deliberate, measured pace, purposefully drawing them out so that the words can be heard and consciously engaged. Though faster songs often grace the latter slots in devotional services (where one often hears such gospel standards as "Jesus on the Mainline" and "Soldier in the Army of the Lord"), the opening songs usually proceed with stately dignity.[15]

By starting slow, devotional leaders deliberately invite the saints to contemplate the lyrics and begin the focusing process. As Branchette Lena Mae Perry says, they're trying to get folks to "roll those thoughts over in their mind":

When you sing a song slow,
    people sit and listen.
Then the thoughts are rolling over and over in their mind.
    And things will pop up in their mind that they have experienced.
    And that song will touch right at the appointed time.
When you sing that song fast—
    now this is what I've experienced—
        all right, you got a beat,
        and all you try and do is keep up with the beat.

At this point, Sister Perry claps her hands together just long enough to establish a fast tempo. Then she continues her explanation.

You aren't really *hearing*, you know.
You don't really hear the words.
  But you're just keeping up with the beat.
    Because it just sounds so good.
And, you know, in the ears of lots of people now,
  that's what they're used to hearing.
    The beat.
    And, "I'm going to keep up with the beat."
But as soon as the beat stops,
  you done forgot the song and everything else.
You see.
But that old slow song is like—
  it just winds, [here she deliberately slows and stretches her words]
    and it winds,
    and it gets right to the core of whatever is happening to you.[16]

The slow songs wind their way into consciousness, setting memory into motion and thoughts—to use Sister Perry's phrase—to rolling. That's why Sister Perry refers to these pieces as "getting-close-to-you gospel." With no distracting "beat" to turn the mind aside, they confront the singer with their words, inviting reflection that grounds the lyrics in personal experience. The words penetrate; the memory stirs. The obvious next step in the process is praise.

The most common devotional songs at gospel programs are not only slow. They are also old. Note that Deacon Denkins and Sister Perry both specifically mention this feature, talking about the "*old* familiar hymns" and the "*old* slow songs." Devotional repertoires certainly confirm this reading; most of the pieces already cited date back at least a hundred years, with many stretching back twice that long. For the saints, these "old" songs carry a particular cachet of depth and time-tested truth. Hailing from a time when tribulation dogged every step taken by Black feet, these are the hymns and spirituals that brought the ancestors through. They fueled hope around down-turned pots in slavery-time hush harbors, shouted freedom in the early days of jubilee, toughened resolve in seasons of drought and desolation, granted strength during reigns of robed and uniformed terror, promised better days in the face of habitual humiliation and everyday abuse. These songs rang from plantation fields, whispered from big-house kitchens, echoed from grimy factories, chorused from country churches. They carried countless troubles to the Lord and returned countless times bearing the sustaining touch of grace. They bore up the "good old way" and buoyed the "old-time religion."

As soon as the first notes of these old standards sound, an entire framework of historical association falls into place. The hymns and spirituals tacitly reference a shared past, situating the singing saints in a historical continuum that links their worship to that of the generations that preceded them. The tie that binds present to past is song; the broader field of which it is a part, however, is the "old-time religion."

Give me that old-time religion,
Give me that old-time religion,
Give me that old-time religion,
    It's good enough for me.

This is the faith that "was good for the Hebrew children," "was good for Paul and Silas," "was good for my old mother," and, as sanctified folk have declared for generations, "is good enough for me." The lines of lineage charted in the familiar spiritual are quite clear: the same faith that inspired the Hebrew children and sustained the biblical apostles stretches across the ages to the saints' own "foreparents" and then to the saints themselves. The line is continuous, unbroken, and ongoing; with each new generation, the "old-time" gathers unto itself a host of new meanings, adding richness and depth to those already in place. Hence in the years after the Civil War, saints told how the "old-time religion" "brought me out of bondage," while almost a century later they would chorus those same lines and add "it kept us strong in the jailhouse."[17] At the heart of these shifting meanings—and tacitly invoked every time the old songs ring forth—is the conviction that faith in those "back yonder days" was stronger than it is today.

Every few years, another gospel singer records a version of the old congregational favorite "People Don't Do Like they Used to Do." The lyrics succinctly address the declining faith that saints have so long decried:

Oh the people don't sing like they used to sing,
The mourner's don't moan like they used to moan,
The preachers don't pray like they used to pray,
That's what's wrong with the church today.

Precisely what *is* wrong with the church has apparently been plaguing it for years, for this call to faith seems to sound anew in every generation. As early as 1870, when southern saints were still jubilantly creating their own independent congregations, some believers were already finding reason to contrast present-day practice with the "good old way." One disillusioned sister complained: "I go to some churches, and I see all the folks sitting quiet and still, like they don't know what the Holy Spirit is. But I find in my Bible that when a man or a woman gets full of the Holy Spirit, if they should hold their peace, the stones would cry out! And if the power of God can make the stones cry out, how can it help making us poor creatures cry out, who feel to praise Him for His mercy? Not make a noise! Why, we make a noise about everything else, but they tell us we mustn't make no noise to praise the Lord. I don't want no such religion as that! I want to go to heaven in the good old way."[18]

Over the course of the next half century, African American saints meticulously crafted the rhetoric of devotional decline. The holiness revival rode to prominence in the late 1800s with a call for sanctification and a return to "that old-time religion." Less than two decades later, Pentecostalism challenged believers to renew their spirits and revive the "old apostolic way." Appeals for revival filled the air, carrying with them an implicit romanticizing of the devotional past. In the minds of saints across a wide denominational spectrum, the time of the ancestors became a time of "true religion."[19]

If anything, churchfolks' talk about the "holier" past has increased in recent decades. One can hardly speak with elder saints about the current state of the church without hearing remarks about how faith was deeper—and believers "more real"—in the "way-back days." All seem to agree with gospel radio announcer James Thomas's assessment that "most of the churchgoing people—and most of the really true religious people—have gone on."[20]

Just as comments of this sort pepper conversations with elder saints, so too do they permeate every aspect of gospel presentation. Program announcers and performers constantly invoke images of the past, rhetorically constructing a mythic landscape of historical holiness. Singers sing about "The Way We Used to Have Church," complain that "People Don't Do Like They Used to Do," reminisce about "The Little Wooden Church on the Hill," lament that "Time Has Made a Change," call saints to "Go Back to the Old Land Mark," and rejoice in the knowledge that "I've Got that Old-time Religion All Over Me." Before and between their songs, performers poetically recall the "old country church," with its "amen corner," "mourner's bench," and "old-time mothers" who "knew how to get a prayer through." They talk about times when "folks *knew* how to have church," when "saints weren't ashamed to shout," back before "modern days pushed the Spirit out of the church-house."[21]

Elder singers tend to locate this past in their own childhoods. Younger ones invoke the memories of their "foreparents," referencing a time they know only through story and song. What matters in their words is not so much the *experience* of this past as the *awareness* of its one-time existence. With this awareness comes a tacit claim to knowing the truths of the "old-time way" and to possessing the spiritual insight that allows one to differentiate between worship then and worship now. By publicly articulating this awareness, singers both pay tribute to a collectively imagined past and claim a place in the present-day community of saints. Their words, in essence, draw them into a shared symbolic stream whose banks are fashioned by memory and whose waters course toward holiness.

The "old songs" chorused by congregations draw worshipers into this same symbolic stream. Though most saints in the pews may not initiate the songs, when they join them, they find the referential waters of the "old-time religion" lapping at their feet. The associations are simply too pervasive and the references too frequent for saints to avoid getting wet.

* * * * *

Let us all go back to the old land mark,
Let us all go back to the old land mark,

Let us all go back to the old land mark,
And then stay in the service of the Lord.

Let us blend our voices in the old time way.
Let us blend our voices in the old time way.
Let us blend our voices in the old time way.
    Common meter,
        yes they're sweeter,
    When you stop singing,
        they'll keep ringing,
They'll keep lingering way down in your soul.

When Baptist preacher and songwriter W. Herbert Brewster wrote "Let Us Go Back to the Old Land Mark" in 1949, churchgoers still knew the meaning of "common meter." Many saints were still singing from songbooks that showed no notes, books that instead suggested tempo and tune family with a simple note about "meter" above the lyrics; many others sang from works that included "supplements" of such words-only pieces. The hymns that bore the common meter designation were all slow; most were also old, with a long history of lining out in African American churches. The very mention of "common meter" called these traditional songs to mind, filling out the image of the "old time way" that Rev. Brewster hoped to evoke.[22]

But Rev. Brewster wasn't content to merely call for a revival of ways gone by. He had a deeper message to convey, a message *about* those "old-time" songs, a message that tacitly critiqued many contemporary pieces he was hearing. "When you stop singing, they'll keep ringing," he wrote. "They'll keep lingering way down in your soul." That's the goal—Rev. Brewster seems to be saying—of truly spirited congregational singing. To sing so that when singing stops, thinking goes on. The sung messages should "keep on ringing," "keep on lingering," working their way into the soul. Just as the tongue caresses words when they ring forth in song, so should the mind caress thoughts when the tongue's movement has ceased.

In his letter to the saints at Ephesus, Paul encourages believers to "be filled with the Spirit; speaking to yourselves in psalms and hymns and spiritual songs, singing and making melody in your heart to the Lord" (Ephesians 5:18–19). For the saints, good congregational singing—singing that, as Sister Perry says, just "winds and winds its way to the core"—enables this "singing in the heart." The read scriptures offer the psalms; the chorused songs offer the hymns and spirituals. Together, they provide the contemplative substance that sparks the internal dialogues of praise.

Chapter 10

Praise

"Up Above My Head, I Hear Singing in the Air"

One morning soon,	Lord, I was down on my knees,
One morning soon,	Down on my knees,
One morning soon,	Down on my knees,
I heard the angels singing.	I heard the angels singing.
All in my room,	Lord, it was all over my head,
All in my room,	All over my head,
All in my room,	All over my head,
I heard the angels singing.	I heard the angels singing.[1]

When saints sing about the celestial chorus, they aren't simply painting a metaphorical picture. Instead, they are voicing a deeply held conviction that heaven rings with the songs of Zion. Inspiring and delighting in this singing is the Lord Himself, who reigns over all as the ultimate master of music.

Within this frame, song ranks as much more than "just another" realm of expression. Song stands apart, vaulted to the very pinnacle of heavenly favor. In the eyes of the saints, song reigns as the chosen channel of celestial expression. Sounding from the mouths of countless angels, it fills heaven with the tuneful sounds of praise. For this to be, it must accord with God's will, for He both created the angels and granted them the gift of song. He also granted this gift to those here below and called upon them to fill their worship with song and the joyous strains of music. "Sing unto the Lord a new song, and his praise in the congregation of saints," declares the psalmist. "Let them praise his name in the dance: let them sing praises unto him with the timbrel and harp. For the Lord taketh pleasure in his people" (Psalm 149:1, 3–4).

For the saints, pleasuring the Lord is the frame within which all sacred song falls. Whenever one joins the choruses of a congregation, sings as a performer before a church audience, hums melodic praises in a moment of privacy, or simply listens to sacred songs on the radio, one enters a sphere imbued with associations of celestial agency and godly delight. Engaging with song thus entails more than just engaging in praise. It also entails, if only in a limited way, partaking of the holy. As Isaac Watts declared in a hymn that was likely chorused by the earliest African American saints, singing draws saints into a relationship of "kindred" with the angels:

> We bring our mortal pow'rs to God,
>   And worship with our tongues;
> We claim some kindred with the skies,
>   And join th' angelic songs.[2]

Even more important than "claiming this kindred," however, is the simple fact that singing involves the singer in a kind of service that the Lord Himself deems particularly pleasing. The equation, as holiness deacon Joe Vereen points out, is quite simple: "God loves music. He loves to see us worship and praise Him. And we love—and live—to please Him."[3]

When saints speak about music, their first and final reference is always the Bible. Herein lies source and answer, foundation of faith and cradle of understanding. Herein also lies justification for belief in the celestial wellsprings of song. Though specific references are relatively few, their words are widely known and their ramifications are far-ranging. The saints point to the Old Testament, for example, for stories of the heavens singing forth, sounding joyous praises that sweep over the earth. In the New Testament, these praises find themselves in the mouths of angels, serenading the shepherds with news of Christ's birth (Luke 2:13–14). Angelic song also sounds forth in the final days of judgment, when "ten thousand times ten thousand, and thousands of thousands" of angels will sing hosannas before the Lamb (Revelation 5:8–13), when the blessed 144,000, accompanied by "harpers harping with their harps," will chorus a "new song" with a voice like "many waters" and "great thunder" (Revelation 14:1–3), and when those who gain victory over the beast will "sing the song of Moses the servant of God, and the song of the Lamb" (Revelation 15:2–3). At this time also shall ring from heaven the calming sounds of celestial harps (Revelation 15:2), and the fearsome blasts of the seven trumpets of judgment (Revelation 8:2–11:15). The saints affirm that from the very birth of creation (Ezekiel 28:13) until the final days of glory, the heavens have echoed and will continue to echo with the hallowed songs of God.[4]

Just as song fills the mouths of angels, so too, says the Bible, should it fill the mouths of saints. In verse after verse, the writers of the Word enjoin believers to "sing praise to the Lord God of Israel" (Judges 5:3), to "sing forth the honour of his name" (Psalm 66:2), to "sing with the spirit" and "with the understanding also" (1 Corinthians 14:15). Sometimes the Lord Himself provides the song, as He did for Moses and the psalmist David (Deuteronomy 31:19, Psalm 40:1–3). At other times, He endows saints with the gifts of composition and performance (see, e.g., 1 Samuel 16:12–13, 2 Samuel 23:1–2). Many singers say that this special endowment is precisely what the prophets Moses, David, and Isaiah each referred to when they proclaimed, "The Lord is my strength and song" (Exodus 15:2, Psalm 118:14, Isaiah 12:2). Clearly, worshipful singing is an activity that bears heaven's absolute endorsement.

In conversations with sanctified singers, these verses often flow without prompting, spilling forth one after another in a jumble of referenced citation. Many singers—particularly the elders—call these passages to the tongue with casual ease, suggesting both the depth of their study and the seriousness with which they treat their gifts. Few of those whom I've heard "ramble the Bible" on this topic say they've ever seen these matters addressed in biblical commentaries or Sunday school lessons. Instead, most credit their knowledge to personal study of the Bible, to conversations with preachers and other singers, and to careful hearings of the preached Word. They clearly suggest that at least among the community of singers, the specific biblical grounding of song is commonplace knowledge.

The general association of heaven with singing, of course, has deep roots in vernacular Christianity. When Africans in the New World first encountered the teachings of Protestant preachers, they undoubtedly heard hymns that pointedly celebrated this musical link. Though most of these pieces probably plodded at tempos that must have sounded markedly *un*celebratory to West African ears, their lyrics nonetheless invoked the joys of celestial praise. (Isaac Watts's highly popular *Hymns and Spiritual Songs*, for example, included scores of references to singing angels.) Such portraits in song undoubtedly found elaboration in the antebellum teachings of white ministers, many of whom preached at length about the joys of heaven. Such preachings promised a happy future as the reward for trials faced here on earth, thus encouraging an ethic of passivity and submission. Given this end, and given the widespread perception among whites that Africans, to use the words of one eighteenth-century minister, "have an ear for music and [take] a kind of ecstatic delight in Psalmody," one can assume that many preachers probably featured singing and music-making prominently in their descriptions of heaven.[5]

This feature of the preached descriptions almost certainly fell upon receptive ears. For African peoples who treated singing as integral to the lived artistry of everyday existence, images of celestial choruses and singing angels must have seemed eminently plausible. If heaven indeed did exist, and if it indeed was a realm of unceasing joy, then surely it rang with song. Any other state of existence, particularly given the belief that angelic activities fundamentally mirrored activities on earth, was simply inconceivable. Given this frame of understanding, it should come as no surprise to discover that when nineteenth century African Americans sang of heaven, they filled their songs with references to celestial singing.

"I've got a song, you've got a song, all God's children got a song," sang the saints. "And when I get to heaven, I'm going to sing that song! I'm going to sing all over God's heaven!" Saints told of how they would "sing all along the way" to Zion, and then would

> Shout over all our sorrows,
>   And sing forever more,
> With Christ and all his army,
>   On that celestial shore.

Anticipating that great day, the saints declared, "I've a harp up in the Kingdom, Ain't that good news!" Having joined the celestial fellowship, they would surely "join that heavenly band," and would "hear the trumpet sound" and "ring them bells at heaven's door."[6] Whether recounting stories from the biblical past, describing the glories of an anticipated future, or foretelling the final fateful days of judgment, the saints filled their heavens with song.

The cited lyrics might lead one to assume that the saints' association between heaven and song is purely a matter of faith. Most of the lyrics either reference the Bible or address an expected future; they seem to present a knowledge grounded more in traditions of talk than in experience. A few songs, however, offer a tellingly different perspective. One piece, for example, sets celestial singing in the frame of an experienced present, declaring, "I hear archangels a-rocking Jerusalem, I hear archangels a-ringing them bells." Others set such singing in an experienced past. The song that opened this chapter, for example, declares, "Lord, it was all over my head, I heard the angels singing." Another proclaims, "The trumpet sounds in the other bright land, I heard from heaven today!"[7] All of these songs ground knowledge in actual encounter. All claim that the singer *actually heard* the celestial chorus.

Perhaps no song makes this assertion more strongly than "Up Above My Head," a traditional piece that boasts a long history of commercially recorded renditions and that remains to this day a congregational favorite:

Up above my head, I hear singing in the air.
Up above my head, I hear singing in the air.
Up above my head, I hear singing in the air.
Well, I really do believe,
  Yes, I really do believe,
    That there's a heaven somewhere.

In this piece, the songwriter not only tells of hearing singing in the heavens, but also uses this experience to ground belief. For the songwriter, the heard singing provides empirical proof of heaven's existence. Far from being taken for granted as a matter of faith, the singing offers evidence of faith's validity.

It would be easy to discount these references as exercises in poetic license, arguing that they flow rather predictably from a broader tradition of religious talk and thus tell us nothing about actual experience. But when we set these lyrics within the field of sanctified *testimony*, they reassert their significance, for here they find telling narrative confirmation. The church's narrative tradition reveals that generations of saints have testified to actually *hearing* celestial song. Some of these testimonies set this experience within a visionary frame, with the tellers describing how they found themselves divinely transported to an alternate reality, where they heard angels singing.[8] Others recount dreams in which the angels revealed to the sleeping mind songs "no human ear had ever heard before."[9] But many narratives locate the experience of hearing celestial song firmly in the world

9. "I don't have a background with me," announced Brother Kenneth Nichols when he stepped into the cross-aisle. "So I'm looking at it!" he added with a smile, pointing to the congregation. As Brother Nichols presses into his second song, the roles of singer and congregation dissolve, yielding a single body joined in soulful praise. Brother Nichols, visiting the Branchettes' twenty-sixth anniversary from Landover, Maryland, is Sister Perry's cousin. (Photo by Roland L. Freeman)

of wakeful consciousness. One Tennessee saint, for example, testified in the late 1920s: "I remember one night—Oh, I used to love good times!—I was lying down after a dance. I felt so wicked. I laid and prayed and while laying there the prettiest music came to me. I told the Lord I wanted to see where the music came from and I looked above me and saw many angels and heard the flapping of their wings. I woke my children up to listen to the music. It was the prettiest I had ever heard. I wanted them to hear it."[10] Not only did this saint *hear* the music, but she also *saw* the angels and then *woke up her children so that they might hear it, too.* Although she never says whether the children shared her experience, she certainly suggests that she was hearing the singing even as she awakened them.

An even more compelling testimony comes from songwriter Kenneth Morris, one of gospel music's most influential composers and publishers. Describing the birth of his song, "I Feel the Spirit," Morris wrote: "One Thursday night, in the midst of my choir rehearsal, this song came to me. The 'voices' sang this song in my ear so loud and clear that I forgot where I was and what I was doing. When I came to myself, I was at the piano singing and playing this song. I immediately taught it to my choir and they sang it the following Sunday."[11] Interestingly, a few years before this experience, Morris wrote the song "Heaven Bells," whose chorus repeats the present-tense assertion, "I hear those heaven bells ringing."

One needn't look far to discover the ongoing strength of this popular association between heaven and song, for it regularly reemerges in the lyrics of commercial gospel releases. The Canton Spirituals' 1984 release, "Heavenly Choir," for example, tells the story of an elder saint whose cracking voice kept him out of his church choir but did not prevent him from singing with the angels when he passed away. Indeed, the song recounts how the deceased elder actually sings back to his congregation, letting them know that he's now "singing with that heavenly choir."[12]

Perhaps the most telling link between the earthly practice of singing and its celestial analogue appears in the Gospel Keynotes' immensely popular "Just a Rehearsal," a song that continues to enjoy regular gospel airplay more than a decade after its initial release. In this up-tempo piece, the Keynotes proclaim that the singing they are doing now is "just a rehearsal" for the "real" singing they hope to do in heaven:

I love to sing, each and every night.
 Sometimes this old voice just won't act right.
I want to keep on singing, so the world will see,
 When I make it to heaven, I'll sing in perfect harmony!
This is just a rehearsal.
 When we get to heaven,
 We're going to really sing! [13]

The notion that present-day performance is but a rehearsal for singing in heaven brings us full circle to the special significance accorded to song by the saints.

The singing done here on earth not only pleases God, and not only partakes of the holy, but also prepares the singer for life everlasting. And, one might well add, for song everlasting.

*　*　*　*　*

"When I finish on this earth, I'm hoping—I'm looking to live eternally," says Smiley Fletcher, longtime singing partner of Deacon Edward Denkins. "Singing with the heavenly choir. Because they tell me it won't be no preaching up there. Everything will [just] be singing and having a good time. With the Lord."[14]

Saints have long contended that "there will be no preaching in heaven." Much the same is said about prayer. But not so singing. In the minds of the saints, song and praise-giving will forever reign as heaven's principal activities. Singing in this life thus readies saints for the inevitability of singing in the next. Perhaps this explains why so many gospel groups—singers who presumably are more "rehearsed" than their fellow saints—give themselves names clearly associated with heaven. Smiley Fletcher, for example, sings with the Sensational Cherubims. Others sing (or have sung) as the Angelic Gospel Singers, the Echoes of Zion, the Gospel Angels, the Wings Over Jordan Choir, the Voices of Heaven, the Pearly Gates Choir, the Angelic Supremes, the Heavenly Echoes, the Tones of Heaven, and the Sensational Angels. All these singers proclaim, by virtue of their titles, that they are readying themselves for an eternal afterlife of song.

If God reigns as the supreme master of music, and heaven as the ultimate source of song, then how do saints explain the earthly rule of *worldly* music and the insidious ascendancy of profane performance that wears the guise of sanctity? The answer, say the saints, is simple. Satan, too, is a master of music. Not *the* master, but certainly *a* master. After all, as saved singers are quick to point out, Satan himself was once an angel. This means that he was also a singer. Indeed, many saints cite the Book of Ezekiel to suggest that Satan was once heaven's premier singer. In the referenced passage, Ezekiel allegorically describes the creation of an "anointed cherub" who was banished from heaven. Ezekiel cites the Lord as saying, "the workmanship of thy tabrets and of thy pipes was prepared in thee in the day that thou wast created. Thou art the anointed cherub that covereth; and I have set thee so. . . . Thou wast perfect in thy ways from the day that thou wast created, till iniquity was found in thee. . . . therefore I will cast thee as profane out of the mountain of God" (Ezekiel 28:13–16).

The link to music lies in the references to "tabrets" and "pipes," terms that many saints interpret as instrumental metaphors for the ability to create rhythm and tune. This passage clearly identifies these "instruments" as central to this particular cherub's perfection. It also notes that this angel, described in an earlier line as having once been in Eden and in a later one as having been "cast to the ground," bore a special anointing. This combination of features leads many to suggest that this angel, inferentially identified as Satan, once reigned as heaven's chief musician. When banished from the angelic ranks, Satan presumably kept his special skills, which he continues to employ in his ongoing struggle to turn humans away from God.[15]

* * * * *

The Badgett Sisters, an a cappella duo from North Carolina's northern Piedmont, had just completed a recording session when we started joking about the devil. As we walked away from the studio, the younger sister, Connie Steadman, asked how my writing was going. I told her that at the moment I was writing about Satan's skill at music. "You shouldn't have to study too hard on *that*," teased Celester Sellars, the other sister. When she raised her eyebrows in a show of mock innocence, we all laughed, and then began to talk about the devil's attributes. Thinking about a verse from one of the Badgetts' more playful songs,

Oh I wonder what the devil keeps on grumbling about,
    He's way down in hell and he can't get out.
There's just one thing I can't understand,
    He once was in the heavens, but he wouldn't join the band!

I mentioned that I'd heard the devil was a fine fiddler. Celester turned toward me and said, "Now I don't know nothing about no fiddling, but they say he was a top singer. Say he had golden pipes in his throat, and could outsing all the other angels in heaven!"

"Pipes in his throat?" I repeated, pulling out a pen and a piece of paper. "I've never heard it like that."

"You better watch out," kidded Connie upon seeing me reach for my pen. "He's gone to writing it down again!"

Celester chuckled at Connie's playful warning, and then continued: "Yeah, they say he was the top angel when it comes to singing. He was created that way. He was created a perfect angel, and he had a golden voice."

"You think he's still got it?" I asked.

"Well, it's nowhere in the Bible that tells you God took anything He created from him, when He cast him down," Celester answered. "So I guess he's singing right on."

"That would sure explain a lot of things," I added with a grin.

"Well, you know, there are a lot of folks out there singing in church that sure aren't singing for God," responded Celester, picking up on my inference. "You don't have to figure too hard to know who they *are* singing for!"[16]

* * * * *

The belief that Satan is a master of music boasts a long history in African American lore. For generations, musicians both inside and outside of the church have spoken of musical instruments as the "devil's playthings." This association undoubtedly has its roots in the antebellum preachings of white ministers, many of whom branded all instruments as tools of devilish pleasure. Nineteenth-century accounts suggest that many African Americans wholeheartedly endorsed this pro-scription and banished banjos, fiddles, fifes, and other instruments from the world of plantation worship. These instruments' very association with worldly ways seemed to cloak them in condemnation. At the same time, this association ce-mented their identification with Satan, whom saints saw as the master of worldli-ness. Just as the presence of song in heaven was taken to indicate the Lord's ap-proval of singing, so was the association of musical instruments with worldly dance and "base emotions" widely interpreted as evidence of satanic endorsement.[17]

Not all saints were so willing to assign agency on the basis of simple association. Many nineteenth- and early twentieth-century accounts tell of musicians who continued to play their instruments long after they were converted. While some of these musicians cast all worldly songs out of their repertoires, many others cer-tainly did not.[18] By the late 1800s, with the blossoming of independent holiness congregations, instruments earned a new, biblically justified status in the fellow-ship of saints. The very speed with which holiness congregations incorporated instrumental music into their worship suggests that beliefs about the devil's intrin-sic ties to instruments were neither as homogeneous nor as deeply seated as many have argued.[19] Nonetheless, there can be little doubt that vernacular associations between Satan and music—whether believed or not—were certainly widely known throughout working-class African America.

Many of the beliefs cited thus far testify more to Satan's involvement with rather than mastery of music. When we look to stories about actual encounters with the devil, however, explicit evidence of musical mastery comes to the fore. Perhaps most telling are the recurrent narratives about musicians who sell their soul to Satan in order to gain supernatural proficiency upon their chosen instrument. Typically, such encounters are said to be initiated by musicians, who recognize in the devil a force that can bestow uncanny musical prowess. Many of these accounts describe a series of crossroads encounters that culminates when Satan takes, tunes, and then returns the musician's instrument. The passing back into human hands both confers the musical mastery and seals the contract for the soul. The fact that Satan is the source of this competence, and that he himself demonstrates mirac-ulous musical facility, clearly suggests his mastery in the realm of music.[20]

Interestingly, some of these narratives about soul-selling close with the devil's demand that the musician play a *sacred* tune.[21] Such stories clearly imply that Satan expects his charges to master not only worldly songs, but also religious ones. This mastery grants the contracted singers the ability to cloak themselves in robes of sanctity, thus serving the devil's deceitful ends. As we have already seen, many saints contend that such devilish deceivers are common in the world of gospel.

Many present-day saints reject stories about crossroads compacts as worldly "superstition" and imaginative "tales." Nonetheless, they endorse the underlying premise about the devil's musical skills. Further, they admit that these skills, in the hands of one as powerful as Satan, pose a very real danger to the church. As Bishop

Frizelle Yelverton often reminds his congregation, the devil is not one to be trifled with. "We must remember," says the bishop, "there's two powers in this world. You got God, who is a power. You got Satan, who is a power. But God is almighty. Satan is mighty, but God is *al*mighty. He controls the devil. But that doesn't mean the devil isn't always on the job. Everything that he can get going his way, he's going to get going his way."[22]

Chief among the "things" that Satan tries to "get going his way" are the "things" of the Lord. If he can infiltrate the pulpit, the choir-stand, the cross-aisle, or the amen corner, then he can more effectively undermine God's ministry. To effect this infiltration, the devil is said to focus his considerable powers on imitation. He becomes, in effect, a spiritual chameleon, an unholy mimic even capable of working miracles in the falsely invoked name of God. Assuming the guise of holiness, the devil can preach, sing, and pray. Indeed, as Christ pointed out to His disciples, he can show "signs and wonders" so great as to almost fool the elect (Matthew 24:24, Mark 13:22). He too has "wonder-working power"; he too, as Bishop Yelverton reminds us, is mighty. When Satan channels this power into his God-perfected talents as a singer, he becomes a formidable adversary indeed.

* * * * *

When Rev. Z. D. Harris talks, people listen. As the longtime pastor of Durham's Oak Grove Free Will Baptist Church, Rev. Harris is one of those preachers whose rich voice and stately countenance command attention both in and out of the pulpit. Widely known for the ease with which he rambles the Bible, Rev. Harris is also celebrated for his quick wit and his skill at fitting a story to every situation. On many occasions, I had been impressed with his mastery behind the pulpit. It was not until I saw a printed prophecy in one of Oak Grove's Sunday-morning bulletins, however, that I decided to pursue a private audience. Two days later, on a chilly winter morning, I was sitting in Rev. Harris's church office.

We spent the first hour renewing our acquaintance (I've known Rev. Harris on a casual basis for almost twenty years) and talking about the many ways that the Lord speaks through mortal mouths. I then asked where song fits in the framework of revealed knowledge. Are some songs, I wondered, also the products of revelation? Indeed they are, Rev. Harris affirmed. The Spirit puts words in the heart of a chosen saint, and then that saint writes those words as song. They simply "come to him," Rev. Harris explained, flowing with an ease that tacitly testifies to their celestial origin. "So, see how God works?" the pastor concluded, closing his explanation. I nodded and voiced a word of affirmation.

"Now, all right," Rev. Harris continued, "then say, 'Well, if God revealed the songs in the hearts of the Christians, where are all these other fellows getting—where do they get their songs from?'"

"That's the next question," I laughed, happy to see that our thoughts were following the same path.

"The next question?" Rev. Harris smiled and continued. "All right. It comes in the heart. But who gives it to them? *Satan*." Here he paused, letting the name stand alone. When he began anew, his words were slow and measured.

> See, he is the one
>   who uses *his* children,
>   like God is using His children.
> See?
> He's an imitator.
> So he reveals all these foolish songs
>   and all this kind of stuff to them.
> They sits down;
>   they writes it out.
> Yeah.
> Because he reveals it to them.
> See?
> See, Satan has imps.
> Satan has people working for him,
>   as well as Christ has some working for Him.
> That's where they come from.
> There's a higher power putting it in their hearts.

"How does one tell the difference?" I wondered aloud. I was thinking about the frequent complaints voiced by elder saints about many "contemporary gospel" songs whose lyrics are criticized for being overly worldly. "Well, now . . ." Rev. Harris began, but I cut him off in an effort to further focus the question. ". . . If Satan is such a good imitator?"

"Oh, he's a good imitator," Rev. Harris affirmed. "But that's how come He said, 'Study the Word, so ye will know.'"

> See, that's how come He was saying that.
> "You are the children—
>   you're not of the darkness,
>   but you are the light."
> Which means, then,
>   that you *know* the difference:
>   that which is real;
>   and that which is phony.
> But if you hadn't been borned again,
>   you wouldn't know that.

"Right," I nodded. The answer, like so many others, rests in the mysteries of membership. The saved believer will simply "know" the difference, feeling it inside, knowing that its source is Spirit rather than intuition. Satan is indeed mighty,

Rev. Harris infers, but God gives His children ways to know when Satan's wiles are at work.

"So that's what's got to be done," Rev. Harris continued, his fingers traveling across the open Bible on his desk. "You got to be of Him. You got to be of the children of the light."

For the next few minutes, Rev. Harris grounded his words in the Bible, citing 1 Thessalonians to show the source of spiritual discernment and then Revelation to demonstrate the devil's duplicitous might. "See, now that's what we got to watch," he said, speaking of Satan's power to deceive and mislead. "Satan can have his men working power, as God have *His* men working power."

This brought us full circle to the pastor's opening words. He had started by comparing the devil's children to those of God. Then I had asked about telling the two apart. This time, however, he posed the follow-up question himself.

So well, how do you know?
All right,
    let's go back to the book of Exodus.
When Moses was standing before Pharaoh,
    and was saying to him that God said let his peoples go.
And God said,
    "Moses, throw down your rod, so he can see."
He throwed that rod down,
    and the rod turned to a snake.
"Oh," he [Pharaoh] said, "you ain't done nothing.
    We got mens can do that!"
So they throwed theirs down,
    and here come *two* snakes!
But Moses' snake done what?
    Turned around and swallowed them whole.
You get what I'm saying?

At this point, Rev. Harris began to laugh. Nodding in response to his question, I smiled a smile of understanding. In the end, the greater power would prevail. And the lesser would vanish. My mind recalled Evangelist Yarborough's remarks about the inherent transience of the world's works and Rev. Brewster's comments on the "staying power" of the old hymns. That which was of God would survive the assaults of "the enemy" and would endure in a world of false promises and falsely stirred hopes.

Time itself thus becomes a measure of truth. The Spirit grants to each generation of saints the power to discern between darkness and light, between truth and trickery, between the real and the imitation. That which survives the tests gets passed from generation to generation, becoming tradition, joining the ranks of the "old-time." Perhaps this accounts, at least in part, for the saints' oft-voiced reverence for the past.

Rev. Harris broke my train of thought, and the lengthening pause, with a few words of summation. His closing remarks suggested that once again, we were thinking on the same track.

"So therefore then, what I'm trying to say is that the devil, he does the same thing that Christ does. But see, the only thing about it—it won't hold long. It's phony."[23]

*   *   *   *   *

According to Rev. Harris, the devil exercises his musical prowess through his mortal "children." He acts, in essence, as a master conductor, directing his workers on earth to play his music and sing his songs. As agents of his will, these workers become living vessels of deception. They too are "inspired" by stirrings within; they too receive words and songs authored from beyond. They too feel the emotional epiphanies of sermon and song. Many never pause to question the source, assuming that all skill derives from self and all ecstasy issues from God. Such are the ways of deception.

Saints say that the pews are filled with Satan's workers. Some are fully aware of their soul's status; others are wholly deceived, mistakenly confident that the path they follow is the Lord's. Together, they pray with the saved, sing with the saved, sometimes preach to the saved, ever wearing the guise of holiness. Some can even rightfully claim the status of "saint," having been born again but having somewhere strayed, their weaknesses unwittingly allowing the devil entry. Many saints contend that these are the most dangerous deceivers, for their past commands a measure of respect not merited by their present. But saints say that like all of Satan's workers, their imposture will eventually come to light. Their rendition of holiness is, after all, but an act, an imitation, a mask that must sometimes fall away. "It won't hold long," asserts Rev. Harris, suggesting that the performance of sanctity, the putting on of a persona that's not the self, will always be flawed, and thus will always be revealed for its true nature. The devil's creations may be mighty, say the saints, but they cannot be perfect. For those with eyes to see, for the "children of the light," the darkness will eventually make itself known.

Again, time emerges as the measure of truth. Now, however, it need not cross generations, as it does when saints pay homage to a "holier" past. Time also reveals truths within the measure of one's life, betraying those whose performances cannot meet the demands of everyday holiness. "Just watch and wait," the saints seem to be saying; "if Satan is there, he will eventually make a mistake and show himself." He is, after all, an imitator; his public acts are all facsimiles, modeled on those of the saints. But life is too capricious and social interaction too unpredictable for modeled behavior to serve as one's only guide. When saints face the novel and the unexpected, they turn to the tenets of holiness; but when those only *acting* as saints face the novel and unexpected, they turn to remembered responses and the rules of the role, searching for models. When those models aren't there, they must turn to the self beneath the role, seeking guidance in worldly principle.

Caught off guard and forced to improvise, Satan the imitator thus shows his hand. Time, say the saints, is always on the side of the Lord.

For all his mightiness, the devil can only imitate when acting within the sphere of the church. Outside of "the world," his power to create, to fashion anew, is limited. The church, in essence, binds him, restricting the scope of his actions. His performances and the products thereof are thus necessarily derivative. In the realm of song, of course, this derivation comes with particular ease, as Satan well knew—and some suggest, perhaps even led—the singing of the angels. Saints often say the same thing about the devil's musicianship. Indeed, members of holiness churches have been making this argument since the 1880s, when they first broke away from their parent denominations and invited what their mainstream counterparts branded as the "devil's instruments" into the church. Citing biblical passages calling for instrumental praise, holiness believers asserted that the ban on instruments was in fact a ploy of the devil and that *all* music rightfully belonged to God. These saints (and their Pentecostal successors) contended that by reclaiming music on behalf of the church, they were in fact reinstating it to its rightful place. The fact that instrumental music seemed "out of place" in worship simply testified to the success of the devil's imitation, which had been so thorough that it had convinced many believers that music was Satan's realm.

"You see, music belongs to the church," declares holiness bishop Frizelle Yelverton, testifying to the ongoing strength of this argument. Bishop Yelverton, whose position as overseer for all of North Carolina's Mount Calvary Holy churches lends his words particular force, addresses this issue with a sense of deep certainty. "The music that Satan is using, it belongs to [the] church. It don't belong to him. But he has it. See? And what they [i.e., the unsaved] are doing, they're praising their God with that music. And we, in turn, turn it around and praise the Lord with the same music—the guitar, the drums, the organ, the piano."[24]

This argument effectively sets the contributions of all musical instruments firmly in the Lord's corner. In so doing, it not only endorses musical "borrowing" from the worldly sphere, but also sanctions such borrowing as an act of holy reclamation.[25] Of course, as the previous chapter's discussion of "the beat" makes clear, such reclamation is not without its dangers. Indeed, some saints argue that bringing instrumental music back into the church so angered Satan that he directed all his energies to perverting its use, making it a vehicle of distraction and emotional excitement. Though music clearly does serve these ends, it also serves as a vehicle for reflection and devotional focus. One needs only note the ubiquity of instruments in gospel programs to tell where most saints currently stand on this issue.

So song and its musical accompaniments originate, at least conceptually, in heaven, while Satan and his minions operate on earth to corrupt their every use. The popular reign of worldly music offers ample testimony to the devil's creative genius. Clearly, his powers are at their peak in this realm. How do saints combat this devilish mastery? How do they tap into the streams of heavenly praise, so that saints might join the angels in bringing forth songs that speak with holy power? The simplest answer, of course, is the same as that which governs all creative expression within the church—simply that faith and prayerful sincerity will guide appropriate creation. But as the already-cited testimonies of many songs, the account of gospel songwriter Kenneth Morris, and the opening words of Rev. Z. D. Harris all suggest, this is by no means the only way that song finds its way into the mouths of saints. Some songs are said to come directly from the heavens above. For these pieces, the act of singing becomes an act of holy quotation. This adds yet another dimension to the significance of singing in the community of saints, transforming not only the way that songs are *sung*, but also the way that they're *heard*. Saints know that at least *some* of the songs being sung carry the express approval of God. With this knowledge comes the expectation that these songs carry a special power to touch the soul.

Chapter 11

Welcome

"Not for the Appointment, but for the Anointment"

As Mother Nixon steps back to the amen corner and the guitarist fingers a wandering melody, Sister Lena Mae Perry stands from her place behind the registration table. A short woman with a sturdy build and radiant face, Sister Perry turns to the congregation and begins what the printed program simply calls a "Welcome." Sounding a bit winded from the singing, she opens in a conversational tone, neatly connecting her words to the praises that preceded them by beginning with "Praise our God!" Without waiting for a response, she moves right into a statement of thanks.

"We want to thank our mothers for the wonderful devotional service, that they have rendered to us for this afternoon." ("Thank you," murmurs a sister in the amen corner.) "We are so glad to be here." (Sister Perry smiles and pauses to gaze over the congregation, as if to make sure that her eyes meet those of everyone gathered here. Two "Amens" quickly fill the momentary silence.) "And to see all of you here." ("Thank You, Lord," adds another sister.) Sister Perry's slightly husky voice grows louder as she speaks, and her words begin edging to a higher tone at the close of each phrase.

Knowing that the Lord has so wonderfully blessed,	(Yes Lord!)
that we were able to get out to our anniversary	
one more time.	(Oh yes)
Because the Lord has been good to all of us,	(Jesus!/My Lord)
we ought to give God the honor and the praises,	(Yes!)
for *every*thing that He has done for us.	(Yes!)

The organist begins his soft phrasings, laying a slow foundation for Sister Perry's accelerating words. A few lines later, the bass player adds his resonant ramblings to the words of welcome and praise. Sister Perry continues as if the musicians were silent.

Praise God,
   we're here to welcome you,
praise God,
   to our twentieth anniversary.   (Amen)
Praise God,
   we know that you loved us,
      because you are here!   (Amen!)
Praise our God!
As I heard one brother say—
   and I think it was the brother of the William Coley
      Trio,
      when I talked with him on the phone—
He said, "We're coming *not* for the *appointment*,
   but for the *anointment*!"   (Amen!/Alright!)

A chorus of enthusiastic "Amens" and "Alrights" sounds through the church. The congregation clearly appreciates the cleverness—and the sentiment—of the rhyme.

   Sister Perry's reference to anointment marks the service's second call for the Spirit's visitation. Deacon Eldridge had prayed, "Lord, we're looking for Your blessings again this evening"; now Sister Perry declares, "we're here for the anointment." Both statements explicitly evoke the frame of devotional expectation that has been tacitly referenced by every act of worship thus far in the service. The saints' swift and loud response suggests that all are looking forward to the Spirit's visit. Voicing her agreement, Sister Perry joins the chorus of affirmation, adding her own ardent cry of "Praise God!"

We're coming to have a good time in the name of the
      Lord!   (Amen!)
We welcome you to this, our twentieth anniversary.
Praise God,
   and when we say twenty,
praise God,
   we have traveled up and down the dangerous highways,
praise God,
   through rain, through snow,
   through sleet, through the storm,
      but the Lord has yet kept us.   (Alright!/Amen!)
We're just so happy to praise our God,
   to be here celebrating our twentieth anniversary,
      and to have you here with us!   (Amen!)
To welcome you to *enjoy* in the name of *Jesus*!   (Praise Him!)
Praise our God!

Sister Perry's cries of "Praise God" roll one after another, emphatically punctuating her remarks. They remind listeners at every turn that the purpose of this gathering is not to celebrate the Branchettes' accomplishments, but to praise the many and wondrous achievements of the Lord. As Sister Perry makes clear, such praise is itself a thing of enjoyment. "We're coming to have a good time in the name of the Lord!" she declares at the beginning of this segment. "We're happy to welcome you to *enjoy* in the name of *Jesus*!" she announces at its close. Both references firmly set "enjoyment" in a devotional frame. This is not the "enjoyment" one finds in worldly engagement, not the "good time" one experiences when being "entertained." Instead, these are "good times *in the name of the Lord*," where pleasure arises not from worldly amusement or sensual arousal, but from the joyous communion of worship, from "having church."

Without pausing in her welcome, Sister Perry hastens on, her words now tumbling forth in an excited rush. Though she's not using a microphone, there's little doubt that those at the rear of the church can hear her clearly. Her hands, which started out with outstretched fingers pressed against the table top, are now both raised—palms outward—to her sides.

We were able to get out,	(Yes!)
we all walked in here,	(Thank You, Jesus)
we all have our hands,	(Amen!/That's right!)
we were able to come together to know the *glory* of	
God!	

Chorused cries of "Amen!" and "Yes!" once again ring through the church. Churchgoers know these phrases and those that earlier invoked "the dangerous highways" quite well, as they often appear in testimonies. Here, however, the words give thanks for a collective "we" rather than the testimony's "I." The saints' enthusiastic responses signal their approval.

The voiced approval in no way slows Sister Perry, who presses on with only the slightest of pauses.

Praise God!	
If there's anything that we can help you with,	
you let us know.	(Praise God!)
And as I always say during our anniversary,	
if there is somebody here,	(Yes)
praise God,	
and they want to, you know,	
turn their lives over to Jesus,	(Have mercy!)
praise God,	
we can have a station break!	(Alright!/Amen!)
In the name of our God!	
And we can pray for somebody!	(Yes!)
Praise God!	
Somebody might want to be saved this evening!	(Amen!)

10. "Somebody might want to be saved this evening!" cries Sister Lena Mae Perry, one of the Branchettes. "We can always change it from anniversary to a revival!" The Branchettes always extend an invitation for spiritual revival at their anniversaries, hoping that the message in the music might touch some listener's heart. (Photo by Roland L. Freeman)

We can always change it from anniversary to a	
revival!	(Oh yes! / Amen!)
It doesn't matter with me!	(Alright! / Amen!)
Praise God,	
'cause we're here to have a good time!	(Yeah! / That's right!)

By the time Sister Perry shouts, "It doesn't matter with me," her voice has jumped to a noticeably higher pitch. This remark climaxes a sequence that begins with her invitation ("And as I always say . . .") and grows in intensity with each subsequent line, the words ever quickening and the phrases growing ever more emphatic. As Sister Perry's voice gets more animated, so too do her arms. Held loosely in front of her body, both are pumping up and down, with elbows bent, fists clenched, and palms facing forward. The movements seem to drive every phrase, pushing them forcefully on their taut trajectory.

The congregation is clearly riding the same wave of enthusiasm. Their cries and handclaps grow louder and louder, until finally, when Sister Perry talks of turning the meeting to a revival, they overpower her words altogether. The next three lines are lost to all but those sitting near the amen corner. As the noise subsides, so does Sister Perry's voice, which drops to a conversational tone as she continues.

"So again, I'd like to say on behalf of our pastor, Reverend David N. Atkinson, from our deacons, mothers, from our saints and friends here at Long Branch, and especially [from] the Branchettes, we do welcome you here, to our twentieth anniversary."

A round of "Amens" greets her closing words and sets the entire church to clapping. As Sister Perry sits down, the guitarist—who has been quietly improvising throughout her remarks—fills the approaching silence with a clearly articulated, up-tempo melody. A toddler sitting behind me yells out "Come on!" apparently directing his remark to the guitarist. The child's words seem to capture the mood of the entire congregation, who wait in hushed anticipation, knowing that the anniversary singing will soon begin.

✶　✶　✶　✶　✶

Paving the way for congregational accord, the "welcome address" formally welcomes gathered programgoers to the service. While rarely heard at commercial programs, such "welcomes" have long been a part of church-based events that draw their participants from beyond the host church's regular membership (e.g., gospel programs, anniversaries of various sorts, men's and women's day programs). In essence, their purpose is to minimize any perceived differences of membership, practice, and denomination that might divide churchgoers, and to invite all to join the communion of worship. "The church doors hang on welcome hinges," says an old church adage; the welcome address simply elaborates on this sentiment, making sure that everyone present feels welcome.[1]

At the beginning and ends of these addresses, speakers traditionally extend the "right hand of fellowship" to all in attendance. This is precisely the format followed by Sister Perry, who both opens and closes with an explicit statement of welcome, the former on behalf of the Branchettes, and the latter on behalf of both the church and the group. The middle of the address, in turn, traditionally offers speakers much freer rein. Some skip this section altogether, fusing beginning and end together in a rather perfunctory and formulaic welcome. Most, however, take this opening as an opportunity for words of encouragement and exhortation, turning the welcome address into a platform for lay preaching. Again, this is Sister Perry's strategy. After twice welcoming the assembly, and after invoking words of testimony that firmly identified the Branchettes (and thus herself) with the congregation, she pushes the address to its emotional climax, passionately calling sinners in the crowd to "turn their lives over to Jesus." The moment's intensity—as evidenced by the fervor of congregational response and the manifest passion of Sister Perry's performance—easily equals that achieved during the deacon's prayer. Then, just as suddenly as during the prayer, the moment passes, leaving sparks of energy virtually sizzling in the air. Sister Perry is once again speaking conversationally, restating her welcome with friendly informality. Just as she had begun.

Sister Perry's welcome follows a clear—and increasingly familiar—pattern. From conversational start to conversational finish, the address describes a cycle of devotional ebb and flow, delineating a pattern that is beginning to characterize not only the flow of talk, but also the entire service. Start low; rise high; return to low. The worshipful act—be it prayer or preaching, welcome or song—seems to mirror the whole in which it is embedded. Both act and service follow the same trajectory. Turn up the fire; let it sizzle; then turn it down. But never turn it down all the way. Never fully return to the last point of rest. Instead, keep raising the bottom, ever boosting the ambient energy, ever bringing the sustaining lows closer to the fiery peaks. Make the circle of praise a spiral, giving the whole an ascendant spin. Herein lies the dynamic that fuels the gospel program.

To insure its realization, saints must be able to freely manipulate the program's parts, ever tailoring them to meet the needs of the moment. This suggests that the component parts must be flexible. Like the welcome address. Like the prayer. Like the songs. Each act offers itself as frame rather than as fixed text, actively courting creativity, actively inviting situation-specific elaboration. The pieces emerge not as discrete parts in a predetermined whole, but as interlocking elements whose sequenced emergence defines that whole while moving it toward its novel realization.

Traditionally, a member of the host church gives the welcome address. In turn, a visiting member of the congregation offers its response. At the Branchettes' anniversary, Sister Perry acts as representative of both the church and the sponsoring group. Both roles fall squarely within the devotional convention of congregational control. Standing in the amen corner, Sister Perry speaks only as a gifted peer. Neither church mother nor deacon, she claims no special church authority. Yet as *saint*, she can claim the authority of sanctification, an authority grounded in the knowledge that she is one of God's elect.

This authority is quite different from that offered by rank. While the latter draws its power from status and singularity, the former draws power from its essential collectivity. *All* saints are said to share the authority of sainthood; all carry the Spirit's special certification. Hence every born-again believer can preach with a measure of wisdom and insight; every saint can pray with passion and power; every saint can witness with understanding and grace. While freely admitting that some believers' gifts are more developed than others, most saints contend that *every* saint bears the blessings of basic devotional competence. Sanctification brings with it a measure of mastery; competence comes with the commission. Furthermore, as Deacon Eldridge reminds us, being born again also makes every saint a candidate for divine vesselhood. Every born-again believer thus speaks with the realized authority of sanctification and the potential authority of Holy Ghost revelation. Hence *any* saint could appropriately extend the welcome, and *any* saint could stretch that welcome into exhortation, not only greeting the saved, but also urging the unsaved to change the status of their souls. The congregation responds to Sister Perry's words not because she sings and faithfully attends church, but because she is saved and thus can appropriately speak on behalf of the gathered saints.

Underlining this spirit of collectivity are the welcome address's many allusions to testimonies and its use of such phrases as "having a good time in the Lord"; both presume familiarity with the mysteries of sainthood and the conventions of sanctified talk. The welcome thus seems to address a congregation of "insiders," of churchgoers who share both beliefs and ways of worship. At the same time, however, the welcome explicitly recognizes the presence of those who are *not* saved, who are not members of the sanctified fellowship. This leads us to question precisely who *does* make up the audience at gospel programs. Who, in other words, is being welcomed?

I've already suggested that congregational makeup varies dramatically with the type of program being presented. Saints say, for example, that you'll find far more folks looking for "entertainment" at professional "ticket programs" than you will at small church-sponsored events and at local anniversaries. At programs like that at Long Branch, the expected audience seems to be more narrowly defined. Though some are clearly there for "form and fashion" (as suggested by Deacon Eldridge's tacit plea for spiritual authenticity) and some are clearly unsaved (as inferred by Sister Perry's invitation), most are thought to be born-again believers. The very designation of "saint"—the term most often used by devotional leaders and performers when referring to members of the congregation—suggests a set of shared beliefs that transcends doctrinal differences and denominational affiliation. Biblically grounded and experientially confirmed, these beliefs forge an unaddressed, undefined bond between the worshipers, reducing matters that might seem of importance on Sunday morning to a state of relative insignificance. What "counts" at programs like that at Long Branch is not one's church home or the particulars of one's belief, but the state of one's soul.

The gospel program is one of the few events in the African American church community that is characterized by cross-denominational attendance. Most other services tend to be congregation-specific, drawing their numbers from the body of members and "regulars" who attend Sunday morning worship. Prayer meetings, evening services, Bible study sessions, choir rehearsals, and the various events sponsored by church auxiliaries all rely on this core group for attendance. Only revival meetings—events whose evangelical thrust impels them to move beyond the confines of single congregations—begin to approach the gospel program's denominational catholicism.

Like gospel programs, revivals self-consciously attempt to draw in the widest possible public, encouraging saints, backsliders, and sinners alike to fill the pews. Revivals' focus on soul salvation, like gospel programs' focus on praise, overrides specific doctrinal concerns, cementing a cross-denominational bond between revival meetings and gospel events. More than any other services, revivals and gospel programs deliberately downplay the concept of denomination, arguing that one's place in the pews is ultimately less important than one's place in the heavenly band.

＊　＊　＊　＊　＊

The big program at the Durham Civic Center is well into its second hour when Willie Neal Johnson and the Gospel Keynotes finally take the stage. Hundreds in the audience have come out on this Monday night specifically to see the Keynotes, the acknowledged "master showmen" of quartet performance. Programgoers want to hear Paul Beasley hit his high falsetto, to see Jeffrey Newberry do his holy dance, to watch group leader Willie Neal Johnson playfully hit his hesitant singers with his hankie. Programgoers hope to hear a few of the Keynotes' latest hits, to witness the dramatic testimonies with which these self-proclaimed "country boys from Tyler, Texas," weave together their songs, to experience the intensity of a Keynotes' performance. Fans in the audience are not disappointed. Coming on as the evening's fourth group, the Keynotes are in high form.

By the close of the opening song's first verse, two singers are already off the stage and into the center aisle. They're back onstage by the beginning of the second song, though they and a third vocalist are back off when the song struts into its thrumming drive, a hypnotic repeat of the phrase, "I thank You, Jesus." The Keynotes close the song with voices pitched in sweet harmony.

Then Brother Newberry—still on the floor—begins to address the crowd, using the gruffly staccato tones of a sanctified preacher. He opens by berating those who haven't "changed the expressions on [their] face since we've been up here." He then chides programgoers who are afraid to say "Amen" because their next-door neighbors, "sitting two or three seats down," might hear them and "talk about" them tomorrow. Next he scolds the sisters who are afraid to shout because they might "mess up" their new dresses and the brothers who are afraid to shout because they might "scratch up" their new shoes. The sequence culminates in a masterful series of antiphonal cries, with two Keynotes trading falsetto "Yeahs," each pushing the other to higher and more strained peaks.

Jeffrey Newberry jumps back to the foreground with a roughly shouted, "I feel pretty good now!" Focusing his gaze on the audience, he quickly lets them know that he's not yet through with them, as he calls, "I'm still looking at you!" Then, to the chorus of Paul Beasley's piercing falsetto, sporadically echoed by Willie Neal Johnson's gruff tenor, he starts talking about denomination.

Some of you saying,	
"I'm from the Baptist church.	/ Church!
And in my church,	
they don't carry on like that!"	/ Church!
Some of you saying,	
"I'm from the Methodist church.	/ Yes!
And in my church,	
they don't carry on like this!"	/ Oooooh, my God!
Some of you may be from the Catholic church,	/ Yes!
"And they sure don't act like this in my church!"	
But I want to let you know something tonight!	
I don't care if you're Baptist,	/ Ye-e-e-e-es!
I don't care if you're Methodist,	/ Yes Sir!
I don't care if you're Catholic—	/ Ye-e-e-e-es!
In order to see Jesus,	/ Jesus!
In order to see Jesus,	/ Jesus!
you've got to be saved!	/ Saved!/Ye-e-e-e-es!
You've got to be sanctified!	/ Sanctified!/Yes Sir!
You've got to be wrapped up!	/ Wrapped up!/Ye-e-es!
Ti-i-i-ied up!	/ Tied up!/Yes!
Tangled up!	/ Tangled up!/Yes!
Ye-e-e-e-eah!	/ Yes!

By this point, Brother Newberry is wiping away the sweat that streams down his forehead with a large, white handkerchief. Having stalked eight rows into the audience, he suddenly pivots to face the stage and lets out a long falsetto moan. Paul Beasley immediately overlays the cry with a higher falsetto "Ye-e-e-e-es!" The drummer, who has been punctuating each of Brother Newberry's lines with a double beat, rides the cymbals and punches the bass drum again and again.

Jeffrey Newberry pulls out of his moan with a shouted "Yes Sir!" The two onstage guitars churn out a wall of sound as he goes back to preaching, once again in his gruff, exhortative tone. Dozens of audience members are clapping and yelling encouragement back to the stage.

How many ever read your Bibles?	
Do you read the Bibles in the building tonight?	
If you don't mind,	
will you turn the pages in your Bible with me,	/ Church!
to the Book of Acts,	
two and one.	/ Church!

On the day of the Pentecost, / Yeah!
   when the Holy Ghost came, / Yes!
      they were all in the upper room. / Yes!
Everyone there was on one accord. / Yes they were!
They tell me, when the Holy Ghost filled the room, / Yes!
   it moved like a mighty rushing wind! / Yes Sir!
They tell me, when it filled the room, / Yes!
   they began to speak in an unknown tongue! / Yes Sir!
Some of them began to stagger in the Spirit! / Ye-e-es!
But you know, we got a crowd of bystanders,
   that just don't believe nothing. / Ye-e-es!
Some of them said, "Look at those people, / Go on, Jeffrey!
   acting like they drunk!" / Drunk!
But Peter said, / But Peter said!
   "Oh no, they not! / Oh no!
When the Holy Ghost comes, / Yes!
when the Holy Ghost comes, / Holy Ghost comes!
   it'll make you rock! / Ye-e-e-e-e-e-eah!
   It'll make you leap! / Le-e-e-eap! / Yes Sir!
   It'll make you shout! / Yes! / Ye-e-e-e-es!
Ye-e-eah!

Again Brother Newberry climaxes his preached words with a melismatic shout. Paul Beasley, whose falsetto cries have gradually moved from staccato accents to piercing wails, responds with an overlapped "Ye-e-e-e-eah!" Then Brother Newberry cries out a second time, leading Brother Beasley to launch another, even longer falsetto yell. Willie Neal Johnson answers with a quavering, highly ornamented "Ye-e-eah!" Closing on a descending note, he sets the stage for Brother Newberry's preached return.

Y'all know
   that the Lord will be good to you. / Yes!
And you're not ashamed to be a witness for Him. / Yeah!
If you don't mind being a witness for Him, / For Him!
   let me see you stand on your feet tonight! / Yeah!
Raise your hands!
Tell him "Ye-e-e-es!"

By the third vibrato quaver in Brother Newberry's "Yes," the other Keynotes are adding a counterpoint "Yes" of their own, singing in tight and crystal-clear harmony. Seamlessly, with no one sounding the least bit winded, they ease into the slow praises of "Yes, Lord," a favorite song among the sanctified.[2]

The preached sequence is a masterpiece of argument and execution. Beginning by scolding programgoers who were unwilling to "let go and let God," it renounces the doctrinal overlays and expressive restraints of denomination, arguing that in order to "see Jesus," believers must be saved, sanctified, and "wrapped, tied, and tangled" in the Word of God. As if to dramatize the experiential depths of this involvement, the singers join in a shouted chorus, actualizing intensity as they enact personal epiphany.

Coming out of this dramatized fervor, Brother Newberry grounds his argument in the biblical account of Pentecost, paraphrasing the second chapter of Acts. For a brief moment, he steps into the historical present, suggesting that audience members who cling to denominational guidelines are a "crowd of bystanders that just don't believe nothing." Then he shifts back to the past and links these folk to those who long ago mistook the Spirit's ministrations for simple drunkenness. The segue climaxes by collapsing past and present in the timelessness of divine action, as Brother Newberry lists physical manifestations of the holy touch. The cited source is purposefully ambiguous; the words could be Saint Peter's, or they could be Brother Newberry's. The point, of course, is that source doesn't matter, for the message's truth transcends time. As before, the singers immediately dramatize this truth, following the declaration "It'll make you shout!" with a series of piercing, counterpoint cries.

Brother Newberry next moves from enactment to invitation, turning his attention to those who are "not ashamed to be a witness" for the Lord. Implicitly contrasting these believers with those who hide behind denomination, he invites them to stand and offer witness through a song that is clearly identified with Pentecostal worship (and was in fact composed by Bishop Charles H. Mason, founder of the Church of God in Christ). The song itself ties the gathering on the day of Pentecost to contemporary sanctified services, setting the two on the same experiential plane. Brother Newberry's message is clear: to see Jesus, and to feel the holy fire, believers must follow the sanctified path. Though Brother Newberry names denominations whose practices might lead believers *away from* this path, he never specifies those that lead them *toward* it. Instead, he leaves the issue open, inferring that shared faith blurs all denominational lines in the fellowship of saints.

*   *   *   *   *

One hears this same message again and again in gospel programs. From small church-sponsored events to grand, commercial productions, the same disclaimer rings forth, always denying the overlays of denominational doctrine, always welcoming programgoers to the single body of Christ. At issue, as Evangelist Hattie Lofton declared during her invitation at the Branchettes' anniversary, is not membership in "any particular church," but rather membership in "*the* church—the church of the living God."

"*The* church," as envisioned by these saints, would not in fact include many of the mainstream denominations whose practice denies the ongoing revelation of the Holy Ghost. Congregations deemed "too stylish to shout," whose "seditty ways" show more concern with formality and decorum than with rebirth in the

Spirit, tend to be left out of saints' descriptions of the "apostolic fellowship."[3] In the eyes of the sanctified, these "nonshouting" churches (often associated with the middle and upper classes) have abandoned the "old-time religion" and have adopted in its stead a more "comfortable," worldly version of Christian practice. Yet Christ never promised a "comfortable" faith, say the saints. Nor did He ever suggest that the Spirit would someday cease moving among the faithful. Instead, say the saints, He declared that "the Comforter" would abide with believers forever (John 14:16). Those who deny this presence, or who interpretively shrink it to a mere "feeling," are seen as standing outside the true circle of faith.

So who's in the circle? All those who are "saved, sanctified, and filled with the Holy Ghost." Holiness folk, Pentecostals, Disciples, believers from a host of independent sanctified congregations, lots of Baptists, and a generous sampling of Methodists. Denominational labels, as Brother Newberry and Evangelist Lofton suggest, really aren't very useful, as they reveal little about the actual practice of faith. Church membership doth not a saint make. Faith, holiness, and a relationship with the indwelling Spirit do.[4]

The preferred music of this sanctified circle is clearly gospel. But gospel, as a popular form, also transcends denominational lines. Even the most formal, middle-class churches boast gospel choirs and often host gospel performances. Nonetheless, the music's heart—and certainly its commercial face—is sanctified. References to holiness and the moving Spirit, and unfettered displays of shouting, holy dancing, and other Spirit-driven behaviors, have come to characterize most gospel performances. Even gospel singers who are *not* saved (whose numbers, say the saints, are legion) regularly make a point of "showing" spiritual signs and "playing holy." They run the aisles, shout "in the Spirit," burst into tongues, testify with tear-filled eyes, and cut their showy steps. The fact that these behaviors lend themselves to dramatic simulation in no way diminishes the message that they convey about belief. Whatever their source—whether self or Spirit—holiness nonetheless emerges as the reigning frame of performance. The gospel program's overriding message—conveyed over and over again in song and preached words—is that only by being saved, sanctified, and filled with the Holy Ghost will one ever be assured a place in the heavenly choir.[5]

To further ground the transdenominational nature of gospel performance, we need only look to the groups that sang at the Branchettes' twentieth anniversary. Of the twenty-three soloists and ensembles that performed over the two-day event, only three (including the Branchettes) hailed from Disciple churches. Nine of the ten choirs came from Free Will Baptist, Missionary Baptist, Holiness, Holiness New Birth, and United Church of Christ churches, and from a range of independent sanctified congregations. Members of trios, quartets and family ensembles expanded the denominational roster to include Church of God in Christ, A.M.E., and A.M.E.Z. assemblies.

"We don't care about denomination at our anniversary," explained Sister Ethel Elliott, when I asked her about this denominational breakdown. "Because denomination doesn't have nothing to do with getting to heaven. What *does* is living holy. And holiness is not about denomination." After a short pause, she continued:

"You know, it won't be all Disciples up in heaven. It won't be all Baptists up in heaven. And it won't be all Presbyterians up in heaven, unless they live holy. That's what matters—living holy. God ain't studying about no denomination. He's looking at your heart."[6]

What of those who don't live holy? They too attend gospel programs. Indeed, the constant calls to holiness, the frequent invitations to receive Christ, and the recurrent warnings against "form and fashion" all testify to the expected presence of the unsaved. Saints say that the programs' overriding focus on music insures this presence, for it invites interest from many whose sole goal is entertainment. It also attracts those whose goals are less worthy. Satan, you will recall, loves music. And he loves to corrupt—or silence—the sounds of praise.

As I've already suggested, the perceived percentage of the unsaved and the nonworshipful varies with the type of program being presented. Most saints contend that audiences at commercial "ticket programs," unlike those at noncommercial events like the Branchettes' anniversary, consist in large part of entertainment-seekers. Some saints, like Fayetteville gospel announcer and evangelist Dorothy Jackson, maintain that at least a third of the audiences at commercial programs come just "expecting to see a show." Others, like Raleigh gospel promoter James Thomas, put this number as high as 70 percent. Still others suggest that the percentage may even be higher. Whatever the exact figure (something which, as all of these believers point out, can be known only by God), most saints with whom I spoke agreed with Jojo Wallace's assessment that commercial programs tend to draw both the "auditorium crowd"—"those just looking to be entertained"—and the "church folk."[7]

*　*　*　*　*

Rev. Z. D. Harris and I were talking about the "entertainment crowd" when he first told me the parable of the poll parrot. I had just asked for his reaction to some comments by gospel songwriter Thomas Dorsey, in which Dorsey likened the emotions felt in church to those experienced while listening to the blues. I had been taken aback by Dorsey's rather facile comparison and wondered whether Rev. Harris would respond the same way. Instead of answering directly, he told a story that gently explained precisely who might experience the same feelings from these musics. Key to the parable's meaning is the doubt cast on the sincerity of many who "carry on" in church.

"It's sort of like the poll parrot was," Rev. Harris began. "Where the man said, 'Here, here's a poll parrot [that] I want to sell you.' Said, 'He'll talk.' "

"Well [this other man] said, 'You sure he'll talk?' Said, 'Yeah, he'll talk.' "

" 'So how much he'll cost?' He said, 'He cost a dollar and a half.' "

"He say, 'And you sure he'll talk?' Say, 'Yeah, he'll talk.' "

"He say, 'All right.' Say, 'If he'll talk, I'll buy him.' So he bought the poll parrot. Paid a dollar and a half for him."

"And on the way home—the poll parrot hadn't said nothing. So he was saying then, said, 'Now this man said this thing'll talk, but he hasn't said a word! Since we've been on our way home.'

"But after a while, the poll parrot looked and saw—he said, '*Shoe-shop!*' " (Here Rev. Harris affects a shrill pitch, mimicking the parrot.)

" 'Mmmm!' the man said. 'He *will* talk, won't he!' "

"And he goes on, and goes on. And after a while he said, 'Well, now, he just said one word, but he ain't said nothing else.' "

"Then after a while [the poll parrot] come along and he said, '*Theater!*' " (Again Rev. Harris takes on the parrot's pitch.)

"The man said, 'Oh yeah! I believe I got my money's worth now!' Said, 'There's one more place I want you to name. If you name *that*, I know I got my money's worth.' Cause he paid a dollar and a half for him—so it means it's fifty cents for every voice he done, in times in the conversation. So he knew he had his money's worth. He said, '[There's] one more place I want you to name.' "

"So he come along there, and [the poll parrot] said, '*Nightclub!*' "

"The man said, 'I got my money's worth! But I tell you what I'm going to do. I going to take you to church tomorrow morning, and let you see what that is.' "

"So he went to church. The preacher was preaching. And after a while, folk got happy, shouting and carrying on, and falling over benches. And the poll parrot hadn't said a word. And the man said, 'What's this place?' [The poll parrot] said, '*Nightclub!*' "

"He said, "*This* ain't no nightclub! This is *church!*' "

" '*Same crowd!*' " Having assumed the parrot's screech one last time, Rev. Harris burst into laughter. His point needed no further elaboration.[8]

* * * * *

By identifying the congregation as a club crowd, the parrot pointedly pierces the illusion of congregational sanctity. One could easily interpret this parable as a critique of so-called "saints" who shout on Sunday morning but frolic on Saturday night. The context of our conversation, however, gives the story an even more telling point. Rev. Harris and I had been talking about people who attend gospel programs seeking only entertainment. This parable suggests rather clearly that this number includes many who falsely assume the behavioral guise of sanctification, who "shout" and "carry on" in church without ever feeling the Spirit. "The same crowd," Rev. Harris explains, "that goes to that nightclub and does all this carrying on and everything, is also the same crowd on Sunday morning in the church—*doing the same thing*. So that's how come it's hard to tell sometimes, the Christians from the worldly people. Because you got a lot of *so-called* Christians is in things [in the] other world, and then on Sunday morning they come back and do their thing *again*."[9] Like their "form and fashion" counterparts in the cross-aisle, in the pulpit, and on the stage, these churchgoers are merely performing sanctity.

Saints have long talked about churchgoers who shout for show. Generations of singers have cautioned that "everybody talking about heaven ain't going there." Their songs tell of those who "go to meeting to sing and shout," and then add that their real purpose is just "to put on pretense."[10] This theme surfaces again and again in conversations, sermons, public prayers, and cross-aisle commentary. Every congregation seems to have members who earn a reputation for "playing church"; every program seems to include folks who can be counted on to "fall out" at the slightest cue; every community seems to have members who win the tongue-in-cheek designation of "shoutingest." These folk *always* seem to shout, even though their lives outside of church often fail to suggest any particular holiness. "Same crowd," said the parrot; "same crowd as the nightclub." If they're not *living* the faith, then why are they *acting* it in the church-house? Why do churchgoers fake their shouts?

The first answer that many saints give is the most charitable, suggesting that many of these pew performers simply don't know better. In essence, they are following tradition, doing what they see others around them doing, and getting from their actions an emotional reward. Many saints tell how they once *thought* themselves saved, how they sincerely *believed* that what they felt in church represented the wholeness of Holy Ghost encounter. Not knowing that a deeper fulfillment could be achieved, they contented themselves with what they knew. They saw others shouting and doing the holy dance; they saw the behavioral signals of triumph and joy; they witnessed the release, the relief, the final calm. So they struggled to copy that which they saw, attempting to translate seen behavior into felt experience. With no understanding of the mysteries of holiness, they treated shouting as a behavioral equation whose "solution" lay entirely in the plane of calculation and practice.

When tracing the roots of such calculation, many saints point to childhood experiences at the mourner's bench. They tell of feeling the pressure to convert, of watching their friends "come through," and finally of responding to the pressure by acting out the appropriate behaviors themselves.[11] Others locate the process in their adult lives, telling about finding themselves called from the pulpit to declare the state of their souls. Facing the preacher's exhortations and the congregation's clapped and cried encouragements, some step straightaway into the Lord's embrace. Others, however, bow to the pressure, responding to emotion rather than grace. They are literally *driven* to confess their faith—before the eyes and ears of the full congregation.

Some of these "converts" recognize immediately that they haven't truly been saved. Yet they've made a public commitment that many find hard to deny. To admit to feeling nothing is to admit deception, which is to lose face. So many stay silent, having unwittingly begun what often becomes a pattern of pretense. Other "converts" convince themselves that they indeed *have* been saved. As our discussion of "emotional" shouting suggested, they may well have felt a moment of deep emotional fullness. The intensity of expectation, coupled with surging emotion and the keenness of remembered example, may indeed have fueled an epiphany unlike anything they had ever experienced. For many, this stands as sufficient "proof" of transcendence's touch. After all, in a tradition where descriptions of divine encounter are usually cloaked in metaphor, there are few standards against which one can measure such experience. The epiphany may indeed feel like "fire in one's bones"; it may indeed seem to be authored from without. Believers who have long heard about the certain "knowing" of born-again holiness simply interpret this as that.

Thus begins the cycle of misinterpretation. If believers begin by equating self-generated epiphany with the divine touch, they might well continue to do so, interpreting every subsequent shout (and perhaps even every rush of good feeling) as a sign of celestial approval. Over the years, I've met many such believers, all of whom claim sanctification, and yet all of whom describe the Spirit solely in terms of human emotion. "The Spirit is a feeling," explained one such "saint," himself a professional gospel singer. "It's just a feeling, a good feeling."[12] Saints say that the very appearance of the modifier "just" in such remarks immediately casts doubt on the believer's experience. When I've pressed such self-professed "saints" for further details about the Spirit, all have resorted to markedly impersonal description, speaking of Spirit as emotional force rather than as transcendent entity. All sense of divine will and personality vanish in the vague language of human "feeling" and sensation.

Some churchgoers undoubtedly become quite adept at inducing the epiphanies they interpret as transcendence. They learn how to throw themselves into the music, how to ride the rhythms of praise, how to catch the contagion of emotion. These believers often earn reputations as the "shoutingest" sisters or brothers, for they can always be counted on to "fall out," seemingly feeling the touch with even greater frequency than the most devout saints. *But,* say the saints, all this shouting counts for naught when these believers stand before the gates of judgment.

Saints in central South Carolina illustrate this point with a telling anecdote about the "outshoutingest" member of a local Baptist congregation, "the only man in the church who could outshout the sisters." Convinced that his shouts showed divine approval, this brother was certain that he would "walk the golden streets when he got to heaven." His fellow church members apparently felt the same way. But when he finally crossed death's threshold, the shouting brother found not only that heaven's gates didn't fly open in instant welcome, but that he had to knock to even get anyone's attention. A watching angel finally asked what he had done to deserve entry. "Saint Peter knows all about me!" the confident believer replied. "Ask *him* about what I've done." The angel did just that. But Saint Peter couldn't remember ever having heard much about this particular brother. So he summoned Saint James, who looked in the record book and finally declared, "He didn't do much of nothing!" In the end, the angelic host sent the disappointed brother packing, traveling dejectedly down the winding path to hell.[13]

The church members in this story clearly accepted the brother's shouts as real. The story itself, however, suggests the merit of doubt, encouraging a healthy skepticism about shouting's source. Yet the tale offers no means of evaluation. The cited churchgoers remain forever in the dark. This leads us to ask what measures saints use to differentiate between true and false shouting. How can they *know* that others' profound experiences are merely exercises in emotion? How can they be sure that some believers are deceiving themselves when they claim the status of "saved"?

When asked these questions, most saints immediately qualify their answers, saying that they can rightfully stand in judgment of no one. Many promptly cite Christ's admonition to "judge not, that ye be not judged" (Matthew 7:1). Having said this, saints often go on to tell of the "gift of discernment," the mystical endowment that allows select believers to distinguish between inspired and uninspired behavior. They also speak of contextual understanding, saying that those who are in the Spirit (those whom Rev. Z. D. Harris earlier spoke of as "children of the light") will know the Spirit, and suggesting that if the evinced "spirit" fails to flow, then its source merits a measure of suspicion. The most telling evidence offered by saints, however, rests in personal history. Many born-again believers tell how they themselves were once deceived, how they themselves were once satisfied with the lesser glories of emotion, honestly believing that their experiences were manifestations of God's abundant grace. Only *after* they were saved did these saints recognize the depths of their self-deception. This recognition made them ever more wary of the devil's duplicity and led them to speak freely of those "before" days, hoping that their testimony might keep others from making the same mistake. Rather than judging specific others, these saints first judge themselves, and then issue a general caution so that all with ears to hear may hear.[14]

✶ ✶ ✶ ✶ ✶

Evangelist Dorothy Jackson is one of those preachers who exudes the infectious excitement of holiness. I first saw her in action at a commercial "ticket program" in Raleigh, where she served as the afternoon's emcee. Unlike most emcees at such events, she constantly called on program goers to reject the "form and fashion" antics of the program's professional singers. "It's time to stop playing church," she told the audience. "Playing time is out! These are *real* times, and we need to get real for Jesus!" Every time a group started "jumping and hollering" to capture audience acclaim, Evangelist Jackson followed them on stage with strong words of caution. Everyone could tell that she disapproved of those who "trifled with God."[15]

A few weeks after the program, I was sitting with Evangelist Jackson in her comfortable Fayetteville home, talking about believers who "played church." To open our conversation, I played back a recording of some of the remarks she had made in Raleigh and asked for further elaboration on the issues she had raised there. She replied with ease and eloquence, confidently moving from one point to another, allowing me to just listen and learn. At one point she spoke about knowing "the difference between showmanship and when the Spirit takes over." I asked her how she could tell. She proceeded to talk about the calmness of the Spirit, about how it never raged out of control, about how Satan used showmanship to mimic the Spirit's ways. Then she revealed that she herself had once performed professionally, singing backup with Evangelist Shirley Caesar. During that time, before she was saved, she herself had been guilty of "putting on" the shouted guise of sanctity. But when the Spirit really *did* come, everything suddenly changed. Now she *knew*, she explained with quiet conviction, what she had been missing.

> One thing Shirley [Caesar] used to tell us:
>   "You don't shout,
>   if the Spirit does not make you shout."
> You know.
> And I remember that I used to try to shout.
> And *every* time I would try to shout,
>   I would break a shoe-heel!
> God, I thank you!
> I would break a shoe-heel.
> Yes I would!
> Yes I would.
> I would break a shoe-heel.

I couldn't help but laugh at this subtle sign of divine displeasure. Evangelist Jackson smiled at the memory, and then continued.

> And my father told me one time,
>   "Dorothy,
>   one thing you don't ever play with,
>   is to play with the Spirit of God.
>   Don't ever play with it.
>   If you don't know it,
>   if you don't feel it,
>   leave it alone.
>   Don't ever play with it.
>   Don't pretend.
>   Don't act like you see somebody else acting.
>   Because you don't know *what* they're feeling.
>   It could be right,
>   and it could be wrong.
>   You don't know *what* they're feeling.
>   But wait—
>   if you desire it,
>   if you wait on it,
>   it'll come."
> You know.
> So I waited.

Evangelist Jackson paused. Her words had quickened as she recounted her father's warning. By the close of his quoted remarks, the words were rolling freely from her tongue, each phrase poetically referencing that which had come before. I remember thinking that she certainly *sounded* like a preacher. Then she slowed, momentarily reliving the time of waiting. When she began anew, her words were once again measured and calm. At least for a moment . . .

And when the Spirit really did come,
   it like to scared me,
      crazy.
Yes, it was—
I can't express it,
I can't put it in words.
I *knew* that it was the Lord.
Cause I've *never felt nothing like that in my life.*
The joy!
The fulfillment!
The explosion!
The everything—
   was there!
And I had longed for that.
So . . .

Again Evangelist Jackson paused. Again her words had started slow, speeded up, and then abruptly returned to slow. Her pauses seemed to mark moments of reflective resolution. She left the pause by returning to the point on which she began.

And the shout that I used to be around my house trying to do—
   because we were going to [the] stage—
when the Holy Spirit truly came,
   I had no more control of my feet.
   I couldn't control them.
      They were moving by the Spirit.
My handclap—
   I couldn't clap anymore.
      The Spirit controlled my hand.
In the praises,
   you know, the Spirit just totally began to control my praises.
And then when I see somebody that does this—
   this, this "show" thing—
     it's very disturbing.
     It's very frightening.
       Very, very frightening.
       For me.

Another pause. This time I interrupted, asking why the showiness frightened her. She answered by telling how the anointing carried with it a powerful "authority," a sense of depth and command that born-again believers could "feel." Saints could tell, she explained, that it was "real." But not so the showiness.

> Because it's just *not* real.
> You know.
> And when it's not real,
>   you can feel that too.
> It's just like—
> it's like words just flapping off of your ears.[16]

Words flapping off your ears. Words with no power. Words with no penetration. Words with form but no substance. Words spoken with fashion but no passion. Words, as the saints say, that are mere "form and fashion." The fright comes from the realization that these words keep the speaker away from the truth. They lure with shallow satisfaction and convince that this contentment represents the fullness of grace. In so doing, they suspend the search for sanctification, persuading believers—as they did the "shoutingest" brother denied entry to heaven—that all is well in the eyes of God. This self-deception, in turn, yields condemnation, consigning deceived believers to the fate of that same shouting brother.

Hence Evangelist Jackson's fear. She knows that she once traveled the path of deception and came close to missing the fulfillment that she ultimately found in Christ. When she sees others walking that same path, she fears for their souls. And so she speaks forth, never condemning, but always warning, always letting others know that a greater fulfillment awaits them, always hoping that her words will help save some souls.

* * * * *

Not all churchgoers who shout in self do so out of unawareness. Saints say that many shout with full consciousness of their deception. Others shout with a qualified awareness, knowing that they are not in the Spirit, but not seeing anything particularly "wrong" with their pretense. Some of these find temporary emotional release in shouting and use this to justify their actions, pointing out that they are not purposefully deceiving anybody. But saints say that most of those who falsely shout do so for the same reason that once motivated Evangelist Jackson—for "show." In essence, they are trying to draw attention to themselves.

Given the egalitarian dynamics of most services, this should come as no surprise. Saints constantly remind each other that the church knows "no big 'I's' and little 'you's.'" All are equal, they say, in the eyes of God. Devotional services invite enactment of this equality, granting center-stage focus to anyone who seizes the performative lead. Anyone can testify; anyone can lead congregational singing; anyone can respond to the welcome. This same spirit extends throughout the service, even marking the sermon, the point where rank seems most clearly defined. For even though the preacher seems to stand apart, the distance lessens the moment the Spirit begins to guide the preacher's tongue. From this point forward, the preacher—though physical vehicle for the preached Word—is hearing the message for the first time just like everyone else in the church-house. For a moment, all are equals in the face of revelation. Even when the preacher is *not* speaking in the Spirit, all others in the congregation—whether in the pews, the choir stand, or the deacon's corner—are equal participants in the voiced conversations of worship. Anyone can clap; anyone can call out; anyone can shout.[17]

While encouraging a spirit of equality, the saints make no attempt to standardize or flatten self-expression. Indeed, quite the opposite is true. Sanctified worship celebrates the creatively individual voice; it welcomes artful expressions of the self. Within this frame, every act of public worship becomes an act of explicitly personalized artistry.[18] The testimonies that generate the greatest response, for example, are those that stray from formula and cliché to ground praises in the particularities of personal experience. The song leads that prompt the loudest acclaim are those that freely personalize text and melody to capture the intimacies of praise. The prayers that earn the most spirited "Amens" are those that frankly admit personal hardship and then eloquently build praises on proofs of hardships transcended. And the sermons that call forth the most enthusiastic affirmations are those that ground their lessons in experiential anecdote and then convey them with the poetic singularity of the preacher's personal style. The motivating aesthetic seems to demand more than mere improvisation; it calls for improvisation that *personalizes*, transforming each act of worship into an act of artfully intimate testimony. Hence the prevalence of such terms as "prayingest," "singingest," and "preachingest." Each testifies to saints' abilities to make prayers, songs, and sermons uniquely and artistically their own.[19]

How does shouting fit within this frame of expected artistry? Most saints argue that "real" shouting doesn't fit at all, because the outward signs of the touch are controlled by the Spirit rather than the self. At the moment of anointment, the self ceases to be a player. The only "artist" in this devotional drama is the Spirit, whose actions, say the saints, transcend all mortal evaluation.

But not all churchgoers are saints. And not all saints can resist the lure of artful display. Hence the temptation to transform shouting into performance, to make the shout a show. Finding themselves caught between the service's voiced calls for egalitarian selflessness and its unvoiced invitation to artful self-expression, many churchgoers make shouting a way of publicly declaring their personhood. The dramatic shout momentarily breaks the frame of congregational parity, thrusting the shouter to the center of congregational attention. Saints' ears hear the rapturous cries; their eyes search to find the source; their hands clap in spirited encouragement. For an instant, the shouter claims sole possession of the devotional center-stage.[20]

Why do false shouters seek this center-stage position? Most saints would agree with Branchette Lena Mae Perry when she answers, "They just want to be seen. That's all it is—for other people to see them."[21] The false shouters simply want the attention. They want to stand apart, to feel the eyes upon them, to relish the moment of focus. Saints are always trading anecdotes that elaborate on this desire, telling of sisters who shout to draw attention to their new dresses, of brothers who shout to show off their sharp suits, of sisters and brothers who shout to catch the eyes of potential sweethearts. Some stories tell of folks who shout just to outdo the shouts of shouting others. Others tell of women who "fall out" in revealing ways, hoping that bared flesh or a flash of underwear will spark some brother's (or sister's) interest.[22] An entire body of tales describes "shouting saints" who "miraculously" manage to keep their wigs from falling off or their clothes from being dirtied in even the most rambunctious shouts. Another cluster of stories tells of pranks played on false shouters to reveal their self-serving imposture. In all these narratives, the shouts' key purpose is garnering attention.[23]

The quest for prestige also plays a role in false shouting. After all, every shout outwardly suggests a measure of divine approval. The Spirit presumably graces only those who are "living right," who are "holy" and "sanctified." By assuming the outward signs of anointment, crafty churchgoers can thus publicly claim an internal state of grace. Their shouts, in essence, symbolically testify to their holiness. This testimony, in turn, grants shouters status in the eyes of their peers, all of whom are themselves presumably seeking spiritual fulfillment. (Not all churchgoers, of course, *are* in fact seeking the Spirit. Saints say that some shout solely for one-upmanship, competitively claiming a greater holiness than those who shouted before. This spirit of rivalry sometimes yields what amounts to shouting "contests," where churchgoers enact ever more flamboyant and seemingly out-of-control shouts in order to "outshout" others in the congregation. While prestige still ranks as the "reward" in such contests, the motivating force seems to be simple competition.)[24] The heightened status afforded by frequent shouting often translates directly into increased power within the individual church. Manifesting itself in arenas as diverse as officerships in church auxiliaries and increased attention from the pastor, such prestige carries a clear political edge.[25]

✷ ✷ ✷ ✷ ✷

In 1946, Baptist preacher William Walker wrote the poem "I Wonder Is Everybody Happy That Shouts?" He often recited this piece in Chicago churches and distributed it in a privately printed booklet that he sold at personal appearances and church conventions. More than five decades later, the poem is still available in Chicago-area stores that specialize in gospel music. Saints apparently still find the message tellingly relevant.

It's not out of place to shout,
　　but don't shout for fun.
Don't be a false pretender,
　　just shout when the Spirit comes.

Be perfect in everything you do,
    and stay in a Christian's place.
God is tired of men and women playing church,
    and putting on a long, sad face.
Pretending that you are happy,
    before you take your seat.
Hollering all over the church,
    clapping your hands and stomping your feet.
Now I don't believe in quenching the Spirit,
    when it comes in, let it out.
But I wonder, yes, I wonder,
    is everybody happy that shouts?
To the ones who shout all the time,
    these words to you are hard.
But the day has really come,
    for man to stop playing with God.
The Spirit doesn't stay on one person all the time,
    like some of us pretend.
This jumping and shouting, and tearing up benches
    without the Spirit, it's a sin.
Hypocrisy has ruined the world,
    I mean in every way.
In singing, preaching, and praying,
    men are taking Christianity for play.
It's bad to be a hypocrite,
    to pretend that what you are not.
Shouting without the Spirit,
    your soul will end up where it's hot.
I've seen some in my life,
    until I really got my fill.
I know God is tired of men jumping and shouting,
    and breath smelling like a whiskey still.
That's why the sinner is so hard to repent,
    the Christian keeps him in doubt.
It keeps me wondering, yes, Lord wondering,
    is everybody happy that shouts?[26]

* * * * *

In the course of his poem, Rev. Walker warns false shouters that their souls "will end up where it's hot." In part, this fate is the basic cost of deceit. Rev. Walker also suggests that it comes as repayment for the impostor's role in keeping sinners "in doubt," by blurring the boundaries between worldliness and holiness. A third, unspoken reason for this hellish fate rests with Satan himself. "Learning how to fake—now that is a gift from Satan," asserts Baptist preacher Sam McCrary. "You see, Satan will teach you how to do that." Once again, Satan shows his face as the master imitator. Rev. McCrary and many other saints contend that the devil "teaches" his charges how to shout so that they might sow confusion among the saints. The ability to shout thus becomes a "gift," a matter of endowed competence, a skill honed under the watchful eye of Satan. Those who accept the gift become active agents of duplicity, garnering temporary worldly advantage from a pact that will eventually land them in hell.[27]

The shouters actively working for Satan stand at the end of a continuum that begins with those who honestly believe that their shouts are sincere and of the Spirit. Saints say that Satan rambles the continuum's full length, deceiving at one end and encouraging others to deceive at the other. Whatever one's place on the line, the immediate result is the same. The shout comes from self, but acts like it comes from the Spirit. In the eyes of the saints, all such shouts are inauthentic. And inauthenticity, as the old congregational song "You Better Mind" assures, will surely prevent false shouters from entering the land of "comfort and glory":

You better mind how you shout.
    You better mind what you're shouting about.
If you want to live in the comfort and glory,
    You better mind.[28]

✶ ✶ ✶ ✶ ✶

When Sister Perry stood to speak, she welcomed *everyone*—saints and sinners alike—to the service. She knew, from looking over the congregation, that many in the pews were saved. Some were members of Long Branch; others were family and close friends; still others were singers from the invited groups. She also knew, with equal certainty, that many of the programgoers were unsaved. Again, some were church members, some were family, some were friends. Sister Perry did *not* know, however, the status of many familiar faces at the anniversary. Nor did she know that of the many strangers. Some were certainly children of God. Others were just as certainly agents of Satan. But none of this mattered. All were equally welcome. Sister Perry invited the saints to join the communion of praise and the sinners to witness and experience the joy of worshipful accord. She also invited the sinners to consider crossing the threshold of holiness. Having done so, Sister Perry sat down, confident that the service now rested in the hands of God. As she was to note at a later time, she didn't have to wait long for the first indication of where God planned to take it.

Chapter 12

Response

"God Ain't Coming into No Dead Heart"

As Sister Perry sits down, Sister Ethel Elliott rises from behind the registration table. Resting her fingers on the tabletop, she purses her lips and slowly scans the congregation. "Ummm," she begins, sounding somewhat pensive, "is there someone here like to respond?" Still surveying the pews, Sister Elliott smiles and adds, "before I appoint somebody?" Chuckles ripple through the church, and a toddler begins to cry. The guitarist plays quietly in the background.

Less than three seconds pass before a voice behind me cries, "Praise the Lord!" I turn in time to see a thin, middle-aged woman wearing a bright fuchsia blouse literally jump from her place in the pews. "Hallelujah!" she shouts as she sidles toward the center aisle. "Amen!" chorus the saints. "Praise God!" cries Sister Perry.

Having now reached the aisle, this energetic sister—whom I later discover is Sister Mary Bracey, a member of the Bracey Singers—launches into her "response." The words literally leap from her mouth, the lines excitedly tumbling one after another. As she speaks, she moves toward the front of the church.

I'm just so glad—	
I'm just so glad to be in the number!	(Yes!/Alright!)
One more time!	(Amen!)
And after hearing that warm welcome—	(Alright!/Amen!)
Whooo!—	(That's alright!)
till I feel like just giving Him *praise*!	(Amen!)
It's just good to be in the number!	(Amen!/Yes!)
One more time!	(Yes it is!)

By her third line, Sister Bracey's shoulders are visibly twitching, jerking upward as if acting on their own accord. The twitches match neither her words nor her steps, and instead set a rhythm of their own. I instantly recognize them as possible signs of the Spirit. Sister Bracey's loud, piercing "*Whooo!*" adds to this impression, as does the sharply rising tone of her voice. Though she started off at a heightened pitch, she's now gone even higher. "She's jumping right into high gear," I think to myself, mentally contrasting her pitched excitement with the conversational openings of those who spoke before her.

As Sister Bracey reaches the church-front, she turns to face the congregation. Her shoulders are still twitching, and the words are still tumbling forth. Two sisters in the amen corner have begun to clap, sharply punctuating Sister Bracey's remarks. The overall level of excitement continues to rise.

It could have been the other way!	(Yes it could!)
We could not have been able to walk in here!	(Alright!)
We could not be able to clap our hands!	(Yes!)
We could not be able to sing!	(Yeah!)
But we're here today!	(Ye-e-es!)
And Branchettes, we want you to know,	(Lord Jesus!)
we felt welcome anyway!	(Yes!)
'Cause we know who you all are!	(Yes!)
We know who you're serving!	(Yes!)
We just came to help you lift up the name of Jesus!	

"Praise God!" cries Sister Perry. "Yes!" chorus the saints. If anything, Sister Bracey's words have speeded up. They've also taken on a distinct tonal contour, starting sharply, rising through each line, and then dropping abruptly on the final syllable. From high to higher to low, high to higher to low, the lines surge like breaking waves, pausing only long enough to grant a gasped breath and a shouted response. Though the syllable count varies with each line, the words stretch and shrink to yield a precise interval, giving Sister Bracey's comments the rhythmic regularity of a metronome. The shoulder twitches establish a clear counterrhythm, while her slender arms, now pumping up and down in front of her body, define yet a third. Sister Bracey's face is radiant but tightly drawn, its muscles trembling with strained intensity.

And I would like to say	(Alright!)
that we're just glad to be here!	(Yes!)
We do accept your welcome.	(Oh Lord!)
And on behalf of all the groups—	
I would like all the groups to stand!	(Alright!)
Stand up on your feet!	(Praise the Lord!)
And let's give the Branchettes a stroke!	(Yeah!)
We are so glad to be here!	(Yes!)
Praise the Lord!	(Praise the Lord!)
Thank You, Jesus!	(Thank You!/Yeah!)

When Sister Bracey calls for a "stroke" for the Branchettes, the congregation breaks out in enthusiastic applause. Sister Bracey has to raise her strained voice even higher to be heard over the clapping. As scores of singers stand and clap, she begins to make her way back to her seat. But after only a few short steps, her feet stall. The saints continue clapping, while Sister Bracey presses her eyes shut and clenches her raised hands into fists. For a moment, she seems suspended in time, oblivious to all around her. Then, suddenly, Sister Bracey's head jerks backward and a piercing "Oooooh!" wells up from her throat. At the same instant, her feet leap into the inspired rhythms of the holy dance. Her eyes remain closed, while her face stays pointed to heaven.

Though the applause masks Sister Bracey's stepped tempo, saints who see her body and hear her shout quickly channel their clapping into the syncopated rhythms of the "holy clap." Exuberant cries of "My Lord!" "Hallelujah!" "Amen!" and "Thank You, Jesus!" ring from the pews. The entire church seems caught in a moment of deep praise.

Still feeling the touch, Sister Bracey cries out a second time. She follows her shout with a shrill "Hallelujah!" The saints continue calling and clapping their encouragement. "Go ahead!" cries one. "Glory to God!" calls another. A young sister starts shaking her tambourine, adding a droning sizzle to the rhythmic clapping. The guitarist, who has not stopped playing since the beginning of devotions, subtly slips his melodic wanderings into the new tempo.

Then, without warning, the shout ends. Sister Bracey's feet are once again still. After only a few brief seconds, the Spirit has left. Though the holy clap extends for a few seconds longer, it soon rambles into irregular clapping, which itself quickly begins to thin. Sister Bracey makes her way back to the pew, murmuring "Glory!" and "Praise Jesus!" under her breath. As she sits down, her face now lit with a beatific smile, the saints continue to offer quiet praises. "Praise our God!" says Sister Lena Mae Perry from the amen corner. She too is now seated. "Thank You, Jesus!" she adds. "Praise our God." Sister Perry's winded words grow gradually quieter, as do the sounds of clapping. The sister with the tambourine silences its insistent hiss; the voiced praises hush to a whisper. For a brief moment, the sighing guitar once again claims the foreground.

Sister Perry breaks the moment with a cry of "Thank You, Jesus!" Then the floor suddenly rings with the quickened beat of dancing feet. I turn just in time to see Sister Bracey, still sitting in the pew, raise her hands and cry an elongated "Ye-e-e-eah!" Instantly the saints are clapping again. Sister Bracey, again feeling the holy touch, cries "Yeah!" a second time. "Praise God!" calls a sister sitting nearby. "Jesus!" cries the woman with the tambourine, starting its sizzle once again. Again Sister Bracey cries out, "Yes! My Lord!"

Just as the applause begins to marshal itself into a holy clap, the moment passes, and Sister Bracey is once again alone in self. Shaking her head from side to side, and showing clear signs of tiredness, she mutters, "Thank You! Thank You, Lord Jesus! Thank You, Jesus!"

As the claps slow and the tambourine falls silent, Sister Perry stands and continues the litany of comments she has been voicing throughout the response. "Jesus! Praise our God!" she begins.

| We want to thank Sister Bracey | (Uh-huh) |
| for the beautiful response. | (Yes!) |

Putting all she had	(That's alright!)
into the response.	(Amen!)
A-a-all right,	
I feel a little bit better now.	(Praise God! / Amen!)
Knowing that the presence of the Lord	(Praise Him!)
is in the building!	(Amen!)

Sister Perry's thanks, unlike her encouragements of a few seconds earlier, are slow and relaxed. They momentarily return the service to an informal, conversational frame. But as she talks of the Lord's presence, Sister Perry picks up the pace and throws her voice into a noticeably higher pitch. The congregation responds with clapping and a chorus of enthusiastic "Amens." One sister utters a piercing, staccato "Oh-oh, oh-oh-oh!" Sister Perry herself joins the praises with "Hallelujah! Glory be to God!" As the clapping subsides, Sister Perry continues, her voice once again quietly calm.

| Lord, we say, "Thank You!" | (Thank You, Lord!) |
| Praise our God. | (Thank You, Jesus!) |

Somewhere in the pews, a young sister begins to whisper "Thank You, Jesus!" again and again, the words tumbling one after another as if in a single rushed sentence, the whole utterance pitched in a gently sharp soprano. Someone else is feeling the holy touch. One saint starts to clap; another starts to rattle a tambourine. But again the moment passes quickly. The thankful sister begins to moan a quiet "Mmmmmm," her descending tone suggesting the Spirit's departure. As she moans, Sister Perry continues her calming words of encouragement.

Thank You, Jesus.	(My Lord!)
Thank You, Lord Jesus.	(Thank You, Jesus.)
Thank You, Lord Jesus.	(Yeah!)
Praise our God.	(Praise Him)

Again the service eases toward a moment of quietude. The guitarist starts bending his stretched notes, capturing the sound of a gentle moan. Under his sweetly voiced notes, I hear the faint sigh of whispered praises. But most are silent. Devotions have come to an end. With the Lord "in the building"—as Sister Perry noted—and with accord steadily becoming a reality. Now the saints wait expectantly to meet the anniversary's emcee. And they await, with a sense of muted eagerness, the further ministrations of the Spirit.

* * * * *

While the "welcome" usually comes from a member of the host church, the "response" always comes from a visitor. Any visitor. Hence Sister Elliott offers the floor to *anyone* who wishes to respond, naming no special qualifications. Church-goers know that the respondent's only obligation is to "accept" the welcome and to thank the hosts for their hospitality. Churchgoers also know, however, that the response need not be nearly this simple. Like its devotional counterparts, the response invites creative elaboration; it opens a space, in essence, for congregational commentary.

In some services, program hosts apparently ask visitors to prepare their responses in advance. This frees hosts from the potential embarrassment of having nobody answer their invitation, and supposedly insures a fluent, carefully worded statement.[1] Though some saints with whom I've spoken say they've heard of this practice, none have ever requested or given a prepared response. All say instead that they prefer to leave this matter to the Spirit, who will guide selection of an appropriate respondent and insure the appropriate words. Like the ability to extend a fitting welcome, competence to craft a suitable response is said to come with the commission of sainthood. Trust in Jesus, say the saints, and the words will be there. If Sister Bracey's comments are in any way representative (and I would contend that they are), then the fear of a poorly worded response seems rather misguided. Among the saints, spontaneity seems to be a wellspring of eloquence.

Sister Mary Bracey's poetic skills shine throughout her brief response. Opening with quick words of praise, she immediately links her words with the world of song, referencing the familiar lyric "I want to be in that number, one more time." She then acknowledges the welcome—her only real obligation as a respondent—by describing how it made her *feel*. In so doing, Sister Bracey both personalizes her response and frames it in the language of experience. Next she again references song, neatly tying her words together in a bounded unit.

Upon reaching the cross-aisle, Sister Bracey quickly invokes a frame of testimonial thanksgiving, much as Sister Perry had done in the welcome. Like Sister Perry, Sister Bracey sets phrases typical to testimony in the context of a collective "we." Giving thanks for being able to walk, clap, and sing, she tacitly declares her identity with the congregation. Unlike Sister Perry, however, Sister Bracey cloaks her thanks in rhetorical indirection, suggesting *what might have been* had the saints not been "in the holy number." This strategy allows her to triumphantly transcend the thrice-stated negations with a declaration of victory. "We're here today!" she cries, suggesting that the saints' mere presence marks a defeat for Satan. This itself, she implies, is worthy of thanks.

Having established her identity as peer and proxy, Sister Bracey responds once again to the welcome, this time speaking for the collective. Whereas earlier she told how the welcome made *her* feel, she now tells how it made the *congregation* feel. This conflation of self and collective allows her to turn her focus to the Branch-ettes. "We know who you are!" she declares, tacitly acknowledging the last remaining we/you division. "We know who you're serving!" Each comment sets the stage for dramatic resolution. "We came to help you lift the name of Jesus!" With this remark, Sister Bracey steps toward resolution, momentarily uniting the "we" and "you" in the shared pursuit of praise.

Sister Bracey next accepts the welcome and calls for a round of applause for the

Branchettes; both acts symbolically cement her identification with the congregation. Then, by asking the singers to rise and by giving thanks on their behalf, she associates herself with yet a third group—the performers. In so doing, she establishes, through her own example, their oneness with the congregation. The fact that the standing singers are scattered throughout the sanctuary only confirms this sense of coincidence.

As the singers rise, so too do the Branchettes, who thus become one with the gathered performers, who in turn become one with the broader congregation. The stage is thus set for the final resolution, which Sister Bracey finesses by inviting *everyone*—and not just those standing—to join. The clapping quickly shifts from applause for the Branchettes to applause for the Lord, a shift that Sister Bracey first signals with her shouted cry, "We are so glad to be here!" Once again she speaks for the collective, the "we" that are "here today," the "we" that Sister Perry identified in her welcome as having "come together to know the glory of God." By the time Sister Bracey shouts "Praise the Lord!" and "Thank You, Jesus!" the entire congregation has joined in the communion of worship.

In fitting manner, the response closes by dissolving the very divisions that called for its enactment in the first place. As everyone unites in praise, all distinctions between hosts and guests vanish. Devotions thus end on a chord of accord. In this particular service, the accord finds quick confirmation in the flowing presence of the Spirit.

✳ ✳ ✳ ✳ ✳

After Sister Mary Bracey twice feels the Spirit, Lena Mae Perry stands to thank her for her response. Then Sister Perry salutes her for "putting *all* she had into the response." This remark immediately calls to mind the issue of displayed intensity, and the familiar adage "The more you put into it, the more you'll get out of it." Sister Bracey didn't *just* respond to the welcome. She didn't just recite words that met minimum expectations. Instead, she put *all* she had into her response, infusing her performance with obvious passion. With words sizzling with poetic fire, she praised and testified and preached. Rather than merely *accepting* the opportunity to speak, she *seized* and then *engaged* it, throwing herself fully into the response. Sister Bracey used the occasion not to perform—to be seen and judged by others—but to intensify her devotional focus. Her intended audience clearly included the saints *and* the Lord.

When discussing congregational song, I spoke about how accord—and by extension, "church"—is a condition that must be actively achieved. Saints say that accord never simply "happens"; "having church" is never a devotional "given." Both demand sincere effort. This effort, in turn, is both cognitive and communal, beginning with personal focus and then pressing toward devotional communion. As we've seen, congregational singing facilitates this focus, demanding a creative involvement that far transcends mere enactment and response. But singing is by no means the only vehicle of devotional engagement. The saints don't say "The more you put into *song*, the more you'll get out of it." They leave the adage open, referencing *every* act of worship. Recall for a moment the recitation of Evangelist Rachel Green, whose spoken recalling of song lyrics precipitated a shout. Then think again about Sister Bracey, whose impassioned response climaxed in ecstasy. Neither woman was singing. Yet both threw themselves wholly into worship, talking and moving and actively encouraging the saints to join the praise. They "put all they had" into their words, engaging the message both physically and mentally. Moving beyond mere reflection, both women transformed their bodies into spirited vessels of praise.

Listen closely to the conversations between cross-aisle and pew and you'll discover that saints actively encourage such full-bodied engagement. "Go ahead!" cry churchgoers when believers show the slightest signs of "getting into" praise. "Don't hold back!" call some. "Let go and let God!" shout others. Even cries of "Praise God!" can be heard as encouragements, particularly when set alongside such comments as "Go on and praise Him!" More than merely supporting and commenting on others' worship, these remarks actively spur praise on, urging believers to deepen their involvement.

Just as believers in the pews encourage engagement, so too do saints in the pulpit and cross-aisle. Devotional leaders are constantly calling on churchgoers to clap their hands, to pat their feet, to "make some noise for the Lord." "If you're a witness for Him tonight, let me see you stand on your feet!" calls the singer. "Come on and give the Lord a hand!" prompts the preacher. "If you know God's been good to you, let me hear you say, 'Yes!' " cries the emcee. At every turn, saints encourage a level of sensory engagement that brings both body and mind into spiritual consonance. In much the same manner, worship leaders chide congregations with such remarks as "You all don't hear what I'm saying!" or "Come on and say 'Amen!' " Each such comment calls for an involvement that eschews the ease of passive receipt, deepening the experience of hearing with the complementary experience of *doing*. More than just soliciting a response, saints voicing these words are encouraging believers to immerse themselves in active worship, fully aware that each added measure of sensory engagement deepens the praise experience.[2]

Note that all these comments call for involvement by *all* the saints. In so doing, they create the same conditions of engaged community that give group singing much of its devotional force. Take, for example, the invitation to "Give the Lord a hand!" In extending this call, devotional leaders are hoping for more than a simple exercise in joint activity. They recognize that clapping is *felt* and *seen* and *heard* by every churchgoer, that it sends ripples of rhythm through both body and mind. These rhythms in turn resonate with thoughts of praise, often triggering other, associated forms of worship. The body might sway; the hands might wave slowly through the air; the voice might cry "Hallelujah!" The praising vibrates through the entire self, drawing the individual more fully into the experience of being "wrapped, tied, and tangled in the Holy Word."[3]

"When I got saved, the Lord filled me from the crown of my head to the soles of my feet." Again and again, this testimony sounds from the pews and cross-aisle during sanctified services. "He didn't only save my soul," affirm the testifying saints. "He saved my hands, He saved my feet, He saved my whole body!"[4] The same message echoes from the mouths of singers, many of whom set it directly in song. In her popular piece "I'd Sho' Shout It," for example, gospel singer Louise "Candy" Davis sings:

> Folks act like they're dead and in the grave,
>> Like they ashamed that they've been saved.
> Act like the Holy Ghost has gone out of style,
>> they take Him out of church, and put on file.
>
> How can you sing of Amazing Grace,
>> and not make a noise anytime, anyplace?
> When my soul got saved, through and through,
>> my hands and my feet got saved too.
>
> Now when I go to church, I just shout and sing,
>> I praise the Lord for everything.
> I clap my hands, I pat my feet,
>> for the love of God runs so sweet.[5]

The blessings of anointment wash not only over the soul, but over the entire self, immersing body, mind, and spirit in rapturous baptism. In like manner, say the saints, the entire self should return thanks. Not just the hands, not just the voice, but the whole self. To achieve this focused fullness, believers must first draw themselves out of the layered conversations in which they're engaging. On one hand, they're offering praises to the Lord, initiating intimate conversations with the divine. On the other hand, they're communicating with fellow believers, engaging in exchanges of tone, word, glance, and motion. By "putting all they have" into praise, saints ease out of the latter and slide more fully into the former, rebalancing the direction of attention to achieve greater focus.

The very nature of saint-to-saint exchange seems to encourage this focusing. Conversations in the pews are fueled by a dynamic that presses them toward greater intensity. One "Thank You, Jesus!" begets another; one burst of clapping draws another set of hands into supportive motion. As we have seen, these exchanges often take the form of explicit encouragement, with saints urging fellow praise-givers to turn their thoughts wholly toward God. These acts of encouragement, in turn, often turn back to touch the thoughts of the encouragers, working to further deepen their own involvement, tacitly advising them to heed their own words. Cries of "Praise Him!" that are initially directed toward the pews thus transform themselves into cries of "Praise God!" directed toward heaven. In this manner, the very cycle of praise, a cycle born in supportive communion, works to dissolve the doubled dialogues of worship. By creating and riding the waves of worship, believers thus move conversations that begin as split and simultaneous toward the focused wholeness of intimate praise.

At first glance, this process might seem paradoxical. To achieve accord, saints must apparently disengage themselves from the communion of worship. To focus their praise, they must remove themselves from their praising peers. To truly "get into the service," they must affectively and intellectually get *out of* the service, in order to get *into* the intimacy of praise. Called both to personalize their focus and to come to accord, saints seem to be pulled in two different directions.

These dichotomies fail to acknowledge the complex and fluid relationship between praise and accord. They also limit saints' engagement to a single devotional realm, presuming an either/or relationship between personal and collective worship. Saints do say that the conversational focusing of praise brings thoughts to a kind of consonance. They also say that this internal accord yields a degree of disengagement. This disengagement, however, rarely obscures saints' awareness of what is happening around them. Though believers often speak of being "lost in praise," they freely admit that only in moments of rapture do they actually lose consciousness of their environment. These moments, in turn, tend to be fleeting (as was evidenced by the abrupt brevity of Sister Bracey's two shouts). They come and go, as one saint suggested, "like a sharp-edged sword, hitting you right and hitting you left, and then [they're] gone."[6] At all other times, praising saints only partially remove themselves from their surround. In essence, they focus on the internal while still attending to the external. Though struggling to minimize distractions, they nonetheless hear and join the ambient activity of worship, recognizing that this activity may well foster (rather than obstruct) their own focus.

Saints also recognize that at any moment their actions might help *someone else* to focus *their* praises. That call to "Go ahead!" might be just the encouragement another believer needs to take that additional step. Hence saints remain flexibly engaged with worship, moving inward at one moment and outward at another, always mindful that awareness of others may itself be an important act of stewardship.

Even when believers reach the point of greatest disengagement, when focus gives way to anointment, they continue to contribute to the communion of accord. Indeed, one might argue that their contribution climaxes at this moment, for now the Spirit joins the congregational conversation. Sending waves of knowing flowing through the pews, the Spirit silently informs saints that the anointing is at hand. Most saints say they need no behavioral proofs to know this moment. They don't need to hear a shout; they don't need to see some tears. Yet they nonetheless *know*, feeling that familiar feeling of certainty that comes from the Spirit. "Faith," say the saints, citing Hebrews 11:1, "is the evidence of things not seen." One needn't see, they continue, to know without a shadow of doubt. This knowledge, in turn, intensifies saints' praises, giving reason for thanks on behalf of others, and charting for self the path of potential. As the feeling flows through the church, it draws saints together in a fellowship of experience and expectation. Thus the momentary disengagement of anointed saints actually yields a *greater* engagement on the part of their congregational peers. Though believers feeling the touch are not the agents of this engagement (that role belonging to the Spirit), they nonetheless serve as its triggers. In the final analysis, their focused praises foster a public engagement far deeper than any that could be willfully achieved by their fuller

11. With a loud cry of "Thank You, Jesus!" Cedric Perry—Sister Lena Mae Perry's son—leaps to the floor, propelled by the Spirit's touch. As praises roll from his mouth, the Grace A.M.E. Male Chorus sings with renewed fervor. Then Cedric's maternal grandmother—seventy-seven-year-old Orlena Bennett—joins him in the cross-aisle, where her feet quickly move into a fast-stepping holy dance. Soon the two are arm in arm, both caught up in the Spirit. (Photo by Roland L. Freeman)

involvement in the service. Their disengagement, in other words, ultimately furthers rather than inhibits accord.

While exploring the apparent paradox, we should consider again the swiftness and flow of anointment. As noted earlier, the Spirit often comes and goes in the measure of an instant. "And, behold, I come quickly," the Lord declares, "and my reward is with me" (Revelation 22:12). Saints rarely dwell at length in the experiential removal of anointment. More commonly, they step into—and then out of—bliss. They focus their praise, feel the moment of rapture, and then give thanks, rejoining their peers in joyous worship. As one experiences the touch, another might be just beginning to focus, while a third might be giving praise for a moment passed. All are focusing their thoughts in different directions; all are experiencing different degrees of engagement. These degrees and directions, in turn, are themselves constantly in flux. Some saints might never feel the Spirit in the course of a service; others might feel it more than once. Some might never move beyond the shallow concerns of self-interest; others might wade again and again into the deep waters of praise. Most will move betwixt and between, engaging the words of a devotional leader at one moment, the unspoken intimacies of praise at another, the cries of a shouting saint at a third, the worldly worries of work at a fourth, and any combination of these layered one on another at yet a fifth. Accord emerges not when these engagements fall in lockstep unison, but when they come into loose harmony, giving rise to a worshipful spirit that far exceeds the sum of its parts.

Just as the *kinds* of engagement that contribute to accord differ, so also do their *manifestations*. As the Branchettes' anniversary makes clear, the saints prescribe no single path to achieving spiritual communion. Even during congregational performance, all are encouraged to forge their own way, crafting participation to their particular needs, abilities, and desires. In group singing, for example, some sing melody, some sing harmony, some moan. Some clap on every beat, some on every other beat, some only between beats. Some pat their feet, some clap their hands, some strike palms to sides. Some sing the standard words; others improvise freely. Some pause during the rests; others fill them with tuneful interpolations. Some enunciate every syllable; others bend and slur them. All chart their own path, contributing in the ways that they find most satisfactory and meaningful.

Not surprisingly, these paths themselves are full of twists and turns. Moving one way at one instant and a second way at another, they constantly shift to meet the mandates of the moment. Though their general direction may remain constant, their route is infinitely variable, with no single course mapping a way to the end. Hence a saint might sing melody at one point, sing harmony at another, and hum melody or harmony at a third, all in the course of a single song. This same saint might begin the song by patting her feet on every beat, then start clapping on the two and four, then start adding some sharp offbeat accents, and finally ease out of the clapping altogether to pat her sides. Like so many other aspects of the service, the governing dynamic is conversational. Saints listen (both internally and externally) and respond; they hear the other, feel the self, assess the needs, gauge the broad bounds of appropriateness, and then creatively contribute to the devotional flow. Sometimes their contributions are guided by the demands of artistry, sometimes by the appraisal of others' needs, sometimes by the counsel of the Spirit, and most times by these and host of other motives, all layered and shifting and simultaneous. The only constant is an overriding spirit of devotional freedom, a spirit grounded in the belief that each individual establishes a distinctly personal relationship with the Lord and that each path leading toward the fulfillment of this relationship is unique.

This spirit of intimately personalized performance complements the belief that all are equal in the eyes of God. Though some are specially "called" and others are recognizably "gifted," all will stand as peers before the gates of heaven. This canon of equality dissolves the distance between cross-aisle and pew, stealing from foregrounded performance much of the status that would otherwise set it apart. In so doing, it acknowledges that every contribution—no matter from whom it comes or what form it takes—potentially carries deep spiritual significance. The Lord could deliver a message from the pews as easily as from the pulpit; that message could ride on a single word as easily as on an entire sermon. Hence saints encourage every churchgoer to freely participate in worship, recognizing that no contribution is inherently less significant than any other and that all are important. Whether a waved hand or a testimony, a simple sway or a song, every act of worship contributes to the devotional whole, engaging every other worship act in the multilayered, multisensory conversations that ultimately lead to accord.[7]

*　*　*　*　*

Elder Lawrence Richardson and I were discussing sermons when he started talking about "dead folk." Not "dead folk" cold and laid under, but "dead folk" in the church. Folks who won't clap their hands; folks who won't say "Amen!"; folks who won't put "expression" in their singing. Folks who *act like* they're dead.

The topic came up when I asked Elder Richardson to plot the course of an anointed sermon, moving from his introduction in self to his climax in Spirit. He started by noting, "I'm never willing to get out there on my own." At first, I thought he was alluding to his prayerful preparation before mounting the pulpit. I soon discovered, however, that the Lord wasn't his only support. He explained that before every sermon, he first assessed the congregation, trying to determine how "live" they were. If they seemed "dead," he would open by trying to stir some spirit. "You see," he explained, "God don't want nothing dead. He wants you alive." Only if you're alive, he suggested, can the conversation begin.

"So I look over the congregation," Elder Richardson continued, "and see how the people are looking—see if somebody's there, but their mind is maybe someplace else."

"Well, I might say, 'Let me hear the church say, "Amen."' Everybody—or I would say, part [of the folks]—say, 'Amen.'" The quoted response was dull and expressionless.

"I say, 'What about the *whole* congregation?' I say, 'Let everybody say, *Amen!*' I put an *expression* with it. Then I get a response, '*Amen!*'" This time the word rang with spirit.

"I say, 'Well, you about to come alive.' And then maybe I'll use the words, 'Everybody here [that's] dead, raise your hand.'" Elder Richardson paused to chuckle, and then continued. "So one or two raise their hand."

"I say, 'Well, deacons, I think it's time for us to stop right here, and to go out with our pick and shovel, dig a grave and bury those two that raised their hand.'" The elder laughed again.

"So, then the church starts to opening up, to get some kind of in-feeling, [thinking,] 'I'm in church. So I got to be *part* of the church. And I can't be *dead* during this!' Sitting, you know, just waiting to accept the Word of God."

Waiting by itself won't bring on the Word. Waiting without seeking won't bring on the joy. Because this kind of waiting is passive. This kind of waiting is what dead folks do. And dead folks aren't even *thinking* about coming to accord.

Elder Richardson hardly paused as he continued his description of the sermon. He spoke about grounding his message in scripture, about leading a hymn to remind saints that God wants them to make noise joyfully, and then about moving the message through the geared stages of exposition, ever inviting the Spirit to shift the sermon into high gear. A full half hour later, Elder Richardson brought the conversation full circle and returned to the topic of those who just wouldn't join the conversation.

"God ain't coming into no dead heart," he declared, pausing to let his words sink in. He clearly intended this as a coda to his long and eloquent description. "It's got to be *live*. So I feel." Elder Richardson paused one last time. "If you're a child of God," he concluded, "get into it."[8]

* * * * *

God won't come into a dead heart. Nor will He come into a dead congregation. The congregation has got to be "live." And it has to show its aliveness, making it manifest through spirited activity. Just as individual saints must "put all they have" into worship, so too must the congregation as a whole. Hands must clap, feet must tap, bodies must sway, voices must cry out. Fueling this activity are the countless and simultaneous conversations of praise, conversations between saint and saint, between saint and Spirit, between saint and sinner, and between all combinations and variations thereof. Extending far beyond the boundaries of worded sound, these exchanges flow through channels of glance and gesture, tone and touch, voiced melody and sounded rhythm, unvoiced thought and the fluent phrasings of instruments. Some conversations consummate in an instant; others stretch throughout the service. Some involve only two parties; others embrace the entire congregation. When the church comes "alive," these conversations flow with artful simultaneity, engaging one another within and across channels to yield a 'spirited sense of spiritual interlock. Far from fostering confusion, the overlapping exchanges come together in balanced complementarity, eloquently testifying to a shared devotional purpose.[9]

Among the saints, the interlock that signifies "aliveness" becomes a stylistic measure of accord. Deemed an external sign of internal consonance, congruity of communication is said to reflect congruity of consciousness. "Only when hearts beat in unison," say the saints, "can hands clap in tune." Hands in tune suggest minds in tune. When pressed for elaboration, saints quickly point out that the referenced clapping stands for much more than the timely beating of hands. "Clapping hands," they say, really means hands, feet, hearts and minds. When everything comes together, when the myriad conversations yield a harmony that is heard and seen and, perhaps most importantly, *felt*, then accord is at hand. At that point, the Spirit joins the fellowship, giving further evidence of union and further reason for praise. The testimony of transcendent presence lets saints know not only that the Lord acknowledges their praises, but also that He has chosen to participate. In quick consequence, the spirit of accord becomes even deeper.

Chapter 13

The Emcee

"If You Have a Dry Emcee, You Have a Dry Anniversary"

Sister Lena Mae Perry's pause marks an important moment of transition. After whispering calming phrases as the wave of anointment ebbed, she shifts her eyes from heaven to the pews. Still standing behind the registration table, Sister Perry once again addresses the congregation, now speaking as one of the afternoon's honorees. "At this time," she begins in a voice full of friendly warmth, "we're going to introduce our emcee for the afternoon."

As she speaks, one of the singers who set up the microphones slides toward the front, picks up the mike resting on the choir loft rail, and whispers "Check, check" to test its sound. His hushed words boom through the sanctuary, leading him to quickly cut the volume on a nearby amp. As Sister Perry continues, he hands her the mike.

> Praise the Lord.
>> And some of you might know her.
>> And some of you may not.
> Praise God.
>> But she will present herself to you,   (Amen)
>> as she emcees this anniversary on this afternoon.

For the most part, the congregation remains quiet. Folks are waiting for the service's next step and aren't talking back. The guitarist, however, continues to fill the silences between Sister Perry's lines. Sister Perry herself, meanwhile, offers a kind of running response to her own words with her repeated pronouncements of "Praise God." The rolling phrase not only lends her remarks a clear rhythm, but also sets them firmly within a frame of praise.

> Praise God.
>> You know, anniversaries
>> has a lot to do with your emcees.   (Yes)
> Praise the Lord.

If you have a dry emcee,
I know from experience, you have a dry anniversary!

Quiet laughter ripples through the pews. For the saints, "dry" is like "dead," suggesting both a sense of lifelessness and a parched removal from the "living water" of the Word. A "dry" emcee is one withered by the winds of indifference; a "dry" service, in turn, never knows the anointing flow. These saints clearly don't want a "dry" anniversary. Almost as if hearing the quip as a caution, folks in the pews start talking back to Sister Perry.

Meanwhile, one of the guest quartet singers huddles near the guitarist, apparently conferring on the key of an upcoming song. While Sister Perry speaks into one mike, this singer sings into another, his voice low but clearly audible. The guitarist quickly catches his key and turns his improvisations toward the suggested melody. Sister Perry pays the two no mind and keeps on talking.

Praise God.	
You got to have somebody that's *full*	(Well!)
of the Holy Ghost.	(Amen!/That's right!)
Praise our God!	(Alright)
We thank God this evening for a person	
whom we know,	
whom we *love* so dearly.	(Yes we do)
We want you to give a great big round of applause	
to Evangelist Hattie Lofton!	(Alright!/Amen!)

Many in the congregation know Evangelist Lofton—some from previous anniversaries, some from other services that she's led—and they clearly welcome her presence. As hearty applause rings through the sanctuary, the guitarist ups his volume and plays an introductory flourish. Midway through this musical preface, as Evangelist Lofton stands from her place in the pew directly next to my recorder, the keyboards join the guitar and seize the melodic lead. I later discover that the keyboard player, who has remained silent for most of the talking thus far, is Evangelist Lofton's husband, Glenn. Both are members of a neighboring Disciples congregation, where Glenn serves as a deacon.

Taking the microphone offered her by Sister Perry, Evangelist Lofton eases around the table and steps to the center of the cross-aisle. A slim woman with a smooth, youthful face, an elegantly tailored blue suit, and piercing eyes, she seems to be bursting with energy. Her opening words confirm this initial impression. As soon as the clapping starts to slow, she calls out, "Praise the Lord, saints!" The congregation responds with a chorused "Praise the Lord!" While their response still hangs in the air, Evangelist Lofton calls out again, this time louder and with a sharply rising tone, "Praise the Lord!" More saints seem to respond this time, their voices ringing with enthusiasm as they answer, "Praise the Lord!" Again the evangelist jumps in, her words now pushing to yet a higher pitch. "Praise the Lord!" she cries. "Praise the Lord!" return the saints.

With each repetition, the congregation's words—like Evangelist Lofton's—grow louder and more fervent. Some saints have started clapping again; many are on their feet. Evangelist Lofton calls out a fourth time, her words again overlapping theirs, her voice now straining in its upper range. "Praise the Lord!" she shouts. The word "Lord" bursts out with a vibrato growl, further sparking the spirit of intensity. "Praise the Lord!" cry the saints. "Hallelujah!" calls Evangelist Lofton, her voice still at its strained peak. "Ye-e-es!" cries a sister in the amen corner. "He's worthy!" shouts Evangelist Lofton. "Yes!" choruses a host of saints.

The tone of Evangelist Lofton's last two words plunges from high to low, returning her to a pitch just slightly higher than that of her opening call. Up to this point, the overlapped, back-and-forth conversation had charted an unbroken, ascendant path, rising like a single sentence jointly constructed by the entire congregation. Evangelist Lofton's deliberate slide both slows the pace and sets the tone for the ongoing message. Her words, though not as strained as a moment before, still tumble forth with infectious enthusiasm. Now, however, they suggest the advent of a fuller, more developed message.

Praise God.	
We give honor to our most high God,	
for the Lord directing our path.	(Yes!)
Amen! It was not known to me,	
but I tell you what—	
the Lord has a way.	(Yes!)
That is mighty sweet.	(Yes!)
We're here to uplift the name of Jesus.	(Yes!)
Amen, and also to give honor	
to whom honor is due.	

Though Evangelist Lofton's words fall into a clear pattern of pauses, they're flowing so swiftly that few in the congregation can fit a word in edgewise. What *does* fill every rest are the fluent phrasings of the organ, which seem to echo the emcee's every sentiment. As Evangelist Lofton continues, her remarks subtly begin to pick up speed and intensity. The guitarist apparently senses this gradual shift, and kicks in with a series of descending runs, dramatically concluding each line. The evangelist's right hand, meanwhile, starts punctuating her words with sharp, forward-moving jabs.

It's nothing wrong with having an anniversary.	(Lord Jesus!)
Amen, but we did not come this afternoon	
for a program.	(Lord Jesus!)
Hallelujah, but we come for a *service!*	(Yes!/Alright!)
There's a difference in a program and in a service,	
cause in a program you go by a piece of paper!	(Uh-huh.)
But according to the anointing of the Lord,	
when you're in his presence,	
hallelujah, you let the *Holy Ghost* have His way!	(Yes!)

A chorus of shouted affirmations ring from the pews, while a number of saints—including both Sisters Perry and Elliott—begin clapping. Evangelist Lofton's voice has again edged toward fervent passion. As she shifts into a higher gear, I scribble in my field log the note "Starts off with spirited preaching!" Evangelist Lofton, meanwhile, presses right on.

Therefore you're in a *service*!	(Yes!)
Hallelujah, and not a program!	(Praise God!)
But we're here to uplift the name of Jesus!	(Yes!)
Glory to God, and we're going to have a good time!	

Evangelist Lofton's pitch peaks as she contrasts "service" and "program." So too does the vigor of her thrusting right hand. Her next line keeps its strong emphasis, but drops in tone. The fourth line follows precisely the same pattern, leaving listeners raptly involved but not quite as close to the edge of their seats. The organist echoes the descending tonal contour, while the guitarist drops his downward runs to a lower key. Congregational clapping, meanwhile, dwindles and finally dies. Though no less involved, the saints too are pausing, confident that the spirit will soon rise once again.

* * * * *

The "success" of devotions—a success measured by the degree to which the fires of holiness kindle—depends in large part on the skills, sincerity, and spirituality of the devotional leaders. These saints serve simultaneously as conductors, composers, and players in the orchestrated flow of soul and Spirit. Their words set the pitch; their pacing sets the tempo; their direction blends the parts in subtle harmony. At times, they call fellow believers to assume the lead role, inviting them to pray and sing and testify. At times, they take this role themselves, leading the assembly in voiced and unvoiced praise. At times, they simply add their voices to the polyphonic whole, surrendering to the simultaneity of private dialogue and public exaltation.

Leading at one moment and following at the next, devotional leaders claim sainthood as the only source of their authority. Their words and actions ever remind worshipers that the prerogatives of leadership shift with the moment and that all saints have an equal "right" to lead. Divisions of "you" and "I," as we have seen, perpetually press toward the unity of "we." Yet despite this spirit of oneness, devotional leaders must nonetheless assume a measure of authority. They are, after all, the managers of worship. If nothing else, they must guide the saints toward accord and thus toward the point where mortal guidance is no longer needed. Their jurisdiction ends when the Spirit's begins—and, I might add, when their time runs out. For when devotions end, so do their responsibilities. From this moment forward, they are but peers in the pews.

At the Branchettes' anniversary, Mothers Nixon and Lofton, Sisters Elliott, Perry, and Bracey, and Deacon Eldridge have all rejoined the congregation. When Sister Perry introduces Evangelist Lofton as the afternoon's master of ceremonies, devotions formally come to a close. From this point on, the responsibilities of leadership rest with the emcee, the singers, and the Spirit.[1]

Unlike their predecessors in the cross-aisle, emcees usually step to the church-front on the heels of a formal introduction. The very fact of introduction sets these speakers apart from their devotional counterparts, signaling a somewhat different status. At the Branchettes' anniversary, for example, Mother Lofton, Mother Nixon, and Deacon Eldridge received only the tersest of introductions, consisting of little more than a mention of their names. No one welcomed them to the cross-aisle; no one saluted their qualifications for leadership; no one called for a round of applause on their behalf. The passage from one to another flowed quickly and matter-of-factly, underlining their collective status as congregational equals. But not so with Evangelist Lofton. Not only does she receive an elaborate introduction, but she also earns the kind of stylized remarks that are usually reserved for visiting preachers. The fact that Evangelist Lofton happens to be a preacher has little bearing here. She could just as well be a deaconess, a radio announcer, a singer. What matters is that she is the emcee and that emcees bear gifts that set them apart, gifts worthy of special respect. That's why they're chosen for this role.

What are these special gifts? What qualifies someone to serve as a master of ceremonies? Sister Perry herself suggests the primary consideration when she notes, "If you have a dry emcee, you have a dry anniversary!" When she adds, "you got to have somebody that's full of the Holy Ghost," she flatly announces that the cardinal criterion is holiness. Put simply, sanctified hosts seek emcees who know the Spirit. Avoiding those who haven't "been to the water," who are artfully eloquent but spiritually "dry," they look for emcees who can be trusted to keep the proceedings on a high spiritual plane. As we have seen, the temptation to treat praise as "performance" and to let the trappings of "show business" obscure the workings of "God's business" is ever present in gospel. The master of ceremonies—the only constant in a steadily changing lineup of performers—is charged with keeping these temptations at bay. The emcee can succumb to the lures of showmanship or pursue the calls of stewardship; she can turn the program into a "show" or further it as a service. Returning to the cross-aisle after every singer's presentation, the emcee alone can set praises back on track after they've been derailed by "form and fashion" flashiness. By the same token, she alone can keep praises rolling during the lull between performances. Both acts call for devotional discernment and spiritual fortitude. Both demand an emcee who is truly "right with the Lord."

* * * * *

Unlike many of her commercial counterparts, Evangelist Dorothy Jackson doesn't just call for applause and fill the space between sets with stage patter when she emcees a gospel program. Instead, she *preaches*, refusing at every turn to hide her holiness under the proverbial bushel. Again and again between acts, she praises and testifies and admonishes, always giving God the glory, always reminding programgoers that the service is "church."

In my first visit with Evangelist Jackson, we began our conversation by talking about a recent program and about her spiritual calling. Almost two hours later, I asked her about the responsibilities of an emcee.

"What do you see as your job—as a saved emcee—when someone calls you to emcee a program?" I inquire. "What do you see as your duty?"

"As far as I see it, my duty is that . . ." Evangelist Jackson pauses for a second to catch the words, and then continues with a tone of certainty. "The Spirit is going to speak. And it's somebody there—you have people come to singings and funerals that *never* put their foot in a church. And this is why I say that singing is a very sacred thing, because it's a ministry. And during that emcee[ing], the Spirit is going to speak. Somewhere in there. It's going to come. And somebody's going to *hear*."

"So, God has a purpose for all of it. It falls right into place. You know. All He wants is the realness. That's all."

"So, if something is out of order, He'll let it be known. You know. And there's going to be somebody there to witness it; [and] somebody's going to be there to knock it. But that truth is going to outweigh it all. So . . ."

Again she pauses, searching for direction. I nod but say nothing. When she starts again, Evangelist Jackson has switched the frame from *her* understanding of an emcee's duties to that of many *programgoers*.

> And it's some that come to gospel singings
> *looking* for a "real" emcees,
> [for] spiritual field emcees.
> You'd be surprised at people saying,
> "Well, honey, who's going to emcee this?"
> "Well, Reverend So-and-so."
> "Oh yeah? Then I'll go."

Evangelist Jackson claps her hands after the "yeah," suggesting that the decision is made at that instant, based not only on the scheduled performers, but also on the choice of emcee. Nodding in mild surprise at this scenario, I comment, "That's interesting." "Yeah," she affirms. "I'm serious." Then she rejoins the imaginary conversation midstream, this time offering a different answer to the already-voiced question.

> And it has been [that way] down through the years.
> "What's-his-name."
> "Girl, I ain't going *nowhere* to hear him emcee nothing!
> I just seen him last night out there drunk."
> So, it goes that way with gospel singers;
> it goes that way with the emcees.

You know.
They weigh it out.
They weigh it out, you know.

When quoting the second speaker, Evangelist Jackson sours her tone and purses her face to convey the speaker's deep disgust. I've seen the exact same reaction—and heard the exact same reason given—when talking with saints about non-sanctified singers. So too has Evangelist Jackson, as her next lines indicate. Saints hold emcees, she suggests, to the same high standards that they hold singers. Both have to be "real."

So, I'm just there to emcee and give God the glory.
And so He just tell me,
  "Long as you keep it in *order*,
    I'll be there with you.
  But now you get out of order . . ."

Instead of finishing the sentence, Evangelist Jackson just laughs. The caution is clear enough. Getting out of order *oneself* or willfully letting *the service* get out of order means not only that the Lord will leave, but also that He will hold the disorderly servant responsible for the souls that might otherwise have been saved.

Evangelist Jackson had already suggested the magnitude of this responsibility when she noted that many who come to singings attend no other form of church. Song services, she explained, offer special opportunities for witness and ministry, opportunities realized in both the performers' singing and the emcee's speaking. To ignore these opportunities, and to welcome disorder, is to taint one's hands with the blood of the unsaved.

Evangelist Jackson could let this message slide with a laugh only because she had elaborated on it earlier in our conversation. She had told how the Lord once commanded her to go to the house of a friend who was "professing and proclaiming the Holy Ghost, but had it not." The Lord wanted Evangelist Jackson to witness to her and to tell the friend that she could indeed receive the Holy Ghost if she confessed and repented of her false claims. But Evangelist Jackson didn't obey. Instead, she went out of her way to *avoid* the decreed encounter. When she finally did go to her friend's house, she discovered that the Lord had already moved in her friend's heart, and that she now wanted to be saved.

"But now if that lady would have *died*," Evangelist Jackson explained, "and by me being disobedient, and she came up and missed from seeing God's face face-to-face, He would have took me out of line and put me in her place. Because He says, 'Now *you're* going to carry this blood. You're going to carry it on *you*. Because I *told* you what to do.' Now, you talking about fasting and praying and asking God to forgive me! But if he tells me to do something *now*, if it's a thousand *miles* from here—oh yes!—*I will go!*"[2]

Evangelist Jackson bears this same responsibility every time she witnesses, every time she preaches, every time she sings—and every time she emcees a program.

Such ministry is one of the basic duties of sainthood. To deny it is to invite God's wrath.

Evangelist Jackson conveys all this in a single, long laugh, letting what had already been said fill in the unspoken space. As the laugh winds down, I check to confirm my emergent understanding, saying, "So [in] emceeing, it sounds like your job is to—that you become not merely a *presenter*, at all, but [that] you become a devotional *leader*."

"Yeah," she answers, nodding her head.

"You become the one who keeps the program, a service," I continue.

"That's right," she agrees. "That's the difference." Smiling now, Evangelist Jackson repeats herself to underline the point.

> *That* is the difference.
> Because God does not have a "program."
> > God always has a service.
> > > It's never a "program" for God.
> And when you hear emcees getting up,
> > talking about "programs,"
> > > something is out of order.
> Because God don't need a "program."
> > *He's the program all by Himself.*
> > > So He don't need no "program."
> But what it is—
> > He joins us in the *service.*
> So, that's the difference.

Evangelist Jackson nods, smiles, and pauses once again. "And then as an emcee," I add, "you're able to keep it . . ." "As a *service*," she says, finishing the sentence for me. "Yes."[3]

* * * * *

Evangelist Jackson hints at the second qualification required of emcees when she speaks of keeping the service "in order." On one hand, this reference suggests the basic orderliness of worship, the same order addressed by Deacon Eldridge when he prayed that all things in the service "be done decent and in order." Interpreting order as "sequence," this suggests that saints should always place God first, giving all other considerations a lesser priority. Interpreting order as "condition," it suggests that services should flow with the Spirit's guidance and without the showy "disorder" of self-serving performance. Maintaining both types of "order" is a matter of spiritual competence and thus falls under the broad rubric of an emcee's first qualification. On the other hand, "order" refers to the more mundane matter of procedural sequence. The master of ceremonies' most obvious duty is to keep the service "moving," making sure the singers know the order of performance and then keeping them to the scheduled number of songs. In some services, the emcee's responsibility extends to include the actual sequencing of performers. (At the Branchettes' anniversary, as at most such events, the sequence was determined by the order in which the groups "signed in" at the registration table.) Even when the hosts determine the sequence, the emcee must nonetheless see to its enactment, a task that demands tact, firmness, organizational skill, and a spirit of flexibility.

Of these qualities, flexibility ranks as perhaps the most important. Even when programs follow the order of performer sign-up, emcees must always be ready to make changes. On a purely pragmatic level, this arises in part from singers' common practice of scheduling themselves for more than one program in a single day. Taking to heart the belief that they should present their gifts whenever the opportunity arises, many performers piggyback their appearances, leaving one program only to rush to another. Caught in a bind for time, such singers often ask for special scheduling consideration, thus forcing the emcee to do some creative juggling.[4]

A far more important reason for flexibility rests with the essential unpredictability of the Spirit. Saints often say that the Spirit doesn't follow human clocks. Rather than acting to serve the temporal needs of believers, the Lord serves needs that *transcend* time. And does so *according to His own schedule.* Hence Evangelist Lofton's distinction between a program and a service. The former, she says, follows "a piece of paper." The latter, in contrast, "lets the Holy Ghost have His way." The emcee must be ever open to this way and ever aware that the Spirit might take the service in directions that the hosts and emcee never predicted, much less planned for.[5]

✶ ✶ ✶ ✶ ✶

Sister Murphy faced a list of more than twenty registered ensembles when she stood to emcee the Gospel Express's fourteenth anniversary. Knowing that more singers were undoubtedly on their way, she asked the groups to limit their performances to two selections. She realized that even with two songs—particularly when considering the Spirit's hoped-for intercession—the afternoon service would stretch well into the night.

She was right. By the time the fifth group had completed its set, ninety minutes had already passed. And the special ceremony for the honorees was yet to come.

When she called for the fifth group's applause, Sister Murphy reminded singers about the song limit. Then she quickly added that such constraints meant nothing if the Spirit decreed differently.

"Singers," she began, "please give us two selections. Now if you want to give us your theme and one selection, fine. If you want to omit your theme and give us your two *best* selections, fine. And as I always say, if the Spirit of the Lord takes *over*, that's *always* appropriate! Amen?"

The pews rang with cries of "Amen!" and "Praise God!" as scores of saints clapped their approval. When Sister Murphy began again, she immediately differentiated between singing under the guidance of the Spirit and singing in self.

"But as long as we're *in ourself*, let us be governed, and let us be mindful of the next group in line."

Courtesy calls for attention to time. But *ministry* calls for an open-endedness that makes time meaningless. If the Spirit directs singers to sing beyond the two-song limit, then they should sing until the Spirit says "stop." Whatever the Spirit wills, as Sister Murphy reminds the saints, is "always appropriate."

Her point made, Sister Murphy thanked the singers and introduced the afternoon's sixth group. They marched to the front singing their "theme," a song declaring that Jesus answers prayer "not in man's time," but always "on time."[6]

* * * * *

This openness to transcendent direction marks all services among the saints. Generations of believers have spoken of the Lord as an "on-time God" who "follows the counsel of His own will."[7] In like manner, saints have long sung

He's a God you can't hurry,
He'll be there, don't you worry.
He may not come when you want Him,
But He's always right on time.

The referenced "on time" is clearly a time measured by celestial rather than worldly clocks. It's a time that follows only God's rules, a time that cannot be hurried, a time that resists being programmed. When emcees and singers declare that the event is a "service" and not a "program," they are acknowledging their submission to God's time. Hence if the Spirit wills a group to sing more than the allocated "a-and-b selection," the emcee gives them room. If the Spirit stretches a song from three to twenty-five minutes or inspires a singer to launch into a lengthy "sermonette" between songs, programgoers offer no complaints.[8] And if the Spirit chooses to flow with so much power that further performance becomes impossible (just as preaching became impossible in the service described in Chapter 9), saints still leave the sanctuary talking about what "good church" they had. Through it all, the emcee acts as provisional caretaker, facilitating flow when the service rests in human hands, and ceding control when the Spirit steps in.

The flexibility that this caretaking demands hinges in large part on the emcee's powers of spiritual discernment. The master of ceremonies must be sensitive enough to know when the Spirit is taking control, alert enough to know when control is being returned to mortal hands, and discriminating enough to know when apparent spiritual signs are products of pretense. Such discernment comes only with spiritual depth. Even maintaining order thus becomes an issue of devotional competence, returning us once again to the key criterion of spirituality.

Another aspect of maintaining order is insuring a smooth flow between performances, a flow that proceeds primarily on the power of words. This suggests a third qualification for emcees, that they be artful masters of language. Given the eloquence that seems to suffuse sanctified services, this would almost appear to be a given, a characteristic shared by all in the pulpit and cross-aisle, and by many in the pews.[9] None can deny that poetic talk and artistic tone are realms in which the saints have few equals. But while prowess in these spheres is widely shared, the special demands of emceeing call for an extra measure of ability. In addition to challenging the mind with fluent form and poetic argument, in addition to tickling the ears with rippling rhythm and contoured tone, the emcee must speak spontaneously, matching words to moment and style to spirit. Singers come and singers go; songs ring forth and Spirit flows; and the emcee must tie it all together, maintaining the flow of both substance and mood with artful words.

The immediate context for these words is song. Every lyric offers opportunities for deft restatement; every message furnishes fuel for creative elaboration. The skilled master of ceremonies searches for the core meanings of each group's presentation and then crafts these into a succinct devotional message, a message that both summarizes what listeners have just heard and prepares them for what is to come. Complicating this process is the constant question of when the next singers will be ready to sing. The emcee must hold the flow while performers move to the cross-aisle, set up their equipment, test microphones and cable connections, and often even tune their instruments. Not uncommonly, the emcee must also keep talking while group members round up fellow singers who are chatting outside the church or are still donning their uniforms. The possibilities for delay, just like the possibilities for songs from which the emcee must draw messages, are endless. The master of ceremonies must thus be eminently flexible, able both to craft words quickly and to extend them effectively to fill the available time.

Not all emcees are quick with words. Not all can keep the service flowing and "in order." And not all are filled with the Holy Ghost. Sanctified folk often trade stories about masters of ceremonies who lack one or more of these qualities. They tell of emcees who stumble through every transition, of talkers who fill breaks with jokes, announcements, and cheerleading-style encouragements instead of devotional commentary, of announcers who leave long, gaping pauses when faced with delays. Saints also talk about emcees who treat the role solely as an opportunity for personal display. Like many of their singing counterparts, these emcees are said to appear only for "form and fashion." Though they may step to the stage "looking sharp," they often bring little more than sartorial sharpness and a facility with words to their place before the congregation.

Not surprisingly, the most blatantly showy of these emcees tend to appear at large commercial programs, where audience percentages favor the unsaved. Many who attend these events expect the emcee to display all the trappings of secular entertainment, the most obvious of which is stylish dress. Audiences want their emcees, to use the words of one program host, "so clean you need a haircut just to shake their hand." Needless to say, many emcees are quick to oblige.

Raleigh gospel promoter James Thomas often tells a story about how he once numbered in this group. "Ten years ago," he recalls, "and down the road from that, if I'd go emcee a program, I'd have me five or six different suits. Depends upon how many groups were there, because I'd change with every group that came out to sing. I would change in a different uniform. And the people would just rave over it.... Whenever I'd walk out, they'd start to applauding just like they would for the group that was fixing to come out there to sing.

"So I started thinking about that. It wasn't *religion* that they was clapping for. It was just a show. And that's all I was doing at that time—a show. Because I was back there hurrying as quick as I could, and having somebody help me dress, to get ready to come back out on stage.

"And then ten years ago, I started just wearing one particular suit, and [would] get up there. And the religious people would still clap their hands. . . . But you could look through the audience and just tell it had slowed down from the last time that I had changed all them suits. I could tell a big difference there. That [first] day was just like they was in another program. And I said, 'No need of me doing all this. Because it's just a frolic, and I'm not into no frolic.' And I stopped it."[10]

It's important to note that although Thomas stopped *changing* suits in the programs he emceed, he nonetheless always steps onstage dressed at the very height of style. I don't want to suggest that the saints in any way *reject* stylish attire. Indeed, if one is to judge from the emphasis that singers place on introducing elegant new "uniforms" at each year's anniversary, one might well argue just the opposite.[11] Style clearly plays an important role in the sanctified community. Saints *expect* singers and emcees to dress tastefully and strikingly. And they most certainly talk about them when they don't.[12] But saints demand *substance* with their style. They treat style of dress, like style of performance, as a kind of performative overlay, a means of conveying self while imparting the deeper messages of faith. As such, style becomes a way of personalizing one's witness. While the fact of witness remains paramount, the style of dress grounds it more firmly in the personality of the witnessing saint.

With the grounding of faith assured, saints can openly celebrate the joys of fine attire, cloaking their choirs in dramatic robes, counting on quartet members to sing in stylish suits, expecting emcees to cut striking figures at the church-front. Combinations of color and cut free individuals (and ensembles) to proclaim their individuality within the shared frame of community, much as do the infinite performative options of words, tone, and motion. At the same time, clothes send messages beyond the community of saints, where they catch the eyes of spiritual outsiders, perhaps hooking just enough attention to open the ears, and then potentially drawing these listeners closer to the Word. Hence while style testifies to *selfhood* inside the fellowship of saints, it testifies to *faith* outside that fellowship, opening yet another channel for personal witness.[13]

With these various qualifications for emceeing now set forth, we are left with the question of candidacy. Whom do saints traditionally choose to fill this role? Whom do they deem qualified? Among the most frequent candidates are evangelists, ministers who are called to preach but not to pastor. Evangelists easily meet all of the emcee qualifications: as individuals called by God, they bring to the program deep spiritual insight; as evangelists, they bring skill in "managing" the worship of diverse congregations; as preachers, they bring the gift of eloquence. Further, they are usually more available than pastors, whose busy schedule of worship, home and hospital visits, and business meetings often keeps them from attending gospel programs. Many program hosts say that evangelists are always their preferred choice for the emcee role.

Pastors also sometimes officiate at gospel programs. They bring to the event all the advantages of evangelists, plus the added benefit of a congregational following. Emceeing preachers frequently have reputations as singers in their own right, with many of them boasting gospel backgrounds that far predate their calls to preach. This special combination of expertise and authority tends to keep their services in constant demand.

A host of other saints also fill the emcee role. Program hosts often hand the directorial reins to deacons, mothers, or other church officers. This is particularly common at church-sponsored events; the emcee for the first night of the Branchettes' anniversary, for example, was a deacon from a nearby congregation. Given the sense of spiritual parity that such a selection implies, the criteria for emcee election shift to place extra emphasis on eloquence and managerial skill. In essence, those saints deemed better talkers and better managers are chosen to conduct the program's second half.

This same reasoning often lands gospel singers in emcee roles. Singers, like church officers, are not set apart from the congregation by any spiritual authority. Saints certainly do not equate their gift with any special anointing. Yet the gift does often grant them eloquence, and their experience gives them practical knowledge in running a program. Furthermore, their position as performers commands a measure of respect from the nonperforming public, lending singers a kind of tacit authority to oversee other people's singing. This same position also garners respect from fellow singers, presumably making program management somewhat easier. One final factor in singers' favor is their public visibility. Believers from a variety of churches have heard them perform; their community visibility is often as high as— and sometimes higher than—that of local preachers. This broad-based familiarity, when coupled with a sanctified status and these other qualifying factors, often eases singers right into the cross-aisle.

As should by now be obvious to anyone who regularly attends commercial gospel programs, I've saved until last the group of emcees that have the highest profile in the African American church community—the gospel radio announcers. These masters of the airwaves probably officiate more professional programs than all the other camps combined.[14] Though many radio announcers also serve as evangelists, deaconesses, or deacons, it is their role as "announcers" that earns them invitations to the stage.

Why are gospel announcers accorded this special privilege? The answer lies in the special relationship between gospel radio and the saints and in the announcer's unique role in this relationship. Most churchgoers hear gospel through two main channels: live performance and radio. Though records, tapes, and CDs claim a significant share of listening time, most saints put them a distant third on the list. This suggests that most of the gospel singing that believers hear outside of the church comes over the airwaves. The person presenting this music—the one playing the favorite songs, dedicating the selections to "the sick and shut-in," and murmuring the spoken "Amens" over the recorded tracks—is the radio announcer.

Gospel announcers thus emerge as important musical intermediaries, both as devotional facilitators who bring recorded praises to listening saints and as commercial go-betweens who link the worlds of professional gospel and everyday worship. Radio listeners come to identify with their friendly chatter, their devotional asides, and their words of prayer and encouragement. Listeners also come to respect their musical expertise and are undeniably impressed by their easy familiarity with gospel's top-name artists. Saints particularly appreciate the fact that gospel announcers carry the sounds of praise far beyond the walls of the church. Even if the announcers themselves are not saved, saints say that they are nonetheless doing the Lord's work. Finally, for those announcers who *are* saved, believers respect their ability to work worldly jobs while still freely witnessing to their faith. All of these factors—factors that tie radio announcers to both sanctified and unsanctified listeners, to the market, and to the singers whose voices ring out over the radio—give gospel announcers special stature in the community.

A host of additional factors help to parlay this special status into invitations to emcee. The most obvious is the radio announcer's mastery of words. In a community where artful talk is highly valued and where radio positions are few and far between, the very fact of employment as a gospel announcer testifies to an individual's verbal skills. The premium placed on creative expression is evident in the title of the position itself; gospel announcers refer to themselves not as "disc jockeys," but as "announcers," as if to say that spinning records is the least of their duties. As acknowledged word-masters, radio announcers build their reputations on their ability to speak fluently, poetically, and spontaneously. While this gift can in many ways be likened to that of the preacher, it differs in one essential respect: the gospel announcer is practiced at extemporaneously filling in stretches of silence, a skill demanded more in programming radio than in conducting services. This adroitness at fill-in commentary proves particularly helpful when negotiating the flux and flow of gospel programs.[15]

The radio announcer further brings to the stage a tested ability to manage time, a skill that many saints say is often sorely lacking in preachers. Radio work demands a constant awareness of airplay times, verbal pacing, and audience attention span. This same sensitivity, translated to the gospel stage, facilitates easy transitions and a smooth flow.

The final—and most pragmatic—factor favoring gospel announcers' selection is simply that they can promote a program more effectively than anyone else. Such promotion is particularly important for commercial programs, where sponsors are contractually bound to insure artists' payment—whether or not that money is earned at the door. Since radio is gospel's primary advertising outlet, promoters will often hire announcers in hopes of getting some free promotion, both through on-air plugs and through increased airplay of scheduled artists' songs. For many promoters, this possibility alone justifies hiring gospel announcers as emcees.[16]

＊　＊　＊　＊　＊

"Glory to God, and we're going to have a good time!" Evangelist Hattie Lofton's words continue to stream forth in a rush of poetic eloquence. Though her pitch has dropped somewhat, it still remains high, clearly straining her voice. Yet she doesn't pause for a second. Instead, she fixes her gaze on the congregation and challenges them with a rapid-fire question. "But guess what?" Sister Perry barely has time to utter a confirming "Uh-huh" when Evangelist Lofton launches into the answer.

You are here!	(Yes!)
And *they* are here.	(Yes!)
And when you get up there singing,	
we're going to sing!	(Yes!)
And when you go up there singing,	
we're going to sing!	(Yes!)
Hallelujah,	
it's no "*your* group" and "*my* group"!	(Alright now!)
'Cause we're *all* here	(All here!)
to give the name of Jesus the highest praise!	(Yes! Yes!)

Evangelist Lofton quickly breaks down the groupings of "you" and "they" with which she begins this section, transforming them immediately into "you" and "we." For her first, "When you get up there singing," she motions to the pews on her left; for her second, she motions to her right. She closes both with a broad sweep of her hand, suggesting a "we" of everybody else. For a brief moment, everyone is both "you" and "we." Then, just as Sister Bracey had done before her, Evangelist Lofton collapses the distinction, triumphantly declaring the unity of praise.

When Evangelist Lofton denies the difference between "your group" and "my group," the young sister with the tambourine starts its sizzle. At the next line's affirmation of oneness, scattered handclaps sound throughout the pews. The guitar and organ, meanwhile, are accenting the close of every couplet with a dramatic, descending phrase. Paying no heed to the clapping, Evangelist Lofton pushes on.

And if you come with that attitude,	
you're going to have a good time.	(Yes!)
But if you're holding back	
and waiting for *your* group to go up,	(Jesus!)

and holding back on somebody else,
  then you going to be disappointed!   (Yes!)
For I want you to know,
  the *anointing* breaks the yoke!   (Yes!)
Hallelujah!

"Yes!" cry the saints. Evangelist Lofton's pitch is rising again, moving to the upper ranges of her register. She shouts the next lines with strained intensity.

And if you need *healing*,   (Yes!)
  it may be in somebody else's song!   (Yes!)
If you need *deliverance*,
  it may be in somebody else's song!   (Yes!)
But I want you to know,
  whatever you want from the Lord,
    it's here this afternoon.   (Yes!)
Give Jesus the highest praise,
  and that's "Hallelujah!"   (Hallelujah!)
Hallelujah!   (Hallelujah!)
Hallelujah!   (Hallelujah!)
Oh glory!   (Glory to God!)
Glory!   (Amen!)

Evangelist Lofton's tone peaks with the close of the second couplet. The next three lines tumble downward, finding calm resolution in the reassuring words "whatever you want, it's here this afternoon." The organ follows the descent phrase by phrase, swooping downward in a single extended run, as if following a well-worn path.

The moment of resolution passes quickly, as Evangelist Lofton leaps into a rising litany of "Hallelujah!" Just as she had opened with a fourfold call to "Praise the Lord!" so now she summons the saints to "give Jesus the highest praise." This time, however, the saints are with her from the very beginning. By the first syllable of her first "Hallelujah," a tambourine is already shaking. By the end of the word, scores of saints are clapping and crying "Hallelujah!" themselves. Each of the three times Evangelist Lofton shouts "Hallelujah!" her voice jumps a step higher. By the third "Hallelujah!" the entire church is on fire, with dozens of saints on their feet, everyone clapping, and shouted cries mingling one with another in a fervent outpouring of praise.

As the praises continue, Evangelist Lofton drops her voice and murmurs, "Oh glory!" With the mike away from her mouth, the words are but a whisper. The programgoers recognize the cue and begin to quiet their praises. Again Evangelist Lofton says, "Glory," this time with the mike raised. Her tone is calm, her voice sounding winded.

For the first time in the service, I notice several saints fanning themselves with the church's paper fans. Provided by a local insurance agent or by one of two nearby funeral homes, most of the fans picture a scene from the Last Supper. Many are ripped where the thin stick attaches to the paper; all are deeply creased across the middle, a sure sign of heavy use. As folks fan themselves, the fans' upper halves flap rather limply, providing a kind of visual counterpoint to the moving arms. The fans waving the most vigorously are all wielded by youngsters. I later discover that most of the fans bear a penciled message on their backs, noting simply, "Please don't give to the children."

As the clapping winds down, Evangelist Lofton comes back with a triplet that builds on the statement of purpose she voiced before the round of "Hallelujahs." Quickly reestablishing the strained peak with which she began her last crescendos, she holds her tone steady.

We're here to break the yokes, aha!	(Yes!)
We're here to break tradition!	(Yes!)
We're here to cast aside "ism" and "schism"!	(Yeah Lord!)
Hallelujah, in the name of Jesus!	(It is!)
For this service is anointed unto Him.	(Yes!)
There's an old hymn say, "Consecrate me now Lord.	(Yes!)
To your *service*, Lord!"	(Yes!)
That's what we need to ask the Lord to do right now!	(Glory!)
"Search *my* heart, Lord!	(Uh-huh!)
If You find anything that isn't right, aha!	(Yes!)
If You find something that will bind this service,	(Yes!)
Change it right now, Lord!	(Right now, Lord!)
Before I go up there in that choir stand	(Lord Jesus!)
and sing a song,	(Yes!)
change me right now, Lord!	(Right now, Lord!)
If I got a problem with somebody,	
change me right now, Lord!"	(Right now, Lord!)
See, it's time out for playing church, you all!	(Yes!)
It's time out for us to look—	
for us looking so pretty	
just to sing a song!	(Ye-e-e-es!)
But we got to *live the life we sing about*!	(Ye-e-e-es!)
In our song!	(That's right!)
Hallelujah! Whoo!	(Yes!/Glory!)
Glory to God!	(Glory! Glory!)
[I'm] feeling right churchly now!	(Yeah!)
Feeling right *holy*!	(Yeah!)
Glory to God!	(Hallelujah!)

The steady tone of Evangelist Lofton's voice belies the buildup evident in her layered sets of parallels. Her opening triplet ("We're here to . . .") celebrates the "we" of shared purpose. Her next—built around the thrice-repeated "Change me right now, Lord!"—reframes her words as prayer. Then suddenly the implied "we" of entreaty becomes the plural "you" of exhortation, as Evangelist Lofton chastises those who would "play church" and scolds those overly concerned with "looking pretty" (a clear reference to the singers' stylish outfits). Throughout this set of parallel remarks, her tone is edging higher and higher, finally climaxing as she once again dissolves the "me/you" division into the unity of "we."[17] "We got to live the life we sing about!" she cries, her voice returning to its strained peak. "In our song!" she adds, now shouting over the tambourine and the cries of the congregation. With her cry of "Hallelujah!" Evangelist Lofton is right back at the very top of her register. Then, with a short, sharp burst of breath, she cries a soprano "Whoo!"

(At this point, I remember wondering, "Where did she get that extra breath?" The "Hallelujah!" had been long, loud, and hard. And yet the "Whoo!"—which was every bit as forceful—followed it without a pause. As I started to note this moment in my log, I chided myself for getting caught up in the mechanics of talk. Most saints would "read" that "Whoo!" as a sign of the Spirit, as a fleeting acknowledgment of experience. At such moments, the normal rules of vocal "mechanics" simply don't apply.)

From the very beginning of this section, saints have been punctuating Evangelist Lofton's words with short bursts of handclapping. One or another tambourine has added further accenting, connecting word to word and line to line with a sustaining hiss. The organ and guitar, meanwhile, are enunciating every shift of tone and emphasis, prefacing some lines with suspenseful arpeggios and concluding others with dramatic flourishes. At Evangelist Lofton's shouted "Hallelujah!" the scattered handclaps come together in a solid and sustained burst of sound. The claps continue right through the evangelist's two-line testimony and begin to waver only when she utters her pitch-dropping "Glory to God!" With eyes closed, Evangelist Lofton gives her head a single sharp shake, as if still feeling the lingering effects of the touch. Then she pauses and lets the guitar finish out the line, signaling a momentary shift of topic, tone, and pace.

* * * * *

As Evangelist Lofton moves the service toward the singing, she articulates two central themes. The first addresses the importance of accord. Again and again, she stresses the need for shared purpose and unified worship. "It's no 'your group' and 'my group,'" she reminds the saints. "Because we're all here to give the name of Jesus the highest praise." One by one, she details the divisions that might sunder the congregation—between group and group, between individual and group, between individual and individual—only to dissolve them in the oneness of a praising "we." The second theme concerns the power of the Spirit—acting through song—to enlighten and save. Evangelist Lofton clearly sees singing as more than just a one-way giving of praise. For her, singing is a ministry, a sacred channel through which people can be touched and souls can be saved. "If you need healing," she declares, "it may be in someone's song." "If you need deliverance," she adds, "that too may be in a song." "*Whatever* you want from the Lord," she concludes, "it's here this afternoon." When she later declares, "We're here to break the yokes!" after having already attributed such breaking to "the anointing," she makes clear the agent of the promised deliverance. Evangelist Lofton is saying, in essence, that the Lord will act through singers (and, implicitly, through the emcee) to touch and to save souls.

Speaking in another context, Evangelist Dorothy Jackson made precisely the same point. In the conversation cited earlier in this chapter, Evangelist Jackson spoke of singing as a special ministry. "Sometimes people can get touched by a song, where a preacher can preach all day long and do nothing," she explained. "And a song—maybe a line or a phrase in that song—can actually touch the heart of man. . . . Many souls have been saved through singing."[18]

Gospel programs often openly acknowledge this potential by including a formal altar call in their schedule. In the eyes of many saints, this call is another of the features that transforms a "program" into a "service." Later in the Branchettes' anniversary, for example, when Evangelist Lofton extends an invitation to all those "standing outside the arc of safety," she notes that "no service should be without an invitation being extended, for therefore your blood won't be required to our hands." Many singers wholeheartedly agree with this sentiment; some even regularly include an altar call in their performances. Such is the case, for example, with the nationally renowned Sensational Nightingales, who *never* perform without extending an invitation. "We should be having revivals, [and] not entertaining," says Jojo Wallace, the Nightingales' tenor singer and one of the principal architects of their "Word Through Song" ministry. "Every time we get through with our singing, we should come together and have an altar call."[19]

While some singers and emcees always extend an invitation, many others leave it as an open option, recognizing that if the Spirit so wills, an altar call can always be added to the program. This seems to be the spirit of Sister Perry's welcoming remarks when she asserted, "If there is somebody here, and they want to turn their lives over to Jesus, we can have a station break! . . . We can always change it from anniversary to a revival!" Sister Perry's words suggest that the altar call is a tacit part of the service, a structure always present in mind even if not always invoked. The fact that the first night of the Branchettes' anniversary did *not* include an invitation tends to support this interpretation. So too do the many gospel songs that explicitly invite sinners to accept Christ as their savior. Later in the Branchettes' anniversary, for example, the Davis Singers of Lillington, North Carolina, sing a driving rendition of "The Doors of the Church Are Open":

The doors of the church is open,
　Come on in.
The doors of the church is open,
　Come on in.
The preacher's got outstretched hands,
　Saying, "Join us while you can."
You got a standing invitation,
　Come on in!

Hundreds—perhaps thousands—of gospel songs convey this same invitational message. Though most congregations still sing traditional hymns during formal altar calls (where slow pieces like "Just As I Am" or "I Surrender All" remain favorites), these other invitationals live a life of their own in gospel services, where they often stand in lieu of formal, spoken invitations. If, however, their message strikes someone's heart, they may well lead to a traditional altar call. Saints say that in such cases, the Spirit will mystically inform someone else in the service that a candidate is ready to receive Christ, and an invitation will usually result. The same thing happens if the Spirit takes the initiative and notifies some saint—a singer, an emcee, perhaps a visiting preacher—that a particular soul needs saving or a back-slider needs to be called back into the church and that the time is right. I've spoken with many preachers and singers who have heard such a message and who subsequently steered the service toward just the kind of "station break" that Sister Perry invited in her welcome. As Evangelist Lofton reminded the saints at Long Branch, a service doesn't follow "a piece of paper," but instead follows "the anointing of the Lord." For the saints to most effectively serve and for the singing to truly become a service, believers must be always attuned to the Spirit's Word and ever open to shifting the service "from an anniversary to a revival."

Not surprisingly, few *professional* programs allow this degree of flexibility. When asked about this matter, promoters often claim that there's simply not enough time to "take time out" for an altar call. Hidden behind their words is an admission that many of their paying programgoers might feel uncomfortable with such a sequence. Though sung invitations are acceptable and expected, many sponsors fear that their entertainment-minded audiences might find an altar call too much like "church."

Nonetheless, singers in professional programs sometimes *do* extend impromptu invitations. As often as not, however, these "invitations" are little more than formal exercises in fueling audience involvement. What begin as announced altar calls often end with singers calling people forward to "Come shake my hand!"—as if a handshake alone confers some special spiritual power. Rarely do such "altar calls" include any devotional follow-through; rarely do they invite preachers to counsel and pray for those who step forward. For most saints, such observances are little more than hollow rituals, ceremonies whose only function is allowing singers to publicly proclaim their holiness. Like feigned shouts, they offer lots of form but little depth.

Another aspect of Evangelist Lofton's words that merits comment is her skillful incorporation of song lyrics into her remarks. Such lyric references punctuate virtually all talk among the saints, ever blurring the boundary between song and prose. But such citations rarely occur with the frequency that they achieve in gospel programs, where they pepper the remarks of devotional leaders, singers, and emcees.[20] Of all these speakers, the emcee emerges as the most artful, for the emcee must transform the lyric messages of each singer into the fluent commentary that links set to set. Whereas singers can tailor their between-song remarks to a known repertoire, emcees must craft theirs to whatever songs singers choose to sing.

Just as emcees fill the spaces between sets with lyric citations, so also do they often season their opening remarks with references to song. Evangelist Lofton, for example, deftly uses two lines from "an old hymn" to introduce her remarks about personal responsibility. Two lines later, she quotes another line, "Search my heart, Lord," that frequently appears in song. Then, as she brings the section to its tonal and textual climax, she closes by paraphrasing the familiar Thomas A. Dorsey piece, "I'm Going to Live the Life I Sing About in My Song." Of the eighteen lines that make up this thematic unit, fully one-third allude to song. Each of these does so in a way that calls to mind all of the referenced song's associated lyrics, thus lending each citation a connotative depth barely suggested by its brevity. Simple mention of the Dorsey piece, for example, invokes the entire debate about singers who "sing holy" but lead worldly lives.[21] In the context of this service, the reference also calls to mind both the gentle cautions of Deacon Eldridge and the tacit admonitions of Sister Perry. The practice of lyric citation thus serves as a form of artful shorthand, giving speakers an effective tool for saying more by saying less.

*   *   *   *   *

As the guitar completes its run, Evangelist Lofton begins anew, her voice now a bit calmer and more conversational. Up to this point, she has been praising, exhorting, and testifying. Now, however, it's time to address procedure. Many singers still don't know where they're to appear on the program; some might also not know how many songs they're expected to sing. As the clapping winds down, Evangelist Lofton answers these unvoiced questions.

And we got several groups,	(Glory to God!)
and they're asking that you sing	
a theme song and two.	(Praise God.)
And I tell you, we're going to keep it going—	
I'll call one group, and I'll tell the next group,	
and so,	
you all won't have to be sitting there wondering	
who's next and everything.	
We're going to keep the anointing flowing.	(Yeah!/Amen!)
Glory to God!	

Though her words are still tumbling out, the announcements lose the rhythmic regularity that has marked Evangelist Lofton's remarks thus far. As her tone evens out and her comments take on a more mundane character, congregational response slackens. The talking back dwindles; the clapping stops; the organ silences. Even the ever-present guitar mutes its contribution.

But the lull lasts only a moment. With hardly a pause, Evangelist Lofton once again presses her words toward preaching.

And I'll tell you what—
    When the sister came up here to give the response,
        I like that spirit!   (Yes!)
I believe in being *noisy* for the Lord!   (Yes!/Yes! Yes!)
Glory to God!
And I don't have to go into too much of my past
    but let me tell you—
        I was *loud*!   (Uh-huh.)
And I'll tell you what—
    I don't mind being loud for the Lord!   (Jesus!/Alright!)
Hallelujah!
'Cause when I get to thinking about the goodness
    of Jesus—   (Yes!)
Hallelujah!   (Glory!/Yes!)
    And *all* He's done for me!   (Yes!/My Lord!)
Huh?   (Yes!/Praise God!)
Glory to God!

Again Evangelist Lofton builds toward tonal climax, gradually rising from a conversational foundation to the heights of strained intensity. As she speaks of being "noisy for the Lord," her voice grows louder and more emphatic. It continues to rise as she talks of being "loud," her words now clearly referencing the psalmist's call to "make a joyful noise unto the Lord, all the earth: make a loud noise, and rejoice, and sing praise" (Psalm 98:4). As if following the psalm singer's counsel, she immediately quotes a song of praise (the very same song, by the way, whose citation in another context led Evangelist Rachel Green to feel the holy touch—see Chapter 9). Evangelist Lofton's voice rises sharply as she paraphrases the song's first line and finally explodes in a shouted "Hallelujah!" Joining the praise, the saints chorus and clap their enthusiastic affirmation.

The same fervor that fueled Evangelist Lofton's "Hallelujah!" stretches through her next line, also drawn from the song. There's clearly no need to cite the lyric's third line—"My soul cries out 'Hallelujah!'"—for Evangelist Lofton has already experienced its spontaneous enactment. Instead, as the congregation cries its praises, she fixes her gaze on the pews and utters a drawn-out "Huh?," clearly inviting their further response. As a host of saints answer, she drops her tone with a quickly uttered "Glory to God!" Then, after a fleeting pause, she jumps right back with a heightened tone.

Done brought us through the storm!   (Uh-huh.)
Done brought us through the rain!   (Jesus!)
Sitting up here with a roof over our heads!   (Yes!)
Glory to God, we got a lot to be thankful for. (Sure do!)

Evangelist Lofton's voice stays steady but strained through the emphatic opening triplet. Her entire body seems to testify to the depth of her involvement. When her words are calm, she shifts her weight from foot to foot, gently rocking her body from side to side. But when the passion rises, her feet move forward, pushing her toward the congregation, down the center aisle. At these moments, the muscles in her face and arms are as taut as her voice. But they loosen as her words relax, visibly shedding the tension and replacing it with a serene calmness. For example, when Evangelist Lofton cried "Hallelujah!" both of her hands leapt into the air and her head shot backward, pushing her eyes toward heaven. Her hands stayed above her head for the next two lines, though her face turned toward the saints as she shouted her thanks and challenged them to do the same. Then, with her tone-dropping "Glory to God!" her hands fell to her side and her face burst into a radiant smile, her teeth flashing in a gleam of pure joy. This same smile returns as Evangelist Lofton closes with yet another "Glory to God," drawing her words back to a relaxed, conversational mode. Now her voice is calm and unhurried, as she returns to procedural announcements.

We got plenty of musicians.	(Glory!)
God bless.	(Yes!)
We got plenty of musicians that can play	
all kinds of music.	(Yes!/Lord!)
So if you don't have a musician,	
don't worry about that.	(Glory!/Yes!)
We got plenty of microphones.	(Amen!)
If your voice is too hoarse because of cold,	(Alright!)
don't worry about that.	(Jesus!/Alright!)
But it's up to you, now, to bring the anointing!	(Yeah!/Yes!)
For the anointing to flow, now!	(Uh-huh/Jesus!)
Glory to God!	(Praise God!/Amen!)
Amen!	(Thank you Jesus!)

With even tones, Evangelist Lofton returns to her earlier-stated theme of worshipful unity, reminding saints that all will be helping each other and that no one will sit in a seat of judgment. Those worries, she implies, are too insignificant, too petty, to divert attention from the service's *real* purpose, which is "to uplift Jesus' name" and to invite the anointing's flow.

Following her "Amen!" Evangelist Lofton pauses for the longest interval thus far in her remarks. Saints fill the silence with calls of "Thank You, Jesus!" "Amen!" and "Praise God!" After glancing toward Sisters Perry and Elliott, Evangelist Lofton asks the congregation in a relaxed tone, "Do we have any other groups that have not registered?" When no one but the guitar answers, she continues, "All right, we got St. James Gospel Choir, all the way from Benson—number one. Then we're going to have the Bracey singers—number two. Benson Chapel Choir, Father and Sons, Davis Singers, Gospel Tones, Smith Chapel, South Johnston High School. That's eight groups. Got any more? Come on up and tell me!"

A number of saints laugh at the playfully melismatic stretch that Evangelist Lofton puts into her invitation. As they chuckle, the evangelist adds a section-

12. "We got plenty of musicians that can play all kinds of music," proclaims Evangelist Lofton. "So if you don't have a musician, don't worry about that!" William Coley, lead singer and guitarist with the William Coley Trio, bears out the emcee's words as he plays guitar for the Ebenezer Gospel Choir. Members of the Grace A.M.E. Mass Choir sit in the deacon's corner, awaiting their turn to sing. (Photo by Roland L. Freeman)

marking "Glory to God!" and "Amen!"—again stretching out her words. Sister Perry responds with a quick "Praise God!" Then, with a smile, Evangelist Lofton poses a second joking question, again eliciting laughter in the pews.

Anybody got to change places with anybody?
    Come on up here and tell me!
    Glory to God.
    All right then.
    Now we're going to start our service—
        no, we're going to *continue* our service,
            cause the service has already started!   (Yeah!/Amen!)
    Huh?!   (That's right!)
    Glory to God!   (Praise God!)
    We're going to have St. James Gospel Choir,
        come all the way from Benson—
        came through that snow!   (Alright!)
    Hallelujah! From Benson!

The saints clap to welcome the choir and laugh a bit at the emcee's emphasis on the snow, particularly given the bright sun shining through the church's amber windows. The entire tone of the service has changed, with folks suddenly looser, more willing to laugh, more inclined to exchange smiles among themselves. It would be wrong to suggest that focus has in any way faded, for the fires of deep praise can be rekindled at the snap of a finger. Instead, I would suggest that focus— and more particularly, the special focus of accord—brings with it a freedom to experience a full spectrum of moods, without worry that they will somehow distract from the praise or diminish the intensity. While the press toward accord admittedly demands a letting-go of worldly concerns, it does so only to usher the saints into a realm whose experiential and emotional fullness is in no way attenuated from that of everyday encounter. The Lord, say the saints, doesn't *take away* from the self. Instead, He *adds to*, broadening horizons while expanding the potential for self-expression. Services among the saints are marked neither by the stolid sobriety that characterizes many of their nonsanctified counterparts nor by the single-minded "frenzy" that stereotype attributes to them. Instead, they celebrate a full and ever-shifting range of spirit and mood, balancing solemnity with laughter, sobriety with joy, deep reflection with shouted praise. At one moment, the saints are listening pensively. At another, they're crying enthusiastic praises. At yet another, they're simply crying. And at a fourth, they're laughing. The spirit of accord is a spirit of openness and potentiality, a spirit that frees individuals from worrying about what others might think, and thus frees them to be more fully themselves. Instead of stifling self-expression, accord liberates it. Instead of restricting options, it increases them. In essence, accord's move toward oneness ultimately enables individuality to blossom.

Evangelist Lofton's demeanor is relaxed, her voice warm and welcoming, as she calls for the St. James Gospel Choir. "And after them we're going to have the Bracey

Singers," she says, drawing a quick "Praise the Lord!" from the pews. "All right!" adds Evangelist Lofton, now beginning to clap her own hands. "So let's give St. James Gospel Choir a hand!"

The clapping intensifies, a tambourine starts to rattle, and Evangelist Lofton cries "Ye-e-es! That's our choir! Come on, St. James!" Five women, all looking to be in their twenties and thirties and all dressed in flowing white robes with brilliant burgundy trim, stand in one of the pews a few rows behind me. They hail from the St. James Disciple Church, a nearby neighbor of Long Branch. As they make their way to the center aisle, Evangelist Lofton stays at the microphone, keeping the praises flowing. "Glory to God!" she exclaims. "Yeah! Clap like they're *your* choir, now!" This last appeal, reminding the saints that "it's no 'your group' and 'my group,'" draws a cry of "Glory! Glory!" from the pews. Evangelist Lofton answers with an enthusiastic "Come on! Yes! Ye-e-es!"—each phrase rising to a higher pitch and volume. Once again, the clapping grows louder.

When the choir reaches the cross-aisle, Evangelist Lofton utters a tone-dropping "Hallelujah!" Then when they step around to the choir loft, she says, "St. James! Thank the Lord!" her voice falling back to conversational levels. "Praise the Lord!" cries one saint. "Thank the Lord Jesus!" echoes another. The clapping, meanwhile, winds down, and the shaking tambourine stills. With the choir almost in place, Evangelist Lofton steps back toward the registration table and her place in the pews. Before laying her mike on the front pew, she utters a final "Amen!" "Praise the Lord!" declares Sister Perry. "Praise God!" answers Sister Elliott. "Thank you, Jesus!" adds Sister Perry. Then, as a choir member reaches for the microphone that rests on the choir loft rail, the saints fall silent, waiting expectantly for the singing to begin.

Chapter 14

Format

"Let's Give the Lord a Praise"

The five members of the St. James Gospel Choir stand side by side, their matched robes mutely testifying to their unity of purpose. As the singer nearest the Branchettes lifts the microphone, the others smile and exchange glances, showing no sign of uneasiness at being the first group to sing. Their apparent confidence is echoed in Sister Phyllis Love's introductory words.

"We give honor to God for our first being here," she begins, her voice strong and steady. The saints respond with calls of "Amen!" and "Praise God!" "And are praising God," she continues, "because God truly has been good to us." "Yes He has!" cries one sister in the pews. "Amen!" affirms another.

Those of us in front can easily hear Sister Love's words. Those at the rear, however, are straining, as the microphone is not turned on. Immediately diagnosing the problem, a quartet singer slips to the choir loft, reaches for the mike, and flips it on. As he does so, a saint fills the pause with a loud, "Thank You, Jesus!" With the microphone restored to her hand, Sister Love, the choir's "president," repeats her introduction, changing the words but expressing the same thought.

We thank God for enabling us to be here,	(Alright!/Yeah!)
and for giving us a mind to come this way.	(Lord Jesus!)
We are few in number today, but nevertheless	(Yes!/That's alright!)
I think about the ladies whose anniversary	
we are celebrating.	(Alright!/Jesus!)
We've bumped into them so many times,	(Lord Jesus!)
and seen them on the highway—	(Lord Jesus!)
just *two* of them!	
But nevertheless, we're not going to complain.	(Lord Jesus!)
We going to go on and do what	(Alright!)
thus saith the Lord!	(Amen!/Alright!)
We'd like to say to you,	

```
        we from Saint James,
        we love you!                                    (Amen!/Praise God!)
        Happy anniversary!                              (Thank You, Jesus!)
```

Like Sister Bracey and Sister Perry before her, Sister Love opens with words that sound like testimony. She then immediately apologizes for the choir's small size, suggesting that more members are usually present. As she says this, I can't help but think about the Branchettes, who themselves came together as a group only after they found themselves singing at a program for which none of their fellow choir members had shown up. But numbers, say the saints, don't really matter. Nor, for that matter, does the particular excellence of one's singing. (Though, of course, special excellence *does* earn special acclaim.) What *really* matters are sincerity and spirit. That's why, when the speaker says that the choir is not complaining and that they're going to do what "the Lord saith," the saints respond so enthusiastically. Programgoers from every corner of the church cry words of encouragement, letting the singers know that they don't care if the choir numbers five or fifty. As long as they're truly doing the Lord's work . . .

Upon wishing the Branchettes a happy anniversary, Sister Love lays the microphone back on the railing and steps back into line. For a moment, all is silent. Then, with a quick glance to make sure everyone is ready, she launches into an up-tempo rendition of "Give the Lord a Praise." The first line is hers alone; the second rings with all five voices, joined in loose but inspired harmony. As the voices come together, so too do the choir members' enthusiastically clapping hands. Instantly, the women are swaying in tight unison, their movements punctuating every other clapped beat. By the third line, dozens of saints in the congregation are singing along.

```
        Give the Lord a praise!
          GIVE THE LORD A PRAISE!
            LET'S GIVE THE LORD A PRAISE!              (Go ahead!)
          THE LORD IS WORTHY!
            OH YES, HE'S WORTHY!
              LET'S GIVE THE LORD A PRAISE!            (Yeah!)
```

As if to confirm the emcee's assurance that singers without musicians "needn't worry," a full complement of accompanists have already joined the singing. A tambourine player eases in first, adding a double-timed sizzle before the end of the second line. The electric organ slips in midway through the next line, while the bass joins during the fourth. Next comes the guitar, introduced by a shriek of electronic feedback. Within seconds, the guitarist brings the feedback under control and is adding a stream of slurred notes to the thickening musical texture. By the end of the chorus, a teenage boy has joined on the drums, while a second tambourine has started to sound. Saints are crying out "Yeah!" "Go ahead!" and "Alright! Alright!"

```
        Give the Lord a praise!
          GIVE THE LORD A PRAISE!
```

Give the Lord a praise!
GIVE THE LORD A PRAISE!
LET'S GIVE THE LORD A PRAISE!   (Alright! Alright!)
THE LORD IS WORTHY!
OH YES, HE'S WORTHY!
LET'S GIVE THE LORD A PRAISE!

As the voices of choir and congregation flow together, I can't help but appreciate the appropriateness of this opening song. The primary purpose of sanctified programs—whatever their announced aim—is always praise. Ask any gospel singer what the singing is all about, and the answer is invariably the same. Though some songs exhort and admonish, and others offer testimony or prayer, praise always emerges as the single most cited function. Listen, for example, to the response of Rev. Sam McCrary, the longtime lead with the Fairfield Four. "When you're singing," Rev. McCrary states simply, "you're singing praises to the Lord." Rev. McCrary's singing partner, Elder Lawrence Richardson, restates the equation with even greater simplicity. "Praise *is* singing," he declares. "And because you're singing, you're praising the greater power of all powers." Jojo Wallace, tenor singer with the Sensational Nightingales, couldn't agree more. "I want everybody to know what God ordained us for as singers," he says. "We are gifted. God wants us to use the gift *for His glory*. That's what it is. That's the whole bottom nutshell."[1]

Certainly that's been the main message thus far in the Branchettes' anniversary. Virtually everyone who has stood in the cross-aisle has stressed the centrality of praise. Now the St. James Gospel Choir is doing the same thing in song. "Give the Lord a praise!" the singers chorus, their voices brimming with joy. "Let's give the Lord a praise!"

Somebody PRAYED FOR ME,   (Yes!)
    HAD ME ON THEIR MIND,
        TOOK OUT TIME AND PRAYED FOR ME.   (Oh yes!)
I'M SO GLAD THEY PRAYED,
    I'M SO GLAD THEY PRAYED,
        I'M SO GLAD THEY PRAYED FOR ME.

Though praise reigns supreme in gospel programs, it never stands alone. Instead, it stands alongside and becomes part of many other frames of worship, weaving its way into prayer, preaching, testimony, and the reading of scripture. In like manner, these other frames weave their way into praise. This intermingling becomes particularly evident in song, where the lyrics often shift from one worship frame to another, switching voice and direction in the process. "Give the Lord a Praise," for example, begins as exhortation, with the singers urging their hearers to give praise. The lyrics' imperative structure makes the congregational "you" the subject of the choir's address. As the choir swings into the third verse, however, the frame changes from exhortation to testimony, with the first-person "I" replacing the tacit "you." Now the singers are personalizing their praise, reflecting on self rather than exhorting the other. In so doing, they are both tightening their own focus and implicitly inviting their hearers to do the same. The overriding end is still praise. Now, however, the singers are taking a different path to get there.

Some mother PRAYED FOR ME,	(Yes!)
HAD ME ON HER MIND,	(Ye-e-es!)
TOOK OUT TIME AND PRAYED FOR ME.	(Alright!/Go ahead!)
I'M SO GLAD THEY PRAYED,	(Come on!)
I'M SO GLAD THEY PRAYED,	
I'M SO GLAD THEY PRAYED FOR ME.	(Oh yes!)

From the broad anonymity of "somebody" to the focused anonymity of "some mother," the verses repeat and build. Such repetition is never merely additive. If anything, it pushes the song's power exponentially, the familiar framing prompting both deepened reflection and expressive fervor. Singers say that the path is always easier to follow the second time around. Freed from worrying about the travels of the tongue, they can focus more intently on the meaning of the lyric. Each such verse thus presses its message deeper and deeper into the consciousness, playing with the memory, talking with the soul. As the message's grounding in self grows more profound, the words roll with greater ease and increased passion. In this performance, the choir's performance grows noticeably more exuberant, their voices a bit louder and their handclaps a bit sharper. The congregation responds in kind with off-time clapping and fiery cries of encouragement.

Then the singers push the frame a bit further. Instead of adding to the catalog of those who prayed, they flip the focus from thanksgiving to triumphant declaration of victory. The saints in the pews immediately recognize the familiar verse and enthusiastically join the singing.

O-o-o-oh, VICTORY IS MINE,	(Yes!)
VICTORY IS MINE,	
VICTORY TODAY IS MINE.	
I TOLD SATAN	
TO "GET THEE BEHIND!"	
O-o-o-oh, VICTORY TODAY IS MINE!	

From an earnest call for praise, to a joyous cry of thanksgiving, to a jubilant assertion of triumph, the song charts a familiar spiritual journey. At the same time, it captures the full course of a service, taking singers from the devotion's call to the invitation's victory. With victory now declared, the circle comes to completion. And with completion comes reason for further praise. So the singers conclude by starting the journey anew, drawing on the knowledge of victory to fuel renewed praises.

Give the Lord a praise!
GIVE THE LORD A PRAISE!

Give the Lord a praise!
GIVE THE LORD A PRAISE!
LET'S GIVE THE LORD A PRAISE!
THE LORD IS WORTHY!
OH YES, HE'S WORTHY!
LET'S GIVE THE LORD A PRAISE!

Midway through the verse, the songleader glances and nods at the watchful musicians, signaling the song's impending end. As the final words ring out, the guitarist closes the melody with a fancy fingerpicked tag. The other musicians quickly follow suit, while the singers still their sway and dissolve their rhythmic clapping into general applause. The saints do the same, layering the final instrumental phrases with loud cries of "Glory to God!" "Amen!" and "Praise His name!" The choir members are themselves calling out God's praises, following their sung advice with claps and cries not for self, but for the Lord. Throughout, one of the congregational tambourines keeps up its sibilant chatter, while the bass riffs on the recent melody.

As the clapping subsides, a sister in the amen corner utters a loud "Thank You, Jesus!" As if in response, Sister Love says "Praise the Lord." She has ceded her position at line's end to another singer, who now holds the mike. With no further pause and with no words of introduction, this second singer launches into the choir's second song.

✶ ✶ ✶ ✶ ✶

And so it goes, from song to song. "A theme song and two," the emcee had advised. So three songs ring forth, and the group melts back into the congregation. The master of ceremonies rises, offers words of connection and praise, and calls for the next ensemble, who step to the cross-aisle or choir loft. They sing their three and then make room for their singing peers, who follow the pattern until the emcee introduces the service's honorees, calls for an offering, or extends an invitation. Or until the Spirit intervenes with a different agenda. At this second service of the Branchettes' twentieth anniversary, the Spirit flowed but did not transform the program's structure. By evening's end, ten groups and two soloists had offered praises through song.

Programs such as this typically unfold as spirited celebrations of musical diversity. Instead of featuring a single style or sound, they purposefully vary musical textures, thus acknowledging in their programming the many faces of praise. Saints say that just as the Lord blesses His children with different gifts, so also does He bless His singers with different skills and different sounds. This diversity, in turn, increases the likelihood that sung messages will reach more ears and touch more souls. After all, say the saints, no single set of words will touch every heart. No song will spur every mind to reflection. No style will lead every ear to listen.

And no voice can speak for the whole. Hence the need for diversity. By bringing varied voices into the church, saints hope to catch more ears and draw more believers into the communion of accord. In so doing, they celebrate not only the diversity of Christian song, but also the essential parity of Christian singers.

One need only survey the broad compass of gospel singing to recognize the many forms that gospel takes. Standing side by side in the cross-aisle are full-voiced soloists and sweet-singing duos, close harmony quartets and strident, instrumentally accompanied ensembles, jubilee choruses and shouting choirs. Some groups are all women; some are all men; some are mixed. Some sing with the authority of advanced age, their voices straining to capture notes that once flowed without effort. Others sing with the callowness of youth, their voices trembling with pride and anxiety and inexperience. Some sing for praise, others for pleasure, still others for prestige. All are hoping to touch the hearts, minds, and/or souls of their hearers.

Cutting across vocal organization, gender, and age are broad variations in song style. Among quartets, for example, some groups still favor the measured pacing and tightly blended harmonies of the old "spiritual" (or "harmony") style. Others prefer the upbeat tempos and narrative leads of "jubilee" singing. Most quartets, however, now embrace the instrumental framing and improvisatory freedom of "quartet gospel," a style marked by impassioned lead vocals, subtle melodic colorations, and constantly shifting vocal textures. "Gospel" also reigns as the preferred style among most soloists, non-quartet ensembles, and choirs, the singers who originally brought this sanctified-based sound to vernacular popularity. In sharp contrast to these saints' improvisatory stylings, some sanctified singers favor the restrained precision and trained harmonies of the Western classical tradition. And an ever-growing body of artists (in every vocal combination) embrace "contemporary gospel," a broad, loosely defined style whose smooth vocals, nontraditional harmonies and melodic structures, layered orchestration, and complex rhythms owe as much to African American styles on the *Billboard* charts as they do to church tradition.[2]

Complicating this portrait of musical diversity is the fact that each of these styles admits a wide range of internal variation. Further confusing the picture is singers' tendency to include more than one style in their repertoires, thus allowing them to accommodate different tastes and to address different congregational needs. Finally, we must take into account gospel's penchant for drawing features from different styles to create stylistic blends that are uniquely a singer's own. Here the aesthetic of personalization once again comes into play, actively encouraging gospel artists to forge singular (and, ideally, singularly identifiable) sonic identities. Stylistic boundaries can't help but blur when choir singers inject operatic roulades into hard gospel leads, or when "contemporary" quartets burst into four-part falsetto harmony. Nonetheless, despite this canon of diversity, most singers tend to associate themselves with one of three broad styles—"quartet," "gospel," or "contemporary." These designations add one more factor to the performed diversity that manifests itself in the cross-aisle.

The Branchettes' anniversary itself offers telling testimony to this diversity. Ap-

13. "Something got a-hold of me!" sings the director of the St. Amanda Gospel Choir, voicing lyrics that testify to the emotion that is sweeping over her. Congregation members urge her on with cries of "Sing now!" and "Tell it! Tell it!" (Photo by Roland L. Freeman)

pearing on that Sunday program were four choirs, three gospel groups, two male quartets, one husband and wife duo, and two soloists. Of the choirs, the first—the St. James Gospel Choir—was a small women's group that favored a traditional, congregational repertoire. The second and fourth were larger, mixed ensembles who sang straight gospel and songs drawn from quartet gospel sources. The third was a six-man "father and son" chorus who harmonized old quartet standards in a modified jubilee fashion.

The afternoon's first gospel group consisted of four women singers, a male guitarist, and a male bass player. They sang in a fiery, tightly harmonized gospel style. The other two gospel groups were both women's duos. The first was the Branchettes, an older ensemble whose full-voiced style, a cappella harmonies, and time-honored repertoire testify to the early roots of sanctified song. The second duo, in contrast, were two high school students who sang a carefully modulated, rather thinly voiced contemporary piece. A third duo, this one a husband-and-wife team, added to the variety by performing traditional congregational pieces in a warm, loosely harmonized a cappella style.

The anniversary's two male quartets offered yet another set of sounds. The first fit squarely within the current quartet tradition, with "sweet-" and "hard-singing" lead vocalists, a tightly harmonized backup line, and accompaniment of lead guitar, bass guitar, and drums. The second "quartet," in contrast, was an unaccompanied trio of men in their early twenties. Instead of singing in a traditional quartet style, they combined the contemporary harmonies of a cappella stylists like Take 6 with a repertoire that stretched from contemporary pieces to the congregational classic "What a Friend We Have in Jesus."

Finally come the soloists, one male and one female. The male soloist sang two classic hymns with a rich, tightly controlled baritone. The young woman also chose a familiar hymn for her single solo. Like her male counterpart, she began the song in a straightforward, controlled style. As she moved into the lyric, however, her singing grew "harder" and more impassioned, ultimately transforming the hymn into a gospel tour de force. For those who might predict that the choirs and quartets would provoke the fullest flow of the Spirit, I should note that this teenage sister's solo brought as much Spirit into the church as any group that performed at the entire anniversary.

The variety evident in this roster of twelve is by no means unusual, particularly for community-based programs. Indeed, one could well argue that the sheer diversity of gospel styles and sanctified voices virtually mandates such variation. Even when groups with similar configurations dominate a program, variety still reigns supreme. At the first night of the Branchettes' anniversary, for example, fully eight of the thirteen groups were choirs. This figure proves deceptive, however, when we consider that some were small and others large, some were elders and others youth, some sang hymns and others shout songs, some sang in loose unison and others with tightly arranged harmonies, some performed with cool poise and others with fiery passion. The fact that they were all choirs in no way lessens the realized significance of their differences. I can assure you that no one left that anniversary complaining about sameness of sound.

14. "There is going to be a mighty storm!" warn the Clouds of Harmony, predicting clouds of a very different order from those that mark the harmony of congregational accord. The lead shifts from singer to singer as this six-man quartet—singing from the cross-aisle—draws its set to a powerful close. (Photo by Roland L. Freeman)

Every rule, of course, has its exceptions. Some programs actively seek stylistic sameness, filling their roster with ensembles who share both sound and structure. This is particularly true for commercial "ticket programs," many of which fill their bills with professional touring quartets.[3] Not infrequently, these quartets boast comparable vocal lineups and identical instrumentation and would undoubtedly strike community outsiders as markedly similar. Nonetheless, few audience members would ever level the charge of sameness. As any quartet fan will testify, even the narrow boundaries of a tightly defined style still allow for wide variations in sound, texture, and spirit. The aesthetic press toward musical personalization, toward "having your own sound" and "singing like yourself," insures that few quartets end up sounding the same. Singing like someone else, say many quartet singers, is the quickest way to lose your listeners.[4]

Nonetheless, many saints steadfastly refuse to attend commercial quartet programs. When asked why, the first response almost always addresses not stylistic narrowness, but rather the "form and fashion" showmanship that such programs seem to foster. When pressed further, many saints *do* eventually point to the programs' sameness, but only to say that the groups' similarities—however different their sounds—invariably invite comparison and competition. The very structure encourages groups to try to set themselves apart, to proclaim their singularity before a discriminating audience. The obvious measure of success, of course, is audience acclaim. In the effort to win such acclaim, and thus to mark their success, many singers start singing more for the audience than for the Lord. As they focus more on "outsinging" (and, in a more general sense, "outperforming") their counterparts, they grow less concerned with bringing the assembly "to one accord." The spirit of competition, in essence, annuls the spirit of communion.[5]

Such rivalry is by no means restricted to quartets. Programs featuring choirs or gospel groups are subject to precisely the same pressures. Jackie Jackson, a St. Louis choir director, describes this rivalry as a constant inducement to "rise and fly." "A lot of times nowadays, you have services where there's going to be an evening of gospel music," Sister Jackson explains. "And it just becomes too competitive. When you go to a gospel program these days—I call it 'rise and fly.' These groups, these young people, these choirs go from church to church to church. And it's, 'Who can outfly, outdance' [the other]. . . . Consequently, [with] my choir at church, I tell them that we're not here for form or fashion, that we don't come to entertain. We come to lift up the name of Jesus. So therefore, I decline a lot of invitations. Because I view them as 'rise and fly.' And we don't do that."[6]

Many gospel promoters clearly don't share these sentiments and actively encourage performative rivalry. Figuring that nothing lures crowds like the promise of competition, promoters often bill their programs as "song battles." Using posters and promotional handbills, they readily adopt the rhetoric of conflict to "sell" sacred song. "Battle of the Giants—It's Been a Long Time Coming" proclaims one recent handbill; "Song Battle of the Decade" declares another; "Hear the Heavy Weights of Gospel Battle for the Crown" announces a third. Although most such "battles" are not as formally structured as their counterparts in the 1940s, 1950s and 1960s (when community "judges" actually measured applause and declared "winners"), they nonetheless celebrate competition as an appropriate frame of performance.[7] The singers who perform under the banners of such "battles," in turn, often sing so as to realize the rhetoric. Enacting carefully developed strategies of vocal and physical theatrics, they vie to make theirs the "showiest" in the contest of "shows."

As if to further encourage this spirit of rivalry, most commercial promoters sequence their programs so that the least popular singers come first and the most popular come last. At first glance, this strategy seems to make eminent sense: if you want to keep an audience, then save the "best" for last. This is precisely the advice offered by the various manuals available in gospel circles on "how to conduct a program." Gospel composer Kenneth Morris's popular guidebook, for example, advises:

There is only one way of sustaining the interest of the audience until a climax is attained and that is by "BUILDING UP THE PROGRAM." This means GRADING THE PERFORMERS ACCORDING TO ABILITY so that each succeeding performer will be a little better than the preceding performer until the STAR of STARS of the program appear at the climax or end of the program. In this way, the program progressively gets better as it goes along.

Morris concludes his section on "arrangement according to grade" by noting that "the best laid plans may have to be altered instantaneously by the successful program-giver because of one important DETAIL. THERE IS NO WAY TO GRADE THE 'SPIRIT.' "[8] Though this postscript somewhat tempers the advice, the message remains quite clear: program-givers should "grade" performers and schedule them accordingly. One need only canvass the bills of commercial programs to realize how this "grading" is done. The singers with the biggest "hit" on the gospel charts, or the ones currently riding the crest of national popularity, invariably close the program, with those who were perhaps the "most popular" a few months ago now filling the next-to-the-last spot. And so it goes, all the way down to the opening slot, which usually falls to a local, nonprofessional group. The message conveyed by such programming is that crowd-pleasing artistry is the cardinal measure of ability. Sincerity and spirituality don't seem to figure into the equation.

For the most part, saints reject this programming rationale. Arguing that "grading" by artistry alone fosters competition and invites showmanship, they tend to schedule programs with a flexible hand, often letting the order of arrival determine the order of performance. When emcees *do* shift this order, they usually do so not to program the best for last, but rather to insure a greater degree of diversity. For example, they might shuffle the roster a bit to avoid scheduling two like-sounding groups back-to-back. Or they might schedule special guests—singers whose stature issues not so much from particular artistry as from distance traveled—near the program's end as a mark of respect. Beyond these changes, however, the programming tends to flow without the imposed constraints of rank. I've attended scores of programs where the closing act was an aging soloist, a group of out-of-tune teenagers, or a choir composed entirely of children under six. In virtually every case, the congregation responded with as much enthusiasm as they did to the most talented singers on the program. What seemed to matter most to these saints was not the singers' sound, but rather the singers' *spirit*.[9]

* * * * *

When I first began attending community programs, I couldn't understand why their scheduling didn't acknowledge obvious differences in talent. Why didn't they follow the format of their commercial counterparts? Why didn't they program with an eye toward intensification and climax? After all, even Sunday morning services follow this familiar trajectory. Such services typically start low (in the scattered worldliness of early devotions), build in intensity (in the mind-focusing engagement of prayer, praise, and testimony), and rise toward an emotion-filled climax (in the revelatory power of the sermon). Most gospel programs begin in precisely the same manner. They too move from division to accord; they too seem to push toward climax. Why, then, don't they extend the trajectory by scheduling the most overtly passionate and passion-invoking singers for last?

The very question speaks volumes about my assumptions. Not only was I wrongly equating artistry with passion, and equating passion *displayed* with passion *felt*, but I was presuming that spiritual climax was something that could be programmed and achieved. In essence, I was measuring climax by performance instead of by Spirit. All of this was brought home to me in a late-night conversation with Wilson Waters, longtime tenor singer with the Fairfield Four. We were sitting together in Waters's hotel room, talking about the group's singing schedule for the upcoming week, when our conversation turned toward talk of competition and performance strategy. Brother Waters pointed out that the Spirit lent a constant note of unpredictability to gospel performance, making "strategy" something of a moot point. If you're truly "living the life you sing about," he explained, then the Spirit might touch at *any* point in a given performance. No matter what the singers' plans. And that touch, he added, has nothing to do with one's skill in singing. The key lies not in the singing, but in the life that gives it rise.

"We got a guy there [in Nashville]," Brother Waters continued, "an old man, Eli Cheeks. The old man have lived such a life that—well, I haven't never seen him do anything wrong. And, no doubt, the other people around have never seen him do anything wrong."

Brother Waters paused, looked straight at me, and then said quietly, "*He can't sing.*" This time the pause stretched even longer as Brother Waters smiled and gently shook his head. "What I'm saying [when I say he] can't sing—he don't have a good voice. He might have used to had [one] years ago." Again Waters shook his head. "But *anything he do*," Brother Waters continued, his voice quickening, "he can open his mouth and *the Spirit's there!*" Suddenly Waters's right hand was waving in the air, as if to stress the immediacy of the Spirit's presence. "Huh?"

"Now, his background [singers]," he continued, "[it] seem like they just—well, they all know *how* to sing, but I'm saying . . ." Again Brother Waters hesitated, clearly searching for words, clearly not wanting to criticize. "It seems like it ain't all together. But whatever *they* do," he added, the note of surprise and respect again in his voice, "just seem like it's right! You understand? I mean, it's just the way people carry themselves sometimes. [And] the Spirit [will] come out of nowhere."

"So it *is* a lot more than . . ." I began to ask, nodding at the realization that skill is no indicator of Spirit.

"Right!" exclaimed Brother Waters before I could even finish my sentence. "It ain't *all* singing. See, it ain't all singing."[10]

✳ ✳ ✳ ✳ ✳

Eli Cheeks would probably never be invited to sing on a commercial program. If he were, his group would probably be asked to perform first. After all, such programs should "build"—as Kenneth Morris reminds us—to the gospel "stars." But *if* this scenario were ever enacted and *if* the audience included a goodly number of saints, then I suspect that the unwitting promoter might well find his carefully plotted trajectory summarily shattered. Not by Brother Cheeks, but by the Spirit. For if the Spirit does indeed flow almost every time that Brother Cheeks sings, as Wilson Waters suggests, then the service might well reach an early climax. This is not to suggest that additional climaxes are either improbable or impossible. It *does* suggest, however, that any plans for linear intensification—at least when dealing with sanctified performers—are always subject to the Spirit's will.

Though the spiritual trajectory of gospel programs can be likened to that of Sunday morning services, the comparison ends when the program's first group of singers returns to the pews. From this point forward, the linear rise toward climax loops back into itself to become a cycle. Whereas Sunday morning devotions prepare saints to receive the preached Word, starting them on a journey that ideally culminates in spiritual revelation, the devotions in gospel services lead saints to a high state of praise that ebbs and flows with every singer that steps to the church-front. Instead of the single climax of an ascendant sermon, saints experience the multiple climaxes of songs and sets, one following another in a cycle that rolls from the emcee's introduction to the final benediction. Every group starts at a low point in the cycle, struggling to "read" the congregation's needs, listening for inspiration's silent voice, prayerfully preparing themselves to sing. But as they move into song, the powers of praise draw forth the passion, setting the cycle of focus and intensification into motion. Powered by faith and the hidden dynamic of prayerful conversation, the set climbs inexorably toward climax.

This climax is not something measured or marked by an obvious peak moment, as when a singer shouts or a listener leaps into holy dance. Instead, it's simply the set's affective high point, however that might be expressed or experienced. Many groups anticipate it by arranging their sets to close with their fastest or most emotionally wrenching piece; others sing whatever seems appropriate, trusting their tightening internal focus to bring the set to a devotional peak. Whatever the strategy, sanctified singers say that their prayerful conversations, combined with the emotional enmeshment and elevation of performance, invariably move their singing—like the proverbial rounds of Jacob's ladder—"higher and higher."

As group follows group, climax follows climax, with the emcee providing the link that joins each reached peak with each new beginning. One might well envision the program as charting a kind of spiritual spiral, with each group adding one or more rounds to the ascending whole. Some rounds stretch high and others crest low, but all extend the spiral, adding cycle to cycle in the procession of praise. As the program proceeds, these cycles take a distinctly upward tilt. Each new beginning starts at a slightly higher point than that which came before. The cycles, like same-sounding lines in preaching and kindred verses in song, don't merely repeat themselves; they don't just extend the whole while holding the affective tone steady. Instead, they build from one to another, every cycle stoking the flames of worship a bit higher. Whereas devotions chart a path that transforms worldly concern into devotional passion, the succession of singers presses that path along an ascendant journey of intensification. Through climax after climax, the singers and congregation move ever deeper into the fullness of focused praise.

This trajectory, of course, describes a devotional ideal. Reality doesn't always follow such a neatly ordered course. Singers singing for "form and fashion," for example, can stall the devotional journey, momentarily stifling the passion with their pretense. When one such group follows on the heels of another, the once-kindled flames subside even further. But saints know that "God's Word will never return unto Him void"; they realize that even when cloaked in the trappings of pretense, the Word will have an impact. "Jesus said His Word was strong," reminds Rev. Sam McCrary. "*Even if* it comes out of hellish mouths." So the fires don't die, and the saints hold onto their passion, secure in the knowledge that the Spirit—unlike them—is not distracted by worldly ways. When the "form and fashion" passes and the praises again ring true, the spiral starts anew, quickly regaining the momentum of its upward journey. Though momentarily dampened, the smoldering fires are quick to burst back into flame.[11]

Chapter 15

Purpose

"The Anointing of God Breaks the Yokes"

Sister Mary Bracey once again stands in the cross-aisle, addressing the congregation. When she and her husband, Brother Samuel Bracey, were called to follow the St. James Gospel Choir, they rose from the pews singing. Sister Bracey's powerful voice swallowed the closing words of Evangelist Lofton's introduction, and the passion has yet to subside. After marching forward to the rousing choruses of "If the Lord Needs Somebody," the Bracey Singers had launched into a driving rendition of "Everything Is Moving by the Power of God." The entire congregation had joined in the exuberant "shout-time" singing. Then the musicians had pushed the song—and the clapping saints—into an extra, instrumental verse. Now fans are flapping throughout the pews, and winded saints are crying "Glory!" and "Praise God!"

As the guitarist whips the melody to a frothy crescendo, Sister Bracey wails, "Thank You, Jesus!" No longer do her words craft a simple statement of praise. Instead, they flow with the shifting contours of chant. Sister Bracey is shaking her head, clenching her fists by her side, clearly feeling the power. As the guitarist plays on, her words begin to roll, threatening at every moment to burst into song. She seems to be straining to hold herself back, struggling to keep the passion in check.

We're getting ready to leave you now!	(That's alright!)
We ask that you pray for us,	(Yeah!)
and we'll do the same for you.	(Alright now!)
I'm feeling all right!	(Yes!/Amen!)
Knowing that God is a good God!	(Yes He is!)
Thinking about [the] way God cares for us!	(Uh-huh!)
May He help me right now!	(Yeah!)
We ask that you pray for us,	(Glory! Glory!)
and we'll do the same for you.	(Thank You, Lord Jesus!)
We're going to leave you in God's hands,	(Uh-huh!)
the one that will take care of . . .	(Glory to God!)

Sister Bracey's words fade in her plunging tone, the final "you" lost to a sharp shake of the head that leaves her face facing heaven. Her chanted remarks chart a singsong pattern that pulls every opening line to a tonal rise, and then sends its counterpart into a breathy dive. The lines rise and fall, rise and fall, the pattern broken only by the cried affirmation "I'm feeling all right!" which begins at a voice-cracking pitch even higher than its close. If this was a sermon, the sound alone would suggest climax.[1]

But the words carry no sustained message. Nor do they link themselves to the songs sung or yet to be sung. Instead, they just pour out, freely mixing praise, prayer, announcement, and testimony in an exuberant jumble. Watching her rapt delivery, I realize that Sister Bracey doesn't need to say anything more than she's said. Her tone—and more important, her entire body—convey her message for her.

As another "Praise God!" rings from the amen corner, Sister Bracey's husband steps to the microphone. "Branchettes, I'm going to sing my last song for you," he promises, his resonant baritone sounding a sharp contrast to his wife's piercing soprano. "Lord Jesus!" cries Sister Perry. Brother Samuel Bracey continues with a quick "Hallelujah, search my soul!" tagged by a sudden, rising "Hey!" Then *he* shakes his head, signaling to all the fleeting touch of the Spirit. Cries of "Glory!" and "Go ahead!" ring from the pews, as Brother Bracey utters a brief, falsetto "Whoo!" Then, with another shake of the head and a swift shrug of his shoulders, he shouts "Hallelujah!" Scattered claps erupt from the congregation, accompanied by another wave of enthusiastic affirmation.

When the saints finally fall silent, Brother Bracey again addresses the Branchettes, saying, "On down the line, you all are doing just what I'm going to sing about!" "Lord Jesus!" responds Sister Perry. Deacon Eldridge adds an "Oh yes!" while the drummer strikes a single-beat accent on the snare. Then Brother Bracey says, "If you . . ." This time, however, he can't finish, the "feeling" rising too high to allow him to proceed. As he shakes his head in silence, the guitarist plays a quiet, calming phrase. "Thank You, Jesus," whispers Sister Bracey. "Jesus!" calls Sister Perry.

Suddenly, Brother Bracey starts to sing. His richly textured voice fills the church with quavering passion, as he slides his opening word in and around the emergent melody, stretching it for two full measures. The musicians remain silent, not knowing where he plans to take the song, not even knowing what song he plans to sing. Someone in the pews, clearly impressed by Brother Bracey's melismatic wanderings, cries "Bless Him! Bless Him!" Then Brother Bracey closes the line, causing the church to erupt with claps and cries of recognition. He has chosen to conclude the set with the old spiritual "I Done Done What You Told Me to Do."

Lo-o-o-o-o-o-o-ord, I done done,	(Yeah!/Eh-hey!)
Lo-o-o-o-ord, I done done,	(Jesus!/Go ahead!)
Lo-o-o-o-ord, I done done,	(Yes!)
Lord, I DONE DONE WHAT YOU TOLD ME TO DO.	(Alright now!)

The first three lines ring out as impassioned solo, accompanied only by the congregation's cries and the organ's dramatic phrasings. On the fourth line, however, Sister Bracey joins the singing, as does the entire congregation. A tambourine jumps in on the first congregational "done," the drums start at the close of the "what," and the bass and guitar enter on the chorused "You." The bass quickly pushes its way to the instrumental lead, churning out a slow, rolling riff that echoes the deep resonance of Brother Bracey's voice.

> I'm saying, Lo-o-o-ord, Lord, I DONE DONE,   (Yes!/Well, well!)
> LO-O-O-ORD, I DONE DONE,
> Oh LO-O-O-ORD, I DONE DONE,   (You alright now!)
> I DONE DONE WHAT YOU TOLD ME TO DO.

Though Brother Bracey leads the song, the refrain clearly belongs to the congregation, who sing with such fervor that the Braceys' amplified voices are lost in the chorus. But when Brother Bracey introduces the next verse, he does so with an emphatic shout, the first word literally bursting from his mouth.

> Told me to pray, Lord, I done that too.   (Yes!/Help me!)
>   Lord, I DONE DONE WHAT YOU TOLD ME TO DO.
> Told me to pray, and I done that too.   (Alright now!)
>   Lord, I DONE DONE WHAT YOU TOLD ME TO DO.
> I'm saying, Lo-o-o-ord, You know, I DONE DONE,
>   LO-O-O-ORD, I DONE DONE,   (Ye-e-es!)
>   Oh! LO-O-O-ORD, I DONE DONE,   (Oh yes!)
> Yes, I DONE DONE WHAT YOU TOLD ME TO DO.

Mary and Samuel Bracey are standing side by side, both singing into a single microphone positioned at the center of the cross-aisle. Like the choir before them, and like the saints in the pews, they are swaying as they sing, moving back and forth in loose unison. Though their hands rest at their sides, one or another often rises to pointedly accent their testimonial message. Whenever one hand moves up to shake and point, its counterpart invariably pulls to the hip, as if the two were connected by an invisible thread. The final stance, though rarely sustained for more than a few seconds, instantly calls to mind the preaching preacher.[2]

When Brother Bracey swings into the next verse, he starts the additive ascent of parallel statement, substituting "singing" for "praying" as the subject of the Lord's command. Sister Bracey, meanwhile, shifts her accompaniment to a high-pitched moan.

> Told me to sing, Lord, I'm doing that too,   (Alright now!)
>   Lord, I DONE DONE WHAT YOU TOLD ME TO DO.
> Told me to sing, I'm doing that too,
>   Lord, I DONE DONE WHAT YOU TOLD ME TO DO.
> I'm saying, LORD, You know, I DONE DONE,   (Yeah!/Glory)
> LO-O-O-ORD, I DONE DONE,   (Yes Lord!)
> LO-O-O-ORD, I DONE DONE,
> We-e-ell, I DONE DONE WHAT YOU TOLD ME TO DO.

As the chorus draws to a close, Brother Bracey suddenly steps away from the mike and launches into a line that more than doubles the song's tempo. Both he and Sister Bracey immediately start clapping in this quickened rhythm, signaling musicians and singers alike that they're pushing the song into a new phase. The musicians, caught off guard by the sudden shift, momentarily stumble. But they recover almost instantly, with the organ and bass jumping on the new, "shout-time" beat. The congregation isn't far behind. Following Sister Bracey's lead, they leap right into the second line, taking it up with an ease that earns my instant admiration. I would expect a singing group to fall in this easily; but for an entire congregation to do it—and particularly such a diverse congregation—is a feat of a very different order. I make a quick, appreciative note in my field log, and then enthusiastically join the singing.

> I done done,
>> I done done what YOU TOLD ME TO DO!
> I done done,
>> I DONE DONE WHAT YOU TOLD ME TO DO!
> I done done,
>> I DONE DONE WHAT YOU TOLD ME TO DO!
> I done done,
>> I DONE DONE WHAT YOU TOLD ME TO DO!

Quartet and gospel singers often call this rise the "elevation," referencing the point where the lead "elevates" the song to a quickened rhythm and heightened pitch. Preachers use the same term when speaking of the shift from "natural voice" to "elevated voice." Both groups are using the term in precisely the same way. To "elevate" is to step up the intensity, to shift into higher gear, to push performance into an entirely new realm. A realm of both expression and experience. Saints say that elevation not only changes the rules; it also changes the feeling. Or perhaps it occurs *in response to* a change in feeling. Either way, elevation and heightened engagement go hand in hand. When a preacher elevates a sermon or a singer elevates a song, the message conveyed is that the presenting saint is truly "getting into" the presentation.

When Sister Bracey closed the previous song, her words and tone eloquently testified to her own elevation. Gone was the sharp, staccato phrasing that marked her comments after the group's first song; in its place was the musical flow of chant, the sanctified "moaning" of the elevated Word. Now Brother Bracey is doing the elevating. As was the case with his wife, his entire body bears witness to his "getting into" the song. Having pulled to the side of the microphone, he's moved into a kind of standing crouch, with knees flexed, back bent forward, shoulders hunched high, and head thrust toward the front. His sinewy arms, both rigidly bent at the elbow, are pumping slowly by his sides, moving back and forth, back and forth. Mirroring the arms, and keeping perfect time with the music, are Brother Bracey's feet, which press him forward in a slow, low-stepping march. His fluid advance and gentle side-to-side sway pose a striking contrast to the rigid angles of his arms and body and to the choppy rhythms of the song.[3]

Without a moment's hesitation, Sister Bracey falls in behind her husband, her posture and motion loosely mirroring his. As the two move past the first pew, Brother Bracey moves the elevation from chorus to verse. His lead words, which leap toward a high tenor, are little more than a shouted moan.

> Lo-o-o-ord, Lord, Lord, Lord!
>> I DONE DONE WHAT YOU TOLD ME TO DO!
> Oh Lo-o-o-ord, Lord, Lord, Lord!
>> I DONE DONE WHAT YOU TOLD ME TO DO!

With tambourine and drums pressing the driving rhythm, the Braceys slowly make their way down the center aisle. Sweat streams from Brother Bracey's forehead, rolling past his intense eyes, flowing down his taut cheeks, dripping to the carpet below. A sister in the pews responds to his testimony with a shouted "Yes you did!" Another utters an impassioned "Ye-e-e-e-e-es!" Beneath the chorused cries, the keyboardist switches from organ to piano. Now every pause rings with the piano's rolling flourishes and the tambourine's emphatic hiss.

As Brother Bracey gets closer to his seat, he reprises the elevated chorus. I can hardly hear his words over the pounding music.

> I done done,
>> I DONE DONE WHAT YOU TOLD ME TO DO!   (Yes! Yes!)
> I done done,
>> I DONE DONE WHAT YOU TOLD ME TO DO!
> I done done,
>> I DONE DONE WHAT YOU TOLD ME TO DO!
> I done done,
>> I DONE DONE WHAT YOU TOLD ME TO DO!

The rhythms and words seem to animate the entire church. Saints are swaying, clapping, waving outstretched hands, leaping to their feet. Brother Bracey reaches his pew and pauses there, still crouched, his feet now stepping steadily in place. Looking up, he cries out one last verse, rushing the words to fit them in the clipped metrical space. I can make them out only by watching his mouth.

> Told me to move, and I done that too!   (Go ahead!)
>> I DONE DONE WHAT YOU TOLD ME TO DO!   (I hear you!)
> Told me to move, and I done that too!
>> I DONE DONE WHAT YOU TOLD ME TO DO!

Finishing the verse, Brother and Sister Bracey sidle past three standing saints into their pew. Though they both sit down, the music gives no indication of stopping. The song is now rolling on its own volition. Instantly reprising the chorus, the congregation repeats "I done done what you told me to do!" four more times. Two saints yell "Alright!" at the break where the new verse would fall, but no one seizes the lead. The Bracey's are both seated, seemingly caught up in rapt praises of their own. So the musicians skip the verse and slide right into the repeated "I done done . . ." riff. All semblance of song structure vanishes as they roll the riff again and again, keeping the praises high and drawing even more saints to their feet.

Only a few programgoers are singing now, their voices wholly swallowed by the music. Most, however, are still clapping and many are calling loud hosannas. One sister in the amen corner has both hands raised in the air, her fingers outstretched, her mouth whispering a quiet litany of praise. Sister Elliott sits nearby, with eyes closed and a blissful smile lighting her face. The musicians just keep on playing, praising in their own way.

When I turn to look at the Braceys, I notice that both are now clapping along with the music. Nothing distinguishes them from their peers in the pews. Just as they had emerged from the pews singing, so too did they return, melting right back into the congregation. Now they are joining the saints in the praises that they themselves had initiated. The circle is complete.[4]

As the singing fades, the saints' attention turns toward the four musicians, who are deftly shifting the voicing of each repeated riff. First the keyboardist takes the lead, pounding out a flashy, improvised melody over the chorded base. Then the guitarist, who's still sitting in the front pew, claims the musical foreground; he overlays the riff with searing flurries of fingerpicked fire. When the keyboardist returns, he's shifted his instrument back to the organ tonality. As he wraps warm chords around the guitar's fiery notes, the drummer accelerates the rhythm even further. A standing saint cries out, "Glory! Glory! Glory!" Another shouts, "Praise Him! Praise Him, you all!" while waving an outstretched arm toward the musicians. Many others are simply calling out, "Yes!" and "Go ahead!"

After twelve soundings of the riff, Evangelist Lofton stands and tentatively steps toward the center aisle. Gazing over the praising congregation, she pauses, making no attempt to speak. She knows that the Psalms say to praise the Lord "with stringed instruments and organs" and to "praise him upon the loud cymbals" (Psalm 150:4–5). So she lets the musical phrase roll eleven more times before even approaching the microphone. When she finally does so, the guitar and keyboards immediately cut their volume, thrusting the churning bass into the musical foreground. "Come on, Benson Chapel," she calls, inviting up the next choir. "Praise God!"

The bass and drums seem oblivious to her presence. So too do many saints, who are still crying "Hallelujah!" and "Glory!" Two riffs later, the guitarist eases out of the musical conversation with a flurry of descending notes. Then the organist hits a long sustained tone, setting up his closing phrase. The drums and bass catch the signal, and the three instruments go out as one. As they close, Sister Perry calls, "Glory to God! Praise our God!"

"Amen!" says Evangelist Lofton. "We thank God for the Bracey Singers! And as

15. "Told me to move, and I done that too!" cries Brother Samuel Bracey, as he begins his slow march down the center aisle. "I done done what you told me to do!" Behind him, his wife and singing partner, Sister Mary Bracey, feels the Spirit's touch and moves into the rapturous rhythms of holy dance. (Photo by Roland L. Freeman)

Benson Chapel is coming to the stand, let's give Bracey Singers another hand! Praise God!" The pews burst into quick applause, and the choir members start to move toward the front. While the saints are still clapping, Evangelist Lofton reviews the Bracey Singers' songs, quoting from each to draw the key messages from their three-song set.

Say, "If the Lord needs somebody,	(Amen!)
here am I—send me!"	(Yes!/Yes!)
Amen!	
Then they say, "Everything is going to be moving,	(Hallelujah!)
by the *power* of God!"	(Power of God!/Yes!)
Amen!	
And then they say, "I done done	(What you told me to do!)
what you told me to do, Lord!"	(Sure enough!)
Too many of us is doing what *man* telling us to do!	(Yeah!)
Time for us to do what the *Lord* will have us	
to do!	

Sister Perry responds with a loud, "That's right!" Evangelist Lofton, meanwhile, turns toward the singers assembling in the choir loft. "Here come another one of our choirs!" she exclaims. "Let's support Benson Chapel! Amen!" Evangelist Lofton no longer needs to prompt the applause, for the clapping begins as soon as she utters the church's name. "Praise God!" she adds as she steps back to her place in the pew.

As the applause subsides, the guitarist fills the growing quiet with a hushed melody, and one of the choir's singers takes the mike. Now it's *their* turn to stoke the fires of praise.

＊　＊　＊　＊　＊

"You told me to sing," says Brother Bracey, "and I'm doing that too. Lord, I done done what you told me to do." The singer steps to the church-front with no doubts about why he is there. His purpose is clear. Singing is the Lord's will. More precisely, it's the Lord's *command*. The song doesn't say, "You *asked* me to sing." Nor does it say, "*I* wanted to sing." Instead, it says, "You *told* me to sing." Singing stands as a *duty*, a holy obligation to follow the Lord's bidding. As Evangelist Lofton reminds the saints, worldly concerns should play no part in this equation. Only the will of God.

If singing is a duty, then what ends does it serve? What do gospel singers see as their purpose? The singers' answers are easily ascertained. One need only listen to the words they utter when standing before the congregation. At the Branchettes' anniversary, for example, Sister Mary Bracey declared, "We're here to lift up the name of Jesus!" Sister Lena Mae Perry announced, "We're coming to have a good time in the name of the Lord!" One of the Davis Singers proclaimed, "We're here tonight to have church!" And Evangelist Lofton asserted, "We're all here to give the name of Jesus the highest praise." Though taking many forms, these proclamations of purpose—like those voiced at most gospel programs—show a striking unanimity. All profess praise and ministry as the program's paramount goals. "I am not just singing and wasting time," explains Sister Perry of the Branchettes. "We are singing, first of all, to please God. [And] second of all, we're singing to help the people."[5]

These familiar goals immediately call to mind both the urgings of devotional leaders and the stated purposes of testimony. When coupled with singers' denials of self-serving "performance," they invite programgoers to hear songs not merely as artistic products or overheard dispatches to heaven, but also as conversation with the pews, as sung commentary that bears immediate relevance to the hearers' lives. "We sing not only for God," singers are tacitly saying. "We're also singing for you." They thus remind programgoers that song is *ministry* as well as *praise*, and that its messages merit special attention.

Nonetheless, it is praise that dominates the sung conversation, with singers typically defining themselves first and foremost as praise-givers and praise-leaders. They treat praise as a devotional duty and as a way of acknowledging the many blessings for which they are thankful. One of these blessings, of course, is the gift of song. Like all of the Lord's gifts, song is seen as a holy endowment, a talent that can be nurtured but not learned, a gift that separates "natural artists" from simple "practitioners." In the case of singing, the gift is that which distinguishes true "singers" from those who "just sing."

This blessing alone, explains Durham evangelist Evelyn Gilchrist, gives ample reason for praise. "You go [to programs] to sing to the glory of God," she says, "lifting Him up, giving God the praises. For He's the one that has *allowed you* to be able to sing. He's the one that has *anointed your voice* to sing. This is a great blessing, a gift from God, that you're able to sing. See, 'cause everybody can't sing. Some people *think* they can sing, and some people *try* to sing, and some go to school to *learn* to sing. But everybody's not *gifted* to sing."[6]

Those who are so blessed, like their praying, preaching and testifying counterparts, stand apart from their peers—in both skill *and* power. The first of these endowments, that of skill, is the most easily discerned. Saints say that the gift brings an easy command of tempo and tune, a deftness in improvisation, a nimbleness with harmony, a facility for learning by ear. This skill, in turn, marks the receiver for special service, for it gives the bearer a singular tool for touching the emotions. As I've already suggested, many saints contend that song can reach hearers in ways that spoken words cannot. Song's alluring artistry is said to break through the barriers of reason and logic so as to "open the doors of the heart," clearing a path for receipt of the lyrical message. With the way thus cleared, the message strikes deep, evoking response in even the most hardened of hearers. This response, in turn, promotes reflection. And reflection, say the saints, is the first step on the path to worship.

Hence the *power* of the gift, a power of affective effect, a power to touch. With this power comes a special responsibility, because the power comes with no constraints. *Any* gifted singer can stir the emotions. Toward any purpose. For evil or for good. For deception or for truth. For the soul's condemnation or for the soul's redemption. Just as with prayer, the Lord grants the gift but doesn't dictate its use. That decision rests wholly with the gift's receiver. Hence the sanctified singers' special charge. Recognizing the gift's affective power, singers must always be mindful of its use, always aware that stirred emotions must be *guided*, always careful to steer reflection toward worship. Toward this end, singers must do more than simply bear a spiritual message. They must also sing with spiritual intent. Only then can they "minister to the soul." Only then can they fulfill the gift's special mandate.

When speaking about prayer, I cited Elder Richardson's comments about the Spirit "riding" anointed words, giving them an affective impact that eloquence alone could never achieve. He likened the difference to that between a half and a full stick of dynamite. The gift alone—the rhetorical half stick—would rattle and shake, leaving a clear mark on the emotional landscape. But the gift with the anointing—the dynamite's full stick—would *explode*, shaking the soul to its very foundation. This is precisely what happens, say the saints, when the anointing empowers song. The anointing so magnifies the gift's affective impact that the gift alone seems feeble by comparison. Hence singing saints need not worry about being overpowered in the ongoing battle for listeners' souls. They know that the anointing gives them greater power. Those who "misuse" the gift, who appeal to the emotions but don't minister to the soul, can never use song quite as effectively as those who sing with the anointing. The anointing, in essence, gives saints the clear advantage.

＊　＊　＊　＊　＊

For a long time, I didn't understand the difference between the gift and the anointing. Having heard many singers speak about the "gift of song," I had assumed that the gift came *with* the anointing. Just like with preachers and the call. Saints have long said that preachers, when truly called by God, are mystically endowed with the ability to preach. They don't have to learn to preach; nor need they attend school to be certified to preach. Instead, they need only be *called*. The Lord is said to have declared, "Those whom I call, I qualify." Hence, at least in preaching, competence comes with the calling.[7] I assumed the same held true for singing. I was wrong.

What I hadn't taken into account was the unique nature of the call and the freedom that comes with the gift. This must have been evident in my questions during a conversation with Pastor Rosie Wallace Brown. Pastor Brown is the founder and pastor of Philadelphia's First Church of Love, Faith and Deliverance; she's also a gifted singer, having recorded many albums with both the Imperial Singers and her own choir. We were sitting in Pastor Brown's church office, talking about the "flow" that comes when the Spirit provides a preacher's words, a flow she likened to a faucet, a flow that also marks prayer, testimony, and songwriting.

She explained that she had seen people "delivered by the power of God" through all of these forms. Then she paused.

"And you know, [there's] something else I wanted to say too," she remarked. I looked up from the notes I was writing and saw that she was gazing right at me, her eyes testifying to the importance of what she was about to say. I laid down my pen and listened. Then Pastor Brown's calm, quiet voice filled the room, her words conveying the same serene assurance that is so evident in her preaching. "You know," she began,

> Just like you have preachers,
>> you have *preachers*.
> You have teachers,
>> you have *teachers*.
> You have singers,
>> you have *singers*.
> By that I mean,
>> you have some that sing just because they have a voice,
>> or they're getting good money for it,
>> or whatever.

Pastor Brown chuckled at the thought of gospel singers getting "good money" for their singing and added, "If you get good money for gospel singing!" Then she was once again serious.

> But then you have others
>> who have really committed their lives to Jesus Christ.
>>> And they walk with Him.
> They have *consecrated* lives.
> These are the individuals whom God trusts his anointing on.

Perhaps sensing the look of emergent understanding on my face, Pastor Brown rushed to elaborate, her voice quickening.

> Everybody don't possess the anointing of God,
>> and the power of God.
> They might have good *voices*—
> We got preachers who are very articulate.
> Okay?
> They know this Bible from Genesis to Revelation,
>> and they can tell you about every patriarch that ever lived!
> But they have *no anointing*.
> There's a difference in the *anointing* and the *gift*.
> You have people who are gifted to speak,
>> gifted to sing,
>> gifted to play instruments.
> But they don't have the *anointing of God*.

And it's the anointing of God that *destroys* the yoke.
There is a difference there.
And then you have those that are gifted *and* anointed.
You follow me.

Though Pastor Brown phrased her last comment more like a statement than a question, I nodded and murmured an affirmation. I *was* following her and was finally beginning to see the complexity in the Spirit's workings.

And then you have those
    who don't necessarily have a gift to play or to sing—
        they might sing and their voices might be cracking.
But they have such an *anointing*.
    Until yokes are broken.
People are *encouraged*!
People are *lifted*!
The power of God just *takes over* the congregation!
You follow what I'm saying?

Again I nodded, thinking about the many feeble-voiced singers whom I'd seen openly move a churchful of saints. But Pastor Brown wasn't yet finished.

I've seen this many times.
I've *experienced* this—
There've been times when my voice was just completely *gone*, Glenn.
Hoarse.
Couldn't talk.
Couldn't sing.
But I *had to minister*.
And the Lord would anoint me—
    believe me, you talk about depending on the anointing!

Once again, Pastor Brown broke into laughter. This time, I did too. And once again, when she resumed talking, her voice was slow and serious.

But the Lord would *anoint so*,
    because I would be doing *nothing* in self.
It would be *totally* God!
And when God can have *full control* of an individual—
    man, woman, boy, or girl—
        we'll see *exploits*.
He will do *exploits* through their lives!
He will do *great* things.
    And people will be *blessed*,
        and helped,

when God has full charge.
That's what He wants—*full charge*.
So there is a *difference*,
   for one who is anointed.

This time Pastor Brown's pause suggested closure. After waiting a few seconds, I pressed the point, still searching for understanding. The question I asked suggests how little I understood at the time. Caught up in the distinction between the gift and the anointing, I completely overlooked all that I'd heard about the soul-jarring intensity of conversion. For some reason, I wasn't linking the *anointing* with *being saved*. Instead, I was thinking of anointment as an extension of the gift, as a kind of "ritual stage" through which gifted saints passed on their journey toward holiness. I didn't yet understand the deep and certain "knowing" that saints say marks communion with the Spirit.

"When did you realize . . . ," I began, groping for words. "Or, when did you. . . . In looking back on your life as a singer, before you were called to preach, when did you realize that you were anointed as well as gifted?"

"Well," answered Pastor Brown, the sigh evident in her voice, "for a long while, all I knew [was] that the Lord was using my life."

But as I began to get in the Word more,
   and talked with others,
     who had pioneered,
     and started before me,
     and the Lord was using their lives—
   and I saw the difference,
     in watching the lives of others.
I saw people who were extremely talented,
   but with something missing.
And I would see another one that wasn't quite as talented,
   but looked like they had *everything*.
And that's when the Lord—
   when I got into the Word—
     the Lord began to open it up to me.
And then the Lord showed me my place that I had in Him.
   And how He was *entrusting* this,
     as I walked with Him.
It was based on my walking with Him,
   my staying in the Word,
   my wanting to be *consecrated* and be *separated*.
And the Lord said, "If you choose"—
   this is what He told me—
     "If you chose to walk with me,
       I'll anoint you.
       And I'll give you *power*."

And He said, "Not only for you,
　　but [for all] those who will walk with Me."
So it's for *anybody* who wants to yield their lives totally to God.
　　For God's purpose,
　　for God's will.

With this closing couplet, Pastor Brown leaned back in her chair and gently smiled. Before she was saved, she had noticed the difference between gifted and anointed singers, noticed that "something was missing" in the lives of those with only the gift. She had also realized that she was among their number. And so she studied the Word and sought the Lord, hoping to cross that threshold of difference. In the course of her seeking, the Lord told her—in clear and unambiguous terms—that if she walked with Him, He would not only anoint her, but would also grant her *power*. The power that was missing in her singing. The power that would break the yoke.

Pastor Brown's words hit to the heart of my misunderstanding. Without ever pointing out my error, she turned my question from one asking her when she realized she was anointed, to one asking when she realized that she *wasn't* anointed. At the time, however, I didn't grasp the significance of her shift. And judging by her answer to my next question, she knew that I didn't. So when I asked her when in her career did she actually hear the Lord's message, she made sure that I understood that the anointing came the moment she was saved.

"Now when the Lord revealed that to you," I asked, "was that prior to your really becoming a singer, on a more or less semiprofessional basis, or was that at the point when you decided that you would go into the ministry?" "Well," she explained, the sound of resolution in her voice,

I had the experience of singing because I had the *talent*.
And it was during my singing career that the Lord saved me.
I wasn't saved when I first started singing.
I was singing because I had the talent,
　　and I was playing [the piano] because I had the talent.
That's why I know the difference.
I had the personal *experience*.
And it's when I let the Lord come into my life,
　　when I accepted Christ,
　　　　and started conforming to His Word,
　　　　and allowed Him to become the Lord of my life,
　　is when the Lord *revealed* to me the difference
　　　　between the gift and the anointing,
　　　　　　the talent and the anointing.
And the gift *with* the anointing is great.

There it was. Like Evangelist Dorothy Jackson, many years her junior, Pastor Rosie Wallace Brown sang with the gift but not the anointing. She sang because she had the talent, because she enjoyed singing, because she was drawn to the music of the Wards and the Davis Sisters and other gospel artists. But not because she saw her singing as a form of ministry. Not because she wanted to make the fullest possible use of her God-given gift. These weren't even considerations. Pastor Brown's reasons for singing were far more mundane.

All this changed when she was saved, for then she realized both her mandate and her potential. She also realized that she had contented herself with performances that in retrospect seemed shallow and lacking in power. Now Pastor Brown could look back and tell the difference. And now she could more easily distinguish between singers who were anointed, those who were singing with good intent but without understanding (like she once was), and those who exploited the *appearances* of anointment without having the power themselves.

This was the next topic in our conversation. After speaking a bit more about song as ministry, I asked Pastor Brown about the overt "enactment" of anointment in gospel. For outsiders like myself, I suggested, this enactment—the shouting, the crying, the running down the aisles—has become one of the defining features of gospel performance. "Could you talk about *that*," I inquired, "in light of what you said about 'anointment' versus merely 'gifted but not anointed'?"

Smiling in response to my question, Pastor Brown leaned forward and rested both hands on the large, open Bible laying on her desk. Her words, elegant in their simplicity, struck to the very heart of the matter. More than a decade later, after countless conversations with saints about this very issue, I have yet to hear a more eloquent explanation. "Well, you know," she began,

> There's one scripture that speaks of having a *form* of godliness.
> But denying the power thereof.
> Now there are many who are very serious about what they're doing.
> But there are many who are not.
> And they've learned how to do it.
> They can do it very well.
> Some are professionals in emotionally exciting the group, the congregation, or the audience.
> They know how to do this very well.
> Others are very, very serious.
> They're motivated by the Spirit.
> As it is in gospel singing,
> so it is in preaching,
> and—you name it![8]

Though Pastor Brown chuckled a bit at her assertion that those who specialize in "emotional excitement" pervade *all* realms of the church, her eyes remained deadly serious. As she cataloged the categories of false performance, reprising the list with which she began the conversation, she slowly shook her head, as if to convey a sense of deep disappointment. Her head was still shaking when she began talking again.

You have those who have a form of godliness,
　but [are] denying the power thereof.
Then you have those who are *full* of the *Spirit* of God.
　They're full of the Spirit of God.
And those that are,
　they more or less minister *to the spirit*.
Those who have a form of godliness,
　they more or less minister *to the emotions*.
You know, they get people emotionally excited and that kind of thing.
　But they don't *give* them anything
　　to meditate on,
　　　you know.
When your spirit is ministered to,
　your spirit will *grasp* whatever is going forth.
It'll *leave* with you when you leave that place.
　And it'll get with you in your car,
　　and go home with you,
　　　and you'll meditate on that thing.
You understand.
That's when you have *really been reached*,
　and you'll *apply* that thing.
There's a difference.[9]

Pastor Brown uttered this closing line with an air of finality. Her point was made. Just as there is a difference between those singing with only the gift and those singing with the anointing, so too is there a difference in their impact. Those *without* the anointing can only minister to the *emotions*. They can excite their hearers, stir their passion, perhaps even elicit a shout. But the feelings they evoke, as Evangelist Deborah Yarborough asserted in remarks I've already cited, "won't be with you long." They're too shallow, too grounded in self, too easily displaced by worldly concern. As Pastor Brown declares, they give you nothing to meditate on.

In contrast, singers *with* the anointing minister to the *spirit*. Their messages are filled with meditative substance, giving saints something far greater than mere "feeling." This elusive "something" is also greater than the words that convey it, for it carries the mysterious power of Spirit, a power that saints say penetrates far beyond emotion. Such is the special power of the anointing. And such is the special responsibility of the anointed singer.

＊　＊　＊　＊　＊

Pastor Brown's remarks neatly chart the essential relationship between praise and ministry. Singers praise to celebrate God's goodness, to give thanks for their blessings, to joyfully acknowledge their special gift. With this acknowledgment comes an awareness of responsibility, a realization that the gift carries with it an obligation for appropriate use. The most appropriate such use is ministry. Saints say that God doesn't grant the gift merely to hear His own praises. Rather, He grants it so that saints might be strengthened, so that burdens might be relieved, so that souls might be saved. Hence when singers describe their purpose in singing, they almost always frame their remarks in terms of gospel's power to touch, teach, soothe, inspire, lift burdens, and bring joy. They speak of song not merely as *artistry* with the power to stir emotions, but as *ministry* with the power to effect real change. In essence, sanctified singers treat song as a devotional *tool*, as an instrument of impact and influence. From the singers' perspective, programgoers are never merely listeners who appreciate and applaud. Instead, they are *targets* of the Word. Singers aren't only singing *to* and *with* them; they are also singing *for* them.

This sense of purpose hinges, as Pastor Brown points out, on whether singers are "gifted and anointed" or merely "gifted." After reviewing Pastor Brown's remarks, Evangelist Evelyn Gilchrist—one of my key consultants and readers—suggested that perhaps I ought to add a bit more on the different impact that these two groups of singers have on programgoers. The difference, she explained, lies in congregation members' *experience*. When I asked for elaboration, Evangelist Gilchrist offered to bring me the explanation that she had already written so that I could add it to the discussion.

"Many singers that are gifted (or have talent to sing) sing without repentance," she writes. "We are known to sing because we came from families of great singers of old, singing notes with just the pat of the foot for time and music.

"This kind of singing with feeling and emotions can and will cause you to clap your hands, pat your feet, cry if you want to, close your eyes and dance a little—this is that getting under your skin. That's why you will sometime see and hear singers put their hands upon their heads and rub their face as though there may be an itch, or even wring their hands, or get down on their knees singing with many expressions of the song. Now this kind of feeling sometimes will cause the people in any congregation to stand and yell out 'Sing y'all!' or say 'Come on now!' And when the singing is all over and the people are shaking hands with the singers, you will hear them say 'Your singing really made me feel good' or 'Wooo-wee, man, you sang up something tonight!'

"Now here is the difference with repentance.

"First of all, you really know the Lord for yourself, because He is your Lord and Savior. He's the one that anointed and cultivated your voice for singing, and that's awesome and deep. Now when you sing, you sing with the anointing of the Holy Ghost and fire—the *words* are *powerful*, and the *sound* is out of this world (heavenly), and this anointing destroys every yoke of bondage. While you are singing with the anointing, the spirit of God will touch that person or those that are going through great tests of pain and sickness, depression, loneliness, broken hearts, no finance, living in poverty, etc. As they hear the words of the song, for example:

He's the joy of my salvation,
    Yes He is.

He's the joy of my salvation,
  Yes He is.
Just to know He died for me
  Now my soul's been set free
He's the joy of my salvation,
  Yes He is.

"People *will* relate to the *words*—not the music only. The pain and sickness just goes away, [yielding] an outcry of 'I thank you, Jesus, for healing me!' Another will say, 'God, I just want to thank you for my deliverance! Thank you, Jesus, for loving me and giving me another chance to be ready for your coming.'

"It's not under the skin any more. It's not an itch or a wringing of the hands. It's the praises to God in the highest of 'Hallelujah,' glory from the depth of your heart and soul, praises going up and blessings coming down, that will cause you to run when ain't nobody chasing you. You will even continue to dance on after the music stops. You are drunk now in the Spirit with joy, unspeakable joy—a sweet peace, love and happiness you've longed for—it's all yours, a little heaven on earth. Only Jesus can do things like these, with a song through the songster. Amen."

Singing with the anointing gives the words *power*, Evangelist Gilchrist declares. Power to break the yokes, erase the pain, invite the joy. With this power comes responsibility, as song becomes a tool of ministry and singing becomes strategy. Most sanctified singers say that they rarely sing without first prayerfully considering the specifics of the singing situation. They don't just go into a program with an "a-and-b selection" already in mind, and then sing those selections without regard to the moment. Instead, they step into the church with eyes and ears open, trying to discern what the congregation "needs." They listen to the testimonies, look at the faces, assess the overall spirit. Then they choose their songs accordingly. Hence even song sets eschew predetermined "programs." Like the services of which they are a part, they are not written "on a piece of paper." Instead, most are tailored to the occasion, strategically crafted to minister to perceived needs.

* * * * *

When I first asked the Branchettes about song selection, Sister Lena Mae Perry answered by talking about ministry. Instead of talking about style or repertoire or the songs performed by other groups, she spoke first about the congregation.

"There are people in every church that might have a problem," she began, speaking reflectively and then pausing. "Now the Branchettes are a little bit different from some groups. Some groups go to church for *competition*. Like some of our younger choirs that are singing—they go for competition. But when we go to a church, we go to . . ." Again she paused.

"If there is somebody there that might have a problem, somebody might not feel well, somebody might be financially burdened, somebody might be lonely, somebody might seem like they don't have a friend [and] that nobody cares, and the songs that we try to pick to sing—we try to sing songs that will lift the burdens of each one of those individuals.

"I have been on an occasion where I had gone in this church, and I was hesitant to go because I had visited [there] once before, and it seemed as though there was not too much spirit in the church. It was just *dry*. The preacher preached, people prayed, people sang—[but] everybody was just sitting *still*. Just sitting there *looking*. Nobody praising the Lord. So later, some of them [at that church] sent word for me; they wanted me to come, and be on a program there.

"I said, 'Now Lord, I don't want to tell the people I can't come.' I said, 'But Lord, now, how am I going to go in this church, and I'm looking in the face of this great big audience, and they're so dry, and not moving? And the ladies with their white gloves on, and their hands in their lap? And the men just sitting so still? And nobody saying "Amen" or "Praise the Lord"?' I said, 'Now Lord'—I consulted the Lord about it. I said, 'Lord, what can I do? How can I get *through* to these folk? What am I going to *sing*?'

"So I went on there that Sunday morning. And as time grew near for me to sing, I said, 'Mmmm!' I was steady talking to the Lord. Said, 'Now Lord, am I in the right place today?' Said, 'Lord, I know there's a reason You have me here.' You know, sometimes you just got to talk to God like a natural man! I said, 'Lord, I'm trusting in you, Lord.'

"So as I began to get up and sing—and I knew in that church that there were problem people. There was kids there that needed something that they hadn't been used to getting, something from the Lord.

"So I got up there and I began to sing. And I saw women and men with their hands in their laps as if they couldn't move. They were sitting there as if they—you know—were so proud that nothing could move them. And I began to sing the song, 'Because He Lives, I Can Face Tomorrow.' And I sang it with all I had! I put everything in it! And I said, 'Lord'—to myself, I said—'Lord, this song isn't moving, Lord! Why did you give me this one? This is not moving these folk!'

"I *sang*, and after a while, I looked back there—and I don't know where them white gloves went, but them hands was up in the air!" So too were both of Sister Perry's as she reached this point in the story. Waving her hands back and forth, she continued. "I mean, that church just *come alive*! Then I said, 'Lord, I thank You!' It just came *alive*!"

"That's the way the Branchettes do. You can just about tell a problem person when you start singing. Because they're totally quiet. But when the song that you sing satisfies their condition, they begin to *move*. And then you know you have gained something by this song that you have sang.

"[For] some people, it takes a slow song with lots of meaning. For some, it takes a faster beat, as to get them stirred. And once you accomplish this, once you see the reactions—because when I'm singing, I watch the reactions of people. And Ethel and I have certainly seen a lot of hands go up in the air. We've certainly sang to people that have really cried. We have sang to peoples that has confessed that they felt bad when they come to church, but after we had sang they felt so much better.

"So singing is like a lawyer, a doctor, a teacher, and a nurse. Because it's sort of like a healing process. For those that feel real bad, those songs can be as a doctor— it removes the pain. They get into the Spirit till they forget about the pain. Somebody might need to be soothed, as if a nurse tried to sort of smooth out their condition. Or a lawyer, where maybe somebody was in trouble, and the song we sang made them forget all the trouble. And they could sort of smile again. And some of it is like burning fire—because we sing sometime until it's so hot under their seats, they have to get up!"

Both Sister Perry and Sister Elliott started laughing at this point. Then Sister Perry went on, pressing toward her conclusion.

"It's just several things. It's just a picture that's painted there while you're up front singing, and you watch the audience. There's a picture painted of their minds, and you can tell if this person's had a problem, or if they were sick, or if the children weren't acting right, or if something just didn't go right on their jobs. That song will sort of just *lift*, and they get up—and when you know anything, they're just going! They're just going! And the reason we know that it has helped is because once we're outside, several people come to us and express this thing to us. And then when Ethel and I leave this church, we feel like we have accomplished something."

As Sister Elliott nodded in agreement, Sister Perry stopped talking. The length of her pause indicated that she had said all that needed to be said. I, too, nodded, satisfied that she had done just that.[10]

* * * * *

"It's like a picture," Sister Perry explained, "a picture painted before you while you're up front singing." A picture of faces, perhaps, but also a portrait of minds. A portrait that captures more than mere facade. A portrait that reveals to the discerning eye inner condition, testifying to sorrow, to pain, to worry, to anger, to confusion. Singers say that the Spirit grants saints the ability to "read" the picture that stretches before them, sharpening their perceptions, endowing them with mystical insight. "Something inside" lets them know the congregation's needs; "something inside" guides their song selection to meet these needs. I've heard many singers say they don't know *why* they're led to sing certain songs. But they sing them anyway, wondering all the while about the songs' travels, watching for a response in the congregation. Sometimes, as Sister Perry's story attests, the consequences are obvious. Those gloveless hands rising in the air amply testified to the song's impact. At other times, the consequences remain hidden, perhaps revealed only after the service's conclusion, perhaps never revealed at all. Many a time, Sister Perry explains, "somebody will come [up after a service] and say, 'I don't know how you all knew it, but that song was just for me.'" But even when no one testifies to the songs' impact, singers say that they still don't worry. For they *know* that their songs moved out to minister. "God's Word does not return void," they remind each other. "*Somebody* got a blessing through those songs."[11]

Though singers often cloak their talk of ministry in terms of "lifting burdens" and "easing troubles," they readily acknowledge that their singing also serves a host of other ministerial functions. Perhaps foremost among these is simply bringing joy. The songs don't only touch those who are particularly burdened; they also touch those who are not. Saints often say that songs raise spirits even when spirits aren't low, that they strike chords of recognition and resonance that send delight cascading through the body. While this joy is often sparked by the Spirit, it just as often is not, rising instead from simple emotions, from the "mental" as opposed to the "spiritual" part of the self. But this joy too, the saints remind us, is to be valued. Both for itself and for the praises it elicits, which themselves can set in motion the reflective cycle that invites the Spirit. When tempered with spiritual understanding, even this joy—however temporary—is precious.

Many singers also cite *teaching* as an important aspect of their singing ministry. Sister Lena Mae Perry, for example, likens song to "a teacher," saying that it often provides answers to questions that human friends and counselors cannot resolve. In like manner, Nightingales singer Jojo Wallace contends that the Spirit uses anointed singers to teach the Word through song. Like many of his songwriting counterparts, Brother Wallace maintains that the most effective teaching songs are those in which the Spirit Himself had a hand in writing. "All of [those songs] got messages that folk can draw from," he says. "Every one of them. But they come from God—[they] don't come from man. We're not smart enough."[12] But the Lord, say the saints, certainly *is*. That's why He helps with the songwriting—not only to give songs uplifting power, but also to make them instructional. Saints say that songs can elaborate on biblical lessons in a particularly inviting manner, thus reminding listeners of their immediate relevance. In this regard, singers often cite the apostle Paul's advice to "let the word of Christ dwell in you richly in all wisdom; teaching and admonishing one another in psalms and hymns and spiritual songs, singing with grace in your hearts to the Lord" (Colossians 3:16).

Just as saints use songs to teach "one another," so too do they use them to reach the unsaved. I've already mentioned the widespread belief that many who attend programs would "never put their foot in a church." Saints often say that singing can reach these listeners in ways that preaching cannot, if only because many programgoers would never sit through a sermon. They *will*, however, listen to singing and even go out of their way to hear it. Hence singing's special effectiveness. Well aware that many listeners attend programs solely to be entertained, sanctified singers fill their "entertainment" with clearly-stated Biblical messages, thus effectively "preaching" in song. This way, singers reason, even if listeners won't read the Word or hear it preached, they will still be exposed to its power.

* * * * *

"You know, a lot of times you don't even have to hear a sermon," asserts Sister Ethel Elliott during a conversation about the power of song. "You can just hear a song, and that'll just lift you right up! Seems just like it'll just pick you on up. I know a lot of times [when] we go sing, sometimes I tell Lena Mae, I say, 'Let's don't sing today. Let's just give a donation, and go on.' Because I be feeling so *bad*, you know. But I tell you the truth—when we get up there and get started, seems like everything just lift right off of me!"

"The songs are for us too," adds Sister Lena Mae Perry, nodding in agreement.

"Just lift right off of me!" repeats Sister Elliott. "And I can just go right on with the program, and just *sing all I want to!*"

" 'Cause sometimes the songs are for *us*," concludes Sister Perry. "As well as for those other people."[13]

* * * * *

Thus far, our discussion of ministry has focused on outreach, on singers ministering to others. Yet when singers talk about the target of their efforts, they're usually quick to include themselves. After all, they too need strength and counsel; they too find relief, uplift, and inspiration in song. I've heard scores of singers close their sets by remarking that when they first stepped up to sing, they were feeling "low and downhearted." But by the time they finished singing, they felt uplifted and revived. Such testimony echoes words that often come from the pews, when congregation members tell of feeling so bad that they even considered not coming to church. But when they got in the car and started singing to themselves, they could feel their burdens "rolling away." The process is precisely the same for gifted singer and ungifted saint; the special attributes of the gift have no bearing on the outcome. All that matters is the conversation of praise that singing begins.

Singing for self-ministry *does* assume special significance, however, when the singer is singing before a congregation. If only because any evidence of deep absorption or spiritual "signs" becomes part of the communicated message. Though not *intended* as messages, these behaviors nonetheless suggest involvement and intensity. Every private tear, every head-bowed wave, every eye-closed shake of the head becomes a public statement. So too does every shout, every holy step, every moment of speechless ecstasy. When saints in the pews show these signs, attention focuses and then turns away. But when singers at the church-front show them, attention focuses and abides. The signs become part of the enacted whole, referencing and tempering the messages conveyed by text and tune. While singers may say that they're simply "singing until they feel it," and thus are not *trying* to communicate anything through their actions, saints in the pews are reading every enacted cue and assigning them explicit meanings.

Of the many messages conveyed by singers' actions, none carry greater weight than those that suggest the Spirit's ministrations. Each such sign becomes an indicator of personal holiness, a statement that declares, in effect, "This singer bears the Lord's approval." Many such messages, of course, are not accepted at face value, their veracity cast in doubt by factors suggesting fakery (e.g., knowledge that the singer is "not living the life," or signs indicating that the evidenced behaviors are in fact consciously controlled). But many such messages *are* taken as truth. These, in turn, command sanctified hearers' complete attention, for they suggest spiritual endorsement of the sung or spoken message. Awareness of such "approval" maximizes the message's impact, prompting an extra measure of reflection, perhaps encouraging extra efforts toward application. Signs of the Spirit thus effectively empower the words they accompany, driving them deeper into the consciousness of hearing (and believing) saints.

Needless to say, this is precisely the outcome that sanctified singers seek. Singers *want* their words to touch; they *want* them to prompt reflection. But the intervening mechanism—the appearance of spiritual signs—is out of their hands. They can only sing so as to *invite* the anointing; they can neither cause it to occur nor control the forms it takes. But by sincerely engaging in praise, by singing "until they feel it," by ministering—in effect—to their own souls as well as to those of the congregation, they *can* extend the invitation. If the Spirit does then choose to touch and does so in a way that makes the touch publicly evident, the cycle of spiritual purpose is complete. Thus by ministering to themselves, singers can ultimately (if inadvertently) increase the effectiveness of their ministry to others.

What of those singers who don't know the Spirit, but choreograph their performances to suggest that they do? Certainly the temptation for such manipulation is great. The lure of prestige, enhanced reputation, and audience acclaim draw many a singer down this path. But saints are quick to point out that the path's final destination is damnation. They say that those who travel this road sow confusion all along their way, claiming ministry with their mouths but mocking it with their lives. In so doing, they condemn themselves not only for their deception, but also for the seeds they have sown—the souls turned from the path of righteousness, the souls lost in bewilderment and uncertainty.

"A lot of your audience [at gospel programs] come for showmanship," laments Evangelist Dorothy Jackson, speaking from the vantage point of a once-unsaved singer. "And then there are some that come to really be lifted up through the sung praises. [But] when you get the ones that do all of this 'performing,' [then] when the real ones come along—[the ones] giving the glory to God instead of man—then there's a *confusion*. Because [many audience members] want their showmanship instead of the real thing. For them, it's kind of hard to detect the real from the unreal. And this is why so many people are confused."[14]

Evangelist Jackson suggests that those who can't tell the difference between the real and the unreal don't know whom to follow. They *do* know, however, that the showmanship is exciting. Hence this is what they pursue, perhaps assuming that the Spirit lies behind the show, and that the experience observed (and maybe even felt) represents the fullness of grace. Saints say that these confused hearers run the risk of contenting themselves with what they know, of confusing "ministry to the emotions" with "ministry to the soul." If, as a result, they fail to find salvation, then their blood will stain the hands of those who falsely guided them. As Evangelist Jackson observed in her remarks on spiritual duty, misused gifts and denied ministry can yield only condemnation.

Many a saint has earnestly asked the Lord to "not let me say or do anything that would disencourage anybody." Many others have chorused the old congregational favorite that declares:

I don't want nobody stumbling over my life,
  stumbling over my life, stumbling over my life.
I don't want nobody stumbling over my life.
  That is why I pray so hard.

The prayer and the song both convey the same message. Let me live a life that others can follow to holiness. Let me live a life that won't lead others to stumble. Or, for singers, let me live the life that I sing about. Saints often say that they are called to be living examples of God's way, proofs of the possibility of holiness in an unholy world. Realizing that they are always being watched by the unsaved, they try to live their lives "without spot or wrinkle." This responsibility rests particularly heavily on the shoulders of singers, for they have been given a gift and a mission that constantly brings them before the public, thus casting the harsh spotlight of scrutiny on both their public and private lives. Not faking on stage, say sanctified singers, is not enough to keep others from stumbling. They must "live holy" *every* moment of their lives, realizing that the respect accorded to their artistry means that *there is no offstage.* Every misstep, every stumble—no matter how private—potentially invites emulation. That's why singers ask the Lord to help them live their entire lives as ministry. Knowing that they're always on somebody's stage, they strive to make their lives living lessons in holiness.[15]

✷　✷　✷　✷　✷

Quartet lead Smiley Fletcher was talking about his years as an unsaved singer when he contrasted his onstage appearance with his offstage life. After admitting that his "main objective" at that time was "just to go out and have a good time" and "maybe to try to impress some girl," Brother Fletcher declared, "I was straddling the fence. I was what you call a 'great pretender.' Which was nothing but phony. No sooner you get through singing and come out of church, [than] you was looking for the first nightclub, the first bar, or a speakeasy."

Having heard Brother Fletcher's testimony many times before, I wondered aloud about the precedent for his actions, given that his quartet was still quite young and inexperienced at that time.

"See," he responded, "the little local group wasn't the only one doing it. The big-time professional groups was doing it. They was out there singing for a living. They were singing for a living. They'd have a big concert, and get eight hundred, nine hundred dollars. And then they'd find them a club. Or go to a hotel. And have a party in their hotel. Passing around a bottle and all that! I've been right there with them."

Shaking his head at the memory, he added, "I could name some of them. But it wouldn't be right for me to do that."

"And this is what they was doing," he continued, returning to the story. "So by me being young—[and] they was the big-timers, professional groups—I thought *that's what you were supposed to do*. Until I found out better."

At the time, Brother Fletcher was an aspiring young singer. Impressed by the fame of the "big groups," he readily followed their lead, joining them at their parties, emulating their lifestyles. After all, *they were successful*. They boasted fine clothes, adoring audiences, record contracts, and lives that must have appeared decidedly exotic. And best of all, they were making their living by singing! Surely, he thought, they were blessed.

But then, Brother Fletcher explained, the Lord started to "really deal" with him. Soon thereafter, he accepted Christ into his life and was saved, sanctified, and filled with the Holy Ghost. Then he discovered, as he put it, that "I wasn't having the fun that I thought I was when I was out in the world." Then he discovered, he explained, what being blessed *really* meant.

"As they say, the Lord takes care of all babies and fools," Brother Fletcher added, speaking after a moment of quiet reflection. "I was a fool then. [And] He took care of me. Now I just thank God that He spared me to live as long as I did and gave me a chance to get my life together. Now I'm doing whatever *He* wants me to do."[16]

* * * * *

Brother Smiley Fletcher closed our conversation by declaring that he was now doing whatever the Lord wanted him to do. Samuel and Mary Bracey closed their performance at the Branchettes' anniversary by singing the same thing. Their words echo a prayerful petition that runs throughout sanctified song, prayer, and preaching, a request that saints be "consecrated to the Lord's service." Saved singers often say that they keep this prayer on their tongue every time they are called to sing. Knowing that every situation is different and that every congregation has different needs, they pray to the Lord for guidance, asking what He would have them do.

"Very rarely do I go on that stage without consulting Him," testifies Brother Jojo Wallace of the Sensational Nightingales.

I say, "Lord,
   I don't know what to feed your children, Lord."
I talk to Him like I'm talking to you.
"I just don't know it."
I get to myself, most of the time,
   because I can meditate better with myself.
And I say, "I don't know how to feed them.
   You call the words that You want them to hear,
     to be blessed by."

And He do it every night!
Glenn, *every night*!
I don't care where it's at—
   it can be a hallelujah church—
I don't care where—
   a quiet, seditty crowd—
Every night, He calls them, He calls them.
It's a miracle![17]

The "miracle" of which Brother Wallace speaks is the same miracle that envelops Deacon Eldridge when the Spirit provides Him with words of prayer. It's the same miracle that called preachers experience when revelation "rolls" from their mouths, and that inspired songwriters know when lyrics "leap" from their pens. All these saints describe the experience of becoming vessels of the Lord's will. All tell how the Spirit guides them in using their gift, sometimes suggesting choices, sometimes elaborating ideas, sometimes actually providing the words. And all point out that ministry is never a solo process. The Holy Spirit is always present; the anointing is always near at hand. Their ministry is thus always collaborative, with saint and Spirit working hand in hand.

Many sanctified singers say that this collaboration makes itself evident as soon as they step before a congregation. As I suggested earlier, they speak of a mystical knowing that guides their selection of songs and words, often leading them to change the structure of their planned set, sometimes even prompting them to change the arrangement of rehearsed songs. Brother Wallace tells how the Spirit provides the words for his cross-aisle testimonies; Sister Perry testifies how the Spirit guides her choice of songs. Neither account is in any way unusual. If anything, they represent the norm. Virtually all saved singers tell the same story, describing how they come prepared to sing one thing and then find themselves singing another, knowing that Spirit has willed the change.

"When we're riding, going to the church, we'll sit there and we'll say, 'What are we going to sing when we get there?'" says Sister Lena Mae Perry, telling her version of this often-heard narrative. "But, Glenn, do you know that we never know what we're going to sing when we get there? We'll write down something. But most of the time we sing *opposite* of what we write down. Ethel will tell me, say, 'Lena Mae, I *asked* you what we were going to sing!'"

Both of the Branchettes laugh at this point, recalling what is clearly a common scene. Then Sister Perry continues. "And when we get up there, we just sing. We get up there, and we just sing. And as you sing, then deep on the inside in your mind, songs just start *rolling*. You know. Songs just start rolling over in your mind; they start rolling over in your mind. And you hit the right song. And you know that it's no one but the Lord doing that!"[18]

The songs start to roll, churning in the mind, shuttling from one to another and finally stopping at the one that is "right." The one that will draw a tear; the one that will lift a burden; the one that will stir a soul. The Spirit knows what songs lie in the mind—Sister Perry suggests—and knows what needs lie in the congregation. So the

Spirit puts the two together and reveals the appropriate choices to the singer. The singer then completes the collaboration by singing what the Spirit reveals. "You told me to sing, and I'm doing that too," says the old song. At least one singer has suggested to me that the verse "You told me *what* to sing, and I'm doing that too" would be just as apt.

The Spirit grants the gift; the singer nurtures and develops it. The singer crafts a repertoire; the Spirit helps guide its use. The Spirit suggests songs for specific occasions; and the singer sings them, filling them with a soulful spirit that is uniquely the singer's own. Throughout, the singer stays prayerfully alert, always listening for guidance, always ready to change course as the Spirit decrees. "That comes under the heading of being flexible in the Spirit," declares Pastor Rosie Wallace Brown. "You must be. Because only God knows the needs of the people."[19]

Chapter 16

False Purpose

"We Didn't Come for No Form or Fashion"

At Evangelist Lofton's call and the congregation's warm applause, the four Jerusalem Travelers stride down the center aisle. Dressed for the occasion in sharply tailored purple suits, the Travelers hail from the Greater Six Run Missionary Baptist Church in the nearby town of Turkey. They've been singing together for twenty-six years and are long-time friends of the Branchettes. Three of the four are brothers.

The front two men quickly move toward the deacons' corner, where they retrieve a guitar and bass from their black plastic cases. As they each move toward amplifiers on opposite sides of the center aisle, the quartet's other two members busy themselves aligning four chrome mike stands. While they're moving mikes, the guitarist and bass player check their tunings. A baby in the pews starts to cry. Somebody calls out, "Thank You, Jesus."

"Check one, check one." The lead's deep voice booms from the working microphones. "Test one, test one." The baritone's does the same. "Thank You, Jesus," says the sister in the pews once again, adding a passing note of praise to the cross-aisle's mundane workings. "Check." The guitarist starts to finger a quiet, wandering melody. "Thank You, Jesus," whispers the baritone singer into his mike.

Then the quartet's lead, Brother Sonnie Stevens, starts to speak. His voice is soft, humble, almost hesitant. Echoing the opening words of Sister Love and the St. James Gospel Choir, he begins on a note of praise and tribute.

Giving honor to our Lord and savior Jesus Christ,	(Thank You, Lord)
We're happy to be here on the Branchettes'— I think they say, twentieth anniversary.	(Amen!/Amen!)
Praise God!	
God certainly have been good to us.	(Oh yes!/Yes He has!)
And we are *happy* to be here.	(Praise God!/Well!)
We didn't come this afternoon for no form or fashion.	(Alright then!)

16. "We didn't come for no form or fashion," declared Brother Sonnie Stevens as the Jerusalem Travelers stepped into the cross-aisle. "We came to lift up Jesus!" Those prefacing words invite the saints to recognize Brother Stevens's impassioned singing as *real* and to read his emotion as heartfelt. (Photo by Roland L. Freeman)

Neither did we come for outside show,	(Lord Jesus!)
like be in the world.	
We came to lift up Jesus!	(Yes!)
We don't want to be like that old rich man,	(Alright!)
who prayed, but his prayer was too late.	(Too late!/Alright!)

As Brother Stevens utters the last line, the guitarist strums his strings, setting the key for the Jerusalem Travelers' first song. Before the final note fades, the four voices lock together in sweet, high tenor harmony. Their opening song is the slow Nightingales' piece "He Prayed, but His Prayer Was Too Late."

＊　＊　＊　＊　＊

"We didn't come for no form or fashion. We didn't come for outside show," declares Brother Stevens. "We came to lift up Jesus!" Even before offering the familiar statement of purpose, Brother Stevens extends two emphatic disclaimers, announcing to all what the group is *not* here to do. He recognizes the honorees, gives thanks for being at the program, and then twice *denies false purpose.* Before talking about praise, before talking about ministry, before talking about "having church." The disclaimers come first. As if to say, "We may be here as *singers,* but first we're here as *saints.* Judge us by our faith rather than our artistry."

Such denials of "form, fashion, and outside show" are almost as pervasive in gospel services as declarations of praise and ministry. Some programs include dozens of such disclaimers, often all from different speakers. They show up in prayers, in testimonies, in the comments of devotional leaders and emcees, and— with the greatest frequency—in the introductory remarks of singers.

"We're not here for no *performance,*" proclaims Evangelist Evelyn Gilchrist at her family's fifteenth singing anniversary. "We're not here to be seen or heard by man, nor for any form or fashion! We're here to give *God* the *glory,* and to have a *hallelujah* good time!"

"We're not here for a *program,*" echoes emcee Josephine Booth at a Durham gospel service. "And we're not here to entertain you! This is your time to just praise God!"

"And I tell you, we didn't come for no *show!*" adds the lead singer with Sanford's United Choral Ensemble. "Didn't come for no form or fashion. We come to uplift Jesus! We come to let the world know that Jesus lives!"

"We didn't come here to play church," declares Rev. David Bell at a yet another gospel service. "Playing time is over! And we didn't come to entertain you. Entertaining time is over too! We came to praise the Lord, and to get soul-saved!"[1]

Though the words may differ, the meaning is always the same. The message always leads listeners from the "wrong" way of hearing to the "right," from the worldly to the worshipful, from "performance" to "praise." "Form and fashion" emerges as the negation of "sincerity," "entertainment" as the opposite of "worship," "show" as the inverse of "church."

A closer look at the words that reference worldliness in these disclaimers reveals a complex tangle of relationship and association. Perhaps the most common such term is "form or fashion," a phrase that church elders say has seen routine use at least since the 1920s. As a phrase, the term has no exact analogue in the Bible. Its component parts, however, readily invoke a host of biblical citations. The word on whose derivation all seem to agree is "fashion." When saints talk about singers singing for "fashion," they're usually speaking of *style.* More particularly, they're speaking of *current* style, of that which is "fashionable," of that which will one day pass away. The key issue here seems to be the shallowness of transient trends. "The fashion of this world passeth away," declares the apostle Paul (1 Corinthians 7:31). "And the world passeth away, and the lust thereof," adds Saint John, "but he that doeth the will of God abideth forever" (1 John 2:17). Styles change, echo the saints, but the Word stays the same.

On the first night of the Branchettes' twentieth anniversary, the William Coley Trio sang a song that cautioned, "Now the devil, he will tempt you—*he'll pull you away with style.*" At the song's close, the singer, William Coley, commented:

You know, we're not that kind of group can sing	
a shouting song every time.	(That's alright)
We sing that one that soaks in.	(Alright!/Yeah!)
Way on the inside.	(Amen!/That's right!)
All the way through you.	(Praise our God!)
I look at that young adult choir,	
and the young people singing,	(Yes)
I say, "If you all were old as I was,	
you probably wouldn't sing it just like that."	(Alright!/Jesus!)
Thirty-nine years ago, we haven't done much	
changing in our singing.	
You know, God don't change.	(No He don't!)
He's the same today He was thirty-nine years ago.	(Oh yes!/Thank You!)[2]

Brother Coley's remarks clearly link "style" to the "shouting songs of the young people," drawing them together in the familiar rhetorical net of devotional decline and the "old-time way." The changeability of fashion—here represented by musical style—becomes a mark of worldly capriciousness, an indication, perhaps, of the distractions that Satan sets in the paths of the faithful. This critique echoes one leveled in the 1930s by church elders who lamented that "style has crowded all the grace out of religion today."[3] All these saints see "fashion" as a diversion, something that lures the mind toward worldly concern and thus weakens its focus on holiness. To sing for "fashion" is to sing with one's mind on "show" rather than on Spirit.

✳ ✳ ✳ ✳ ✳

Rev. Samuel McCrary and Isaac "Dickie" Freeman, both longtime singers with the Fairfield Four, were relaxing in their Arlington hotel room after a grueling day of outdoor performances. Earlier that afternoon, Rev. McCrary and I had talked about "form and fashion" in preaching. Now that the day was winding down, we were continuing the conversation.

Sitting across from Rev. McCrary at the tiny, hotel room table, I asked about the role of "style" in preaching, wondering whether style—like the words it often

17. "We're not that kind of group can sing a shouting song every time," declares gospel veteran William Coley. "We sing that one that soaks in, way on the inside." Having sung together since 1954, the members of the William Coley Trio build their repertoire on gospel standards and old congregational songs. Here Sister Mary Lewis closes their set with "My Life Will Be Sweeter By and By." (Photo by Roland L. Freeman)

carried—was a gift of the Spirit. "Does style," I asked, "come with the calling?" Did a preacher have to develop a way of preaching, or was that given, like the gift of song? Rev. McCrary's response suggested that he'd heard a different question from the one I'd asked, for he associated the word "style" not with ways of talking, but with "form and fashion." For him, "style" was something "put on," something "for show," something that anointed preachers avoided.

"You're supposed to speak with understanding and sing with understanding," he explained, his words both careful and measured. "That's what you're there for. Not to just say it for *style*. Because the Bible says [that] form and fashion—which is style—shall be done away with. Nothing will stand but His pure Word."

Realizing that Rev. McCrary was using the word "style" differently than I was, I rephrased the question and asked it again. This time I simply asked about the different ways that preachers preached, leaving out all mention of "style." Noting that preachers who preached under the anointing all "sounded different," I asked if the "difference" in sound was something the preachers controlled, or if this too were part of the gift.

"Well," he responded, seeming somewhat confused by my question, "if the Spirit is in you—you don't have no control over the Spirit. You just do it like the Spirit *wants* you to do it. But if it's *yourself*, [your preaching] has no effect. It's just words. But if it's the Spirit, it will affect somebody."

Just as I had avoided using the word "style" in my question, so did Rev. McCrary avoid it in his response. But we still seemed to talking about two different issues. So I tried once again, this time asking whether the lack of control in anointed preaching suggested that the Spirit "wanted" different preachers to preach in different ways. Rev. McCrary's answer leaped right over the specifics of my question to draw our two lines of thought together in eloquent union. In retrospect, I could see that he had been answering my question all along, but was assuming that I understood the interim steps. I didn't, and thus kept pressing the issue. But the story that Rev. McCrary proceeded to tell quickly set me straight, explaining that any concern about one's way of speaking—any concern about one's sound—was a concern that got in the way of one's duty. Put simply, attention to "style" (or "fashion") focused one's thoughts on "form" rather than substance.

There was three men [that] once preached the same sermon.
   About "the Lord is my shepherd."
And one of them men—the first man—
   he preached it,
   and he knew what he was doing.
     He knew the *letter*.
The second man preached—
   and he did it with all *style*.
And the last man preached—
   he never went to school,
   he never been nowhere—
     but he did it from *experience*.

See, his *experience* was "the Lord is my shepherd."
  But he knew that the Lord *was* his.
And the first man, see,
  didn't know whether the Lord was his or not.
    But he just *said* it.
And he said it ,
  people applauded.
And the second man,
  they looked at him,
    and congratulated him by saying it,
      because he was such a *smart* man.
And the other man—
  when *he* was saying it,
    tears fell from their eyes.
      Because he did it with the Spirit.

Rev. McCrary paused, his eyes searching my face for understanding. When I nodded, he smiled and continued.

They all three of them had a different meaning.
So that is the Spirit.
Yeah.
The Spirit say, "Ye that are led by the Spirit are the sons of God."
And everybody that get up there to preach or sing are not the sons of God.

"There are those with a form of godliness . . ."—the words echoed in my mind as Rev. McCrary concluded his story. The first preacher preached with *erudition*, letting "learning" guide his carefully chosen words. The congregation applauded his intelligence. The second preacher preached with *style*, letting tone and lyrical grace guide his deftly chosen words. The congregation applauded his eloquence. The third preacher, however, preached with *understanding*. Not worrying about reason or artistry, he let the Spirit guide his words. And the congregation cried. The preacher without "learning" or "style"—the one without "form or fashion"—was clearly the one who numbered among the "children of God."[4]

✶ ✶ ✶ ✶ ✶

If the "fashion" in "form or fashion" alludes to the fickleness of time, then the "form" alludes to the shallowness of appearance. When saints talk of those who sing "just for form," they are speaking about singers who don false robes of reverence in order to gain something for themselves. These are the "false prophets" who wear a "form of godliness," the ones who "put on" holiness so as to "minister to the emotions," the ones who cloak selfish motives in an aura of righteousness.

Their "form" is their projection of self, a deliberately crafted persona that gives no hint of the soul beneath the shell. Hence the saints speak of those who "put on form." "Form" becomes a mask, something that can be "put on" (and, implicitly, taken off) at will.[5]

It's easy to see how talk of "putting on *form*" slides into talk of "putting on a *performance*." Or simply of "*performing*." Look again at Evangelist Evelyn Gilchrist's remarks at her family group's fifteenth anniversary. "We're not here for no *performance*," she declared. "We're not here to be seen or heard by man." Then recall Evangelist Dorothy Jackson's comments in the previous chapter, when she contrasted "real" singers with "the ones that do all of this 'performing.' " Finally, think back to the conversation with Deacon Willie Eldridge, when he labeled his early attempts at leading worship—attempts that were wholly determined by self, with little counsel from the Spirit—as "performing." All of these saints, and countless others like them, use the word "perform" to suggest spiritual theatricality. Often cloaking the term in verbal italics, or prefacing it with a disparaging "just" (as in "they weren't real; they were just performing"), they speak of "performance" as the enactment of a put-on role for the purpose of "entertaining" an audience. Within this frame, a "performer" is an actor, one who "puts on form," one who portrays something other than self. In the words of Free Will Baptist minister Rev. Z. D. Harris, a "performer" is a "pretender."

When singers say, "We're not here to perform," Rev. Harris explains, "they're saying that 'we are not here pretending. We are real. We are not here to pure give you a show. We're here to give you a service.' " To *perform* is thus to *pretend*. And to pretend, Rev. Harris suggests, is to be insincere. "When you're saved," he continues, "the whole thing changes. See, you're not going over what you used to do. [Then] it's not performing. It's not acting. It's being *sincere*." Saints say that sincerity destroys the pretense of "performance." Because when singers are sincere, when they are living the life that they sing about, they don't *need* to perform. They don't need to "put anything on." Their sincerity—their authenticity—will carry the message.[6]

The theatrical implications of the term "performance" find full confirmation in the cluster of terms that often accompany it. Many singers open their disclaimers by saying that they're "not here to put on an act" or are "not doing a stage act." Many others declare, "We didn't come for no show!" Even more deny singing for "outside show," thus combining the sense of surface appearance implied by "form" with the spirit of stagecraft suggested by "show." Finally, many say that they don't come to "play church," using the term "play" in the sense of "playacting." All of these terms suggest a clear sense of distance between speaker and hearer; all present the performer as one who plays *to*—rather than *with*—the audience. And all pose the performer's primary concern as pleasing the audience—rather than *ministering* to the audience, and *pleasing the Lord*.[7]

Hence when singers stand before a congregation and declare that they are "not here to perform," they aren't saying that they're not going to sing. Rather, they're saying that they're not going to "put on an act," that they're not singing "just to entertain." In so doing, they are telling congregation members precisely how to interpret their presentation. By invoking and then denying the frame of self-conscious, theatrical performance, singers are asking the audience not to judge them on the basis of artistry alone. "We may be singing artfully," they are suggesting, "but we're not here as artists. So don't judge us as if we were." They want congregation members to know that the artistry displayed is artistry *in service of.* In essence, they want it treated as a means to an end rather than as an end in itself.

This is not to suggest that sanctified singers in any way denigrate their artistry, or that they aren't constantly working to develop and perfect it. One needs only consider the emphasis that groups place on formal rehearsals—an emphasis that often extends to imposing monetary fines on members who miss meetings—to recognize the deep seriousness with which most singers treat their art.[8] Yet this seriousness ideally rests on a foundation of humility. Singers are quick to point out that their artistry is not theirs to claim. "It's really the Lord's," they say. "We're just its vessels." By denying their role as "performers," singers thus deflect any acclaim their singing might garner, tacitly giving the credit to God.

Another term that regularly appears in singers' disclaimers, and another one closely associated with "form," is "formality." When saints use "formality" in this context, they're speaking about hollow ceremony, about formalized routines that have no meaning. Elder Lawrence Richardson, for example, uses the term when talking about singers who choreograph their shouts. "But I sing it out of my heart," he asserts. "I don't get up there for no formality." In like manner, Rev. David Bell—cited earlier for his comments on "playing church"—says that when he sees a singer "take his coat and sling it out into the congregation," then he knows that "it's a formality. It's just a form to get the congregation applauding and going on." Both of these saints and many of their peers use "formality" not to signify stiff decorum, but rather to suggest showy dramatics. Such "formality," in essence, takes "form" and turns it into a tradition.[9]

What, then, is this tradition? What forms does "form and fashion" most often take? We've already encountered many of its manifestations in the reminiscences of saved singers. Evangelist Dorothy Jackson, for example, talked about when she used to "put on" shouts, leaping and crying out as if she had felt the Spirit's touch. Rev. William Walker told of those who "played church" by "clapping [their] hands and stomping [their] feet," "hollering all over the church," "jumping and shouting, and tearing up benches." And Smiley Fletcher spoke of simply singing without worshipful intent, of "putting on an act" not through showmanship, but through the lived lie of a sinful life. Others tell of singers who leap off of stages, who sing on their knees, who run down the aisles in theatrical displays of spiritual abandon. All agree that these dramatics have become so routine in gospel performance that programgoers have almost come to *expect* them. Indeed, saints say that at commercial programs, there's no need for the "almost." Everybody at these events—saint and sinner alike—expects a hearty dose of theater. Though most saints will deny that they come for this purpose, many others freely admit that this is why they slide their dollars across the ticket counter. They come expecting to see a "good show."

Older saints used to say that "the empty cart is always the one that makes the most fuss."[10] "Fuss" is still the word that many use to describe the empty showmanship of "form and fashion" performance. When discussing such "fuss," saints often point first to the realm of sound. More specifically, they point to the vocal and musical strategies that singers use to "get a house." I've already discussed the role that displayed intensity plays in performance, suggesting that it modulates the message conveyed by words. When singers "sing for show," however, intensity often *becomes* the message, displacing text altogether. What matters is the *appearance* of impassioned engagement. Many singers convey this intensity through extraordinary vocal pyrotechnics, techniques that they themselves call "tricks." They stretch falsetto cries to seemingly impossible lengths; they swoop from growling bass to screaming falsetto in the course of a single syllable; they leap into driving, polyrhythmic exchanges whose layered rhythms amaze and baffle the ears. And they cry; they shout; they stop singing midverse in apparent, enacted surrender to the Spirit. The conveyed message is always the same: "We are profoundly involved, 'caught up' in praise, 'wrapped, tied, and tangled' in worship. You, as audience, should be too."[11]

The affective dramatics of tone find a ready partner in the impassioned appeals of text. Freely acknowledging that they're playing to audience emotions, many singers fill their performances with tearful tributes to "mother" and heart-wrenching tales of disease and disaster. Such between-song (and sometimes in-song) testimonies can stretch for more than ten minutes, their affective impact boosted by artful poetics and a fluent lyricism. Like their sanctified counterparts, unsaved singers readily adopt the tonal and structural styles of the preacher, constantly referencing the *sounds* of anointment. Unlike the saints, however, their use of style tends to be both studied and rehearsed. Every mournful cry, every touching phrase, every head-shaking, response-inviting complaint that "You all don't know what I'm talking about!" is calculated to elicit an emotional response.

Further adding to the testimonies' impact is their apparent spontaneity. Singers will often pull out of a song by testifying that it reminds them of some dramatic incident in their lives. They then launch into rehearsed—but nonetheless impassioned—testimony, making the shift seem completely ad-libbed. Or they will acknowledge that their time is up but will nonetheless ask the audience, "Would y'all let me tell *my* testimony?" suggesting that the "feeling" won't let them leave until they bear witness. Such strategic "spontaneity" particularly marks the performances of commercial touring ensembles, whose infrequent appearances in any given area virtually insure that their "spontaneity" won't be recognized as routine. (Not surprisingly, most of those whom I've heard talk about the programmed sameness of commercial performance are gospel emcees and professional singers—presenters who see the same performance, and thus the same "spontaneity," night after night.)

Always standing alongside talk and tone in the "form and fashion" repertoire are the physical enactments of intensity and anointment. Saints have long asserted that when transcendence touches, "you got to move." "When the Spirit comes, it's not a 'performance,'" explains Evangelist Dorothy Jackson, speaking about the outward signs of anointment. "The Spirit is not a performer. But you still get that *uplift*. Sometime it'll make you move. Sometime it'll make you stand still. But it's still there. The realness is there."[12] Even when the "realness" is *not* there, however, its physical manifestations—the dramatic shouts, the quick-stepping dances, the runs down the aisle—thrive in the theater of "form and fashion." Spiritual "performers" needn't look far for inspiration, for the drama is already at hand, amply provided by the saints. They need only to transform the inspired into the mundane, making art out of that which transcends art, twisting the adage "let go and let God" into a worldly "let go and let *me*."

The enacted range of "outside show" is every bit as broad as gospel's stylistic spectrum. At one end are simple signals of intensity—an emphatically loosened tie, a handkerchief-wiped brow, a cast-off jacket. None of these signs necessarily indicates pretense. Indeed, many of them regularly appear in sanctified pulpits and cross-aisles, showing up when preachers and singers "get into" worship. This ubiquity cloaks them in a guise of familiarity, thus strengthening their power as signals when singers "put them on" as part of their "performance."[13]

As we move further along the continuum, the enactments become decidedly more showy. The tie gets pulled entirely off; the handkerchief starts to wave in the air; the jacket gets flung into the congregation. Some singers bend into a strained crouch; some begin to roam the aisles; some drop to their knees. At this point the false signs of anointment begin to make their appearance. Singers burst into loud shouts; they leap into the "holy" dance; they may break into tongues. Underlying all these actions is an apparent loss of control, signaling growing surrender to the Spirit. When these signs appear in the course of a song , the singing usually goes on, with the background filling in while the lead "lets go." After a quick, eye-catching enactment, the lead usually rejoins the song, invariably jumping in right back on beat.

At the far end of the spectrum, the signs suggest an even greater abandonment of control. Sometimes singers lay their mikes down and stop singing altogether, apparently unable to continue. Sometimes they run from aisle to aisle, shouting all the while, until other singers restrain them. And sometimes, in classic demonstrations of intense engagement, they act like they can't *stop* singing.

This last strategy is a quartet favorite. Here's how it goes. The lead singer is singing in the center aisle, stretching the song far beyond its usual length, showing all the signs of deep and impassioned involvement. Silently suggesting that it's time to go, another singer takes his microphone and starts nudging him toward the cross-aisle. But the lead pushes away and keeps on singing, now without amplification. At this point, the lead often talks about not *needing* the mike, and about singing "like we *used to do* back home." Then another backup singer joins the first in trying to restrain him. Grabbing the lead's jacket, they start pulling him out of the aisle. Before he leaves the floor, however, the lead somehow slips out of his coat and runs back to his original position, still singing. Finally, the other singers wrestle him back to the church-front, where the entire sequence typically concludes with all the singers closing the song in tight harmony.

Even though this routine bears striking parallels to similar sequences on the rhythm-and-blues stage (James Brown's cape-shedding routine immediately comes to mind), the sanctified frame of self-surrender and celestial control draws it into the realm of distinct spiritual possibility.[14] As the Book says, only the Lord can predict how the Lord will act. Hence *anything* is possible. Even this seemingly stagy bit of showmanship. The saints' admission of the Lord's inscrutability, coupled with their unwillingness to judge, seems to give "form and fashion performers" an almost unfettered hand in crafting such strategies of spiritual simulation.

But saints *do* judge, and they *do* reject the excesses of gospel "performance." When showmanship reaches these levels, saints label it with yet another term drawn from the world of entertainment, calling it "clowning." The term "clowning" carries all the theatrical implications captured in "entertainment" and "outside show," and then adds to them a sense of manifest foolishness. Clowning is acting that wears pretense on its sleeve, making no attempt to be anything other than what it obviously is. To call performance "clowning" is thus to declare its obviousness, as if to say that it stretches the boundaries of spiritual probability so far that even those who aren't saints can see its fakery.[15]

Many saints suggest that the only ones who fail to recognize this are the "clowns" themselves. They still see themselves as clever actors, unaware that their "cleverness" has caused them to lose all semblance of credibility. Saints say that this blindness to outside perception is the subtle work of Satan, who clouds singers' judgment so that he can better control their actions. "Clowning" singers thus become more than just players who wear the mask of sainthood. They also become *playthings* who are unwittingly doing the bidding of a crafty master. Hence they are doubly "clowns," both *playing the fool* and *being played as fools*. As such, say the saints, they should be received not with contempt, but with prayer.

* * * * *

Joseph "Jojo" Wallace is one of the few professional gospel singers whom I would say truly exudes holiness. He always seems to carry with him an aura of warmth and compassion, instantly setting at ease all who come in his presence, instantly letting them know that he holds love in his heart. Saints across the country seem to agree with this assessment. In years of conversations about gospel, I've heard his name invoked more often than any other when saints talk about professionals who are "real." After meeting him, I understood why. Jojo Wallace truly lives his life as a testimony to his faith.

Every time I'd seen Brother Wallace on stage with the Sensational Nightingales, I had been struck by the humility and joy that he conveyed in his testifying, singing, and guitar playing. I felt this same spirit as we sat together in his living room in Durham, North Carolina. What doesn't come across as much on stage, I thought, was his enthusiasm. Brother Wallace's words ring with the exuberance of a recent convert, as they've no doubt done for the nearly three decades since he committed his life to Christ. When we started talking about this book, his story seemed to roll from his mouth with an eager exhilaration, as if it had been waiting to be told, pent-up and ready for release. I barely needed to pose a single question. Brother Wallace knew *exactly* what he wanted to say.

He started by telling how the Holy Spirit "teaches" him things that he can hardly speak, things that he knows need be said to singers "in the world," things that the Spirit will reveal "in His own time." He came to know that if he just "let his light shine," then Jesus would draw the misguided many in. "Just pray for them and keep living it," he explained. And they'll be drawn in.

Then Brother Wallace began to talk about his own experience as an unsaved singer. "We've been singing for forty-six years, with the same group—the Nightingales," he began. "Maybe a couple years more."

> And [for years], nobody was saved.
>> Nobody thought about Christ.
>> I mean—couldn't have cared less.
> We were making up songs to make folk—
>> to try to make folk shout.
> We was making up songs trying to get on their sympathy.
> Like "My mama dead and gone,"
>> and "Took my mama to the graveyard,"
>> you know, "Way over yonder"—
> You know, *our mama was living.*
> Just lying.
> In other words, we were singing *lies.*
> Didn't care.
> Running around, you know, in the world.
> Just like the sinnerman.
> You understand?
> And here we are trying to tell somebody else—
>> call ourselves, "trying to sing gospel."
> *We didn't know what the gospel were.*
> None of us did.

Brother Wallace shook his head as he thought back on those years. That was during the so-called "golden age of gospel," when quartets dominated the field and ruled the gospel airwaves. For years, the Nightingales rode the tops of radio playlists, producing hit after gospel hit. Every time they sang, they brought down the house. Folks shouting everywhere. The group's legendary front man, June Cheeks, running down the aisles with his impossibly "hard," shouting lead. The Nights' guitarist, Jojo Wallace, running right behind him with his fancy choreographed steps. And folks just "falling out." Back then, people called the Nightingales "sure enough house-wreckers." And not one of them was saved.

All this is now the stuff of gospel legend, the stories told and retold by singers who remember the incredible power of those performances. Brother Wallace knew that he didn't need to tell the stories again, knew that I'd probably already heard them. And I had, from singer after singer, all across the country. But I had *not* heard that none of the Nightingales had been saved. My surprise must have shown on my face, for Brother Wallace came out of his pause by assuring me that the same thing was happening now. "And I'm going to say something here, Brother Glenn—" His words were rushed, his eyes gazing intently into mine.

That's happening right today.
I hate to say it, and [to] tell the truth—
   I can tell you the singers that [are] doing the same thing today.
They need to accept Jesus Christ—
   just like I did—
      before it's too late.
Because what the enemy does,
   he plays tricks on their mind.
He plays tricks on their mind,
   make you *think* you're right.
That's the way that *seems* right to man.
You understand?
End up, because God is so merciful,
   they take that for His [mercy]—
      Many of them, *too many of them* have told me about,
        "Brother Wallace, Brother Jojo—
         God been good to me!
         God blessing me!"
   And I *know* they haven't been born again!—
   But they're using God's mercy, or His blessings.
He rains mercy on everybody, the just as well as the unjust.
So you can't *hide* behind that.
Jesus said, "*You must be born again.*"
See what I'm talking about?
You *must* be.
So my point is—singers—now—

For a moment, Brother Wallace struggled for words, wondering how to say what needed to be said. Then he breathed a slow, deep sigh. When he began again, his voice was much quieter than before, barely above a whisper. Now he was right back where he started, talking about his own experience, telling his own story.

I was out there with them, Brother Glenn,
   for year after year.
Lying.
Singing lies.
And my mother—
   I'll never forget it as long as I live . . .

It was a long while before I found out exactly *what* his mother did. The mere mention launched Brother Wallace into a long reminiscence about how he started singing. He told about being "raised up in the country," about sneaking his brother's guitar and learning how to play, about moving to Philadelphia and forming his first quartet. "We enjoyed it, and could blend our voices together," he explained. "And Glenn—hear me real carefully—[we knew] nothing about Christ. We couldn't have cared less."

Inspired by the Golden Gates, the quartet developed their own smooth sound. But by the time Gotham Records expressed an interest in recording them, Brother Wallace had been invited to join the Nightingales. So he returned to North Carolina, where he, June Cheeks, Carl Coates, and Bill Woodruff developed the Nightingales' unique sound. "We would sound like skyscrapers, boy, scraping the sky!" Brother Wallace declared, recalling Cheeks's hard lead and his and Woodruff's high, powerful harmonies. "And we excited folk everywhere we went."

I still hadn't said anything beyond a few words of affirmation. Brother Wallace spoke for a while about June Cheeks's "amazing" ability to stir up people's emotions and "what they call 'bust a house.'" Then he started talking about his own "performance."

> And I used to carry my guitar myself,
>   and run down the aisle, you know,
>   up and down like I was—
>   I would just call out like I was shouting!
>   Putting shouts on,
>   fake shouts—
>   and folks just shouting besides me,
>   and I [was] just boogying up there shouting!
> And the whole house—they'd go in an uproar.
> And then we done that night after night.
> Night after night.
> And didn't know nothing about Christ's word!
> Didn't know nothing about Jesus.
> See my point now?

I nodded and made a sound of affirmation. Brother Wallace answered by exclaiming, "Don't tell me it's no different spirits!" Then, as he laughed, he added, "It is! Cause God let us experience *all that*, Glenn, to bring us to this point here."

Captivated by Brother Wallace's testimony, I still didn't say anything. After a moment's pause, he continued.

> So, to make a long story short—if I can—
>   we done that year after year,
>   year after year.
> Till twenty-eight years ago . . .

At this point, Brother Wallace began talking about long-ago personnel changes in the Nights. Realizing, however, that he was getting ahead of his story, he pulled the narrative back on track, returning to his mother.

Right after I got saved—
    follow me carefully—
        I was anointed by the Word.
Now it come from my mama.
    'Cause Mama kept praying—
Many times I would come home,
    I thought I was, you know—
        "I'm with the Nightingales,"
        and had folks shouting,
        and talking about us—
And Mama, she said, "Son,
    don't play with God like that."
And I *knew* she was *right*.
She said,
    "It's too dangerous, you know."
I knew she was right, now.
And it began to irritate me a little bit, you know.
And then she said,
    "You know, you can sing a lie as good as you can tell one."
Like that.
And I mean—and you know what I done, Glenn?
I thank God He saved me to testify to what my mama told me,
    and folk know it all over everywhere now!
And see, I'm hopeful it will *help*—
    the choirs, the singers, everybody, you know—
        that you can live one [thing] and say something else, you know.
So [in] other words,
    so she told me that, Glenn,
        and it *affected* me.
And I began to study the Word.

Brother Wallace later described his attitude as "puffed up with pride." He was proud of his accomplishments and convinced that success was his just reward. Hard work had made him a "star," one whom singers like Smiley Fletcher would emulate, one who would set an example for an entire generation. "I'm with the Nightingales!" he could boast. "I can make whole auditoriums jump up and shout!" Yet his mother saw it all as a charade. In her eyes, he was simply living a lie. And *that* bothered him. So he began to study the Word.

This was the turning point in Brother Wallace's narrative, the point at which pride in the accomplishments of self began giving way to acknowledgment of

God's merciful guidance. Studying the Word was the first step. The second was rethinking his approach to performance. With the Nightingales, he had always relied on hard singing and flashy showmanship to arouse the crowds. But now he was beginning to think that perhaps all this wasn't necessary.

> And I started to travel with a preacher,
>> a guy called Anthony Butler.
> He used to tell me,
>> he said, "Brother"—
>>> God was doing this here!
>>> I know he was!—
>> He said, "Son,
>>> I'm going to show you how much power the Word got."
>> Said, "You ain't got to be screaming and hollering.
>>> Let me show you."
>> He said, "Come with me and read with me."
> So I went with him.
> 'Cause I was concerned, for some reason.
>> I weren't saved, now—
>> I hadn't catched up with Christ.
> But I was concerned.
> *God was molding me.*
> So I used to read with him.
> And he says, "Read."
> He'd be talking, teaching the Word, and focusing in on it, you know.
> And I reads.
> And I say, "And Jesus said—"
>> "and Jesus said such and such a thing—"
> And then he'd take it and explain it.
> And after a while,
>> after a while I saw folk [crying],
>>> "Praise the Lord!"
>>> "Oh, Praise Him!"

As Brother Wallace quoted the two congregation members, he lifted his hands and eyes to the sky, acting out gentle praises. But as he said the next line, he shifted his tone to a rough, strained shout and squinched his face into a taut mask. For a moment, he played the role of a hard quartet lead. And then he burst into laughter.

> Without "Yaaah! Yaaah!"
> You know, without any shouting!
> See, I saw the *Word* doing it!

Though Brother Wallace had certainly seen this before—the praises following the calm delivery of the Word—he had never *thought about what was happening.*

18. "When you sing a song slow, people sit and listen," notes Sister Lena Mae Perry. "The thoughts are rolling over and over in their mind. . . . And that song will touch right at the appointed time." Judging from congregational response, this is precisely what happened at the Branchettes' anniversary, where quiet, slower songs never failed to draw the saints to their feet. Here, church sisters stand to the hushed harmonies of "No Tears in Heaven." (Photo by Roland L. Freeman)

As a singer, he had convinced himself that the only way to move a crowd was to "rip and run." Such "outside show" always got the shouts and grabbed the acclaim. What Brother Wallace did *not* understand was how this gentle preaching seemed to light the same kind of fire. Perhaps, he reasoned, he was missing something.

"And I said to myself," he continued, " 'Lord, I wonder will I *ever* get the chance where I'll be able to stand and see the effect of Your—' "

Before he could finish—while sitting right there in his living room—Brother Wallace felt the Spirit's touch. His face burst into a radiant smile, as he uttered a quiet, "Praise the Lord!" A single tear rolled down his cheek. A moment later, with joy still radiating from his face, Brother Wallace finished his sentence.

" '—to see the effect of Your Spirit working through the people? Your sacred spirit that's in every man, already.' "

"To *stand* and see the effect," Brother Wallace had said. Not to *run*. Not to *shout*. But to *stand*, and to sing with the power that was so evident in the preaching of Rev. Butler. This question would come to chart the course of the Nightingales' future, as they gradually moved away from "form and fashion" and toward the Word.[16]

* * * * *

Every time the Nightingales sing, Brother Wallace makes some reference to his testimony. Sometimes he tells the whole story, setting the "form and fashion" issue squarely before the congregation, forcing them to confront the difference between worship and entertainment. At other times, he tells only the story's bare outline. Even in the shortened versions, however, he makes sure that programgoers know he once lived a life of lies.

Brother Wallace is by no means the only singer who regularly includes such testimonies in performance. Many other singers—particularly those who sing noncommercially—do precisely the same thing. These testimonies, when coupled with the appeals of prayer-givers, the admonitions of emcees, and the introductory disclaimers of singers, effectively keep the issue of spiritual fakery in the devotional foreground. Congregation members can't help but hear the message. At every turn, they are being cautioned to shun "outside show."

With all these cautions in the air, one might think that singers would avoid "form and fashion." But saints say that this assumption seriously underestimates Satan's power. The lures of the world are simply too enticing—they argue—and the world's rewards too great to keep singers from the path of deception. I've already discussed some of these temptations. Like false shouters in the pews, "showy" singers want to be seen, want to stand apart from their peers, want to attract somebody's eye. Further, they want the prestige that comes with the *appearance* of divine approval. Finally, as Smiley Fletcher's testimony aptly reminds us, these singers want the special *status* that comes with the spotlight.

When asked *why* they performed before they were saved, most saints simply say that they enjoyed singing before a crowd. "I used to sing with quite a few groups, and I sang for quite a few many years, because I liked to sing," testifies quartet lead Robert Faulk. "We went because we loved to sing," adds Smiley Fletcher. "Our main objective was just to go out and have a good time."[17] Often implied in these explanations is the admission that singers performed not only because it "felt good," but also because it put them at the center of attention. Their "good times" were the product of public acclaim, the ego-boosting result of standing in the spotlight. Within this frame, the quickest way to increase one's "good time" is to magnify the spotlight's intensity. Which can easily be achieved by putting on a more flamboyant "show." The equation is quite simple: the more one plays to the audience, the greater the audience's response; the greater their response, in turn, the greater one's personal satisfaction. "Putting on a show" thus becomes a vehicle for "getting the praises" and serving the self.

This is precisely the reason that Jojo Wallace offers for his one-time showmanship. "*I* was the one that was doing it," he explains. "'Cause I was playing, and folks was giving *me* the praises. You understand? God wasn't getting none of it. [They would say,] 'Jojo—boy, you sure can play that guitar!' And then they'd get down: 'Jojo went down the aisle when he came out, and the folk—you should have saw them folk shouting! Boy, they was boogying!' That's all I was hearing. You see my point now? *I* was doing it. *I* was getting the glory out of it."[18] And that glory, he adds, "felt good" at the time. Good enough, at least, to keep him searching for new ways to arouse the audience and garner even more acclaim.

Among professional singers, acclaim translates into increased opportunities for performance, higher performance fees, greater radio airplay, and larger tape and CD sales. It also brings personal perks, not the least of which is increased interest from members of the opposite sex. Many singers freely admit that they've sung with hopes of catching someone's eye. Judging from the stories told in the gospel community, many audience members are apparently quick to oblige. Indeed, references to clandestine trysts between singers and their admirers—typically cloaked in words of stern admonition—regularly pepper the remarks of emcees and singers.[19]

Of all the reasons given for "form and fashion" performance, perhaps the most telling is the one given by Jojo Wallace at the beginning of his already-cited testimony. "We were making up songs," he says, "to try to make folk shout." This statement of purpose runs like a litany through the talk of unsaved singers. They boast about "shouting the church," about "getting a house," about "turning the house out." They brag about how they "killed the crowd," how they "didn't leaving nothing standing but the dust." And they call groups with particularly "effective" routines "house-wreckers." All of these terms pose performers as the agents of congregational excitement. And all present singers as the *cause* of the shouts.[20]

This claim to agency becomes particularly apparent when singers talk about "shouting" a church. Here "shout" becomes a transitive verb, a term whose meaning hinges upon the naming of someone or something to receive the designated action. Hence singers are not merely shouting; they are "shouting" *somebody*. Or to use Brother Wallace's phrase, they are "making folk shout." There's no mention of the Spirit, no reference to focus and invitation, no suggestion of stewardship. Instead, all agency rests in the hands of the singers.

★ ★ ★ ★ ★

Another hotel room. Another morning after an evening's impassioned performance. This time I was talking with one of the legends of quartet gospel, a singer whom I shall identify only as Brother Hardsinger.[21] Brother Hardsinger is a classic "hard gospel" lead, an intense singer whose growling vocals have carried his group to international acclaim. Though he's been on the road for more than forty-five years, he shows no sign of tiring and still fills his calendar with a grueling schedule of one-night stands. Unlike in his early years, however, Brother Hardsinger's bookings now include colleges and festivals as often as they do gospel programs. Yet his popularity with hard-core gospel audiences remains undiminished. His quartet still places songs on the gospel charts with easy regularity.

We were talking about strategy in singing and about the techniques that groups use to "involve" their audiences. When I asked Brother Hardsinger about invitational comments of the "Stand up on your feet!" and "Let me hear you say 'Yeah!' " variety, he explained that he uses these to get the audience "to feel something."

"We know that God is a spirit," Brother Hardsinger noted, "and we are trying to touch the spiritual part of God that's in them. Our theory is that when God breathed into man's nostrils the breath of life and he became a living soul, then we believe that we can touch that part. 'Cause I don't care if you're agnostic or what-are-you, you still got that part of God in you. . . . So we try to draw [the audience] into our net, and make them feel something that they've never felt before."

"So what is it that they're feeling?" I asked, somewhat surprised at the stress on "feeling" without any mention of "understanding."

"Spirit," he responded. "And God is a spirit. So we're making them feel God."

Again Brother Hardsinger emphasized the "making." "Touching" the spiritual part of the self and then "making" the audience members "feel God." The process he was describing was somewhat different from that which I'd heard explained by other saints. The singers' role here seemed much more active. But I didn't press the issue. The conversation eventually turned to talk about the power of song.

Then, as Brother Hardsinger explained how different kinds of songs appealed to different denominations, the conversation veered right back to the issue of agency. After remarking that his group tried to please *all* churchfolk, he declared, "The most important thing, especially in church, is to get them to shout. You know, because that's the most important thing. In the other field, in the rock field and the jazz and the blues field, you just want them to feel good, to feel something that they never felt before."

"But you say the most important thing in the church is to get them to shout?" I asked, wanting to make sure that I'd heard correctly. Before I could even finish the question, Brother Hardsinger answered with a flat "They will."

"They will?" I repeated, somewhat taken aback by his sense of certainty. "Oh yes," he replied. "And I've seen it happen in the clubs. Seen it happen at the jazz festivals. We was out there in California—had twenty-five thousand inside and twenty thousand on the outside. And everybody got involved. And you talk about—we couldn't get off the stage, you know!"

Somehow we'd moved from churches to festivals, and from "shouting" to "getting involved." Trying to determine the connections, I asked, "Now is the shout that you're getting in that auditorium and the shout that you're getting in the church the same thing?"

"I think so," he asserted without hesitation. "Because we're still talking about God. Now, I've seen it happen in the rock-and-roll field. Where the devil come in and he make women just scream and tear their clothes off. You know, you've seen that before."

"Right," I answered, nodding.

"All right. So it's the same thing. Now the main important thing is to get people *involved* in whatever you're doing. If you're singing the blues—I've seen B. B. King tear the house down! You understand? Just have women screaming and falling out. You understand? So *the same thing is in the gospel field*. Ain't no difference. That's what you're aiming for. Anyway, that's what *we're* aiming for! To do the same thing that rock and roll do."

So the shouts are the same. B. B. King can "tear a house down" just as effectively as a gospel group. But it's the devil that makes the women tear their clothes. And God, presumably, makes the churchfolk shout. But it's the artist who's *causing* the feeling. The different spirits apparently just give it form.

I had one more question. I wondered what satisfaction *he* derived from "making" folk shout. "What does that do for you?" I asked.

"O-o-oh!" Brother Hardsinger replied with an animated tone. "For us, it makes us feel like we've done something, you know, [other than] just going out there singing a song. We feel that we have accomplished our aim, and our aim is to make people *feel* good."

So we ended up right back where we started. He sings to make others "feel good" and to make the churchfolk shout. When they show their feelings, then *he* feels good, secure in the knowledge that his artistry can sway people's emotions, reassured that his voice still carries power. For Brother Hardsinger—and for many others like him—the artist is the agent of affect. The Spirit—as a "part of God" in all beings—is merely the force that responds when the message is a spiritual one.

* * * * *

I suspect that many born-again singers would find this explanation quite familiar. Many times, I've asked such singers what they used to think was happening—in the years before they were saved—when people shouted to their singing. Their answers show a striking unanimity. Virtually all of them believed that *they* were "causing" the shouts, that they were—as Jojo Wallace puts it—"addling the people's spirits." Though they acknowledged the involvement of the Holy Ghost, they always minimized His role, reducing Spirit to a "feeling," never treating Him as an active agent. By the same token, they simplified the human side of the equation, leaving out the processes of reflection and invitation, and treating shouting as an unthinking abandonment to one's emotions. Not surprisingly, comparisons with "falling out" at secular performances run through all these accounts. Before they were saved, these singers firmly believed that the mechanism was essentially the same.

And in a sense, it is. At least for the shouts that are *not* in the Spirit. Remember, not all congregational shouts are spiritually "real." Some are merely "shouts for show," conscious displays enacted to attract attention. Others are "emotional shouts," spontaneous outbursts that feed on the emotions. Neither of these forms are informed or induced by the Spirit. And both are subject to human manipulation. "Form and fashion" singers can indeed generate these kinds of shouts, often by "performing" shouts themselves. What results is thus a dialogue of deception, with singers "putting on" shouts in order to provoke false (or simply misguided) shouts from the audience. These shouts, in turn, trigger others like them in the pews. They also encourage "performing" singers to put even more effort into their "performance." The conversation thus becomes a cycle. With the Spirit nowhere to be found.

"Now I can stand there and *teach* you first," explains Jojo Wallace, describing how many unsaved singers build their sets to a shouting climax. "Nice and calm. But until I start to yelling, you don't respond. So I'm going to get used to this. See, I'm going to feel like, eventually, *this is what you want me to do*. Is yell. So I'm going to yell and make fancy runs that make you say, 'Go ahead!' It will enhance me to keep on doing it, because I see you're enjoying that. More so than if I was just singing a message song, a song with a message."[22]

Saints contend that the author of the singer's misunderstanding—and the director of the hollow dialogue—is Satan himself. Actively struggling to keep the Spirit out of the conversation, he encourages singers to rely on the vocal and physical "tricks" that elicit emotional rather than spiritual responses. Some say that Satan even *teaches* these tricks. (African American lore has long labeled Satan a master of "trickeration.") Whatever his exact role, saints agree that Satan is in fact the one doing the "tricking." "He plays tricks on your mind," Brother Wallace said in his testimony, "to make you *think* you're right."

The devil's mode of operation thus becomes clear. He limits singers' understandings, helps them to imitate the ways of the saints, encourages audience members to applaud and "shout" to these imitations, convinces singers that they are indeed walking a "spiritual" path, and then rewards them (through enhanced prestige, monetary gains, sexual favors, and so on) for their deception. On the surface, the deal seems sweet. This explains, say the saints, the widespread currency of "form and fashion." The factor that remains hidden in this equation, however, is the singers' souls. By joining forces with the "master of deception"—whether wittingly or unwittingly—singers step onto the path of condemnation. Only by turning toward grace and turning their backs on "form and fashion" can they avoid this fiery fate.

"Beloved, believe not every spirit," cautioned the disciple John. "But try the spirits whether they are of God: because many false prophets are gone out into the world. . . . They are of the world: therefore speak they of the world, and the world heareth them. We are of God: he that knoweth God heareth us; he that is not of God heareth not us. Hereby know we the spirit of truth, and the spirit of error" (1 John 4:1, 5–6).

False prophets are *of the world* and speak *to the world*, declared the apostle. The saints, in contrast, are *of God*. Only others who are also of God will truly *hear* their words. Yet false prophets will seek this same audience. Assuming the guise of God's children, they will speak to the saints *and* to the world. Hence John cautions the saints to "believe not every spirit, but try the spirits whether they are of God." The responsibility for distinguishing between true and false prophets—and, by extension, between true and false *singers*—thus rests with the saints. They must separate the real from the unreal.

But how does one "try the spirits"? How can saints tell when performance is merely "performance"? When asked this question, saints offer many answers, suggesting a range of evaluative means. Some point to the guidance of inner feelings; some to assessment of the performance itself; some to appraisal of the performance's impact; some to knowledge about the performer's life. Every aspect of the presentation—the performer, the performance, the witnessed reaction, the felt response—offers clues for evaluation. Taken together, these clues guide the saints to a qualified judgment. Not, they note, to *certainty*, but only to a *considered opinion*. Certainty—like the right to judge—is said to rest only with God.[23]

The most frequently mentioned means of assessment looks not outward to the performance, but inward to a simple, mystical knowing. Saints say that those who are truly "born again" can usually *feel* when someone is faking. They pose this "feeling" as a kind of spiritual intuition, an inner sense that subtly informs their understanding. When asked to explain the workings of this special awareness, most saints with whom I've spoken describe it in terms of spirit meeting spirit. The process is essentially the same as that set forth by Elder Richardson when he discussed how the soul's "vibrations" flow from heart to heart (see Chapter 7). In essence, the spirit of every saint is said to reach beyond the body when the saint joins in worship. When this spirit touches the spirit of another, the two connect, resonating in a moment of communion. Sometimes this connection makes itself felt as a quick shiver, abruptly pushing its way into consciousness. Sometimes it comes as a general tingling, a feeling that many saints describe as "like electricity." And sometimes it just comes as a deep, calm knowing. Whatever form it takes, saints say that they instantly *know* its meaning.

Saints also know the meaning when there is *no* feeling, when the praises of another just flap—as Evangelist Jackson suggested—off the ears. No feeling means no connection. And no connection suggests no spirit. Which in turn raises questions about the performance's "realness." This is what is meant, say the saints, by "trying the spirits." When the spirit tries the spirit and finds it wanting, the message is clear.

"He tells us to try the spirit by the spirit," explains Evangelist Dorothy Jackson. "And so what He means by that—to 'try the spirit by the Spirit'—when we have the Spirit of God within us, then God will let us know when it's real. He said, 'Because I will not withhold any good thing from you. I will not allow anything to slip from you. I will always make you aware. So when Satan's there, I will let you know!' And all you have to do is just sit there and look."[24]

"Just sit there and look," Evangelist Jackson says. "*Look*, and the Spirit will make you aware." Her phrasing suggests that *knowing* can't always be separated from *seeing*, and that awareness may result from *guided* assessment. Saints say that revelation need not always take the form of instant, full-blown exposition. Sometimes, the process is collaborative, with the Spirit steering saints' senses and helping them to discern the real from the unreal. In essence, the Spirit guides both their eyes and their evaluations. The knowing that results is no less full than that granted by inner revelation; it still bears the full authority of the Spirit. This knowing, however, carries with it an added sense of *involvement*. The saints actively participate in its unfolding. And in so doing, they sharpen their powers of discernment, thus making each future assessment that much easier.

One of the key criteria that saints cite when speaking of inspired appraisal is the cross-aisle presence of "confusion." "God is not the author of confusion," they say, quoting 1 Corinthians 14:33. "Neither does God lead you to act unseemly," they add, drawing from 1 Corinthians 13:4–5. Saints often apply these verses to singers' "showy" antics, suggesting that the "show" is nothing but "confusion," and that its author is other than the Spirit. This holds particularly true for performances that suggest an absolute loss of control, as when singers leap off stages or run the aisles shouting. Saints say that most such routines testify to their own falsity. First, because they suggest that the Spirit itself is out of control (a virtual impossibility). Second, because they typically stretch the apparent "anointing" far beyond the brief interval it usually assumes ("The word of God is quick," says the apostle Paul in Hebrews 4:12). And third, because such routines suggest that the performer's will is wholly suppressed, overwhelmed by the greater power of transcendence. But saints say that the Spirit *joins* rather than *displaces* the believer's spirit. The resultant spirit/Spirit balance rarely swings so far as to obliterate the human will. Some aspect of the will always remains, ever wary of "unseemliness" and the attendant possibility that the reigning spirits might *not*, in fact, be of God. This, in turn, means that "showy" singers could always reign in their actions, easily avoiding the "confusion" their performances suggest.

"I always say that if the Holy Ghost would really hit one of them [singers] out there clowning, it would *scare him to death!*" declares Evangelist Dorothy Jackson. "If the Spirit were to really come to one of them, while they're in this high emotional thing of showmanship—if the Spirit would come and touch them with the meekness and the calmness—they'd probably have a heart attack. Because He's meek. And He's calm. . . . [And He] never lets you lose control. Never. He *keeps* you *in* control."[25]

Evangelist Jackson suggests that the Spirit never lets singers who are "in the Spirit" lose control. But if the Spirit were to touch singers who were *not* "in the Spirit" but were acting as if they were, they would be terrified. Because they would experience the very loss of control they were feigning. And because they would realize, as they felt the deep calmness of the Spirit, the hollowness of their fakery. They would recognize, as Evangelist Jackson said a few minutes after these comments, that only Satan "needs to show himself. . . . God doesn't need no show."

A second criterion that believers mention when they speak about guided assessment is *sameness*. Saints say that the Spirit will never touch one of His children in precisely the same manner more than once. Hence if a singer shows the same spiritual signs—the same shouts, the same waves, the same dance—at the same place in the same song on more than one occasion, or if that singer offers the same tearful testimony—repeating every word, every gesture, every tear—night after night, then the singer is enacting a rehearsed sequence. As the saints often say, "God don't work like that."[26]

Quartet lead John Landis, lead singer with the Franklinton, North Carolina, quartet the Golden Echoes, explains how sameness can serve as a measure of authenticity. "If you are sitting out in an audience, and you go to hear a group one time," he suggests, "go back and hear them a second time. And watch the leader, because he's the one that's going to be exposed more than anyone else. You watch that leader, and just watch his reaction from the first time to the second time. And if he puts on the same show the second time that he did the first time, and uses the same little gimmicks and everything the second time [that] he did the first time—go back and listen to him one more time. If he does it the *third* time, he's putting on a show."

"Because you don't *practice* what you're singing about in the gospel," Brother Landis explains. "If you *mean* what you're doing, you don't practice that. That comes—it just comes natural. Just like in my singing, up there. I can't tell you what I'm going to say when I get on stage. I can't tell you what I'm going to say, because *I don't know*. Words come to me. And when words come to me, I'll say them.

"Now if you would sit up there and *practice* what you're going to say when you get on the stage—[if you were to] say, 'Now what am I going to say to these people? I'm going to say this and I'm going to say that'—and [if] you rehearsed it over at rehearsal, [then] when you get up to say that, you know what will happen? *You'll forget it all.* It'll all leave you. Because once upon a time, I have tried that. But that's not the way it's supposed to be done. See, that's putting on a show."[27]

Brother Landis's words are tellingly similar to those of Deacon Eldridge, who also testified to the futility of practice when delivering the Lord's Word (see Chapter 8). Both men offer living testimony to Christ's decree that saints should "take no thought beforehand what ye shall speak, neither do ye premeditate: but whatsoever shall be given you in that hour, that speak ye: for it is not ye that speak, but the Holy Ghost" (Mark 13:11). In so doing, both men attest that sincerity needs no rehearsal. Both suggest that practice yields only self-serving "form." (Deacon Eldridge speaks of "performing"; Brother Landis calls it "putting on a show.") And both agree that performances that are prepared and rehearsed leave no room for the Spirit.

When asked for further biblical grounding for the measure of sameness, most saints with whom I've spoken frame their response in terms of predictability. Citing Jesus' declaration that "ye know not what hour your Lord doth come" (Matthew 24:42), they point out that mortals can never predict the Spirit's ways. Sameness in the Spirit's touch would suggest that one *could* make such predictions. Following this same line of reasoning, believers also cite Genesis 6:3, where God declares, "My spirit shall not always strive with man." Saints say that if the Spirit *does* always seem to strive with certain performers, then the spirit involved is probably not a holy one.

Beyond these citations, of course, the saints rely on the revelation of experience. The measure of sameness is simply something they *know*, something that the Spirit has revealed to generations of saints, something that has become part of the general knowledge. When preachers decry the "formality" of manuscript preaching, when emcees declare that gospel events are not "programs," when singers describe how the Spirit guides their words—all are testifying to the rule of spiritual spontaneity. Every occasion poses a different constellation of congregational needs; every situation invites a differently crafted response. When these responses are the same, needs aren't being met. And when needs aren't being met, say the saints, then the Spirit is probably not part of the performance.

* * * * *

Members of Durham's Oak Grove Free Will Baptist Church often find a single xeroxed sheet slipped into their Sunday morning bulletins. The top of the sheet bears the words "MESSAGE FROM THE LORD," followed by a recent date. Below the title flows a single-spaced stream of words, words that spill down the page and sometimes onto its flip side. These are words of prophecy, words uttered in tongues and interpreted in the Spirit, words offered for the edification of the saints. Every time such words grace a service, a sister in the assembly reviews the church's recording and transcribes the prophecy. "These are messages directly from the Lord," declares the church's pastor, Rev. Z. D. Harris. "When [the sister who utters them] gets through, she don't even know what she has said. Until somebody types it out. . . . These are not prepared messages."

Late in the fourth week of October 1992, the scribe brought Rev. Harris a prophecy that had been revealed the previous Monday night at a Bible study and praise service. The two-page prophecy opens with the following words:

"Never the same. Never the same. I never come the same. Never the same. I never come the same. I never come the same. No, I never come the same, for I'm carrying you into things just to teach you how to move with Me—just to teach you how to flow with My Spirit. Never the same. I carry you deeper. There are reasons, but they are Mine and I may not always explain them, but just flow with Me. Yes, flow with *My* Spirit. Yes, flow, flow."[28]

✶　✶　✶　✶　✶

"Flow with Me," say the words of prophecy. "Flow with My Spirit." This gentle invitation suggests yet another means of assessing spiritual authenticity. Saints believe that if the Spirit is truly in the performance, then He will also flow through the pews. If the Spirit manifests itself *there*, then the performance is probably "real." This measure thus encourages saints to shift their eyes from the *singer*— where they probe for "confusion" and "sameness"—to the *congregation*. There they search for fulfillment of the Book's promise that the anointing will flow "from heart to heart and breast to breast." The very commonness of this promised diffusion leads saints to expect its presence. They know that when the anointing touches one, then the "mysterious drops of the Holy Spirit" will rain onto others also. What saints do not know, however, is whom the droplets might touch. This, says quartet lead Smiley Fletcher, is a "thing you can't predict."

"Sometimes [the Spirit] flows just like water," Brother Fletcher explains. "It'll *run*. It might hit me, and it might miss you, [and] might go over there and hit my wife. And then it might just hit the whole congregation at once. That is something you just can't tell."[29] Believers realize that the Spirit does not always dwell with every saint. And they recognize that they themselves might not always feel the spirit-to-Spirit connection. But they know that *somebody* will feel the flow, and that *somebody* will show some signs. This much is promised by the Book. Hence their willingness to trust the flow as a measure of "realness." Though they themselves might feel nothing, the evidence of others being blessed testifies that the Spirit is truly at hand.

When measuring "confusion" and "flow," the interpretive clues come in the course of a single performance. When assessing "sameness," the clues become clear only after observing several performances. In yet another measure of "realness," clues to spiritual authenticity come from a realm wholly separated from presentation. They lie instead in the "lives" of the singers. More specifically, they lie in whether or not the singers are "living the life they sing about." As the debate over "performance" and "outside show" makes clear, saints are well aware that singers who seem "right" in the church may be living "wrong" outside its walls. Though they can clearly "talk the talk," standing before the congregation with "excellency of speech" and "enticing words" (1 Corinthians 2:1, 4), they will not be able to walk the corresponding walk. *Because*, say the saints, in the tangled pursuit of day-to-day life, the devil will always slip and show his hand. His skills at deception—

however mighty—will always falter. As Evangelist Dorothy Jackson puts it, "Satan always has to show himself. 'Cause he cannot be real to save his life."[30]

*　*　*　*　*

Robert Faulk knows well the wiles of Satan. For more than four decades, he "performed" gospel leads with a range of choirs and quartets. Though a dedicated Baptist, a respected member of his church, and an esteemed figure in Durham's gospel community, he wasn't saved. Then, one afternoon in the early 1980s, he happened to turn his radio to a church broadcast. The preacher was preaching; the saints were crying hosannas. And Brother Faulk realized that he didn't really *know* the joy that he heard coming from that church. So he said to himself, "Lord, if I could receive the Holy Spirit and enjoy myself like I think those people are doing . . ." Before he could finish, he heard a voice asking, "If I was to let you receive Me, would you keep it?" Trembling, Brother Faulk answered, "Yes, Lord." Instantly, he felt his soul flooded with the wondrous power of the Spirit, leading him to shout and cry and praise the Lord. At that moment, he knew that he would finally live up to the promise he had so often made when he sang, "I'm going to live the life I sing about in my song." From that day forward, he would be a "changed" man.

One afternoon shortly after his encounter with the Spirit, Brother Faulk and I were sitting in his living room, talking about the change. Though I had known Brother Faulk for many years, I had never before heard the passionate conviction that now filled his voice. As we spoke about his new life in Christ, he began to muse on the life he led before the change, thinking about how completely Satan had been able to deceive him. I wondered aloud whether his new understanding would help him to better discern the "realness" of other singers. He responded by asserting that Satan will *always* show a flaw. Hence one need only look at singers' lives. "You'll notice," he began,

If I mock and take after you long enough,
　　I can get it *almost* perfect like you.
Almost.
But there'll *always* be one flaw.
Now one thing about the devil—
　　he can shout like you,
　　he can preach like you,
　　he can almost *look* like you.
But there's one thing he can't do.
He cannot live a true Christian life.
　　He can't do that.
　　See, that's not his makeup.

But he can "perform" like you.
  He can act like you.
  He can do like you.
But he cannot *live* a Christian life like you.
  That's his bad mistake.
  He can't do that.
He can do everything like you—
  jump and run and holler and shout—
    but he cannot live a Christian life.
    He can't do that.
He can act and make you think he's got what *you* got,
  but it won't live it out.
Yeah, it'll catch him on down the road somewhere.
  He won't live it out.

After a short pause, Brother Faulk began speaking of specifics, citing incidents that led him to wonder if certain singers (always unnamed) were "living the life." About five minutes later, his examples led him right back to where he started, yielding a second poetic litany of what the devil can and cannot do. This time, however, he brought the listing to a different close. After asserting that Satan can't "carry out the truth," Brother Faulk paused and then remarked, "And all you got to do is go on and let the Lord fix it."

This quiet, closing comment led me to wonder about the purpose of all this evaluation. If singers' unholy lives truly proved those singers to be liars, then how should a saint *use* this knowledge? Should the saint confront them? Denounce their falseness? Or just leave the matter to the Lord? Brother Faulk gently pointed out that the first two of these alternatives placed the saint in the judgment seat. And that particular seat, he reminded me, belonged only to the Lord.

A lot of times,
  we are quick to say, you know,
    "They are not doing this"
    and "They are not doing that."
If *they* say they are,
  and we say they are *not*,
    don't try to condemn them.
'Cause, it's a funny thing about the truth—
  you can stomp it,
  you can stamp it,
  you can get on it,
  you can do this,
  you can throw it out and do that,
    but when you bring it back,
      it's *still* the truth.

You can't harm it.
You can't hurt it.
It's just like a bright light—
    you just can't put it out.
It'll *always* shine.
No matter what you do to it,
    it'll shine right on.
So that's the way the Spirit is in an individual.
If *you* try to condemn them,
    somebody else can come along and try to condemn *you*.
So that's the reason it says,
    the Bible says itself,
        "Judge ye not,
            because the same judgment that you judge,
            you shall be judged."
See, the Bible is telling you that—
    don't judge an individual.
Just go ahead on and live your life from day to day.
    And ask the Lord to keep you the best way that you know how.
    And you try to live as close to Him as you can.
    And don't try to judge that man.
Now he's doing things that you don't particularly like,
    or he's doing things that you don't particularly say it goes with Christianity,
        but, just let him be and go his way,
        and you keep on going.
        You just keep on going.
And *sooner or later*, all that thing he did in the dark going to be brought right
    to light!
And then he going to show himself up right then.
And where he thought he was such a big man—
    he was this and he was that—
        and the Lord [will] just show everybody
            that he ain't what he said he was.
Because just like I said back again—back to the same thing—
You can *do* these things,
    but you can't *live the life* unless you really got the Holy Spirit.

As Brother Faulk paused, I couldn't help but think about the old congregational song, "I'm Going to Leave You in the Hands of the Lord." That's precisely what Brother Faulk was recommending. It's appropriate, he suggests, to *assess* the saints who seem to be holy. After all, the Book does say to "prove all things; [and] hold fast that which is good" (1 Thessalonians 5:21). The assessment is the necessary "proving," the "trying of spirits," that will guide one's actions, turning one away from deception and toward that which is holy. But this assessment, however well founded, is still only a guess, an unproven assumption, a conclusion reached by reason rather than revelation. Without the certainty that only God can provide, evaluation must stop with the saint, never broadcast, never publicly proclaimed. Brother Faulk suggests that censure—if it is truly due—*will* eventually come. But it will come only in the Lord's own time. Until that moment, or until God grants the certain knowing that reveals truth, saints can only act upon their uncertainty, testing but not judging, considering their conclusions but not denouncing. Without spiritual revelation, the truth about deception remains elusive.[31]

✳   ✳   ✳   ✳   ✳

So after all is said and done, saints are still left with a measure of ambiguity. They still do not *know*—with absolute certainty—whether or not performers are "real." Because all of their measures are subject to human misperception or the imponderable vagaries of spiritual choice. Sometimes, saints explain, the "feeling" isn't there to grant insight. Sometimes the "connection" simply doesn't happen. Perhaps the assessing saint's mind is not focused on worship; perhaps the devil is testing the saint's faith; perhaps, for some reason, the Spirit doesn't *want* the connection to occur. All would cast the reliability of this measure into doubt.

What, then, of the tests of "confusion" and "sameness." What if a sequence that *seems* to be "confusion" is indeed willed by God? And what if the Spirit *does* choose to act in similar ways in subsequent performances? After all, the Bible declares that the Spirit "worketh all things after the counsel of his own will" (Ephesians 1:11). That "will" remains a mystery to those here on earth, an imponderable that, as the saints say, is "not ours to know." The appraisal of sameness also raises questions of definition and perception. Who is to decide the difference between "same" and "similar"? And how much can memory be trusted from performance to performance? This link in the chain is clearly weak.

Next comes assessment of the Spirit's "flow." Again we face the failings of human perception. We've already established the fact that many who seem "touched" are feeling only emotion or are "acting" for the eyes of others. And Brother Jojo Wallace reminded us that "false" singers will draw "false" shouts, setting up a dialogue of deception that can deceive all but the most discerning eye. The "flow" itself thus might be false. Furthermore, if the true flow *is* indeed present, it need not manifest itself overtly. Saints say that the touch yields private tears and silent praises as often as it does shouts and holy dancing. Since the *form* that the flow takes is decided solely by the Spirit, it might well remain invisible to the evaluating saint. This potential for invisibility further adds to this measure's ambiguity.

The final measure of authenticity—and the one that saints rely on more than any other—is the "life" that singers lead. But this test too has its limitations. The most obvious is churchgoers' simple unfamiliarity with the lives that lie behind the songs. In small, closely knit communities, saints tend to know the habits and ways of local singers. But when singers come from afar, their out-of-church conduct remains something of a mystery. Saints freely admit that gossip fills many of the informational gaps created by distance. They also acknowledge, however, that gossip does not grant reliable grounds for judgment. Though it can caution saints to listen with a critical ear, it offers no proof of singers' "outside lives." Particularly since gossip—say the saints—is one of Satan's favorite tools. If he can use it to cast doubt on the holy, then he will surely do just that, crafting yet another barrier to the delivery of the Word. Saints are thus left with only their direct experience and with God's guidance when assessing singers' "realness."

This catalog of uncertainties brings us full circle to the question that began this quest: how can saints tell when performance is merely "performance"? Must assessment *always* end in uncertainty? When asked this question, saints quickly point out that the Spirit can—and will—grant certain knowledge when *any* of these criteria are called into play. Though all these tests admittedly have their limitations, all are also subject to the Spirit's guidance. If the Spirit wills that saints should know of a singer's "realness," then those saints will *know* beyond a shadow of a doubt.

For some saints, such knowing stretches beyond the specifics of situation to stand as an abiding ability. These saints are said to be endowed with the "gift of discernment," a gift that brings penetrating insight in matters of the Spirit. One of the nine spiritual gifts named by the apostle Paul, the "discerning of spirits" allows chosen saints to look beyond surface appearance to gaze at the soul within.[32] Those who bear this gift speak of the separation of real from unreal as but one of its wondrous facets. Bishop Frizelle Yelverton, for example, tells how the gift lets him walk the aisles of unfamiliar churches and call forth those who haven't been saved. And Evangelist Dorothy Jackson explains how the gift enables her to "see"—with a "spiritual eye"—the terrible, immaterial form of sicknesses that call for healing. All those who bear the gift say that it allows them to see through "form and fashion," granting insight into the status of a performer's faith.

Though the gift of discernment brings knowledge, it does not call saints to publicly announce that knowledge. Saints with discernment speak of it as a quiet, private gift, one whose understandings are to be conveyed not to the assembly as a whole (unless the Spirit so directs), but to the specific individuals involved. "You don't stand up and talk about it in a congregation," explains Evangelist Evelyn Gilchrist. "You know, [saying] 'I see that so and so . . .' Because, as you know, Jesus Christ, while on earth, never embarrassed a soul. He never embarrassed a soul. And to those of us that He called into the ministry, we are not to embarrass a soul. We are supposed to throw our arms around [false singers] and say, 'Hey brother, God loves you and I do to.' And you *encourage* each other; you don't try to pull them down. Because we're trying to win their souls for the Lord! Because we want them to go to heaven, and live eternally there, and sing in that great choir."[33]

Evangelist Gilchrist's gentle words offer a perfect coda for this discussion of "form and fashion." When discerning saints see through "performance"—indeed, when they realize that even the disclaimer of "form and fashion" is itself a formula spoken for "show"—they should not publicly condemn. Instead, say the saints, they should act with gentle compassion. On one hand, they should personally heed that which has been revealed. Perhaps by no longer attending programs featuring the questionable singers. Perhaps by simply becoming more watchful for the "enemy's" subtle wiles. On the other hand, if at all possible, they should confront false performers with words of encouragement and concern, bearing witness to the joys that await them when "church" becomes more than "show." Saints contend that "form and fashion" will always be in the world. Indeed, they say that as the final days draw closer, "form and fashion" will increase. "Many false prophets shall rise, and shall deceive many," Jesus prophesied on the Mount of Olives. "Take heed that no man deceive you" (Matthew 24:11, 4). With scripture in mind, the saints do just this—watching, taking heed, and singing with "minds stayed on Jesus." As "form and fashion" claims an ever-increasing role in gospel, sanctified singers want their listeners to *know* that they're singing to "have church."

Chapter 17

Elevation

"Go Slow, Rise High, Catch on Fire, and Sit Down"

As the anniversary service rolls into its third hour, Evangelist Lofton calls the Gospel Tones to the cross-aisle. Singing in the evening's seventh slot, this Raleigh quartet stands before a congregation that is both "live" and "on fire." The Spirit has already swept through the pews many times, and the saints are clearly ready for His blessings once again. An air of joyous anticipation seems to pervade the sanctuary. While the Tones walk to the church-front, resplendent in their powder-blue jackets and charcoal-gray pants, I see saints around me edging ever so slightly forward on the pews, as if expecting to soon be drawn to their feet. They have good reason to be hopeful. The Spirit had blessed many in their number mere moments before, when the Branchettes had sung an extended and deeply spiritual set. Now the Gospel Tones will do their best to keep the spirit high.

As the Tones arrange themselves, the drummer, guitarist (the same one who has been playing throughout the anniversary from the front pew), two vocalists, and bass player form the back line. At the mouth of the center aisle, in front of the "background," stands Johnnie Faison, the quartet's "hard" lead. A bricklayer by trade, Brother Faison has been singing with the Gospel Tones for twenty-one of the group's twenty-three years. He's a sturdy man, with thick arms, slightly graying hair, and a warm, round face. Upon reaching the church-front, he removes his microphone from its clip and pushes the chrome stand back toward the pulpit. Every aspect of his "uniform"—from the folded hankie in his chest pocket to his glossy black shoes—perfectly matches those of his fellow singers.

The Gospel Tones open their set with quiet words of thanks and praise. Brother Faison speaks intimately and conversationally, as if talking to a close friend rather than to a church full of saints. His relaxed intimacy sharply contrasts with the emcee's enthusiastic introduction and the preceding set's spiritual fervor. He is starting the set slowly, as if opening a new conversation.

After remarking that the Gospel Tones would sing the requested two songs and a theme, Brother Faison introduces the group's first selection. "I want to sing a song," he comments gently, "that says, 'Will the Lord be with me when I go through the valley? Will He walk beside me, will He hold my hand?'" His humble,

19. "When it's time to cross that chilly Jordan," sings Johnnie Faison, standing at the end of the Gospel Tones' line. "Will He guide my feet and hold my trembling hand?" choruses the full front line, their voices locked in sweet harmony. The set's slow, impassioned opening has already brought many saints to their feet; the Branchettes' Sister Perry can be seen standing in the amen corner. (Photo by Roland L. Freeman)

hushed tone and slightly downcast eyes almost suggest that he's asking the congregation for their permission. When a sister in the pews voices an acknowledging "Amen," he asks, "You all know that song, don't you?" The saints chorus "Yes!" and Brother Faison adds, "'Cause I want you all to sing along with us." Again, his eyes and tone suggest modest entreaty.

Without further words, the Gospel Tones launch into their introductory "theme." Brother Faison opens the slow song by singing the verse rather than the chorus, carefully articulating the questions he has already posed to the congregation. His rich baritone seems to caress every word, giving each of the lyric's questions an easily understood fullness. While he sings, the guitar and bass offer a softly understated backup, as if to avoid muddying the lyric message. The four men in the back line simply stand and sway, their movements locked in tight unison.

When Brother Faison swings into the chorus, three other Gospel Tones join the singing, following every lead phrase with their delayed harmonies. Like the instruments, their voices stay in the background, never challenging the lead. Meanwhile, Brother Faison's baritone starts edging toward graininess, growing slightly louder and slightly raspier. As he presses into the second verse, the shift grows decidedly more apparent. Though the words are still clear, they lose their rounded edges and relaxed tone. In their stead come echoes of strain. Brother Faison's vocal attack begins to sharpen, while his fluid fullness increasingly assumes a gravelly undertone. As if to accentuate this shift, the backup abandons the phrase-for-phrase restatement that marked the chorus and pushes the verse's first two lines with a sharp, percussive repeat. For the third line, they replace this phrase with a wordless, harmonized moan, thus foregrounding the lead even further. On the fourth line, the backup returns to responsive restatement, thus closing the verse much as they had the chorus.

Twice more Brother Faison repeats the chorus, his voice maintaining its sounded strain. Both times, the backup follows the pattern established in the previous verse. As the second singing of the chorus draws to a close, all the vocalists join in tight harmony, easing out on a "sweet" note that draws the lead fully back into the vocal blend.

Now the saints are clapping and crying "Amen!" The guitar and drums sound a brief, rising phrase, effectively prefacing Brother Johnnie Faison's remarks. "May the Lord be with me," he says, restating the entreaty posed in the theme, "when I go through the valley." His words show none of the grainy tautness so evident mere moments before. Instead, they once again sound relaxed and conversational. Now, however, there's a slight edge in their tone, a subtle sharpness that blunts the appearance of calm. Brother Faison's appearance conveys this same edge. Whereas his earlier comments came with a relaxed smile, these come with a look of studied earnestness. Eyes that once played across the pews now gaze forward with purposeful intent. And Brother Faison's relaxed, foot-shifting stance has now given way to a flat-footed solidity. Though his words still sound conversational, his body suggests that he has a definite message to convey.

The song say, "Get right with God,	(Uh-huh)
and do it now."	(Yes!/Alright!)
Better not wait for tomorrow,	(Alright now!)
for tomorrow may be too late.	(Yes!/Sure enough!)
"Get right with God."	

Inflecting his closing words to suggest that he's quoting a song title rather than actually calling the saints to "get right," Brother Faison keeps his tone conversational. Before the saints can respond, the guitarist strums the song's opening chord. The drums immediately sound a quick triplet, drawing the guitar and bass in on the third beat. Four times the drummer repeats the pattern, and four times the guitarists offer a chorded answer, each time raising the pitch. The drummed lead and dramatic, up-tempo introduction suggest that this will be a "shout song."

The song's first line bursts from Brother Faison's mouth with shouted ferocity. Gone are the careful articulation and gentle tone that marked his introduction. In their place is a percussive insistence, a roughly voiced fervor that commands the congregation's attention. Gone also are the long, word-filled lines of the opening theme. In their stead is a string of terse declarations, each one instantly echoed by tenor harmonies. Before the backup can close each echoing line, Brother Faison jumps right back with another, layering every phrase on both ends. The overlapped back-and-forth gives the song a pulsing swing, driving the message home with each rolling repetition.

You ought to get right,	/ GET RIGHT WITH GOD!
A-a-a-and do it now!	/ AND DO IT NOW!
Get right!	/ GET RIGHT WITH GOD!
He will show you how!	/ HE WILL SHOW YOU HOW!
Down at the cross,	/ RIGHT DOWN AT THE CROSS
Well, down at the cross,	/ RIGHT DOWN AT THE CROSS
Down at the cross,	/ RIGHT DOWN AT THE CROSS
He gave His blood!	/ JESUS SHED HIS BLOOD!
Get right!	/ GET RIGHT WITH GOD!
A-a-a-and	/ AND DO IT NOW!

Brother Faison launches his second line with a growl far deeper than anything uttered in his first song. His gravelly, vibrato "A-a-a-and" sets the tone for the shouted "Get right!" that fills the next line, instantly casting Brother Faison in the role of "hard" exhorter.[1] His voice's commanding fullness completely dominates the singing, reducing the backup to the status of attending chorus. Though their high harmonies are effectively carrying the melody, Brother Faison's lead is clearly carrying the message.

The lead's first four lines, stretching over eight measures, fall into a familiar pattern of split statement. Each set of two lines forms a poetic whole; these two wholes, in turn, rhyme to complete the stretched couplet ("You ought to get right, and do it now! / Get right, [and] He will show you how!"). The song's melody suggests that the singers will repeat this structure to close out the verse, yielding a sixteen-bar lyric with two four-line couplets. But at the opening of the second couplet, Brother Faison stalls the song's progress. Instead of completing the two-part line, he repeats the phrase "Down at the cross" a second and then a third time, each time giving the words the same melodic profile. The backup does precisely the same thing, as if caught in a repeating loop. Except for a prefacing "Well," the three lead and three backup lines exactly duplicate each other.

As soon as Brother Faison signals the stall, a few saints in the congregation wave their hands and cry "Yes!" They're clearly expecting a shift to yet a higher "elevation." But Brother Faison quickly slips back into the verse. Giving no indication of anything out of the ordinary, he completes the stalled couplet and slides into the next, closing the verse precisely as he began it. The stall came and then passed, a mere trick of arrangement, perhaps a suggestion of things to come. But it *did* grab the saints' attention, building expectation while compelling them to *listen* to the lyrics. As I sit in the pews, I wonder if this was precisely its purpose.

Brother Faison never completes the verse's closing line. All he gets out is the opening word, a simple "A-a-a-and" that stretches into a strained shout. Before the backup can even complete their response, he's already launched into the next verse, a close repetition of the first. Just as he ended with a grainy cry, so too does he begin, overlapping the backup's "now" with a gravelly, rising "Wo-o-o-o-o!" This opening shout, with its upward tonal slide, marks a further narrowing of Brother Faison's register. All semblance of his full, resonant baritone is now gone. In its place is the coarse intensity of his constricted, shouted vocals.

Wo-o-o-o-o, you ought to get right,	/ GET RIGHT WITH GOD!
A-a-a-and do it now!	/ LORD, AND DO IT NOW!
Get right!	/ GET RIGHT WITH GOD!
He will show you how!	/ HE WILL SHOW YOU HOW!
Well, right down,	/ RIGHT DOWN AT THE CROSS
Down at the cross,	/ RIGHT DOWN AT THE CROSS
Down at the cross,	/ RIGHT DOWN AT THE CROSS
He gave His blood!	/ JESUS SHED HIS BLOOD!
Get right!	/ GET RIGHT WITH GOD!
A-a-a-and	/ AND DO IT NOW!

The blue-suited singers in the back line present a single figure of tightly harmonized motion. Their gentle sway is unerringly precise—one beat with the weight on the right foot, one beat with it on the left, back and forth, back and forth. The two center vocalists have bent their arms at their sides and are moving them one after another, as if briskly marching in place. The lead, however, stands wholly apart, freed from the strictures of symmetry. Sometimes his sway matches theirs; more often, it does not. While their arms pump up and down, his show far more restraint. His right hand holds the mike close to his mouth, while his left gestures only for slight accents, its range limited by the two loops of microphone cable in its grasp.

Now Brother Faison moves slightly down the center aisle, taking two steps into the pews, singing directly to the saints that now surround him. Beads of sweat start to mark his brow. Dropping the mike cable, he grabs a handkerchief from his rear pocket and drags it across his forehead. The white hankie stays clenched in his broad left fist as he continues to sing.

Just as he had done in the first chorus, Brother Faison stalls the second. Again the saints respond with waved hands and cries of encouragement. And again the words slip seamlessly back into line. Then, with another closing-and-opening set of growled shouts, Brother Faison introduces a new verse. This time, the background vocals drop out entirely, leaving brief pauses at the close of each voiced line. Saints quickly leap in to fill the spaces, showing a degree of vocal involvement that until now has been masked by the backup harmonies.

Wo-o-o-o-o, I was a lonely island;	(Go ahead!)
I was a sinner too.	(Yes!)
I heard a voice from heaven,	(Yes!)
saying, "There is work to do."	(Alright!)
I took the Master's hand,	
I joined the Christian band.	(Christian band!)
And ever since that day,	
I've been holding to His hand.	

The verse stands out in its starkness, its simple text commanding the sounded foreground. The guitar and bass both limit themselves to unembellished statements of the melody, while the drums push a spartan bass-and-snare beat. Brother Faison's voice, meanwhile, maintains both its sharp attack and its coarse raspiness. Signs of strain are now becoming apparent in every aspect of his performance. Sweat beads on his forehead; muscles stand taut in his neck; breathy gasps preface every shouted line. Yet his singing loses none of its power.

Brother Faison barely breathes between the verse's last line and the chorus's first, pulling the two phrases together into a single, long sentence. Right on cue, the backup singers jump into place, adding their propulsive echo. Brother Faison's gasps are audible even over their harmonies.

You ought to get right,	/ GET RIGHT WITH GOD!
A-a-a-and do it now!	/ AND DO IT NOW!
Get right!	/ GET RIGHT WITH GOD!
The Lord will show you how!	/ HE WILL SHOW YOU HOW!

Now comes the time for the melodic stall, the part that many singers simply call the "hang-up." This time, however, Brother Faison doesn't return to the chorus. Instead, after twice voicing the "Down at the cross" line, he begins to improvise, "running" the song, putting it into "drive." As before, the backup singers put themselves on vocal hold, repeating the same percussive phrase again and again. Shifting neither its melodic nor harmonic structure, they simply reiterate "Right down at the cross." This time, however, *they keep on repeating it*, freeing Brother Faison from the constraints of lyric structure, freeing him to tell the story.

Wo-o-o-o-o, right down,	/ RIGHT DOWN AT THE CROSS
Down at the cross,	/ RIGHT DOWN AT THE CROSS
He died for you,	/ RIGHT DOWN AT THE CROSS
And He died for me!	/ RIGHT DOWN AT THE CROSS
It was at the cross,	/ RIGHT DOWN AT THE CROSS
He shed His blood!	/ RIGHT DOWN AT THE CROSS

Put thorns on His head—	/ RIGHT DOWN AT THE CROSS
It was down at the cross.	/ RIGHT DOWN AT THE CROSS
He died for you!	/ RIGHT DOWN AT THE CROSS
He hung right there,	/ RIGHT DOWN AT THE CROSS
From the sixth to the ninth hour!	/ RIGHT DOWN AT THE CROSS
He gave His Blood!	/ JESUS SHED HIS BLOOD
Get right!	/ GET RIGHT WITH GOD!
Ye-e-e-eah	/ AND DO IT NOW!

When Brother Faison twice sang the *chorus* of "Get Right with God," his stance was firmly exhortative. "Get right!" he declared; "*you* ought to get right!" Then when he sang the *verse*, his words shifted to testimony. The testifying "I" replaced the imperative "you" as his subject, almost as if to ground his sung counsel in a foundation of personal experience. "*I* was a sinner," he explained, "and *I* took the Master's hand." In the *drive*, Brother Faison switches orientation once again, now becoming the teller of sacred history. Lines that earlier served only to anchor admonition now blossom into imagistic narrative, graphically capturing the scene on Calvary's hill. The piercing thorns, the dripping blood, the long, hanging hours all push their way to the lyric foreground. The subject is Jesus; the scene—as the droning background repeats again and again—is "right down at the cross." Now Brother Faison is telling listeners *why* they need to "get right." Just as his sung testimony established *his* right—as a saved believer—to speak, this narrative establishes why *others* need to listen. "He died for *you*!" Brother Faison cries. Then, when he's told the story, he slips back into the chorus and returns to exhortation. Having given the reason, Brother Faison now urges his hearers to act.

While the backup holds the melody steady during the drive, Brother Faison overlays a tonal pattern of his own, pressing his lines into a rising and falling structure that tonally suggests the split sentences of the chorus. The pattern begins with the drive's third line ("He died for you"), when Brother Faison starts the phrase low and then pushes it high, crafting a clear rising contour. On the next line ("And He died for me"), he starts the phrase high and then drops it low, thus ending at his tonal beginning point. In so doing, he draws the two phrases together into a single tonal unit. Every two lines for the rest of the drive fall into this same up-and-down structure. As if to punctuate—and echo—this pattern, the drive phrase itself (the backup's repeated "Right down at the cross") adopts a rising and falling contour *within* the line, peaking at the word "down" and then dropping to tonal resolution at the line-ending "cross." The entire drive is thus pushed by an overlapping structure of seesawing tones, a structure that repeatedly raises expectations and then effects their resolution. The product of this alternation is a sense of rushing dynamism, a feeling that aptly attests to the appropriateness of the term "drive."[2]

Having eased the drive back into the chorus, Brother Faison begins what seems like another refrain. Opening with a coarse shout, he sings the chorus's first line. This time, however, the backup responds with a hard, punchy "Get right!" Instantly, Brother Faison assumes the role of exhorter, shouting "Sinnerman!" Back

20. "Down at the cross, He died for you, and He died for me!" Pushing into the drive, where the background's percussive response punctuates each phrase, Brother Johnnie Faison seems lost in song. With eyes pressed shut, he takes on the role of sacred storyteller, recounting the passion of Calvary. (Photo by Roland L. Freeman)

comes the backup with their percussive, "Get right!" And so begins what might be termed the "overdrive," as the singers *elevate the drive itself*, raising the song to an even higher level of intensity.

O-o-o-oh, you ought to get right!	/ GET RIGHT!	(Go ahead!)
Sinnerman!	/ GET RIGHT!	
Somebody!	/ GET RIGHT!	(Go on!)
Each of you!	/ GET RIGHT!	(Yes!)
Get right!	/ GET RIGHT!	
Mothers,	/ GET RIGHT!	
Get right!	/ GET RIGHT!	
Daughters,	/ GET RIGHT!	
Get right!	/ GET RIGHT!	
Sons,	/ GET RIGHT!	(Yes!)
Get right!	/ GET RIGHT!	(Yes!)
Fathers,	/ GET RIGHT!	
Get right!	/ GET RIGHT!	
He's calling,	/ GET RIGHT!	
For the sinners,	/ GET RIGHT!	
To get right!	/ GET RIGHT!	
Get right!	/ GET RIGHT!	
Get right!	/ GET RIGHT!	

Now the song is rolling of its own accord, the phrases careening with machine-gun intensity. The backup cries "Get right!" with staccato crispness, punching the phrase into the final two beats of every bar. Brother Faison, in turn, squeezes most of his message in each measure's first half. Working with half the space he had in the earlier drive, he cuts his phrases to their exhortative core. No longer telling a story, Brother Faison is now *preaching*.

As the drive's turnaround time diminishes, its melodic form simplifies. The "overdrive" phrase assumes a simple, ascending contour, rising every time from low to high. This insistent, unresolved rise grabs the listener's ear, building up expectations but never bringing them down. Brother Faison layers this percussive rise with the ascending and descending pattern established in the previous drive.

His first three cries—"Sinnerman!" "Somebody!" and "Each of you!"—all effect a rising tone, while "Get right!" concludes them with a tonal drop. Each double phrase in the next set of four ("Mothers, get right!" "Daughters, get right!" and so on) climbs and then tumbles, while the set that concludes the naming repeats the double rise (climbing on both "He's calling" and "For the sinners") before falling on "Get right!" As if to emphasize his point, Brother Faison twice more shouts "Get right!"—each time dropping its final tone.

As Brother Faison pushes the drive to its exhortative conclusion, he drops everything but the song's key message. Now the command to "Get right!" fills *both* halves of the rising and falling sequence. On the falling side, however, Brother Faison starts adding an extra syllable, making the injunction sound like "Get *it* right!" The slight difference gives the entire phrase an extra measure of momentum.

Get right!	/ GET RIGHT!	
Get right!	/ GET RIGHT!	
Get right!	/ GET RIGHT!	
Get right!	/ GET RIGHT!	
You,	/ GET RIGHT!	
Get right!	/ GET RIGHT!	
You,	/ GET RIGHT!	
Get right!	/ GET RIGHT!	
He's telling you,	/ GET RIGHT!	(Yes!)
To get right!	/ GET RIGHT!	
God is calling	/ GET RIGHT!	
Everybody	/ GET RIGHT!	
To get right!	/ GET RIGHT!	(Alright!)
Get right!	/ GET RIGHT!	
Get right!	/ GET RIGHT!	

The first time Brother Faison cries "You!" he points his open hand toward the pews on his left. At the second "You!" he points toward his right. Then when he declares that "God is calling *everybody*," his hand describes a rough circle, suggesting that *all* need to hear the message.

As Brother Faison pushes toward the drive's end, I can hear his mounting exhaustion. His lines are losing their sharp edges; his gasps are growing louder; his words are sounding more winded. But his coarse, shouting vocals lose none of their intensity.

Just as Brother Faison closed the first half of the "overdrive" by thrice repeating "Get right!," so too does he end the second. This time, however, he raises his left hand to shoulder level and gives a slight shake of his head. The singers instantly stop singing, leaving the instrumentalists to carry the song to its conclusion. Brother Faison slowly turns and steps back toward the cross-aisle, wiping his sweaty forehead. The saints, meanwhile, clap and call out "Alright!" and "Praise the Lord!" And the musicians play on, taking the opportunity to let *their* praises be heard.

After sixteen bars of improvisation, the musicians sound a closing phrase. "Yes! Yes!" cries Sister Perry from the amen corner. "Praise God!" calls another sister, as the congregation breaks into applause. Underneath the clapping, the three musicians continue to play in hushed tones. Without a note's rest, they are already laying a musical foundation for the lead's next remarks. Once again facing the congregation, Brother Faison looks remarkably more rested than he did mere moments before. Lifting the microphone to his mouth, as the saints continue clapping, he humbly reminds them to "Give the honor to God." He wants to make sure, even before he introduces the next song, that the saints give credit where credit is *really* due.

✳   ✳   ✳   ✳   ✳

While certainly giving honor to God, the handclaps in the Long Branch pews also acknowledge the masterful construction of the Gospel Tones' set. The careful "elevation," moving from conversational beginnings to the "high-gear" fire of the drive, carried both singers and seated saints on a journey of devotional intensification. Though the course is certainly familiar (recall, for example, the Bracey Singers' "rising high"), this particular unfolding—as all such unfoldings—is just as certainly unique. This uniqueness aptly reflects the range of factors that shape each song set.

I've already discussed the Spirit's role in guiding song selection. But as Sister Perry reminded us in an earlier chapter, the *potential* of such guidance does not preclude careful set preparation. Sanctified singers realize that the Spirit might *not* guide their song choices on a particular occasion; hence the care they put into preparation. They'll often try, for example, to match song themes to the event at hand; when singing at an anniversary, for instance, they might sing pieces like "We've Come Too Far to Turn Around" or "It's Another Day's Journey, and I'm Glad About It." They survey the other groups singing at the program and steer away from songs that are considered those groups' "specialties." They assess the pieces that they've most recently practiced and gauge the strength of their voices to meet the demands that each of those songs poses. They consider the special requests made by churchgoers and try to recall whether the honorees or sponsors have ever stated a preference for particular songs in their repertoire. And, of course, they reflect on the special needs that they believe lay with members of the expected congregation, needs that the singers feel their songs might be able to meet.

Sanctified singers set all these factors within a frame of deepening personal involvement. Most would agree with quartet lead Robert Faulk when he declares, "I don't only want to sing to the audience and make *them* feel good. *I* want to feel good while I'm up there singing."[3] Realizing that the more they focus their thoughts on praise, the greater the chances that the Lord will use their performance for His ends, many singers thus prepare sets with an eye toward intensifying *their own involvement*. In other words, they order their songs so as to gradually sharpen their focus. The "starting low" and "rising high" trajectory thus emerges not only as a strategy of congregational inducement, but also as one of personal engagement.

This sense of heightening involvement is aptly captured in an advisory adage that gospel singers often trade among themselves. I first heard this saying from Isaac "Dickie" Freeman, the longtime bass singer with Nashville's Fairfield Four. While recounting a conversation held many years earlier with an older quartet singer, Brother Freeman told how the elder singer offered him these words of advice:

"You're young in the field. And you don't have but one thing to remember, inasmuch as singing these gospel songs. And that is this: whenever you're featuring numbers, the basic of it, of what you need to do, is—remember, when you sing a song, always go slow, rise high, catch on fire, and sit down."[4]

Brother Freeman offered these words as if nothing more needed to be said about singing. "Go slow, rise high, catch on fire, and sit down." The adage is elegant in its simplicity and far-reaching in its scope. Contained in those four clauses is a model for building both song sets and individual songs, a model that charts the performed passage from the mundane to the transcendent. Start low and in self, it implies, but rise high toward the Spirit. Then when the fires start burning, let go. Let God take control. And when the fire passes, sit down. Don't stretch the singing. Don't try to scale heights that self alone can never scale. All such efforts would be futile. Not to mention anticlimactic. Instead, be content with the Spirit's blessing. Simply sit down, and give thanks.

For singers outside the faith, the elder's advice seems a simple statement of presentational pragmatics. "You start your performance slow," it seems to suggest, "and then build to a climax." The charted strategy is a theatrical given, a taken-for-granted trajectory that merits no special mention. What lends these words special significance, however, is their subtle emphasis on the *experience*—rather than on the simple presentation—of singing. The subtlety lays in the words themselves. When saints speak about "rising high," they are referring to the personal journey of elevation, the soulful journey that begins in reflection and ends in a joyous connecting of spirits. And when they talk about "catching on fire," they are pointing to the fires of transcendence, the holy flames that burn "like fire in the bones." Within this spiritual frame, "rising high and catching on fire" does not mean "putting on a good show" and then "wrecking the house." Instead, it means pursuing a path of personal focus that invites the blessings of the Spirit. To "go slow, rise high, and catch on fire" is thus to transform one's singing into a worshipful vehicle for "calling down the fire."

This is precisely the way that Brother Freeman interpreted the elder's words. As he unfolded their meaning, he explained how singers begin their sets by engaging in a two-pronged process of focus. On one hand, they focus their own minds, beginning the devotional conversation just as if they were singing in the congregation. On the other hand, they try to catch their listeners' attention so that *they too* can begin the process of focus. Realizing that many listen solely for sound, singers often begin their sets by singing pieces that deliberately foreground the lyrics. This thrusts the song's message into listeners' minds, encouraging them to confront the words. "When you start a song, you're telling a story," explains Brother Freeman. "Any song that you sing carries a message. [So] you want to start [the set] off real slow; you go slow. And then . . . you get everybody's attention."[5]

Start it slow. Start it low. The two directives stand side by side, each one elaborating on the other. To start low is to lay a foundation, crafting a base upon which the singers can slowly "build." Adding layer upon reflective layer, they then "work" the set, drawing it higher and higher, moving toward climax. But for this "building" to proceed, the foundation must be firm. It cannot rest in the "shifting sands" of rhythm and emotion.[6] Hence the call for slowness. Just as devotional leaders begin devotions with pieces that, as Sister Lena Mae Perry suggested, set "the thoughts to rolling in people's minds," so too do singers typically begin their sets. The opening song, with unhurried pace and accessible words, invites program-goers to reflect upon its message.

✳   ✳   ✳   ✳   ✳

Sitting in the pastor's office at the First Church of Love, Faith and Deliverance, I was asking Pastor Rosie Wallace Brown about the "effectiveness" of the "drive." At that time, I thought of the drive solely as a strategy for pushing people's emotions, as a way of somehow "triggering" the Spirit's touch. I was thinking, I now realize, much like Brother Hardsinger, assuming that song could "make people feel God."[7]

Pastor Brown heard this assumption in my questions and gently moved to correct it. "People love to be excited," she explained. "And the kind of songs that have leads to them *do* excite the people. Those are the kinds of song that catch their ear." *But*, she continued, those songs don't necessarily foster *understanding*. Those pieces often touch only the emotions.

> [But] the slower songs,
>   the slower paced songs,
>   temple songs,
>   are songs that the audience will have to sit and listen to.

And once you get people to listening—
    not *emotional*, but *listening*—
        then you can get a definite message across.
Because so many people that are emotionally excited by the songs that take a
    lead are not really listening to the words.
Many of them don't know the words,
    unless they're into gospel singing,
        and maybe their particular group might sing that song.
But when it's slowed down,
    and they sit,
        they start *listening*.
When they start listening,
    then they start *hearing the words*.
And that's when the Spirit will begin to deal with them.

Pastor Brown paused to let her words sink in. Then she reminded me again of the service I had attended the previous week, where the Spirit had flowed and the songs were all slow. "It's the same process," she said gently. "It's the same Spirit."[8]

*   *   *   *   *

Pastor Brown's implied contrast between "temple songs" and "songs with leads" raises yet another point about most gospel groups' opening songs. Singers don't only sing *slow* pieces when laying their set's foundation. They also tend to sing "sweet" pieces, songs that stress harmony and vocal subtlety, songs that "soothe" and "invite." Such pieces typically favor group harmonies over lead vocals, and vocal lines over instrumental ones. Their foregrounded harmonies accentuate the ensemble's unity, tacitly turning ears away from the contributions of individual singers. Singers who "start sweet" open by *inviting* rather than *attempting to impress*, by *showing accord* rather than *showing off*. They begin with crafted eloquence, starting praises on a note that catches the ear with its tuneful elegance and catches the mind with its clearly stated message. "You want to get everybody's attention," explains Brother Freeman. "You want to get the people's minds focusing."

The blended harmonies of the opening song also challenge singers to focus their own energies. Singers often say that "you've got to be right" when harmony carries the song. There's no room for distraction, no room for error. The harmonizing must stand by itself, without foregrounded instruments or lengthy leads to hide behind. Further underscoring the importance of a smooth blend is the slow pacing of most opening songs. Every off-note in such pieces stands out, calling attention to itself at the very moment when singers want all attention focused on the message. Hence singers struggle for harmonized precision, trying to sing with an ease that discounts its own artistry, trying to convey a sense of effortlessness that slides listeners right past the sound and to the words. Achieving this apparent ease—and doing so on the first song—is anything but easy. But it *does* force singers to start their set with focused minds. The group itself, asserts Rev. Samuel McCrary, must be "on one accord." "That means agreeing in mind, agreeing in Spirit," he explains, "so your sound can come together."[9] This agreement ideally pulls the group together as a devotional unit, bringing singers' spirits into worshipful accord while extending a joint invitation to the Spirit.

✳ ✳ ✳ ✳ ✳

Brother Hardsinger again. We were talking about the makeup of song sets, discussing how sets for secular audiences differed from those sung for church audiences. When I asked about up-tempo songs, Brother Hardsinger assured me that he always saved pieces "with the best beat" for the performance's end.

"If I was in church," he explained, "I'd probably sing two or three mess-around songs . . ." I must have looked puzzled at the term "mess-around," for he quickly offered a definition. "You know," he said, "[songs] sung just to stay on the floor and keep things moving. And then we'd get into the upbeat part."

A few seconds later, Brother Hardsinger repeated his definition, once again relegating opening songs to a relatively trivial status. "In church we would place the *better* songs after we get through messing around. You know, singing a tune just to stay up there and get involved in the audience."[10]

Brother Hardsinger's words stand in sharp contrast to those of Pastor Brown. For her, and for countless other sanctified singers, the slow opening songs begin the process of reflection. For Brother Hardsinger and his "performing" counterparts, they serve only to bide time and "keep things moving." For one group, the songs are invitations. For the other, they are merely introductions.

✳ ✳ ✳ ✳ ✳

As services proceed and congregational accord solidifies, the need for slow, "sweet" beginnings gradually lessens. Singers appearing early in the program typically travel the full low-to-high path, always trying to focus congregational thoughts on worship. Those performing later, however, often find themselves facing programgoers already "caught up" in praise. Such singers also find *themselves* "caught up," having themselves been part of the worshiping congregation. As I've already mentioned, saints speak of this spiritual intensification as if it were a rising spiral, with every performance advancing worship to a higher level. In the ideal program, where all singers are "real" and all saints are in accord, each ensemble would thus start at a higher devotional pitch than its predecessor and would push the praises to a new climax. Even when this ideal is not realized, however, the program's ascendant tone allows late-singing groups to move right into the "rising high" phase of their performance. They might, for example, replace their "theme" with a song normally slated for later in the set. They might open with exhortation instead of praise. Or, like the Gospel Tones, they might accelerate their ascent toward "hard," intense performance. Alternately, they might do nothing at all, satisfied that their messages of praise will simply resonate at a deeper level in their hearers' souls. Whatever the chosen strategy, the options increase as the singing proceeds.

Many singers say that as their first song nears its end, they're preparing for the second. This is the moment that Sister Perry describes when she tells of songs "rolling" in her mind, silently guiding her to the next piece. Countless other singers describe much the same phenomenon. Durham's Rev. Liggonia Young, for example, tells of being guided by spiritual "vibrations" that she feels from the congregation. "It's not a matter of reading somebody's mind," she explains, "but it's just a matter of feeling certain *vibrations* from them. . . . And you just, kind of *listen*, and let God do with you what He wants to do." Pastor Rosie Wallace Brown, in contrast, describes the process as being even more direct, with the Spirit specifying the precise songs to be sung. "So many times the Lord would speak to my heart and say, 'this song is necessary,'" she attests. "And it would be the very song the people would need."[11]

All of these singers admit, however, that the Spirit does not *always* provide guidance. When the vibrations aren't felt or the songs don't roll, they consider again all the factors already considered when planning the set. Now, however, they add the factor of congregational response, taking into account reaction from the pews. That's why singers often say that the discerning eye is one of their most valuable tools. Watching programgoers' responses—particularly when spiritual insight is not forthcoming—helps them to steer their set toward greater efficacy.

Working within the frames of spiritual guidance and congregational response, many singers consciously vary the tones and textures of their words and songs. Just as program hosts try to bring variety to their lineups, so do singers strive for variety in their sets. Both attempt to diversify their presentation in order to reach the broadest possible public. In song sets, this diversity manifests itself in many ways. For example, singers will often switch song styles during their sets, perhaps moving from harmony singing to hard gospel, or from traditional to contemporary. Or they might vary their tempos, shifting from slow to mid-tempo to fast. At the same time, they might shift vocal textures, sliding (as did the Gospel Tones in their first two songs) from smooth, "sweet" singing to gravelly, "hard" shouting. In so doing, they might also vary their songs' themes and functions, perhaps cycling from a praise song to one posed as testimony, or from prayer to exhortation (as the Gospel Tones did when they followed "Will the Lord Be with Me" with "Get Right with God"). Such shifts in function often yield corresponding shifts in emotional tone, as songs move from joyful to solemn, or stern to sentimental. The governing "rule" seems to be constant and conscious variation and contrast.[12]

When assessing all these shifts, we must also take into account the remarks between songs, for these too figure into the drama of variation. They too move from slow to fast, from conversational to chanted, from "sweet" to "hard," from testimony to exhortation. Sometimes they do so as simple bridges, effecting the stylistic and thematic slide from song to song. Just as often, however, they stand as independent players in the devotional drama, corresponding in style and function to neither of the songs that frame them. This holds particularly true for between-song testimonies, many of which stretch as long as—or longer than—the songs themselves. Such remarks greatly magnify the potential for contrastive variation, granting singers even more options within the boundaries of the typical three-song set.

Just as any of these shifts can occur within the course of a singer's remarks, so too can they occur within the course of a single song. We need only look back at the Gospel Tones' performance of "Get Right with God" to see how seamlessly these shifts can occur. Brother Johnnie Faison's voice moved from the gentle, conversational tones of his spoken introduction to the coarse insistence of his singing to the even coarser intensity of his drives. The song's opening choruses conveyed an exhortative message; then the verse offered first-person testimony. The first drive told an abstract narrative; the second leapt into "hard" exhortation. Furthermore, the piece started fast (in contrast to its mid-tempo predecessor) and then got faster. Even when taken alone, this song stands as a model of elevation and internal contrast.

But no song stands alone. Nor do the words that precede or follow it. Instead, songs and commentary flow together, creating a whole only when heard as a set. Each part of the set—every song, every introduction, every testimony—offers itself as a frame for creative elaboration; each part invites the crafting of its own unique trajectory. At the same time, the set itself emerges as a frame; its loose structure also invites a singular and situation-specific realization. The difference between the two is that the set follows a logic of intensification. Whether this logic is internally enacted (as when singing saints tighten their devotional focus) or externally imposed (as when singers press toward a crowd-pleasing climax), the product remains the same: the set slides inexorably toward spiritual and/or emotional crescendo. Within this overarching frame, the individual parts—though not themselves subject to the set's logic—nonetheless contribute to its ultimate realization.[13]

When saints talk about the gradual intensification of performance, they tend to use the term "elevation." Congregations are said to "elevate" songs when they quicken their tempo and begin to layer their rhythms. Preachers are said to "elevate" sermons when they move from the "low gear" of conversational teaching to the "high gear" of chanted preaching. Gospel singers are said to "elevate" performance when they shift from the "sweet" to the "hard." In all of these instances, believers pose the "elevation" as both strategic action and submissive receipt. In other words, saints both *elevate* and *are elevated*. On one hand, they are actively *doing* the elevating, consciously tightening their devotional focus and heightening the intensity of their presentation. On the other hand, the elevating *is being done unto them*, as the Spirit joins the conversation and blesses the saints with inspiration, succor, and experiential uplift. As the term "elevation" suggests, this process of spiritual intercession is often gradual and cumulative. As the conversation deepens, the Spirit's role grows greater, while that of the worshiping saint diminishes. Saints say that the Spirit rarely pushes believers from "starting low" directly to "catching on fire." In between usually comes the "rising high" of gradual self-surrender.

Perhaps the simplest and most familiar form of elevation is that which manifests itself in congregational singing. Generations of saints and outsiders have remarked upon the way that sanctified congregations often intensify songs in the course of their singing. Sometimes this intensification takes the form of a gradual speeding up; sometimes it entails an additive layering of rhythms; sometimes it manifests itself in a shortening of lyric lines and a subsequent acceleration of call-and-response pacing. Sometimes it takes all of these forms; sometimes it takes others. When asked *why* the singing changes, saints simply say that the "feeling" starts stirring and the conversations begin. When this happens, as Deacon Denkins has already explained, the *vibrations* of accord draw saints more fully "into the service," leading them to sing with greater spirit.[14]

But elevation takes a somewhat different course when saints step into positions of devotional leadership. Saints who stand before the congregation to lead worship—be they preachers, prayer leaders, testimony givers, or simply singers—describe elevation as a process of emergent spiritual collaboration. In essence, they tell of experiences that chart a continuum of spiritual intercession, with the Spirit playing an increasingly larger role as the elevation proceeds.[15]

We've already encountered the Spirit's contributions in the early stages of intercession, when the Spirit inspires and empowers. As we've seen, the Spirit inspires by granting knowledge or guiding thought. This is the process that leads singers to know the proper songs to sing, that leads emcees to deliver the words that programgoers need to hear, that leads preachers to construct the arguments that will draw sinners to salvation. "The Spirit is talking within you about His people out there," explains Elder Lawrence Richardson. "God lets [you] know, 'My people need to know so-and-so and so-and-so.' . . . He'll point you *to* it, and then He'll guide you *into* it, to His Word."[16]

Just as the Spirit inspires, so too does He empower, infusing saints' words with affective force. This is the same power already addressed in the discussion about prayer, a power that doesn't change words or the way they are spoken, but instead changes *the way they are received*. "They're [still] your words," asserts Deacon Edward Denkins. "The Spirit's just helping them along. It builds, putting a little *process* on them. Just like a cylinder goes up and down."[17] This mystical "process" grants human words the authority of transcendence, giving them the "power to move." As a force of consequence rather than creation, the empowerment is authored solely by the Spirit.

In inspiration, the Spirit guides (but doesn't provide) saints' words. In empowerment, the Spirit fills those words with spiritual authority. As these processes occur, the speaking or singing saints themselves begin to feel the Spirit's ministrations. They experience the elevation, feel the mysterious tingling, embrace the upwelling joy. These feelings, in turn, cry out for expression. Saints say that you can't talk in the "calmness of conversation" when the "feeling is on you." Something has got to change. The elevation has got to show itself. And it does so in the realm of style, transforming the way that words roll from the mouth, changing their delivery and their sound. As a holiness deacon once told me, "You can hear the change—the change from natural to supernatural, from the natural voice to a spiritual one. And you just *know* that the Spirit is working with that saint."[18]

✶ ✶ ✶ ✶ ✶

I had asked Bishop Frizelle Yelverton about the Spirit's role in preaching when I first heard him use the word "zooning." I knew that "zooning" referred to a particularly musical form of preaching. I also knew, from many Sunday services, that Bishop Yelverton's anointed sermons often soared to heights of melodic mastery. So when he mentioned "zooning," I thought that a definition was worth pursuing.

Chuckling at my question, Bishop Yelverton responded, "Well, we call that something like a little *gravy* in your sermon, you know. That's something that kind of *brings you up*. When you zoon or squall or something like that—is that what you're talking about?" When I nodded, he continued. "Well, it's just something in it that has a tendency to lift the people. You know. When you zoon home, it'll lift the people."

So the zooning both "brings up" the preacher and "lifts" the congregation, I thought to myself. That leaves open the question of authorship. Who is actually *causing* the zooning, I wondered. But before I could ask the question, Bishop Yelverton was offering the answer. He began by grounding his explanation in the Bible, referring to the "crying" of John the Baptist. "I don't know how John did it when he was down in the wilderness," the bishop said,

> But he said,
>   "I'm a voice,
>   down here *crying* in the wilderness."
> He cried down there so,
>   till Jerusalem and Judea went out to see him.
> I don't know *what* he was hollering out.
> He was down there *hollering*.
> And they wanted to know,
>   "Who is you?"
> He said,
>   "I'm just a voice,
>   crying in the wilderness."
> He didn't claim to be nothing but a voice.
> So, he must have been—
>   I don't know whether he was zooning,

whether he was moaning,
    but he's *crying*.
Not *natural*, not natural crying with tears.
But he cried out with his voice.

When the bishop paused, I nudged the explanation home, asking about his *own* experience with "crying out." "When that happens," I asked, "when you're in a sermon, and you begin to . . ."

"You're getting elevated in the Spirit," he declared, answering my question before I could even ask it.

You're getting elevated.
You notice that when the preacher start preaching,
    he don't start off zooning.
But as he go on in the sermon,
    as he feel that *impact* of the Spirit of the Lord,
        then he [is] lifted up to that point.

"So is the Spirit, then, more or less the 'director' of the zooning?" I asked. "Yeah," he replied, obviously somewhat hesitant about my use of the word "director." "It would be." Then, as he thought about the term's implications, he nodded and repeated with more assurance, "Yeah, it would be."

"So that's not something that you would *consciously* begin doing?" I continued. "No," he answered flatly. "No. I got to build up my sermon. I got to build it up until where I begin to *feel* it. See? You can't *preach* until you *feel* the sermon yourself."

Bishop Yelverton proceeded to describe the Word of God as "spiritual food" that feeds both the congregation and the preacher. Then, by way of a coda, he returned to the issue of control.

"It's a certain peak in your sermon that you reach," he explained. "When you reach that place, then maybe the zooning comes on. Or the moaning. Or the voice lifted. . . . It's not me. But it's God. God is having control of the service this way."[19]

* * * * *

Bishop Yelverton leaves no doubt about the source of his style. His voice elevates, he explains, when *he* elevates. And *he* elevates when he begins to feel the Spirit in his words. And when he feels the Spirit, then his hearers too are elevated. For the Spirit rides his words to touch *their* spirits. Then *they* cry out; they say "Amen"; they acknowledge the feeling. And *this*, as the bishop explained later in our conversation, comes right back to the preacher, pushing him or her further along the rising spiral of epiphany. Bishop Yelverton likened this process to that of a ball attached to a paddle by a rubber band. "Every time you hit the ball out, it comes back," he explained. "So as you throw the *Word* out, *it* comes back." And when it comes back, it further focuses the preacher's mind, opening more space for the Spirit, inviting the elevation to proceed. And setting the entire cycle into motion once again.

Bishop Yelverton asserts that his words begin to elevate when the Spirit begins to elevate him. He does *not* say, however, that the Spirit is actually controlling his particular style of zooning. Controlling the *service*, perhaps, and controlling the *elevation*, certainly, but not necessarily controlling the *style*. When pressed on this matter, most sanctified preachers with whom I've spoken say that style is a gift that comes with the calling (or, in the case of saints who aren't preachers, with the anointing). The Spirit doesn't so much guide the tongue (at least at this point in the elevation) as provide the pathways for the tongue to follow. Then when elevation occurs, the tongue naturally and unconsciously follows these paths, starting to zoon, falling in tune. Saints say there's no need for forethought, no reason for practice. The pathways are provided; the tongue need only follow.

Note that "pathways" is plural. Believers are quick to point out that elevation finds voice in many different ways. As with the gift of song, everyone's style is unique. "There can be a million leaves on a tree," explains quartet lead Robert Faulk, "and not a one of them is shaped alike. So that's what I'm saying [about preaching]—God got a whole lot of preachers, and a whole lot of preachers that was called to preach His Word, but all of them have a different style."[20]

Brother Faulk's closing phrases also make an important point about style's relationship to anointing. By carefully distinguishing between called and noncalled preachers, and then indicating that all of them have distinct styles, he subtly suggests that *anyone* can preach with the *sound* of elevation. "The loud tone and the upstairs voice—that don't always be the Spirit," he explained later in our conversation. "That can just be the way you was trained to preach! It don't always be the Spirit." This carries us right back to Chapter 7's discussion about style in prayer, when I spoke of saints' wariness in linking sounded style with spiritual state. The association is certainly there, forged both by tradition and by the untold times that elevated words have yielded a felt touch or a witnessed flow. But association does not establish cause. And sound does not testify to Spirit. After all, as the saints remind us, Satan is the world's greatest imitator.

But saints admit that they aren't always vigilant. They don't go into services *looking* for Satan. If they did, there would be little need for so many reminders about "form or fashion." The very constancy of these cautions suggests saints' own acknowledgment that they sometimes aren't watchful enough. And, perhaps, that they don't challenge enough of their own assumptions, one of which links elevated style with elevated experience. When questioned on this matter, most saints are like Brother Faulk—though quick to deny causal connection, they'll admit that the connection is nonetheless there, always tacitly in mind, always present as an unaddressed "given." When they hear the sounds of elevation, they simply assume—unless given reason to think otherwise—that the Spirit is at hand.

What, then, *are* these "sounds" of elevation? They're as diverse as the leaves on a tree, says Brother Faulk. But like those leaves, they show some fundamental similarities. Enough so, at least, to allow for a rough description.[21] We've already encountered most of these features in the speaking and singing of saints at the Branchettes' anniversary. The one that comes across most clearly on the printed page is the grouping of words into tight, percussive phrases, phrases shorter than those of most nonelevated, congregational exchange, and much shorter than those of everyday conversation. These phrases often assume a poetic elegance that manifests itself in parallel structure and incremental repetition. As the phrases grow shorter and more poetic, the voice tends to grow louder and more insistent. At the same time, the overall pitch often shifts, typically sliding upward. (Hence Brother Faulk's reference to preachers' "loud tone and upstairs voice.") With this slide, the speaker's tonal range tends to narrow, settling into a band whose outer edges are much closer together than those of everyday speech.

Saints note that the degree and direction of elevation's sound shift vary from speaker to speaker. What tends to remain the same is the simple fact of change. As Brother Freeman observes, when speaking about elevation in prayer, "The more [the prayer-giver] enters into the Spirit, his voice will change. Usually, he'll go up. Sometimes he gets a high-pitched voice. Sometimes he gets a low voice. Sometimes he starts quivering in his voice. So it changes. Everybody's different . . . but his voice *will* change."[22]

Perhaps the most remarked-upon aspect of this change is its move toward music. As we've seen in the cross-aisle comments at the Branchettes' anniversary, elevated words tend to ride the contours of recurring melodic patterns, rising and falling with a predictability unique to each saint. The tuneful combination and contrast of these passages often gives elevated words a distinctly musical lilt. Churchgoers openly acknowledge this tunefulness in the names they give to elevated speaking, calling it "tuning" (or "tuning up"), "zooning," "groaning," "whooping," and "crying." As saints are quick to say, elevation tends to move talk into song and song into talk, pulling the two realms together in the harmonious service of the Word.

Saints' use of the term "groaning" to describe heightened style also hints at the strain that often makes itself apparent during elevation. This too is part of elevation's sound. We've already encountered such strain many times at the Branchettes' anniversary: in the tense tautness of Deacon Eldridge's delivery, in the staccato urgency of Sister Bracey's praises, in the strained sharpness of Evangelist Lofton's urgings, in the gravelly hoarseness of Brother Faison's singing. Almost as if to accentuate this evidenced exertion, many saints close their elevated lines with a sharp expulsion of breath, typically heard as a grunt or explosive "Ha!" Other saints punctuate their lines with a gasped intake of breath, as did Brother Faison when he rolled into his song's drive. All of these signs convey a clear message of intensity and deep engagement.

✳   ✳   ✳   ✳   ✳

Just a few weeks before the Branchettes' twentieth anniversary, I was sitting with Ethel Elliott and Lena Mae Perry at Sister Perry's home in southeastern Raleigh.

We had been talking about the easy flow of songs in performance, and about the way the Spirit guided their singing, when I asked about the term "hard." "What does it mean," I asked, "to say that someone sings 'hard'?"

Sister Elliott immediately posed the analogy of ballplayers who "put everything they had into their playing." "And when you get up to do something for the Lord," she concluded, "He wants you to put everything you got into it. He don't like no slowing around." She paused for a moment, and then clarified her meaning. "You know," she added, "[He don't like] this messing around."

"So a lot of times," Sister Elliott continued, "I might tell Mae, I say, 'Well, we sure sang *hard* today.' I mean, that's just a word we use. *Meaning* . . ." Again she paused, this time for dramatic effect. ". . . that we put everything in it . . ."

". . . that we had," murmured Sister Perry.

". . . that we had," agreed Sister Elliott. "And so when you do that, I believe the Lord is pleased."

"I do too," concurred Sister Perry.

This wasn't the answer I had anticipated. When Sister Elliott brought up the baseball analogy, I expected her to say something about effort and exertion, riffing on the notion of "playing hard." Instead, she defined "hard" wholly in terms of engagement. "Exertion" seemed to play no role in her definition.

At first, this puzzled me. Most saints whom I'd questioned about "hard singing" spoke first about its sound, pointing to its characteristic "strained voice" and fast, labored vocals. The Branchettes, however, said nothing about strain. Nor did they as they kept talking, elaborating on their definition. I just listened, saying nothing.

Then Sister Perry offered an answer to my unasked question. She started by subtly acknowledging that other people's definition of "hard" might differ from their own. "Wherever we go," she explained, "people tell us, 'You all sing *so* hard.'"

But what they don't understand is,
   it's not that you're really singing *hard*.
[But] as Ethel said,
   you're putting all you got in it.
And then when the Spirit of the Lord gets on you—
   they don't understand that.
See?
   They don't really understand that.
To *us*, it doesn't *seem* hard.
But to *them*, it might *look* hard.
See?
To us, it isn't that hard to sing.[23]

There was the answer. The Branchettes don't link "hard singing" with strain not because they don't *show* strain (as indeed they sometimes do), but because they don't *feel* strain. As Sister Perry went on to explain, when they submit their singing to the Spirit, the words flow with ease. No matter *what* it may look like.

21. While closing their anniversary set with "Oh Lord, You've Been Good to Me," the Branchettes' Lena Mae Perry seems lost on the Spirit's passionate embrace. "We put everything in it that we have," Sister Elliott explains. "And so when you do that, I believe the Lord is pleased." (Photo by Roland L. Freeman)

When I got home that evening, I searched through my field notes to see if other singers had made this same point, and I had let it pass unaddressed. At first, I found example after example of *preachers* describing precisely this same experience in preaching. Then I came across the notes from a conversation held almost ten years earlier with Rev. Liggonia Young, the young lead singer with Durham's Everready Singers. Listening back to the tape, I discovered that her words were even more explicit than Sister Perry's.

We hadn't even been talking about "hard singing." Instead, Rev. Young had been describing how she felt when the Spirit began to "deal with her." First she spoke of "thinking about the words" of her songs, and then about "really getting into" what she was singing. Then Rev. Young described the anointing, portraying it as a feeling of deep relaxation that washed over her body as she sang. "You become relaxed in your songs, and relaxed in your music, " she explained. "And the Spirit is bringing about this relaxation. Then you *know* that you're singing with a very special anointing."

As she continued, she began to talk about watching other singers sing. "If you'll notice," she remarked,

> A lot of people,
>   they have to kind of *push* to get their words out,
>   to make it sound right.
> It's like they're straining,
>   and they're pulling so hard.
> [But] the anointing will permit you to just—
>   *sing.*
> I mean, it's not a lot of stress,
>   it's not a lot of strain.
> Of course, you must think to make your words sound correct,
>   or to go with the music.
>   You know, so that it will be in harmony together.
> But it's not a strenuous thing.
> It's not hard.[24]

Again the emphasis on engagement. And again the emphasis on ease. Rev. Young and the Branchettes both portray elevation not as a state that saints must "work" to attain, but rather as one that saints slide into as they submit to the Spirit. And both contend that there's nothing "hard" about singing when singers are singing with the Spirit.

* * * * *

When Bishop Yelverton addressed the shift into zooning, he described it as a gradual "lifting." When Rev. Young spoke of "getting into" her singing, she described it as a gradual "easing." Both saints described elevation in terms of *emergence*; both suggested that the Spirit wielded the guiding hand. Yet when Brother Faison flipped his song into drive, he seemed to forsake emergence in favor of quick action. He was clearly controlling the elevation. Furthermore, the other Gospel Tones knew precisely what he was doing and instantly jumped to their prearranged parts. Rather than waiting *until* they were "raised," Brother Faison and the other Gospel Tones seemed to be doing the "raising."

A review of Brother Dickie Freeman's "go slow, rise high" remarks suggests that he advised much the same course. After establishing the need for slow, low beginnings, he recommended that "your next step is—you raise. You rise high. In other words, the level. You come on up, and on up." You raise the *level*, he suggests. You come on up. In light of elevation's characteristic pitch and volume rise—indeed, in light of Brother Freeman's own comments about elevation often yielding a "high-pitched voice"—this sounds more like strategy than submission.

And this is precisely what it is, as many singers freely admit. Elevation, they explain, takes many forms. Spiritual elevation is something that *is done to* a saint; the Spirit is the author. But what might be called "strategic" elevation is something that *the saint does*; here, the saint is the author. When asked to explain the purpose of self-authored elevation, most sanctified singers with whom I've spoken describe it as *elevation in service of elevation*. They say that they consciously adopt some of elevation's stylistic features in order to more effectively focus both their praises and those of the congregation. In other words, they elevate their own intensity so as to invite the intensity of anointment. Strategic elevation thus becomes a tool for inviting spiritual elevation.

The process works in two ways. On one hand, strategic elevation pulls singers into a structured intensification, drawing them into a forceful, driving phase of performance. With fellow singers pushing the melody and the musicians (or clapping churchgoers) pushing the rhythm, the process is much like that enacted in shout songs, when the demands of engagement force a tight focus on the task at hand. Singers say that elevation compels them to concentrate on their singing, that it pushes them to confront the lyrics and the message. In so doing, it sharpens their spiritual focus.

On the other hand, strategic elevation—again like shout songs—"excites" the congregation and ideally moves *them* toward greater focus. By conveying the appearance of engagement, it ideally stirs them to reflection and invites them to deepen their own involvement. As congregation members become more involved, their conversations with both the cross-aisle and the Spirit become more animated, prompting even more cries of "Amen!" and "Thank You, Jesus!" These cries, in turn, echo in the ears of the singers, inspiring them to "dig on down a little deeper," encouraging them to further their own reflective centering. Singers thus benefit from their own engagement and that of the congregation, with both fostering the focus that invites anointment.[25]

Of course, intentional elevation also has its dangers. Sanctified singers admit that "the beat" always stands ready to lure the emotions and distract the spirit. Just as shout songs can sometimes lead thoughts away from the lyric's message, so too can the intensity of elevation. Furthermore—say the saints—self-willed elevation invites singers to flirt with falsity. Though most singers treat such elevation solely as a mode of personal intensification, some get caught up in the excitement of congregational arousal. As Jojo Wallace cautioned in the previous chapter, the exhilaration of sparking "Amens" and "getting the crowd" can draw singers further and further into "performance," tempting singers to exaggerate their engagement and to push their enactments to new crowd-pleasing heights. Saints say that singers with "minds stayed on Jesus" needn't worry about these temptations, as their faith gives them strength to resist. Those whose faith is weak, however, unwittingly woo Satan every time they flip a song into elevation.

Of all the ways that elevation can be strategically enacted, the most common among sanctified singers are sharp, in-song elevations (the "flip" mentioned in the previous sentence) and the more gradual escalations that come from sequencing songs in a set. Both follow the "start low, rise high" trajectory, and both are arranged in advance (though these arrangements are always subject to change). Since the former stands in service of the latter, we'll start there.

When introducing the concept of elevation, I offered congregational song as a model, pointing to the way that congregations often intensify singing as they press songs to their conclusion. For the most part, this intensification is gradual and unconscious; saints say that it "just happens" as songs begin to wind themselves into the soul. Sometimes, however, congregation members deliberately and abruptly push the singing to a higher level. The saint singing lead, for example, might suddenly shift the melody to a markedly faster pace. Or an instrumentalist might double-time the song's tempo. The effect of these shifts, particularly if they are "borne up" by the congregation, is instant elevation. Intensity crackles through the church like an electric current, sparking praises in every pew. The singing grows more exuberant; the clapping becomes more forceful; the tapped and tambourined rhythms grow thicker. Such elevations palpably transform the tone of worship.

Elder saints with whom I've spoken claim that churchgoers have been elevating singing in this manner as long as they can remember. Elder singers say much the same thing about gospel performers, noting that quartets and gospel groups have long pushed their songs with abrupt elevations. Sometimes they elevate their singing by cutting the line length and accelerating the tempo, swinging the song into a driving roll. At other times, singers elevate by suddenly shifting the lead and harmonies to a higher pitch, forcing the entire group to push their voices to their upper limits. Both strategies dramatically disrupt the song's flow, creating "before" and "after" segments that stand sharply apart.

Both shifts achieve this break by switching to styles that openly reference elevated speech. The first does so by slashing the lead lines into short, punchy phrases, thus accelerating the call-and-response turnaround and giving the elevation a percussive drive. The second alludes to elevated style by sharply hiking the pitch, thus connotatively capturing the "upstairs voice" of the preacher. (Singers tacitly acknowledge this allusion when they call this pitch switch "raising the voice" or "raising the tone," terms typically applied to the preacher's elevation.)[26] Both style shifts effectively capture listeners' attention, compelling them—as quartet lead Smiley Fletcher suggests—to "focus on the song":

"When you start it down, a lot of people is not aware—well, I would say they're not paying much attention. Then when you raise it, and really get the beat and the swing to it, then it *clicks in mind* of what you're doing. *Then you got their whole attention focused on that one song*, and on what you're doing."[27]

The elevation "clicks in mind," Brother Fletcher says. It snaps programgoers to attention. And then it thrusts the song's message to the foreground of their minds.

✶ ✶ ✶ ✶ ✶

A breezy wind had swept away the afternoon sultriness, and the outdoors offered a rare respite from the Carolina summer. So the four of us—brothers John and Claude Landis, their mother Bertha Landis, and myself—pulled the chairs outside to Ms. Landis's narrow front porch. The Landis brothers had recently celebrated their twenty-third singing anniversary with the Golden Echoes, a Granville County quartet widely respected for both their singing skills and the seriousness with which they take their music. Bertha Landis, herself an active singer in church, was the one initially responsible for steering her sons toward music.

That afternoon, we had gathered at Ms. Landis's to talk about "form or fashion." John Landis and I had discussed this topic on other occasions, and I wanted to get his thoughts on tape. When I called to set up the meeting, he suggested that the views of three singers might be better than those of one. I heartily agreed. So now there were four of us.

It didn't take long for the conversation to move from the general to the specific. Within minutes, we were talking about professional quartets and their showy flamboyance. At this point, I mentioned the "drive," remarking that this section seemed to invite an extra measure of showiness. John Landis—the Echoes' lead singer—quickly agreed, though he cautioned against assuming that what I was seeing was all "show." Things *do* change, he assured me, when you start "running a song." Because when the song builds up, it takes you right along with it.

A song builds itself up.
You can start singing a song—
you can start off with it,
    and maybe you're not really *into* that song
      when you start singing.
But the more you sing it,
    and listen at yourself,
    and listen to the words,
      you can *build yourself up*.

Until where you can just—
   you can start *running* that song.
And if people enjoy it,
   people out there will help you.
If *they* enjoying it,
   you ought to be getting something out of it.

Claude Landis and his mother had been murmuring agreement throughout Brother John's words. Then Ms. Landis interceded, saying, "And then the Spirit— the Spirit will just build up . . ."

Before she could finish, John Landis was talking again, his words rushing to complete his point.

It's just like a *whirlwind*.
The farther it go,
   the more it builds up.
     In there.
And then you—
   you just keep rolling.

The other two Landises nodded their heads. But John wanted to make sure that I had heard his mother's comment, and that I realized that what was "building" was not just "emotion."

I've seen people sing,
   that get to singing a song,
     until where *they can't sing anymore.*
   And they just sit there.
     Filled up.
Maybe they get to shouting then;
   maybe it leads to a shout.
You see what I'm saying?

Again we all nodded, and John Landis went on to compare such songs to a hurricane, saying that they "get more powerful the further they go." "That Spirit will build up in you," Ms. Landis inserted. "Because in your singing, you're supposed to be led by the Spirit," added Brother Claude, the Golden Echoes' baritone. "And when you're led by the Spirit and the people together, then you . . ." As his words trailed off, Claude gently shook his head, momentarily stalled in his effort to describe the indescribable.

Brother John quickly came to his assistance. "That's something that—it's hard to explain what it is," he explained. "It's just something that comes over on you, and it . . ." He too paused, searching for words.

"Well, it's the *Spirit*," interjected Ms. Landis, her voice filled with certainty. "The

Spirit, I think [the Bible] says, is like the wind. You don't know where it come from or where it going, but you know when it's *there*! You know when it's there."[28]

* * * * *

The song "builds," John Landis declared, "like a whirlwind." The more you sing it, and the more you "listen to the words," the stronger the feeling gets. Until finally you can "run" the song. And then, Brother Landis declares, "you just keep rolling." Because then you are fully focused. And then, as a result of this focus, you often have the help of the Spirit.

The vehicle for the improvisatory "run" that John Landis describes is often called the "drive." Like the intentional pitch shift of elevation, the drive is an instrument of intensification, a carefully arranged song section that stalls melodic progress while freeing the lead to improvise over a static, repetitive background. Typically following a song's regular verses, this section transforms the lead-backup relationship into one of contrasting freedom and fixity. The backup's duty during the drive is to repeat a single, brief, percussive phrase (e.g., the Gospel Tones' "Right down at the cross"), restating the same passage again and again without shifting its melodic or harmonic structure. The backup singers, in other words, put themselves on vocal hold. With this steady "repeat" as a foundation, the lead singer can improvise at will.

As soon as the backup slides into the drive, the lead can cast off all the constraints imposed by the song's predrive melody and predrive lyrics. From this point forward, the lead singer faces a vista of lyric freedom. The only limitation is that imposed by the cadences of the backup, a restriction that does little more than keep the lead's lines relatively short. But as Johnnie Faison's improvisations suggest, the lead can circumvent even this constraint by simply dividing long statements into short parts, and then uttering the whole over the course of two, three, or more "repeats." (For example, Brother Faison extended the line, "He died for you, and He died for me," over two cycles of the drive phrase, while he stretched "He's calling for the sinners to get right!" over three.) The lead's freedom even extends to determining when the drive will end. Until the backup singers get the cue to close, they just sing on and on. Then, when the signal comes, they drop their repeated phrase and either close the song (as the Gospel Tones did on their second drive) or jump back into the melody, adding a quick coda to close out the verse (as the Gospel Tones did on their first drive).[29]

The experienced features of this song section are aptly captured in the many names bestowed on it by gospel singers. One set of terms alludes to the backup singers' melodic stall and repeated phrase; hence the terms "hang-up," "riff," "working section," and "repeat." When singers describe this section as *process* rather than *thing*, they speak about "working the song," "rotating," or "hanging the song." A second set of terms points to the driving intensity and spirited freedom of the lead. Hence the terms "drive," "free-style," and "stretch-out," and their processual counterparts, "running the song" (or "running the note," "running the lead part"), "ad libbing," "putting the song in drive," "riffing," and "stretching out." A third set of terms points to this section's place in the trajectory of elevation, with singers talking about "working the song up" or simply "climaxing." All of these names tacitly acknowledge the formal and strategic structure of the drive.

Gospel veterans generally agree that the drive evolved as a popular strategy of song intensification sometime in the mid to late 1940s. Its earliest architects, by all accounts, were quartets, who treated it as a second-stage elevation, using it to further focus the attention already captured by a "raised" pitch.[30] The dramatic shift of form, the driving roll of the "repeat," and the dynamic contrast between a free-singing lead and a droning background all seemed to catch congregational ears and fire congregational excitement. In the drive's early years, lead singers tended to overlay the background phrase with couplets drawn from tradition and with rhymed lines composed specifically for the hang-up. As the drive grew more popular, however, singers began to explore its lyric possibilities. They soon came to view it as an ideal vehicle for improvisation, as a section where they could "stretch out" and effectively "work the song." At the same time, they discovered that the drive offered an unparalleled opportunity for sharpening their *own* devotional focus.

The dynamic at work here—the "whirlwind" quality to which John Landis referred—is easily understood. Whether singers start their songs low or in elevation, they remain bound by the song's structure. The potential for textual improvisation (particularly given the vocal presence of the backup) is rather limited. But when the lead signals the shift into drive, the constraints of text and tune fall away. Suddenly the lead singer stands alone, free to praise, preach, challenge, and testify, all over the churning backdrop of the drive. The quick turnaround of the drive phrase forces the lead to shorten the lead lines and voice them quickly. The percussive loudness of the overlapping backup pressures the lead to utter the lines at a heightened volume. And the elevated pitch plateau from which many drives begin compels the lead to forcibly project each phrase, giving them a particularly explosive quality. These features should by now sound familiar. All are sounded characteristics of elevated speech. But in the drive, they emerge not as the natural products of experienced elevation, but as the shaped products of elevated structure. The drive, in essence, coerces the lead's words into the *sound* and *form* of elevation.

This likeness is certainly not lost on lead singers. Suddenly they find themselves in a position where their words *sound* like heightened speech, whether or not the singers *feel* "heightened." Furthermore, they find themselves facing a rather insistent lyric void. The familiar options of verse and chorus are gone, wiped away by the structural stall. In their stead is an openness equaled only by that found in singers' between-song remarks and their midsong talked commentary. But unlike those spaces, the drive offers no time for emergence and gradual elevation. The switch to full stylistic elevation occurs with a suddenness that jars the singer, forcing instant "high gear" performance. Granted, the drive usually follows some elevation elsewhere in the song and/or set. Nonetheless, the hang-up marks an elevation of a different order. If, as John Landis suggests, singers aren't particularly *into* a song when they start singing it, the drive quickly snaps them to attention.

When asked about negotiating this sharp shift, lead singers tend to describe one of two courses. John Landis suggests the first when he speaks of riding the elevation and then "rolling" in the drive, letting the words take their own course while trusting the Spirit to provide guidance. Singers who adopt this approach freely admit that they enter the drive with *some* words in mind, but then say that the need for forethought vanishes as the words start to roll. This is precisely the same approach already discussed by a host of other saints for other acts of worship, an approach borne on faith, submission, and trust. A second course often mentioned by singers suggests full reliance on one's own artistry, trusting that one's skills at freestyle improvisation (or at memorization) will meet the drive's demands. Singers in this camp often say that once one "gets the hang of running a song," the rest comes easy. These singers also speak of the words "rolling," though they attribute the "roll" wholly to their own prowess.

Whatever the singer's approach, there seems to be widespread agreement about the drive's effectiveness as an instrument of elevation. Even if the singer doesn't feel elevated, by all appearances, congregations often do. More than in any other sequence in a set, drives regularly coincide with conspicuous displays of apparent spiritual "signs" in the pews. Hands wave; feet dance; programgoers shout. Precisely *what* programgoers are feeling—whether it's the spiritual elevation that comes from worship, or the emotional elevation that comes from a driving beat—remains an open question. The fact remains, however, that drives somehow "move" the congregation.

This manifest "moving," when coupled with the focus that drives foster in sanctified singers, probably accounts for this sequence's widespread popularity. The degree of this popularity becomes evident when one charts the drive's actual appearance in gospel programs. To do this, I surveyed the songs sung at twenty gospel programs over a ten-year period in the north-central Piedmont of North Carolina. Randomly selecting these events from a much larger listing in my field-notes, I ended up with ten programs that featured only community groups and ten that included at least one professional ensemble. Together, they accounted for 142 sets and 585 songs.[31] Of these sets, fully 57 percent (81 performances) included at least one drive. When adjusting the set total to remove soloists and duos (who cannot, for the most part, effectively perform the drive), this number jumps to 65 percent. In the overall analysis, 106 of the 585 songs included a hang-up, suggesting a rough ratio of one drive for every five and a half songs. Given the extraordinary diversity of gospel styles, this number testifies to the high regard with which singers—and, by extension, their audiences—hold the drive.

When we break this figure down according to the professional or nonprofessional status of the artists, the numbers become even more interesting. Of the 112 sets presented by community-based singers, precisely half included one or more drives. Of the 30 professional sets, in turn, this figure jumps to a startling 83 percent (25 sets). Professional groups (and particularly quartets, who make up the majority of the tallied professionals) clearly emerge as the drive's principal purveyors.

Though these numbers make no claim to statistical exactness, they do suggest a pattern of strategic use. Not surprisingly, this pattern is not lost on the saints. When I reviewed these figures with some of my sanctified consultants, they were somewhat surprised that the overall ratio of drive appearances was so high and very surprised that the ratio for professional groups was *only* 83 percent, a figure they considered *low*. Many of these saints specifically associate the drive with professional quartets, who they say commonly use it as a tool of audience manipulation. The reasons for such use should by now be obvious. The drive offers a potent combination of driving rhythm, forceful delivery, and spiritual connotation. Furthermore, as the climactic stage of elevation, it provides an ideal platform for "form and fashion" theater. For groups trying "to get a house," the drive presents itself as a convenient and effective means to an end.

Needless to say, saints look upon such use with disdain. They accuse singers who use the drive manipulatively with perverting a legitimate tool of focus, transforming it—as quartet veteran Wilson Waters puts it—into "a power thing." "That's often the purpose of raising it, of elevating a song and hanging it," Brother Waters asserts, speaking about the drive's misuse. "The power. You're pushing—pushing the audience emotionally. Instead of telling the story." Many professionals and their nonprofessional counterparts would have no argument with Brother Waters's assessment. They freely acknowledge that the drive's purpose is to "excite" the crowd and "drive" them to shout. "You try to get them in a frenzy," admits Brother Hardsinger. "Because once you get the audience involved in the situation, you get them to pay more attention to what you're doing. See, you just use a little *psychology*."[32]

The precise nature of this "psychology" becomes apparent when we examine the drive texts actually used by many quartets. Instead of using this improvisatory space to tell a story, give a testimony, issue a spiritual invitation, or press home a preached point, many singers fill it with pointed references to their own elevation (e.g., "I feel the fire!") and repeated prompts for programgoers to show that they feel it too (e.g., "Let me hear you say 'Yeah!' "). The terse testimonies to the singer's own state serve as rhetorical goads, urging listeners to "feel" what the lead is so obviously feeling. The calls to action, in turn, offer an easy means toward this end, promising programgoers quick epiphany through physical and emotional involvement. Together, they transform the drive into a vehicle of sensuous inducement. All through "a little psychology."

A single text should suffice to show how the psychology of inducement works. At a 1993 "ticket program" in Raleigh, North Carolina, a popular professional quartet stepped into the program's second slot. The emcee had prefaced their appearance by declaring that the time for "playing church" was over. "These are *real* times!" she proclaimed. "And we need to get real for Jesus!" Then, with an instrumental fanfare from the onstage musicians, the five vocalists with a group that I'll call the "Gospel Drivers" strode onto the stage.[33] The singers opened with a slow prayerful theme and followed it with a faster song of praise. In this second piece, the lead singer repeatedly called programgoers to "Stand on your feet!" At the song's close, he urged those who knew that the Lord had been good to them to wave their hands in the air. With this as his preface, the lead plunged into a slow, soulful song about humanity's debt to Jesus, broken in the middle by a heart-wrenching, chanted description of the crucifixion. Midway through this piece, while singing on his knees, the lead passed the microphone to his brother, who stepped off the stage and into the congregation. The original lead soon followed him onto the floor, and the two closed the song there, both singing into the same mike.

Without a moment's pause, the second lead three times called the congregation to "Say 'Ye-e-e-es!'" As the programgoers responded, the first lead took back the mike and shouted, "I feel better now! I feel good now! I wonder do you feel all right, children?" Again the crowd answered, and again he urged them to wave their hands and "tell God, 'Thank You!' Wave your hand and say 'Yes!'" Then the guitars and drums kicked in, churning out a tune far faster (and with a beat decidedly more pronounced) than any other piece in the Gospel Drivers' set. Now shouting into the mike, the lead again commanded the congregation's engagement, calling them to put their hands together, to "give Him praise," to say "Yes!" and to wave their hands. After twice declaring, "I feel like shouting!" he called the group's tenor to swing the song into its chorus.

Twice more the lead repeated the same pattern, filling the verse space with shouted commands for audience involvement and then calling for the chorus. At the close of the third chorus, the backup singers uttered a quick, falsetto "Whooo!" The lead followed with a rough, shouted "Come on," launching into yet another rushing sequence of audience invitation. This time, his phrases assumed the rising and falling tones of elevation, sliding upward in one line and dropping down in the next. After each gruffly barked phrase, the Drivers' tenor added a strained falsetto echo, throwing the two into pointedly percussive conversation.

I need somebody,	
that been born again!	/ Born again!
To come on down here,	/ Come on down!
and help me praise Him!	/ Come on down!
Come on down here,	/ Come on down!
and help me praise Him!	/ Help me praise Him!
If you know He been good to you,	/ Come on down!
get up out of your seat tonight!	/ Come on down!
Walk on down!	/ Walk on down!
Just come on down!	/ Come on down!
And help me praise Him!	/ Praise Jesus!
If He been your bread,	/ Praise Jesus!
you ought to come on down!	/ Praise Jesus!

If He been your water, / Ye-e-eah!
    you ought to come on down! / Come on down!
If He been your doctor,
    you ought to give Him the praise tonight!

By this point, dozens of programgoers were heeding the singer's call and were streaming to the front of the stage, where the lead gave their hands a quick, spirited shake. Despite the distraction, his singing never lost a beat. As he shook the waiting hands, he began to speak of his own conversion, telling the story in a four-line series of short, staccato outbursts.[34] The guitarist answered each line with a searing instrumental phrase, thus setting up the call-and-response structure that slid the song into drive.

One Thursday,
    one Thursday evening,
He filled me
    with the Holy Ghost! / HOLY GHOST FIRE!
Does anybody here, / HOLY GHOST FIRE!
    Anybody got it? / HOLY GHOST FIRE!
    Has anybody got it? / HOLY GHOST FIRE!
Is there anybody in this building, / HOLY GHOST FIRE!
    Got the Holy Ghost? / HOLY GHOST FIRE!
I wonder can you feel it? / HOLY GHOST FIRE!
    I wonder can you feel it? / HOLY GHOST FIRE!
I wonder can you feel it? / HOLY GHOST FIRE!
    I wonder can you feel it? / HOLY GHOST FIRE!
If you feel all right, / HOLY GHOST FIRE!
    Then wave your hands! / HOLY GHOST FIRE!
Wave your hands! / HOLY GHOST FIRE!
Let me hear you say, "Yeah!" / HOLY GHOST FIRE!
    Let me hear you say, "Yeah!" / HOLY GHOST FIRE!
I feel the fire! / FEEL THE FIRE!
    I feel the fire! / HOLY GHOST FIRE!
I feel the fire! / FEEL THE FIRE!
    I wonder can you feel it? / HOLY GHOST FIRE!
Doesn't anybody here? / HOLY GHOST FIRE!
Doesn't anybody here? / HOLY GHOST FIRE!
How can you sit there, / HOLY GHOST FIRE!
    And hold your peace, / HOLY GHOST FIRE!
        When you know He been good to you? / HOLY GHOST FIRE!
If you know He been good to you, / HOLY GHOST FIRE!
    You oughtn't to mind, / HOLY GHOST FIRE!
        Giving Him the praises! / HOLY GHOST FIRE!
Has anybody got it? / HOLY GHOST FIRE!
Has anybody got it? / HOLY GHOST FIRE!

Anybody got it?	/ HOLY GHOST FIRE!
My feet feel light,	/ HOLY GHOST FIRE!
With the Holy Ghost!	/ HOLY GHOST FIRE!
With the Holy Ghost!	/ HOLY GHOST FIRE!
It'll make you walk right!	/ HOLY GHOST FIRE!
It'll make you talk right!	/ HOLY GHOST FIRE!
It'll make you love,	/ HOLY GHOST FIRE!
Love everybody!	/ HOLY GHOST FIRE!
It'll make you love,	/ HOLY GHOST FIRE!
Love everybody!	/ HOLY GHOST FIRE!
It'll make you cry!	/ HOLY GHOST FIRE!
It'll set your soul,	/ HOLY GHOST FIRE!
Your soul on fire!	/ HOLY GHOST FIRE!
I wonder have you got it?	/ HOLY GHOST FIRE!
I wonder have you got it?	/ HOLY GHOST FIRE!
I wonder have you got it?	/ HOLY GHOST FIRE!
Got it down on your knees, children?	/ HOLY GHOST FIRE!
Got it down on your knees?	/ HOLY GHOST FIRE!
Got the Holy Ghost?	/ HOLY GHOST FIRE!
Somebody got it!	/ HOLY GHOST FIRE!

When the lead stayed silent after the backup's final "Holy Ghost fire!" the guitarist stepped in, filling the next eight bars with loud, descending phrases. Then the tenor shouted a piercing "Ye-e-eah!" The lead immediately responded, setting up an exchange much like that which introduced the drive, except even faster.

Ye-e-eah!	/ Ye-e-eah!
Ain't He all right!	/ Ye-eah!
Ain't He all right!	/ Ye-eah!
Can I get a witness!	/ Ye-eah!
Wave your hands!	/ Ye-eah!
Wave your hands!	
Let me hear you say, "Yeah!"	
Let me hear you say, "Yeah!"	
Let me hear you say, "Yeah!"	
I feel all right now!	
I feel all right!	

With this closing line, the lead singer pulled the microphone from his mouth, leaving the lead to the churning guitar. Eight bars later, the musicians ended the song.

After listening to this piece, an outsider might well assume that the term "drive" means "to drive the emotions." Or perhaps, to use Brother Hardsinger's terms, "to drive into a frenzy." Because there's little else here. This drive's clear purpose is to push programgoers toward experience and the expression thereof. Of the forty-nine lines in this rhetorical tour de force, fully twenty-one pose a single question to the congregation: "Has anybody got it?" (or, in its other form, "I wonder can you feel it?"). The referenced "it," of course, is the insistently repeated "Holy Ghost fire!" as the lead makes clear in his final query ("Got the Holy Ghost?").[35] After asking the question again and again, the lead singer urges programgoers to give their feelings demonstrative form. "If you feel all right," he cries, "then wave your hands!" Twice he asks them to wave; twice he commands them to say "Yeah!" And then, in a set of linked triplets, he presses them to give praise. These urgings account for another eleven lines.

Such insistence would lose much of its authority if the singer himself didn't appear to be feeling what he was calling others to feel. So he leaves no question about his own experience. In the song's introduction, he twice declares "I feel good now!" As the music begins, he suggests that the "good feeling" is elevating to another stage as he twice cries "I feel like shouting!" Then, in the midst of the drive, the elevation apparently reaches climax. Three times the lead shouts "I feel the fire!" The backup singers, apparently expecting this line, seamlessly shift their phrase from "Holy Ghost fire!" to a "Feel the fire!" echo. In so doing, they effectively accentuate the lead's announcement of epiphany. Thirteen lines later, the lead singer again claims the Spirit's touch, this time by inserting a triplet declaring that his feet have been lightened by the Holy Ghost. Finally, as he concludes the song, he twice shouts "I feel all right!" These final cries return him to the state of elevation at which the song began, effectively framing both the song and the professed rise to climax. Within the drive itself, the assertions of epiphany fill six lines.

So what's left? Questions, commands, and claims fill thirty-eight of the drive's forty-nine lines. The introductory line—which itself is a claim to experience, though set in an earlier time—accounts for another, as does the closing declaration that *somebody* feels the Holy Ghost. The remaining nine lines, all clustered near the drive's end, describe attributes of the Spirit that the singer is so urgently trying to get people to "feel." These nine lines convey the only message not conveyed elsewhere in the song. As such, they might be said to constitute the drive's core. But when set in the context of the surrounding lines, their seeming singularity quickly fades. Before them come three lines of questions and three lines of claims; after them come six more lines of questions. Within this frame, this sequence becomes but a rhetorical preface, a seductive bit of bait for the climactic questioning hook. "It'll set your soul on fire!" the singer shouts. "I wonder have you got it?" He's already told you that *he* does. And he told you how good it feels. "Now," he seems to be saying, "all that's left is for *you* to feel it too."

Given the persuasive insistence of this elevation and drive, singers' claims about "shouting the house" become more understandable. Singers such as the Gospel Drivers actively pursue "shouts" by constructing talk and song sequences that are carefully calculated to arouse the emotions and excite the body. Filling their performances with "psychological" hooks, they appeal to the unconscious and impulsive elements of self, purposefully bypassing the reflective in order to stir the deep currents that lie beneath it. As Rev. Z. D. Harris would say, such singers seduce the mental and the physical, but don't even talk to the spiritual.

That their seductions prove profitable finds testament in the "shouts" they often produce. Saints are quick to remind us, however, that most such shouts are *not* shouts in Spirit. Instead, they're authored wholly by the self. Yet this distinction is lost on "performing" singers (like our Brother Hardsinger), for whom these *may be the only kinds of shouts that they know*. Given this partial understanding, one can certainly understand their satisfaction in "getting" such responses.

Another aspect of these drives that merits mention is the insistently repeated phrase that "hangs" behind the improvised lead. Though the lead lines clearly serve as the drive's main message-bearers, the droning background also carries a message. And unlike the utterances of the lead, this one refuses to be ignored. While the lead's lines emerge and then vanish, the drive phrase rolls on and on, pushing itself deeper into consciousness with each repetition. On one hand, this phrase becomes the drive's reference point, providing an interpretive center for the improvisations that swirl around it. On the other hand, the phrase itself becomes an agent of persuasion.

A survey of commonly used drive phrases quickly reveals the importance of this rhetorical task. The most frequent phrases are those that explicitly mention the Holy Ghost; among the favorites are "Holy Ghost fire!" "Holy Ghost power!" and "Got the Holy Ghost!" (All of these phrases regularly get shortened in "overdrives" to "Holy Ghost!" "Power!" or "Fire!") Other common variants include the double-drive phrases "Holy Ghost/doctor!" and "Send it on down/Send the Holy Ghost down!"[36] Countless other phrases also reference the anointing, though often without mentioning the Holy Ghost. Many seem to brazenly command the Lord's intercession (e.g., "Lord, I want you to move!" "Lord, lift me higher!" and the double-drive demand "Come on Jesus/we need you!"). Others advise listeners to seek the Spirit (e.g., "You got to be ready/ready when Jesus comes!" "You ought to call Him/you ought to call Him up" and the simple command, "Shout!"). Still other phrases convey the same message with a bit more subtlety. For example, when the backup sings "Ain't going to hold back!" listeners instantly recognize the reference to shouting. And when singers repeat, "Going to walk that holy highway!" programgoers know the journey's path rises high. All of these phrases compel listeners to at least *think* about the holy touch. When set in the context of insistent rhythms and apparent elevation, most of them go one step further and actively encourage their listeners to shout.

Not all drive phrases are so clearly manipulative. And not all lead singers are "trying to get a house." As I tried to establish earlier in this discussion, most sanctified singers treat the drive as a legitimate tool of personal and congregational focus. They say that the hang-up allows them to "get into" their message, that it sharpens their devotional vision, that it frees them to develop the song's message. And that it often carries them to spiritual climax. Note that they don't pose themselves as the agents of this elevation. Saints claim only to elevate the song's *structure*. But they say that this structural elevation often yields a spiritual one. Not because of any intrinsic link between song and Spirit, but because the singing both tightens their already-tightened focus and pulls them into a lyric space that invites submission to the Word. Facing the void, saints say, "Have Your way, Lord." And by all accounts, the Lord often does just that. The Spirit, saints say, simply takes over. Though the singers may be *voicing* the words, the Spirit often ends up *providing* them.

Singers describe this experience in precisely the same way that Deacon Eldridge described anointed prayer and that generations of preachers have described anointed preaching. All report experiencing a gradual spiritual elevation. All tell of eventually "letting go and letting God." All describe how the words "come" of their own accord. And all testify to *knowing* that the words' source is the Spirit.

Saints say that this anointing is essentially the same as that which leads to tears or a shout. But it manifests itself in a different way. Saints still feel the overwhelming rapture. And they still respond with a willful yielding. This time, however, the Spirit chooses a different course. Instead of a shout comes a flow of words—word after word after word, rolling, as the saints say, "just like a wheel." Saints report no struggling for thoughts, no searching for words, no sense of control. Instead, they tell how they "let go," and then listen to what is being said through their mouths. All agree that the words become fully known only as they are *heard*.

＊　＊　＊　＊　＊

Rev. Samuel McCrary, Elder Lawrence Richardson, and I sat down together one night to talk about preaching. Though we had held many long conversations over the previous two years, I had never really asked these two preachers about their *preaching*. We had always talked about singing. But earlier that afternoon, the two of them had described the experience of preaching under the anointing. I asked them if we could revisit the matter when I had my recorder handy. They both graciously agreed.

What I particularly wanted to catch on tape was their comparison between the elevation in anointed preaching and the shifting gears in an automobile. They explained how preachers begin to preach in low gear, in what Elder Richardson called "the calmness of conversation," speaking to the saints with "low tone" and deliberate, carefully chosen words. But as preachers reflect upon those words, they begin to speak with more spontaneity and spirit. This marks the shift into second gear, into an elevated plane of spiritual communion. Preachers begin to feel the guidance of the Spirit, to sense the silent messages of inspiration, to experience the flow of ideas. As the "Amens" begin to ring and the Spirit starts to flow, the gears ease into third. At this point, Rev. McCrary explained, the words are flowing almost effortlessly, naturally falling into patterns of elevated sound and form. The ideas are flowing too, tumbling into the preacher's mind and freeing it to focus ever more clearly on the preached message. The path is thus cleared for the final shift, when the Holy Ghost is said to reach down and throw the gears into high. From this point on, the preacher can just drive and drive and drive. Because from this point on, the Spirit is behind the wheel.[37]

That evening, as the three of us sat down to re-create our earlier conversation, the talk took a different course. I was asking about the *experience* of the shifting gears and about the *feeling* of the flowing words. Though they had both talked about elevation's euphoric joy, I pressed them on the issue of the rolling words. "What does *that* feel like?" I asked. "How does that feel *inside* of you?"

Rev. McCrary was the first to answer. He opened by immediately linking the elevation in preaching with that in singing, making sure that I realized they were the same. "Well, the Spirit comes to you in preaching *or* singing," he began, "and the Bible says that when we come to preach, we preach not of ourselves, but the Spirit that's with us. He say, 'You open your mouth and I'll speak for you.'"

I murmured affirmation, recognizing Rev. McCrary's paraphrase as a promise that appears in both the Old and the New Testaments.

"It's just like in singing," Rev. McCrary continued. "Now I have did this so many times—I started the song and we got so much in a climax until I—it seems like you be—" For a moment, he was at a loss for words. Then came the car analogy, with Rev. McCrary likening elevation to an automatic transmission.

"You know, you ever drive a car, and be driving along the road and it'll switch over? You mash on it and it'll switch over in high?" "Yeah," I answered, nodding. "It's just like that," he continued. "You see, when the Spirit takes over, you can *operate.*"

"Right!" agreed Elder Richardson.

"But before the Spirit comes on—if the Spirit don't never come, you're *guessing* what you're going to do. But if you give over to the Spirit, the Spirit will just take over—"

"Take over!" repeated Elder Richardson.

"And let you *motivate*, and you don't worry about the next word. It'll just come."

Throughout this description, Elder Richardson had been moving toward the edge of his seat, clearly anxious to have his say. As soon as Rev. McCrary paused, Elder Richardson jumped in, his tone already raised and his words ready to flow.

"Yes!" he declared, "It'll come! God will *give* you the next word. In other words, if I'm thinking about what the next word is going to be—" For an instant, Elder Richardson paused, seeming to realize that this was not the direction he was meant to take. When he started again, his words were rolling with eager eloquence, rushing one after another as if elevation was not only his *subject*, but was also his immediate *experience*.

> But see if I turn it all over
> > after I'm *in* it and God is in me,
> > > God's going to give me words after words after words after words.
> Why?
> Because God done took over!
> Right there's where He done took over.
> And when he *takes over*,
> > man, you don't look back and say,
> > > "I'm tired."
> > > "I'm giving out of breath."

But see, God's *power* is *omnipotent*!
 Yeah, it's omnipotent.
God can give you that power,
 and elevate you in it,
  and, man, when He elevates you,
   man, you just out there *singing*!
You out there—
 as I said, you might forget about,
  you know,
   "I don't have no other word."
But God will place those words,
 just word after word,
  word after word,
  word after word!
And then it'll make you go up,
 up,
 up,
 and *up*!

His face lit by a broad smile, Elder Richardson paused. When he started again, his words had slowed and become more conversational. "So," he began. "So this thing, it's in itself as a *feeling*. And if—" Again he paused, apparently struggling to capture in words an experience so hard to describe. When he resumed, he had shifted his descriptive stance from one who feels the flow to one who witnesses it. Now he was describing how saints *know* when the words are the Lord's.

If a person don't know anything about the power of the Holy Ghost,
 then they absent from knowing what's going on.
But if you *in* the power,
 of the Holy Ghost,
 of your God and my God,
  God's going to let you know,
   "What he doing,
    he doing it from his heart.
   And if he doing it from his heart,
    and [is] a servant of Mine,
     you'll feel it!
    'Cause you're Mine too!"
Then when you feel it—
 Lord have mercy!
Man, *some action going to happen!*
Can't help from to happen!
Why?
Because the Holy Spirit got you in control now.
Takes over.[38]

Elder Richardson uttered his last line as a tone-dropping coda, indicating that no more needed to be said. Perhaps it didn't. Because he had just ended where Rev. McCrary had begun, emphasizing that the Spirit acts through different forms and through different saints in precisely the same way. Just as the Spirit takes the surrendered control in preaching and in singing, so too does He take it in simple hearing. The Spirit lets the saint know, lets the saint feel, and then guides the saint's actions. To a shout, to a dance, to a flow of words. To whatever, Elder Richardson suggests, the saints need.

* * * * *

Rev. McCrary and Elder Richardson's descriptions of the words' flow show remarkable agreement not only with each other, but also with the descriptions of countless other saints voiced over the course of untold generations. "On the morning I stood up to [preach my first sermon]," testified a Tennessee preacher who was called to preach in the late 1860s, "I did not know what I was going to say, but when I started to talk my thoughts came faster than I could speak. I was filled up." "It's just like an automatic transmission," explains North Carolina Baptist preacher Rev. David Bell, speaking in the mid-1980s. "You can tell when it's slipping. And when the Holy Spirit comes, there is no slipping at all. It just flows. It just flows just as sweet as a perfect transmission in an automobile."[39]

Running through all these descriptions is a sense of easy flow, of guided thought and effortless talk. The words are said to roll like a wheel, to flow like running water, to run like a car in high gear. When saints describe this experience, they carefully distinguish it from inspiration and the enablements of elevation. In inspiration, the Spirit provides the ideas, serving as source of the conveyed messages; in elevation, He helps give those messages their form and then fills them with affective power. The flow, however, marks yet a further elevation. And a different degree of spiritual involvement. In prophetic anointing, the Spirit provides both the *messages* and the *words to convey them*. There's no need for saints to rework, restate, or elaborate the rolling talk. Instead, they just let it flow. As Deacon Willie Eldridge explained, "It's His words. We're only just a vessel."[40]

This carries us right back to the adage with which this chapter began. "Go slow, rise high, catch on fire." The words take on new meaning when "catching on fire" signifies more than just feeling the holy touch. Just as "rising high" alludes to elevation, so does "catching on fire" point to the prophetic anointing of the drive. This isn't to say, of course, that the Spirit touches *only* in the drive. Indeed, saints often testify to feeling the Spirit elsewhere in songs. Many tell how the Spirit has led them to *stop* singing and to *talk* over the ongoing background, elaborating on themes raised by the song. Others describe how the Spirit has fed them words as they were singing, yielding spontaneous compositions that followed the song's form but not its known text. Still others tell how the Spirit has led them to sing on and on, repeating known verses but *not being able to stop*. All are examples of prophetic anointing. But none occur with the regularity of prophecy in the drive. It is here, where focus, style, elevation, and opportunity all come together, that the Spirit most often graces singing with revelation.

Upon learning of this phenomenon, nonsaints often ask how one can tell if the words are indeed God's. Do they ring with special eloquence? Do they pulse with special power? Do they openly proclaim their authority? Yes, say the saints, and no. Yes they *do* stand apart—as Elder Richardson explained—*for the sanctified*. But no they *don't*, for those who "don't know anything about the power of the Holy Ghost." These hearers remain "absent from knowing what's going on." (Unless, of course, the Spirit wills otherwise.) Because the words' distinction lies not in their sound *or* their style *or* their syntax. Nor does it lie in any self-referencing declaration of holiness, any more than it does in anointed sermons or prayers or testimonies. In all these forms, awareness of revelation comes only from within, from the feeling inside, from the knowledge imparted by God. For those without this feeling, authorship remains ambiguous. They can only rely on sound, style, and other cues—all of which are subject to worldly manipulation. The only route to certainty, say the saints, is salvation.

When certainty comes—when the feeling is there—saints dramatically shift the way they assess performance. Before the Spirit's arrival, they evaluate performance according to prevailing canons of style, skill, and taste. This holds particularly true for singing, which stands apart from other artful acts of worship in the openness of its claim to artistry. Unlike preachers, prayer-givers, and testifiers, gospel singers present themselves as Christian *artists*. In so doing, they openly invite aesthetic evaluation. While singers admit the importance of their words, they also recognize the significance of the way that they convey these words. Therein lies the special power of song. And therein lies their gift. When singers step into the cross-aisle, they expect to be judged for the way they have nurtured and developed this gift. They expect to be judged, in other words, as artists.

This is precisely how saints typically assess gospel performance. Unless they have reason to dismiss singers as "form and fashion" deceivers, saints evaluate them as artists presenting their gifts. This all begins to change, however, with the first evidence of anointment. As singers begin to show signs of spiritual elevation, they move into an evaluative space quite different from that which measures mortal artistry. In essence, they step *out of* a realm where aesthetic fullness is the final measure and *into* one where measurement is ultimately moot. Now transcendence figures into the equation. The singers no longer stand alone in the cross-aisle; they no longer assume sole responsibility for their singing. Saints realize that as elevation proceeds, the artistry they are witnessing is growing increasingly collaborative. The ideas, the expression, and perhaps even the words themselves are passing into the Spirit's hands. As this shift occurs, singers move further and further *out of* performance. Every degree of surrender nullifies another measure of artistry, because singers are moving into a realm that transcends both art and evaluation. As they gradually give in to the Spirit, their performances give way to revelation.[41]

Of course, not all sanctified singing ends with revelation. Much such singing never even "catches on fire." Saints say that the words flow only when the Spirit so wills. Hence the flow can never be predicted. What *can* be predicted, however, is the Spirit's presence when needs exist. As generations of saints have sung, the Spirit is "always right on time." This "on-timeness" means meeting needs as they need to be met. Which in turn suggests a universe of options. Sometimes needs can be met through simple talking or singing, without any intervention by the Spirit. Sometimes they are met through words or songs *suggested* by the Spirit. Sometimes they are met through words or songs *enabled* by the Spirit. Sometimes they are met through words or songs *revealed* by the Spirit. Sometimes, say the saints, they can even be met by the true words or songs of *unsaved* singers. The *means* by which the Spirit meets needs are clearly less important than the fact that *He meets those needs*.

So singers "let go and let God." They offer their singing as service, trusting that the Lord will use it as He sees fit. Some may never experience the flowing of words. Some may never feel the inspired guiding of songs. But these saints realize that they are no less favored than their sanctified peers. They are simply called to different service. And for this service, they know they will be blessed.

✻ ✻ ✻ ✻ ✻

When the elder singer advised Dickie Freeman to "go slow, rise high, and catch on fire," he was not suggesting that Brother Freeman close all his song sets with a drive. He was simply setting forth a course of engagement, urging Brother Freeman to treat sets like sermons, encouraging him to think of songs as parts of a greater whole. Each song should be a further unfolding of the Word. And each should draw the singer deeper into worship—toward the end of spiritual surrender and the referenced "catching on fire." The elder was not saying that all sets will end with the fires of anointment. Instead, he was advising that all sets be pursued with sincerity and faith, always submitting themselves to the Lord's service, always *inviting* the fire.

And if the fire comes, then singers should let it flow, avoiding all attempts at control, resisting all impulses to "squench the Spirit."[42] Let it come, saints say, and let it go. And when it goes, then singers should observe the maxim's fourth and final phrase, a simple "sit down." Because when the Spirit leaves, the climax has passed. No efforts by saints singing in self can recapture the power. This doesn't mean that the elevation goes away, that the joy doesn't linger and tingle, that the emotions stop overflowing. It simply suggests that any self-willed extension of performance, when compared with what has gone before, would seem labored. Besides, say the saints, there's no real reason to go on. The Spirit has met the needs that He wanted to meet. Now all that remains for singers to do is to pass the mantle on to the next singers in the service.

Chapter 18

Invitation

"The Souls of Many Are Yet Lost"

When the Gospel Tones close "Get Right with God," Brother Johnnie Faison turns to address the congregation.[1] Speaking over the quiet phrasings of the guitar, he recalls how he had recently found himself in a prayer line at the nearby Benson Chapel church. While he stood in that line, praying that his faith might be strengthened, the church choir sang a song that deeply touched him. "I can't sing it like they sang it," he says humbly, "but I want to sing a few verses of it, the way the Lord laid it on my heart." Then, with his voice almost a whisper, he begins to sing "I'm Free, Praise the Lord I'm Free."

Though the hardness soon creeps into Brother Faison's singing, the song maintains its quiet, devotional tone. Twice he sings the chorus, singing alone. The third time through, the background singers join him in sweet, understated harmony. When he eases into the verse, they support him with a high, harmonized hum. Then Brother Faison returns to the chorus, his voice now hoarse from the strain of his gravelly delivery. No longer singing the full lines, he lets the background carry the lyric, limiting his own contribution to short phrases and low, throaty cries. As the singers sing the chorus's final line, Brother Faison shouts "Hallelujah!" five times in quick succession. As he cries the words, his head bows and shakes from side to side.

Once again the background singers repeat the chorus. This time, however, Brother Johnnie Faison adds no more than a few short words. When the chorus closes, he raises his hand and signals the singing's end. As he does so, the guitarist leans down, switches his amp to a lead channel, and steps forward to the center aisle, where he begins to play the chorus. He fills the ensuing solo with quiet, soulful slides and fluid, voice-like phrasings. Some saints in the front pews begin singing along with the music, prompting the guitarist—Eddie Faison—to repeat the instrumental chorus. Midway through his second playing, an elderly sister near the back of the church rises to her feet in a shout. Crying "Hallelujah!" she begins to dance. Brother Eddie Faison keeps playing his slow phrases, acknowledging her with his eyes but not with his music. By the time he closes the chorus, she is seated once again.

The saints applaud both the singing and the playing as the Gospel Tones unplug their instruments and ease back into the congregation. But the Spirit has not yet stopped His flow. Up in the amen corner, Sister Lena Mae Perry begins to cry "I'm free! I'm free! Thank You, Lord! I'm *free!*" At first, her words blend in with the congregation's calls of encouragement. But as the singers move to their seats and the saints' calls wind down, Sister Perry's cries grow louder. Instantly recognizing the Spirit's ministrations, a sister with a tambourine begins to rattle out a thrumming rhythm, quickly drawing the saints into a holy clap. Within seconds, Sister Perry is running down the center aisle, both hands raised above her head, crying "Glory!" and "Hallelujah!" As she rejoices in the Spirit, at least two more saints shout, one standing in her place in the pews and the other staying seated. Meanwhile, the organist, guitarist, and drummer join the praises, laying a mantle of melody over the congregation's fast clapping and the Spirit's gentle flow.

When the clapping begins to wane, the guitarist sounds a closing phrase and Evangelist Lofton steps to the cross-aisle. "Glory to God!" she cries, her face beaming. "Amen!" answer the saints. "Amen!" echoes Evangelist Lofton. "Thank You, Jesus!" adds a sister in the amen corner. Twice more Evangelist Lofton calls "Amen," each time generating an enthusiastic chorus of replies. Then she cries, "Let the church say, 'Amen!'" As the saints respond, Evangelist Lofton repeats her call, this time louder and with more force. "Oh, let the church say, 'Amen!'" "Amen!" shout the saints.

> Hallelujah, if you're free   (Jesus!/Yes!)
>   and you want to make the devil a liar
>   stand up on your feet and say,
>   "Lord, I'm free!"

Instantly, the saints are on their feet, joyfully crying "Lord, I'm free!" As they call and clap, Evangelist Lofton shouts "Hallelujah!"—her voice already scraping the elevated heights reached only at the peaks of her introduction. A second "Hallelujah!" quickly follows the first, leading Evangelist Lofton to cry,

> And when you're a son of God,   (Thank You, Lord!)
>   and set free,   (Uh-huh!/Thank You!)
>   you're free *indeed*!

Recognizing the paraphrase of John 8:36, scores of saints join her in chorusing her final two words, shouting "Free indeed!" Evangelist Lofton responds with another cried "Hallelujah," drawing a quick "Glory!" from Sister Perry. Then the evangelist drops her tone slightly, and continues her reflection on the Gospel Tones' closing song.

> And when you're free indeed,
>   and people look at you funny,
>   you don't lose your freedom, now.   (My Lord!/That's right!)

You *still* stay free!	(Ye-e-es!)
Hallelujah!	(Glory!)
This young generation is looking for some	
kind of *power*,	(Jesus!)
They saying they need Black power,	
or white power.	(Jesus!)
Only thing they need is the *Holy Ghost power*!	(Ye-e-es!)
Hallelujah!	(Yes!)
He'll set you free!	(Yes!/Jesus!)
He'll keep you free!	(Yes!/Hallelujah!)
Amen, I like that song!	(Glory!/Thank the Lord!)
Amen, but he sung the song before he sung	
that one,	(Lord Jesus!)
he said, "Get right,	(Get right!)
right now."	(Right now!)
It's time to get right, now!	(Yes, Lord!)

Before Evangelist Lofton can go any further, one of the church mothers sitting in the amen corner begins to cry "Thank You, Jesus!" Instantly drawn to her feet, she starts to shake uncontrollably, her thin frame fluttering like a leaf in a windstorm. With each shudder comes another cry of "Thank You!," yielding a sharp, shouted litany that stretches for more than two minutes. Shortly after the mother begins to shout, as saints call out "Hallelujah!" and "Glory to God!" the Gospel Tones' guitarist reprises his solo of "I'm Free." Once again playing from the front pew, Brother Eddie Faison fills the church with his soulful phrasings. His fluid notes seem to wrap around the mother's strained shouts, dulling their sharp edges. Within a few bars, a tambourine joins the slow melody. A few bars later, the drums and organ follow. The saints, meanwhile, continue to voice quiet encouragements and praise.

After more than thirty repetitions of the mother's "Thank You!" a piercing "Whooo!" echoes through the sanctuary. Once again Sister Perry is on her feet, slowly shaking her upraised head as she gently cries "Whooo!" a second and then a third time. Her arms are both raised by her sides, bent at the elbows with hands clenched and palms facing forward, slowly moving back and forth, back and forth. Though her eyes are pressed shut, Sister Perry's face glows with a look of deep serenity. Her hushed cries gradually give way to whispers of "Thank You!" and "Thank You, Lord," all murmured in quiet counterpoint to the mother's ongoing shouts.

As Sister Perry's thanksgivings drop to a whisper and the mother's cries begin winding down, I can hear many saints behind me voicing rapturous praises. Before I can turn to look, however, Evangelist Lofton is once again at the mike, her voice brimming with gentle tenderness. "Praise God," she whispers. "While the Spirit of the Lord is yet moving, somebody may not could confess that they are free."

From the rear of the church, I hear another sister feel the touch. Almost as if in response to Evangelist Lofton's words, she begins to cry, "I'm free! I'm free!" Her blissful words slowly fade under the guitar and organ's gentle hosannas. Evangelist Lofton, meanwhile, continues to speak.

At this time, we're going to extend an invitation
    to those who are lost,   (Yes!)
    to those who cannot say they are yet free.   (Thank You, Jesus!)
Time is winding up now.   (Yes it is!)
And many of us are winding up in the time,
    but our souls has not yet been made right with
        the Lord.   (Thank You, Jesus!)
And the anointing of the Holy Ghost is speaking to
    our saints.   (Yes Lord!)
And hearts are being heavy because   (Whooo!)
    the souls of many are yet lost.   (Yes!/Jesus!)
But this afternoon,
    with the permission of your beloved pastor,
        the invitation is now being extended.   (Whooo!)
           To the unsaved!
           To the unchurched!   (Jesus!)
           To them that are lost, ha!
When the blood of Jesus has not yet covered
    your soul,
    you can be set free this evening!   (Yes!)
The invitation is being extended right now.   (Whooo!/Yes!)
Is there a one who's out of the church?   (Whooo!)
Is there a one who's out of the arc of safety? (Yes!)
It is by the Spirit of the Lord that this invitation
    is being extended.
Come to Jesus.   (Yes!)
We're not trying to get you to join no particular
    church.
    But we want you to get in *the* church!   (Amen!)
        The church of the living God!   (Amen!)
Hallelujah!   (Hallelujah!)
Then you can say you are free.   (Yes!)
    Free from your sins!   (Yes!)
    Free from your sickness!
    Free from your peculiar ways!   (Yes!)
        Be free, and be free indeed!   (Yes!)
Hallelujah!
The invitation is being extended.
Praise God!
Is there one
    who's unchurched?
There's one whose soul has not been anchored

22. "Is there one who's unchurched? Is there one whose soul has not been anchored in the Lord? This invitation is being extended to *you*." As Evangelist Lofton extends the invitation, the saints sit in rapt attention, praying that some soul might choose this moment to step into the "arc of safety." (Photo by Roland L. Freeman)

in the Lord?
This invitation is being extended to *you.*
No service should be without an invitation
   being extended.   (Praise the Lord!)
For therefore your blood won't be required to
   our hands.
And you might [be] sitting there,
   "Lord, I wish I had a chance."   (Alright!)
He's going to *remind* you that that second Sunday
   in March,
     March the fourteenth, nineteen ninety-three,
       during the twentieth anniversary of the
        Branchettes,
        you had a chance!   (Alright!)
          To give your soul to the Lord!   (Amen!)
Hallelujah, the invitation is being extended.   (Thank You, Jesus!)
Praise God!
Amen.

Evangelist Lofton's voice rises and falls throughout the invitation, returning to quiet earnestness each of the five times she gently declares that "the invitation is being extended." Her fifth call culminates in a dramatic portrayal of judgment, with God reminding the unsaved petitioner that the opportunity to accept salvation had been extended and heard. When no one steps forward, Evangelist Lofton closes the invitation with a firm "Amen." Then without a pause, she resumes her duties as emcee.

We praise God.   (Praise Him!)
Thank the Lord for the invitation.   (Thank You!)
Thank the Lord for the Gospel Tones.
At this time, we'll ask Smith Chapel to come,
   and we ask the Voices of Praise to be ready.
Amen.
Praise God.   (Jesus!)

In the silence that follows, I can hear murmurs of praise whispering through the church. Hushed cries of "Thank You!" and "Jesus!" float from pew to pew, broken now and then by an ecstatic, sliding "Whooo!" As the keyboards sound a meditative melody, the robed members of the Smith Chapel choir slowly make their way to the church-front. Though the moment is quiet, the praises will soon rise anew.

Chapter 19

Benediction

"May the Grace of God Rest, Rule, and Abide"

The three young men in Solid Foundation chose to close the anniversary's singing much as it had begun, with one of those old, "getting-close-to-you-gospel" songs. So they sang "What a Friend We Have in Jesus." And now, easing out of the final verse with a sweetly harmonized moan, their unaccompanied voices glide to a whispered finale.

Before they've even finished, a sister in the amen corner cries, "Lord Jesus!" Other voices quickly follow, tumbling one after another in a joyful torrent of praise and appreciation. The saints know that the end is at hand, and they seem intent on filling this last moment with all the energy that remains in their hands and throats. "Hallelujah!" they cry. "Glory to God!" "Praise the Lord!"

Evangelist Lofton slowly stands at her place in the front pew. Murmuring quiet "Amens," she gazes over the congregation and takes the offered mike. But this time she doesn't move toward the center aisle. Instead, she holds her place, knowing that her words will be few. With a hushed voice and beaming smile, she names the trio's songs and then asks God's blessings on the congregation. I can hear the emotion stirring as she continues:

I have *enjoyed* myself!	(Glory!)
I don't know about *you*,	
but *I* came to have church.	(Yes!)
And God has blessed me!	(Yes!)
Hallelujah!	(Amen!/Yes!)

The "Hallelujah!" bursts from her lips like an explosion, giving final vent to the pent-up praise. Then, with a happy "Amen!" Evangelist Lofton hands the service back to the Branchettes.

For a long moment, the microphone remains silent. But waves of sound continue to murmur through the church, flowing as if a giant, holy hand were moving over the pews and drawing forth the praises. The peak now past, the thanks are hushed and personal. When Sister Elliott finally takes the mike, her words aptly capture this gentle spirit. She opens by humbly thanking God for allowing her to be here and for blessing the anniversary. But just like Evangelist Lofton before her, she can't hold back the joy that trembles inside.

I don't know about you all,	
but I felt something!	(Hallelujah!)
Glory!	(Jesus!)
Something got in my *feet*—	(Yes!)
I couldn't hold them *down*!	(That's right!)
They got light!	(Yes!)
I had to *move* them!	(Yes!/Glory to God!)

Her tumbling words quickly slide from humble thanks to an exalted shout. And the saints rise right along with her, matching her every phrase with joyous cries of their own.

Though Sister Elliott's tone drops somewhat as she continues, it maintains its emotional elevation as she thanks the congregation, and then again thanks the Lord—for her family, for her friends, for the singers, and for the blessings He has bestowed on the Branchettes over twenty long years. After asking for the saints' prayers, she closes by again mentioning the holy dance that carried her into the cross-aisle earlier in the service. "I think you know," she declares, "that I can't hardly walk! But today these feet had to *move*! And I thank God for it!"

As the saints all clap, Sister Elliott hands Sister Perry the microphone. She too opens by thanking Jesus, declaring that "the Lord is blessing the Branchettes! We been praying a long time! See what the Lord has done!" Sister Perry's words flow even more easily than Sister Elliott's, thanking God for her pastor and the singers and the many saints who helped with the anniversary. Then she gives special thanks for the Gospel Tones, saying:

I praise God—	
when you can sing, and sing your *own self* happy,	
you doing good!	(That's alright!)
You know, when the Spirit of the Lord get upon you,	
you can sing *any way*!	(Alright!/Amen!)
Sometimes you might not be able to carry a tune at	
home,	
but when the Spirit of the Lord takes over,	(Alright!/Yes!)
praise God, you can *move*!	(Yes!)

Sister Perry next asks the saints to pray "one for another," for the Branchettes, and for her parents. Then, to my surprise, she asks *me* to say a few words, explaining the presence of my recording equipment. I stand and do just that, briefly giving my own thanks and then explaining that the tapes will be deposited at the University of North Carolina, where copies will be available for all who wish to hear the Word in song.

Sister Perry closes her remarks with more words of thanks, and then passes the

23. "When you've been singing together as long as we have," declares Sister Ethel Elliott, "you might as well call us *all* family!" At the close of the Branchettes' twenty-sixth anniversary, Sister Elliott calls some family members forward for special recognition. Standing from the left are Sister Elliott's daughters Bridgett Elliott and Willa Elliott, Sister Ethel Elliott, Sister Perry's mother Orlena Bennett, Sister Lena Mae Perry, and Sister Perry's sister Geneva Williams. (Photo by Roland L. Freeman)

service into the hands of her pastor, Elder David N. Atkinson. Elder Atkinson speaks in a quiet, almost hesitant manner, his words showing little of the rushing emotion so evident in the previous speakers. He opens by giving honor to God, and then apologizes for missing the first half of the anniversary, noting that he had to preach a funeral at a nearby church. But he arrived in time to hear the Branchettes and the last five groups. Having established how much he enjoyed what he *did* hear, he too speaks of the Spirit's power.

> So we thank God for all of you,
>> and most of all,
>> and out of all,
>>> is to see you *moved by the Spirit of God*.   (That's right!)

But Elder Atkinson doesn't stop here. He wants to make sure that programgoers know the limits of song. So he reminds them that getting to heaven hinges on "living the life."

> Singing is all right,   (Yes it is!)
>> but you got to live the life!   (Live the life!)
> You know, if singing alone would take you to heaven,   (Lord Jesus!)
>> I'd go back to it.   (Uh-huh)
> But when we finish singing,
>> there's a life,   (There's a life!)
>>> that got to be lived.   (Amen!)
> Amen.
> We must be born again.   (Praise God!)

Elder Atkinson concludes with a few words about Evangelist Lofton's invitation, expressing thanks that the service "didn't forget the sinnerman." Then, with a sly smile, he mentions all the food waiting in the fellowship hall, jokingly suggesting that the saints are probably ready for him to stop talking and give the benediction. Still smiling, he invites the programgoers to stand and raise their hands. When all hands are in the air, Elder Atkinson closes the service.

> Now may the grace of God and sweet communion of his Holy Spirit,
>> rest, rule, and abide with us all,
>>> henceforth and forever more,
> Till we shall all meet again in Jesus' name.
> Let us all say "Amen."

"Amen!" chorus the saints. "Amen!" say many a second time. "Praise the Lord!" adds Sister Perry.

As I lift my head, I see Evangelist Lofton standing beside me, extending her hands to clasp mine and to wish me God's blessings. Returning those blessings, I notice that saints all around me are hugging, kissing cheeks, and squeezing hands,

24. "Singing is all right," declares Elder David N. Atkinson, the pastor of Long Branch Disciple Church. "But you got to live the life!" As he closes the Branchettes' anniversary, Elder Atkinson—who himself sang gospel for many years before being called to preach—reminds programgoers that singing alone won't get them to heaven. (Photo by Roland L. Freeman)

enacting the accord so palpably evident during the service. Though the devotions began almost four and a half hours ago, nobody is moving toward the door. A few saints busy themselves unplugging amps and winding microphone cables; others edge toward the fellowship hall. But most just stand and hug and talk. Because even though the *service* is over, *church* clearly is not.

Before I have a chance to congratulate the Branchettes, one of the church mothers steps from the amen corner and warmly embraces me. Then Deacon Eldridge comes over to shake my hand. He is quickly followed by the young boy who toyed with my microphone before devotions, who now stands before me proudly extending his hand. As I show him the workings of the recorder, I overhear other saints talking about the anniversary—citing favorite songs, remarking on this group's uniforms and that group's harmony, and reflecting on how the Spirit had seen fit to truly bless the service. I can't help but smile and agree with them. The service truly *had* been blessed.

* * * * *

Closing with a spirit of warm fellowship, the Branchettes' anniversary ended much as it had begun. With smiles, with laughter, with a feeling of community. But one need only glance across the sanctuary at Long Branch Church to realize that something had changed. The smiles now seemed buoyed by an inner joy. The laughter seemed to ring from deeper depths. The fellowship seemed tightened by a bond of mystical communion. The church *felt* different.

I suspect that many social scientists would describe this sensed change as a product of "communal catharsis." Others would designate it the lingering manifestation of "communitas" fostered by "ritual drama." The saints, in contrast, simply say that the Spirit moved. When pressed for further unfolding, they point inside, to the mysterious knowing that separates works of self from works of Spirit. Then they remind us that this knowing wasn't always there. Saints freely testify to a time when their knowledge of the Spirit's workings was borne only by belief and the testimony of others. The boundaries between the encountered "natural" and the presumed "supernatural" were vague and undefined. But now, saints declare, those boundaries are clear. Because now their knowledge is grounded in *experience*. Now they *know* when the hand that moves them is holy. From whence comes this certainty? Saints say that they've felt it ever since they received the baptism of the Holy Ghost. At that moment, with that experience, they crossed the threshold into a new reality. And the rules in this reality, saints add with a smile, are simply *different* from those of "the world."

The gospel service stands as a celebration of and testimony to this difference. Saints come to the service to praise God and to share the special gifts that He has bestowed on singers and musicians. When saints join in worship, they expect to leave behind the conflicts and worries of everyday life. At the same time, they look forward to forging a community of singular accord, a community where hearts beat in unison and voices rise in spiritual harmony. With this accord, they hope to invite the Spirit.

This isn't to say that the Spirit will come only in such times of communion, or that the reality in which saints live becomes "real" only when invoked in worship. Theirs is *not* a reality removed from the everyday, not a situational frame into and out of which they freely step. Rather, their reality *is* the everyday; it *is* the reigning realm of experience. One need only listen to congregational testimonies to recognize the absolute prosaicness of spiritual action in the saints' lives. One hears of healings (both modest and dramatic) and calmings, infusions of joy and grantings of insight, unsought visions and extraordinary signs, unprompted words and celestial voices, spiritual gifts and material blessings, and, of course, the touch. Felt when driving the car, talking with friends, cleaning the home, working on the job, conversing over the Internet. Spontaneous and unexpected, the Spirit's visitations frame the saints' "normal," cloaking the whole in a mystery that is as much a part of the everyday as every other experience and eventuality.

Why, then, need saints gather in services of song? If the Spirit's visits transcend the particularities of context, why come expecting a blessing? In response, the saints remind us that they don't *need* to gather; they *want* to gather—to offer praises, to give thanks, to delight in the fellowship of worship. And they come with expectations because they know that accord facilitates focus in a way accomplished by few other modes of engagement. The swirling conversations draw the voice, while the reveries of communion draw the mind, turning thoughts away from self and toward the worshiping whole. Within this whole, attention easily refocuses on the holy, reengaging the self in a conversation both personal and collective. Saints say that *this* conversation—while no less powerful than that felt in solitude—is nonetheless qualitatively different. And this conversation, given the dynamics of the Spirit's flow, is even *more* likely to yield the felt blessings of the touch.

Hence the service begins by openly inviting accord. The first song, typically a piece steeped in history, draws the saints together in memory and collectivity. The very consonance of sound encourages consonance of spirit, laying a devotional foundation for the scripture that follows. The reading, in turn, grounds these soulful stirrings in the Word. Often drawn from the Psalms, it both establishes the fitness of praise and sets the service in a historical continuum that stretches back to biblical times. Next comes supplication and thanks. While a lone voice prays aloud, all others pray in silence, their engagement evinced only by the calls of "Yes, Lord" and "Thank You, Jesus" that murmur through the meetinghouse. The very stillness of led prayer invites conversational involvement, prompting saints to reflect rather than simply accompany. In this reflection, prayer again draws together the personal and the communal, extending thanks on behalf of self and entreaty on behalf of others. These silent thanksgivings, in turn, press for expression. They find it in song.

The service's subsequent songs differ markedly from the first, if only because they build on a communion already established. Saints often say that while the first song catches the attention, those that follow put it to use. By this point, accord is often becoming a palpable reality. Formally acknowledging this emergent sense of community, the welcome and response extend and accept the hand of fellowship. At the same time, they initiate the conversation of purpose, giving the service its shape as they elaborate the references already voiced in prayer and then declare the singular goal of praise. This declaration, in turn, is reaffirmed by the emcee, who typically wraps praise in a mantle of exhortative fire. She also reminds saints that artistry can serve deception as well as truth, and that "Spirit" displayed need not be Spirit felt. The emcee thus both focuses the praises and gives them a critical edge.

By engaging the saints in praise and prayer, devotions kindle the fires of holiness. The song service that follows, in turn, fans these flames to a sanctified blaze. It does so not by simply fanning emotions, but by furthering devotional focus. The instruments of this focus are singers, who enter the cross-aisle as ministers of the Word, trusting their artistry to draw saints' attention and trusting the Lord to guide their art. Unlike preachers (in whose stead they momentarily stand), singers come bringing a gift rather than a calling. This gift nonetheless has the power to touch and convict and lead souls to salvation. Hence the singers' special ministry.

And so the service proceeds, following an ascendant spiral of elevation, starting low, rising high, and hopefully, prayerfully, catching on fire. When the Spirit is high, each song emerges as a dispatch from heaven, its message resonating with hearers' experience and touching hearers' hearts. The guiding hand in this process belongs to the Spirit, who joins the service not as exalted observer, but as full participant. At every turn, the Spirit assists the submissive and sanctified singers, suggesting songs, giving ideas, fueling eloquence, empowering singing, and sometimes even providing the words themselves. Just as the Spirit blesses singers, so too does He bless listening saints, bringing succor, strength, and joy as He flows through the pews. The Spirit-filled service thus unfolds as a sacred celebration of revelation and epiphany.

When the last group steps from the cross-aisle, a spirit of exhilarated calm washes over the congregation. Under it run deep currents of elevation, currents that saints say will linger not for minutes or hours, but for days. The true blessings of the Spirit abide with believers long after the touch has passed. The experience of accord, however, is not so enduring. So saints often tarry, hesitant to sever the spirit of communion. At the Branchettes' anniversary, this hesitation opened space for praise and thanks and public reflection. The course taken by this reflection is worth our attention. The service's four final speakers all found their words pulled to an emotional peak when they spoke of *experiencing the Spirit*. Evangelist Lofton joyfully declared how God had blessed her soul. Sister Elliott excitedly testified to the blessings of holy dance. Sister Perry exuberantly recounted how the Spirit had powered her singing. And Elder Atkinson thanked God "most of all, and out of all" for moving in the service. The theme of holy experience draws these remarks together into a single reflective whole, reminding saints why they came and encouraging them to hold tightly to their faith.

With this message conveyed, the pastor calls for the final act of communion, drawing all to their feet with their hands in the air. "May the grace of God," he prays, "rest, rule and abide." Rest, that the Spirit might sustain. Rule, that the Lord's will might prevail. And abide, that the feeling might endure. Then the saints join together in a choroused "Amen," closing the service in harmonized voice and spirit. Just as they began with shared expectation, so they end with shared affirmation. And before the "Amens" can even fade, they enact their affirmation with smiles and hugs and words of joy. Saints thus close the service by immediately embracing "the life" that the singers called them to live.

Thus ends the service. Fashioned from praise, preaching, testimony, and prayer; constructed by saints, sinners, and Spirit; grounded in the Word, framed by tradition, built by faith, and elevated by God—each component contributes to the structure of devotional meaning. The mortar that binds the whole together, filling every hollow with intent and will and feeling, is spiritual experience. The saints proudly proclaim that such experience separates their reality from that of "the world." That's why they're so quick to define the term "sanctified" as "set apart." Saints say that worldly experience can yield only partial understanding of their apartness, granting insights into system, structure, and behavior but *not* into transcendence. Such insights, they say, obey the logic of a constricted reality. Hence saints liken those who probe holiness with worldly understandings to observers who try to discern a house's inner workings by standing outside. Though these observers can admittedly learn *some* things by peering into windows, they could learn much more by simply stepping inside.

Those unwilling to take this step—and those unwilling to admit that the sanctified reality might indeed be a reality apart—will argue that the hidden "inside" is actually quite predictable. Donning a cloak of "objectivity," they contend that the saints' claimed reality is a perfectly reasonable social construction, a logical product of tradition and belief. This approach—when applied with the expected measure of ethnographic sensitivity—dutifully avoids presenting believers as naive or misguided. Indeed, it poses them as rational actors acting rationally, making commonsense connections between empirical knowledge and the structures of faith. Yet the reasoning that guides these connections—a reasoning whose rules presumably lie well beyond awareness—is itself said to be guided by belief. Herein lies the hidden hand of culture and the invisible evidence of construction. The believers' conviction that their reality is *real*, in turn, is said to issue from this very invisibility. Could it be any other way? For it *is* real—declare the outsiders—*for those inside*. After all, they (and those that came before them) created the rules and fashioned the logic; they constructed reality's walls and then convinced themselves that the world beyond was different from that which those walls enclosed. For those standing outside, however, the "mystery" of insideness poses no mystery at all. In their eyes, the logic of cultural process renders the walls transparent, making the workings therein evident to all.[1]

Saints respond to this argument by once again invoking experience, pointing out that though culture may chart the pathways of cognition, and belief may guide the interpretation of seemingly supernatural encounter, *experience itself* confirms the fullness of their felt reality. "But experience is known only through one's subjectivity," argue the outsiders. "It can't bypass the filters of interpretation; it can't impart knowledge without the mediation of memory and worldview." That may be true, answer the saints, for experiences that are "of the world." Such experiences do indeed engage awareness only after being processed by the mind. But this isn't the case when experience is *holy*. Saints say that such experience is categorically different from that of mundane encounter. Not only does it *feel* different, but it *presents itself differently to the mind*. The very nature of awareness is transformed by the presence of holiness. It's not as if the Spirit simply reaches down—the saints remind us—and bestows a transcendent tap; He doesn't just grant a moment of epiphany and then leave. Instead, He *abides*. Believers say that the Spirit *connects* with the spirit, that the two *come together* as one, that the Spirit *indwells*. All of these terms suggest not only deep communion, but also deep *communication*. In moments of indwelling, the Spirit is said to impart a profound knowing, a penetrating certainty that certifies source and clarifies meaning. *This* is the knowing that bypasses the frameworks of belief; *this* is the knowing that lends holy experience its immediacy and apartness. And this is the knowing that allows saints to proclaim with such confidence the realness of their reality.

(The sense of communion conveyed by this experiential model also helps explain why saints object so strenuously when outsiders describe anointment as "possession." The Spirit does not "take over," say the saints; He does not erase believers' wills and control their actions. Instead, He *engages* them, inviting saints to "give in" so that He might work with and through them.[2] Most action arising from such engagement is thus collaborative, with the self typically maintaining a measure of awareness and involvement. Hence even when preachers describe preaching under the anointing, they typically tell of *hearing* the words as they flow from their mouths. Consciousness—and a measure of control—remains even when most control has been ceded. Saints say that it is precisely this deep level of consciousness that receives the experiential knowing imparted by God.)[3]

Faced with this claim to experiences that transcend cognitive and cultural process, investigators who would confine such experiences to *their* reality find themselves at an impasse. The process that saints describe, of course, could itself be a subjective creation. The deep knowing could itself be a product of mind. The insights of insiders are thus effectively rendered moot; though interesting as ethnographic data, they remain within the interpretive loop, themselves now treated as part of the cultural process. This brings those investigating the saints' world right back to their starting point, with experience reduced to predictable pattern and the walls of reality still transparent. The saints, meanwhile, simply shake their heads. When the urge to explain overrules the desire to learn—they sigh—the victim is understanding.

Thus the conversation ends, the two sides still separated by a chasm of belief. The saints proclaim the fullness of their reality, while investigating outsiders declare its partiality. The saints grant fundamental primacy to experience, while analytic readers treat it as a product of culture. The saints celebrate subjectivity as vital to crafting meaning, while "objective" researchers dismiss it as ephemeral and idiosyncratic. The saints believe in a God who acts in the everyday, while most investigators—though perhaps also believers—dismiss the proofs that saints read as clear evidence of a holy hand. Finally, the saints accept mystery, while disbelieving outsiders prefer answers.

All too often, ethnographic inquiry stops at this point, with believers and ethnographers locked in disagreement over matters of belief. Working from a position of unarticulated disbelief, most ethnographers simply refuse to accept believers' words at face value. To do so, they argue, would be to sacrifice their objectivity, to risk losing their scholarly perspective, to "go native." So they find solace in the mirrored means of relativism. Here, they can hear, probe, question and explain without jeopardizing their grasp on reality. But relativistic inquiry is rarely so benign. Judging from the history of Anthropology and Folklore, most ethnographers have found that relativism in matters of faith offers them a convenient stopping point, a place beyond which they needn't press investigation, a point at which questions cease. Presuming that all additional answers will yield only further evidence of belief, ethnographers simply stop asking, contenting themselves with the "data" at hand while withdrawing into the scholarly removal of analysis.

Just as the questioning stops here, so too do conversations with believers. From this point forward, ethnographic "conversations" typically become elegant fabrications, skewed exchanges where stilled words stand in phantom proxy for consultants. Only rarely do ethnographers invite believers to review and critique their analyses; even more rarely do believers' suggestions find their way back into the text.[4] In their stead stands eloquent theory, "objectively" voiced and usually nuanced by disbelief. Should it come as any surprise that experiential testimonies are among the first victims of such conversational substitution? The particularities of subjective encounter—and the passion with which they are often conveyed—seem to lose their primacy when removed from the contexts of faith and conversation. Distance dulls the immediacy, while experience—so vital in its initial telling—evolves into "behavior." The subtleties of the supernatural, meanwhile, all but disappear.

This, of course, is not the only available approach. Ethnographers can pursue the capricious paths of experience without inscribing them on a map and then offering that map as sufficient portrayal of lived truth. They can probe the ways of faith without themselves adopting faith's tenets. They can explore the edges of another reality without (wholly) leaving their own reality behind. And they can work with believers to tell their stories and unfold their meanings without losing their own voice. To do so, ethnographers must challenge many of the assumptions that have long governed their enterprise—assumptions of disbelief, of the generalizability of experience, of the interpretive shallowness of consultant analysis (evidenced, for example, in the post-fieldwork closure of conversation), of the relative primacy of objective portrayal over subjective story. At the same time, they must surrender the interpretive authority they have historically assumed, seeking instead a collaboration that draws consultants into the analysis as equal partners and then creates textual space for the ensuing conversation. As this conversation unfolds, experience—in all of its complexity and connectedness—will reassert its centrality to the study of lived reality.

In this work, I've attempted to capture some of this conversation. Throughout the process of writing, consultants in the church have read, commented upon, and contributed to my observations. When they've pointed out errors in logic or interpretation, I've made the suggested changes. When they've suggested issues that deserved elaboration, I've tried to elaborate. And when they've offered anecdotal assessments that brought new insights, I've tried to incorporate the insights—and often the anecdotes themselves—into the text. Together, we've tried to present the(ir) lived logic of sanctified meaning.

This logic charts a fullness that might never have been evident had the saints not repeatedly grounded our conversations in the experiences that set their world apart. Every testimony told of spiritual encounter; every story suggested the taken-for-grantedness of grace; every song alluded to epiphany. These references, in turn, opened the door to a new domain of understanding. Silence now revealed itself as reflective conversation. Congregational comments showed themselves as steps to accord. Shouts presented themselves as received joy. Elevated speech suggested the presence of revelation. And the Holy Spirit—the invisible, immanent force so often overlooked by those outside the community of faith—revealed Himself as the principal actor in the lived drama of holiness.

"If you really want to understand gospel singing," say the saints, "you've first got to understand the *Word*." Studying *singing* alone isn't enough. That might give insight into patterns of performance and perhaps into community aesthetics. But it will tell little of intent and less of personal meaning. The saints would call such study—as they do songs without spirit—"dead." To enliven the inquiry, song must be restored to the mouths and minds of believers, where faith fans the flames of passion. Not passion of the *world*, but passion of the *Word*—a passion that issues from emotion's embrace of knowledge, with both emotion and knowledge "wrapped, tied, and tangled" in reverence and praise. Inquiry must thus press beyond song to the Word, where it quickly finds itself following the same path that saints tread when they sing about "singing till their feeling comes." And it's at this "feeling" that the search for understanding ends, for the feeling is the fire—the fire in the bones—that testifies to the communion of saint and Spirit. In the heat of these sanctified flames, knowledge, belief, experience, and artistry all join together as one.

Appendix

Stepping Around Experience and the Supernatural

One doesn't have to step far into the annals of ethnography to realize that experience is a domain often invoked but rarely engaged. The invocation is everywhere apparent: experience lurks at the edges of ethnographic portrayal, guides passage through thickly described vignettes, and claims its tacit place at the heart of most analyses. But this "invoked" experience is generally of a different order than the experiences recounted by consultants; it seems to chart a domain curiously removed from the individual, a realm where all subjective encounter is pressed into the service of cultural portrayal. The particularities of self—the history and happenstance that lend each individual's experience its singularity—somehow vanish from the ethnographic equation, replaced by vague outlines that reflect experience much as a fun house mirror reflects truth. The mirror-master's hand, in this case, belongs to the ethnographer, whose selective twisting of the reflective surface yields portraits that all seem to convey a distorted sameness. It's this sameness, in turn, that catches the eye, suggesting patterns that often lie more in the distortion than in the singularity initially brought to the mirror. Yet these convoluted mirrorings nonetheless come to stand for experience in the ethnographic text; they come to represent the lived realities of our consultants. The experience of the individual, meanwhile, disappears in the distortion.

Yet *this* experiential realm—the eminently subjective encounter with the everyday—ultimately fires the machinery of meaning and activates human awareness. *Individual* experience—rather than that presumably held in common—charts the frame of personal reality and defines the everyday within those bounds; as such, it functions as a critical and irreducible denominator of existence.[1] Both uniquely singular and—through the lens of that singularity—uniquely shared, experience demarcates self and circumscribes the self's understanding of the other. In so doing, it provides the elemental material for the construction of meaning.

The paradigm-challenging approaches of contemporary ethnography have led many ethnographers to reexamine experience as a wellspring of cultural insight.[2] Some approach experience through a reflexive lens, probing self to better understand other; others build on the intellectual foundations laid by phenomenology and the American pragmatist school, exploring perception and the framing powers of worldview. All of these scholars call for an ethnography that looks beyond "behavior"—as reflected and observed experience—to confront lived experience in what one anthropologist calls its "full existential immediacy."[3]

Yet despite this call for all-out encounter with subjectivity, few ethnographers actually accept the challenge. Instead, most of those claiming an experiential approach explore what some have called "structures of experience," a strategy that still allows them to treat experience at a collective rather than a personal level.[4] In their analyses, experience becomes that which is shared and structured, that which emerges from the shaping forces of culture, that which follows culturally decreed contours of emotion, encounter, and interpretation. This is experience writ large, experience of pattern rather than personality, experience without the idiosyncratic variables of particularity. As such, this experience ever stands a step removed from the individual. All sense of engagement, of immediacy, has vanished.

Inquiries into collective experience do, in fact, draw us a bit closer to the immediacy of lived encounter. But they still keep their distance, seeming unwilling to surrender the analytic prerogative of description from afar. Consequently, the individuals they claim to represent lose face and features, while the particularizing moments that break the mundane vanish in a sea of generality. To recover this particularity and to confront the subjective engagement of those rendered faceless by ethnographic generalization, we must listen more closely to the testimonies of our consultants, letting their words chart the maps of meaning. They, after all, are the experiencers whose experience we are seeking to understand.

In order to *hear* the testimonies proffered, we must first jettison the assumption that our consultants' accounts are wholly crafted products of culture. This forces us to treat tellers not as persons bound by cultural prescription, but as individuals who daily face the unexpected and extraordinary. Next we must listen closely to our consultants' words, accepting their descriptions at face value while engaging them as colleagues in the search for realized meaning. The experiences they describe, each emerging from a memory and interpretive structure unique to the individual, deny collective characterization. Favoring fortuity over pattern, such told experiences reaffirm the subjectivity of significance. At the same time, they restore a much-lacking human dimension to ethnography, granting it a vitality and immediacy that ground it more firmly in lived truth.[5]

This grounding leads me to use the term "testimony" when speaking of experiential description. In the community of saints, a "testimony" is any expression whose focused referent is lived experience. Unlike the academic designations "personal experience narrative" and "memorate" (with the latter's specific reference to belief accounts), "testimony" knows no restriction of form. In its most common usage, it refers to a personal account of experience and thanksgiving presented before a gathering of saints. This recounting often assumes a highly elaborated form, poetically detailing the particularities of experience. Yet just as often, the account is sharply abbreviated, referencing experience but never publicly revealing the details. Whatever the form, testimony's core feature is the telling of experience.[6] Hence personal stories related in conversation are also called testimonies, as are songs whose words resonate with personal history. Linking all these expressions is a focus on testified truth. This quality, in turn, echoes with undertones of passion and heartfelt witness. A testimony thus stands as much more than a simple telling; it is a telling imbued with the authority of truth.

This is not to imply, of course, that testimony offers unmediated encounter with experience. Or that truth speaks with a single voice. The very act of transposition between the lived (in real time) and the relived (in narrative time) entails the mediation of memory and reflection, of will and words, of tradition and the available repertoires of talk. The recounting of experience necessarily involves both conscious and unconscious editing, as the narrator shapes the telling in accordance with the norms of appropriate talk, the canons of artful statement, the reading of audience receptivity, and the talk's intent. Testimony is thus inherently creative; it is always a "making."[7] And it is precisely this creativity, this quality of "madeness," that makes testimony such an effective guide to experience, for it reveals not only what happened but also what emerges from that happening as *tellable*. Herein lies the idiosyncratic, the extraordinary, the meaningful. Testimony defines the remarkable (that which is worthy of remark) while implicitly circumscribing the routine. In so doing, it sheds light on both individual and community canons of significance, offering an exegesis of experience that is simultaneously subjective and shared. The sorting of these realms becomes the task of dialogue, as ethnographer and consultant press testimony to reveal the assumed and unsaid—and, as is often the case in talk of transcendence, to address the unsayable.

Just as talk mediates between experience and its telling, so also does hearing mediate between experience as told and experience as imagined by the hearer. This secondary mediation is every bit as complex as the first, for it engages the hearer in a kind of co-creation, calling into play the processes of assessment, interpretation, and invention.[8] Grounding all of these processes is a fundamental comparison with one's *own* experience. This measurement provides the essential basis for understanding, lending narrated experience an immediacy and imaginative fullness it could otherwise never achieve. The hearer's personal experience infuses heard narrative with a kind of ideational reality, a creative actualizing that fills in unspoken details and allows the hearer to empathically share experiences as they unfold in talk. Without this self-referential grounding (or without its proxy analogue, the known traditions of described experience), testimony loses much of its effectiveness, becoming but so many uprooted words. As experiential distance grows and the comparative base shrinks, layers of intended meaning fall away, lost to the hearer's nonunderstanding.[9]

In order to capture some of this understanding, ethnographers have long struggled to establish some experiential common ground with their consultants. Hence they take up residence in their consultants' communities, participate in the day-to-day activities of community life, develop close relationships with new friends and families. By so doing, they hope to develop a basis for experiential comparison, encountering and assimilating the experiential reference points that will ideally expose their assumptions, guide their inquiries, and foster their understanding.

While such ethnographic experience is admittedly partial and circumscribed, it nonetheless moves the ethnographer one step closer toward the understandings of community membership. And it helps the ethnographer to at least imagine—if not to feel—some of the fullness of consultants' reported experiences.

But the experience-based extrapolations of ethnography tend to break down when recounted experience draws the ethnographer toward the supernatural. Shared experience is fine, it seems, until that sharing challenges the ethnographer's reality. Then it's time to step away, to affirm the relativity of belief, to invoke the "explanatory" mechanisms of psychology and cultural pattern. Suddenly reports of experience that in other areas of life are accepted at face value lose their credibility; suddenly they no longer reference the real, or at least not a "real" that isn't sharply circumscribed by the consciousness-shaping forces of culture. It's as if the very association with belief somehow taints told experience, drawing it out of the realm of the objective and authentic and into that of the subjective and imaginary. Supernatural experience is thus consigned to a reality apart, a realm where the "real" is defined only within the narrow parameters of belief. "That's what they believe," most ethnographers seem to say, "and thus it's real *for them*." What remains unsaid—but certainly not misunderstood—is the concluding codicil "but not for us, for we can see *beyond* the boundaries of their belief." Thus slips away any guise of ethnographic objectivity, only to be replaced by implicit claims to a fuller knowledge and a more real reality. Accounts of supernatural experience, in turn, get treated as artifacts of belief, interesting for the light they shed on culture, but meaningless as testaments to authentic encounter.[10]

This is not to say, of course, that all ethnographers find refuge in rationalism when confronting accounts of supernatural encounter. A growing number of investigators are treating such accounts as unproblematized testimony and are thus granting experience the same ontological status accorded it by believers.[11] Some of these have themselves traveled the pathways of encounter, seeking to more fully share the experiential world of their consultants. But most ethnographers still respond to the supernatural's challenge by stepping back to the ontologically secure foundation of known experience. They retreat, in essence, to the seemingly stable ground of disbelief.[12]

As folklorist David Hufford has so lucidly chronicled, this strategic retreat takes many forms.[13] Perhaps the most common entails simple disregard—not paying attention to accounts of supernatural encounter, dismissing claimed experience as a realm not worthy of investigation. This is not to say that ethnographers don't carefully probe the cognitive frameworks and behavioral manifestations of belief; ethnography has long deemed these realms central to holistic cultural portrayal. But the experiences that give rise to belief and grant meaning to behavior are consistently ignored. Not so much by design, I suspect, as by assumption. Most ethnographers encountering supernatural belief assume that they are dealing with a *conditional* reality and hence need only address those factors that actually effect the conditioning. In other words, they need only attend to the *structures of belief*, presuming that experience is the product thereof. So stories of experience become but building blocks of structure (and perhaps subjects of narrative analysis), while the experiences that lie at their heart get overlooked.[14]

Disregard is an act of omission, of not paying attention to reported experience. Other strategies of analytic retreat are not nearly so passive. Or nearly so benign. While disregard at least leaves open the possibility of *eventually* addressing supernatural experience, strategies of ethnographic "explanation" close discussion by flatly claiming to know "what really happens." Their practitioners directly address accounts of numinous encounter but attempt to "explain away" the accounts' phenomenological foundations. In so doing, ethnographers substitute *their* explanations—and their vision of reality—for those of their consultants, thus implicitly asserting the inherent superiority of their "more studied" understandings. What results is a kind of ontological colonialism, where consultant testimony gets pressed into the service of ethnography's analytic ends.

Ethnographic "explanations" of supernatural encounter take many forms. One common strategy involves outright denial, with the ethnographer asserting that testimony is either patently false or so cloaked in figurative speech that its experiential referents are obscured. Students of this "explanatory" school often focus on those who claim to be agents of the supernatural, the diviners and preachers and shamans who see themselves as vessels for a higher power. Dismissing the mystical without a second thought, many ethnographers portray these agents as artful actors in the high theater of ritual. Their skill is said to lie not in crossing from one reality to another but in cleverly maintaining that fiction through trickery. In essence, this "explanation" exposes ritual specialists as adroit hoaxers. Their audiences, in turn, become naive believers who suspend all judgment when faced with the forces of tradition.[15]

This claimed suspension of judgment opens the door for a second strategy of explanatory denial. This one, however, is far more subtle. Instead of openly discrediting the experiencers, this "explanation" focuses on testimony, arguing that belief and its narrative tradition inevitably shape both the telling and the hearing of experiential accounts. After all, no narrative stands alone; all emerge from a world of dialogue, with tradition providing the models for appropriate narration. Though these models might not be consciously recognized by community members, they nonetheless are tacitly known. This knowing, in turn, subtly directs all tellings, informing memory, guiding word choice, and shaping narrative structure. The resultant narratives, say ethnographic explainers, are crafted products of tradition, accounts that owe more to the elaborating powers of custom than to any actual supernatural experience. Those experiences, meanwhile, vanish from the analytic discussion, dismissed with a shrug and the clear implication that they "weren't real anyway."

The beauty of this explanatory strategy lies in its immunity to narrative numbers. The more accounts one encounters—be they of visionary meetings with spirits, of dramatic spiritual conversions, or of fleeting moments of ecstasy—the easier it is to attribute them to tradition. Hence, instead of taking recurrent testimony as evidence of real experience (as would be the case with most nonsupernatural accounts), ethnography treats it as proof of the shaping powers of culture. Disbelief simply turns the normal diagnostic process on its head, making a singular exception for the supernatural.[16]

Strategies of denial "explain" narratives of supernatural encounter by discrediting the experiencers or attributing the narrative substance to tradition. In essence, they question whether any real experience ever occurred. Another set of explanatory strategies—one that might be termed "assimilative"—takes a different approach. Ethnographers adopting this strategy admit the phenomenal reality of experiences that yield narratives of numinous encounter but deny these experiences' supernatural nature. Hence, while accepting the genuineness of the *experience*, they reject its supernatural *interpretation*.

This rebalancing of the belief/experience equation is simply effected. It begins by acknowledging that believers claiming numinous encounter experience *something* out of the ordinary. This "something," however, is presumed to fall within the "rational" universe of everyday life. With supernatural explanations thus dismissed, ethnographers try to determine the exact nature of the experience and the rational grounds which gave it rise; they then attempt to identify the cultural factors that shaped its interpretation and led to the particular claim. Analytic focus thus makes what by now should be a familiar move—turning away from experience per se and toward the cultural forces that allegedly give it perceptual and discursive form.

Now begin the final moves toward analytic assimilation, as supernatural claims are pressed into an acceptable "scientific" frame. This assimilation itself takes many forms.[17] Ethnographers "explain" some accounts by contending that they are rooted in illusion, in the misperception of ordinary (or at least otherwise explainable) events. This approach suggests that supernatural explanations often ensue when individuals encounter phenomena that they perceive in only a partial manner and then struggle to extract from their partial understanding a workable explanation. In the passage from partiality to wholeness, the perceived "something" often becomes "something supernatural," thus giving rise to "misguided" tales of numinous encounter.

A second assimilative strategy attributes supernatural accounts to interpretive rather than to perceptive failings, suggesting that the misinterpretation of ordinary events often fosters creative (if unintended) fabrication. Here the grounds of error shift from perception to assessment. Though the senses do their job well, the interpretive faculties intervene, transforming the everyday into the extraordinary and the natural into the supernatural. The culprits in this misdiagnosis, of course, are our old friends tradition and belief. In essence, this approach assumes that where belief would suggest the presence of the supernatural, there the believer will locate it, bypassing what some would consider the more "rational"—and non-supernatural—explanation.[18]

A third class of "explanation" situates experience entirely within the individual, bypassing outside referents and ascribing supernatural reports to hallucination. Here everything is said to happen in the believer's mind, with outside stimuli acting only to trigger the mental flights that actually construct the experience.

Whether the influencing agents are psychotropic drugs, severe physical and/or psychological stress, the mental convolutions of psychosis, or the mind-numbing actuators of trance, it is ultimately the forces of the unconscious that "explainers" credit with crafting supernatural fantasy and molding it to the convenient models provided by culture. The expedience of this "explanation," of course, rests in its freedom from outside referents and thus in its ultimate unprovability. Since both cause and effect—the construction of experience and the experiencer's interpretation—are situated in the mind, the validity of this "explanation" cannot be tested. Hence, it simply becomes a given. The explanatory credo is thus quite straightforward: when no "rational" explanation suffices, attribute it to the unconscious.

Somewhat surprisingly, it is to a variation of this final class of "explanation" that ethnographers have most often turned when *they themselves* experience something that best lends itself to a supernatural explanation. After ruling out the standard categories of cause, ethnographers have tended to look inward to themselves, questioning their experiences and often deciding that they must have been tricks of the mind. But this still leaves the task of explaining their experiences' disturbing coincidence with their consultants' beliefs. Ethnographers often end up attributing this correspondence to their immersion in fieldwork and to the pressures this immersion exerts on their objectivity. They reason that just as culture shapes experience for their consultants, so too does it shape that of outsiders attempting to submerge themselves in an alien setting.[19]

Of course, this is a different kind of shaping, as belief rarely plays a role in the experiential equation. Some ethnographers opt for a simple cognitive explanation, likening supernatural encounter to the alternate "reality" experienced in a theater, with disbelief momentarily suspended in order to more fully engage the emergent drama. Such encounter presumably unfolds as a consequence of familiarity and the *desire* to experience (even though the latter may be wholly unconscious).[20] A far more common explanation, however, attributes "supernatural" experience to a host of mitigating factors—physical debilitation, sensory saturation, the stress of fieldwork, the buffeting forces of fervent testimony. Working singly or in conjunction, these factors are said to fuel the fires of fantasy, provoking experience that only *seems* to be supernaturally induced. But the distance of time and the comforting surround of a shared (and disbelieving) worldview eventually expose this seeming encounter as nothing more than a bit of mental trickery a momentary lapse of lucidity prompted by extenuating circumstance.[21] In essence, most experiencing ethnographers, like Ebenezer Scrooge in his encounter with the ghost of Marley, attribute supernatural experience to that "undigested bit of beef," never considering that on this one occasion their minds might *not* be playing tricks with them.[22]

Denial, disregard, and assimilation—the strategies of disbelief and ontological substitution pervade ethnographies of belief and religious action. Though employing different means, all tacitly work toward the common end of rationalizing the supernatural. They reach this point not so much through intention as through assumption, not so much through the overt denial of believers' realities as through the tacit affirmation of the ethnographer's own. Herein lies their subtle deception.

The objectivity they herald in fact disguises a form of conceptual imposition, as native frameworks of understanding are silently shaped by the subjectivity of the researcher's worldview. In some realms of inquiry, this analytic overlay may be of little consequence. When applied to supernatural belief and experience, however, it becomes crucially important. Conceptual substitution in this domain transforms our understanding of the very mechanisms that believers use to frame their reality, distorting not only their thoughts, but also the sense-making and sensory-receiving processes that underlie them. The resultant understandings suffer from a distortion far greater than the simple blurring occasioned by seeing the world through different interpretive lenses. These understandings address an *entirely different reality*, a world apart from that experienced by believers. Though still peopled by our friends and consultants, the conceptual landscape now belongs to the ethnographer.

In presenting these strategies of testing and explanation, I do not mean to imply that they have no place whatsoever in the ethnography of belief. Deception sometimes *does* occur in the presentation of supernatural encounter; belief and narrative convention often *do* shape the telling of experience; believers sometimes *do* misperceive and misinterpret naturally occurring phenomena. Our consultants are the first to admit this. After all, every tradition of belief fosters traditions of disbelief; every claim of supernatural encounter invites a measure of doubt. The questioning, the testing, the calling for evidence already occur in our consultants' communities. Yet instead of looking to these established structures of assessment and evaluation, ethnographers have tended to impose their own. And they have often done so in a rather heavy-handed fashion, treating belief as an either/or proposition, without admitting the possibility of degree. Questioning accounts of supernatural experience need not entail the a priori assumption that these accounts are wholly in error; testing need not always be conducted from a stance of absolute disbelief. These strategies of inquiry are useful only if applied in a spirit of openness to alternative explanations. To weight them with disbelief is to destroy their effectiveness and to abandon all claims to objectivity. But to buoy them with openness is to invite dialogue, drawing our consultants fully into the search for understanding. With consultants as colleagues and with our demand for total "explanation" dismissed as an exercise in imposed authority, we can jointly chart new paths of inquiry, drawing on collective strengths to explore the experienced realities of belief.

Notes

Chapter 1. Seeking Understanding: "You Got to Be in It to Feel It"

1. From a conversation with Elder W. Lawrence Richardson (1986). Elder Richardson began his long and distinguished career as a gospel singer in the mid-1920s and brought his Spirit-filled singing to the public for more than six decades. He sang lead with the Nashville quartet the Fairfield Four from 1982 until his passing—shortly before his eighty-first birthday—in 1993.

2. Though rarely addressed in the literature on African American religious experience, such spontaneous touches are in fact a familiar feature of sanctified life. References to such moments regularly appear in church testimonies, and evidence of their frequency confronts anyone who speaks with saints about spiritual means. For historical examples, see Harrison (1893:366) and the 1920s testimony of Sister Kelley (in Egypt, Masuoka, and Johnson 1945:161–68); a fuller discussion of this phenomenon in sanctified talk appears in Hinson (1988). For examples of analogous (but by no means identical) phenomena in other African diaspora traditions, see Sheila Walker's discussion of nonceremonial possession in Haitian Vodoun (1972:43–44). Arguing from a stance of positivistic disbelief, Walker locates the cause of such possessions in human psychology rather than supernatural agency. She describes nonceremonial possession as a kind of psychological coping mechanism called into play when a believer experiences "extreme personal stress, fear, pain, or fatigue, or when the honor, interest, or life of the subject is threatened" (1972:43). Unfortunately, Walker never addresses the causal explanations *offered by believers*, and thus gives us no basis for comparing the processes of spiritual invocation with those used by the saints.

3. From a conversation with Elder Lawrence Richardson and Rev. Samuel McCrary (1985). The same emphasis on song, prayer, and preaching appears in a traditional aphorism often heard among African American Baptists: "The Church consists of three books—the hymnbook, the prayer book, and the Bible." Comparable comments are voiced by Baptist theologian Wyatt Tee Walker (1979:22) and Rev. William Herbert Brewster (in Reagon 1992a:196).

4. From a conversation with Lena Mae Perry and Ethel Elliott (1993). Sister Perry, as we shall see, sings with the North Carolina gospel duo the Branchettes.

5. From a sermon delivered by Rev. W. A. Daye (1993).

6. Many saints reserve a closet in their homes for deep prayer, thus following Christ's injunction to pray in private (see Matthew 6:6). Such "prayer closets" were once common in

sanctified homes, though their use seems to have decreased in recent decades. Nonetheless, references to prayer closets still abound in testimonies and devotional remarks.

7. For further discussion of expression as a register of options not chosen, see Hymes (1974:104–5). Both Tedlock (1976) and Urban (1982) discuss the connotative cross-referencing of communicative acts within an experiential frame.

8. For detailed discussions on multisubjectivity and the need to present an event's "reality" as contested and negotiated rather than as monologically decreed, see Clifford (1983: 118–46); Tyler (1986:122–40); and Marcus and Fischer (1986:30–32, 67–73).

9. The ethnography of communication approach, pioneered by Dell Hymes (see esp. 1962, 1974), encourages ethnographers to simultaneously address the broadest spheres of context and the most intimate spheres of feeling. In setting forth this approach, Hymes divides communicative inquiry into four levels of ethnographic specificity (1964:13–25; 1974:9–25). The first level focuses on the communicative event and the community's designation thereof. Noting that the range of features deemed diacritically significant for the definition of each event varies with community and situation, Hymes offers a heuristic guide for identifying relevant components (see esp. 1974:53–62). The second level details the systematic relations of communicative components, focusing on patterns of co-occurrence and the relative integration of communicative features in the conduct of culture. In essence, this level charts the norms of combination, examining which components go with which others and how the combined wholes engage. Moving beyond relationships to consider capacity and function, Hymes's third level addresses the culturally and situationally defined capabilities of components. This level focuses attention on differential competence and performance evaluation, issues that are particularly relevant to the study of religious communication. Drawing these three realms together in the working interlock of culture, the fourth level addresses the activity of the full system.

For situated analyses utilizing an ethnography of communication approach, see Baugh and Sherzer (1984), Bauman (1977), Bauman and Sherzer (1974), Gumperz and Hymes (1964), and Gumperz and Hymes (1972). See also the essays in the journal *Language in Society*.

Chapter 2. Belief, Knowledge, and Experience: "The Lord Can Be Mysterious"

1. This account, credited to Susan S. McPherson of Fayetteville, Ala., appears in Harrison (1893:366). In the original, Jack's words are conveyed with dialect spelling, such that "the" appears as "de" and "bless" as "bress." In that this dialectal respelling carries no morphological significance, and in fact describes a predictable phonological deviation (*if* it represents a deviation at all, and is not just an attempt at eye-dialect for the sake of narrative "color"), I have chosen to present the words in standard orthography. In like manner, I will respell all subsequent citations of dialectal speech where phonological transcription is neither crucial to an understanding of the text nor central to the text's poetic structure (as would be the case, for example, with deliberate elision or syllabic extension in song and sermon). By so doing, I hope to avoid the ethnocentric stigma that accompanies nonstandard spelling in the transcribed speech of minority communities, a stigma that implicitly links phonological deviation with cultural inferiority. For a detailed discussion of lingua-centric attitudes in dialectal renderings and a set of suggested rules for transcription, see Preston (1982, 1983). I will indicate all subsequent respelled quotations by appending the word "Respelled" to the note citation.

2. This formulation draws upon the insights of Donald Brenneis, whose investigations into the matrix of social aesthetics, emotion, and performance in the Fijian village of Bhatgaon led him to conclude that: "The language of emotion and aesthetics in Bhatgaon . . . provides the primary medium through which villagers conceptualize and articulate their experience" (1987:247). In describing the articulation of experience in Bhatgaon,

Brenneis paints a markedly nonindividualistic picture, arguing that community members conceptualize experience in a collective frame, with shared mood taking precedence over individual feelings. This stands in stark contrast to discursive conventions among the saints, where experience ultimately references the individual, and where testimonies—as public accounts of private experience—constitute an important and valued genre.

3. In her insightful discussion of subjective sources of knowledge among birthing mothers, Bonnie O'Connor (1993) presents a secular, nontranscendent analogue to this category of knowing. Calling the phenomenon "just knowing," O'Connor notes how many mothers who are giving birth experience a sudden, intellectual knowledge that carries with it complete authority. Like the "knowing" reported by the saints, this knowledge brings with it certainty and understanding.

4. The opening comment comes from Stephen McCray, an elder interviewed by Works Progress Administration workers in Oklahoma City, Okla., in the late 1930s (cited in Rawick, vol. 7 [1972:209] of the Oklahoma narratives). The latter two passages come from unidentified saints interviewed in Nashville, Tenn., in the late 1920s (in C. S. Johnson 1945:57, 16, with emphasis added).

5. From Rawick, vol. 4, part 1 (1972:4). Respelled, with emphasis added.

6. For those interested in further exploring this approach to the ethnography of belief and in probing the place it occupies within the broader history of ethnography, see the discussion in the Appendix.

Chapter 3. Experiencing the Holy: "Just Like Fire Shut Up in My Bones"

1. A pioneering Baptist preacher, Elder David George helped establish many African American congregations during the late 1700s. Born a slave in Essex County, Va., he fled the South during the Revolutionary War and made his way to Nova Scotia, where he preached to both Blacks and whites. In 1792, Elder George led a migration of more than a thousand followers to Sierra Leone. The quoted passages come from a letter published in the 1794 *Baptist Register* (Rippon 1794:478–80). Throughout this account, Elder George speaks of saints who "gave" their experiences to the church prior to baptism.

Throughout the text, I have capitalized the term "Black " to acknowledge the distinct cultural legacy shared by African Americans. I have not, however, done the same for "white," where the reference seems to point more to skin color than to a singularly shared cultural heritage.

2. Rev. Charles Raymond (1863:680) spent fourteen years preaching in the antebellum South. The account from which these comments are drawn includes a brief, rather stereotyped conversion narrative, offered as a characteristic "experience." The term "Negro" is not capitalized in the original.

3. Sister Kelley, a saint born in 1821 and converted twelve years later, told the story of her conversion to a Fisk University researcher in 1929 or 1930. These comments appear in Egypt, Masuoka, and Johnson (1945:161–68). Respelled and repunctuated.

4. White evangelicals of this same period—including Baptists, Methodists, and revivalist Presbyterians—also held "experience meetings," a practice apparently carried over from the eighteenth-century Evangelical Awakening in England and Wales (see, for example, the Welsh poet and hymn-writer William Williams's 1777 work, *The Experience Meeting* [Williams 1973]). While Baptists gathered in "experience meetings," American Methodists typically told their "experiences" in class meetings and, more particularly, at quarterly love feasts. By all accounts, these Methodist gatherings were on the wane—at least among whites—by the 1830s and 1840s; analogous gatherings among other white evangelicals had already ceased by this time (R. O. Johnson 1981; Holsclaw 1979; Wigger 1998:84–88, 185–87). African Americans, however, continued to hold "experience meetings" well into the twentieth century. See, for example, the accounts in Tybout (1904:289); Davenport (1905: 50); Adams ([1928] 1987:274); Hurston, who documents both Baptist experience meetings

and Methodist class meetings in Florida ([1935] 1963:253); and J. Lomax (1947:228). Brewer (1953:41, 44, 54) suggests that some Texas saints termed these gatherings "speaking meetings," but still called the featured conversion stories "experiences."

Two such "experiences" actually made their way onto a commercial recording in the late 1920s, when a team from the Okeh Phonograph Corp. invited Deacon Leon Davis and Sisters Jordan and Norman to record an "experience meeting" in the crew's makeshift Atlanta studio. The resulting disc, recorded on October 6, 1927, and released as "Experience Meeting" on Okeh 8527, featured Deacon Davis introducing "what you call a genuine experience meeting," followed by the sisters' conversion narratives. For more on this recording, see Oliver (1984:165–66).

5. Rev. Lockheart's words appear in Steiner (1900:68); Fanny Roberts's testimony comes from Rawick, supplement series 1, vol. 4 (1977:537). Respelled. See also Edward C. L. Adams's fictionalized account linking "experience giving" and church membership ([1927] 1987:58–59).

6. Some have suggested that the prospect of narration itself fosters the drama of conversion, that the expectation of future telling shapes the experience so as to render it more tellable (see, for example, Raymond [1863:680–82] and Powdermaker [1939:260]). Not surprisingly, believers reject this interpretation, arguing that it rather cavalierly shifts experience from the domain of divine induction to that of mortal creation. In so doing, it ignores the mystical sense of certainty that pervades conversion, the profound knowledge that the encounter's author is none other than the Lord. The depth of this knowing validates the experience and confirms its intrinsic insulation from cultural process.

This is not to suggest, however, that this special knowing is always present or that conversion is always real. The saints freely admit that many churchgoers *believe* they have been saved but do not *know* it. And others know they have *not* been saved but yet *claim* it. These false converts *have to* embellish their stories; they *have to* follow the guidelines of tradition, for they have no other basis upon which to build testimony. For them, the act of telling and the hearing of the told determine their "experience."

7. See, for example, Elder David George's repeated use of this lexical combination in Rippon (1794:479–80), and Elizabeth Kilham's account of saints "giving their 'experience' " between songs during devotions, a practice analogous to the "giving of testimonies" in contemporary services (1870:305). See also the references to saints who "give in"—rather than simply "give"—their experiences in Dooley (1906:43) and Tybout (1904:35–36 and passim).

8. Many community outsiders who wrote about "experience meetings" commented on this link between experiential telling and reexperience. Among these was Rev. William Barton, a minister whose description of African American congregational practices in Kentucky included the note: "not infrequently there are people to be received into membership with ecstatic experiences proved by a repetition of them on the spot" (1899:715). See also the accounts in Davenport (1905:50–51) and Raymond (1863:681).

9. The first citation comes from an unidentified saint cited in C. S. Johnson (1945:85–86); the second comes from the Tennessee saint Susanna Hall, cited in Egypt, Masuoka, and Johnson (1945:321). See also Egypt, Masuoka, and Johnson (1945:149), and Brother Julius's testimony in Raymond (1863:681). For analogous accounts linking "experience" telling and religious ecstasy among white Methodists at love feasts and class meetings, see R. O. Johnson (1981:81–82) and Wigger (1998:85–86).

10. See Hufford (1976:18–19) for a discussion of the inadequate language and ambiguity that typically plague descriptions of supernatural encounter.

11. From a conversation with Rev. Samuel McCrary and Elder Lawrence Richardson (1985). This description of the holy touch, likening it to "fire shut up in my bones," runs throughout sanctified songs, sermons, prayers, and testimonies. Its biblical source is Jeremiah 20:9, where the prophet says, "But his word was in mine heart as a burning fire shut up in my bones, and I was weary with forbearing, and I could not stay."

12. From a conversation with Rev. Carolyn Bryant (1985).

13. From remarks by Evangelist Evelyn Gilchrist (1993); and conversations with Edward Denkins (1985), Claude Landis (1984), and Lawrence Richardson (1986). The final citation comes from an anonymous account in C. S. Johnson (1945:79).

14. The ubiquity of this interpretation in writings about African American faith prohibits me from citing but a few representative examples. All of the authors I cite below reject the once-common attribution of religious practice to some inherent racial "disposition." At the same time, however, they tend to interpret religious behavior in highly functional terms, stressing the cathartic role that emotional expression plays in relieving social, political, and economic stress. While not denying the fact that religious *community* does meet certain psychosocial needs, I reject the reductionist strategy that reduces all experience to emotion and then "explains" emotion in terms of individual and cultural function.

Among those adopting this approach is theologian Joseph R. Washington Jr., who once labeled Black "folk churches" as "amusement centers for the entertainment of disengaged Negroes" and dismissed gospel singers as opportunists who "lead the masses down the road of religious frenzy and escapism" (1964:45, 52; see also 95–104). Washington's stress on escapist "frenzy" echoes the writings of W. E. B. Du Bois, who lists "the Frenzy" as one of the three central "characteristics" of slave religion—and the "one most devoutly believed in" (1903:190–191). Unfortunately, Du Bois never explored the nature of this belief.

Theologians C. Eric Lincoln and Lawrence H. Mamiya set out to rectify this oversight and claim as one of their goals "a deciphering of the frenzy" (1990:5). Ultimately, however, their "explanation" hinges on the functional "answer" of catharsis: "The highlight of the service was to worship and glorify God by achieving the experience of mass catharsis; a purifying explosion of emotions that eclipses the harshness of reality for a season and leaves both the preacher and the congregation drained in a moment of spiritual ecstasy" (1990:6; see also 175 and passim). See also the references to emotional "frenzy" in the works of Frazier (1963:56–57, 62) and M. Williams (1974:51, 54, 106).

15. From remarks by Evangelist Deborah Yarborough (1988), citing 1 John 4:4; for comparable comments contrasting God's power *on* you versus *in* you, see Caesar (1998:41). The lines in this transcription are entirely determined by congregational and/or musical response. In some instances, as in the line beginning with "'Cause I'm telling you," Evangelist Yarborough rushes her words to convey a more complete thought before pausing for breath. In others, as in the lines comprised of a simple "Huh?," she purposely pauses to draw the saints' reply. Only once, in the line beginning with "And I tell you," does the organ stand alone in percussively filling her pause. The clear patterning of Evangelist Yarborough's words, highlighting a host of parallel and contrastive constructions, testifies to the artistry that pervades all talk in the service.

The congregational commentary in the right column captures only a fragment of the saints' simultaneously voiced remarks. These are the comments most audible on the tape, suggesting that they were either the loudest or the ones voiced by saints sitting nearest to me. When more than one remark stands out, I include a selection. I make no claim for the comprehensiveness of this congregational transcription, as this would be impossible in a church filled with concurrent utterances. Yet this at least gives a *feel* for the dialogic nature of performed speech in the sanctified church, accenting the back-and-forth that draws all talk into conversation. Henceforth, I will use this format whenever I transcribe speech in congregational settings.

Within the congregation's comments, I have chosen to spell "alright" as a single word, thus acknowledging the voiced elision that draws its syllables so closely together. When consultants reviewed a draft that spelled the response as "all right," they remarked that the two-word construction suggested a pause that simply wasn't there.

16. Paraphrased from the comments of an unnamed preacher cited in Wyman (1891: 786).

17. From a sermon preached by Evangelist Wendell Spivey (1988). Evangelist Spivey's

words, and those of Evangelist Yarborough, both reference the sanctified adage "You can't go to heaven on a shout."

18. From a conversation with Rev. Zebedee D. Harris (1993).

Chapter 4. A Conversation: "You've Got to Open the Door"

1. This transcription by pause and parallel draws its inspiration from the ethnopoetic work of Dell Hymes and Dennis Tedlock, though it does not strictly follow either of the transcriptive strategies that they set forth. For Hymes's pioneering discussion of rhetorical structure in performed narrative, see Hymes (1975, 1977, 1981). For Tedlock's discussion of the "practical poetics" of talk, in which he poses the goal of a "performable translation," see Tedlock (1971, 1983). My recognition of poetic patterning in nonnarrative talk owes a particular debt to Henry Glassie's discussion of vernacular poetics (1982:35–40). Glassie's lucid discussion of poetic emergence led me to listen differently to the words of my consultants, prompting the poetic presentation that I use throughout this book.

2. From a conversation with Bishop Frizelle Yelverton (1987). For a telling testimony to the power of Bishop Yelverton's preaching, see Caesar (1998:24).

Chapter 5. Beginnings: "Happy to Be in the House of Worship"

1. When identifying church members, I will preface their names with the titles "Brother" or "Sister," in accordance with community usage. My consultants felt that the titles "Mr.," "Mrs.," or "Ms." were too distancing. They also expressed concern that the use of un-prefaced last names might be taken as disrespectful. Hence we opted for the titles accepted in the church.

2. "At the Cross," along with a host of other eighteenth-century hymns penned by Dr. Isaac Watts, has long been a favorite among African American congregations. Not surprisingly, its lyrics have changed slightly from the original, with the opening line's "alas," for example, becoming a clearly articulated "at last."

3. The Branchettes' twentieth anniversary took place on March 13 and 14, 1993, at Long Branch Disciple Church in rural Johnston County, N.C. All descriptions of the anniversary are drawn from the March 14 service.

4. "Devotional services" are alternately called "devotion services," "devotions," or, in services that include testimonies, "song and testimony services." Most saints use these terms interchangeably.

5. For a fuller discussion of the range of devotional services, see musicologist and gospel singer Horace Boyer's comparative study of Black church music (1973:208 and passim). Detailed descriptions of sanctified devotional services appear in Paris (1982:54–61), McIntyre (1976:30–31), and Pitts (1993:11–18). See also Allen (1991:82–86).

6. Such sermonettes usually grace only the devotions of services that otherwise do not include preaching. Hence, one might expect to hear them at gospel programs but not at revival meetings or Sunday morning services. When they do occur, the delivering preachers often explicitly define them as part of devotions. At the thirty-ninth anniversary of the Sensational Nightingales, for example, the presiding preacher followed congregational singing with altar prayer and a ten-minute "sermonette." As if to affirm that his preaching was a preface to the singing, he explicitly declared that this was all "part of the devotion service" (Bell 1985b).

7. From a conversation with Lawrence Richardson (1985b). Compare Elder Richardson's actions with Deborah Barney's fascinating account of gospel announcers who sequence the songs in their radio shows to replicate the order of church services (1994:132–33).

8. In distinguishing the source and purpose of devotional words, I don't mean to imply that the Spirit speaks only through "called" preachers. The saints are quick to point out that

the Spirit also animates the mouths and bodies of churchgoers in the pews. Yet when the Spirit guides these saints' words, the messages usually maintain a heavenbound orientation. They are still addressed, in other words, to God. Hence, even though anointed churchgoers are "receiving" the words of prayer, they still stretch their entreaties toward heaven—making God both source and recipient. In contrast, when a minister preaches "in the Spirit," the words are directed to the assembly (a body that explicitly includes the preacher). Thus while the preacher's anointed words address the saints, the congregation member's do so only rarely, and instead address the Almighty. The key exceptions to this rule are congregational prophecies (including interpreted tongue-speaking) and the "Amens" that saints say are sometimes elicited by the Spirit.

9. In his ethnography of a Pittsburgh Pentecostal fellowship, Melvin Williams includes this cross-aisle center point in what he terms the church's "sacred inner space" (1974:146–51 and passim; see also the map on p. 144). This symbolically marked area extends outward in a rough circle from the pastor's seat behind the rostrum, encompassing the pulpit, the communion and offering tables, the middle stretch of the cross-aisle, and the pew positions at the front corners of the center aisle. Williams argues that the church's "most sacred" activities—from preaching to communion—occur in this arena, giving it an air of special sanctity. This quality of set-apartness restricts regular activity in this space to the church elite.

While this space's connotative significance certainly lingers at church-based gospel programs, I would argue that its different use transforms the envelope of meaning. In most programs, the church elite get no special place; they sit in the pews alongside the performers and other saints. The pulpit and the seats behind it remain empty, and the communion (and often the offertory) tables remain unused. When the program occurs outside of a church structure, the spatial markers of pulpit, dais and tables simply don't exist. What does remain, however, is the cross-aisle. Whatever the structure, this space becomes the program's locus of significance.

Chapter 6. Scripture: "It's About Being Sincere in Your Heart"

1. This verse in Psalms finds a host of counterparts throughout the Old and New Testaments. See, for example, Exodus 4:10–15, Deuteronomy 18:18, Isaiah 51:16 and 59:21, Jeremiah 1:9, and the oft-cited words of Christ in Matthew 10:19–20, Mark 13:11, and Luke 12:12.

2. From a Sunday morning sermon by Bishop Yelverton (1988).

3. This is not to suggest that all devotions include scripture; many reserve this for later in the service. As Horace Boyer suggests in his comparative survey of Black church liturgies, the difference is often denominational (1973:209 and passim). See Boggs (1977:32), McIntyre (1976:30), and Paris (1982:54–55) for descriptions of scripture reading in Church of God in Christ (C.O.G.I.C.) and Mount Calvary Holy devotions.

4. Remarks voiced during a performance by the Greater Joy Ensemble (1987). For analogous remarks, all of which include some form of the adage "The more you put into it, the more you get out of it," see Allen (1991:85), Reagon (1989:15), and John Watson's comments in A. Young (1997:139). The "theme" mentioned in this description refers to the special song with which a gospel group typically opens its sets; such pieces, usually repeated at every performance, come to be closely identified with particular ensembles.

5. From a conversation with Elder Lawrence Richardson and Rev. Samuel McCrary (1985). At the time of this conversation, both Elder Richardson and Rev. McCrary were singing lead with the Nashville-based quartet the Fairfield Four. For a historical synopsis of their role with this quartet, see Seroff (1988:12–18).

6. The special respect accorded to overtly intense performance calls to mind Robert Farris Thompson's discussion of "vital aliveness" in West African aesthetics (1974:9). In gospel events, a comparable aesthetic of intensity governs both performance style and

congregational engagement. Folklorist Mellonee Burnim, in her pioneering inquiries into gospel aesthetics, addresses the importance of impassioned involvement by discussing the essential physicality of gospel performance. "Over and over again," she notes, " . . . respondents indicated to me that the voice must transmit intensity, fullness, and the sense that tremendous energy is being expelled. The singer must convey complete and unequivocal absorption in the presentation, thereby *compelling* the audience to respond" (1985:156–57, emphasis in original). See also the discussions of devotional "aliveness" in Burnim (1980: 142, 148–53; 1988:115), Allen (1991:152–55), and H. Phillips (1969:37–38, 66–67), and of expressed intensity in blues performances in Keil (1966:161).

7. From a sermon by Evangelist Susan Massenburg (1988).

Chapter 7. Prayer: "The Vibrations of the Holy Spirit Go Out There"

1. When discussing the conversational nature of African American worship, sociolinguist J. L. Dillard notes a similar disparity between churchgoers' comments during sermons and the message to which they are apparently addressed. Citing an instance in which a church sister says "Thank the Lord" when the preacher is talking about sin, Dillard concludes that "Her comment applies to the sermon context as a whole—Thank the Lord that the sermon is being preached, that the people are gathered in church—and not to the immediate sentence the preacher happens to have uttered. . . . Here, as in so many cases, the discourse and not the individual sentence is the unit to which primary attention must be given" (1977:55). Dillard is correct in pointing to the "discourse" rather than the "sentence" as the trigger for the sister's comment. His contention that the referenced "discourse" is the *sermon*, however, is rather presumptuous. Most saints would say that the sister's "Thank the Lord" was probably part of a separate, largely silent conversation, one in which the sermon figured only tangentially.

2. From a conversation with Joseph "Jojo" Wallace (1993).

3. One such testimony appears in the conversion account of the already-introduced Sister Kelley. "Well, I still didn't know nothing about praying," she says, recounting the morning of her conversion, "but I says, 'Oooh, my good and holy Father, what can I say to Thee for Thy blessings?' And He said in a voice that shook me like a storm, 'Open your mouth and I will fill it with all the elements from on high.' " According to her testimony, the Lord did just that, providing words that "just came . . . from nowhere" (in Egypt, Masuoka, and Johnson 1945:166, 164.) Respelled and repunctuated.

4. "Prayingest" stands alongside "singingest" and "preachingest" as a vernacular measure of devotional skill. With all three terms, saints deem the named ability more a product of supernatural endowment than of human competence. In essence, the Spirit gives the gifts, and then gives receivers the freedom to use them as they see fit.

5. From a conversation with Deacon Willie H. Eldridge (1994).

6. From a prayer delivered by Sister Rachel Williams (1988).

7. From a prayer delivered by Rev. Louis Cash (1987).

8. From a conversation with Deacon Edward Denkins (1985).

9. Zora Neale Hurston alludes to the self-serving quality of worship performance when she talks about the artistry inherent in prayers, sermons, and testimonies, and notes that "there is a lively rivalry in the technical artistry in all of these fields" (1983:83).

10. From "Stop That Putting On," in Walker (1969:47). Born in rural Arkansas, William Walker moved to Chicago in 1919, where he quickly established a reputation as a community poet. In addition to writing secular pieces, he penned many poems directly inspired by the Spirit. He often recited these inspired poems in churches, at gospel programs, and on gospel radio broadcasts. He also distributed his poems in broadsheet and booklet form.

11. Mellonee Burnim makes much this same point about the broader gospel music

tradition when she poses music as a potent "symbol of ethnicity." Noting that gospel "attracts many supporters who identify with its message as much for its communication of Black values, experiences and beliefs as for its communication of religion," she argues that the music holds deep meanings for churchgoers and nonchurchgoers alike (1980:2; see also pp. 85–87, 189–98; Burnim 1985:147). Though Burnim focuses on gospel's performative universe, her arguments apply equally well to its component parts. What she does not pursue in her analysis, however, are the meanings that transcend those shared by co-cultural peers, those that saints say are experienced only by the saved. Anointed believers argue that this realm of experienced significance renders the broader symbolic meanings rather shallow.

12. From a conversation with Elder Lawrence Richardson (1985b).

13. From a conversation with Deacon Edward Denkins (1985).

14. Frederick Law Olmsted (1856:449) credits this account to the owner of a rice plantation in South Carolina or Georgia.

15. Just as saints tend to associate the stylistic features of elevation with preached sermons, so too, apparently, do most scholars. Consequently, the most detailed analyses of this stylistic complex appear in studies of African American preaching. Particularly valuable are the works of Gerald Davis (1985) and Bruce Rosenberg (1970, 1974, 1975, 1988), both of whom examine the syntactic, metrical, and (to a lesser degree) tonal aspects of preaching. For a detailed analysis of preached sermons' tonal and rhythmic characteristics, see McIntyre (1976:74–77 and passim). Less detailed stylistic analyses appear in Gold (1981:178–197), Joyce Jackson (1981:213–16), Holt (1972:191–94), Hurston (1983:81–84), and Mitchell (1970:162–77). See also Kroll-Smith's analysis of elevation in testimonies (1980), and Smitherman's insightful discussion of "tonal semantics" and "talk singing" beyond the pulpit (1977:134–39).

One of the few scholars to explore elevation across communicative genres is ethnomusicologist Morton Marks, who compares stylistic traits in preaching and gospel performances (1974:87–98, 106–9; 1982:313–16).

16. In an essay relating performance style to spiritual status, Kroll-Smith (1980) suggests that this co-occurrence is so well established that the elevated style actually serves as a way of publicly declaring the depth of one's relationship with the Spirit. Drawing upon research in a C.O.G.I.C. congregation, he argues that believers fully expect church "mothers"—whose spiritual status has earned them respect and honor—to testify in a heightened style, while expecting younger and less-experienced "sisters" to testify in a more conversational, non-demonstrative manner. While accepting the frequency of correlation, I am unwilling to draw style and status into a rule-bound relationship, particularly given saints' frequent conversations about those who manipulate style for their own ends.

17. Saints often tell believers that if they *think* they've been saved, but don't *know* it beyond a shadow of a doubt, then they have *not* been saved. Being saved, as I suggested in Chapter 2, is said to bring with it a sense of deep certainty, a "knowing" whose intensity far transcends that of mundane knowledge. Saints say that this "knowing" *always* accompanies the status of sainthood. Nonetheless, saints admit that many church members who sincerely believe themselves to be saved are in fact not. These believers only *think* that they know, mistaking self-generated feelings for the mystical "knowing" of holiness. When these misguided believers do get saved, they are quick to declare the difference between knowledge *before* and knowledge *after*.

This issue of "thinking" oneself converted shows up in a short but telling reference in Goreau's biography of Mahalia Jackson. When the young Mahalia asked a neighbor what it "feels like" to get converted, the neighbor answered, "Some people don't have no real conversion; they just think they do, tell theyself they do." Overhearing the conversation, Mahalia's aunt declared, "Halie's not going to *think* it, she's going [to] *know* she has it!" (1975:44; emphasis in original).

18. From a conversation with Deacon Edward Denkins (1985).

Chapter 8. A Conversation: "It's the Words of Him That's Speaking Through Me"

1. The text that follows is transcribed verbatim from my conversation with Deacon Eldridge (1994).

2. Deacon Eldridge here refers to 1 Corinthians 1:17–27, where Paul tells the saints at Corinth that the unsaved will always view the words of preaching as mere "foolishness." At the heart of this passage is verse 18, which reads, "For the preaching of the cross is to them that perish [i.e., the unsaved] foolishness, but unto us which are saved it is the power of God." Perhaps the deacon's reference (and his subsequent chuckle) points to my attempt to interpret the transcribed prayer. The written words alone, he implies, are partial; only when heard in the context of performance and faith do they achieve full meaning.

Chapter 9. Song: "Sing Till the Power of the Lord Comes Down"

1. This spirit of layered simultaneity invariably calls to mind the shifting textures of jazz, a performative realm that also values collective improvisation and that also draws music, movement, and voice together in unity. Among the many who have remarked on these jazz/worship parallels is sociologist Arthur Paris (1982:73–78), who discusses aural similarities and the shared shifting of performative focus. But Paris focuses only upon those actors who "play" to the full congregation (e.g., preachers or praying deacons), treating them as soloists while relegating all others to a "supportive" role. At no point does he address the experience of individual worshipers, examining how their unique contributions shape the emergent whole or how they too become "soloists" in the dialogues of personal praise. Further, when discussing the collective improvisation of the supporting "section," Paris examines only their aural contribution, never looking beyond sound to the harmonized flow of motion and emotion.

2. From an unnamed Tennessee preacher, cited in C. S. Johnson (1945:153, 156).

3. I don't mean to suggest that other worship acts cannot elicit analogous involvement. The conversational commentary that punctuates prayers, testimonies, and sermons, for example, also bears witness to reflection and creativity and certainly embodies a spirit of communion. But this conversational participation, though often interlocked, is not as consistently or redundantly patterned as group song. In free moments of praise and response, congregation members act independently, with each individual helping to shape—but not defining—the expressive result. In group prayer, for example, the prayer leader's words define the path of thanksgiving and entreaty. Though the thoughts of individual worshipers might follow different paths and yield comments that might ultimately effect the prayer's course, the foregrounded message remains that voiced by the prayer leader. In song, however, lyrics, melody, and rhythm limit expressive independence, insuring a degree of consonance not found in most other worship acts. Though the mind is still free to wander, the demands of participation keep drawing it back to the song. Only group recitations (responsive readings, collective benedictions, and so on) occasion a similar unity of voice. These acts, however, often unfold as rote exercises, offering little opportunity for improvisation and embellishment. Recitations *can* stir souls, admit the saints, but they don't do so as predictably or as powerfully as song.

4. From a conversation with Bishop Frizelle Yelverton (1987).

5. From a conversation with Deacon Edward Denkins (1985). Similar comments from another deacon and gospel singer appear in Robinson (1997:410).

6. While recognizing the popularity of this congregational standard, quartet singer Jojo Wallace—one of the manuscript's initial readers—noted that its text could lead readers to misunderstanding. "It should say, 'sing until His presence *overflows* in you,' and not 'till the power comes down,'" he wrote. "Because He is already—and always—here."

7. The words of Evangelist Rachel Green and the ensuing commentary are drawn from

fieldnotes written during and after the May 1, 1988, service at Durham's Mount Calvary Holy Church.

8. Addressing this process of condensation, Mary Catherine Bateson coined the term "praxon" to describe communicative commonplaces "whose meaning is not deducible from their structure" (1974:159).

9. Of course, meanings that attach themselves to a song as a whole, wholly apart from its lyrics, might themselves prompt reflection and engagement. All songs, after all, exist in a world of memory and association. The acts of retrieval and performance might well spark memories that link particular songs with people, places, and/or events that hold special significance for the singer. These memories might then trigger praises every bit as deep as those prompted in another singer by the lyrics. Hence, though the singing might be rote, devotional engagement might nonetheless be intense.

10. From the remarks of an unidentified speaker at the Famous Jordanaires' thirty-first anniversary on August 8, 1988, in Durham, North Carolina.

11. This definition is purposefully loose, as is the use of this term among the saints. Many churchgoers use the term "shout song" to designate any fast piece that folks regularly "shout off of." And most agree that *any* song can be transformed into a shout song. Even traditionally slow pieces like "Amazing Grace" and "Precious Lord," when given up-tempo arrangements, earn this designation. The critical factor seems to be the song's "beat." See, for example, the definitions offered by Baptist songstress Cleonia Graves (in Hinson 1990), quartet lead Rev. Burnell Offlee (in Joyce Jackson 1988:277), and gospel scholar Horace Boyer (1992a:95; 1992b:224).

12. Saints' descriptions of "emotional" shouting bear an intriguing resemblance to Gilbert Rouget's categories of "excitational" and "emotional trance"—the former arises from deliberately induced bodily excitation, and the latter issues from a strong emotional response to music and sung words (1985:284–317). "Emotional shouts" seem to share characteristics with both of Rouget's categories, in that they involve both intense physical and intense emotional engagement. At the same time, however, they blur Rouget's distinctions, in that they can be prompted by the "beat" *or* by lyrics, by spoken words *or* by other shouts; further, even when spurred by words, they can be maintained by music and congregational clapping. In the final analysis, the distinctions that Rouget makes on the basis of behavior prove far less flexible and nuanced than those made by the saints, which rely more on subjective references to emotions and spirit.

13. From conversations with Rev. Zebedee D. Harris (1993) and Joseph "Jojo" Wallace (1993). For more on this issue, see Joyce Jackson's insightful discussion of lyric articulation in quartet performance (1988:163–66, 277).

14. From a conversation with Pastor Rosie Wallace Brown (1983). For closely parallel accounts, see Heilbut (1985:xviii) and Caesar (1998:37).

15. Published descriptions of African American devotional services tend to confirm this general outline. See, for example, Boyer (1964:28), Rubman (1980:98), and Allen (1991:81, 84). Anthropologist Walter Pitts Jr. contends that the presence of older hymns and spirituals in devotions is best explained by the binary framing of African American services, wherein the first part of the service (devotions) sets a frame for the Spirit's descent, while the second (the post-devotional service) actualizes this frame and brings on what he describes as "trance." Arguing that devotions replicate the opening stages of West African initiation rituals, Pitts attests that "non-trancing" songs appear in the devotional frame, while "only those songs that are conducive to trance are placed in the second frame." He then describes a process whereby songs that hold primary "emotional significance" (those that, presumably, will "cause" trance) remain in the main part of the service, while those that have lost this meaningful centrality cycle into devotions (1993:145–53).

Unfortunately, in his effort to present a blanket schema for African-based ritual, Pitts ignores actual practice. Though the devotions in the Baptist church in which he conducted most of his fieldwork might indeed have been "lugubrious" and "archaic," and though the emergence of a shout during devotions might indeed have been deemed "embarrassing," this is certainly not the devotional norm (1993:31, 15–16). Indeed, in most churches that celebrate the gifts of the Spirit, the descent of the Holy Ghost during devotions is a goal actively *sought* by the saints. Far from "disturbing" the service, most saints argue that the Spirit's presence enlivens and fulfills it.

16. From a conversation with Lena Mae Perry and Ethel Elliott (1992). Gospel composer Thomas A. Dorsey makes much the same point in M. Harris (1992:73, 22), as does singer and gospel radio announcer Rev. J. W. Shaw in A. Young (1997:177).

17. The verses cited here draw from J. W. Johnson (1925:76–77), Odum and Johnson (1925:143), Marsh (1880:158), and the reminiscences of saints in Durham, N.C. Respelled.

18. These comments, voiced by an unidentified speaker in a devotional service, appear in Kilham (1870:306). Respelled and repunctuated. For a tellingly similar testimony, recorded three decades later, see Dooley (1906:41–42).

19. Rambling through the thousands of "transcribed" interviews conducted by Writers' Project workers with ex-slaves in the 1930s reveals the breadth of this rhetoric of decline. Showing a remarkable uniformity of opinion, hundreds of saints echoed the trenchant critique of Oklahoman Prince Bee: "That religion I got in the way-back days is still with me. And it ain't this 'pie crust' religion such as the folks are getting these days. The old-time religion had some filling between the crusts, [and there] wasn't so many empty words like there is today" (in Rawick 1972, vol. 7, Oklahoma narratives, p. 15; respelled and repunctuated). Whether or not the interviewed elders expressed a fondness for the past, they invariably criticized the present-day practices of faith.

20. From a conversation with James Thomas (1993). Brother Thomas presided over one of North Carolina's most popular and widely heard gospel radio programs for more than three decades.

21. Anthony Heilbut notes that, "As early as 1926 Sister Sallie Sanders begins her recording 'Shall These Cheeks Be Dried' with the admonition 'Let's go back to the old-time singing of our grandfathers and grandmothers'" (1985:xx). Folklorist Ray Allen offers a much fuller discussion of these themes, treating them as expressions of "cultural revitalization" among gospel communities in the urban North (1991:186–203). Focusing primarily upon gospel singers' invocations of the old-time South, Allen argues that performers "use these symbolic expressions to remind churchgoers of the joys and sorrows of their southern heritage and to preserve the old religious value and practices that brought them and their forebears through arduous times" (1991:203). References to a southern past undoubtedly do remind many northern African Americans of their Southern roots. Yet by focusing on the southerness of these images, Allen gives short shrift to the factor of *age*. The fact that southern singers invoke the *same* images as their northern counterparts suggests that southern imagery is but one factor in a broader symbolic complex whose significance ultimately transcends region. Further examples of past-oriented evocation in gospel performances appear in Marks (1982:311–13, 325–27).

22. In the same year that Rev. Brewster wrote "Let Us Go Back to the Old Land Mark," Thomas Dorsey published "The Little Wooden Church on the Hill," another song whose lyrics explicitly linked "meter singing" with the worship practices of an earlier era. After an opening verse that sets the referenced time as "in my childhood . . . many years ago," the song's chorus says: "When that old fashioned preacher gave out that meter hymn / Then each heart with the Holy Ghost was filled / And the people would be shouting, 'Praise God,' I hear them still, / In that little wooden church on the hill." In keeping with this retrospective framing, Dorsey dedicated the song "to the memory of the old country churches attended by our forefathers and mothers" (1949).

Although the meter designation formally specifies only the poetic structure of a lyric, and not its tempo, saints have long associated the term "meter hymn"—and specifically "common meter hymn"—with slow, measured singing. When I've asked both elder and younger singers to define "common meter," most do so first in terms of tempo. Ethnomusicologist William Tallmadge reported a similar finding in 1961, though he found that churchgoers differentiated between the tempos indicated by the terms "long meter" and "short meter." Interestingly, Tallmadge described the tempos performed with these meters as "regular" (for short meter) and "slow" (for long meter); no meter hymn moved at a fast tempo.

Chapter 10. Praise: "Up Above My Head, I Hear Singing in the Air"

1. This version of "One Morning Soon," sung by saints in the Georgia Sea Islands in the early decades of this century, appears in Parrish ([1942] 1992:140–41; respelled); see also Pinkston (1975:192). Among recorded renditions of this congregational favorite are a short version by Rev. C. J. Johnson (on *African American Congregational Singing: Nineteenth-Century Roots*, Smithsonian/Folkways CD SF 40073, 1994) and a masterfully elaborated rendition by Rev. Gary Davis (which appears as "I Heard the Angels Singing," on *From Blues to Gospel*, Biograph BCD 123 ADD, 1992).

2. From "The Glories of My Maker, God," book 2, hymn 71 in Watts (1793:221).

3. From a conversation with Joe Vereen (1988), a deacon at Durham's Mount Calvary Holy Church.

4. In the Old Testament, see, e.g., Job 38:7, Isaiah 44:23, 49:13, and 51:11, and Jeremiah 51:48. Additional New Testament descriptions appear in 1 Corinthians 15:52 and Revelation 15:3 and 19:6. For a fuller discussion of the role of song and music in the Bible, addressed from a sanctified perspective, see Noble (1986:3–42).

5. The comment on psalmody, cited in Foote (1850:286), comes from an oft-quoted letter written in 1755 by Presbyterian minister Samuel Davies to John Wesley of the Society for Promoting Religious Knowledge among the Poor. In the letter, Rev. Davies requested that the society send him a shipment of Bibles and Isaac Watts's *Psalms and Hymns*.

6. From "Going to Shout All Over God's Heav'n," in Work (1940:180); "Gwinter Sing All Along de Way," in J. Johnson (1925:128–29); "Ain't That Good News" and "I'm Agoing to Join the Band," in Work (1940:195, 196); "I Hear from Heaven To-Day," in Allen, Ware, and Garrison ([1867] 1951:2); and "Go Ring Them Bells," in White (1928:83). Respelled and repunctuated. To get some idea of the ubiquity of this imagery, see also the song texts on pp. 58, 109, 117, 158, 176, 189, 190, 194, 215, and 226 in Work (1940).

7. From "Rockin' Jerusalem," in Work (1940:226); "I Heard the Angels Singing," in Parrish ([1942] 1992:140–41); and "I Hear from Heaven To-day," in Allen, Ware and Garrison (1951:2). Respelled.

8. Charles Johnson's *God Struck Me Dead* narratives, recorded in Tennessee in the late 1920s, are full of such accounts. In one narrative, for example, an unnamed saint tells of seeing the very "brink of hell" and then being turned away toward a narrow path: "Then I heard the heavenly host sing the 'Canaan Fair and Happy Land Where My Possessions Lie.' It was the prettiest song I ever heard" (1945:91; see also the accounts on pp. 14, 17, 36, 50, 53–54, 57, and 88).

9. David MacRae ([1870] 1952:353–54) tells of one such testimony in which an Andersonville, Georgia, saint stands before his congregation, recounts his dream, and then sings the song heard from the angels. MacRae includes the song's first verse. See also the dream-song accounts and texts from South Carolina saint Washington Dozier (in Rawick, vol. 2, part 1 [1972:331–32]) and from gospel composer Kenneth Morris (1944:18), and the contemporary accounts cited in Hinson (1995) and Allen (1991:62).

10. From the testimony of an unnamed saint, as printed in C. Johnson (1945:69–70). For other accounts of wakeful hearings in this same collection, see pp. 59, 83, and 92.

11. This account of musical inspiration appears in Morris (1944:22). George Ricks ([1960] 1977:141) quotes a similar account from gospel singer Alex Bradford, who tells of a "melody [that] floated to my ear on whispered tones from beyond." In words uncannily like Morris's, Bradford continues: "I lost track of what I was doing or even where I was and when I came to, I found myself at the piano singing and playing this song." See also the

accounts of singers Dorothy Love Coates (in McAllister 1995:63–64), Connie Steadman (in Hinson 1992b), and Jessie Mae Hemphill (in A. Young 1997:62).

12. "Heavenly Choir" first appeared on the Canton Spirituals' album *Mississippi Poor Boy* (J & B 069); a later version graces the Canton Spirituals' 1993 release, *Live in Memphis* (Blackberry BBD-1600).

13. From Willie Neal Johnson and the Gospel Keynotes' *Just a Rehearsal* (Malaco 4403), 1985.

14. From a conversation with Smiley Fletcher (1988).

15. For a published version of this vernacular line of reasoning, see Noble (1986:59–61).

16. From a conversation with Celester Sellars and Connie Steadman (1994). The verse comes from "Michael and the Devil," a song that the Badgetts learned from their father; it appears on their 1992 cassette, *The Voice That Refused to Die* (Global Village C-222).

Shortly before her death in 1994, gospel singer Marion Williams made much the same point to journalist Lenore Yarger. "Scripture says the morning star sang to God and all the angels in heaven," she explained. "So music started with God. When the devil was thrown out of heaven, he exploited everything. He took all the music because he was a chorister, master of songs, and he exploited it. And here comes the blues, here comes the jazz. The devil took music out of context and did it his way" (in Yarger 1994:27).

17. Dozens of accounts set in antebellum times tell of fiddlers who laid down their fiddles, or banjo players who spurned their banjos, when they "got religion." See, for example, the reports cited in Epstein (1977:207–15) and Ricks ([1960] 1977:85–86). See also the testimonies of Texas fiddlers Bill Thomas and Willis Winn, the latter of whom burned his fiddle upon joining the church, and Oregon fiddler Lou Southworth, in Rawick, vol. 5, part 4 (1972:86, 206); and supplement series 1, vol. 2 (1977:273–75). Some believers apparently even viewed such renunciation as a subject worthy of song. In the North Carolina ballad "I Picked My Banjo Too," for example, the protagonist—who claims to have been "raised up a slave"—tells of going to church after having been struck down by a severe fever. There he was converted, leading him to sing, "I went home rejoicing, And I burned my banjo up." In the song's closing verse, he extols heaven's "delightful shore . . . Where banjos are no more" (in Belden and Hudson 1952:637–38). For more on the link between the devil and the instruments of secular music, see "Negro Superstition" (1892) and Levine (1977:177–79).

18. See, for example, the 1930s accounts of Texas elders Louis Fowler and Louis Jones, both of whom tell of preachers who continued to play their fiddles (and, in the latter case, also the banjo) after joining the ministry (in Rawick, vol. 4, part 2 [1972:51, 238]). See also North Carolina elder Alice Baugh's narrative about slaves who sang spirituals to banjo accompaniment (in Rawick, vol. 14 [1972:83]).

Further evidence for the diversity of sanctified opinions about musical instruments lies in the very existence of church-sponsored bands in the immediate postbellum years, bands that boasted a host of "worldly" instruments and yet regularly played for church functions. Elder songsters in west-central Alabama, for example, tell of brass ensembles organized in, and even taking their names from, local churches (Ramsey 1960:67, 72). African American churchgoers in North Carolina's mountainous southwestern counties report a parallel tradition, and describe church-sponsored "Sunday School marches" led by ensembles of fifes, drums, jawharps, and fiddles. One resident, who was born only thirteen years after the Civil War's close, counted these marches among her earliest memories, noting that even her parents deemed them "an old tradition" (Stewart 1978). The bands that played for these North Carolina events were based in Baptist and A.M.E. Zion churches, both of which hosted what local churchgoers now characterize as "shouting" congregations.

19. Although evidence of this musical development is limited, some clues can be found in early church records and in the testimonies of elder saints. Church historian William Turner, for example, reports that Holy Temple Church, founded in Wilmington, N.C., in the late 1880s, quickly earned the community's designation as a "band room" due to its spirited music-making. Almost immediately after the church's founding, it boasted

music on piano, drums, and tambourines (1984:54). Other congregations apparently followed a similar pattern; by the turn of the century, ensemble instrumentation characterized holiness worship across the South. The very rapidity of this transformation, coupled with the wide geographic area over which it quickly stretched, suggests that the musical roots of vernacular instrumental praise were already well in place by the advent of the holiness revival.

20. The ubiquity of this belief in the devil's musicianship and of narratives recounting specific instances of attempted or achieved soul-selling becomes apparent when one looks through collections of African American narratives and songs and when one speaks to elder saints and blues artists. See, for example, the multiple references in Hyatt (1970:99–100, 4003–14), Hand (1964:151–52), and Puckett (1926:553–54). For specific narratives, see Bastin (1973:190), Brewer (1968:281–82), Evans (1971:22–23), Hinson (1989a:6, 13), and Amanda Styles's account in Rawick, vol. 13, part 3 (1972:345). See also Jon Michael Spencer's detailed "theomusicological" interpretation of the crossroads tradition (1993:26–30), and Robert Farris Thompson's telling analysis of the crossroads' symbolic significance in African American lore and Kongo cosmology (Thompson and Cornet 1981:151–52).

21. See, for example, Puckett (1926:553), where the devil-taught musician "was not able to play reels until he had mastered the tune, 'Gimme Jesus.'" I have heard this same stipulation, without a specific song title, mentioned by a number of consultants in the northern Piedmont of North Carolina.

22. From a conversation with Bishop Frizelle Yelverton (1987).

23. From a conversation with Rev. Z. D. Harris (1993). The referenced Bible passages are 2 Timothy 2:15 (concerning the need for study) and 1 Thessalonians 5:4–5 (citing the saints as children of light). The story of Moses and Pharaoh appears in Exodus 7:10–12.

24. From a conversation with Bishop Frizelle Yelverton (1987). Mahalia Jackson made much this same point when a white musicologist suggested that her music owed a debt to jazz. She replied, "Baby, don't you know the Devil stole the beat from the *Lord*?" (cited in Goreau 1975:150; emphasis in original). A few years earlier, an unidentified church elder alluded to this same interpretation when he declared, "The devil should not be allowed to keep all this good rhythm" (cited in Work 1949:140). On its surface, this statement seems to echo a much earlier query—variously attributed to Martin Luther, John Wesley, the eighteenth-century English preacher Rowland Hill, and Salvation Army founder General William Booth—asking "Why should the devil have all the good tunes?" The difference lies in the holiness elder's use of the word "keep," implying that the music in question never really *belonged* to Satan, but was in fact property of the Lord. Though Luther, Wesley, and Hill advocated using secular tunes for sacred purposes, they never claimed that all music was intrinsically divine.

25. This attitude of musical acceptance ranks as one of the holiness movement's most important legacies to African American sacred song. Forged in the fires of schism, it fostered a musical tradition that quickly set holiness and Pentecostal congregations apart from the broader community of saints. Though churchgoers in established nineteenth-century denominations largely rejected the nascent sanctified sound, decrying it as heretical surrender to Satan's wiles, the new churches held fast to their musical beliefs, citing Biblical precedent while claiming the world's gifts as their own. In the decades surrounding the century's turn, this attitude was to profoundly influence the development of religious song. Opening musical doors long closed by uncatholic saints, it ushered in a new era of sanctified creativity, freeing the forces of creolization to mold new traditions of sacred performance. Principal among these was a spirited style of song and accompaniment that found expression among soloists and small ensembles, a style that increasingly drew performers out of the congregation and set them before their peers in positions of featured artistry. Developing through the 1910s and 1920s, this style assumed a range of performative faces, synthetically drawing upon diverse musical traditions to achieve a multifaceted singularity all of its own. By the late 1920s, this new music was being called "gospel."

Chapter 11. Welcome: "Not for the Appointment, but for the Anointment"

1. By all accounts, such addresses were once far more common than they are today. Indeed, from the 1930s to the 1960s, many gospel publishers marketed booklets that printed model addresses (and model "responses," the formal replies to welcomes) for speakers uncertain of their extemporaneous skills. See, for example, the "welcome addresses" and "responses" printed in Saulter (1939), Morris (1983, 1985), and William Walker (1946b, 1946c, 1971). Most often, however, those giving the welcomes simply improvised, drawing liberally from more developed traditions of church talk to craft brief, situation-specific speeches.

2. From remarks by Jeffrey Newberry (1988). Gospel groups often use "Yes, Lord" to close their sets, thus balancing performed intensity with concluding calm (cf. Boyer 1995:23).

3. The split in African American churches between the more mainstream, "emotionally restrained" congregations and their shouting counterparts is often traced to the years immediately following emancipation, when many denominational leaders sought to free their churches from beliefs and behaviors deemed "superstitious" and "emotional." In the subsequent routinization of denominational practice, belief in spiritual activity was tempered, and celebrations of the Spirit's touch (as manifested in shouting, holy dancing, and so on) were stilled. Perhaps the clearest statement of this effort at "spiritual reform" appears in the memoirs of Bishop Daniel Payne, one of the most eminent bishops in the A.M.E. Church (see Payne 1888, esp. pp. 253–56). For a broader discussion of this schism in the church, see Levine (1977:160–66).

Saints often use the term "seditty" to describe churchgoers whose worship practices bear a closer resemblance to the "restrained" norms of most white congregations than to the "old-time ways" of African American believers. This usage highlights the probable root of the term, the word "sedate," which perfectly describes the enforced stoicism of much mainstream worship. In a broader sense, the term "seditty" refers to those whose actions and attitudes seem calculated to set them apart from—and pretentiously "above"—other community members. People who act "above their raising," who consistently "put on airs," are often deemed "seditty." For further discussion of this term, see Mitchell (1970:169) and Andrew and Owens (1973:91).

4. This is precisely the point that sanctified preacher and singer Washington Phillips conveyed with such telling power in his 1927 recordings, *Denomination Blues—Parts 1 and 2* (Columbia 14333-D). Rev. Phillips, who identifies himself on another recording as an anointed preacher "born to preach the gospel," criticizes denominations for their reliance on doctrine instead of on Jesus. In the first half of his two-part recording, he declares: "Well, denominations have no right to fight, / They ought to just treat each other right. / And that's all, I tell you that's all. / But you better have Jesus—I tell you that's all." As the song continues, Rev. Phillips cites the doctrinal narrowness of Primitive Baptists, Missionary Baptists, A.M.E. Methodists, African Methodists, Holiness people, and Church of God believers, concluding in every instance that "you better have Jesus—I tell you that's all." In the midst of this listing, he asserts rather pointedly, "You know denominations ain't a thing but a name." For a fuller discussion of Washington Phillips's singing, see Oliver (1984:199–200). For later restatements of Rev. Phillips's sentiments, see the 1937 comments of South Carolina preacher George Briggs (in Rawick, vol. 2, part 1 [1972:84]) and the 1992 remarks of Mississippi preacher Roma Wilson (in A. Young 1997:29).

5. Taking note of this sanctified thrust in gospel, theologians C. Eric Lincoln and Lawrence H. Mamiya remark that "there is probably a denominational bias against gospel in some churches because of its strong Pentecostal identification" (1990:377). By far, the most thorough and insightful discussion of the emergence of sanctified style and beliefs in gospel appears in Boyer (1995:16–29, 36–44, and passim); see also Heilbut (1985:202–11 and passim), Hinson (1989b:129–33), Allen (1991:30–31, 34–37, 100–1, 213–15), and Lornell (1995:27–29, 127–28, 153–54).

6. From a conversation with Ethel Elliott (1994).

7. From conversations with Evangelist Dorothy Jackson (1993b), James Thomas (1993), and Joseph Wallace (1993).

8. From conversations with Rev. Z. D. Harris (1993, 1994). After I transcribed Rev. Harris's initial telling of this tale, we reviewed the transcript to clarify some details. This telling is the result of that revision.

This story fits into a broad cycle of African American parrot tales, many of which close with the parrot's telling observations on human ways. Gospel singer Connie Steadman tells a variant of this story in which the parrot's owner takes him to a liquor store, and the parrot squawks, "*Liquor store! Liquor store!*" The next day, the owner brings the parrot to church, and the parrot again cries, "*Liquor store! Liquor store!*" When the owner corrects him, the parrot answers, "*Same folks! Same folks!*" (Steadman 1994). A printed version of this story appears as "Same Old Crowd" in Dance (1978:69); many other parrot tales, most set in slavery times, appear in Dorson (1967:120–23).

9. From a conversation with Rev. Z. D. Harris (1994).

10. See, for example, the texts to the traditional congregational songs "Heaven" and "Forty Days and Nights," in Odum and Johnson (1925:98, 128).

11. Stories of false childhood "conversions" abound in the sanctified community. One such account appears in Powdermaker (1939:265–66), telling of a ten-year-old girl who went with a friend to the mourner's bench and pretended to "get religion" when her friend began shouting. The ten-year-old's pretense earned her an unintended blow from the shouting girl's flinging arms, an outcome the saints would no doubt interpret as just reward for her duplicity.

12. For obvious reasons, this singer shall remain anonymous; suffice it to say that the conversation took place in Arlington, Virginia, on July 1, 1986. Interestingly, another singer participating in this same conversation took the opposite approach to description. Every time the first singer portrayed the Spirit as "just a feeling," the second singer plunged into detailed, highly personalized description of the Spirit's workings and goals. To this second singer, the Spirit was much more than a simple "feeling." His descriptions included such terms as "comforter" and "friend" and always presumed that the Spirit acted with a clear sense of will.

13. J. Mason Brewer heard this tale in 1945 from Rev. P. H. Carmichael in Clarendon County, S.C.; it appears in Brewer (1945:44). Quoted sections are respelled and repunctuated, with italics added. The likely biblical source for this tale is Matthew 7:21–23, where Jesus declares that not everyone who comes to heaven crying "Lord, Lord" will gain entrance. The "false prophets" who claim to have "prophesied," "cast out devils," and "done many wonderful works" in the Lord's name will all be turned away, with the Lord declaring, "I never knew you." This is precisely the same message conveyed to the shouting brother.

14. When addressing the forces that motivate shouting, theologian Henry Mitchell suggests that "Black congregations can unerringly sense a put-on, and an insincere shouter is almost always chilled into silence by a disapproving congregation" (1970:44). My own conversations with saints suggest that the certainty Mitchell presumes is rarely articulated; most saints seem to reserve judgment in all but the most blatant cases of fakery. The story about the "shoutingest" brother seems to confirm this assessment, in that none of the brother's fellow churchgoers ever sensed his deception. I discuss the issue of discernment and spiritual evaluation further in Chapter 16.

15. From remarks voiced by Evangelist Dorothy Jackson (1993a); cf. the comments of Memphis singer Clara Anderson, cited in Joyce Jackson (1988:92).

16. From a conversation with Evangelist Dorothy Jackson (1993b).

17. Affirming this sense of congregational parity, Mahalia Jackson once remarked in one of her performances, "There is no great and no small among us; we [are] great when we got God's love, and we [are] small only when we reject Him" (cited in Goreau 1975:282).

18. Hurston makes much the same point when she speaks of the artistry inherent in sanctified worship. Noting that sermons, prayers, moans, and testimonies each follow their own set of rules, she adds that "Any new and original elaboration is welcomed, however, and

this brings out the fact that all religious expression among Negroes is regarded as art, and ability is recognized as definitely as in any other art. The beautiful prayer receives the acolade [sic] as well as the beautiful song. It is merely a form of expression which people generally are not accustomed to think of as art" (1983:83).

19. For a discussion of personalization in testimony, see Kroll-Smith (1980:20–23); he argues that personalization particularly marks the testimonies of saints who are spiritually mature, a feature that itself draws congregational acclaim. Making a similar point for song, Mellonee Burnim contends that audiences expect gospel artists to sing in a manner that conveys "the totality of personal involvement in performance" (1980:145). Theologian Henry Mitchell adds that stylistic personalization is also central to the success of African American preaching (1970:163).

20. This discussion owes a debt to the insights of Dan Rose, whose analysis of the street as a place of biographical enactment led me to question how the church—as a public space that actively *discourages* such enactment—nonetheless comes to serve as a stage. Rose speaks of the street as a site of continuous, evolving, and self-defining performance, where nonperformance momentarily breaks the frame and demands immediate performative "healing" (1987:139, 181). Sanctified services also enact a frame of constant performance, with churchgoers engaging at every moment in the performed conversations of worship (through singing, clapping, calling back to the focused singer or speaker, and so on). When these conversations slow or cease, devotional leaders chide churchgoers for their nonperformance, calling the service "dead" and urging the congregation to "liven things up." Within this frame, however, leaders are constantly discouraging what Rose calls the individual "performance of biography." (The exception to this rule, of course, is the testimony service, when believers are *encouraged* to take a center-stage role with their stories and/or songs. Even here, however, the self is ultimately *not* the focus of attention; rather, it serves only as a jumping-off point, on a journey that turns narrative focus away from the individual and toward God's grace.) Whatever the frame, the proclaimed purpose of performance is not to celebrate or elaborate self, but rather to create a communal spirit (i.e., "accord") that minimizes the self's importance. One might thus say that the service moves toward the "performance of community." Saints contend that concern for one's own performance ultimately hinders the achievement of accord and prevents performing believers from fully opening themselves to the touch of the Spirit.

21. From a conversation with Lena Mae Perry and Ethel Elliott (1993).

22. For example, Sister Bernice Franklin recounts how Mahalia Jackson would sometimes sit with her in church and point out the sisters who were shouting for attention. "[We'd] be in church," recalls Sister Franklin, "[and] she'd say, 'See that lady? She always wears good underwear because she knows when she shouts, she's going to pull up her dress.' Or she'd poke me when the women landed in the men ushers' arms: 'They're not really shouting; they just want to land there' " (cited in Goreau 1975:89). J. J. Farley, the longtime bass for the Soul Stirrers, suggests much the same thing when he tells of the "eager women" who shout to the soulful singing of quartet leads. "The ladies would start a different shout," he says, "and the way they shouted, they'd be trying to say something" (cited in Heilbut 1985:85–86). See also the account of Caesar Burton, whose girlfriend's "shouting" to catch the eye of another suitor led to a fight in the church-house (in Hendricks 1943:121–26).

23. Over the years, I've heard scores of anecdotes about false shouters in the pews. Perhaps the most common such stories are those that describe shouting churchgoers' concern over their personal appearance. Tales about wigs seem to be particular favorites. The late Elder Lawrence Richardson, for example, enjoyed telling the story of a wig-wearing sister who shouted to impress a quartet singer. "I was over at church," he recounted, "[and] a lady had a wig on. A quartet was up there singing. They were singing on and on and on. After a while she's going to put this false shout in there. I was sitting right behind her. I'm looking at her, right at her back. After a while, she goes, 'We-e-eow!' " (Elder Richardson threw his arms in the air, and made the sound of a shout.) "You know, 'We-e-eow!' And after a while the wig came off and fell down between the pews. And man, she stopped

shouting! If you're in the Spirit—I'm talking sure enough—[you're] going to continue going on in the Spirit! But that woman stopped shouting, and reached down there, and put her head down there, and put that wig back on! I said, 'That was nothing but false.' It's an act, to get the attention of a man singing in the group" (1986).

More than four decades before this telling, WPA workers in Louisiana recorded a similar story from eighty-six-year-old Frances Lewis. Speaking of her youth, she recalled, "When a sinner got converted, she'd sing like this: 'You may hold my hat, / You may hold my shawl, / But don't you touch / My waterfall!' You see, when I was young, Negro girls wore what was called a 'waterfall' It was made of real hair and fixed on a thin wire. They was expensive, too, and that's why they was so careful with them. When they got religion they'd faint and swoon and all, but they was careful not to hurt that waterfall" (cited in Saxon, Dreyer, and Tallant 1945:473). For a similar story, in which a shouting singer purposefully "falls out" to hide the *loss* of her wig (which had been dislodged by her initially "real" shout), see Caesar (1998:74–75).

24. This calls to mind the account of Colorado elder Charles Harris, who told a WPA interviewer that his mother "boasted of her ability to raise children and out-shout all other mothers at the annual revival meeting" (cited in Rawick, supplement series 1, vol. 2 [1977:47]; repunctuated). The very fact that the term "out-shout" continues to claim a place in vernacular talk suggests the perceived frequency of this competitive practice.

25. Anthropologist Sheila Walker makes a similar point when speaking of possession-based faiths in the African diaspora. Citing Bastide's remarks on "sociological possession," she suggests that feigned possession can serve many psychological ends, including the desire to "play act, be the center of attention, and gain prestige" (1972:79). Anthropologist Peter Gardner cites specific examples of such possession imposture among the Paliyans, a foraging people of South India. After noting that "mock possession is part of the culture," Gardner tells of speaking with an elder who described how people faked possession to gain prestige, hoping that possession would lead others to deem them "important people" (1991:379). In citing these references, I am making no comparison between anointment and what these authors describe as "possession." Rather, I am simply demonstrating that religious imposture is by no means unique to the sanctified church.

26. From William Walker (1946a:18). Rev. Walker apparently considered this theme important enough to address in a number of his published poems. See, for example, "Stop Playing with God" (1946a:7), and "Stop That Putting On" (1969:46–47).

27. From a conversation with Rev. Samuel McCrary and Elder Lawrence Richardson (1985). This calls to mind Georgia saint and singer Bessie Jones's comments on the devil's teachings: "The devil's got so much he can teach you although it ain't nothing more than trying to prank with God. . . . 'Cause if you're working for the devil and working for him right he's going to show you many points and many things although ain't none of them good" (cited in Jones 1983:171; respelled).

28. As sung at Ruffin Nichols Memorial A.M.E. Church, Philadelphia, Pa., on November 20, 1983. The traditional song "King David" also addresses this subject, with the verse:

You got a true way to find / Mr. Hypocrite out.
At the first thing [he's] going / to church and shout.

(As sung by Rich Amerson and Earthy Anne Coleman on *Negro Folk Music of Alabama, Vol. 4: Rich Amerson, 2*, Ethnic Folkways Library P 472, 1956; a full transcription appears in Courlander 1963:46–49).

Chapter 12. Response: "God Ain't Coming into No Dead Heart"

1. Chicago's Rev. William Walker, who published many model "responses" for church use, formally advocated this practice. "The response must be given by a visitor. One who has

been notified in advance of the program," he advised. "Don't call or ask some one to give the response at a spur of a moment. To do so causes stage-fright and some times embarrassment" (1974:5).

2. In his study of formulaic structure in African American sermons, Rosenberg treats these phrases as formulaic "stimulants" that preachers often use "unreflectively." Though he admits that they're sometimes used to prompt congregational response, Rosenberg suggests that most often they serve as "stall formulas" that give preachers time to compose the next sermonic line. At no point does Rosenberg set these phrases within the broader context of experiential invitation; nor does he link conversational engagement with devotional focus. See Rosenberg (1988:78–81, 150–51; 1975:76–78); for further discussion of congregational engagement, see Mitchell (1970:108).

3. This sense of intensified personal engagement calls to mind Kapferer's 1986 analysis of group experience in Sinhalese exorcisms. Kapferer suggests that music and dance draw ritual participants into an alternative experiential reality whose structure is framed by the flow of performance. He contends that active involvement in ritual dancing draws individuals out of the realm of everyday encounter and into an individuating, "recontextualized" world of sensory experience. He then argues that within this "recontextualized" realm, participants temporarily lose the ability to reflectively address their experience, casting them into the reality posed by ritual (1986:197–99).

This conclusion presumes that reflection and performative engagement stand in an either/or relationship. Most saints reject this dichotomy, arguing instead that engagement is actually deepened by simultaneous reflection. Both contribute to the meaningfulness of experiential encounter, with full sensory involvement potentially sparking (but not overriding or distorting) the reflective dimensions of praise-giving.

4. For similar comments from gospel singers Willie Mae Ford Smith and Mahalia Jackson, see Heilbut (1985:196) and Jackson and Wylie (1966:66).

5. From Louise "Candy" Davis's *Then These Trials* (Malaco LP/cassette 4418), 1987.

6. From a conversation with Henry "Duke" Thrower (1982), a longtime quartet bass singer. Thrower draws his metaphor from Hebrews 4:12.

7. This interpretation of sanctified performance patterns closely parallels the conclusions reached by Alan Lomax and his associates in their cantometric studies of sub-Saharan African and African diaspora musics. Lomax contends that these musics show an "extraordinary homogeneity" of style and structure, at the heart of which lies a shared emphasis on the integrating, cohesion-inducing features of group song. An openness of text and tune, coupled with a stress on layered performance, "facilitate group participation, opening the door for anyone present to make a contrastive and complementary personal contribution to the song-dance performance" (1970:193). African-based song thus emerges as a democratized art, performed in an aesthetic arena that not only invites co-performance, but that in fact achieves its ultimate expression only when such performance shapes its artistic contours. (See also Lomax and Erickson 1968:91–95, and other essays in A. Lomax 1968a.)

These same principles of layering and group engagement reappear in the stylistic canons of many other African-based performance traditions. In his studies of African dance, for example, R. F. Thompson points to an aesthetics of "apart dancing," whereby each dancer moves in solo dialogue with the music, shaping in space and sound a personalized contribution to a polymetric, fluidly shifting whole (1966:93). In like manner, Karl Reisman's analysis of speech patterning in Antigua reveals a tradition of "contrapuntal conversation," whereby many voices sound forth simultaneously, neither surrendering the floor in the face of polyvocality nor overtly acknowledging the entry of another voice (1974:111–15, 123–24). In both traditions, a sense of structured oneness invites personal contribution to a multilayered performative gestalt. The essence of wholeness seems to lie in preserving the integrity of the individual voice. The drama of unity emerges as these voices join in harmonized complementarity.

8. From a conversation with Elder Lawrence Richardson (1986).

9. Alan Lomax's concept of "interlock" proves quite useful when probing the workings of

this devotional complementarity (1968b). Lomax uses this term to describe what he calls the "highest" form of choral organization, a "maximally individualized and leaderless style" that simultaneously supports a range of distinct melodic, rhythmic and/or harmonic paths within a given song performance (1968b:156). If we extend this concept to encompass the expressive contours of sanctified worship, we might well speak of *expressive interlock*, suggesting balanced simultaneity in a range of complementary communicative realms.

Folklorist Roger Abrahams hints at this expressive harmony in his incisive survey of African performance patterns (1976). Defining "interlock" as the practice whereby "the distinction between performer and audience is made meaningless, for all perform to some degree," Abrahams discusses the interlock not only of performers (the realm charted by Lomax), but also of all participants in musical events (1976:37–38). For richly detailed discussions of interlock at this broadened level, see Chernoff's 1979 exploration of West African drumming (esp. pp. 160–62), and Richard and Sally Price's 1991 analysis of tale-telling at Saramaka funerals (esp. pp. 4–8, 12–14).

Chapter 13. The Emcee: "If You Have a Dry Emcee, You Have a Dry Anniversary"

1. Programgoers usually refer to the song service's leader as "master of ceremonies" or "emcee." (The term "master" still dominates vernacular usage, regardless of the announcer's gender). In keeping with this terminological convention, I shall use these terms when referring to the announcer.

2. When asked about purpose, most of the sanctified preachers and singers with whom I've spoken immediately invoke this special responsibility to do the Lord's bidding. While asserting that *all* believers are accountable for the souls they mislead, saints endowed with gifts that they're called to share with the public see this duty as particularly pressing. They tend to ground this commission in the prophetic words of Ezekiel, who cites the Lord as saying that when the anointed "givest [the wicked] not warning, nor speakest to warn the wicked from his wicked way, to save his life; the same wicked man shall die in his iniquity; but his blood will I require at thine hand" (Ezekiel 3:18; see also 3:20–21 and 33:7–9). Not following the Lord's command—in Evangelist Jackson's case, not telling the friend that she was "playing" with God—is tantamount to "not warning the wicked from their wicked ways."

3. From a conversation with Evangelist Dorothy Jackson (1993b).

4. Such double-booking is quite common among singers who travel in an active gospel circuit. In large part, it arises from their attempts to satisfy norms of reciprocity. Community-based singers often agree to appear at other singers' programs in return for a like commitment. Hence, when presentational creditors call, debtor groups are obliged to respond, even if they have already scheduled a performance for the same date. Devotional commitment also figures rather importantly in such double-booking. Saints see singing as service and say that God calls all believers to serve "in season [and] out of season" (2 Timothy 4:2). To reject an invitation simply because one has another booking or because one might be tired from an earlier performance is considered tantamount to giving human needs precedence over God's will. I have known singers to accept as many as three engagements for the same evening and to perform at all three of them, even though the distances between program sites were sometimes as much as sixty miles.

5. The distinction between "program" and "service," articulated by Evangelists Lofton and Jackson, is often heard at gospel events. Voiced by emcees, singers, and devotional leaders, the rhetorical contrast of the two terms suggests both an openness to spiritual guidance and a rejection of any "entertainment" associations carried by the word "program." (See, for example, Pastor Shirley Caesar's comments in Harrington 1992:34.) Despite the pronounced difference, the same speakers who declare "This is not a 'program'" tend to use the term themselves when referring to gospel events.

6. From remarks made by Sister Murphy (1983).

7. From the comments of an unnamed Tennessee saint in C. Johnson (1945:20; see also pp. 7, 99). For a discussion setting these passages in the framework of a West African worldview, see Sobel (1988:125–26).

8. Note that I specify the Spirit as the active agent here. Programgoers *do* complain when they feel that *singers* are stretching a song or set solely to "get a house." Saints say that such performers push the boundaries of their allocated time only to elicit an emotional response from their listeners.

Time concerns also plague gospel singers who perform in nonchurch settings, where they're often forced to conform to schedules that don't take the Spirit—or the need to "sing until one feels it"—into account. Mahalia Jackson, for example, earned quite a reputation among television and record producers for singing beyond the tight time constraints imposed by the studio. "I'm used to singing in church where they don't stop me until the Lord comes," she used to complain (in Jackson and Wylie 1966:108; cf. Schwerin 1992:106).

9. The artful talk of the church is but one expression of a broader African-based tradition of respect for the artistically shaped word. Zora Neale Hurston spoke of this trend toward eloquence as the "conscious artistry" of African American expression (1963:81). Roger Abrahams, who traces the tradition across the creole world of African America, calls it "African eloquence speaking" (1983:39). And Molefi Kete Asante describes it as a "lyrical" approach to language, a quality that emerges as African Americans' "basic poetic and narrative response to reality" (1987:43). For more detailed discussion of African American vernacular verbal artistry, see Smitherman (1977:94–166), Asante (1983:37–80), Abrahams (1983:1–39), and Kochman (1970, 1972); for an insightful analysis of verbal artistry in gospel announcing, both on the air and in gospel services, see Barney (1994:229–46).

10. From a conversation with James Thomas (1993). When Brother Thomas first told me this story, I asked what led him to change the suits in the first place. He explained that he "had seen a lot of the big emcees do it" and was simply following their example. For another example of emcee outfit-changing in gospel programs, see Hannerz (1969:155).

11. John Landis, the lead singer with the Golden Echoes, goes so far as to suggest that dress is one of the first things on programgoers' minds when they attend anniversaries. "Fifty percent of your singing or how far you'll ever get in singing is the way you dress," he asserts. "They're not curious over who you get [to perform at the anniversary], or what's going on in there, or how many songs you're going to sing, or what songs you're going to sing, or whatever. They're curious of what you have on when you come through the door" (in Patterson 1988:98). See also the comments of Katie Davis Watson, second lead with Mississippi's Golden Stars, in A. Young (1997:137). For discerning discussion of the care that gospel announcers put into selecting their outfits, see Barney (1994:185, 188–89, 192, 196–201).

12. This calls to mind a 1982 Philadelphia appearance by the Mighty Clouds of Joy. Booked as headliners in a program that featured largely local performers, the Clouds were scheduled to close the service. But when their time came, one of their members strode onstage and announced that the quartet would not sing. He explained that the promoter was claiming low ticket sales (though the huge church was clearly packed) and wouldn't pay the agreed-upon fee. For the next fifteen minutes, the church rocked with accusation and counteraccusation, as promoter and group members both publicly defended their positions, and the emcee tried in vain to ease tempers. Finally, the Clouds agreed to sing an abbreviated set "for the good folks who paid good money to hear us." They then proceeded to perform *in their street clothes*, without changing into their uniforms. I could hear the buzz of critique as soon as they began their first song. "Aren't they even going to change?" puzzled one surprised programgoer. "Those boys got no respect at all, singing like that in church!" muttered a second. The incident fueled conversations for the entire week, as word of the Clouds' intransigence sped through the community. All the secondhand accounts that I later heard gave prominent play to the Clouds' sartorial slight, dwelling with far greater detail on their clothes than on the group's uncharacteristically lackluster performance.

13. Folklorist Joyce Jackson makes a similar point when she discusses quartets' "colorful and visually stimulating" uniforms: "When the quartet walks to the front of the church or onto the stage, they immediately command the attention of their audience before uttering a sound. Their visual image gives the group individuality and distinguishes them from other groups" (1988:193–94). Mellonee Burnim presses this point further by suggesting that singers' clothes manifest the same sense of "aliveness" that performers strive to infuse in their music. As such, clothes become markers of intensity and personal involvement (1988:115–16). For further discussion of clothing's significance at gospel programs, see Burnim (1980:161), Patterson (1988:98–99), Barney (1994:196–201), and A. Young (1997: 61–62).

14. Radio announcers' involvement with live gospel programming dates back to the 1930s, when radio stations sponsored gospel programs as a means of promotion in the local African American community. These semicommercial events usually featured singers who broadcast live, regularly scheduled performances from the sponsoring station. The announcers for these broadcasts, in turn, often served as program emcees. As stations gradually switched from live performance to records, they expanded their promotional programs to include nonlocal recording artists, many of whom were just beginning to make the move to professional status. The masters of ceremonies at these increasingly commercial events were also often announcers. For both types of programs, radio personnel traditionally served as booking agents, promoters, and emcees.

In the 1950s, as the ranks of professional gospel artists swelled, a growing number of independent promoters began booking gospel programs. Radio stations, in turn, eased out of the booking business. Although many radio announcers still act as booking agents, and some stations still sponsor gospel events, most radio station involvement is now limited to on-air promotion and program officiation.

For the most part, the history of radio's complex relationship with gospel performance remains to be written, with Barney's 1994 contribution thus far the most thorough. For a detailed account of gospel broadcasting and station-sponsored programs in 1930s–1960s Memphis, see Lornell (1995:177–85). See also A. Young (1997:141–52), Heilbut (1985: 265–70), and Hannerz (1969:154–55).

15. I am indebted to Deborah Barney for pointing out the distinction between the terms "disc jockey" and "gospel announcer." Barney, who herself is a gospel announcer, skillfully unpacks the components of announcers' verbal artistry in her dissertation (1994:229–46).

16. The degree to which this concern governs emcee selection becomes particularly apparent in communities serviced by more than one gospel radio station. Promoters in these markets often engage multiple emcees for a single program, inviting at least one announcer from each station to stand on the stage.

17. As should be evident by now, the parallel structures that pepper Evangelist Lofton's remarks distinguish most forms of sanctified talk. Though the scholarly discussion of parallelisms in worship has focused almost exclusively on sermons, the same discussion could easily be extended to include prayers, testimonies, between-song remarks, praise commentary, and even informal conversations. Perhaps the most developed analysis of sermonic parallelism is that of Gerald Davis, who suggests that parallel structures emerge from the preacher's efforts to generate meaningful frames for textual elaboration and to create an overarching "rhythmic environment" (1985:53–56). While Davis focuses on the creative processes that give rise to parallels, Bruce Rosenberg addresses their emotional impact, pointing out that sermonic parallelisms "can have a profound cumulative dramatic impact" (1988:168, 151–54). Neither of these scholars address the essential *artistry* of parallel statement, exploring its role within an aesthetics of artful talk. When I've asked saints about passages such as Evangelist Lofton's "We're here to break . . ." triplet, they invariably say that such statements are the mark of a "good talker," one who might merit the designation "preachingest," "prayingest," or simply "talkingest." The speaker who consistently creates and uses such structures demonstrates a command of language that itself draws appreciation and acclaim from the community of listeners.

18. From a conversation with Evangelist Dorothy Jackson (1993b). Folklorist Ray Allen suggests that there's no consensus on this issue, noting, "There remains some question . . . as to whether an individual can actually be saved through singing or whether this can only be accomplished through the preached Word. Further, the gospel program provides no built-in structure for prompting the sinner to come forward and accept Christ, a function carried out through the altar call in a Sunday morning service" (1991:102). One need only listen to the countless stories that saints tell about sinners saved through song to realize that this isn't much of an issue among sanctified congregations. See, for example, the accounts in Goreau (1975:57) and Jones (1983:163–67), and the comments of Marion Williams in Yarger (1994:30). As the ensuing discussion makes clear, the "built-in structure" that Allen mentions is in fact always present as *potential*, ready to be invoked at any moment.

19. From a conversation with Joseph "Jojo" Wallace (1993). Wallace also noted that the Nightingales try to include an invitational hymn on every album that they release. (For analogous comments from gospel singer Shirley Caesar, who also includes altar calls in all her performances, see Caesar 1998:199).

20. In his analysis of African American preaching, Bruce Rosenberg notes that "a surprising number of sermon lines" are taken from spirituals, gospel songs, and Baptist hymns (1988:46, 145–46). While treating such citations as formulaic components in folk preachers' "poetic grammar," Rosenberg never addresses the meanings that they convey—as pieces of familiar songs—to the listening congregation. Much the same can be said of Peter Gold's discussion of the role song citations play in sermons. Instead of addressing their textual and connotative meanings, Gold suggests only that they are "recited in order to elicit a musically affective response from the congregation" (1981:178). Since both Rosenberg and Gold focus on sermons, neither address the degree to which such citations mark other genres of African American religious speech.

21. Variations on the title of this Dorsey favorite have been a part of the gospel vernacular since the song was introduced in 1941. Whenever saints speak of performers who sing for reasons other than praise and ministry, they invariably talk about singers who "aren't living the life they sing about." This was precisely the message Dorsey was trying to convey; he composed this piece as a protest against the corrosive effects of commercialism on gospel (Heilbut 1985:33). An insightful discussion of this phrase's significance within the gospel community appears in Feintuch (1980:42, 46–48).

Chapter 14. Format: "Let's Give the Lord a Praise"

1. From conversations with Rev. Sam McCrary and Elder Lawrence Richardson (1985) and with Joseph "Jojo" Wallace (1993).

2. Many detailed descriptions of these and other gospel styles, along with analyses of their musicological and performative characteristics, have appeared in the past two decades. For insightful discussions of the development of quartet harmony and performance styles, see Seroff (1985), Rubman (1980), and Lornell (1995). For musicological analyses of "gospel" (as opposed to "quartet") stylings, see particularly the writings of Boyer (1979:22–34; 1985) and William-Jones (1970:210–15). Perhaps the best overview of gospel's stylistic diversity appears in Boyer (1995).

Gospel scholars have paid less attention to "contemporary" gospel, though this style easily commands the largest audience among young African American churchgoers and certainly accounts for most of commercial gospel's major-label exposure. The most thorough discussion of "contemporary" style appears in Boyer (1985). Most other writings about this style take the form of biographical portraits of its major artists; see, for example, Heilbut (1985:316–22) and Broughton (1985:116–31).

3. Quartets have historically maintained a larger and more faithful following than any other type of gospel ensemble. Some of this appeal can be attributed to the remarkable vocal skills the quartet tradition has fostered; some must also be credited to the youth, charisma

and showmanship of many quartet singers. Whatever the reason, professional quartets regularly draw large crowds, with many in their audiences hailing from outside the sanctified fold. This fact is certainly not lost on gospel promoters. Since larger crowds mean larger profits, commercial agents often assemble "package" tours comprised entirely of professional quartets. They then offer these "packages" to local promoters, who typically fill out the bills with hometown quartets.

4. For a detailed and insightful discussion of the aesthetics of personalization among quartet singers, see Allen (1991:143–48).

5. The programmatic roots of such rivalry probably rest in the "quartet contests" that were popular in African American communities from the 1920s through the 1950s. Drawing large audiences to churches, auditoriums, and other public halls, these programs pitted quartet against quartet in formal competition. Panels of community "judges"—many of whom were singers themselves—meticulously measured each performance, often using scorecards that clearly set forth the criteria of evaluation. "Time, harmony, and articulation" are the measures most often remembered by quartet veterans, many of whom vividly recall the emphasis placed on precise, even rhythm; close, balanced harmony; and clear enunciation. Some singers also tell of judgments based on the stance of quartet members, on the "sharpness" and uniformity of their outfits, and on the close coordination of their movements. Needless to say, all of these criteria favored style over substance, technique over spirit, and appearance over intention. In short, they appear to have rewarded the very "form and fashion" otherwise spurned by the saints.

This consideration undoubtedly kept many saints away from these "contests" and almost certainly helped to discourage their sponsorship by church organizations. Such sponsorship had already ended in many communities by the mid-1930s; in others, it extended into the early 1950s. Whatever the date, congregational withdrawal effectively passed the mantle of sponsorship to commercial promoters, who kept contests alive as long as they remained financially viable. By the turn of the century's fifth decade, however, such competitions were increasingly giving way to "song battles," events that declared "victory" less on the basis of formal, "judged" evaluation and more on that of simple congregational acclaim.

This capsule description of quartet contests owes a deep debt to the research of Doug Seroff, who first brought these events to my attention; see Seroff (1980a:3; 1980b:48–49). See also Joyce Jackson (1988:148–54), Lornell (1995:129–31), Allen (1991:79), and Hinson (1989b:165–72).

6. From a conversation with Jackie Jackson (1992). Sister Jackson is the daughter of the late Willie Mae Ford Smith, longtime head of the Soloists Bureau of Dorsey's National Convention of Gospel Choirs and Choruses.

7. Such formal "song battles" seem to have emerged out of quartet contests in the late 1940s and early 1950s. These commercial events replaced the carefully articulated criteria of quartet contests with the simpler measure of audience acclaim. Gone were the panels of judges listening for every nuance of time and tone; in their stead stood the audience, whose applause and "shouts" determined the battle's "winner." In the early days of such competition, judges still rendered a final decision, publicly proclaiming the crowd's will. As years passed, however, even this token ruling was abandoned, leaving all conclusions to the individual programgoers. With this final transformation, all semblance of judged competition vanished.

The terminological shift from "contest" to "battle" suggests a degree of escalation, implying passage from rule-governed competition to unrestrained encounter. On one level, this title change succinctly captures these events' performative metamorphosis, as the deliberate comparison of preset criteria gave way to a more general assessment of performance. On another level, the shift also suggests intensification, hinting at a deepening of involvement, a sharpening of encounter. This too occurred during this period, though the quickened engagement had little to do with competition. Instead, it lay in the arena of expressed anointment. The move away from quartet contests coincided with the emergence of quartet gospel, a style that actively acknowledges the participation of the Spirit. The tightly regulated balance of voices and the carefully rehearsed coordination of movement seemed to lessen in importance as quartet harmonizers finally began acting upon the saints' longstanding dictum to "let go and let God." After almost three decades of singing in the shadow of secular performance norms, quartets began performing in a style that invited rather than "squenched" the overt display of the Spirit. Stressing passion over control, quartet gospel encouraged singers to submit their singing to spiritual will.

Ironically, this new spirit of spiritual surrender also nurtured a parallel tradition of spiritual simulation. The shouts and holy dancing of the saints, the chanted preaching and center-aisle "walk" of sanctified preachers, the leaps and laughs, tears and tongues of sanctified believers all became tools of gospel theater. Nonsanctified singers swiftly seized this opportunity to augment their performative repertoires, boosting their potential for flamboyance while opening whole new realms of showmanship. Needless to say, "song battles"— with their emphasis on audience appeal—proved the perfect forum for this new simulation.

8. From Morris (1949:59, 60); for comparable advice in another "how-to" guidebook, see William Walker (1974:3).

9. Ray Allen seems to miss this point when describing sponsors' tendency to invite "anyone from elderly soloists to pre-teen youth choirs" to perform at noncommercial community programs. "This non-restrictive policy sometimes results in an inordinate number of low quality performances," he remarks, "but these are generally tolerated if the singers are judged to be sincere in their religious commitment" (1991:91). The very suggestion that saints "tolerate" "low quality" singers ignores singing's function as worship and suggests that the program's prevailing frame is aesthetic rather than devotional. Allen's repeated references to gospel as "spiritual entertainment" seem to sanction this interpretation. While some saints do indeed speak of gospel in this way, most temper their comments by granting quick priority to worship, saying that the balance of faith and art must always weigh toward faith.

10. From a conversation with Wilson Waters (Waters and Hamlett 1986). To avoid potential offense, I have changed the name of the singer to whom Brother Waters refers.

11. The conviction that God's Word will never return void finds verification in Isaiah 55:11. Saints often cite this passage when discussing "form and fashion" singers, suggesting that if they are indeed singing God's Word, then their performance is never wholly for naught, for the *Word itself* can touch and transform. The comment on "hellish mouths" comes from a conversation with Rev. McCrary (McCrary and Richardson 1985).

Chapter 15. Purpose: "The Anointing of God Breaks the Yokes"

1. In his analysis of African American preaching, Gerald Davis identifies "hemistich phrases shaped into irrhythmic metrical units" as the sermon's principal morphologic parts (1985:49–50, 59; see also 93–100). In Sister Bracey's comments, these hemistich phrases fall into regular couplets, each of which achieves definition as a single tonal unit. The predictable rise and fall of each two lines grant the whole passage a compelling, forward-moving momentum.

2. This familiar stance graces a range of performances in sanctified services. Typically linked with exhortation or admonition, it often marks the remarks of devotional leaders, the testimonies of congregation members, and the between-song commentary and songs of lead singers. Its most concrete association, however, is with the preacher. When churchgoing children "mock the preacher," for example, they invariably adopt this pose, thus gesturally cementing their assumed identity. The same thing occurs when adults tell tales about preachers. Though it appears in a variety of church settings, the stance's link with preaching remains the dominant one.

This connection with preaching finds intriguing confirmation in the work of R. F. Thompson, who identifies this hand extended/hand on hip stance as a "classical gesture of authority . . . deriving from the lexicon of ancient Kongo gestures, especially those famous contexts of declamation and high oratory—the courts of law" (Thompson and Cornet 1981:123, 175; see also 122–24, 172–76).

3. Brother Bracey's crouched, "get-down" march will be familiar to anyone who has ever observed African American quartet performances. The hunched posture, sometimes accompanied by alternately pumping arms and sometimes by the hand-on-hip, hand-pointing-forward gesture, most often appears during moments of heightened performative intensity, just as it does here. For more on the "get-down" tendency in African and African diaspora song, dance, and iconography, see Thompson (1974:13–14).

4. Gospel singers have long used the singing "walk-up" and "walk-back" to establish their identity with the congregation. Though perhaps most common with soloists, who can strike up a song as soon as the emcee calls their name, the walk-up and walk-back also mark ensemble singing. Group members will sit next to each other in the pews and start singing while still seated, thus momentarily invoking the sound of *congregational* singing; by the same token, they will return to the pews singing, blending again with the surrounding saints. Some ensembles take the walk-up a step further and sing from positions scattered throughout the sanctuary. Quartet veteran Smiley Fletcher remembers that this strategy was once quite common.

"Quite a few groups used to do it," he recalls. "We used to go to a church, and we would spread all over the church. Maybe I'd go over here and sit; one of the fellows [would] sit over here, the baritone [would] sit over there, and the bass [would] sit back there. And when they call us to sing, I would hit the theme song here. When I hit, the tenor hit from over here, and the baritone from over here, and the bass—the people started looking around, you know. And then we all come on and walk on up" (1983).

The frequency of singing walk-ups has decreased as the frequency of instrumentally accompanied performance has increased. Set-up requirements now usually call instrumentalists to the church-front before the singing can begin, thus dulling the drama of unified musical entrances. Nonetheless, the walk-up is still practiced by many soloists, a cappella ensembles, and choirs.

5. From a conversation with Lena Mae Perry (Elliott and Perry 1992).

6. From a conversation with Evangelist Evelyn Gilchrist (1984).

7. The deep-seated faith in the sufficiency of the Lord's call derives in part from the words of the apostle John, who warns saints against those who might falsely seduce them with worldly teachings. "The anointing which ye have received of him abideth in you, and *ye need not that any man teach you*," writes the disciple, ". . . the same anointing teacheth you of all things, and is truth" (1 John 2:27; emphasis added). Sanctified preachers have long echoed this sentiment, with generation after generation specifically denying the need for formal, ministerial education.

One of the most eloquent of these denials comes from Texas preacher and singer Washington Phillips, whose 1927 recording, "Denomination Blues, Part 2" (Columbia 14333-D), includes the following verses: "There's another class of preachers that's high on speech, / They had to go to college to learn how to preach. . . . / But you can go to the college, and you can go to the school, / But if you ain't got Jesus, you an educated fool." The second of these verses is still popular among saints and often finds its way into congregational singing. (Similar verses from other Phillips' recordings appear in Oliver 1984:200.) Compare these lyrics with those of Rev. Dan Smith's more recent composition "I've Never Been to Seminary (But I've Been to Calvary)" on *Just Keep Goin' On* (Word ET 52989, 1991).

For further discussion of this belief, and evidence of its longstanding nature, see Davenport (1905:56), Mays and Nicholson (1933:40), Powdermaker (1939:275), Egypt, Masuoka, and Johnson (1945:308), and the comments of South Carolina preacher George Briggs (in Rawick, vol. 2, part 1 [1972:94]), Texas saint Louis Fowler (vol. 4, part 2 [1972:51]), Oklahoma saint Lou Smith (vol. 7 [1972:303–4]); and Alabama preacher John H. B. Smith (s.s. 1, vol. 1 [1977:370–71]).

8. The scripture that Pastor Brown cites in her opening line is 2 Timothy 3:5, which culminates a four-verse segment cataloging the many sinners who have "a form of godliness." Included in this list are "boasters," "false accusers," "despisers of those that are good," "lovers of pleasures more than lovers of God," and those who are "proud," "blasphemous," "unthankful," "unholy," "heady," and "highminded." The list concludes with the fifth verse: "Having a form of godliness, but denying the power thereof: from such turn away." By using this verse to make her point, Pastor Brown implicitly consigns "false" singers to this sinful company. This association, one that I've heard voiced quite often, speaks volumes about the low regard with which many saints hold those who put on the "forms" of anointment.

9. From a conversation with Pastor Rosie Wallace Brown (1983).

10. From a conversation with Ethel Elliott and Lena Mae Perry (1994).

11. Sister Perry's comment comes from a conversation with her and Ethel Elliott (1992). Offering an alternate perspective on "reading" a congregation, gospel scholar Ray Allen (1991:146) cites the appraisal strategy of Brooklyn Skyways' singer Willie Johnson, who explains that he watches for what other groups "don't do right" (as determined by audience response) and then builds his set accordingly. "You capitalize on [their] mistakes," Johnson suggests. In stark contrast to Sister Perry's approach, this strategy not only relies on overt audience reaction, but also leaves the Spirit out of the set-planning process.

12. From a conversation with Joseph Wallace (1993).

13. From a conversation with Ethel Elliott and Lena Mae Perry (1992). Sister Elliott's mention of "donations" refers to the common practice of giving a monetary gift to an anniversary's honorees. In suggesting that they "give a donation and go on," Sister Elliott was proposing that the Branchettes show up at the anniversary, make their "donation," and then leave without singing.

14. From a conversation with Evangelist Dorothy Jackson (1993b).

15. For eloquent testimony to this regard, see the comments of Kentucky gospel singer Vickie Cross, cited in Feintuch (1980:47).

16. From a conversation with Smiley Fletcher (1988).

17. From a conversation with Joseph Wallace (1993). Not all singers, of course, let the Spirit guide their words in this manner. Many rehearse virtually everything they plan to say—even their testimonies. Ray Allen, for example, describes quartet rehearsals at which "the dramatic recitations and testimonies that connect songs are also rehearsed, with the lead singer (chanter/reciter) working out appropriate call-and-response patterns with the background singers and musicians to accompany her or his chanted words" (1991:58).

18. From a conversation with Ethel Elliott and Lena Mae Perry (1992).

19. From a conversation with Pastor Rosie Wallace Brown (1983).

Chapter 16. False Purpose: "We Didn't Come for No Form or Fashion"

1. From the remarks of Evangelist Evelyn Gilchrist (1986), Sister Josephine Booth (1987), the United Choral Ensemble (1987), and Rev. David Bell (1985a). Compare these with the prayed comments from Sister Rachel Williams (in Chapter 7) and those cited in Drake and Cayton (1945:620), with the gospel announcers' disclaimers in Barney (1994:209–10, 271, 300), and with various singers' denials in Heilbut (1985:xv), Hinson (1989b:141–42), and A. Young (1997:25, 99).

2. From remarks delivered by William Coley (1993).

3. From the comments of Texas elder Ellen Payne, cited in Rawick, vol. 5, part 3 (1972:179). Respelled and repunctuated.

4. From a conversation with Rev. Samuel McCrary and Isaac Freeman (1986). Rev. McCrary's opening comment about speaking and singing "with understanding" references the advice given by the apostle Paul in 1 Corinthians 14:15.

5. That this use of "form" was already familiar by the early 1920s is suggested by the congregational song "After "While," where saints sang:

The world is full of *forms and changes*, / It's just now so confused,
You will find some danger, / In everything you use.

Interestingly, the phrase "forms and changes" closely parallels that of "form and fashion," with "fashion" and "changes" conveying roughly the same meaning. Later in this song, the singers use yet another term from this cluster, criticizing false preachers who "want the whole arrangement to suit their selfish style" (cited in Odum and Johnson 1925:134).

6. From a conversation with Rev. Z. D. Harris (1994). Such prefatory denials of performance call to mind analogous disclaimers in a host of other traditions. See, for example, Elinor Keenan's comments on the disclaimers that plateau Malagasy speakers employ when opening ceremonial speeches (1974:135), and Regna Darnell's remarks on denials of competence among traditional Cree narrators (1974:324–25). In both the Malagasy and Cree examples, performers deny performance in order to shift responsibility away from self and onto tradition; in essence, they are declaring that the words are not their own. Gospel singers, in contrast, are announcing that the words and sentiments conveyed in their performance are *very much their own*. By defining "performance" as "outside show," and then by denying "performance," they declare that what they are about to present represents their deepest beliefs, the "inside faith" rather than the "outside form." The disclaimer thus serves as an affirmation of sincerity (and, by extension, as an affirmation of spiritual competence). At the same time, it denies the importance of message *style* and message *form*, suggesting that these are but overlays on the meaningful core of message content.

Folklorist Richard Bauman suggests that disclaimers of the sort described by Keenan and Darnell serve to "key" performance in communities where "self-assertiveness is disvalued" (1977:21–22). In one sense, the same could be said for gospel disclaimers, in that they serve as denials of the surface self. At the same time, however, they serve as potent acts of self-assertion, in that they pose the singers as "children of God" who proudly claim their status as saved saints. Hence, the disclaimers *devalue* the outer self while *proclaiming the value* of the inner self.

7. Many professional gospel singers flatly reject this wholesale denial of theatricality. They argue that, as professionals, they are duty-bound to present paying audiences with quality entertainment, thus giving *everyone*—saints and sinners alike—"something for their money." What really matters, they suggest, are the performers' motives. If the intent is good, then the means are justified. This perspective is aptly captured in the words of Edwin Hawkins, the C.O.G.I.C.-based singer whose 1969 crossover hit, "Oh Happy Day," led his Edwin Hawkins Singers onto the stages of rock festivals, Las Vegas casinos and Madison Square Garden: "I think that many Christians fear some important words such as 'concert,' 'performance,' or 'show.' But we have to realise that this is a business too, and people are paying money to come and see a performance . . . to see a show. The result has to come from the artists on stage, from their motives and objectives, and ours is to minister. At the same time, we want people to be entertained . . . entertained by the Spirit" (cited in Broughton 1985:124). Needless to say, many saints reject this stance, insisting that it represents a concession to the ways of the world.

8. See, for example, the discussion of quartet rehearsals in Allen (1991:55–59), Patterson (1988:94–96), and Lornell (1995:115–17, 131–32). Particularly telling are the two sets of gospel group "bylaws" that Lornell prints, both of which stress the absolute importance of regular rehearsals (1995:116–117).

9. From conversations with Elder Lawrence Richardson (1986) and Rev. David H. Bell (1986). That this use of "formality" has enjoyed a long history among the saints is suggested by the 1937 comments of Arkansas elder Tom Douglas, who noted, "We don't live right now, [and] don't serve God. Pride, formality and love of money keeps folks from worshiping and [keeps them] away from the old-time religion" (cited in Rawick, vol. 8, part 2, [1972:202]; respelled).

10. See, for example, the adage's appearance in Dooley (1906:43).

11. For an insightful discussion of vocal techniques that gospel singers use to generate

"activity in the audience," see Raichelson (1975:427.–28). Burnim offers a more detailed analysis of one of these techniques, the pitch slide, and describes an incident in which a consulting saint critiqued a singer's quick passage from "heavy chest tones to sweet, lyric falsetto." The saint, Margaret Bryant, dismissed the dramatic vocal slide as "pyrotechnics," and then commented, "They are putting on a show; they are trying to work the audience up—get them excited" (1980:167–69).

12. From a conversation with Evangelist Dorothy Jackson (1993b).

13. In an essay on preaching style, Grace Sims Holt specifically mentions the symbolic significance of the preacher's handkerchief, suggesting that its appearance signals "that the preacher is really going to get down and preach." Acknowledging its symbolic link with intensity, she notes that the preacher traditionally starts to "wipe his face as he builds the utterances in pitch, intensity, and volume" (1972:194, 192).

14. The "can't stop singing" sequence has long been a trademark feature of James Brown's stage revue. At the close of the show, when Brown is on his knees singing, one of the band members taps him on the back and drapes a cape around his shoulder. Brown eases up, begins to move away, and then falls back on his knees, shedding the cape and setting the stage for a repeat of the entire sequence. James Brown says that he developed this routine (borrowed in part from professional wrestler Gorgeous George) to "arouse" his audience (Brown and Tucker 1986:104, 106). Needless to say, this is precisely why gospel singers use it.

15. Offering a very different definition of "clowning," gospel scholar Anthony Heilbut calls it "an ambivalent term among gospel singers. Everyone knows it's wrong to put on, yet every singer or preacher knows it is necessary and well-nigh universal" (1982:102). I suspect that few of the saints with whom I've spoken would care to include themselves in Heilbut's "everyone." Though all admit that "clowning" is universal, few would call it "necessary." Instead, most would agree with Evangelist Dorothy Jackson's assertion that God "don't need no clowners. He needs realness" (1993b).

16. From a conversation with Joseph Wallace (1993).

17. From conversations with B. Robert Faulk (1984) and Smiley Fletcher (1988).

18. From a conversation with Joseph Wallace (1993).

19. For a discussion of the ubiquity of this practice among professional singers, see Heilbut (1985:261–62).

20. This assumption of agency is by no means limited to singers. Saints have long pointed to "false" preachers as fellow culprits. Elder Lawrence Richardson, for example, tells of preachers who "want to do their own thing," and who say, "I'm going in here; I'm going to make these folks shout today." "I'll tell one [of those preachers] in a minute," says Elder Richardson, " 'You don't have *no power* to make *nobody* shout—even a flea!' " Preachers who preach with that intent, he says, have "nonsense in their hearts" (1986).

21. For reasons that will become apparent, I have chosen not to identify this singer. Though I explained to him my purpose in recording the conversation, I did not specify the context in which these remarks might be used. Nor did I ever openly challenge his explanation, thus possibly misleading him about my own stance and that of my principal consultants. Presenting his comments as if I *had* done these things would be unfair. But the comments themselves deserve a hearing, if only because they represent a widely held perspective that runs counter to that presented throughout this work. Hence the singer's anonymity. The conversation took place in Durham, N.C., in 1993.

I've chosen the name "Hardsinger" in accordance with preexisting naming traditions within the African American narrative tradition. Tales told on religious themes often use names that jokingly allude to some aspect of the named characters' communicative skills (e.g., Elder Thunderholler, Rev. Whirlwind Johnson, Elder Cyclone Williams). One of the names that appears in this repertoire is "Sweetsinger" (see, e.g., Talley 1993:172). In the gospel community, the term "sweet" refers to a smooth, fluid style of singing; singers usually characterize "sweet" singing as slow and soothing. The opposite of "sweet" is "hard," a style that features a more overtly intense, often gravelly delivery. "Hard" vocals tend to be louder, rougher, and more strained than "sweet" ones. The classic gospel crooners (like one-time Soul Stirrers' lead Sam Cooke, and his eventual Soul Stirrers' replacement, Willie Rogers) are "sweet singers," while the gospel "shouters" (like one-time Sensational Nightingales' lead Julius Cheeks, or the Mighty Clouds of Joy's Joe Ligon) are "hard singers." The consultant cited in this section is widely acknowledged as a powerful "hard singer." Hence his pseudonym.

22. From a conversation with Joseph Wallace (1993).

23. For further discussion of this issue, see Hinson (1984).

24. From a conversation with Evangelist Dorothy Jackson (1993b). The first part of Evangelist Jackson's citation paraphrases Psalm 84:11.

25. From a conversation with Evangelist Dorothy Jackson (1993b).

26. Folklorist Ray Allen also discusses sameness as a measure of authenticity (1991:148, 171–72).

27. From a conversation with Bertha, Claude, and John Landis (1984). Mississippi gospel singer Rita Watson makes precisely the same point in A. Young (1997:121).

28. Rev. Harris keeps a transcribed copy of every prophecy uttered by members of his church in a notebook in his church office. This particular message was voiced by Sister Vera Turner, one of two women at Oak Grove who regularly serve as vessels for prophecy. Rev. Harris kindly made me copies of many of these prophecies; this one—dated October 26, 1992—was among those he gave me. Rev. Harris's prefacing comments come from a 1993 conversation.

29. From a conversation with Smiley Fletcher (1982).

30. From a conversation with Evangelist Dorothy Jackson (1993b). Sociolinguist Judith Irvine offers other examples in which knowledge of believers' lives outside of ritual contexts plays a significant role in others' interpretation of their seemingly transcendent states. Noting that interpretation often depends on "the observers' knowledge of participants' past histories," she cites examples of diagnostic questioning of both Wolof mediums and inspired Quaker speakers (1982:257, 248, 253–54).

31. From a conversation with B. Robert Faulk (1984). Brother Faulk's eloquent litany of the devil's wiles calls to mind a tale told to folklorist Harold Courlander by an Alabama preacher. In the tale, Satan sends a "small half-sized Devil" up to earth to "corrupt some folks." The little devil gets to town on Sunday morning, and promptly goes into a church to see if he can stir up some trouble. He sits through the entire service in the back row. Then when church adjourns, he runs about trying to corrupt the churchgoers. When they pay him no mind, he gets discouraged and returns to hell. Needless to say, Satan is not pleased with his failure.

After grilling the little devil about his course of action, Satan shakes his head and says, "If you going to church to do your work, you can't sit in the back row. You got to get up on the mourner's bench and shout and moan and groan with the rest of them. If you'd done that, wouldn't nobody have said they hadn't never seen you before. If you playing baseball with the folks, you got to hit a home run to win their respect. If you doing it with music, you got to make them dance. And if you doing it in a church, you really got to get sanctified. Man, you sure got a lot to learn." (From Courlander 1957:95–97; respelled.)

32. The nine spiritual gifts, as set forth in 1 Corinthians 12:8–10, are wisdom, knowledge, faith, healing, the working of miracles, prophecy, the discerning of spirits, divers kinds of tongues, and the interpretation of tongues.

33. From a conversation with Evangelist Evelyn Gilchrist (1984).

Chapter 17. Elevation: "Go Slow, Rise High, Catch on Fire, and Sit Down"

1. Though African American churchgoers often apply the term "hard" to singers, they freely acknowledge that the true masters of vocal "hardness" are preachers. Hence when

preachers' voices begin to take on a harsh, gravelly timbre, churchgoers say that they are starting to "preach hard" (cf. L. Lomax 1962:86).

2. The tonal pattern of the lead's phrases precisely parallels that of Sister Mary Bracey's comments in her "response" (see Chapter 12). As I've already suggested, this rising and falling, hemistich structure is quite common in sanctified discourse. This particular pattern of tonal layering, where the lead lines fall into rising-and-falling couplets and the drive phrase internalizes the same structure in a single line, has become a drive tradition. Though it certainly does not mark *every* drive, it is so commonplace that even children's groups who "drive" their songs make regular use of it.

3. From a conversation with B. Robert Faulk (1984).

4. From a conversation with Isaac Freeman (1985).

5. From a conversation with Isaac Freeman (1985).

6. Saints often use the "building" metaphor to describe strategies of gradual intensification. Preachers typically speak of "building" their sermons; singers, in turn, talk of "building" songs or song sets. Performers often elaborate the metaphor to include detailed processual description, citing metaphorical referents for laying foundations, constructing walls, putting in ceilings, and so on. The trope's logical culmination, of course, lies in its "climax" at the roof. See, for example, Brother Jojo Wallace's comments about singers "building" until they "scraped the sky," in Chapter 16; see also analogous remarks by Marion Williams in Raichelson (1975:195), and Shirley Caesar in Harrington (1992:82–83, 88).

7. The academic champion of this explanation is Morton Marks, who argues that the drive's "trance-generated" features—particularly hyperventilation, stuttering, constriction of the lead's vocal register, and the lead's contrapuntal, "prophetic" phrasing—*induce* "trance" in listeners. "When the singer 'shouts,'" Marks contends, "he often demands a trance response from his congregation; he 'shouts' them. In gospel, the congregation is encouraged and even commanded to enter trance, to 'feel the Spirit'" (1974:97; see also Marks 1982:316–30). By treating selected songs as automatic "trance inducers," and by reducing the experience of transcendence to the vague, generalized category of "trance," Marks ignores the testimony of believers and radically simplifies a complex experiential process. In so doing, he inadvertently places himself in the same camp as the many unsaved singers who claim that they can "use" song to "shout the house." Even these singers, however, admit that shouts can never be guaranteed and that their best efforts to "wreck the house" often yield no shouted results.

8. From a conversation with Pastor Rosie Wallace Brown (1983).

9. From a conversation with Rev. McCrary and Isaac Freeman (1986).

10. From a conversation with the pseudonymous Brother Hardsinger (1993)

11. From conversations with Rev. Liggonia Young (1984) and Pastor Rosie Wallace Brown (1983).

12. Ira Tucker, the lead singer with the Dixie Hummingbirds, succinctly articulates this "rule" when he explains why the "Birds" have maintained their popularity for so many years. "I'm a firm believer in giving people something for their money," Tucker says. "Talent. A variety—fast, slow, something sad, something with a lot of laughs." For Tucker, the key to the Hummingbirds' popularity is the strategic crafting that they put into each performance. After describing a performance in which the Birds had to give three encores, he adds: "This is what keeps the Hummingbirds at our age at the bracket we're in. *Strategy*" (cited in Heilbut 1985:38, 53; emphasis in original). For analogous comments from Joe Ligon, lead singer with the Mighty Clouds of Joy, see Barr (1993); see also Boyer (1964:30–32) and Joyce Jackson (1988:83–84).

13. The juxtaposition of contrasting parts to yield cohesive wholes calls to mind West African and African American textile traditions, where patterns are often purposefully offset and colors intentionally contrasted to challenge the eye and intensify the textile's visual impact. See, for example, Robert Farris Thompson's discussion of contrast and "off-beat phrasing" in Mande textiles (1983:207–22, 290), and Georgia quilter Lucinda Toomer's comments about juxtaposing colors "to make them work" (cited in Wahlman 1993:35).

14. Accounts of elevation in congregational singing have long appeared in outsider descriptions of African American worship. See, for example, the accounts of Harris Barrett (1912:240) and Elizabeth Kilham (1870:306–08); and the descriptions of quickening "ring shouts" by Henry Spaulding (1863:196–97), James Weldon Johnson (1925:33), and John Lomax and Alan Lomax (1947:335). See also folklorist Jonathan David's detailed and insightful discussion of elevation among contemporary singing and praying bands (1992:3–5).

15. My thoughts on collaborative discourse owe a deep debt to many long and fruitful conversations with fellow folklorist Diane Goldstein, whose own inquiries into the matrix of belief, experience, and religious speech helped me to clarify the speaker/Spirit division in inspired and anointed communication. For further discussion of this issue and for a heuristic model charting the spectrum of speaker roles and collaborative states, see Goldstein (1987) and Hinson (1987).

16. From a conversation with Elder Lawrence Richardson (1986).

17. From a conversation with Deacon Edward Denkins (1985).

18. From a conversation with Deacon Joe Vereen (1988).

19. From a conversation with Bishop Frizelle Yelverton (1987).

20. From a conversation with B. Robert Faulk (1986).

21. For more detailed discussion of the stylistic characteristics of elevated speech, see the sources cited in note 15 of Chapter 7.

22. From a conversation with Isaac Freeman (1985).

23. From a conversation with Ethel Elliott and Lena Mae Perry (1993).

24. From a conversation with Rev. Liggonia Young (1984).

25. When singers strategically reference their degree of spiritual engagement by shifting into an elevated style, they are engaging in what sociolinguists Jan-Petter Blom and John Gumperz call "metaphorical switching" (1972:425). The style-shift's effectiveness depends on the degree to which congregation members associate selected stylistic features with a heightened experiential state. "The context in which one set of alternates is regularly used becomes part of its meaning," note Blom and Gumperz, "so that when this form is then employed in a context where it is not normal [or, by extension, where it is *less* normal than another set of alternates], it brings in some of the flavor of this original setting" (1972:425). In gospel programs, the strategic assumption of elevated style metaphorically references the elevated state, suggesting—but not proving—elevation's advent. When saints conclude that the singer is in fact *experiencing* (and not only *referencing*) elevation, then the shifting becomes what Blom and Gumperz call "situational," in that it now changes churchgoers' interpretation of the entire situation (1972:424). In a congregational setting, any instance of stylistic elevation would probably be interpreted in both ways. Since such assessment is ultimately personal, then style shifts treated as metaphor by one saint might well be taken as evidence of actual experiential transformation by another. For further discussion of metaphorical code-switching, see Gumperz (1982), esp. pp. 60–64 and 98–99.

26. Long a favorite technique of quartets, pitch elevation was probably the original "rise high" in the "go slow, rise high, catch on fire" maxim. As such, it marked the second stage in a three-part trajectory of song elevation, the third stage being the drive. Although the adage clearly suggests three separate parts (the low beginning, the elevation, and the drive), many songs include only the first or the last two. When asked about this, quartet elders with whom I've spoken say that the pitch elevation far predates the drive and probably predates the adage (at least as it applies to individual songs). The drive itself hails only from the mid to late 1940s; by this time, "raising the voice" was already a common elevation strategy. As drive arrangements grew increasingly more popular, however, gospel groups began gradually deleting the second-stage elevation, choosing instead to start the appropriate songs at a heightened pitch and then to push them right into drive. The "go slow, rise high" scenario thus emerged in the *set* rather than the *song*, while the "rise high, catch on fire" sequence emerged in both set and song.

27. From a conversation with Smiley Fletcher (1982).

28. From a conversation with Bertha Landis, Claude Landis, and John Landis (1984). For

a detailed history of the Landis family and the Golden Echoes, see Patterson (1988) and Tullos, Patterson, and Davenport (1989b, esp. pp. 4–7 and 21–27). The family is also featured in the documentary film *The Singing Stream*, a transcript of which appears in Tullos, Patterson, and Davenport (1989a).

29. Though most gospel ensembles limit themselves to one "drive" per song, many include two or more. When singing more than one, singers typically shift from elevation into drive, then "demodulate" back to the elevation (as the Gospel Tones did when they closed out the verse after their first drive), move once again into the drive, downshift again, and then close soon thereafter. I have seen quartets who were "high in the Spirit" repeat a drive up to four times—each time concluding it and "demodulating" back to the verse—before bringing the song to a close. For other description of drive arrangements, see Raichelson (1975:417–19), Rubman (1980:85–86), and Allen (1991:119–26, 180–82).

30. Many quartet veterans say that the first quartet to popularize the drive was the Kings of Harmony, a Birmingham-based group that many credit as the "fathers" of "hard gospel." Though the Kings never recorded any drives, they apparently included them in most performances from the late 1940s forward. "They had one or two numbers that they would *always* hang up," recalls Dickie Freeman, "and they had a great response on the way they were doing those numbers. . . . Then in later years, just about everybody started doing it" (Freeman 1985). For more on the Kings of Harmony, see Seroff (1985:42–43) and Funk (1990).

Though the Kings of Harmony can perhaps be credited with popularizing the "hang-up" as a *quartet* strategy, the drive format—a brief, harmonically static phrase chorused under an improvised lead—ranks as one of the most basic structures of African American song. Traditionally found in both worksongs and children's game songs, this structure also marked many ring shouts, where the lead would sing over a percussive burden voiced by the congregation's "basers." As with contemporary "drives," the chorused refrain could be a one- or two-part passage, with the latter alternating textual and/or melodic phrases around the lead's improvisation. Whatever the form, the repeated structure served precisely the same function as gospel drives, though in a congregational rather than an ensemble frame. (For a thorough discussion of ring shout history and a valuable collection of contemporary texts, see Rosenbaum 1998. To actually hear many of the ring shout songs discussed by Rosenbaum, see the 1984 Folkways release, *The McIntosh County Shouters: Slave Shout Songs from the Coast of Georgia* [FE 4344].)

A more direct precursor to the drive lies in the church singing of so-called "jubilee singers," gifted soloists who traveled from church to church in the decades surrounding the turn of the century. By all accounts, these singers (who are not to be confused with singers in "jubilee quartets" and "choruses") specialized in singing extended, at least partially improvised, narratives set within a call-and-response frame. The host congregation joined the singing on the chorus and apparently often intoned a brief, repeated passage at the close of each of the jubilee singer's phrases. While some of these responses fit within an encompassing tune, many apparently held the melody hostage, simply repeating a single passage much in the manner of a contemporary drive. Such was the case, for example, with the singing of "The Christians' Hymn of the Crucifixion," a congregational piece heard by William Barton in the 1880s. Barton says of this song: "it was sung at an evening meeting, [with] a single voice telling the story, repeating twice each line, while the congregation sang a heavy bass 'Ham-mer-ring!'" (1899:713). The ensuing transcript shows the lead lines initially following a rough rhyming structure. Eventually, however, they depart from rhyme altogether, moving instead into free narration. The parallels with contemporary drives are simply too striking to ignore.

Folklorist Harold Courlander offers contemporary examples of these "jubilee song sermons" (to use Willis James's term [1995:118]) in his transcriptions of the congregational pieces "Rock Chariot" and "Job, Job," both of which revolve around steadily intoned "repeats" (1963:50–56, 225–27). The latter text is particularly telling, in that the lead's lines dramatically shorten after the second chorus, moving into terse, three-syllable phrases that call to mind the staccato intensity of the "overdrive."

Given the timing of the drive's emergence in gospel, one also has to consider influences from the secular realm, and particularly from the riff-based dance music of the southwestern swing bands. Jazz musicians say that Walter Page's Blue Devils, an exceptionally influential band based in Oklahoma City, were building songs around repeated riff structures as early as the mid-1920s. (See, for example, pianist Sam Price's recollection of saxophone riffs under Jimmy Rushing's singing, and pianist Jesse Stone's recounting of the Blue Devils' musicians *singing* riffs, cited in Pearson 1987:66, 68.) Musicians from the Blue Devils eventually formed the backbones of the Bennie Moten Orchestra and the Count Basie Orchestra, two bands that transformed the face of big-band swing with their dance-oriented, riff-based arrangements. (Intriguingly, the Kings of Harmony spent a period in the mid-1930s in Houston, Texas, a favorite stomping ground for the riff-based, southwestern "territory" bands. Many of these bands also enjoyed considerable regional and national radio exposure in the 1930s and 1940s.) For a insightfully provocative discussion of the riff/drive connection, see Bowers (1996).

31. In order to avoid any numerical skewing occasioned by unusually long sets (e.g., those presented at single group concerts), I included only multi-ensemble programs in my tally. The 142 performances included 64 by quartets, 33 by family groups and gospel ensembles, 28 by choruses and choirs, 7 by duos, and 10 by soloists. I chose the programs by randomly selecting from ten years of field notes, letting region and type of program set the only parameters. The events considered include anniversaries, church-sponsored singings, commercial "ticket programs," and local programs presented by local promoters and/or ensembles. The professional/nonprofessional balance of ten and ten was itself random; I discovered this breakdown only *after* I had already tallied set numbers and drive frequency.

32. From conversations with Wilson Waters and Robert Hamlett (1986), and with the pseudonymous Brother Hardsinger (1993).

33. Just as I chose not to identify Brother Hardsinger, so too have I chosen not to identify this quartet. The name "Gospel Drivers" is a complete fabrication; the lyrics, however, are quoted precisely as they were performed (Gospel Drivers 1993). In order to maintain the group's anonymity, I have deleted any prefacing comments or verses that would allow identification of the song.

34. Reference to, or the retelling of, one's own conversion story is quite common in pre-drive remarks and the drive itself. Such references both establish the singer's authority as a saint and fashion a frame of congregational expectation, invoking the Spirit's power so as to turn listeners' minds toward the touch.

35. In this and many other drives, questions emerge as the most consistently repeated communicative unit. Their consistency and repetition, coupled with the implication that the singer is already feeling what listeners are being asked to feel, subtly transforms the relationship between the singer and the congregation. What began as a relationship of equality eases toward inequality as the questioner seizes interrogative command and steps into the role of rhetorical exhorter. In essence, the singer starts acting like a preacher, by virtue of stepping into the preacher's communicative shoes. The singer's use of elevated style, of course, further cements this association. For further discussion about the way that questions can change the structure of relationships, see Goody (1978, esp. pp. 28–30, 35–42).

36. In "double-drives," the drive phrase splits itself into two parts, so that a different half follows each lead line. In the transcribed Gospel Drivers' hang-up, for example, the backup momentarily shifted into a double-drive when they split their phrase into "Feel the fire!/ Holy Ghost fire!" Many groups regularly begin their drives with a double phrase, and then shift to a single phrase as they intensify their singing. Not uncommonly, many of these same groups will then press the drive into a third phase with a staccato "overdrive." For example, they might begin with "Send it on down!/Send the Holy Ghost down!," elevate to a simpler "Got the Holy Ghost!," and then climax with a percussive "Holy Ghost!"

37. Saints often liken spiritual elevation to up-shifting gears, particularly when speaking about preaching; I've also heard the analogy used to describe praying, singing, and testifying. A number of gospel songs cleverly incorporate this elevation metaphor into their lyrics;

many versions of "The Christian Automobile," for example, build a verse around each of three cited gears. For descriptions that use this analogy in reference to preaching and praying, see Reagon (1989:3), McKinney (1973:18–19), and A. Young (1997:189–90, 227–28).

38. From a conversation with Rev. Samuel McCrary and Elder Lawrence Richardson (1985).

39. The comments of the Tennessee preacher appear in C. Johnson (1945:153); Rev. Bell's remarks, in turn, come from a 1986 conversation.

40. In essence, inspiration, enablement, and prophetic anointment mark three different stages of communicative collaboration between the Spirit and the saints. In inspiration, the Spirit acts as the message *source*, bestowing the knowledge that gives birth to speech. This knowledge, in turn, must be transposed and translated before it can be conveyed. The receiver thus becomes a re-stater, transforming the thoughts into words. Hence in inspiration, the receiving saint plays a major role in the communicative process.

In the enablements of elevation, the Spirit acts as message *shaper*. In addition to infusing elevated words with spiritual authority, the Spirit helps mold the manner in which these words are uttered, shaping their style rather than their content. As I suggested earlier, this process is not one where the Spirit actually guides the tongue; instead, He provides the pathways for the tongue to follow. Once again, the elevated speaker—who is still conceiving and conveying the words being shaped—plays a leading role in the communicative drama.

In prophetic anointment, however, the degree of human agency is greatly reduced. At this stage, the Spirit acts not only as source and shaper, but also as *talker*. When the words flow, the Spirit provides the message, the style, *and* the actual words being uttered. The collaborative balance thus shifts away from the saint and toward the Spirit, putting full responsibility for the ensuing communication firmly in the Spirit's hands. From this point on, as saints often say, "it's God talking." (For further discussion of these stages of collaborative communication, see Goldstein 1987 and Hinson 1987.)

41. This shift from claimed to ceded responsibility also forces a shift in the way that scholars must study such spiritual performances. Performance, as understood in the ethnographic disciplines, entails both enactment and accountability. Drawing definition from its situational placement, it emerges with what Richard Bauman describes as an "assumption of responsibility to an audience for a display of communicative competence" (1977: 11). To engage in performance is to put oneself "on stage," to subject one's expressive behavior to judgment by that set of aesthetic criteria deemed situationally appropriate by one's audience. Central to this definition is the concept of emergence. Not all presentation is performance. Rather, performance is something achieved, something realized, something entered into with a "breaking through" to accountability. This breakthrough, in turn, ushers the performer into what might be termed (following Hymes) a "continuum of realization," with bare, skeletal performance at one end and full, authoritative performance at the other. Progressing along this continuum, a performer moves from a state of barely meeting aesthetic criteria to one of fully realizing (and perhaps even exceeding) them. The process of performance can thus be said to entail both an initial breakthrough and a gradual achievement of place on the performative continuum. (For a full discussion of performative "breakthrough" and "continuums of realization," see Hymes 1975:15 and passim; 1981:79–259.)

In gospel performance, elevation *removes* performers from the march toward greater performative fullness. It does so by moving them out of the continuum altogether. As the Spirit assumes greater responsibility for a performer's actions, the degree of human accountability lessens. This lessening continues as performance grows increasingly collaborative. Finally, with the advent of prophetic anointment, the balance of performative responsibility completes its shift from saint to Spirit. At this moment, the performer is no longer *performing*. What began as a "breakthrough into performance" thus ends with a "moving out" of performance.

At this point, the term "performance" becomes descriptively inadequate, as saints acting under the anointing no longer bear responsibility for their pronouncements. They cede all such responsibility the moment they cede expressive control. From this point forward, they are but vessels for discourse created and syntactically shaped by a holy Other. Furthermore, knowing congregation members no longer subject this discourse to aesthetic evaluation. All questions of artistic shape, poetic form, and affective essence are dismissed with recognition of the Spirit as author. In effect, assessment of competence is supplanted by acceptance of omnipotence. The anointed saints, meanwhile, enter a sort of holy limbo, a state that might be termed "anointed vesselhood." Until the return of performative control, they—like their peers in the pews—assume the role of hearers.

42. Saints often testify to their ill-fated attempts to "squench the Spirit," telling how they tried to "hold back" the rising emotions and "keep the Spirit in check." Most such stories portray the saints as "holding back" because they felt that shouting wasn't appropriate for the moment or the occasion. Background vocalists in gospel groups, for example, often tell how they tried to "squench the Spirit" so that they wouldn't "disrupt" the flow of the singing. Needless to say, most such stories emerge as cautionary tales, with the tellers detailing how their attempts to give the natural precedence over the supernatural were ultimately futile. When telling such stories, saints often cite the Bible's specific injunction against this practice: "Quench not the Spirit" (1 Thessalonians 5:19).

Chapter 18. Invitation: "The Souls of Many Are Yet Lost"

1. After reading drafts of the preceding chapters, Brother Jojo Wallace—whose testimony appears in Chapter 16 and who served as one of my initial readers—called me to discuss the unfolding manuscript. "Just like my songs will linger here on earth long after I've been called home," he remarked, the enthusiasm rising in his voice, "so too will this book. Sinners crying out in the day of Armageddon will not be able to say, 'I didn't *know* about Christ! Nobody *told* me about the Word!' Because it's *here*. It's here for them to *hear*, and it's here for them to *read*." Then Brother Wallace paused. I let the seconds tick by, knowing from his tone that he had more to say. "But you've got to *call* them, Brother Glenn. *You've got invite them to accept Christ into their lives*. Somewhere in this book."

His request caught me off guard. "How can I do this," I thought to myself, "in an work aimed—at least in part—at academic audiences? Wouldn't this lead many readers to dismiss the book as biased, as somehow 'tainted' by faith? Wouldn't it undercut the challenge I'm trying to mount to conventional perspectives on belief?" I'm sure I murmured something noncommittal; all I can remember now is pondering the responsibilities of collaborative ethnography. Brother Wallace must have caught the hesitation in my voice, for he launched into an explanation of *why* I needed the invitation, arguing that after all my talk about form and fashion and all my words about folks singing lies, I needed to clearly state the alternative. I promised that I would. But when I hung up the phone, I wasn't at all sure *how* to get an invitation in here.

The answer—it turned out—lay in the anniversary itself. Toward the end of the service, Evangelist Lofton had extended an eloquent invitation. I initially hadn't planned on including it in this work, but my conversation with Brother Wallace (and subsequent talks with other sanctified readers) convinced me that without it, my discussion would be incomplete. Hence I present the invitation here, as my consultants suggested, without added commentary.

Chapter 19. Benediction: "May the Grace of God Rest, Rule, and Abide"

1. For a succinct and sensitive statement of this interpretive approach, see Hallowell (1934:393–94, 404); for an equally sensitive updating, see Young and Goulet (1994a).

2. When saints use the term "possession" to refer to supernatural process, they are usually

speaking about possession by the devil or evil spirits, a process that they portray as dramatically different from that of anointment. This is the association, they point out, that typically appears in the Bible (see, e.g., Matthew 4:24, Luke 4:36, Acts 16:16). Nonetheless, scholars writing about African American religious practice continue to impose the term "possession," usually without ever addressing the significant differences between the process that saints describe and that which traditionally earns this anthropological designation. See, e.g., the many index entries under "Possession" and "Spirit Possession" in Allen (1991) and Pitts (1993).

3. Though saints usually describe anointment as a process of human surrender and spiritual intercession, they note that the Spirit can—if He so wills—intervene without invitation. As I've already suggested, this was the scenario in the conversion of Saul, as recounted in the Book of Acts. In like manner, saints say that the Spirit sometimes *does* touch with such power that receiving saints lose all awareness of their surround—as when believers are "slain in the Spirit," or when preachers get "so anointed" that they no longer know what they are preaching, learning what came from their mouths only after listening to recordings of their sermon. Such accounts are clearly the exception rather than the rule. Their currency, however, reminds saints that the Spirit's power knows no bounds, and that within this power all rules are flexible.

4. Among the few that achieve this collaborative end are Lassiter (1998) and Lawless (1993).

Appendix. Stepping Around Experience and the Supernatural

1. The self's definition of the quotidian fosters recognition of the nonquotidian, when the singular, idiosyncratic, or episodic—Wilhelm Dilthey's category of "*an* experience"—emerges from the everyday (Dilthey 1976:210; see also Berger and Luckmann 1966:23–26, V. Turner 1986, and Abrahams 1986). Any attempt to study the fullness of one's lifeworld must address both classes of experience, probing both the ordinary *and* the extraordinary (cf. Abu-Lughod 1993:14; Michael Jackson 1989:13, 1996a:27). In the experiential world of the saints, encounter with the holy—whether through the epiphany of a holy shout or the subtle workings of inspiration—falls into the latter of these categories. Though always *anticipated* (particularly in the course of worship), the experience can be neither predicted nor prepared for. Nonetheless, it wholly frames encounter with the everyday, creating a *context in mind* that shapes interpretation and shepherds action.

2. Among the ethnographies that insightfully address the experience of ethnographic consultants are Abu-Lughod (1993), Glassie (1982), Hufford (1982a), Lassiter (1998), Stoller (1989), and Turner, Blodgett, Kahona and Benwa (1992); see also the essays in Michael Jackson (1996b).

3. From Kapferer (1986:190); see also Michael Jackson (1996a:7–9).

4. Among those using this term is Victor Turner (1982:13), whose 1986 volume with Edward Bruner first gathered ethnographers under the designated rubric of "experience." Most of the essays in this work adopt a generalized approach whose focus on collective expressions sacrifices that which is idiosyncratic and personal. Bruce Kapferer (1986), for example, addresses a presumed experiential isomorphism in Sinhalese exorcism, arguing that the compelling flow of performance and symbol draws ritual participants into a kind of interpretive and experiential alignment; this alignment, in turn, is said to "structure" their experience, leading all participants to face the same existential encounter. Following a different path to a similar end, James Fernandez (1986) offers tropes as the structurers of experience; he argues that the enactment of symbols subconsciously draws ritual participants to the shared sociohistorical domains from which those symbols were derived, thus linking them in an experience of continuity and community. At no point are the actual participants invited to comment on these analyses; indeed, their testimonies are absent

throughout. So too are the particularities—and thus the subjectively meaningful framing—of their experiences.

5. This echoes a call voiced by Renato Rosaldo in a critique of ethnoscience and ethnographic realism. Rosaldo notes that "Neither approach makes central the stories people tell themselves about themselves, and this crucial omission robs a certain human significance from anthropological accounts. Ethnographers can learn much about meaningful action by listening to storytellers as they depict their own lives" (1986:97–98). Among those who have creatively responded to this challenge are Lila Abu-Lughod (1993), Ruth Behar (1993), Karen Brown (1991), and Eric Lassiter (1998).

6. As if to formally cement this connection, many Black and white Protestants in the eighteenth through twentieth centuries used the term "experience" as a synonym for "testimony"; hence they would "give their experiences" before an assembly of believers. For further discussion of this usage, see Chapter 3.

7. I borrow this term from Jeff Titon's lucid discussion of fictive elements in life stories (1980:290)

8. The co-creativity involved in all communication leads Roland Barthes (1977) to speak of Text as charting an inherently *social* space, where authorship is infinitely shared and meaning infinitely variable.

9. This is precisely the chasm that anthropologist Robin Ridington artfully leaps in his side-by-side tellings of Dunne-za narratives, where the second narrative is his *re*-telling with an eye toward "mak[ing] the connection between [the narrator's] world and our own" (1990:22; cf. Abu-Lughod 1993:15–16).

10. I am reminded here of Ghanaian physician F. I. D. Konotey-Ahulu's response to anthropologist Margaret Field's 1937 study of belief on the southern Gold Coast. "I was impressed by her excellent descriptive proclivities," he writes, "but how could she possibly have missed the spiritual side of the whole thing? How could anybody have come so close to the truth behind the fetish sacrifices in Africa and yet be so far away in England in thought? She interpreted everything in strict Western-orientated 'scientific' language." After arguing that Field never removed the ethnocentric "spectacles" of Western rationalism, Konotey-Ahulu quotes Pascal: "There are two excesses: to exclude reason, to admit nothing but reason. . . . The supreme achievement of reason is to realise that there is a limit to reason. Reason's last step is the recognition that there are an infinite number of things which are beyond it. It is merely feeble if it does not go as far as to realise that" (Konotey-Ahulu 1977:1595).

11. I use the term "unproblematized" somewhat guardedly here, not meaning to suggest that believers don't themselves sometimes question the veracity of experiential accounts. Doubt is inherent in any community of belief; the presumption that all claims to experience earn the same measure of acceptance both robs believers of individual will and grants to belief a consciousness-flattening power to dictate homogeneity. No semblance of such homogeneity reigns among the saints, where doubt is integral to the discourse of performance. If the ethnographer grants experience the same status accorded it by believers, then this doubt becomes a natural part of the inquiry.

Few ethnographers have addressed in any detailed manner the issues of doubt and evaluation within religious communities. For a lucidly argued comparative study of assessment in mediumship and possession traditions, see Irvine (1982). I address the historical lack of ethnographic attention to these issues in Hinson (1992a).

12. Among those ethnographers who have willfully stepped into the realm of the supernatural and then written about the understandings accorded therein, are Karen Brown (1991), Bennetta Jules-Rosette (1975), Paul Stoller (Stoller and Olkes 1987), Larry Peters (1981), Edith Turner (Turner et al. 1992, Turner 1994, 1995), and many of the authors in Young and Goulet (1994b). Perhaps the most widely publicized ethnographer to take this step is Carlos Castaneda, whose *Teachings of Don Juan* (1968) and its many sequels captured the imagination of a generation and convinced many that the essence of ethnography was

the search for mystical experience. Though Beals (1978), de Mille (1980), and others have convincingly argued that Castaneda's writings were actually an elaborate ethnographic hoax, much of the public remains convinced of their truthfulness. This widespread belief, when coupled with the implications it holds for public perceptions of the ethnographic enterprise, more than justifies Castaneda's inclusion in this list. So too does Castaneda's substantial impact (as model to be emulated or avoided) on other ethnographers who have pursued experiential forays into the paranormal (in this regard, see Myron 1994).

13. David Hufford, one of the principal architects of the experience-centered approach to belief studies, thoroughly discusses these strategies of retreat (1982a, esp. pp. 12–16; 1982b; and 1983).

14. Even ethnographies of *religious* communication—the very works that would presumably be most sensitive to these issues—often treat belief and experience as nondiacritic features of ethnographic context. The common justification for this restrictive treatment holds that communication—whether in the service of religion or any other cultural system—is a behavioral domain for which belief and experience have little relevance. One of the most articulate proponents of this stance is sociolinguist William Samarin, whose experience-denying argument merits quotation: "Sociolinguistics, the study of language in relation to social realities, examines religion only because it is another domain of human behavior where language is an important component. . . . We start with no different assumptions. For us, religion is no unique domain of experience; we do not begin our examination of religious language *expecting* to find here what we might not find elsewhere. Whatever validity we might claim for religious propositions, we insist on the inescapable fact of the thoroughly human, therefore common and accessible, mediation of religious experience" (1976:3, 5; emphasis in original). Samarin's strategy—one shared by many ethnographers of religious communication—is one of dual disregard: on one hand, he ignores the role language plays in the articulation of belief and experience; on the other, he dismisses the roles belief and experience play in the generation and interpretation of language. In adopting this stance, he allows a narrow focus on communicative means to cripple the study of communicative meaning. (See also Samarin 1972a:18–29; 1972b:xiii, 230–32.)

15. Ethnography's fascination with religious trickery will be quite familiar to anyone who has studied anthropological treatments of religion. Many early ethnographers seemed to take great pleasure in debunking accounts of supernatural encounter. Taking the error of their consultants' claims as a given, they set out to demonstrate how demonstrations of supernatural power were actually clever performances of human legerdemain. The sheer number of these ethnographic exposés prohibits a detailed discussion of individual cases. For two representative examples, see Franz Boas's account of shamanic trickery among the Kwakiutl (1966:124–27), and E. E. Evans-Pritchard's discussion of deceptive practices among Azande "witch-doctors" (1937:186–93).

With the emergence of performance analysis, the drive to debunk has lost some of its prosecutorial edge. Now ritual specialists are increasingly portrayed as skilled actors and as "managers" of audience expectation and perception. Again, the number of such analyses prohibits exhaustive treatment here. See, for example, John Beattie's comments on Nyoro diviners using a highly marked "ghost vocabulary" to script the symbolic "drama" of possession (1964:127–51), and Edward Schieffelin's discussion of Kaluli mediums artistically "managing" seances through their enactment of "spirit characters" (1985:707–24).

16. The claim to the shaping and "stereotyping" power of culture so pervades analyses of supernatural narratives that one can turn to almost any religious narrative tradition that has come under ethnographic scrutiny and find ample examples of this interpretive strategy. In the world of African American sanctified belief, one might begin with Paul Radin's analysis of the *God Struck Me Dead* narratives, in which he attributes the structure and imagery of the conversion accounts to a variety of social forces, never once considering the possibility of truthfully recounted experience (1945:v–viii; for a second social reading of these narratives, see Sobel [1988:108–22]). When anthropologist Hortense Powdermaker addresses African American conversion narratives, she argues that convention shapes both experience

and its narration. After noting that conversion "conforms to a set pattern, and stereotyped phrases have grown up to describe it," she says of the converted believer's experience, "It is part of the convention that he should so feel it" (1939:260).

For a more contemporary application of this strategy, see Jeff Todd Titon's ethnography of white Baptist worship in southwestern Virginia. When speaking of narratives detailing the spiritual call to preach, for example, he notes: "The fact that these narratives conform to a pattern suggests the possibility that they are learned. . . . More likely, though, the body of call-to-preach narratives serves to guide the future preacher's interpretation of his experience. They shape his *perception* of his experiences, and thus, for practical purposes, the experiences themselves, as they come to live in memory and to be shaped in narrative. The same is likely the case with conversion narratives" (1988:321–22, emphasis in original). In other words, the believer internalizes the narrative tradition and perceives experience accordingly. The resultant narrative, in turn, offers little clue to the actual experience that gave it rise. Hence the ethnographer is justified in treating testimony as socially revealing narrative rather than as experiential account.

17. The ensuing discussion relies heavily on the writings of folklorist David Hufford (1976; 1982a:12–14; 1982b:49–53).

18. Evans-Pritchard (1937:34) resorted to this strategy when attempting to explain his own encounter with a strange light in the Sudanese bush. He spied the moving light one night while walking in his garden and judged from its brightness that it must be emanating from a lamp: "I knew that only one man, a member of my household, had a lamp that might have given off so bright a light. . . ." Evans-Pritchard eventually lost sight of the light and retired for the evening. The next morning, he discovered that the lamp-owner had *not* been out the previous night and that the resident of the house toward which the light had been moving had died. Community members quickly determined that the light was the soul of a witch on an evil errand. Evans-Pritchard, not surprisingly, would not accept this explanation. Instead, despite his earlier appraisal of the light's brightness, he concluded that it was more likely "a handful of grass lit by some one on his way to defecate." Hence Evans-Pritchard challenges not the *sensory basis* of the experience—that being his own vision—but rather *any interpretation that would yield the supernatural*. The placement of this account early in his work on Zande belief effectively attributes a credulous subjectivity to the Azande and a rational objectivity to the ethnographer, thus neatly establishing the relations of authority and credibility. (In 1957, twenty years after this account's initial publication, Evans-Pritchard repeated it verbatim in *Tomorrow*, a review of psychical research. His interpretation of the night's happenings had clearly not changed.)

19. Anthropologists David Young and Jean-Guy Goulet best articulate this approach in the conclusion to their edited volume on experiential approaches to "extraordinary experiences." "The ethnographic record shows that when participation in the society of others is maximized," they write, "fieldworkers have experiences in dreams and visions that reflect their absorption of the local realities." Likening the process to that of language acquisition, when learners unconsciously internalize acoustic and semantic schemata that dramatically enhance their speaking and understanding skills, Young and Goulet suggest that ethnographers can internalize the very schemata that shape their consultants' reality. Consequently, they can "transcend their own subjective limitations and cultural prejudices and share a level of reality with their informants not normally available to outsiders" (1994a:313–14, 315). This "reality," however, is wholly situational, a "finite province of meaning" constructed intersubjectively and encountered only fleetingly. The ethnographer's experience thus testifies not to the existence of the supernatural but only to a level of acculturation that invites entry into otherwise hidden worlds of culturally constructed meaning.

20. See Young and Goulet's elaboration of this approach, and their application of it to Goulet's vision of a recently deceased Dene Tha girl (1994a:314–19, 322–23).

21. Many of the ethnographers who employ this strategy experience something dramatically out of the ordinary while probing the beliefs of their consultants. Felicitas Goodman, for example, experienced momentary dissociation and a vision while studying glossolalia

among Pentecostals in Yucatán (1972:71–73). She begins her account by noting that she had foregone breakfast that morning, thus establishing a frame of extenuating circumstances. Goodman then argues that she was merely "obeying a cultural expectation," adding incidentally that she "intentionally blocked subsequent occurrences." In a similar manner, Nancy Owen (1981:19–20) credits the mysterious infection and illness that she contracted while conducting fieldwork in Dominica to stress, though her consultants insisted (and she initially believed) that it was induced by witchcraft. After a local "bush doctor" prescribed a ritual process that seemingly effected a cure, Owen decided that the "real" cause—"given [her] weakened condition"—had been her unintended internalization of Carib beliefs.

Much less willing to dismiss the reality-jarring impact of supernatural encounter is Bruce Grindal (1983), who witnessed the vivification and dancing of a corpse in a Ghanaian death divination ceremony. Grindal compellingly describes both the encounter and his shaken response. Nonetheless, he spends much of the essay detailing his state of exhaustion before and during the ritual, thus offering "rational" grounds for "explaining" his experience.

Finally, mention must be made of Larry Peters (1981:45–50), who twice experienced an altered state of consciousness—the second time accompanied by a vision—when apprenticing to a Tamang shaman in Nepal. Unwilling to accept the shaman's explanations for his experiences, Peters suggests that a "hyperactive automatic state" led to his involuntary movement and visionary travels. Citing Neher's studies linking rhythmic "driving" with trance, he speculates that his experiences were induced by the drumming in which he—as initiate—was participating. At a later point in his initiation, Peters dreamt a vivid dream that the shaman to whom he was apprenticing interpreted as clear evidence of progress on the shamanic path. For a moment, Peters reports, "I experienced a suspension of disbelief" (1981:52). But retrospection apparently erased this moment, leading Peters to frame his dream account by noting that he was hospitalized for hepatitis at the time, thus suggesting a neurophysiological explanation. Peters concludes his experiential narrative by flatly declaring, "I have not experienced cultural conversion" (1981:53), implying that "conversion" would be the only way that he could objectively accept his consultants' beliefs. Short of this, he is only willing to grant their reality a conditional status: "Spirit possession could not exist for me because I don't hold the same animistic beliefs as my informants" (1981:47).

For further discussion of the supposed link between rhythmic "driving" and altered states of consciousness, see Neher (1961, 1962); Needham (1967); Sturtevant (1968); and A. Jackson (1968). Gilbert Rouget deftly deconstructs and then dismantles the rhythm/trance thesis in his 1985 work *Music and Trance* (see esp. pp. 169–83).

22. Dickens's classic 1843 account of the encounter between Scrooge and Marley incisively captures this willingness to deny the evidence of one's senses when facing the supernatural. Seeing the horrible specter of his late partner Marley, Scrooge initially reacted with disbelief.

"You don't believe in me," observed the Ghost.

"I don't," said Scrooge.

"What evidence would you have of my reality beyond that of your senses?"

"I don't know," said Scrooge.

"Why do you doubt your senses?"

"Because," said Scrooge, "a little thing affects them. A slight disorder of the stomach makes them cheats. You may be an undigested bit of beef, a blot of mustard, a crumb of cheese, a fragment of an underdone potatoe. There's more of gravy than of grave about you, whatever you are!" (Dickens 1954:18).

Bibliography

Abrahams, Roger. 1976. Concerning African Performance Patterns. In *Neo-African Literature and Culture: Essays in Memory of Janheinz Jahn*, ed. Bernth Lindfors and Ulla Schild, pp. 32–42. Wiesbaden: B. Heyman.

———. 1983. *The Man-of-Words in the West Indies: Performance and the Emergence of Creole Culture*. Baltimore: Johns Hopkins University Press.

———. 1986. Ordinary and Extraordinary Experience. In *The Anthropology of Experience*, ed. Victor W. Turner and Edward M. Bruner, pp. 45–71. Urbana: University of Illinois Press.

Abu-Lughod, Lila. 1993. *Writing Women's Worlds: Bedouin Stories*. Berkeley: University of California Press.

Adams, Edward C. L. 1987. *Tales of the Congaree*. Edited with an introduction by Robert G. O'Meally. Chapel Hill: University of North Carolina Press.

Allen, Ray. 1991. *Singing in the Spirit: African-American Sacred Quartets in New York City*. Philadelphia: University of Pennsylvania Press.

Allen, William Francis, Charles Pickard Ware, and Lucy McKim Garrison. [1867] 1951. *Slave Songs of the United States*. Reprint, New York: Peter Smith.

Andrews, Malachi, and Paul T. Owens. 1973. *Black Language*. Los Angeles: Seymour-Smith Publisher.

Asante, Molefi Kete. 1987. *The Afrocentric Idea*. Philadelphia: Temple University Press.

Barney, Deborah Verdice Smith. 1994. The Gospel Announcer and the Black Gospel Music Tradition. Ph.D. diss., Michigan State University.

Barr, Robert. 1993. Music Makers: Joe Ligon on Working a Gospel Crowd: When to "Cut the Fool." Associated Press release, August 27.

Barrett, Harris. 1912. Negro Folk Songs. *Southern Workman* 41:238–45.

Barthes, Roland. 1977. *Image, Music, Text*. Trans. Stephen Heath. New York: Hill and Wang.

Barton, William E. 1899. Recent Negro Melodies. *The New England Magazine* n.s. 19:707–19.

Bastin, Bruce. 1973. The Devil's Goin' to Get You. *North Carolina Folklore Journal* 21:189–94.

Bateson, Mary Catherine. 1974. Ritualization: A Study in Texture and Texture Change. In *Religious Movements in Contemporary America*, ed. Irving I. Zaretsky and Mark P. Leone, pp. 150–65. Princeton, N.J.: Princeton University Press.

Baugh, John, and Joel Sherzer, eds. 1984. *Language in Use: Readings in Sociolinguistics*. New York: Prentice-Hall.

Bauman, Richard, ed. 1977. *Verbal Art as Performance*. Rowley, Mass.: Newbury House.

Bauman, Richard, and Joel Sherzer, eds. 1974. *Explorations in the Ethnography of Speaking.* Cambridge: Cambridge University Press.

Beals, Ralph L. 1978. Sonoran Fantasy or Coming of Age? *American Anthropologist* 80:355–62.

Beattie, J. M. H. 1964. The Ghost Cult in Bunyoro. *Ethnology* 3:127–51.

Behar, Ruth. 1993. *Translated Woman: Crossing the Border with Esperanza's Story.* Boston: Beacon Press.

Belden, Henry M., and Arthur Palmer Hudson, eds. 1952. *Folk Songs from North Carolina.* Vol. 3 of *The Frank C. Brown Collection of North Carolina Folklore,* ed. Newman Ivey White. Durham, N.C.: Duke University Press.

Bell, Rev. David H. 1985a. Remarks delivered at Greenfield Baptist Church. Creedmoor, N.C., September 3.

——. 1985b. Remarks at the thirty-ninth anniversary of the Sensational Nightingales. Durham, N.C., November 3.

——. 1986. Personal conversation. Durham, N.C., September 18.

Berger, Peter L., and Thomas Luckmann. 1966. *The Social Construction of Reality: A Treatise in the Sociology of Knowledge.* Garden City, N.Y.: Doubleday.

Blom, Jan-Petter, and John J. Gumperz. 1972. Social Meaning in Linguistic Structure: Code-Switching in Norway. In *Directions in Sociolinguistics: The Ethnography of Communication,* ed. John J. Gumperz and Dell Hymes, pp. 407–34. New York: Holt, Rinehart and Winston.

Boas, Franz. 1966. *Kwakiutl Ethnography.* Ed. Helen Cordere. Chicago: University of Chicago Press.

Boggs, Beverly. 1977. Some Aspects of Worship in a Holiness Church. *New York Folklore* 3:29–44.

Booth, Josephine. 1987. Remarks delivered at a gospel program at the Durham Civic Center. Durham, N.C., December 14.

Bowers, Alexander. 1996. Sacred Meets Secular: The Importance of Kansas City Jazz in Gospel Quartet Singing. Unpublished manuscript, University of North Carolina, Chapel Hill, N.C.

Boyer, Horace Clarence. 1964. The Gospel Song: A Historical and Analytical Study. Master's thesis, Eastman School of Music, University of Rochester.

——. 1973. An Analysis of Black Church Music with Examples Drawn from Services in Rochester, New York. Ph.D. diss., Eastman School of Music, University of Rochester.

——. 1979. Contemporary Gospel Music. *The Black Perspective in Music* 7:5–58.

——. 1985. A Comparative Analysis of Traditional and Contemporary Gospel Music. In *More Than Dancing,* ed. Irene V. Jackson, pp. 127–46. Westport, Conn.: Greenwood Press.

——. 1992a. Lucie E. Campbell: Composer for the National Baptist Convention. In *We'll Understand It Better By and By: Pioneering African American Gospel Composers,* ed. Bernice Johnson Reagon, pp. 81–108. Washington, D.C.: Smithsonian Institution Press.

——. 1992b. William Herbert Brewster: The Eloquent Poet. In *We'll Understand It Better By and By: Pioneering African American Gospel Composers,* ed. Bernice Johnson Reagon, pp. 211–31. Washington, D.C.: Smithsonian Institution Press.

——. 1995. *How Sweet the Sound: The Golden Age of Gospel.* Washington, D.C.: Elliot and Clark.

Brenneis, Donald. 1987. Performing Passions: Aesthetics and Politics in an Occasionally Egalitarian Community. *American Ethnologist.* 14:236–50.

Brewer, J. Mason. 1945. *Humorous Folk Tales of the South Carolina Negro.* Foreword by B. A. Botkin. Publications of the South Carolina Negro Folklore Guild, no. 1. Orangeburg, S.C.: South Carolina Negro Folklore Guild.

——. 1953. *The Word on the Brazos: Negro Preacher Tales from the Brazos Bottoms of Texas.* Austin: University of Texas Press.

——. 1968. *American Negro Folklore.* New York: Quadrangle/ New York Times Book Co.

Brewster, W. Herbert. 1949. *Let Us Go Back to the Old Land Mark*. Memphis: Bowles Music House and W. Herbert Brewster.

Broughton, Viv. 1985. *Black Gospel: An Illustrated History of the Gospel Sound*. Dorset: Blandford Press.

Brown, James, and Bruce Tucker. 1986. *James Brown: The Godfather of Soul*. New York: Macmillan.

Brown, Karen McCarthy. 1991. *Mama Lola: A Vodou Priestess in Brooklyn*. Berkeley: University of California Press.

Brown, Pastor Rosie Wallace. 1983. Personal conversation. Philadelphia, March 23.

Bryant, Rev. Carolyn. 1985. Personal conversation. Philadelphia, October 4.

Burnim, Mellonee Victoria. 1980. The Black Gospel Music Tradition: Symbol of Ethnicity. Ph.D. diss., Indiana University.

——. 1985. The Black Gospel Music Tradition: A Complex of Ideology, Aesthetic, and Behavior. In *More Than Dancing*, ed. Irene V. Jackson, pp. 147–67. Westport, Conn.: Greenwood Press.

——. 1988. Functional Dimensions of Gospel Music Performance. *Western Journal of Black Studies* 12 (2): 112–21.

Caesar, Shirley. 1998. *The Lady, the Melody, & the Word: The Inspirational Story of the First Lady of Gospel*. Nashville: Thomas Nelson Publishers.

Cash, Rev. Louis. 1987. Prayer delivered at the sixteenth anniversary of the Gilchrist Family. Durham, N.C., September 27.

Castaneda, Carlos. 1968. *The Teachings of Don Juan: A Yaqui Way of Knowledge*. New York: Ballantine.

CBS Trumpeteers. 1987. Performance at Orange High School. Hillsborough, N.C., December 7.

Chernoff, John Miller. 1979. *African Rhythm and African Sensibility: Aesthetics and Social Action in African Musical Idioms*. Chicago: University of Chicago Press.

Clifford, James. 1983. On Ethnographic Authority. *Representations* 1 (Spring): 118–46.

Coley, William. 1993. Remarks delivered at the twentieth anniversary of the Branchettes. Newton Grove, N.C., March 13.

Courlander, Harold. 1957. *Terrapin's Pot of Sense*. New York: Henry Holt.

——. 1963. *Negro Folk Music, U.S.A.* New York: Columbia University Press.

Dance, Daryl Cumber. 1978. *Shuckin' and Jivin': Folklore from Contemporary Black Americans*. Bloomington: Indiana University Press.

Darnell, Regna. 1974. Correlates of Cree Narrative Performance. In *Explorations in the Ethnography of Speaking*, ed. Richard Bauman and Joel Sherzer, pp. 315–36. Cambridge: Cambridge University Press.

Davenport, Frederick Morgan. 1905. *Primitive Traits in Religious Revivals: A Study in Mental and Social Evolution*. New York: Macmillan.

David, Jonathan. 1992. *On One Accord: Singing and Praying Bands of Tidewater Maryland and Delaware*. Notes to Global Village CD 225. New York: Global Village Music.

Davis, Gerald L. 1985. *I Got the Word in Me and I Can Sing It, You Know: A Study of the Performed African American Sermon*. Philadelphia: University of Pennsylvania Press.

Daye, Rev. W. A. 1993. Sermon delivered at Peace Missionary Baptist Church. Durham, N.C., February 28.

de Mille, Richard, ed. 1980. *The Don Juan Papers: Further Castaneda Controversies*. Santa Barbara, Calif.: Ross-Erikson Publishers.

Denkins, Edward. 1985. Personal conversation. Philadelphia, October 1.

Dickens, Charles. 1954. *Christmas Books*. Introduction by Eleanor Farjeon. London: Oxford University Press.

Dillard, J. L. 1977. *Lexicon of Black English*. A Continuum Book. New York: Seabury Press.

Dilthey, Wilhelm. 1976. *Selected Writings*, ed. H. P. Rickman. Cambridge: Cambridge University Press.

Dooley, Mrs. James H. 1906. *Dem Good Ole Times*. New York: Doubleday, Page.

Dorsey, Thomas A. 1949. *The Little Wooden Church on the Hill*. Chicago: Thomas A. Dorsey.

Dorson, Richard M. 1967. *American Negro Folktales*. Greenwich, Conn.: Fawcett Publications.

Drake, St. Claire, and Horace R. Cayton. 1945. *Black Metropolis: A Study of Negro Life in a Northern City*. New York: Harcourt, Brace.

Du Bois, W. E. Burghardt. 1903. *The Souls of Black Folk: Essays and Sketches*. Chicago: A. C. McClurg.

Egypt, Ophelia Settle, J. Masuoka, and Charles S. Johnson, eds. 1945. *Unwritten History of Slavery: Autobiographical Accounts of Negro Ex-Slaves*. Social Science Source Documents no. 1. Nashville, Tenn.: Social Science Institute, Fisk University.

Eldridge, Willie H. 1994. Personal conversation. Newton Grove, N.C., January 24.

Elliott, Ethel. 1994. Personal conversation. Benson, N.C., May 27.

Elliott, Ethel, and Lena Mae Perry. 1992. Personal conversation. Raleigh, N.C., August 23.

——. 1993. Personal conversation. Raleigh, N.C., February 27.

——. 1994. Personal conversation. Chapel Hill, N.C., June 23.

Epstein, Dena J. 1977. *Sinful Tunes and Spirituals: Black Folk Music to the Civil War*. Urbana: University of Illinois Press.

Evans, David. 1971. *Tommy Johnson*. London: Studio Vista.

Evans-Pritchard, E. E. 1937. *Witchcraft, Oracles and Magic Among the Azande*. Oxford: Clarendon Press.

——. 1957. A Seance Among the Azande. *Tomorrow* 5 (4): 11–26.

Faulk, B. Robert. 1984. Personal conversation. Durham, N.C., September 13.

——. 1986. Personal conversation. Durham, N.C., September 25.

Feintuch, Burt. 1980. A Noncommercial Gospel Group in Context: We Live the Life We Sing About. *Black Music Research Journal* 1:37–50.

Fernandez, James W. 1986. The Argument of Images and the Experience of Returning to the Whole. In *The Anthropology of Experience*, ed. Victor W. Turner and Edward M. Bruner, pp. 159–87. Urbana: University of Illinois Press.

Field, Margaret J. 1937. *Religion and Medicine of the Ga People*. London: Oxford University Press.

Fletcher, Smiley. 1982. Personal conversation. Philadelphia, March 15.

——. 1983. Personal conversation. Philadelphia, March 16.

——. 1988. Personal conversation. Philadelphia, November 15.

Foote, William Henry. 1850. *Sketches of Virginia: Historical and Biographical*. Philadelphia: William S. Martien.

Frazier, E. Franklin. 1963. *The Negro Church in America*. New York: Schocken Books.

Freeman, Isaac. 1985. Personal conversation. Washington, D.C., July 6.

Funk, Ray. 1990. The Kings of Harmony. *Rejoice* 3 (2):7–12.

Gardner, Peter M. 1991. Pragmatic Meanings of Possession in Paliyan Shamanism. *Anthropos* 86:367–384.

Gilchrist, Evangelist Evelyn. 1984. Personal conversation. Durham, N.C., September 15.

——. 1986. Remarks delivered at the fifteenth anniversary of the Gilchrist Family. Durham, N.C., September 27.

——. 1993. Remarks delivered at the Ecclesia House of Prayer. Durham, N.C., February 7.

Glassie, Henry. 1982. *Passing the Time in Ballymenone: Culture and History of an Ulster Community*. Philadelphia: University of Pennsylvania Press.

Gold, Peter. 1981. The Black Sermon and the Communication of Innovation. In *Discourse in Ethnomusicology II: A Tribute to Alan P. Merriam*, ed. Caroline Card, Jane Cowan, Sally Carr Helton, Carl Rahkonen, and Laurie Kay Sommers, pp. 173–204. Bloomington: Ethnomusicology Publications Group, Indiana University.

Goldstein, Diane E. 1987. Transcending Words, I: Shifting Participant Roles in Religious Speech Events. Paper presented at the annual meeting of the American Folklore Society, Albuquerque, N. Mex.

Goodman, Felicitas D. 1972. *Speaking in Tongues: A Cross-Cultural Study of Glossolalia.* Chicago: University of Chicago Press.

Goody, Esther N. 1978. Toward a Theory of Questions. In *Questions and Politeness: Strategies in Social Interaction*, ed. Esther N. Goody, pp. 17–43. Cambridge Papers in Social Anthropology, no. 8. Cambridge: Cambridge University Press.

Goreau, Laurraine. 1975. *Just Mahalia, Baby.* Waco, Texas: Word Books.

Gospel Drivers [pseud.]. 1993. Performance. Raleigh, N.C., March 7.

Greater Joy Ensemble. 1987. Remarks made at a gospel program at Durham High School. Durham, N.C., November 20.

Green, Evangelist Rachel. 1988. Remarks made at Mount Calvary Holy Church. Durham, N.C., May 1.

Grindal, Bruce. 1983. Into the Heart of Sisala Experience. *Journal of Anthropological Research* 39:60–80.

Gumperz, John J. 1982. *Discourse Strategies.* Cambridge: Cambridge University Press.

Gumperz, John J., and Dell Hymes, eds. 1964. *The Ethnography of Communication.* Washington, D.C.: American Anthropological Association. First issued as *American Anthropologist* 66 (6), part 2.

———. 1972. *Directions in Sociolinguistics: The Ethnography of Communication.* New York: Holt, Rinehart and Winston.

Hallowell, A. I. 1934. Some Empirical Aspects of Northern Salteaux Religion. *American Anthropologist* 36:389–404.

Hand, Wayland, ed. 1964. *Popular Beliefs and Superstitions from North Carolina.* Vol. 7 of *The Frank C. Brown Collection of North Carolina Folklore*, ed. Newman Ivey White. Durham, N.C.: Duke University Press.

Hannerz, Ulf. 1969. *Soulside: Inquiries into Ghetto Culture and Community.* New York: Columbia University Press.

Hardsinger [pseud.]. 1993. Personal conversation. Durham, N.C., April 16.

Harrington, Brooksie Eugene. 1992. Shirley Caesar: A Woman of Words. Ph.D. diss., Ohio State University.

Harris, Michael W. 1992. *The Rise of Gospel Blues: The Music of Thomas Andrew Dorsey in the Urban Church.* New York: Oxford University Press.

Harris, Rev. Zebedee D. 1993. Personal conversation. Durham, N.C., February 16.

———. 1994. Personal conversation. Durham, N.C., July 5.

Harrison, W. P. 1893. *The Gospel Among the Slaves. A Short Account of Missionary Operations Among the African Slaves of the Southern States.* Nashville, Tenn.: Publishing House of the M. E. Church, South.

Heilbut, Anthony. 1982. The Secularization of Gospel Music. In *Folk Music and Modern Sound*, ed. William Ferris and Mary L. Hart, pp. 101–15. Jackson: University Press of Mississippi.

———. 1985. *The Gospel Sound: Good News and Bad Times.* Rev. ed. New York: Limelight Editions.

Hendricks, W. C., ed. 1943. *Bundle of Troubles and Other Tarheel Tales.* Durham, N.C.: Duke University Press.

Hinson, Glenn D. 1984. Not Singing for Form or Fashion: Experience, Aesthetics and Religious Performance. Paper presented at the annual meeting of the American Folklore Society, San Diego, Calif.

———. 1987. Transcending Words, II: Evaluation and the Assignment of Responsibility in Religious Speech Events. Paper presented at the annual meeting of the American Folklore Society, Albuquerque, N. Mex.

———. 1988. Unintended Trips to Transcendence: Spirit and Consequence in Religious Discourse. Paper presented at the annual meeting of the American Folklore Society, Boston, Mass.

———. 1989a. *Eight Hand Sets and Holy Steps.* LP booklet for Longleaf LL001RE. Raleigh: North Carolina Department of Cultural Resources.

——. 1989b. When the Words Roll and the Fire Flows: Spirit, Style, and Experience in African-American Gospel Performance. Ph.D. diss., University of Pennsylvania.

——. 1990. *Just a Little While to Stay Here*, by the Badgett Sisters. Notes to Global Village audiocassette C214. New York: Global Village Music.

——. 1992a. Searching for the "Real" in Realist Ethnography: Assumptions and Avoidance in the Ethnographic Study of Belief. Paper presented at the annual meeting of the American Folklore Society, Jacksonville, Fla.

——. 1992b. *The Voice That Refused to Die*, by the Badgett Sisters. Notes to Global Village audiocassette C222. New York: Global Village Music.

——. 1995. Dream Songs: Exploring the Contours of Transcendent Experience. Paper presented at the annual meeting of the American Folklore Society, Lafayette, La.

Holsclaw, David Francis. 1979. The Demise of Disciplined Christian Fellowship: The Methodist Class Meeting in Nineteenth-century America. Ph.D. diss., University of Califonia, Davis.

Holt, Grace Sims. 1972. Stylin' Outta the Black Pulpit. In *Rappin' and Stylin' Out: Communication in Urban Black America*, ed. Thomas Kochman, pp. 189–204. Urbana: University of Illinois Press.

Hufford, David J. 1976. Ambiguity and the Rhetoric of Belief. *Keystone Folklore* 21:11–24.

——. 1982a. *The Terror That Comes in the Night: An Experience-Centered Study of Supernatural Assault Traditions*. Philadelphia: University of Pennsylvania Press.

——. 1982b. Traditions of Disbelief. *New York Folklore* 8:47–55.

——. 1983. The Supernatural and the Sociology of Knowledge: Explaining Academic Belief. *New York Folklore Quarterly* 9:21–31.

Hurston, Zora Neale. [1935] 1963. *Mules and Men*. Philadelphia: J. B. Lippincott. Reprint, with an introduction by Robert E. Hemenway, Bloomington: Indiana University Press.

——. 1983. Spirituals and Neo-Spirituals. In *The Sanctified Church*, pp. 79–84. Berkeley: Turtle Island.

Hyatt, Henry Middleton. 1970. *Hoodoo-Conjuration-Witchcraft-Rootwork: Beliefs Accepted by Many Negroes and White Persons, These Being Orally Recorded Among Blacks and Whites*. Memoirs of the Alma Egan Hyatt Foundation. Hannibal, Mo.: Western Publishing Company.

Hymes, Dell. 1962. The Ethnography of Speaking. In *Anthropology and Human Behavior*, ed. Thomas Gladwin and William C. Sturtevant, pp. 15–53. Washington, D.C.: Anthropological Society of Washington.

——. 1964. Introduction: Toward Ethnographies of Communication. In *The Ethnography of Communication*, ed. John J. Gumperz and Dell Hymes, pp. 1–34. A special publication of *American Anthropologist* 66 (6), part 2. Washington, D.C.: American Anthropological Association.

——. 1974. *Foundations in Sociolinguistics: An Ethnographic Approach*. Philadelphia: University of Pennsylvania Press.

——. 1975. Breakthrough into Performance. In *Folklore: Performance and Communication*, ed. Dan Ben-Amos and Kenneth S. Goldstein, pp. 11–74. The Hague: Mouton.

——. 1977. Discovering Oral Performance and Measured Verse in American Indian Narrative. *New Literary History* 7:431–57.

——. 1981. *"In Vain I Tried to Tell You": Essays in Native American Ethnopoetics*. Philadelphia: University of Pennsylvania Press.

Irvine, Judith. 1982. The Creation of Identity in Spirit Mediumship and Possession. In *Semantic Anthropology*, ed. David Parkin, pp. 241–60. New York: Academic Press.

Jackson, Anthony. 1968. Sound and Ritual. *Man* n.s. 3:293–99.

Jackson, Evangelist Dorothy. 1993a. Remarks at the "End of Black History Month Gospel Program." Raleigh, N.C., March 7.

——. 1993b. Personal conversation. Fayetteville, N.C., April 29.

Jackson, Irene V. 1974. Afro-American Gospel Music and Its Social Setting with Special Attention to Roberta Martin. Ph.D. diss., Wesleyan University.

Jackson, Jackie. 1992. Personal conversation. St. Louis, Mo., June 7.

Jackson, Joyce Marie. 1981. The Black American Folk Preacher and the Chanted Sermon: Parallels with a West African Tradition. In *Discourse in Ethnomusicology II: A Tribute to Alan P. Merriam*, ed. Caroline Card, Jane Cowan, Sally Carr Helton, Carl Rahkonen, and Laurie Kay Sommers, pp. 205–22. Bloomington: Ethnomusicology Publications Group, Indiana University.

———. 1988. The Performing Black Sacred Quartet: An Expression of Cultural Values and Aesthetics. Ph.D. diss., Indiana University.

Jackson, Mahalia, with Evan McLeod Wylie. 1966. *Movin' On Up*. New York: Hawthorn Books.

Jackson, Michael. 1989. *Paths to a Clearing: Radical Empiricism and Ethnographic Inquiry*. Bloomington: Indiana University Press.

———. 1996a. Introduction: Phenomenology, Radical Empiricism, and Anthropological Critique. In *Things as They Are: New Directions in Phenomenological Anthropology*, ed. Michael Jackson, pp. 1–50. Bloomington: Indiana University Press.

———, ed. 1996b. *Things as They Are: New Directions in Phenomenological Anthropology*. Bloomington: Indiana University Press.

James, Willis Laurence. 1995. *Stars in de Elements: A Study of Negro Folk Music*. Edited by Jon Michael Spencer, with an introduction by Rebecca T. Cureau. A special issue of *Black Sacred Music: A Journal of Theomusicology* 9, nos. 1–2.

Johnson, Charles S., ed. 1945. *God Struck Me Dead: Religious Conversion Experiences and Autobiographies of Ex-Slaves*. Social Science Source Documents no. 2. Nashville, Tenn.: Social Science Institute, Fisk University.

Johnson, James Weldon, ed. 1925. *The Book of American Negro Spirituals*. Musical arrangements by J. Rosamund Johnson. New York: Viking Press.

Johnson, Richard O. 1981. The Development of the Love Feast in Early American Methodism. *Methodist History* 19 (2):67–83.

Jones, Bessie. 1983. *For the Ancestors: Autobiographical Memories*. Collected and edited by John Stewart. Urbana: University of Illinois Press.

Jules-Rosette, Bennetta. 1975. *African Apostles: Ritual and Conversion in the Church of John Maranke*. Ithaca, N.Y.: Cornell University Press.

Kapferer, Bruce. 1986. Performance and the Structuring of Meaning and Experience. In *The Anthropology of Experience*, ed. Victor W. Turner and Edward M. Bruner, pp. 188–203. Urbana: University of Illinois Press.

Keenan, Elinor. 1974. Norm-Makers, Norm-Breakers: Uses of Speech by Men and Women in a Malagasy Community. In *Explorations in the Ethnography of Speaking*, ed. Richard Bauman and Joel Sherzer, pp. 125–43. Cambridge: Cambridge University Press.

Keil, Charles. 1966. *Urban Blues*. Chicago: University of Chicago Press.

Kilham, Elizabeth. 1870. Sketches in Color (Fourth). *Putnam's Monthly Magazine* n.s. 5:304–11.

Kochman, Thomas. 1970. Toward an Ethnography of Black American Speech Behavior. In *Afro-American Anthropology: Contemporary Perspectives*, ed. Norman E. Whitten Jr. and John F. Szwed, pp. 145–62. New York: Free Press.

———, ed. 1972. *Rappin' and Stylin' Out: Communication in Urban Black America*. Urbana: University of Illinois Press.

Konotey-Ahulu, F. I. D. 1977. Personal View. *British Medical Journal* 1 (June 18): 1595.

Kroll-Smith, J. Stephen. 1980. The Testimony as Performance: The Relationship of an Expressive Event to the Belief System of a Holiness Sect. *Journal for the Scientific Study of Religion* 19:16–25.

Landis, Bertha, Claude Landis, and John Landis. 1984. Personal conversation. Creedmoor, N.C., September 12.

Lassiter, Luke E. 1998. *The Power of Kiowa Song: A Collaborative Ethnography*. Tucson: University of Arizona Press.

Lawless, Elaine J. 1993. *Holy Women, Wholly Women: Sharing Ministries of Wholeness*

Through Life Stories and Reciprocal Ethnography. Philadelphia: University of Pennsylvania Press.

Levine, Lawrence W. 1977. *Black Culture and Black Consciousness: Afro-American Folk Thought from Slavery to Freedom*. New York: Oxford University Press.

Lincoln, C. Eric, and Lawrence H. Mamiya. 1990. *The Black Church in the African American Experience*. Durham, N.C.: Duke University Press.

Lofton, Evangelist Hattie. 1993. Remarks at the twentieth anniversary of the Branchettes. Newton Grove, N.C., March 14.

Lomax, Alan, ed. 1968a. *Folk Song Style and Culture*. Washington, D.C.: American Association for the Advancement of Science.

———. 1968b. Song as a Measure of Culture. In *Folk Song Style and Culture*, ed. Alan Lomax, pp. 117–69. Washington, D.C.: American Association for the Advancement of Science.

———. 1970. The Homogeneity of African-Afro-American Musical Style. In *Afro-American Anthropology: Contemporary Perspectives*, ed. Norman E. Whitten Jr. and John F. Szwed, pp. 181–201. New York: Free Press.

Lomax, Alan, and Edwin E. Erickson. 1968. The World Song Style Map. In *Folk Song Style and Culture*, ed. Alan Lomax, pp. 75–110. Washington, D.C.: American Association for the Advancement of Science.

Lomax, John A. 1947. *Adventures of a Ballad Hunter*. New York: Macmillan.

Lomax, John A., and Alan Lomax, eds. 1947. *Folk Song U.S.A.* New York: Duell, Sloan and Pearce.

Lomax, Louis E. 1962. *The Negro Revolt*. New York: Harper and Row.

Lornell, Kip. 1995. *"Happy in the Service of the Lord": African-American Sacred Vocal Harmony Quartets in Memphis*. 2nd ed. Knoxville: University of Tennessee Press.

MacRae, David. [1870] 1952. *The Americans at Home*. Reprint, New York: E. P. Dutton.

Marcus, George E., and Michael M. J. Fischer. 1986. *Anthropology as Cultural Critique: An Experimental Moment in the Human Sciences*. Chicago: University of Chicago Press.

Marks, Morton. 1974. Uncovering Ritual Structures in Afro-American Music. In *Religious Movements in Contemporary America*, ed. Irving I. Zaretsky and Mark P. Leone, pp. 60–134. Princeton, N.J.: Princeton University Press.

———. 1982. "You Can't Sing Unless You're Saved": Reliving the Call in Gospel Music. In *African Religious Groups and Beliefs: Papers in Honor of William R. Bascom*, ed. Simon Ottenberg, pp. 305–31. Meerut, India: Archana Publications (for the Folklore Institute).

Marsh, J. B. T. 1880. *The Story of the Jubilee Singers; With Their Songs*. Rev. ed. Boston: Houghton, Osgood.

Massenburg, Evangelist Susan. 1988. Sermon delivered at Mount Calvary Holy Church. Durham, N.C., July 24.

Maultsby, Portia K. 1981. *Afro-American Religious Music: A Study in Musical Diversity*. Papers of the Hymn Society of America, 35. Springfield, Ohio: Hymn Society of America.

Mays, Benjamin Elijah, and Joseph William Nicholson. 1933. *The Negro's Church*. New York: Institute of Social and Religious Research.

McAllister, Anita Bernadette. 1995. The Musical Legacy of Dorothy Love Coates: African American Female Gospel Singer with Implications for Education and Theater Education. Ph.D. diss., Kansas State University.

McCrary, Rev. Samuel, and Isaac Freeman. 1986. Personal conversation. Arlington, Va., July 1.

McCrary, Rev. Samuel, and W. Lawrence Richardson. 1985. Personal conversation. Washington, D.C., June 28.

McIntyre, Paul. 1976. *Black Pentecostal Music in Windsor*. Canadian Centre for Folk Cultural Studies paper no. 15. Ottawa: National Museum of Man.

McKinney, Samuel Berry. 1973. Getting It Through: Prayer in the Black Church. *Freeing the Spirit* 2 (Fall): 18–19.

Message from the Lord. 1992. Transcription of a prophecy revealed to Vera Turner. Durham, N.C., October 26.

Mitchell, Henry M. 1970. *Black Preaching*. Philadelphia: J. B. Lippincott.

Morris, Kenneth. 1944. *Twelve Gospel Song "Hits" and Their Stories*. Chicago: Martin and Morris Music.

———. 1949. *Improving the Music in the Church*. Chicago: Martin and Morris Music Studio.

———, ed. 1983. *Morris Book of Poems No. 2, With Welcome Addresses; Responses*. Chicago: Martin and Morris Music.

———, ed. 1985. *Morris Book of Poems and Helper, No. 3*. Chicago: Martin and Morris Music.

Murphy, Sister. 1983. Remarks made at the fourteenth anniversary of the Gospel Express. Philadelphia, April 17.

Myron, Yves. 1994. The Experiential Approach to Anthropology and Castaneda's Ambiguous Legacy. In *Being Changed by Cross-Cultural Encounters: The Anthropology of Extraordinary Experience*, ed. David E. Young and Jean-Guy Goulet, pp. 273–97. Peterborough, Ontario: Broadview Press.

Needham, Rodney. 1967. Percussion and Transition. *Man* n.s. 2:606–14.

Negro Superstition Concerning the Violin. 1892. *Journal of American Folklore* 5:329–30.

Neher, Andrew. 1961. Auditory Driving with Scalp Electrodes in Normal Subjects. *Electroencephalography and Clinical Neurophysiology* 13:449–51.

———. 1962. A Physiological Explanation of Unusual Behavior in Ceremonies Involving Drums. *Human Biology* 34:151–60.

Newberry, Jeffrey. 1988. Remarks at a gospel program at the Durham Civic Center, Durham, N.C., May 10.

Noble, E. Myron. 1986. *The Gospel of Music: A Key to Understanding a Major Chord of Ministry*. Washington, D.C.: Middle Atlantic Regional Press of the Apostolic Faith Churches of God.

O'Connor, Bonnie. 1993. The Home Birth Movement in the United States. *Journal of Medicine and Philosophy* 18:147–74.

Odum, Howard W., and Guy B. Johnson. 1925. *The Negro and His Songs: A Study of Typical Negro Songs in the South*. Chapel Hill: University of North Carolina Press.

Oliver, Paul. 1984. *Songsters and Saints: Vocal Traditions on Race Records*. Cambridge: Cambridge University Press.

Olmsted, Frederick Law. 1856. *Journey in the Seaboard Slave States, with Remarks on Their Economy*. New York: Dix and Edwards.

Owen, Nancy H. 1981. Witchcraft in the West Indies: The Anthropologist as Victim. *Anthropology and Humanism Quarterly* 6 (2–3): 15–22.

Paris, Arthur E. 1982. *Black Pentecostalism: Southern Religion in an Urban World*. Amherst: University of Massachusetts Press.

Parrish, Lydia. [1942] 1992. *Slave Songs of the Georgia Sea Islands*. New York: Creative Age Press. Reprint, with a foreword by Art Rosenbaum. A Brown Thrasher Book. Athens: University of Georgia Press.

Patterson, Daniel W. 1988. "Going Up to Meet Him": Songs and Ceremonies of a Black Family's Ascent. In *Diversities of Gifts: Field Studies in Southern Religion*, pp. 91–102. Ed. Ruel W. Tyson Jr., James L. Peacock, and Daniel W. Patterson. Urbana: University of Illinois Press.

Payne, Daniel Alexander. 1888. *Recollections of Seventy Years*. Comp. Sarah C. Bierce Scarborough. Ed. C. S. Smith. Nashville, Tenn.: Publishing House of the A.M.E. Sunday School Union.

Pearson, Nathan W., Jr. 1987. *Goin' to Kansas City*. Urbana: University of Illinois Press.

Peters, Larry. 1981. *Ecstasy and Healing in Nepal: An Ethnopsychiatric Study of Tamang Shamanism. Other Realities*, vol. 4. Malibu, Calif.: Undena Publications.

Phillips, Helen L. 1969. Shouting for the Lord: A Black Rite of Modernization. Master's thesis, University of North Carolina at Chapel Hill.

Phillips, Washington. 1927. *Denomination Blues, Parts 1 and 2*. Columbia 14333-D. Dallas, Texas, December 5.

Pinkston, Alfred Adolphus. 1975. Lined Hymns, Spirituals, and the Associated Lifestyle of Rural Black People in the United States. Ph.D. diss., University of Miami.

Pitts, Walter F., Jr. 1993. *Old Ship of Zion: The Afro-Baptist Ritual in the African Diaspora.* New York: Oxford University Press.

Powdermaker, Hortense. 1939. *After Freedom: A Cultural Study of the Deep South.* New York: Viking Press.

Preston, Dennis R. 1982. 'Ritin' Fowklower Daun "Rong: Folklorists Failures in Phonology. *Journal of American Folklore* 95:304–26.

——. 1983. Mowr Bayad Spellin': A Reply to Fine. *Journal of American Folklore* 96:330–39.

Price, Richard, and Sally Price. 1991. *Two Evenings in Saramaka.* Chicago: University of Chicago Press.

Puckett, Newbell Niles. 1926. *Folk Beliefs of the Southern Negro.* Chapel Hill: University of North Carolina Press.

Raboteau, Albert J. 1978. *Slave Religion: The "Invisible Institution" in the Antebellum South.* Oxford: Oxford University Press.

Radin, Paul. 1945. Status, Phantasy, and the Christian Dogma. In *God Struck Me Dead: Religious Conversion Experiences and Autobiographies of Ex-Slaves,* ed. Charles S. Johnson, pp. iv–xi. Social Science Source Documents no. 2. Nashville, Tenn.: Social Science Institute, Fisk University.

Raichelson, Richard M. 1975. Black Religious Folksong: A Study in Generic and Social Change. Ph.D. diss., University of Pennsylvania.

Ramsey, Frederic, Jr. 1960. *Been Here and Gone.* New Brunswick, N.J.: Rutgers University Press.

Rawick, George P., ed. 1972. *The American Slave: A Composite Autobiography.* 19 vols. Contributions to Afro-American and African Studies, no. 11. Westport, Conn.: Greenwood Publishing Company.

——. 1977. *The American Slave: A Composite Autobiography,* supplement series 1. 12 vols. Contributions to Afro-American and African Studies, no. 35. Westport, Conn.: Greenwood Press.

Raymond, Charles A. 1863. The Religious Life of the Negro Slave. *Harper's New Monthly Magazine* 27:479–85, 676–82, 816–25.

Reagon, Bernice Johnson. 1989. Sing Till the Power: The Survival of the Congregational Singing Tradition. In *Contemporary Black American Congregational Song and Worship Traditions: A Study in Nineteenth- and Twentieth-Century Oral Transmission,* pp. 3–17. Washington, D.C.: Smithsonian Institution.

——. 1992a. William Herbert Brewster: Rememberings. In *We'll Understand It Better By and By: Pioneering African American Gospel Composers,* ed. Bernice Johnson Reagon, pp. 185–209. Washington, D.C.: Smithsonian Institution Press.

——, ed. 1992b. *We'll Understand It Better By and By: Pioneering African American Gospel Composers.* Washington, D.C.: Smithsonian Institution Press.

Reisman, Karl. 1974. Contrapuntal Conversations in an Antiguan Village. In *Explorations in the Ethnography of Speaking,* ed. Richard Bauman and Joel Sherzer, pp. 110–24. Cambridge: Cambridge University Press.

Richardson, W. Lawrence. 1985a. Personal conversation. Washington, D.C., June 29.

——. 1985b. Personal conversation. Washington, D.C., July 3.

——. 1986. Personal conversation. Washington, D.C., July 1.

Ricks, George Robinson. [1960] 1977. *Some Aspects of the Religious Music of the United States Negro: An Ethnomusicological Study with Special Emphasis on the Gospel Tradition.* Ph.D. diss., Northwestern University. Reprint, New York: Arno Press.

Ridington, Robin. 1990. *Little Bit Know Something: Stories in a Language of Anthropology.* Iowa City: University of Iowa Press.

Rippon, John. 1794. *The Baptist Annual Register for 1790, 1791, 1792, and Part of 1794. Including Sketches of the State of Religion Among Different Denominations of Good Men at Home and Abroad.* London: n.p.

Robinson, Beverly J. 1997. Faith Is the Key and Prayer Unlocks the Door: Prayer in African American Life. *Journal of American Folklore* 110:408–14.

Rosaldo, Renato. 1986. Ilongot Hunting as Story and Experience. In *The Anthropology of Experience*, ed. Victor W. Turner and Edward M. Bruner, pp. 97–138. Urbana: University of Illinois Press.

Rose, Dan. 1987. *Black American Street Life: South Philadelphia, 1696–1971*. Philadelphia: University of Pennsylvania Press.

Rosenbaum, Art. 1998. *Shout Because You're Free: The African American Ring Shout Tradition in Coastal Georgia*. Athens: University of Georgia Press.

Rosenberg, Bruce A. 1970. The Formulaic Quality of Spontaneous Sermons. *Journal of American Folklore* 83:3–20.

——. 1974. The Psychology of the Spiritual Sermon. In *Religious Movements in Contemporary America*, ed. Irving I. Zaretsky and Mark P. Leone, pp. 135–49. Princeton, N.J.: Princeton University Press.

——. 1975. Oral Sermons and Oral Narrative. In *Folklore: Performance and Communication*, ed. Dan Ben-Amos and Kenneth S. Goldstein, pp. 75–101. The Hague: Mouton.

——. 1988. *Can These Bones Live? The Art of the American Folk Preacher*. Rev. ed. Urbana: University of Illinois Press.

Rosenberg, Jan. 1991. When Praises Go Up, Blessings Come Down . . . : The Appreciation Service. *TRAHCS: The Newsletter of the Texarkana Regional Arts and Humanities Council, Inc.* 11 (3):12–15.

Rouget, Gilbert. 1985. *Music and Trance: A Theory of the Relations Between Music and Possession*. Revised by Brunhilde Biebuyck and Gilbert Rouget. Trans. Brunhilde Biebuyck. Chicago: University of Chicago Press.

Rubman, Kerill Leslie. 1980. From "Jubilee" to "Gospel" in Black Male Quartet Singing. Master's thesis, University of North Carolina at Chapel Hill.

Samarin, William J. 1972a. Language in Religion and the Study of Religion. *Linguistica Biblica* 20:18–29.

——. 1972b. *Tongues of Men and Angels: The Religious Language of Pentecostalism*. New York: Macmillan.

——. 1976. The Language of Religion. In *Language and Religious Practice*, ed. William J. Samarin, pp. 3–13. Rowley, Mass.: Newbury House.

Saulter, Charles R., ed. 1939. *Bowles Book of Poems for All Occasions, With Welcome Addresses and Responses*. Chicago: Bowles Music House.

Saxon, Lyle, Edward Dreyer, and Robert Tallant, eds. 1945. *Gumbo Ya-Ya: A Collection of Louisiana Folk Tales*. Boston: Houghton Mifflin.

Schieffelin, Edward L. 1985. Performance and the Cultural Construction of Reality. *American Ethnologist* 12:707–24.

Schwerin, Jules. 1992. *Got To Tell It: Mahalia Jackson, Queen of Gospel*. New York: Oxford University Press.

Sellars, Celester, and Connie Steadman. 1994. Personal conversation. Carrboro, N.C., March 29.

Seroff, Doug. 1980a. *Birmingham Quartet Anthology: Jefferson County, Alabama (1926–1953)*. Notes to Clanka Lanka LP albums CL-144,001/002. Stockholm: Clanka Lanka Records.

——. 1980b. Willie Johnson (1913–1980). June record auction list, pp. 48–49. Goodlettsville, Tenn.: Doug Seroff.

——. 1985. On the Battlefield: Gospel Quartets in Jefferson County, Alabama. In *Repercussions: A Celebration of African-American Music*, ed. Geoffrey Haydon and Dennis Marks, pp. 30–53. London: Century Publishing.

——. 1988. *Gospel Arts Day, Nashville: A Special Commemoration*. Nashville: Nashville Gospel Ministries.

Smitherman, Geneva. 1977. *Talkin and Testifyin: The Language of Black America*. Boston: Houghton Mifflin.

Sobel, Mechal. 1988. *Trabelin' On: The Slave Journey to an Afro-Baptist Faith*. Rev. ed. Princeton, N.J.: Princeton University Press.

Spalding, Henry D., ed. 1972. *Encyclopedia of Black Folklore and Humor*. Middle Village, N.Y.: Jonathan David Publishers.

Spaulding, Henry G. 1863. Under the Palmetto. *Continental Monthly* 4:188–203.

Spencer, Jon Michael. 1993. *Blues and Evil*. Knoxville: University of Tennessee Press.

Spivey, Evangelist Wendell. 1988. Sermon delivered at a Mount Calvary Holy Church revival meeting. Durham, N.C., March 3.

Steadman, Connie. 1994. Personal conversation. Chapel Hill, N.C., April 20.

Steiner, Roland. 1900. Sol Lockheart's Call. *Journal of American Folklore* 13:67–70.

Stewart, Carrie. 1978. Personal conversation. Franklin, N.C., November 29.

Stoller, Paul. 1989. *The Taste of Ethnographic Things: The Senses in Anthropology*. Philadelphia: University of Pennsylvania Press.

Stoller, Paul, and Cheryl Olkes. 1987. *In Sorcery's Shadow: A Memoir of Apprenticeship Among the Songhay of Niger*. Chicago: University of Chicago Press.

Sturtevant, William C. 1968. Categories, Percussion and Physiology. *Man* n.s. 3:133–34.

Talley, Thomas W. 1993. *The Negro Traditions*. Edited with an introduction by Charles K. Wolfe and Laura C. Jarmon. Knoxville: University of Tennessee Press.

Tallmadge, William H. 1961. Dr. Watts and Mahalia Jackson—The Development, Decline, and Survival of a Folk Style in America. *Ethnomusicology* 5:95–99.

Tedlock, Dennis. 1971. On the Translation of Style in Oral Narrative. *Journal of American Folklore* 84:114–33.

——. 1976. From Prayer to Reprimand. In *Language in Religious Practice*, ed. William J. Samarin, pp. 72–83. Rowley, Mass.: Newbury House.

——. 1983. *The Spoken Word and the Work of Interpretation*. Philadelphia: University of Pennsylvania Press.

Thomas, James. 1993. Personal conversation. Raleigh, N.C., March 4.

Thompson, Robert Farris. 1966. An Aesthetic of the Cool: West African Dance. *African Forum* 2:85–102.

——. 1974. *African Art in Motion: Icon and Act*. Los Angeles: University of California Press.

——. 1983. *Flash of the Spirit: African and Afro-American Art and Philosophy*. New York: Random House.

Thompson, Robert Farris, and Joseph Cornet. 1981. *The Four Moments of the Sun: Kongo Art in Two Worlds*. Washington, D.C.: National Gallery of Art.

Thrower, Henry "Duke." 1982. Personal conversation. Philadelphia, March 13.

Titon, Jeff Todd. 1980. The Life Story. *Journal of American Folklore* 93:276–92.

——. 1988. *Powerhouse for God: Speech, Chant, and Song in an Appalachian Baptist Church*. Austin: University of Texas Press.

Tullos, Allen, Daniel W. Patterson, and Tom Davenport. 1989a. *A Singing Stream: A Black Family Chronicle*. A special issue of the *North Carolina Folklore Journal* 36:1–62.

——. 1989b. A Singing Stream: A Black Family Chronicle—Background and Commentary. In *A Singing Stream: A Black Family Chronicle*, a special issue of the *North Carolina Folklore Journal* 36:1–36.

Turner, Edith. 1994. A Visible Spirit Form in Zambia. In *Being Changed by Cross-Cultural Encounters: The Anthropology of Extraordinary Experience*, ed. David E. Young and Jean-Guy Goulet, pp. 71–95. Peterborough, Ontario: Broadview Press.

——. 1995. I Refuse to Doubt: An Inuit Healer Finds a Listener. In *Bridges to Humanity: Narratives on Anthropology and Friendship*, ed. Bruce Grindal and Frank Salamone, pp. 231–51. Prospect Heights, Ill.: Waveland Press.

Turner, Edith, with William Blodgett, Singleton Kahona, and Fideli Benwa. 1992. *Experiencing Ritual: A New Interpretation of African Healing*. Philadelphia: University of Pennsylvania Press.

Turner, Victor W. 1982. *From Ritual to Theatre: The Human Seriousness of Play*. New York: Performing Arts Journal Publications.

——. 1986. Dewey, Dilthey, and Drama: An Essay in the Anthropology of Experience. In *The Anthropology of Experience*, ed. Victor W. Turner and Edward M. Bruner, pp. 33–44. Urbana: University of Illinois Press.

Turner, Victor W., and Edward M. Bruner, eds. 1986. *The Anthropology of Experience*. Urbana: University of Illinois Press.

Turner, William Clair, Jr. 1984. The United Holy Church of America: A Study in Black Holiness-Pentecostalism. Ph.D. diss., Duke University.

Tybout, Ella Middleton. 1904. *Poketown People, or Parables in Black*. Philadelphia: J. B. Lippincott.

Tyler, Stephen A. 1986. Post-Modern Ethnography: From Document of the Occult to Occult Document. In *Writing Culture*, ed. James Clifford and George E. Marcus, pp. 122–40. Berkeley: University of California Press.

United Choral Ensemble. 1987. Remarks delivered at the sixteenth anniversary of the Gilchrist Family. Durham, N.C., September 27.

Urban, Greg. 1982. The Semiotics of Two Speech Styles in Shokleng. Sociolinguistic working paper no. 103, Southwest Educational Development Laboratory, Austin, Texas.

Vereen, Joe. 1988. Personal conversation. Durham, N.C., February 9.

Wahlman, Maude Southwell. 1993. *Signs and Symbols: African Images in African-American Quilts*. New York: Studio Books.

Walker, Sheila S. 1972. *Ceremonial Spirit Possession in Africa and Afro-America*. Leiden: E. J. Brill.

Walker, William. 1946a. *Walker's All Religious Poem Book No. 35*. Chicago: William Walker.

——. 1946b. *Walker's Church Special Book No. 26: Welcome Addresses, Responses, Public Speeches and Poems for All Occasions*. Chicago: William Walker.

——. 1946c. *Walker's No. 1 Welcome: 13 Welcomes, 13 Responds for All Occasions*. Chicago: William Walker.

——. 1969. *Walker's Book of Books, Number 2: Poems & Addresses for All Occasions*. Chicago: Walker's House of Poetry.

——. 1971. *Walker's No. 2 Welcome Address and Respond Book: 21 Welcomes and 21 Responds for 21 Different Occasions*. Chicago: William Walker.

——. 1974. *Walker's Program Guide*. Chicago: William Walker.

Walker, Wyatt Tee. 1979. *"Somebody's Calling My Name": Black Sacred Music and Social Change*. Valley Forge, Pa.: Judson Press.

Wallace, Joseph "Jojo." 1993. Personal conversation. Durham, N.C., February 16.

Washington, Joseph R., Jr. 1964. *Black Religion: The Negro and Christianity in the United States*. Boston: Beacon Press.

Waters, Wilson, and Robert Hamlett. 1986. Personal conversation. Arlington, Va., July 1.

Watts, Isaac. 1793. *Hymns and Spiritual Songs, in Three Books*. London: n.p.

White, Newman I. 1928. *American Negro Folk-Songs*. Cambridge: Harvard University Press.

Wigger, John H. 1998. *Taking Heaven by Storm: Methodism and the Rise of Popular Christianity in America*. New York: Oxford University Press.

Williams, Melvin D. 1974. *Community in a Black Pentecostal Church: An Anthropological Study*. Prospect Heights, Ill.: Waveland Press.

Williams, Rachel. 1988. Prayer delivered at a gospel program at Mount Calvary Holy Church. Durham, N.C., February 6.

Williams, William. 1973. *The Experience Meeting*. Trans. B. Lloyd-Jones. London: Evangelical Press.

Williams-Jones, Pearl. 1970. Afro-American Gospel Music: A Brief Historical and Analytical Survey (1930–1970). In *Development of Materials for a One-Year Course in African Music for the General Undergraduate Student*, ed. Vada E. Butcher et al., pp. 199–219. Washington, D.C.: Office of Education, Bureau of Research, U.S. Department of Health, Education, and Welfare.

Work, John W. 1949. Changing Patterns in Negro Folk Songs. *Journal of American Folklore* 62:136–44.

——, ed. 1940. *American Negro Songs and Spirituals*. New York: Howell, Soskin.

Wyman, Lillie B. Chace. 1891. Colored Churches and Schools in the South. *New England Magazine* n.s. 3:785–96.

Yarborough, Evangelist Deborah. 1988. Remarks made at a revival at Mount Calvary Holy Church. Durham, N.C., March 4.

Yarger, Lenore. 1994. The Morning Star Sang to God: Marion William's Ministry of Gospel Music. *The Other Side*, May-June, pp. 24–30.

Yelverton, Bishop Frizelle. 1987. Personal conversation. Durham, N.C., December 9.

——. 1988. Sermon delivered at Mount Calvary Holy Church. Durham, N.C., February 28.

Young, Alan. 1997. *Woke Me Up This Morning: Black Gospel Singers and the Gospel Life*. Jackson: University Press of Mississippi.

Young, David E., and Jean-Guy Goulet. 1994a. Theoretical and Methodological Issues. In *Being Changed by Cross-Cultural Encounters: The Anthropology of Extraordinary Experience*, ed. David E. Young and Jean-Guy Goulet, pp. 298–335. Peterborough, Ontario: Broadview Press.

——, eds. 1994b. *Being Changed by Cross-Cultural Encounters: The Anthropology of Extraordinary Experience*. Peterborough, Ontario: Broadview Press.

Young, Rev. Liggonia. 1984. Personal conversation. Durham, N.C., September 8.

Acknowledgments

This book began with a puzzle and a prophecy. The puzzle arose at the closing of a Tuesday evening service at Philadelphia's First Church of Love, Faith and Deliverance. I had attended the deeply spiritual service with Diane Goldstein, a classmate and close friend. As we were making our way to the exit at the service's close, a young woman stopped us and asked us to wait for a moment. "The pastor has something for you," she said to me. A bit surprised—as I had never before visited the church and knew its pastor, Rosie Wallace Brown, only by reputation—I waited. Within minutes, Pastor Brown was stepping toward me, holding something in her outstretched hand. "You'll need these," she said warmly as she pressed two cassette tapes into my hands. "One is tonight's service; the other is last Sunday's." Looking down at the carefully labeled tapes, I didn't know what to say. "Why was she giving these to me?" I wondered. "Why just me, and not Diane? And why did she say that I'd *need* them?" Stumbling a bit in my thanks, I introduced myself and Diane, and then asked Pastor Brown if I could speak with her further. We set up an appointment for the following week.

Seven days later, Pastor Brown and I sat in her church office and talked for almost two hours. After finally turning off the tape recorder, we chatted for a few more minutes and then joined together in prayer. Standing to leave, I felt awash in the quiet exhilaration that marks those moments when one's understandings have been wholly reframed. But Pastor Brown bade me to sit down, indicating that more needed to be said. "You've stepped onto a new path," she announced, her eyes smiling. "The Spirit has led me to know that your path has changed. I don't know what it was or what it will be, but this day has marked a change. Remember that, Glenn. You'll understand it after a while. You'll know."

I didn't realize what this shift in destiny might entail until about fourteen months later. That was when I called my dissertation adviser and announced that I was changing my topic to gospel—after having spent the previous five years preparing to write about memory, history, and the blues. That's also when I recalled Pastor Brown's words. My path *had* changed.

That path has taken many twists since then. I returned home to North Carolina, finished the dissertation, married my colleague and soulmate, began teaching at Chapel Hill, helped bring two wonderful girls into this world, and pursued the inquiry that yielded this book. But as the book's subject makes evident, the twists haven't turned me from the path. Pastor Brown was right on both counts. The path had changed . . . and I *did* need that tape. As you'll soon see, that taped Tuesday night service makes a welcome appearance in Chapter 9.

Pastor Brown's guidance has found constant confirmation and elaboration in the years since that chance visit in 1983. More saints than I can possibly name—singers, pastors, evangelists, church mothers, radio announcers, emcees, deacons, deaconesses, and many others—have contributed to this work, generously joining as collaborators in a shared effort to unfold the workings of faith and spiritual experience. Their openness to inquiry, patience in answering my clumsily worded questions, willingness to read, comment upon, and add to the emergent manuscript, and gentle support throughout the process have made this as much their work as my own. As a student of their wisdom, I am deeply in their debt.

A few of these friends and co-authors merit special acknowledgment. The Branchettes—Sister Ethel Elliott and Sister Lena Mae Perry—have been particularly generous with their time and counsel, always offering words of encouragement and always inspiring with the anointed power of their singing. Their twentieth anniversary service provided the frame for this work, and their readily offered insights helped keep it on track in the ensuing years. Their families also deserve special thanks, particularly the ever-gracious Willa Elliott and the always smiling Lena Williams. Finally, I must acknowledge my debt to Pastor David N. Atkinson and the congregation at Long Branch Disciple Church, who allowed us to invade their sanctuary with recorder, microphones, flash, and cameras. If anyone can claim this book as their own, it would be the saints at Long Branch.

Evangelist Evelyn Gilchrist has served as a spiritual and intellectual guide throughout the process of writing. As one of the manuscript's initial readers, Evangelist Gilchrist generously agreed to review each chapter as it emerged. Her insights, suggestions, and eloquent words mark nearly every chapter. So too do those of Joseph "Jojo" Wallace, the manuscript's second reader. In many ways, Brother Wallace—longtime guitarist and singer with the Sensational Nightingales—exemplifies the artist who "lives the life he sings about"; his effervescent personality and incisive recommendations subtly framed the entire project. Both of these consultants freely assumed the reins of engaged co-authorship, treating the book as testimony whose mission they wanted to help craft.

I must also thank the late Elder W. Lawrence Richardson, lead singer with the Fairfield Four. In our conversations prior to his passing, Elder Richardson regularly and gently pointed out my many misguided assumptions; I could always depend on him to cut through extraneous talk to get to the spiritual heart of the matter. Much the same could be said of Bishop Frizelle Yelverton, pastor of Durham's Mount Calvary Holy Church. Bishop Yelverton's wise words, piercing insights, and discerning eye have greatly deepened my understanding of the Spirit. In like manner, Evangelist Rachel Green—another Mount Calvary member—has also guided my understanding. Evangelist Green's constant encouragements helped keep the book's message "real," while her Saturday radio broadcasts have been a wellspring of new understandings. I've also learned much from Evangelist Dorothy Jackson, the first emcee I met with the discernment and spiritual confidence to openly scold singers at commercial gospel programs for their "form and fashion" antics. I have often turned to Evangelist Jackson for guidance. Finally, I must thank Deacon Smiley Fletcher and Evangelist Sylvia Fletcher, who "adopted" me as a child of little understanding very early in the research process, and reengaged me as colleague and friend at the writing's close.

These are but a few of the many saints who guided me on this journey. I also owe a special debt to the members of the Fairfield Four (particularly Dickie Freeman, James Hill, Wilson Waters, and the late Rev. Samuel McCrary) of Nashville; the Badgett Sisters of Yanceyville; the Sensational Cherubims and the Carolyn Bryant Ensemble of Philadelphia; the First Cosmopolitan All-Male Chorus and the Gospel Tones (especially lead singer Johnnie Faison) of Raleigh; the Sensational Nightingales, the Gilchrist Family, and the Gospel Jubilators of Durham; and the Golden Echoes of Creedmoor, all of whom taught me how to hear—and, more important, to *feel*—gospel singing. Joining them in this teaching process have been the announcers at radio stations WSRC "Love 1410" and WNNL "The Light" 103.9, who have kept my ears tuned and my spirits high over many long hours behind the wheel.

I also owe special thanks to Rev. David Bell, Rev. Carolyn Bryant, Pastor Ella Jean Burnett, Deacon Willie Eldridge, Robert Faulk, Pastor James Gilchrist, Rev. Z. D. Harris, Jackie Jackson, Mother Bertha Landis, Claude and John Landis, Evangelist Hattie Lofton, Pastor Deborah Yarborough Obie, Myra V. Simmons, James Thomas, Deacon Joe Vereen, Mirdis Walker, and the congregations of Durham's Mount Calvary Holy Church and Ecclesia House of Prayer. Finally, to close this list of saints, I must thank Sister Suphronia Cheek, whose constant smile, generous spirit, and kind counsel truly mark her as a child of God. Sister Cheek's spirit has never failed to provide inspiration.

Just as the saints have served as consultants, collaborators, and co-authors, my colleagues and mentors in the academy have served as my intellectual advisers. When this journey began more than fifteen years ago, Kenny Goldstein, Roger Abrahams, Henry Glassie, Dell Hymes, John Roberts, and Don Yoder—all then at the University of Pennsylvania—helped guide my first faltering steps, encouraging me to engage ethnography with passion, sensitivity, and a radical openness to new understandings. Their words continue to echo in my head these many years later; as I reread the manuscript, I can see each of them stepping silently through the pages, subtly shaping both strategy and prose. The mentor whose steps are perhaps a bit less silent than the rest is David Hufford, whose practical phenomenology has guided my approach to belief and spiritual experience. David offers both a means for exploring and a way of writing about encounters with the sacred; his unshirking commitment to public outreach, coupled with his constant challenge to disbelief that poses as "objectivity," makes him a mentor well worth emulating.

Since I've been teaching at the University of North Carolina, I've benefited from conversations with many valued colleagues. I've learned to expect nothing but encouragement and insight from Dan and Beverly Patterson, whose discerning remarks and gentle spirits never fail to spark reflection while bringing a smile. Terry Zug—the outgoing chair of UNC's Curriculum in Folklore—has done a remarkable job of keeping the hounds of bureaucracy at bay, and in so doing allowed me valuable time to work on this manuscript. For that, for his friendship, and for his good spirits in putting up with my ability to miss every deadline set before me, I am deeply thankful. Assisting Terry in the Herculean task of holding off the bureaucracy has been Debbie Simmons-Cahan, who has often guided me through the arcane world of university governance, always making the journey seem simple. Somehow, Debbie manages to buoy spirits in even the most depressing of times. Much the same could be said of Jim Peacock, whose prodigious knowledge and penetrating insights are grafted onto a most gracious soul. To all of these colleagues and friends, I owe a deep debt of thanks.

Of course, there are many, many others. Laurie Maffly-Kipp has never ceased to amaze me with her easy command of African American religious history; this work has certainly benefited from the classes we've taught together. Diane Goldstein, who joined me at the First Church of Love, Faith and Deliverance when this journey began, has long been a wellspring of intellectual stimulation; many of the thoughts captured on these pages emerged from long (and always challenging) conversations with Diane. I would also have to include Eric Lassiter in this group, as a colleague whose commitment to collaborative ethnography has long served as a source of inspiration; Eric's work with Kiowa singers offers a model for consultant engagement and is helping to chart the future of a truly responsible ethnography. I owe additional thanks to Bruce Winterhalder for lightening the load of departmental responsibility when I most needed to write; Dottie Holland for her encouragement and patience as the writing stretched on; Don Matthews and Russ Richey for their lessons on experience meetings and southern church history; the anonymous reviewers of this manuscript for their remarkably detailed readings and their helpful advice; the reference staffs at Duke's Van Pelt Library and UNC's Davis Library for their persistence, good humor, and constant willingness to find the seemingly unfindable; Rosetta Anderson of Malaco Records for her assistance in securing permissions; Sonya Hamm for keeping the spirit and the praises high in the mornings; and colleagues Bonnie O'Connor, Mal O'Connor, Doug De-Natale, and Peter Lowry for years of valued counsel. I also owe a deep debt to Marti Bowditch, who sustained me through the Philadelphia experience and enthusiastically supported the fieldwork that gave birth to this project. Finally, I want to thank the many students who have joined me in the "Art of Ethnography" seminar; their comments, critiques, and insights have helped shape and re-shape this manuscript in more ways than I could begin to count.

Additionally, I wish to acknowledge the Chapman Family Faculty Fellowship in

Recognition of Distinguished Teaching, from the Institute for the Arts and Humanities in the College of Arts and Sciences at UNC-Chapel Hill; their valuable support made much of this writing possible. I also want to thank UNC's University Research Council, which twice supported this project with publications grants.

When I began this work, I knew that words alone could never convey the spiritual and sensory fullness of worship. I also knew that photographs could capture some of the fullness that prose could barely begin to communicate. That's why I invited photographer Roland Freeman to join the project. Roland's ability to capture the spirit of African American aesthetics and lifeways is unmatched; he brings to his work both a tellingly sensitive eye and a rare ability to personably engage the subjects of his photographic gaze. His images lend a grace to this work that is matched only by the artistry of the singers discussed therein.

I would be remiss if I also didn't express my deepest gratitude to Patricia Smith, acquisitions editor at the University of Pennsylvania Press, who began asking about this manuscript long before it was written, and who gently and patiently shepherded it through creation, revision, and eventual submission. Patricia's faith in the work kept it alive over many long years. I also owe thanks to Noreen O'Connor, who guided my revisions with both grace and good humor.

Of course, none of this work would have been possible without the unflagging support of my parents, Charles and Rosalind Hinson, who laid the moral and spiritual foundation upon which this book was built. Their faith in my abilities far exceeds my own; their willingness to voice that faith has always been a welcome source of sustenance.

Out of all these contributors, this work owes its deepest debt to my love and my center, Sally Peterson. With patience and compassion far beyond what might rightfully be expected from any companion, Sally has stood by me, guided me, and endured me through years of research and writing. Always the first hearer of my thoughts and first reader of my words, she has been both intellectual and spiritual soulmate, walking alongside me on every step of this journey, keeping my spirits high and my soul happy. From caring for our girls when I was off attending gospel programs, to gently editing my wandering prose, to making time for my long hours of isolation at the computer, Sally made this all possible. Her insights wind silently through the manuscript, while her spirit sustains the whole work. My contributions to this manuscript should rightfully be considered *ours* . . .

Finally, highest thanksgiving goes to the Lord, who turned my path in the first place and has guided my steps ever since.

Index

authenticity, assessing spiritual (*cont.*) ion"; performance, inauthentic; performance, assessing authenticity of; shouting, for show; "show"

Badgett Sisters, 117
Barney, Deborah, 340 n.7, 356 nn.9, 11, 357 nn.13–15, 362 n.1
Barthes, Roland, 373 n.8
Bateson, Mary Catherine, 345 n.8
Bauman, Richard, 336 n.9, 363 n.6, 370 n.41
Beasley, Paul, 132–34
beat, 345 n.11; distracts from the sung message, 101–3, 105–6, 123, 276; stirs emotions, 221, 289. *See also* shout songs; "shout-time"
belief: as mystery, 12, 26; relationship to experience and knowledge, 7, 9–11, 25–28
Bell, Rev. David H., 232, 238, 304
benediction, 317, 321–22
Bennett, Orlena, *158*, *316*
Benson Chapel Choir, 185, 208, 210
Bethel Church of Christ Written in Heaven, 18
Bible. *See* scripture; scripture reading
Blom, Jan-Petter, 367 n.25
Booth, Josephine, 232
Bowers, Alexander, 368 n.30
Boyer, Horace C., 340 n.5, 341 n.3, 345 n.11, 345 n.15, 350 n.5, 358 n.2, 366 n.12
Bracey, Mary, 149–51, 153–4, 166, 190, 203–7, *209*, 210, 227, 285, 366 n.2
Bracey, Samuel, 203–8, *209*, 210, 227
Bracey Singers, 185, 187, 203–8, *209*, 210
Branchettes, *iv*, 5, *6*, 32, 126, 150, 189–90, 196, 264, 285–86, *287*, 288, *316*, 317. *See also* Elliott, Ethel; Perry, Lena Mae
Brenneis, Donald, 336 n.2
Brewster, Rev. W. Herbert, 109, 121
Brown, James, 240, 364 n.14
Brown, Pastor Rosie Wallace, 103–5, 212–19, 229, 276, 277, 278
Bryant, Rev. Carolyn, 18–19
Burnim, Mellonee, 341 n.6, 342 n.11, 352 n.19, 357 n.13, 363 n.11

Caesar, Pastor Shirley, 26, 142, 339 n.15, 340 n.2 (Ch. 4), 345 n.14, 352 n.23, 355 n.5, 358 n.19, 366 n.6
call to preach, 41, 78, 80, 160, 175, 212, 283
Canton Spirituals, 115
Cash, Rev. Louis, 64–65
Castaneda, Carlos, 373 n.12
Chernoff, John M., 354 n.9

"Christ Jesus Paid the Debt That I Could Never Pay," 104
church: nonshouting, 136; as state of worshipful communion, 36, 47, 168, 263, 319; sanctified, early history of, 348, n.19, 350 n.3; "*the* church" as sanctified fellowship, 135–36, 311. *See also* fellowship of the saved; "having church"
Church of God in Christ (C.O.G.I.C.), 135–36, 341 n.3, 343 n.16, 363 n.7
Clouds of Harmony, *197*
Coley, William, *186*, 233, *234*
collaborative communication: balance of self and Spirit, 65, 71, 75, 83, 254, 280, 323; degrees of, 280–81, 283, 304–5, 370 n.40, 372 n.3 (Ch. 19); intended audience, 79, 283, 340 n.8; Spirit adds affective power to words, 62, 68–70, 79, 211–12, 221, 236, 281, 283, 305; Spirit speaks to and through, 77–79, 228–29, 302–5, 323. *See also* inspiration; revelation
competition: in shouting, 140, 146, 353 n.24; in singing, 198–200, 220; "song battles" and "quartet contests," 198–99, 359 nn.5, 7
congregations: equality of members, 41–42, 48, 61, 99, 129, 130–31, 144–45, 153, 160, 166, 177, 179, 351 n.17, 361 n.4; diversity of members, 62, 71, 95–96, 136, 148, 168; include deceivers and Satan's workers, 122, 138; seditty, 135, 227, 350 n.3; spirit of hierarchy invoked among, 99–100. *See also* accord; "dead" congregations
contemporary gospel, 120, 358 n.2
conversation: as cultural style, 58, 339 n.15; encouragements to engage in, 49–51, 97–98, 101, 132, 134, 155, 157, 160–61, 164–65, 177–78, 184, 296–99, 354 n.2; includes voices, music, and motion, 88–89, 155–56, 161, 177–80; no single path to communion, 159; pews and cross-aisle, 34–36, 39, 43, 45–46, 48, 52, 53–54, 58, 155, 164–65, 211, 250, 265, 279; "praises go up, blessings come down," 3, 67, 220; silent, with the Spirit, 2–3, 16, 39, 54, 58–59, 202, 325, 342 n.1; simultaneous, with Spirit and saints, 155–57, 161; Spirit and believer, 2, 16, 36–37, 157, 162, 320. *See also* conversational engagement; intensity; music; singing
conversational engagement, 49–50, 59–60, 88–89, 155–56, 159, 325; interlock, 161–

62, 344 nn.1 (Ch. 9), 3, 354 nn.7, 9; and thickening textures, 89, 156. *See also* conversation

conversion, 11, 36, 169; accounts of, 15–16, 258, 297, 338 n.6, 369 n.34; false, 139–40, 169, 338 n.6, 343 n.17, 351 n.11; prerequisite for the flow, 81–82; through song, 80, 212, 223, 358 n.18; ushers in new reality, 319

Courlander, Harold, 353 n.28, 365 n.31, 368 n.30

cross-aisle, 32, 41–42, 341 n.9

crossroads. *See* Satan, selling soul to

dance. *See* holy dance

Darnell, Regna, 363 n.6

David, Jonathan, 367 n.14

Davis Singers, 181, 210

Davis, Gerald L., 343 n.15, 357 n.17, 360 n.1

Davis, Louise "Candy," 156

Daye, Rev. W. A., 5

"dead batteries," 96

"dead" congregations, 50, 72, 90, 97–98, 156, 160–61, 352 n.20. *See also* congregations; services, "dry"

Denkins, Deacon Edward, 19, 65, 70, 73, 91, 93, 106, 116, 280–81

denomination: not indicative of belief, 136; unimportance in worship, 131–37, 350 n.4; variety at Branchettes' anniversary, 136

devil. *See* Satan

devotional leaders, 42, 71, 166, 170; provisionally declaring distance from congregation, 99, 166; as proxy for preacher, 99. *See also* prayer leaders

devotional service (devotions), 34–40, 56–57, 90, 152, 166–67, 201–2, 320–21, 340 nn.4–5, 341 n.3, 345 n.15; congregational singing in, 90, 92, 94; cycle of shifting roles, 99, 166; sequence of, 39, 40, 46–47, 72, 94; structure denies hierarchy, 99, 144; treated as meaningless ritual, 96

Dickens, Charles, 375 n.22

Dillard, J. L., 342 n.1

disbelief: academic strategies of, 330–34; characterizes most ethnographic investigation, 322–24, 330; "explaining away" the supernatural, 11, 331–34, 335 n.2; often precedes conversion, 11

discernment, 222; gift of, 78, 102, 141, 262; of spiritual authenticity, 120–21, 141, 172, 254, 261–62. *See also* gifts of the Spirit

disobedience, punishment for spiritual, 169

"Don't Let Nobody Turn You 'Round," 84–88

"Doors of the Church Are Open, The," 181

Dorsey, Thomas A., 137, 183, 346 n.16, 346 n.22, 358 n.21

doubt, merits of, 140

dreams and visions, 113, 114, 320, 347 n.9

dress, 30, 32–33, 98, 146, 179–80, 264, 319, 357 n.13; as channel for witness, 174; congregational expectations regarding, 173–74, 356 nn.11–12, 358 n.5; as means of conveying individuality, 174

drive ("riff," "repeat," "working section"), 132, 291, 368 n.29; congregational response to, 294; defined, 292; "driving" the emotions, 276, 295–96, 299–300; examples of, 269–70, 272–73, 297–98; frequency of, 295; history of, 293, 367 n.26, 368 n.30; other terms for, 293; "overdrive," 272–73, 300; phrase, 292–93, 299–301, 369 n.36; prophetic anointing in, 294, 301, 304–5; questions posed in, 297–300, 369 n.35; replicates sound and form of elevation, 294; self-referencing in, 296, 297–99, 369 n.34; tonal structure of, 270, 272, 366 n.2; as way to sharpen devotional focus, 294, 301. *See also* elevation; intensity; revelation

Du Bois, W. E. B., 339 n.14

Ebenezer Gospel Choir, *186*

Eldridge, Deacon Willie H., 53–56, 58, 59, 61, 63, 72, 74–83, *76*, 84, 131, 166, 183, 204, 228, 237, 255–56, 285, 305, 319, 344 n.2 (Ch. 8)

elevation: congregation's role in, 289, 291; dangers of self-willed, 289; defined, 206, 280, 370 n.40; elevating and *being* elevated, 280, 282–83, 291–92; feelings linger, 307, 321; guided by God, 282–83, 288, 304–5; in prayer, 54–55, 68, 71–72; in preaching, 71, 206, 282, 290, 301–5; in singing, 202, 206–7, 266–75, 280, 289–90, 302–3, 367 n.26; sounds of, 71–72, 281, 284–85, 290, 294, 343 nn.15–16; as spiritual collaboration, 280–81, 282–83, 286, 288; strategic, 288–90, 293–94, 367 nn.25–26. *See also* drive; experience, of elevation; intensity; singing; singing, congregational

Elliott, Bridgett, *316*

Elliott, Ethel, 32, 34, *35*, 41, 53, 61, 136–37, 149, 152, 166, 208, 222–24, 228, 286, *287*, 314–15, *316*, 321. *See also* Branchettes

Elliott, Willa, *316*

emcee. *See* master of ceremonies

"emotionalism," 20

emotions: deceptive nature of, 20, 22–23, 139–40; functional analyses of, 339 n.14; manipulating, 66, 218, 239–41, 250–51, 295–96, 299–300, 363 n.11, 364 n.20; and the "mental" self, 24, 223; ministering to, 218; not letting override ministry and praise, 104; respond to the beat, 101–3; responsibility to guide, 211–12; shallowness of, 23, 67, 102, 217–18, 276; spiritual description in terms of, 140; trajectory of, in worship, 130, 187; triggering shouts, 22–23, 71, 101, 139–40, 252, 261. *See also* experience; intensity; joy; self, three-part model; sincerity

enjoyment. *See* joy

entertainment, 4, 181, 241, 248, 360 n.9, 363 n.7; disclaimers of, 198, 232, 237; "entertainment crowd," 137; expectation of, 62, 96, 137, 138, 223; as "just performance," 237. *See also* "form or fashion"; performance, inauthentic; "show"

ethnography: avoids experience, 7–8, 12, 324, 327–28, 373 n.3; avoids the supernatural, 330, 333–34, 373 n.10, 375 n.18; collaborative, 324–25, 328, 334, 371 n.1 (Ch. 18); explores experience, 327–28, 372 n.4; and objectivity, 322–24, 328, 334; and relativism, 324, 330, 375 n.19; seeking experiential common-ground, 329–30, 333; strategies of disbelief, 330–34, 374 nn.15–16; unfolds from position of disbelief, 12–13, 324, 333–34, 374 nn.14–15

ethnography of communication, 7, 336 n.9

Evans-Pritchard, E. E., 374 n.15, 375 n.18

Everready Singers, 286

experience, 5–7, 16–19, 23–24, 25, 27, 38, 42; academic approaches to, 327–28, 372 nn.1–2; academic avoidance of, 7–8, 12, 20, 324, 330–31; addressing immediacy of, 328; born of emotion, 23–24, 67, 140; centers worship, 322; critical assessment of source, 24; description hinges on soul's status, 18–19; of elevation, 206, 280–83, 286, 288–89, 291–92, 301–5; explaining away supernatural, 331–34, 374 nn.15–16, 375 n.18; as grounds for knowledge, 7–8, 9–10, 71, 113–14, 319, 322–23; inability to read from "behavior," 38, 139, 142; individual, as irreducible denominator of existence,

327; language of, 9, 15, 25, 153, 321; narrated, measured against own experience, 329; of praising, 155; recounted as testimony, 328–29; relationship to belief and knowledge, 10, 27–28; shaped by tradition and tellability, 331–32, 338 n.6, 374 n.16; of singing, 80–90, 92–93, 100–101, 219; uniqueness of holy, 323; untellability of holy, 17–19. *See also* anointment; elevation; emotions; intensity; knowing; revelation; shouting

experience meetings, 14–16, 337 n.4 (Ch. 3), 338 n.8

experiences. *See* testimonies

Fairfield Four, 40, 200, 233, 274, 341 n.5

Faison, Eddie, 308, 310

Faison, Johnnie, 264–74, *265, 271,* 279, 285, 288, 293, 308

Farley, J. J., 352 n.22

Faulk, B. Robert, 249, 258–61, 274, 283–84

feeling. *See* anointment; emotions; joy

fellowship of the saved, 131, 304, 305. *See also* church; denomination

Fernandez, James, 372 n.4

"fire in my bones," 11, 18, 51, 140, 276, 325, 338 n.11

First Church of Love, Faith and Deliverance, 103–5, 212, 276

Fletcher, Smiley, 116, 226–27, 238, 245, 249, 257, 290, 361 n.4

focus, devotional: and accord, 89, 159–60, 275, 320; and displayed intensity, 50, 289; and emotional tone, 187; and emotional trajectories, 200–202; fostered by conversations in the pews, 156; fostered by prayer and testimony, 58–60, 352 n.20; fostered by song, 3, 58–59, 89–90, 92–93, 105–6, 192, 275, 277, 321; invites the Spirit, 3, 95, 157, 274, 305; passionate engagement as vehicle of, 154; and strategic song elevations, 280, 283, 289–90, 294, 301. *See also* accord; anointment; inviting; conversation; conversational engagement; elevation

"form or fashion," 64, 65, 138, 144, 173, 202, 217–18, 252, 360 n.11, 363 n.11; allure of, 248–49, 289; and "clowning," 241, 254, 364 n.15; in commercial programs, 198, 295, 359 n.5, 359 n.7; dangers of, 144, 147, 225–27, 245, 252–53; disclaimers of, 49, 64, 198, 230–32, 262; and "form," 236–37, 362 n.8, 362 n.5; and "formality," 238, 363 n.9; manifestations of, 238–42, 244; and "style," 232–33, 235–36, 362 n.5; warnings against, 137, 141, 142, 245, 248, 254–55, 284; will increase, 263. *See also* authenticity, assessing spiritual; entertainment; performance, inauthentic; shouting, for show; "show"

Freeman, Isaac, 233, 274–75, 277, 288, 306, 368 n.30

Funk, Ray, 368 n.30

Gardner, Peter, 353 n.25

George, Elder David, 14, 337 n.1

"Get Right with God," 266–73, 279, 308, 310

"getting happy." *See* anointment

gifts of the Spirit, 47–48, 71, 131, 160, 319, 342 n.4, 365 n.32; gift of discernment, 78, 102, 141, 262; gift of prayer, 47, 61, 68, 212; gift of song, 110, 211–12, 321; nature of gifts, 65, 66, 211–12; responsibilities with, 218–19, 262, 355 n.2; without the anointing, 68, 212–20

Gilchrist, Evangelist Evelyn, 19, 211, 219–20, 232, 237, 262

Gilchrist Family, 64, 232

"Give Me That Old-time Religion," 107

"Give the Lord a Praise," 190–93

Glassie, Henry, 340 n.1 (Ch. 4)

"Glories of My Maker God, The," 111

glossolalia. *See* speaking in tongues

"Go slow, rise high, catch on fire, and sit down," 275–76, 278, 280, 288–89, 305, 306, 321, 367 n.26. *See also* elevation; intensity; programs, trajectory of; revelation; services, trajectory of; song sets, trajectory of

Gold, Peter, 343 n.15, 358 n.20

Golden Echoes, 255, 290, 367 n.28

Goldstein, Diane E., 367 n.15, 370 n.40

Goodman, Felicitas D., 375 n.21

Gospel Drivers [pseud.], 296–300

Gospel Express, 171

Gospel Keynotes, 115, 132–35

gospel music: "contemporary," 194; heart is sanctified, 136, 350 n.5; history, 349 n.25; preferred music of saved believers, 136; stylistic diversity, 193–94, 196, 198, 358 n.2; transcends denomination, 136–37

gospel programs. *See* programs; ticket programs

gospel singers: as emcees, 175; link group names with heaven, 116; scheduling per-

formances, 171, 355 n.4; unsaved, 141–43, 213–18, 226–27, 242–46, 248, 258

Gospel Tones, 185, 264–74, *265*, 279, 292–93, 308–9, 313, 315

Goulet, Jean-Guy, 371 n.1 (Ch. 19), 373 n.12, 375 nn.19–20

Grace A.M.E. Mass Choir, *86, 186*

Greater Joy Ensemble, 49–50

Greater Six Run Baptist Church, 230

Green, Evangelist Rachel, 94–95, 155, 184

Grindal, Bruce, 375 n.21

Gumperz, John, 367 n.25

"hard": defined, 285–86, 364 n.20; exertion not a key factor in, 285–86, 288; singing, 32, 103, 196, 242, 250, 267, 279, 285–86; singing, as rhetorical strategy, 246, 252, 268; talking/preaching, 246, 279, 365 n.1

Hardsinger [pseud.], 250–51, 277–78, 295, 300

Harris, Rev. Zebedee D., 24, 67, 101, 102, 119–22, 124, 137–38, 141, 237, 256, 300, 365 n.28

"having a good time in the Lord," 38, 126–27, 129, 210–11

"having church," 36–38, 40, 50, 94, 108, 127, 154, 172, 211, 263, 314

Hawkins, Edwin, 363 n.7

heaven: antebellum descriptions of, 112; invoked in names of gospel groups, 116; no preaching in, 116; singing in, 3, 110–16, 262, 347 n.8; source of song and music, 123. *See also* angels

Heilbut, Anthony, 345 n.14, 346 n.21, 350 n.5, 354 n.4, 358 n.3, 362 n.1, 364 nn.15, 19, 366 n.12

history: collapsing past and present, 135; of declining faith, 107–9, 233, 346 nn.19, 21; rhetorical recounting of, 108, 240, 346 nn.21–22; time as measure of truth, 121. *See also* old-time religion

Holiness Movement, 107, 118, 123, 348 n.19, 349 n.25

Holt, Grace Sims, 343 n.15, 364 n.13

holy clap, 21, 151, 309

holy dance, 3, 21, 22, 23, 94–95, 104, 143, 151, *158, 209*, 240, 242, 308–9, 315. *See also* anointment; joy; shouting

Holy Spirit, 21–22, 36–37, 136, 162, 167, 180, 199, 258, 260; acts according to own will and time, 95, 171–72, 181, 225, 241, 261, 306; always present, 344 n.6; calls saints to witness, 169; calmness of, 141,

narrative: about angelic singing, 113–15; about the half-sized devil, 365 n.31; in song, 270; about the "outshoutingest" brother, 140–41; about parrots, 137–38, 351 n.8; resonance of told experience, 24; about soul-selling, 118; about the three preachers, 235–36; untellability of holy experience, 17–19. *See also* testifying; testimonies

Newberry, Jeffrey, 132–35, 136

Nichols, Kenneth, *114*

Nixon, Mother Eunice, 34–36, *37*, 41, 42, 43, 45, 84–85, 87–88, 125, 166

Oak Grove Free Will Baptist Church, 119, 256

O'Connor, Bonnie, 337 n.3 (Ch. 2)

old-time religion, 106–8; rejected in non-sanctified churches, 136; symbolic power of, 107–8. *See also* history, of declining faith

"One Morning Soon," 110, 347 n.1

on-time God, 172, 306

order: biblical grounding of calls for, 63; as condition, with Spirit's guidance, 170; Lord wants worship in, 63, 168; out of, invites condemnation, 169–70; as sequence, placing God first, 55, 170

Owen, Nancy, 375 n.21

Paul, Saint, 3, 5, 63, 107, 109, 223, 233, 254, 262, 344 n.2 (Ch. 8)

Payne, Daniel Alexander, 350 n.3

Pentecostalism, 123, 135, 136, 349 n.25, 350 n.5

"People Don't Do Like They Used to Do," 107

performance: aesthetic of intensity, 50–52, 72, 154–6; assessing authenticity of, 253–63, 305, 373 n.11; breakthrough into, 370 n.41; competence comes with sainthood, 131, 153; "dead," 51–52, 352 n.20; disclaimers of, 232, 237–38, 363 nn.6–7; evaluating artistry of, 190, 305–6, 360 n.9; expressive interlock, 354 n.9; holiness as reigning frame of, 136; importance of sincerity, 51–52, 190, 237; inauthentic, 62–65, 136, 138–39, 144–48, 167, 182, 217–18, 224–27, 230–63, 360 n.11; moving beyond, with revelation, 306, 370 n.41; as synonym for spiritual theatricality, 237–41; versus intensifying focus, 154. *See also* authenticity, assessing spiritual; competition; elevation; entertainment; "form or fashion"; intensity; "show"

Perry, Cedric, *158*

Perry, Lena Mae, 4, 32, 105–6, 125–30, *128*, 145, 148–49, 151–52, 154, 163–64, 166, 181–82, 183, 190, 204, 210–11, 220–24, 228, 247, *265*, 278, 285–86, *287*, 309–10, 315, *316*, 321

personalization: importance of, 145, 194, 198; in worship, 145, 153, 160, 191, 352 n.19. *See also* improvisation

Peters, Larry, 375 n.21

Phillips, Washington, 350 n.4, 361 n.7

Pitts, Walter F., Jr., 345 n.15, 371 n.2

"playing church," 139, 141, 237–38; warnings against, 142, 147, 179–80, 245, 295. *See also* entertainment; "form or fashion"; performance, inauthentic; shouting, for show; "show"

possession, 323, 371 n.2

praising, 46–47, 60, 61, 126, 134, 155, 157, 184, 211, 218; controlled by the Spirit, 143; encouragement of, 155–56, 164–65, 177–78, 190–93, 296–99; as everyday activity, 5, 112; as preparation to worship, 90, 96; as purpose of programs, 177, 180, 193; relationship to praying, 60–61; seamlessness in song and speech, 104, 134, 191; through song, 3, 90, 92, 103–4, 110. *See also* music; praying; singing; singing, congregational; thanksgiving

prayer closet, 5, 335 n.6

prayer leaders: misusing prayer to glorify self, 65–66; responsibilities of, 58, 61–62, 72; as vessel for Spirit's blessings, 68. *See also* devotional leaders; praying

praying, 53–56, *57*, 60–61, 67, 73, 83, 94, 179, 221, 344 n.3; affective power of, 62, 65–70, 212; appeals for spiritual authenticity, 62–65; balancing entreaty and thanks, 55, 60, 73, 320; in devotions, 39, 56, 58, 60, 71–72, 73, 97, 320; divine authorship, 15, 62, 75–79, 342 n.3; elevation in, 54–55, 68, 71–72; function shifts as authorship changes, 80; gift of prayer/"prayingest," 47, 62, 65, 68, 76, 145; for guidance before singing, 227–28; mortal authorship as ineffective, 70, 75–76, 81, 83; simultaneous audiences for, 62–63, 67–68, 75, 79–80; Spirit renders effective, 82; spiritual ministrations in, 67–70, 79; as spur to reflection, 58–60, 62, 72, 80; style influences congregational engagement, 72. *See also* gifts of the Spirit; prayer closet; prayer leaders

prayingest. *See* praying, gift of prayer

preachers, 42; as congregational equals during anointed preaching, 145; as emcees, 175. *See also* preaching

preaching: ability comes with calling, 212; no need for formal training, 361 n.7; not expected in devotions, 99; in self, 235; in song, 270, 272, 290; stance, 360 n.2; style, 25, 70–71, 233, 235–36, 246, 281–84; trajectory of, 160–61, 302; in the welcome, 130; zooning, 281–83, 285, 288. *See also* elevation; "hard," preaching/ talking; preachers; revelation; speech style

Price, Richard and Sally, 354 n.9

programs, 4; contrasted to "service," 165–66, 170, 172, 181, 355 n.5; cross-denominational attendance of, 131; flow of, 52, 171, 183, 193, 200, 208, 277–78; include entertainment-seekers, 137; order of performance in, 199, 201; purpose is praise and ministry, 177, 180, 193, 211, 319; shifting musical textures in, 193–94, 196, 198–99; special opportunities for ministry, 169; trajectory of, 130, 199–202, 278, 321. *See also* anniversaries; services; ticket programs

prophecy, 119, 256–57, 263, 365 n.28. *See also* revelation

Psalms, 48, 91, 109, 184, 208; special appropriateness of, 46; Twenty-third, 45–46

quartet contests. *See* competition

quartets, 196, 358 n.3; styles, 194, 198, 359 n.7. *See also names of individual ensembles*

radio, gospel, 4, 175–76. *See also* announcers, radio

Raymond, Rev. Charles A., 14, 337 n.2 (Ch. 3)

Reagon, Bernice Johnson, 341 n.4, 369 n.37

reality, sanctified: treated as cultural construction, 322–23, 330–31, 333; different from that of "the world," 322; new, ushered in when saved, 319; not situational, 13, 320–23

reflection, 16, 49, 95, 354 n.3; inviting anointment, 94, 276; and praying, 58–60, 62; and singing, 58–59, 92, 105, 211, 223

rehearsal, 115, 238, 362 n.17; of spiritual signs, 255; foiled by the Spirit, 81, 255–56

Reisman, Karl, 354 n.7

response, 149–51; dissolves distinctions between hosts and guests, 153–54; pre-pared, 153, 350 n.1, 353 n.1; who gives, 152–53. *See also* welcome address

revelation (prophetic anointing), 46–47, 80, 228, 302–5, 340 n.8, 370 n.40; in the Bible, 46; descriptions of the flow, 75, 77–80, 212–13, 286, 288, 301–5; determining authorship of, 305–6; enabled by conversion, 81–82, 131; in the drive, 294, 301; of lyrics and songs, 111, 115, 119, 124, 223, 305, 347 nn.9–11; in praying, 15, 62, 75–76, 78, 228, 342 n.3; in preaching, 79–80, 145, 304–5; in singing, 301–5; in testifying, 77, 79–80; in tongues, 256–57; transcends evaluation, 306, 370 n.41. *See also* anointment; collaborative communication; elevation; prophecy

revival meetings, 20–23, 38, 39; links with gospel programs, 128–29, 132, 181–82

Richardson, Elder W. Lawrence, 1–3, 16, 19, 40, 67–70, 73, 79, 160–61, 191, 212, 238, 253, 281, 301–5, 333 n.1, 352 n.23, 364 n.20

Ridington, Robin, 373 n.9

ring shouts, 367 n.14, 368 n.30

Rosaldo, Renato, 373 n.5

Rose, Dan, 352 n.20

Rosenberg, Bruce A., 343 n.15, 354 n.2, 357 n.17, 358 n.20

Rouget, Gilbert, 345 n.12

"running the song." *See* drive

St. Amanda Gospel Choir, *195*

St. James Gospel Choir, 185, 187–88, 189–92, 196, 203

Samarin, William J., 374 n.14

sanctification ("set apart"), 2, 131, 322; responsibilities of, 226

sanctified church. *See* church

Satan: attacks believers, 21–23, 233; can make people shout, 251, 353 n.28; cannot live a Christian life, 78, 122–23, 258–59; defeat of, 121, 153; and gossip, 262; as masterful imitator of Christian ways, 118–22, 141, 148, 252, 258–59, 284, 365 n.31; as master of music, 116–18, 123, 348 n.16; needs to show himself, 255, 258; performances are derivative, 123; power of, 119–22, 241, 252; reveals worldly songs, 119–20, 122; selling soul to, 118, 349 nn.20–21; as teacher, 148, 252, 353 n.27; as tempter and deceiver, 118, 122, 243, 248, 252, 365 n.31; works are temporary, 122 scripture, 46–47

scripture reading, 45–49, 133–34, 320, 341 n.3; congregational expectations in, 48, 52. *See also* psalms

self: should engage fully in praise, 155–56; three-part model (spiritual, mental, and physical), 24, 67, 101, 102, 300; worship welcomes expression of, 145, 174

Sellars, Celester, 117

Sensational Nightingales, 102, 181, 191, 227, 241–46, 248, 358 n.19, 364 n.21

sermonette, 39, 172, 340 n.6

Seroff, Doug, 341 n.5, 358 n.2, 359 n.5, 368 n.30

services: calls for "order," 55, 63, 169; contrasted with "programs," 165–66, 170, 172, 181, 355 n.5; "dry," 90, 164, 221; flexible structure of, 130, 165, 171–72, 345 n.15; flow of, 22, 61, 104, 130, 187, 344 n.1 (Ch. 9); as performance of community, 352 n.20, 354 n.9; range of, 4, 131–32; shifting authority in, 40, 61; shifting moods in, 187; trajectory of, 130, 200–201, 283; vs. "entertainment," 4. *See also* anniversaries; programs; ticket programs

shout songs, 196, 203, 233, 267; defined, 100–101, 345 n.11; demand the singer's involvement, 100, 289; do not inevitably trigger shouts, 102; experience of singing, 100–101; as vehicles of invitation, 102, 221, 289. *See also* beat; elevation; singing; singing, congregational; song

shouting, 134, 139, 151, 292, 308–11, 364 n.20; ashamed to shout, 132, 156; for competition/to "outshout," 140, 146, 353 n.24; from emotion vs. Spirit, 22–23, 71, 101, 139–40, 252, 300, 345 n.12; to garner prestige, 146, 248–49; to generate shouts, 249–52, 261, 366 n.7; as message from the Spirit, 95; pranks invited by false, 146; self-generated, 139–40, 142; "shoutingest," 139–40, 144; for show, 139, 144–47, 244, 252, 351 n.14, 352 nn.22–23, 353 n.25; without understanding, 139, 148; warnings against false, 142–44, 147–48. *See also* anointment; collaborative communication; discernment; holy dance; joy

"shouting shoes," 33

"shout-time," 101, 203, 206

"show" ("outside show"), 64, 144, 167, 174, 199, 241, 248–49, 255, 263, 363 n.11; affirmations of, 363 n.7; authored by Satan, 255, 258; and "confusion," 254;

deceives the faithful, 143–44, 225; disclaimers of, 49, 231–32, 254; expectations of, 132, 137, 238; manifestations of, 239–41; and put-on "form," 236–37. *See also* entertainment; "form or fashion"; performance, inauthentic; shouting, for show

signs of the Spirit, 149, 180; not proof of Spirit's presence, 71, 73, 172; as symbols, 224–25, 240. *See also* Holy Spirit

sincerity, 4, 82, 190, 199, 307, 363 n.6; associated with intensity, 51–52; needs no rehearsal, 256; and spiritual authenticity, 65–66, 68, 137, 237

singing: anointed, 212, 215–20; biblical references to, 111–12, 347 n.4; brings pleasure to God, 110–11; competence lies beyond sound, 200–201, 211, 214, 360 n.9; as devotional duty, 210–11, 218, 226; as everyday activity, 112; to glorify/satisfy self, 63, 249, 252, 274; in-song intensification of, 206–7, 266–70, 272–74, 276, 279, 289–92; lies, 242–43, 245; as ministry, 168, 171, 180–81, 211–12, 217, 219–23, 274; as praise, 64, 191, 211, 218–19; preceded by prayer, 227–28; for Satan, 117; repetition in, 192, 202, 205, 208, 267–74, 292; rule of constant contrast, 279, 366 nn.12–13; seamlessness with speaking, 104, 285; as self-ministry, 224; for shouts, 242, 244–45, 248–52, 300–301, 356 n.8, 364 n.20, 366 n.7; slow, invites reflection on the words, 105–6, 109, 221, *247*, 275–76; stopping, in surrender to the Spirit, 239–40, 292, 305; teaching through, 223; under the Spirit's guidance, 172, 221; with understanding, 93, 217, 235. *See also* drive; elevation; gospel music; gospel singers; music; musicians; performance; praising; shout songs; singing, congregational; song; song sets; theme song

singing, congregational, 34–36, 39, 40, 42, 43, 45, 58, 85, 87, 103–4; degrees and diversity of engagement, 96–97, 159, 344 n.3, 354 nn.7, 9; demands creative participation, 92; in devotions, 90, 92, 105–6, 320; emotional engagement with, 48–49; engagement with lyrics, 58–59, 92, 96, 105–6, 109, 220; experience of, 89–90, 92–93; facilitates accord, 89–91, 93, 154; intensification of, 35–36, 43, 85, 87, 93, 100, 103, 192, 280, 289–90, 367 n.14; by rote, 96, 345 n.9; shifting leads and thickening conversational textures, 88–89, 94, 354 n.7. *See also* congregations; devotional service; praising; singing; song

smells, 33, 101

Solid Foundation, 314

"Somebody's Knocking at my Door," 28

song: affective power of, 211–12, 221–22, 224; chosen channel of celestial expression, 110; common meter, 109, 346 n.22; as favored form of praise, 3; and healing, 178, 222; lyrics resonate with experience, 92, 105–6, 109, 192, 211, 220, 223, 345 n.9; as means of saving souls, 80, 178, 180–81, 212, 223, 358 n.18; old, 91, 106; provided by the Spirit, 111, 115, 119, 124, 223, 228, 347 nn.9–11; references to lyrics in talk, 153, 179, 182–83, 210, 309–10, 357 n.20; rising and falling structures in, 267, 270, 296–97; shifting frames and orientation in, 87, 191–92, 270, 279; symbolic meanings of old, 106–8, 346 n.21; as vehicle of personal focus, 93, 320. *See also* gospel music; hymns; music; shout songs; singing; singing, congregational; song sets; spirituals; theme song

song sets: open-endedness of, 171; preparing, 228, 274; song choice guided by the Spirit, 220, 222, 228–29, 278; tailoring to the moment, 220, 274, 278–79, 362 n.11; trajectory of, 201–2, 266, 274–77, 280, 296, 306–7; variation in, 279, 366 nn.12–13. *See also* singing; theme song

space, church, 32, 41, 341 n.9. *See also* cross-aisle

speaking in tongues, 134, 240, 256. *See also* gifts of the Spirit; revelation

speech style: assuming style/Spirit link, 71, 284; characteristics of elevated style, 70–72, 150, 204, 280, 284–85, 343 n.15; comes with the gift/calling, 66, 283; elevated style and the Spirit, 71, 282–84, 325; intensification likened to shifting gears, 161, 280, 302, 304, 369 n.37; perceived link with spiritual state, 70–72, 343 n.16; style-switching, 288–90, 294, 367 n.25; as symbol, 66–67, 69–72, 239, 290. *See also* elevation; "hard," preaching/talking; preaching; talk

Spencer, Jon Michael, 349 n.20

Spirit. *See* Holy Spirit

spirit, mortal, 23; meeting Spirit, 67, 253–54, 257, 323; as part of three-part self, 24. *See also* collaborative communication; Holy Spirit

spirituals, 84, 100, 105, 109, 112–13

Spivey, Evangelist Wendell, 339 n.17

spontaneity: futility of planning performance, 81, 228, 255; lack of, as mark of spiritual inauthenticity, 255–56. *See also* improvisation; rehearsal; revelation

"squenching the Spirit," 147, 307, 359 n.7, 371 n.42

Steadman, Connie, 117, 347 n.11, 351 n.8

Stevens, Sonnie, 230–32, *231*

"Stop That Putting On" (William Walker), 66

"style." *See* entertainment; "form or fashion"; "show"

"sweet" singing, 277, 279, 364 n.21

talk: artistry attributed to the Spirit, 153; between songs, 279; eloquence as a diaspora tradition, 356 n.9; intensifying trajectories of, 69–72, 125–29, 142–43, 149–52, 165–66, 183–85, 204; flow of, 26, 33, 65; structured artistry of, 25, 51, 54–56, 65–66, 78, 176, 177–80, 284, 313, 342 n.9, 357 n.17; ubiquity of eloquence among saints, 173, 351 n.18. *See also* conversation; "hard," preaching/talking; narrative; preaching; speech style; testimonies

Tallmadge, William, 346 n.22

Tedlock, Dennis, 340 n.1 (Ch. 4)

temperature, 101, 178–79

testifying: leading to anointment/re-experience, 16, 338 nn.8–9; guided by the Spirit, 77; in song, 87, 270; as solitary act, 92. *See also* speech style; talk; testimonies; thanksgiving

testimonies ("experiences"), 14–19, 39, 71, 92, 145, 239, 279, 373 nn.5–6; about hearing angelic singing, 113–15; as telling imbued with truth, 328–29; mediated by culture and memory, 329, 331–32, 338 n.6, 374 n.16; language of, 127, 130, 131, 153, 190; strategic spontaneity of, 239. *See also* talk; testifying; thanksgiving

thanksgiving: for everyday blessings, 55, 60, 125, 127, 184, 315; in prayer, 55, 60, 73, 320. *See also* praising; praying; testifying

theme song, 49, 171–72, 183, 193, 264–65, 278, 341 n.4. *See also* song; song sets

Thomas, James, 137, 174, 346 n.20, 356 n.10

Thompson, Robert Farris, 341 n.6, 349 n.20, 354 n.7, 360 n.2, 361 n.3, 366 n.13

Thrower, Henry "Duke," 157, 354 n.6

ticket programs, 4, 6, 72, 96, 131, 137, 141, 198–99, 201, 296; congregation sees self as "audience," 96; percentage of unsaved to saved, 96, 137

Titon, Jeff Todd, 373 n.7, 374 n.16

tongue speaking. *See* speaking in tongues

touch of the Spirit. *See* anointment

transcendence. *See* anointment; Holy Spirit; revelation; shouting

transcription, 26, 336 n.1, 339 n.15, 340 n.1 (Ch. 4)

"trying the spirits," 253–54, 260. *See also* authenticity, assessing spiritual

Tucker, Ira, 366 n.12

Turner, Victor W., 372 n.4

Turner, William, 348 n.19

uniforms. *See* dress

United Choral Ensemble, 232

"Up Above My Head," 113

Vereen, Joe, 111, 347 n.3

Walker, Sheila, 353 n.25

Walker, William, 66, 146–47, 238, 342 n.10, 353 n.26, 353 n.1, 360 n.8

"walking sticks of faith," 3, 56, 335 n.3

Wallace, Joseph ("Jojo"), 61, 102–3, 137, 181, 191, 223, 227–28, 241–46, 248–49, 252, 261, 289, 344 n.6, 371 n.1 (Ch. 18)

Washington, Joseph R., Jr., 339 n.14

Waters, Wilson, 200–201, 295

Watts, Isaac, 34, 111–12, 347 n.5

"We Have Come into His House," 90

welcome address, 125–29, 152–53, 350 n.1; insider and outsider language, 131; structure of, 130. *See also* response

"When I Think of the Goodness of Jesus," 94–95, 184

William Coley Trio, 126, 233, *234*

Williams, Geneva, *316*

Williams, Marion, 348 n.16, 358 n.18, 366 n.6

Williams, Melvin, 339 n.14, 341 n.9

Williams, Rachel, 64

worship services. *See* programs; services

Yarborough, Evangelist Deborah, 21–23, 71, 101, 121, 218

Yelverton, Bishop Frizelle, 26–29, 47, 94, 96, 118–19, 123, 262, 281–83, 288, 340 n.2 (Ch. 4)

"You Better Mind," 148

Young, David E., 371 n.1 (Ch. 19), 373 n.12, 375 nn.19–20

Young, Rev. Liggonia, 278, 286, 288